EMERGENT THEORIES OF AGING

James E. Birren, Ph.D., D.Sc., is Brookdale Distinguished Scholar, Director of the Institute for Advanced Study in Gerontology and Geriatrics, and Professor of Gerontology and Psychology at the University of Southern California. He received his M.A. and Ph.D. from Northwestern University, and was invited to be a Visiting Scientist at the University of Cambridge, England. Dr. Birren is past President of the Gerontological Society of America, the Western Gerontological Society, and the Division on Adult Development and Aging of the American Psychological Association. In addition, he has served as Chief of the Section on Aging of the National Institute of Mental Health. Currently, he is a member of the World Health Organization's Expert Advisory Panel on Health of Elderly Persons.

Dr. Birren has published extensively in the area of aging. He is Series Editor of the internationally renowned *Handbooks on Aging* and has over 200 publications in academic journals and books. His many awards include the Brookdale Foundation Award for Gerontological Research, Honorary Doctorates from the University of Gothenberg, Sweden, and Northwestern University, and the Gerontological Society Award for Meritorious Research.

Vern L. Bengtson, Ph.D., is Director of the Andrus Center's Gerontology Research Institute and Professor of Sociology at the University of Southern California. He received his B.A. at North Park College and his M.A. and Ph.D. from the University of Chicago. He directs a longitudinal study of three-generation families at USC as well as continuing research on the sociology of the life course, socialization, ethnicity, and aging. His publications include *The Social Psychology of Aging* (1973), *Youth, Generations, and Social Change* (with Robert Laufer, 1974), *Grandparenthood* (with Joan Robertson, 1985), and *The Measurement of Intergenerational Relations* (with David Mangen and Pierre Landry, 1987), as well as some 100 papers in professional journals and books. He has been elected Chair of the American Sociological Association's Section on Aging, and is Past Chair of the Behavioral and Social Sciences Section of the Gerontological Society of America. He has been a member of review panels for the National Institute of Mental Health and the National Institute on Aging; he has twice won the Reuben Hill Award for outstanding research and theory on the family, presented by the National Council on Family Relations.

Emergent Theories of Aging

James E. Birren
Vern L. Bengtson
Editors

Donna E. Deutchman, *Editorial Coordinator*

SPRINGER PUBLISHING COMPANY
New York

Copyright © 1988 by Springer Publishing Company, Inc.

Springer Publishing Company, Inc.
536 Broadway
New York, NY 10012

88 89 90 91 92 / 5 4 3 2 1

Library of Congress Cataloging-in-Publication Data

Emergent theories of aging.

  Bibliography: p.
  Includes index.
  1. Aging.   I. Birren, James E.   II. Bengtson, Vern L.
III. Deutchman, Donna E.
QP86.E47 1988   612'.67   87-28509
ISBN 0-8261-6250-9

Printed in the United States of America

Contents

PART III.   Psychological Concepts and Theories of Aging

PART IV.   Social Science Concepts and Theories in Aging

Preface

The scientific community is showing increased interest in research on aging. Both basic and applied issues are attracting a remarkable degree of attention; the volume of publications in this area has more than doubled during the last decade. The literature is continuing to grow exponentially as new research programs and centers on aging emerge. It is our feeling that, following a decade of high research activity on particular aspects of the field, there is an increased requirement for the development and refinement of theory that will serve both to integrate what we know and to guide future research.

Two concerns led to the planning of this volume. First, we believe that further development of research on aging and its increased explanatory power requires systematic effort of a theoretical character. The present volume is an attempt by researchers to begin to address the data-rich but theory-poor state of current research on aging, and to encourage cross-disciplinary interchange that focuses on theory development in aging.

Second, we feel it is important that future research in aging does not become hampered by rigid disciplinary boundaries which may limit information exchange and the transfer of important developments in research design and methods of analysis. The wide scope of the field and, more recently, the high level of its activity and research productivity have resulted in the creation of islands of knowledge with little communication between them. Current theories in gerontology are actually microtheories; they do not, in general, embrace larger perspectives or information from the different domains of the behavioral, social, and biological sciences or from the humanities.

This volume represents the fifth in an annual series devoted to special topics in the field of aging, produced by scholars from the United States and other countries who are fellows of the Institute for Advanced Study in Gerontology and Geriatrics at the Andrus Gerontology Center, University of Southern California. In addition to the fellows of the Institute, other leading researchers have contributed chapters that were identified as necessary to a book on *Emergent Theories of Aging* directed at an audience of researchers, professionals, and graduate students.

As a result of a planning meeting held at the 1986 Meetings of the Gerontological Society of America, the decision was made that this book should focus primarily on theories of aging in the social and behavioral sciences. However, the productivity of this enterprise requires contributions from the biological sciences as well.

The Institute for Advanced Study in Gerontology and Geriatrics was established in 1981, funded by an initial grant from the Andrew Norman Foundation. Fellows of the Institute spend ten months at the Andrus Center doing work related to the year's special topic, meeting in a weekly seminar, and preparing chapters for the annual book, as well as pursuing individual research projects.

The goals of the Institute include furthering research in gerontology and geriatrics, and encouraging the exchange of information and the development of collaborative research. The "aging of societies" is one of the most important issues facing all nations in the world today, and the field of gerontology will benefit greatly from cross-cultural and multinational exchanges of information and approaches to issues of aging societies and aging organisms. Basic theoretical principles of the phenomena of aging are needed at several levels of complex organizations. We hope that this volume will provide some guidance and stimulation in filling this need.

Acknowledgments

It is our pleasure to acknowledge the support of the Andrew Norman Foundation and the Andrew Norman Charitable Trust, whose original gift created the Institute for Advanced Study in Gerontology and Geriatrics, and of Dr. Armand Hammer, who each year has provided financial assistance through fellowships. We also acknowledge the generous gift of the Ernest J. Billman Memorial Fellowship which provided international scholarship support. We are grateful to the Brookdale Foundation, whose support of James E. Birren as Brookdale Distinguished Scholar at the University of Southern California provided the opportunity for serving as senior editor of this book.

We would like to thank Drs. Dale Dannefer, Gary Reker, and Marion Perlmutter for serving on the Editorial Review Board and reviewing selected chapters for this volume. Their broad knowledge and experience assisted in maintaining the multidisciplinary exchange that is fundamental to many of the chapters. Ms. Alice M. Moll and Ms. Alexandra Medina assisted in the production of this manuscript. We are grateful for their clerical expertise; and we are grateful to Dr. Jeffrey Clair who compiled the subject index for this book.

J.E.B.
V.L.B.

Acknowledgements

Contributors

Vern L. Bengtson, Ph.D.
Director, Gerontology Research Institute
Andrus Gerontology Center
University of Southern California,
Los Angeles, California

James E. Birren, Ph.D.
Professor and Brookdale Distinguished Scholar
Andrus Gerontology Center
University of Southern California
Los Angeles, California

Richard T. Campbell, Ph.D.
Professor, Department of Sociology
University of Illinois at Chicago
Chicago, Illinois

Gene D. Cohen, M.D., Ph.D.
Director, Program on Aging
National Institute of Mental Health
Rockville, Maryland

Vincent J. Cristofalo, Ph.D.
Director, Center for the Study of Aging
The University of Pennsylvania
Professor, The Wistar Institute
Philadelphia, Pennsylvania

Dale Dannefer, Ph.D.
Associate Professor of Education and Sociology
Graduate School of Education and Human
  Development
University of Rochester
Rochester, New York

Caleb E. Finch, Ph.D.
ARCO and William F. Kieschnick Professor in
  the Neurobiology of Aging
Andrus Gerontology Center and the Department
  of Biological Sciences
University of Southern California
Los Angeles, California

Christine L. Fry, Ph.D.
Professor of Anthropology
Loyola University of Chicago
Chicago, Illinois

John C. Henretta, Ph.D.
Associate Professor, Department of Sociology
University of Florida
Gainesville, Florida

James P. Henry, M.D., Ph.D.
Professor of Psychiatry
Loma Linda University
Fellow, Institute for Advanced Study
  in Gerontology and Geriatrics
Andrus Gerontology Center
University of Southern California
Los Angeles, California

Gary M. Kenyon, Ph.D.
Chair of Gerontology
St. Thomas University
Fredericton, New Brunswick, Canada

Cees P. M. Knipscheer, Ph.D.
Principal Researcher, Department of Sociology
Vrije University
Amsterdam, The Netherlands

Leah Light, Ph.D.
Professor of Psychology
Pitzer College
Claremont, California

Harry R. Moody, Ph.D.
Deputy Director, Brookdale Center on Aging
Hunter College
New York, New York

Angela M. O'Rand, Ph.D.
Associate Professor, Department of Sociology
Duke University
Durham, North Carolina

Patricia M. Passuth, Ph.D.
Postdoctoral Fellow, Andrus Gerontology Center
University of Southern California
Los Angeles, California

Marion Perlmutter, Ph.D.
Professor of Psychology and Research Scientist
Institute of Gerontology and Center for Human
*   Growth and Development*
University of Michigan
Ann Arbor, Michigan

Gary T. Reker, Ph.D.
Professor, Department of Psychology
Trent University
Peterborough, Ontario, Canada

K. Warner Schaie, Ph.D.
Evan Pugh Professor of Human Development
*   and Psychology*
Director, Gerontology Center
The Pennsylvania State University
University Park, Pennsylvania

Johannes J. F. Schroots, Ph.D.
Associate Professor of Gerontology and
*   Coordinator of the Research Program in*
*   Preventive Health Care for the Elderly*
Agricultural University of Wageningen
TNO Institute of Preventive
*   Health Care*
Leiden, The Netherlands

Peter Uhlenberg, Ph.D.
Associate Professor, Department of Sociology
University of North Carolina
Chapel Hill, North Carolina

Paul T. P. Wong, Ph.D.
Professor, Department of Psychology
Trent University and University of Toronto
Peterborough, Ontario, Canada

F. Eugene Yates, M.D.
Ralph and Marjorie Crump Professor of
*   Medical Engineering*
Director, Crump Institute for Medical
*   Engineering*
University of California at Los Angeles
Los Angeles, California

PART I
Bases of Theory Building in Aging

1

Basic Assumptions in Theories of Human Aging

Gary M. Kenyon

> Mais plus la science produit de verités, et mieux demon-
> trées, plus aussi s'éloigne l'horizon de la verité. La tache de
> conquérir de nouvelles verités, et celle de coordoner et
> systematiser en une verité les verités multiples, successives,
> et disparates, qu'engendre la marche de la science, paraissent
> également indefinies.[1] — PHILIBERT (1968)

A major problem in the study of aging is that research consists of a large number of disparate studies and perspectives. Until very recently, researchers in the psychology of aging, and in psychosocial gerontology as a whole, have concerned themselves with narrowly defined variables, or pieces of the aging person, whether these pieces be intelligence, memory, depression, social competence, or life satisfaction (Birren & Cunningham, 1985; Kenyon, 1985b).[2] This tendency has resulted in a situation whereby far less attention has been paid to the ongoing process of interpreting and integrating these diverse findings in order to arrive at a more comprehensive and systematic understanding of both the processes of aging and the older person. It is a working assumption of this chapter that a broad base as well as a synthesis of knowledge about aging is a sine qua non for theory building in the field.

The purpose of this chapter is to indicate the significance that a particular interpretation of human nature, to be termed *personal existence*, has for the development of theory in the psychosocial study of aging. The chapter will proceed by way of an inquiry into basic assumptions contained in selected theoretical perspectives in the field. The outcome of this inquiry is a contribution toward the clarification and explication of these basic assumptions, as well as a contribution to the broadening of the knowledge base through the consideration of an understanding of human nature that has, until very recently, received little attention in the study of aging.

The chapter will consist of four sections. The first section will comprise a discussion of the importance of analyzing assumptions in research on aging. Included under this topic will be a cursory consideration of the epistemological conditions that give rise to the problem of assumptions. The second section will explicate the personal existence view of human nature. This view is based on the insights of a number of contemporary philosophers, mainly from the existentialist and phenomenological traditions.

In the third section, the notion of personal existence will be used as a reference point for the consideration of basic assumptions in selected psychosocial theories of aging. Specifically, basic assumptions are to be understood as referring to the ontological presuppositions that inform various theories. The term *ontological* here refers to basic images, meanings, or structures of human nature and aging. Finally, in the fourth section, a cursory discussion of the implications that this inquiry has for intervention issues will be presented.

THE SIGNIFICANCE OF ASSUMPTIONS

In recent years a number of psychologists, sociologists, and philosophers have indicated that it is important to examine the basic assumptions of research on aging. For example, Eisdorfer (1983) points out that a very important aim of gerontology in the coming years will be the identification and explication of the various *conceptualizations* of aging employed in theory and practice. Maddox and Campbell (1985) refer to the necessity to analyze the *strategic considerations* that inform theories of aging. Philibert (1982) states that, along with empirical studies, there is a need to consider the broader *phenomenological images* of aging in various disciplines. In addition, Cole (1983), in examining this issue from the point of view of cultural and historical values, notes that a number of scientific perspectives on aging suffer from a series of existential evasions, in that they access a limited range of human activity. Birren and Schroots (1984) also identify and address the problem of assumptions by means of an analysis of *metaphors* in the science of aging. Marshall (1980a, 1986) considers various basic assumptions in the sociology of aging and argues for a more interpretive orientation to research. Finally, a volume has recently appeared, entitled *Philosophical Foundations of Gerontology* (McKee, 1982), in which a range of historical and contemporary philosophical and scientific perspectives on aging is presented.

The investigation of basic assumptions in the study of aging is important for at least three reasons. First, there are a number of orientations contained in various empirical and theoretical perspectives in research on aging. That is, there are several disparate starting points for the scientific study of aging that lead to different and competing conclusions about human nature in the later years. For example, aging can be defined as a series of problems, or as a developmentally interesting phenomenon, with significantly different emphases and outcomes for research, practice, and ultimately the quality of life of older persons (Achenbaum, 1985; Tornstam, 1982). This last point refers to the extent to which scientific findings influence public perceptions of aging, particularly in a culture that looks to science for answers to many of its social questions (Gadamer, 1981). Nevertheless, the existence of competing perspectives or multiple orientations is not, in itself, problematic and may even be healthy. It is the uncritical and unreflective acceptance of one orientation over the others that creates an unacceptable situation.

The second reason for investigating basic assumptions is that they are inevitably operative; that is, they are an intrinsic part of what constitutes scientific knowledge (Gadamer, 1976, 1981). This means that scientific activity, and in particular, social science activity, is subject to predisposing influences. As a human activity, social science is both an empirical phenomenon and a sociohistorical phenomenon. This creates a situation in which, paradoxically, there are facts to be interpreted, discovered, and understood. Yet researchers understand these facts at the level of their own individual perspectives (Gadamer, 1976) and at the level of the *collective intellect* (Marton, 1981) or *collective mind* (Scheler, 1980).

As a result, there can be several equally convincing interpretations of a particular phenomenon of aging, based on differing basic assumptions and perceptions. These interpretations reflect such things as academic training and "the interplay of historical forces and varying societal circumstances" (Achenbaum, 1985, p. 145). Additional dialogue or conversation is required in order to better understand the phenomenon. As Labouvie-Vief and Chandler (1978) note, here scientific truth consists of "the inevitable and intricate relationship between scientific knowledge and the context—personal, historical and ideological—from which such knowledge emerges" (p. 183).

The third reason for investigating basic assumptions in research on aging, related to the first, is that assumptions are not only always operative but also often function tacitly. The crucial concern is that these assumptions, implicitly if not explicitly, guide research and therefore require identification and explication. As indicated earlier, assumptions become problematic only when they are not made explicit. Insofar as it is not acknowledged that they are operating, then a vulnerable situation is created in which questionable assumptions may be discovered after the fact. The preponderance of views that argued for exclusive decrement with age, with their attendant implications for public perceptions of age, and intervention with elderly persons is an example of this. In agreement with Achenbaum (1985): "For this reason, continually scrutinizing our assumptions about the nature and dynamics of growing old(er) is imperative" (p. 145).

The foregoing discussion has described the epistemological conditions that give rise to the problem of assumptions in research on aging. However, in addition to the fact that this issue deserves attention because assumptions are inevitably operative in research, and that it is therefore important to consider the relationship between (scientific) thought and its existential base (Simonds, 1978), inquiry into basic assumptions is also a useful way to integrate and systematize disparate findings in the field. Borrowing from Schroots's (1982) discussion of metaphors in science, this approach can provide a deeper understanding of existing theories, which may include the discovery of previously unrecognized aspects and implications of various theories as well as suggest new directions for theorizing.

HUMAN NATURE AS PERSONAL EXISTENCE

The previous section presented a background discussion with respect to the investigation of basic assumptions in research on aging. In this section, a view of human nature as *personal existence* will be presented. It is the claim of this chapter that the personal existence perspective contains basic assumptions about human nature that can serve as useful guidelines both for the synthesis of knowledge and for theory development in the study of aging. It is important to point out that the personal existence view is not a theory of aging per se but a plausible interpretation of human nature that can inform theories of aging. As such, this inquiry operates at the level of informed speculation and argumentation. Therefore, it need not conform to the logical requirements associated with theory construction.

Three basic principles are implicated in the personal existence view of human nature (see also Kenyon, 1985a, b). First, as biological organisms, and therefore part of nature, human beings are embodied and finite. Thus, human beings are born, grow, and die. However, the distinctive aspect of human nature is that human beings are aware that they have bodies (Berger & Luckman, 1966; Heidegger, 1962; Merleau-Ponty, 1962, 1963) As Merleau-Ponty (1963) points out: "For a being who has acquired the consciousness of self and his body, who has reached the dialectic of subject and object, the body is no longer the cause of the structure of consciousness; it has become the object of consciousness" (p. 204).

The second basic principle is that human beings, as embodied and self-aware, or as "being-in-the-world" (*Dasein*), exist in situations (Heidegger, 1962). This means that human beings are fundamentally relational entities who are necessarily involved with other persons and with a physical and social environment (Merleau-Ponty, 1962, 1963). Merleau-Ponty (1962) explains this principle by referring to the human being as an *opening through perception*. The essential idea here is that the human entity is aware of itself and of the world around it, but from a particular perspective. There are aspects of oneself and one's body that are accessible to others but not accessible to one's own perception—for example, the back of the head. In this fundamental sense, the human body is both a physical and social object that "belongs to the world as well as to the self" (Gadow, 1986, p. 240). It follows that part of what "I am" is constituted by another person (see also Sartre, 1956). The notion that human beings to some extent constitute each other leads to the third principle involved in the notion of personal existence.

As self-aware entities, human beings are intentional creatures. This means that they place meanings on things. Thus, one's own body, as well as the world and other persons, are *structures of signification* (Merleau-Ponty, 1962). According to the personal existence view, human beings, as openings through perception, actively constitute their worlds, even as they are constituted *by* that world. The crucial point in the present context is that this view implies that there is a self-determining, self-creative aspect of human nature.

The basic image of human nature contained in the personal existence view is that of an interpersonal entity. This means that human nature is composed of social and psychopersonal dimensions, along with biological dimensions. (The term *psychopersonal* refers to the proactive aspects of human nature that are of interest to both social scientists and philosophers). Consequently, from this point of view, human beings are to be understood as subject to biological and social-structural influences; however, within this context, human beings also engage in decisive interpretations of their physical and social environments. Human beings, as persons, are not conceptualized exclusively as either individual entities nor socially constructed entities. Rather, they are self-creating, but within contexts that involve various kinds of biological and social constraints. The unit of analysis here becomes the dialectical, creating-created process itself.

The foregoing cursory explication of human nature as personal existence is intended as prolegomena to the consideration of this view, in the next section, as a set of guiding assumptions for theorizing in the study of aging. Simultaneously, the personal existence view will be further clarified.

PERSONAL EXISTENCE AND THEORIES OF AGING

Many psychosocial theories of aging presuppose a basic image or understanding of human nature as a biological organism, moreover, a biologically determined organism. Other theories presuppose an image of human nature as an exclusively social, and socially determined, being (for a review of selected theories that reflect these assumptions, see Kenyon, 1985b; Labouvie-Vief, 1977). In these views, human aging becomes either an exclusively biomaturational process or a purely social, production-oriented process. This is the case since either a declining body is assumed to cause decrement in cognitive and social functioning, or the loss of one's occupational role causes inevitable decrements in psychosocial competence, unless somehow replaced in kind. Thus, older persons are portrayed as either declining biological organisms, not very different from any other organism, or as "nothing but a bundle or summation of roles" (Marshall, 1980b, p. 96). These theories, while presenting a case that argues ostensibly for the multidimensionality of human aging and human nature, contain implicit assumptions that are, in effect, unidimensional. This is so to the extent that there is only one *real* mechanism of aging in these views, either biological or social, depending on the theory. Furthermore, these assumptions encourage negative stereotyping of older persons and often lead to paternalistic intervention strategies.

In terms of the present discussion, the crucial point is that the understanding of human nature and human aging just described is indeed based on a particular set of assumptions. As such, it is neither a statement of fact, nor even necessarily an accurate set of assumptions; the assumptions may have been adopted without much reflection on their implications. In contrast to the foregoing view, the remainder of this chapter will explicate an alternative set of assumptions that provides a radically different picture of human nature and aging, with attendant different implications for intervention and public perception of age.

In what follows, selected theories of adult intellectual and social competence will be discussed, the assumptions of which are consistent with the personal existence view. It will be argued that these views contain assumptions that facilitate a comprehensive understanding of human nature and human aging since they accommodate a broad range of human activity and are sensitive to the interactive nature of various aspects of human functioning. These theories reflect the insight that it is one thing to speak about human aging as multidimensional, and quite another to acknowledge in theory and research that the biological, social, and psychopersonal dimensions are all dynamic, interacting forces in human aging and development.

Examples of theoretical perspectives on adult intellectual competence that reflect personal existence assumptions are Dittman-Kohli and Baltes (in press), Holliday and Chandler (1986), and Riegel (1973). Examples of corresponding social competence theories are Riegel (1975, 1976) and Thomae (1980). Riegel's views figure prominently in this section because his work reflects a comprehensive articulation of many of the issues of concern in this chapter. For additional listings of theory, the consideration of which is precluded here by spatial constraints, the reader is referred to other chapters in this volume and to Kenyon and Birren (1986).

Dialectical Operations

Riegel's (1973) perspective on adult intellectual competence expresses the assumptions of personal existence by postulating that, within the context of Piaget's framework, one can identify a level of cognitive functioning beyond the formal operational level. This higher level, *dialectical operations*, emerges from earlier levels of functioning. However, the term *dialectical operations* refers to such things as a capacity to live with contradictions and an ability to synthesize knowledge as a result of greater life experience. In this view, older people may not do well on formal operational measures but may do well on dialectical measures. The fact that older people fail tests of formal operations has been interpreted to indicate intellectual decline by researchers such as Papalia (1972). In contrast, Riegel's claim is that perhaps older persons *should not* do well on formal operational tests since these tests are designed to assess an earlier level of intelligence that may no longer be dominant in older persons, being superseded by the dialectical level.

On the basis of his analysis, Riegel (1973) claims that formal operations cannot represent the measure of mature intelligence. The notion that thinking at any age is essentially dialectic and not equilibrium-oriented leads to a broader interpretation of cognitive aging. That is, "factors of interests and motivations, practical and social significance codetermine operations, originally thought of as being universal qualities" (p. 21). This view reflects a step toward the explicit consideration, in theory, of the actual impact of social-structural and personal factors on the process of adult intellectual ontogeny. The basic image of human nature contained in this theory is that of an entity composed of biological, social, and psychopersonal, that is, self-determining, aspects.

Wisdom

A second example of a view of intellectual competence that reflects personal existence assumptions is that found in the work of Dittman-Kohli and Baltes (in press) and Holliday and Chandler (1986). The first view presents the idea that adult intelligence best can be characterized by a notion of pragmatic wisdom. It is proposed that this concept, as a prototype of intellectual competence, will allow for a more comprehensive understanding of this phenomenon.

Wisdom in this perspective is defined as an "ability to exercise good judgement about important but uncertain matters of life" (Dittman-Kohli & Baltes, in press). Underlying this formulation of adult intelligence is the assumption that "in each individual life course, a pattern of ontogenetic, social-structural, and idiographic conditions jointly define the form of intellectual aging." The important point here is that the understanding of adult intellectual competence is held to presuppose the consideration of the person's past and present circumstances. The suggestion is that in this way it may be possible to interpret observed decrements in intellectual functioning as often involving the measurement of skills and abilities that are superfluous or irrelevant to the further development of a particular person; or abilities that, although subject to decline, are compensated for in a variety of ways by different persons. The understanding of intellectual competence involves an emphasis on such things as expertise, contextual richness, pragmatics of life, uncertainty, and relativism. The focus, then, is on the complexity of the problem and the crucial importance of situational conclusions. In this perspective, as in the previous one, intellectual aging is assumed to be a genuinely biological, psychological, and social process.

In agreement with this view, the basic assumption of the Holliday and Chandler (1986) perspective is that wisdom as a later-life competency involves cognitive, interpersonal, and experiential domains. Nevertheless, there is some disagreement between these views as to the appropriate way to study wisdom. For Holliday and Chandler, since wisdom is "deeply rooted in social practice," there may be a danger in studying wisdom from traditional cognitive and psychometric points of view, the approach employed by Dittman-Kohli and Baltes (in press). The danger is that it might not be wisdom but something else, such as specialized forms of intelligence, that is referenced without a radical contextual or interpretive approach.

Taking this point one step further, the determination of an appropriate approach to the study of wisdom is important insofar as the purpose is to distinguish between wisdom and other phenomena, such as cleverness. Traditional methods may assist in the classification of successful strategies of adaptation. However, these may involve only a manipulation of the physical or human environment on the part of a person and may not indicate wisdom at all. The understanding of wisdom may require a thorough evaluation of the meanings that different people place on situations and interactions, as well as a more subtle assessment of specific person-to-person encounters, including the intentions that different persons bring to these encounters. The reference to intentions points to the moral dimensions that are usually associated with the meaning of wisdom; for example, in the Greek tradition, where the wise man *knows and does the Good*. Nevertheless, having made these qualifying remarks, we may see the study of wisdom as a clear example of a theoretical orientation that reflects personal existence assumptions.

A Life-Event Perspective

A theoretical perspective that reflects personal existence assumptions in the area of social competence is that of Riegel (1975, 1976). It is useful to discuss this perspective in some detail, as it provides an excellent map of the territory for the development of theories of aging that accommodate personal existence assumptions. Riegel's life-event perspective includes an explicit consideration of, broadly speaking, a changing person in a changing social structure. Thus, Riegel advocates a shift away from universal, biologically based, or exclusively socially based claims about one aspect or another of social competence, which result in an oversystematized order being placed on the life cycle. He proposes more context-specific claims about the concrete actions of individuals in a concrete social world (Riegel, 1976).

For Riegel, this change in emphasis allows for the possibility that the entire person-environment situation is *workable*, in that both the person and the society are viewed as changeable through physical, psychological, and social intervention. Furthermore, a comprehensive understanding of social competence is seen to presuppose the consideration of all of these aspects.

According to this perspective, there are progressions along different types of events in the life cycle. First, individuals develop along an inner-biological progression (including maturation and the experience of sensorimotor deficiencies in late life), which gains its social significance in the normative, age-graded system of a particular society. Second, there is an outer-physical progression which involves such things as earthquakes, accidents, and the death of a spouse. Third and fourth are, in turn, the dimensions of individual-psychological and cultural-sociological progressions which involve the *readiness* of a person to interact in particular social situations and the society's expectations for behavior at different points in the life cycle and at different historical periods.

For Riegel (1976), what is interesting about social competence and human development in this context is that there is not a smooth transition from stage to stage in the interaction between the person and the social structure, or at least there is no single prescribed transition route to adjustment. Rather, development occurs through the *asynchronies* among the four dimensions listed above. These asynchronies create crises and catastrophes for individuals and society. Furthermore, these crises should be seen as "meaningful phases in one's life. This is true for incapacitations and even for death" (p. 693).

Riegel's inclusion of the concept of death raises an issue that is important in the present context. Consistent with the personal existence view of human nature as embodied self-awareness, death and dying are, for Riegel, distinctly human phenomena. This is the case insofar as human beings place meanings on their own deaths (Heidegger, 1962; Munnichs, 1966). Moreover, there are many possible meanings that human beings may ascribe to their own deaths and to the deaths of others (Kenyon, 1981). The particular meanings that persons ascribe to death may have an important impact on their understanding of their own aging and on assessments of cognitive and social competence (Reker & Wong, this volume).

Personality as Process

Another perspective on psychosocial competence that presupposes the assumptions of personal existence is that of Thomae (1980). In this view, the emphasis is on process-centered approaches to the understanding of competence. This necessarily involves the inclusion of contextual and personal dimensions per se. In referring to much earlier research, Thomae notes that there has been an "underestimation of situation-specific inconsistencies of behavior and of the discriminative facility of the human actor" (p. 293).

In addition to this, Thomae (1980), in agreement with the foregoing discussion of Riegel's views, argues that the emphasis on the notion of equilibrium or homeostasis may be useful as a guideline in certain situations, but it leads to the danger of assuming that there is a *modal adjustment pattern* that one must live up to in order to be considered competent. Since many older people do not live up to this hypothetical pattern, they are mistakenly seen as deficient or incompetent.

As an alternative to this scenario, Thomae (1980) points to the idea that there are many instances of *cognitive restructurations* that are related to adaptation to situations but do not reflect achievement activity, external adaptation to institutions, and/or aggression. More simply put, people can develop novel and creative competency strategies that reflect genuine choices. Thomae also indicates that it would be possible to identify more of these creative strategies if an appropriate set of assumptions were adopted.

In this view, there is a complex relation between the perceptions of reality of older persons, their coping strategies, the objective features of the environment, and social competence or incompetence; all of which require assessment in a situation. A final remark is that for Thomae (1980) social competence is to be defined as "a global measure for the individual's capacity to meet social and biological demands and the society's capacity to meet individual needs and capacities" (p. 303).

The purpose of this section of the chapter has been to indicate how selected theoretical perspectives in the psychosocial study of aging reflect personal existence assumptions, and to show that they accommodate a comprehensive and genuinely multidimensional basis for theorizing about human aging. In addition, these views encourage an investigation of the links among various levels of human functioning, including the dimension of personal meaning.

DISCUSSION

An important implication of the personal existence view, reflected in the theories of aging just considered, is that this view permits the inclusion of the self-creating aspects of human nature in the development of theories of aging. On the other hand, in construing the human being as an interpersonal entity—which, as discussed earlier, implies that self-creation takes place in a context that involves biological and social-structural constraints—the tendency to view self-creation or *choice* as occurring in some kind of spiritual void is avoided. This interpretation also avoids the problems associated with omitting the self-creating dimension of human nature, which results in a limited understanding of the range of human activity by reducing human nature to exclusively biological and/or social dimensions.

The assumption that human beings are interpersonal entities and therefore not egoistic in this fundamental sense, in conjunction with the assumption that human beings are, to some extent, active in creating their worlds and therefore not totally reactive creatures, leads to a different interpretation of human behavior and human aging. If one assumes that self-creation is an aspect of the basic structure of human nature, or that it is an ontological characteristic, then the claim that age naturally brings with it such things as disengagement, alienation, and incompetence is subject to reassessment, in that these outcomes may be the result of a frustration of that self-creating dimension. The suggestion here is that the picture of human aging as decrement does not necessarily reflect the basic structure of human nature but perhaps reflects a commonly observed form of inauthentic (Heidegger, 1962) or neurotic behavior.

For example, it might be that human beings have their self-constructing (Birren & Hedlund, 1982), self-creating aspect dampened by *habituation* (Kastenbaum, 1980), that is, by social-structural presses imposed from outside and internalized by the person. Thus, many older persons may accept negative images of aging that come to them from the outside, even though the inner image of their own aging does not correspond to the outside image (De Beauvoir, 1973). According to this interpretation, the older person knows that the outside images are questionable, that is, "il les croyait provisoires et revocables mais doit accepter pour vivre et pour agir"[3] (Philibert, 1968, p. 302). If this is the case, then as Riegel (1976) and Thomae (1980) pointed out, both the person and the society could, in principle, be altered so as to facilitate the expression of the self-creating aspect of human nature by emphasizing more positive images.

The example just discussed points to a need for more research and reflection on the nature and dynamics of the inner-aging/outer-aging dialectic. Issues of relevance here are those such as the extent to which inner aging, associated with the self-creating dimension, is capable of adapting to and obviating various deleterious biological occurrences and environmental constraints that are associated with increased age. On the other side of the dialectic, one can ask which environmental conditions could facilitate the harmonizing of one's inner aging with one's outer aging. Again, the assumption here is that human beings are interpersonal and not individual and egoistic. Therefore, the assessment of their physical and social environment is indeed a necessary but not sufficient condition for the understanding of human aging and, ultimately, for the improvement of the quality of life. In other words, personal and social meanings of aging are intricately related; moreover, it is this relationship that requires investigation as part of the agenda of developing theories of aging.

Thus, the adoption of the personal existence interpretation of human nature leads one to ask a different set of questions about aging and theories of aging than would result from views that contain other assumptions. This orientation also suggests that the meanings attributed to human aging in the scientific arena are, to a significant degree, a function of individual and sociocultural interpretations.

A final point of qualification is that the position outlined in this chapter is proposed as a set of alternative guidelines to those views that presuppose exclusively ontogenetic or sociogenic assumptions about human nature and aging. Although a number of good reasons have been put forth for the adoption of these guidelines, they are, of course, open to reflection and critique as further knowledge becomes available. That is, the personal existence view is subject to the same hermeneutic analysis as other orientations.

IMPLICATIONS FOR INTERVENTION

There are two major implications of the discussion contained in this chapter for the area of intervention, whether it be policy, research, treatment, or education. The first implication is that one must be very cautious in making generalized statements about older persons. It would appear that a contextual or situational orientation is warranted since human aging is such a complex phenomenon and since heterogeneity (Dannefer, this volume) is the hallmark of the older population.

It follows that the training of both researchers and practitioners should reflect this orientation and that more emphasis should be placed on critical thinking, in addition to mastering the techniques involved in specific areas of research and practice. Thus, there should be an increased emphasis on exposure to multiple conceptualizations of aging and of older persons, many of which are usually found in only one discipline. In this way, one becomes more aware of one's own assumptions and other possible assumptions, a procedure that facilitates scientifically and ethically responsive intervention. This is not to advocate that everyone undertake interdisciplinary research, but it is to advocate that a broad background tends to make for a better command of the problems found in the psychosocial study of aging.

The second implication of the chapter for intervention issues is that more attention needs to be paid to the higher aspects of human functioning. By this it is meant, for example, that in addition to accommodating to the decrements or deficiency needs associated with age (such as medical care and pensions), policies should be designed to facilitate the expression of the self-creating aspects of human nature throughout the life span. Such an approach might lead to the prevention of many of those decrements.

The situation that needs to be addressed here arises from the contradiction that exists between the linear and unidirectional way that the human life span is currently divided up socially into the three *boxes* of education, work, and retirement, and the actual situation for more and more people who experience such things as early retirement, youth unemployment, and reduced accessibility to the higher education system. At the same time, as a culture, only a small range of production-oriented occupations and life-styles are valued and supported. (Here, *production-oriented* is used in the narrow sense, taken from employment roles.) Increasing numbers of people are having to find alternatives to these main-line activities, with little preparation for such eventualities.

The problem, then, is one of aging, but not only of older people. The situation requires a rethinking of the basic assumptions about human nature that are presupposed in much research and policy. The facilitation, support, and investigation of instrumental social meanings of aging must be complemented by an equal emphasis on personal meanings. The suggestion of an age-irrelevant society (Neugarten & Hagestad, 1976) could go a long way in remedying the current situation. That is, in Western culture, the movement away from age grading might result in a society in which personal and social meanings of aging would support a situation whereby different persons would engage in different kinds of activities (education, work, retirement) throughout the life span as a function of their competencies and interests.

However, in agreement with Moody (1986), such a scenario will not come about in a postindustrial society without the cooperation of those responsible for the design and content of the three boxes mentioned above. The reason for this is that human life is currently under a high degree of social management. Therefore, social policy becomes an integral ingredient in the process of facilitating alternative personal and social meanings of aging.

CONCLUSION

This chapter has provided a reflection on the basic assumptions of selected theories in the psychosocial study of aging. One of the purposes has been to contribute to a broader base for the discussion of theory building in aging.

The chapter first outlined the background and importance of the problem of analyzing assumptions in the study of aging. Following this, a personal existence interpretation of human nature, based on a contemporary philosophical position, was explicated. The personal existence view was then discussed in relation to basic assumptions contained in selected theories of aging that focus on intellectual and social competence. It was indicated that these theories reflect personal existence assumptions and, as such, accommodate an explicitly multidimensional and interactive approach to theorizing about aging. Furthermore, these views include a consideration of the self-creating aspects of human nature. Reference was made to the fact that these assumptions are fundamentally different from those contained in some other theories of aging. Finally, the chapter presented a cursory discussion of the implications that the position outlined in the inquiry has for intervention issues.

As a final remark, the operationalization of personal existence assumptions presents a challenge to researchers involved with the psychosocial study of aging, since the assumptions suggest a rather complex situation. However, the challenge of complexity, which may include the necessity for the development of new methods, should not be replaced in favor of a possibly misguided parsimony.

NOTES

[1]"But the more that science produces truths, and better demonstrates them, the more the horizon of truth extends. The task of conquering new truths, and that of coordinating and systematizing in one truth, truths that are multiple, successive and disparate, a task that constitutes the path of science, appears equally indefinite."

[2]In the interest of manageability, it is beyond the scope of this chapter to consider the basic assumptions of biological theories of aging, except insofar as particular biological assumptions have been adopted by researchers concerned primarily with issues that bear on psychosocial aging.

[3]"He believes them to be tentative and revocable but must accept them in order to act and live."

REFERENCES

Achenbaum, W. A. (1985). Societal perceptions of aging and the aged. In R. Binstock & E. Shanas (Eds.), *Handbook of aging and the social sciences*. New York: Van Nostrand Reinhold. (pp. 129–148).

Berger, P., & Luckman, T. (1966). *The social construction of reality*. New York: Doubleday.

Birren, J., & Cunningham, W. (1985). Research on the psychology of aging: Principles, concepts and theory. In J. Birren & K. W. Schaie (Eds.), *Handbook of the psychology of aging*. New York: Van Nostrand Reinhold. (pp. 3–34).

Birren, J., & Hedlund, B. (1982). *The metaphors of aging and the self-constructing individual*. Paper presented at the Invitational Research Symposium: Metaphors in the Study of Aging. University of British Columbia, Vancouver, Canada, June, 1982.

Birren, J., & Schroots, J. F. (1984). Steps to an ontogenetic psychology. *Academic Psychology Bulletin, 6*, 177–190.

Cole, T. (1983). The "enlightened" view of aging: Victorian morality in a new key. *Hastings Centre Report, 13*, 3:34–40.

De Beauvoir, S. (1973). *The coming of age*. New York: Warner.

Dittman-Kohli, F., & Baltes, P. (in press). Toward a neofunctionalist conception of adult intellectual development: Wisdom as a prototypical case of intellectual growth. In C. Alexander & E. Langer (Eds.), *Beyond formal operations: Alternative endpoints to human development*. New York: Cambridge University Press.

Eisdorfer, C. (1983). Conceptual models of aging: The challenge of a new frontier. *American Psychologist, 38*(2), 197–202.

Gadamer, H. (1976). *Philosophical hermeneutics*. Berkeley, CA: University of California Press.

Gadamer, H. (1981). *Reason in the age of science*. Cambridge, MA: MIT Press.

Gadow, S. (1986). Frailty and strength: The dialectic of aging. In T. Cole & S. Gadow (Eds.), *What does it mean to grow old: Reflections from the humanities*. Durham, NC: Duke University Press.

Heidegger, M. (1962). *Being and time*. New York: Harper & Row.

Holliday, S., & Chandler, M. (1986). *Wisdom: Explorations in adult competence*. Basel: Karger.

Kastenbaum, R. (1980). Habituation as a partial model of human aging. *International Journal of Aging and Human Development, 13*, 159–170.

Kenyon, G. (1981). Human death: A philosophical analysis. *Gnosis, 2*, 2:21–35.

Kenyon, G. (1985a). The meaning of aging: Vital existence vs. personal existence. *Human Values and Aging Newsletter, 8*, 2.

Kenyon, G. (1985b). *A philosophical analysis of scientific meanings of aging in psychosocial gerontology*. Unpublished doctoral dissertation, University of British Columbia, Vancouver, BC.

Kenyon, G., & Birren, J. (Eds.). (1986). *Theories of aging: A selected bibliography*. Los Angeles: Andrus Gerontology Center.

Labouvie-Vief, G. (1977). Adult cognitive development: In search of alternative interpretations. *Merrill-Palmer Quarterly, 23*, 4:227–263.

Labouvie-Vief, G., & Chandler, M. (1978). Cognitive development and life-span developmental theory: Idealistic vs. contextual perspectives. In P. Baltes (Ed.), *Life-span development and behavior* (Vol. 1). New York: Academic Press. (pp. 181–210).

Maddox, G., & Campbell, R. (1985). Scope, concepts, and methods in the study of aging. In R. Binstock & E. Shanas (Eds.), *Handbook of aging and the social sciences*. New York: Van Nostrand Reinhold.

Marshall, V. W. (1980a). *Aging in Canada*. Don Mills, Ontario: Fitzhenry & Whiteside.

Marshall, V. W. (1980b). State of the art lecture: The sociology of aging. In J.

Crawford (Ed.), *Canadian gerontological collection* (Vol. 3). Winnipeg: Canadian Association of Gerontology. (pp. 76–144).

Marshall, V. W. (Ed.). (1986). *Later life: The social psychology of aging.* Beverly Hills, CA: Sage Publications.

Marton, F. (1981). Phenomenography—describing conceptions of the world around us. *Instructional Science, 10,* 177–200.

McKee, P. L. (Ed.). (1982). *Philosophical foundations of gerontology.* New York: Human Sciences Press.

Merleau-Ponty, M. (1962). *Phenomenology of perception.* London: Routledge & Kegan Paul.

Merleau-Ponty, M. (1963). *The structure of behavior.* Boston: Beacon Press.

Moody, H. (1986). The meaning of life and the meaning of old age. In T. Cole & S. Gadow (Eds.), *What does it mean to grow old: Reflections from the humanities.* Durham, NC: Duke University Press.

Munnichs, J. M. A. (1966). *Old age and finitude.* Basel: Karger.

Neugarten, B., & Hagestad, G. (1976). Age and the life course. In R. Binstock & E. Shanas (Eds.), *Handbook of aging and the social sciences.* New York: Van Nostrand Reinhold. (pp. 35–55).

Papalia, D. (1972). The status of several conservation abilities across the lifespan. *Human Development, 15,* 229–243.

Philibert, M. (1968). *L'Echelle des ages.* Paris: Editions du Seuil.

Philibert, M. (1982). The phenomenological approach to images of aging. In P. McKee (Ed.), *Philosophical foundations of gerontology.* New York: Human Sciences Press.

Riegel, K. (1973). Dialectical operations: The final stage of cognitive development. *Human Development, 16,* 346–370.

Riegel, K. (1975). Adult life crises: Toward a dialectical theory of human development. In N. Datan & L. Ginsberg (Eds.), *Life-span developmental psychology: Normative life crises.* New York: Academic Press. (pp. 99–128).

Riegel, K. (1976). The dialectics of human development. *American Psychologist, 31,* 689–700.

Sartre, J. P. (1956). *Being and nothingness.* New York: Simon & Schuster.

Scheler, M. (1980). *Problems of a sociology of knowledge.* London: Routledge & Kegan Paul.

Schroots, J. J. F. (1982). *Metaphors of aging: Reactions, implications and extensions.* Paper presented at the Invitational Research Symposium: Metaphors of Aging. University of British Columbia, Vancouver, Canada, June, 1982.

Simonds, A. P. (1978). *Karl Mannheim's sociology of knowledge.* Oxford: Clarendon Press.

Thomae, H. (1980). Personality and adjustment to old age. In J. Birren & R. Sloane (Eds.), *Handbook of mental health and aging.* Englewood Cliffs, NJ: Prentice-Hall. (pp. 285–309).

Tornstam, L. (1982). Gerontology in a dynamic society. In T. K. Hareven & K. J. Adams (Eds.), *Aging and life course transitions: An interdisciplinary perspective.* New York: Guilford Press. (pp. 183–219).

2

Toward a Critical Gerontology: The Contribution of the Humanities to Theories of Aging

Harry R. Moody

This chapter examines the convergence of two questions in gerontology, namely, (1) the status and contribution of the humanities to studies of aging and (2) the impoverishment of theory in social gerontology. I argue that these two problems are closely related and indeed that without a more humanistic and self-reflexive approach to social gerontology, empirical work is likely to remain fragmented, while social theory, and political advocacy as well, will be limited by lack of self-criticism and broader historical understanding.

Although I offer a plea here for greater attention to the humanities, this essay is not an argument for the elaboration of humanistic gerontology as an end in itself, which is evident in a growing literature on the subject (Cole & Gadow, 1986; Philibert, 1968; Spicker, Woodward, & Van Tassel, 1978; Van Tassel, 1979). On the contrary, instead of urging advances in the humanities that might parallel the construction of theories of social gerontology, I will argue for a more radical solution, namely, that the perspective of the humanities can offer an alternative ground for theories of aging to embrace both the contradictions and the emancipatory possibilities of late life. In this broader view, *both* the humanities and the social sciences should be seen as resources for the construction of theories of aging that correspond to fundamental ideas of time, narrative, and development over the life course. In sketching the outlines of this reconstruction of social gerontology, I will call upon the resources of Critical Theory, as elaborated in the tradition of the Frankfurt

School, and specifically the work of Jurgen Habermas (McCarthy, 1978; Alexander, 1985).

A MULTIPLICITY OF THEORIES

Any effort to speak of the contribution of the humanities to a "theory of aging" must acknowledge, at the very outset, a problem in the construction of any such theory. To put it bluntly, there is, and there can be, no single, overarching "theory of aging" because *aging* as applied to human existence is inherently multidimensional. That is to say, people age as biological beings, social beings, psychological beings, even as spiritual beings. No single theory of aging is likely to take account of all of these levels. On the contrary, one of the most serious problems in gerontology is the question of just how these different levels or domains of theory are related to one another: for example, as causal determination (i.e., reductionism), as boundary conditions for explanatory systems, as ecological levels of connectedness, and so on. It simply will not do to prejudge the problem of theory construction at the outset, for example, by appealing to the older positivist presumption of a "unified science."

When we look at *gerontology* as an actually existing enterprise, what we find, in fact, is that gerontology is not a single, unified discipline—as, say, chemistry or economics might be understood to be. Rather, it is a multidisciplinary assembly of explanatory schemes, each invoking theoretical terms that simply do not move in the same conceptual universe; for example, the DNA-error theory of cellular aging has nothing to do with the application of exchange theory to age relationships among family members. The point here is not that we ought to prefer theories of the middle range instead of grand, overarching theories. It is rather that theoretical terms at all levels of explanation simply talk past one another; they are incommensurable and belong to different conceptual worlds. This incommensurability of theoretical terms is not, as Kuhn (1970) might argue, a portent of some "scientific revolution" that might promise an advance or transformation of existing theoretical discourse. On the contrary, theory construction in the biology, psychology, and sociology of aging all simply move in different conceptual worlds, and the logical relationship among these worlds is not at all clear.

Obviously, this tower of Babel is disappointing for those who hope for more embracing and cumulative results from scientific inquiry. But the problem is not likely to disappear with the sheer accumulation of empirical detail. Indeed, the multiplication of data only makes the problem worse: We have no way of making sense of the new information gathered. The problem is rooted in a basic logical difficulty endemic to our understanding of scientific explanation itself. So, for example, even if we accept in principle an idea that psychology or psychobiology must at some level serve a mediating role, and therefore ultimately set the structural conditions for aging as a sociocultural phenomenon, this presumption carries us no further in constructing a unified "theory of aging." These psychological laws might just as well turn out to be simply boundary conditions—necessary but not sufficient conditions—for the operation of other causal laws intelligible in historical or other terms. It is precisely the relationship among theoretical principles, conceptual levels, explanatory terms, and logical presuppositions in gerontology that calls for clarification. What is needed is an elucidation of the "philosophical foundations of gerontology" (McKee, 1982), which might offer a convincing picture of the relationships among the different domains and theoretical levels of explanation.

These difficulties cannot be wished away by any sort of methodological fiat—the aspiration toward positivistic "rigor" evident in many chapters of this present volume, for example. Nor can dogmatic reductionism help us out here. Indeed, any form of biological or psychological reductionism is simply another as-yet-unsupported presupposition—perhaps more accurately, a sophisticated superstition—that begs as many questions as it answers. Still worse, physical reductionism may turn out to be a form of mystification and ideological distortion that veils existing forms of theory and practice, for example, by appearing to justify biological interventions (e.g., behavior-controlling drugs) that leave social causes of age-related deficits unexamined and therefore unchallenged.

What is at stake in these matters is nothing less than the relationship between theory and practice, between what we know, or think we know, and how we act and choose (Habermas, 1974). Social gerontology and theories of aging are not merely matters of distinguishing multiple levels of causality or elucidating domains of discourse. They are ultimately matters involving our understanding of what it can mean to grow old in a world where technological reason seeks to overcome or transform the boundary conditions of human existence itself: birth, old age, death, the entire course of human life (Cole, 1986).

THE ROLE OF THE HUMANITIES

What then can the humanities contribute? In calling attention to the methodological and theoretical pluralism of gerontology, I have been focusing on the logic of the sciences. But what about the logic of the humanities? What are the humanities and what distinctive form of knowledge do they offer? Frankel (as cited by T. Cole, 1987, personal communication) put it this way:

> The humanities are that form of knowledge in which the knower is revealed. All knowledge becomes humanistic when this effect takes place, when we are

asked to contemplate not only the proposition but the proposer, when we hear the human voice behind what is said.

The epistemological stance of the humanities must be distinguished from the methodology of the social sciences (Commission on the Humanities, 1980). Frankel's definition is helpful in calling attention to the self-reflective structure of knowledge in the humanities, and this perspective in turn allows us to define the methodology of the humanities with more precision. The distinctive perspective of the humanities disciplines were summed up by Levi (1970) as the "three C's": Communication (Language and Literature), Continuity (History), and Criticism (Philosophy). Allied humanities disciplines—such as art history, jurisprudence, or comparative religion—can be conceptually related to the three C's described here. Communication, Continuity, and Criticism are three modes of self-reflexiveness that allow us to understand and explain the human world (*Lebenswelt*).

On this definition, humanistic scholarship does not represent some sort of vague or defective version of science but rather a different mode of knowledge directed toward historical continuity, imaginative communication, and the critical appraisal of assumptions and values. The humanities are not simply complementary perspectives on the facts uncovered by the specialized sciences; rather, the humanities also promise an enlarged picture of aging in our common world. History, literature, and philosophy each introduce a distinct perspective on what it means to grow old (Moody, 1987; Vaughan, 1982). The history, literature, and philosophy of aging are those self-reflexive symbolic forms where the knower is revealed, where the experience of time, narrative, and meaning become at once problematic and transparent.

Thus, the humanities evidently have their own contribution to make to gerontology and, ultimately, to theories of aging. These humanities disciplines can contribute to social gerontology in different ways (Klineberg, 1978): (1) they have a heuristic role—serving as a source of new hypotheses for empirical inquiry; (2) they have a critical role—exposing horizons that lie beyond the limits of existing methods and results in the empirical sciences; and finally, (3) humanistic ideas contribute to praxis (action) by offering reflection on intentions and values realized by human agents in particular cultural settings. The heuristic, critical, and practical interest of the humanities arise "outside" the epistemic structure of the empirical sciences. Yet at the same time, these cognitive interests have a potential for transforming the theoretical structure of science, including theories of aging. To argue for that potential, finally, is the purpose of this chapter. Let me turn briefly to the question of the impoverishment of theory construction in social gerontology before taking up the contribution of the humanities in order to indicate how the heuristic, critical, and practical intent of humanistic knowledge can contribute to theories of aging.

THEORIES OF AGING

The paucity of theory in social gerontology is an embarrassment to academic students of human aging. The causes of this state of affairs remain debatable, but the overall result is not. Theory construction in contemporary social gerontology has ranged from "macro" theories, such as modernization theory or disengagement theory, to "micro" theories, such as role theory, exchange theory, or the concept of habituation, which have each enjoyed their fashion. All of these theories aspire to serve as comprehensive ways of unifying current empirical findings about aging. But in practice, these alternative "theories" oscillate between extremes. On the one hand are global ideological constructions (e.g., disengagement vs. activity "theory"), where covert value commitments are presupposed, and on the other hand are applications derived from seminal concepts in neighboring disciplines ("role" in microsociology, "habit" in learning theory), where value commitments are simply ignored.

There is an added difficulty to be seen when we look back several decades at the lack of cumulative progress associated with these theories (Kastenbaum, 1965). Whether framed in global or piecemeal fashion, none of these different "theories" of aging is susceptible to falsification. They offer restatements of ideology or methodology, but not verifiable (or modifiable) theoretical schemata, such as we find, for example, in Keynesian economics or cognitive dissonance theory in psychology. Both of these theories certainly have their weaknesses and their share of criticism, but their fruitfulness in organizing complex data sets and stimulating further investigation is beyond doubt.

It is not easy to say what the solution to this theoretical impoverishment of social gerontology might be, but certain lines are promising. Proust (as cited in De Beauvoir, 1972) wrote that "of all realities, old age is perhaps that of which we retain a purely abstract notion longest in our lives." Proust's comment points toward the need to recover a less abstract understanding of aging itself, an understanding grounded in lived experience. Instead of ignoring covert value commitments in our theories, perhaps the generativity of theory would be greater if we turned our attention back to these values and to the repressed subjectivity of the life-world. Indeed, this very "return of the repressed," the reconnection of theory with practice in a self-reflexive way, could promise a far deeper style of gerontology than we have seen to date. What is called for is a refocusing of attention on the central phenomena of gerontology—on time, development, and senescence—with bold "conjectures" that could revivify theoretical speculation (Popper, 1972). These bold conjectures exhibit an affinity for the "return of grand theory" in the human sciences (Skinner, 1985). But for the purpose of this chapter it is not the "grandeur" of the theories that is important—gerontology has had enough of those. It is rather the way in which theory construction is rooted, first and last, in the lived experience of human agency within a shared social world. This positive direction for humanistic theories of aging has barely begun to be explored.

The time is now ripe for such a new direction because of the widespread philosophical crisis affecting positivistic modes of explanation in the sciences in general. Indeed, the problem of theory construction in social gerontology must be understood against the background of contemporary trends in post-positivist philosophy of science: for example, the acknowledgment of the "theory-laden" content of empirical observation terms in the natural sciences, as Kuhn (1962) among others, has argued. This acknowledgement has led to a new appreciation for the role of models, metaphors, and interpretation in scientific theories. This epistemological shift amounts to a recovery of the suppressed "hermeneutic dimension" of scientific inquiry and has implications for the behavioral sciences and for social gerontology in particular. This hermeneutic dimension, for example, may give encouragement to proponents of qualitative and interpretative methods in aging research (Neugarten, 1984).

Yet this shift in the philosophy of science generates problems of its own, particularly where theory construction is at stake. For example, it is not clear how this "phenomenological turn" toward interpretive social science can actually contribute to advances in theories of aging. How are we to understand the relationship between quantitative and qualitative methodologies, or among data, instruments, and theories? How do we adjudicate between rival interpretations of the world? We seem to be seeing a proliferation of methods and theories without finding any overarching framework that might integrate these differing perspectives. The danger here is that qualitative methods inspired by the humanities could simply result in further fragmentation and could deepen the spreading relativism in our view of social reality. How is it possible to acknowledge the hermeneutic and historical dimensions of theory construction without falling into skepticism or relativism? These questions have been at the center of recent debate in the philosophy of the social sciences (Bernstein, 1983; Haan et al., 1983; Sabia & Wallulis, 1983), and the questions can be elucidated in the perspective of Critical Theory, to which I now turn.

Critical Theory

It was Horkheimer (1972), in a 1937 essay, who made the distinction between "traditional" and "critical" theory. Traditional theory, he argued, corresponds to the unreflective elaboration of the empirical-analytical sciences. Although the natural and the behavioral sciences differ in certain respects, both share common logical rules and ideal principles of explanation that aim at prediction and control of phenomena. Traditional theory, in this view, presents itself as "value free," as Max Weber urged. It presumes that application of knowledge depends on value judgments or interests entirely distinct from knowledge for its own sake (Bubner, 1982).

By contrast, Critical Theory, originating in Marx's critique of political economy, is grounded in values and human interests that would otherwise be concealed under traditional theory (Roderick, 1986). Above all, these values and interests are those of emancipation of human subjects from domination—for example, from the dominating modes of prediction and control characteristic of social technologies in advanced industrial society. This dialectic between human interest and emancipatory knowledge is of central concern in the writings of the contemporary exponent of Critical Theory, Jurgen Habermas (Furth, 1983, 1984).

In *Knowledge and Human Interests* Habermas (1971) examines the ways in which diverse human interests constitute the motivating and defining elements that distinguish various modes of knowledge (Overend, 1978). To each category of knowledge, there corresponds a special mode of linguistic discourse (theory) and a characteristic style of practice. An outline of those cognitive interests (see Table 2-1) will make their relationships clear.

Habermas (1971) distinguishes the empirical-analytic sciences, which have a *technical* interest in prediction and control, from the historical-hermeneutic sciences, which have a *practical* interest in promoting intersubjective understanding. Put differently, the technical interest arises from humankind's interest in dominating nature, whereas the practical interest expresses the need for communication and interaction with fellow human beings in the various enterprises of human society. From an epistemological standpoint, these two domains correspond, roughly, to the natural and behavioral sciences, on the one hand, and the humanities, on the other hand. The first corresponds to causal understanding of events, the second to meanings tied to symbolic forms.

Insofar as the behavioral sciences embody a theoretical aspiration toward prediction and control, then the behavioral sciences—including social gerontology—are no different in their *cognitive interest* from the natural sciences. The fact that social gerontology is concerned with human actions in no way precludes this fundamental orientation toward domination—that is, toward treating human beings as *objects* of prediction and control. By contrast, we

TABLE 2-1. Cognitive Interests

Category	Mode of discourse	Practice
Technical	Empirical-analytic	Work
Practical	Historical-hermeneutic	Interaction
Emancipatory	Critical	Power

Adapted from Habermas (1971).

could imagine a species of gerontology preoccupied with the fundamental problem of interpretation and intersubjective communication. It is, in fact, this second reconstruction of the study of human aging that may be called *hermeneutic* gerontology, and it is in this second category that the humanities can make their greatest contributions to theories of aging.

What has been said so far about Habermas's table of cognitive interests corresponds to a familiar view of the relationship between the sciences and the humanities. Less familiar, and more difficult to define, is the category Habermas describes as the "emancipatory sciences," which have a cognitive interest in human emancipation through critical self-reflection. The key to appreciating emancipatory knowledge is to see how the enhancement of knowledge through technical means need not necessarily lead to greater freedom. Enhanced prediction and control can be used for purposes of domination and tyranny. The history of the Dialectic of Enlightenment is the story of greater domination unfolding under the facade of knowledge and freedom (Horkheimer & Adorno, 1972). In many ways, this very process is an accurate description of the fate of old age in the modern world. We see a progressive erosion of meaning in the pattern of professionalization and welfare state, tied to the rise of scientific gerontology. The achievement of instrumental reason, through biomedical technology, allows us to prolong life, while the distorted communicative structure of contemporary society leads to a gradual loss of the meaning of old age itself.

What Habermas argues is that neither the technical interest nor the practical interest, neither the empirical-analytic sciences nor the hermeneutic perspective of the humanities, alone can lead us to that form of knowledge that is most desired: namely, emancipatory knowledge. Emancipatory knowledge has as its primary interest the aim of empowerment in the practice of freedom. Of course, this goal is very far from what we see in the organization of science and scholarship in social gerontology or other academic disciplines.

What all of this implies for theories of aging is that such theories cannot be constructed with moral indifference toward the practical horizon of their validation and application in human affairs. Put differently, any theory of aging that settles for *less than* a form of emancipatory knowledge runs the risk that knowledge gained, whether technical or hermeneutic, will be used for purposes that lead not to freedom but to new domination, perhaps a domination exercised ever more skillfully by professionals, bureaucrats, or policymakers. In the image of a positivist gerontology divorced from any emancipatory interest, we can see that this present danger is already clear. In the welfare state of advanced industrialized societies, Habermas has pointed to "the colonization of the life-world" visible in the expansion of technical and professional controls over regions of the life-world hitherto left beyond the marketplace or administrative machinery.

Emancipatory Knowledge

The argument offered so far must face up to a serious difficulty in Habermas's version of Critical Theory. The problem is simply that there are few concrete examples of emancipatory knowledge to be found. Emancipatory knowledge as a goal sounds utopian or vacuous, as well as subversive of what "value-free" social science should be. How indeed can gerontology be reconstituted as a critical or emancipatory discourse if we lack any concrete example of where this has so far been achieved? Habermas does offer the examples of Marxism and psychoanalysis as instances of attempts at critical modes of knowledge. But both examples, Habermas himself acknowledges, are inadequate since, in each case, the subsequent development of these doctrines has led them to become new "scientistic" ideologies. Each doctrine has become a new ortho-doxy and even has provided new tools of domination. Failing to achieve either science or freedom, both psychoanalysis and Marxism remain flawed instances of the attempt at critical modes of knowledge.

More disturbingly, how are we to recognize the attainment of the goal of emancipation itself? The act of knowing and the activity of self-criticism must be wedded in some way to a normative foundation in a concept of human nature, whether covertly assumed or overtly defended. At least in the case of theories of moral development, this demand for a continuing mode of self-criticism, self-interpretation, and critical consciousness seems to be a defining characteristic of *emancipation* or *development*.

But this point concerning self-interpretation or the interrogation of "meaning" cannot be pressed too far. In fact, Habermas rejects the purely herme-neutic approach of philosophers like Gadamer or Ricoeur (as cited in Men-delsohn, 1979). On the one hand, Habermas retains the view that there is a fundamental difference between explanations that depend on "meaning" and those that are causal-reductive in their structure. But it seems clear that a critical discourse — for example, a critical gerontology — could not be identified *either* with hermeneutics or with causal-reductive sciences. The difference is that a critical gerontology must contain an *emancipatory ideal*, and we still have no clear account of where that emancipatory ideal is to be found.

Nor is the emancipatory content of critical gerontology to be found in some new "stage theory," such as Erikson's (1963) "Ages of Man" or Kohlberg's (1981) stage theory of moral development, where the highest stage might be thought to consist of "self-actualization," "ego-integrity," or "ego-transcendence." The covert ideology contained in such stage theories has been criticized (Moody, 1986b). These stage theories are, to many people today, attractive ideals, but to the extent that they are separated from some specific mode of *praxis*, they run the risk of becoming merely idealized or sentimental projec-tions of human fulfillment, where the highest stage of consciousness turns out to coincide with the last stage of life. There is no shortage of such positive images of late-life development, but it is important to stress here that the enterprise of a Critical Gerontology does not depend on acceptance of any of them in advance.

What is essential instead is that the *idea* of life-span development, like the ideas of human time and narrative, remains at the center of our attention. We need to uphold their epistemological validity as norms for knowing and norms for acting. Without that "utopian" ideal of development, old age risks becoming a self-fulfilling prophecy of decline, a public burden or a private despair. The delineation of a positive content for meaning and late-life development is a task for the future. In the elaboration of a positive content for emancipatory knowledge, we must envisage a dialectical interplay between critical and scientific discourse. Critical gerontology, or any critical science, must begin by challenging the dichotomy between fact and value, interpretation and explanation. Challenging that dichotomy means refusing to accept any irrevocable gulf between meaning and causality, action and behavior (Giddens, 1976, 1984).

Taken seriously, this demand would revolutionize the academic content of gerontology by introducing ideas from the humanities—literature, philosophy, and history—into a discourse distorted by positivistic models of understanding. Without greater complementarity between the humanities and the sciences, between meanings and causes, emancipatory interests are likely to be eclipsed, and gerontology will serve only as a new tool for dehumanized technique and domination. Yet, important as it is, this principle of complementarity is not enough. It is only a necessary, not sufficient, condition for a critical gerontology.

The further condition is to be found in concrete historical experiences of emancipation—of what it means for the last stage of life to be a period of freedom and fulfillment. Those concrete historical experiences will always have a dialectical character; that is, they will exhibit features of emancipation along with opportunities for new forms of domination and passivity. To understand this point we need think only of the history of the social institution of retirement and pension policies. Were these steps toward freedom or new devices for social control—for example, to remove workers from the labor market (Graebner, 1980)? We can only say that, for better or for worse, the institution of retirement was a distinctive historical achievement of industrial society and the welfare state. Retirement, as a social institution, opens up new historical possibilities, the consequences and contradictions of which are still not entirely foreseen.

In constructing theories of aging with emancipatory intent, the categories of historicity and emancipation cannot be separated. The *ideal* old age is not an uncritical subjective preference but depends on concrete historical possibilities. Historicizing the content of emancipation means looking at concrete lived experience: at the life events and the life chances of particular age cohorts and at the political economy of aging. These structural conditions set the background for individual and collective choices.

However, historicizing has its dangers. If emancipation is entirely relative to history and circumstance, then how are we finally to know that what purports to be emancipation is really that? Must we not have recourse, if only covertly, to some standard, some universal criterion that would allow us to know that a "good age" is possible under specific historical conditions? And without knowledge of those conditions, do we really have a critical standard by which to appraise particular social policies—retirement policies, for example, or lifelong learning, or the distribution of geriatric health care? These questions disclose both a theoretical and practical intent and demand further reflection on the quasi-transcendental idea of *life-span development* as a fundamental category for critical gerontology.

THE LOGIC OF THE HUMANITIES

We are now at a point where we can return to the initial question posed in this discussion, namely, the contribution of the humanities to theories of aging. In Table 2-2, I have summarized the three major humanities disciplines and then exhibited their relationship to other elements, which are explained briefly.

Dialectical Gerontology

The term *dialectic* appears in a wide range of philosophical systems, from Socrates and Plato down through Kant, Hegel, and Marx. In gerontology, it was Riegel (1972, 1975, 1976) who made a major contribution in demonstrating the role of a dialectical approach to the psychology of human development as well as in the history of the behavioral sciences. A still broader understanding of dialectic is apparent from the effort to link together dialectical features of theory, practice, lived experience, and social policy (Gurvitch, 1962; Warren, 1984). A *dialectical gerontology* signifies an approach to the study of human aging that acknowledges the contradictory features of old age and tries to locate those contradictions within a developmental or historical framework. Instead of seeking theories of aging that immediately eliminate contradictions, a dialectical gerontology would highlight contradictions (Wershow, 1981).

It is here that history plays a crucial role, as suggested in Table 2-2. History, the study of human activity over multiple generations, is, finally, the study of human time in its collective dimension. Since Hegel's (1979) *Phenomenology of Mind*, there has been a significant philosophical view that the "logic of temporality" must be a *dialectical* account that somehow acknowledges time as something more than a simple metric or a mere variable. Indeed, if there is

TABLE 2-2. Summary of Major Humanities Disciplines

Humanities discipline	Basic category	Intellectual source	Illustrative problem	Duality
History— continuity	Time	K. Riegel	Age–period– cohort issue	Generation vs. social structure: dialectical gerontology
Literature— communication	Narrative	H. G. Gadamer	Interpretation of qualitative data	Life-world vs. symbolic forms: hermeneutic gerontology
Philosophy— criticism	Development	J. Habermas	Disengagement vs. activity	Fact/value, theory/prac- tice: critical gerontology

one outstanding generalization about the progress of social gerontology over the past forty years, it is the recognition that mere chronological age explains virtually nothing about human aging (Kastenbaum, 1978).

Yet gerontology paradoxically remains, supremely, the science of human time (Reichenbach & Mathern, 1959). We cannot understand *aging* unless we already presuppose a concept of human time (Jaques, 1982). Despite this obvious point, time and temporality, as philosophical questions, are repeated-ly ignored or misunderstood in gerontology. A strange "structuralist tempta-tion" in gerontology has repeatedly led to a theoretical reification of lived time and a neglect of historical time—for example, into a timeless succession of life stages (Erikson, 1963; Levinson, 1978). Even where sophisticated statistical methodology tries to "banish" time, it returns to confound the analysis of data: for example, in the age-period-cohort question much discussed in the last decade (Bengtson, Cutler, Mangen, & Marshall, 1985).

The individual time of chronological age and the collective time of cohort membership remain in contradiction, not only in theory but in the lived experience of successive generations. A task of a dialectical gerontology is to thematize—to make explicit and conscious—the sources of contradictions in lived experience, above all the experience of time, whether historical time or individual time. We can speak of a "dialectical gerontology" precisely where certain logical and methodological problems can no longer be suppressed—for example, in the interpretation of longitudinal research data or in problems of age, period, and cohort. What these overt, methodological debates actually manifest is a deeper duality in the life-world itself—namely, the conflict between successive generations and explanatory structures that purport to be "timeless." The humanities, in particular the study of history, cannot solve this problem in the sense of supplying a missing link that would permit the technical cognitive interest of instrumental reason to achieve its final success by predicting and controlling the structure of the life course through historical time. The very notion of such prediction or control seems fantastic, nor is it what historical understanding tries to achieve in the first place.

What history, as a hermeneutic discipline, can achieve is a degree of insight into the dialectical problem of human time across historical generations, including the paradoxical understanding that, despite history, the future itself remains open. This understanding was never more essential for political praxis than today when cultural pessimism and technological determinism serve to cloud our image of the future and make us believe that outcomes are "inevitable." For critical gerontology, there is a more specific implication for our understanding of the structure of the life course itself and the "social construction" of old age. Today—before our eyes, so to speak—the structure of the life course itself is changing in unforeseeable ways.

To speak of a "dialectical gerontology," then, is simply to acknowledge that today there is no escape from this "historicist" dilemma in the construction of theories of aging. The acknowledgment of an ineluctable factor of temporality leads to a new appreciation for the role of history, not only in theories of aging but in the way that data in social gerontology are construed in the first place. History serves to relativize any timeless "covering-law" generalizations about aging and therefore finally serves to relativize the life course itself (Hempel, 1965).

Hermeneutic Gerontology

What theories of aging require is an explicit acknowledgment of the hermeneutic dimension in their own construction. In fact, contemporary scholarship in the humanities has been stimulated by the movement of hermeneutics, or the theory of interpretation (Ricoeur, 1981; Shapiro & Sica, 1984). This trend has already had important implications for the philosophy of the social sciences (Bauman, 1978; Bernstein, 1983): for example, Gadamer's revival of philosophical hermeneutics raises old questions concerning the relation between explanation and "understanding" (*Verstehen*) (Gadamer, 1975a, 1975b, 1976).

Empirical science exhibits an unavoidable hermeneutical dimension because of the relationship between theory-laden observation statements and the meaning of scientific terms contained in larger theoretical paradigms (Bleicher, 1982; Taylor, 1979). For the social sciences, the situation is made more difficult because there are no "social facts" independent of the prior construction or interpretative meanings. The relationship between observation statements (data) and theoretical terms is what demands explication or interpretation. In periods of what Kuhn (1970) calls "normal" science, questions of interpretation are more or less adequately resolved or taken for granted, so much so that the hermeneutical dimension remains in the background. However, in periods of scientific crisis, when old theories break down, questions of interpretation come to the fore and the hermeneutic problem demands attention.

For social gerontology, as in the social sciences, we face the problem that the social sciences describe a "preinterpreted" world of intersubjective meanings. The abstract language of social science and the ordinary language of daily experience are tied in ways that demand explication or interpretation. To cite an example from the field of gerontology, we can ask the deceptively simple question: What is it that constitutes retirement? How do we know, for example, how many people are retired at any given time or how retirement behavior has changed over time? Answering these questions is not easy because, to some extent, *retirement* is a shared meaning of social events, an interpretation of *why* an individual no longer participates in the paid labor force. One and the same individual may have been laid off or be partially disabled and may then describe him or herself to a survey researcher as "retired," whereas others might describe the individual as "unemployed."

The theoretical question of how to define retirement is not simply an idle inquiry (Kohli, 1984). When it comes to measuring labor force participation of older minority group members, it turns out that this question has crucial policy consequences—for disability insurance, worker retraining programs, health care entitlements, and so on. The failure of researchers to acknowledge the preinterpreted world is no innocent error. The uncritical acceptance of retirement rates as an unambiguous "fact" about the social world becomes a kind of mystification of the lived experience of unemployment and chronic illness, and this mystification has political and ideological consequences.

The point is that, for the social sciences, we find a "double hermeneutic" (Giddens, 1976). The double hermeneutic means that a hermeneutic or interpretive element is found in *both* the relationship of theory and fact and the relationship of meaning and social behavior. But beyond this, for the study of aging, we find a "triple hermeneutic": namely, the realization that aging is *not* something remote from one's own experience of time and selfhood. One is *oneself* caught up in time and aging and therefore cannot deny possessing access (or perhaps distorting bias).

For theories of aging, this triple hermeneutic then must address three distinct forms of interpretation: (1) the interpretation of theory-laden empirical observation terms by theories of aging; (2) the interpretation of prereflective judgments about old age in society—shared meanings that demand deeper scrutiny; and finally, (3) the self-reflexive interpretation of one's own aging, to which an individual has unique access through consciousness of memory, the body, and personal history. All three moments of this triple hermeneutic must come into play in theories of aging, and it is precisely here that the humanities make an indispensable contribution. For example, immense resources for this triple hermeneutic are to be found in analysis of narrative in contemporary literary theory, especially treatments of biography and autobiography.

Earlier I described a heuristic function for the humanities disciplines, and there is a natural tendency to think of literature—poetry, fiction, drama, autobiography—in just this light. Literature is heuristic because it gives us "inspiration" for new ways of thinking about aging and life-span development. This heuristic function for the humanities is sometimes described as the "coffee cup" theory of hermeneutics, where the act of interpretation becomes a mere source of inspiration or insight—insight that could just as easily come from drinking a cup of coffee. In this view, empirical science becomes the final judge and arbiter of knowledge, and so the humanities become, like philosophy in the Middle Ages, the handmaiden to a superior discipline.

There is no question that literature can play a role of this kind, but it is rarely a serious role. Far more significant, I believe, is the revived interest in qualitative data in the social sciences: for example, in interpretive sociology, grounded theory, ethnomethodology, symbolic interactionism, and other varieties of social science where communication through the intersubjective vehicle of language takes the place of behavior in other philosophies of the social science. With this interpretive or phenomenological turn in the study of aging, attention shifts to those narratives or life stories that the subjects themselves use to organize their experience of the life-world (Freeman, 1984; Prado, 1983). This new interest in narrative is certainly to be applauded. In fact, attention to the role of narrative here coincides with a broader revival of interest in the role of narrative as the organizing principle for complex cognitive processes (Bruner, 1986).

Critical Gerontology

Finally, I turn to the ideal of a *critical gerontology*, that is, theories of aging that contain self-reflexive rules for their construction, interpretation, and application to the life-world. We can understand best what critical gerontology is in terms of its opposite: *instrumental gerontology*. Instrumental gerontology, the domain of conventional social science research, acts to reify the status quo and provide new tools to predict and control human behavior. The hegemony of instrumental gerontology also serves to legitimate professional interventions that reinforce a pattern of domination in both theory and practice of the bureaucratic state.

However, this negative moment of critical gerontology as critique of ideology alone is not sufficient. A critical gerontology must also offer a positive ideal of human development: that is, aging as movement toward freedom beyond domination (autonomy, wisdom, transcendence). Without this emancipatory discourse (i.e., an expanded image of aging) we have no means to orient ourselves in struggling against current forms of domination (Kenyon, 1985). An undistorted apprehension of what it means to grow old would include both positive and negative elements, both joy and suffering, as imaginative literature confirms for us. Here again, the humanities offer us a touchstone for the future possibilities of critical gerontology. The humanities supply principles of interpretation to connect the findings of the empirical sciences with the life world. They also provide a framework to appraise both theory and practice and to defend a mode of rationality distinct from instrumental reason. But the fundamental category for a Critical Gerontology remains the ideal of human development itself, and it is to this ideal that I turn in conclusion.

THE IDEA OF HUMAN DEVELOPMENT

If the category of emancipatory knowledge is not to be empty or purely utopian, then some of its features must already be available in the life-world, in our practical experience of what growing old might mean. It is this prereflective standard—call it wisdom, freedom, or self-fulfillment—that serves as a criterion for the construction of theories of aging with an emancipatory intent (Staude, 1981). An emancipatory view of the course of life would be governed by an overall human interest in *development* itself: that is, a progressive and cumulative unfolding of capacities of the human state.

What *counts* as development, of course, is a normative question, never purely empirical. The concept of *development*, after all, like the concept of *disease*, presupposes certain values and meanings. It is not neutral or value-free at all, and to pretend otherwise only mystifies the question at hand. There are, in short, normative presuppositions to the idea of a life course that we encounter in our actual historical experience: institutional structures such as the state, the economy, the educational system, and so on. Human lives enmeshed in these structures encounter unavoidable contradictions.

The positivistic self-understanding of the social sciences, and of social gerontology, has repeatedly obscured these contradictions in favor of a narrowly instrumental picture of human agency and public policy (Dannefer, 1984; Rosenmayr, 1981). In this respect, social gerontology has simply adopted an uncritical picture of development promised by technological reason. In that uncritical picture, *development* means, purely and simply, an expansion of energy or capacity to act. For the modern world, development is understood to be the opposite of aging and finitude. Naturally, this picture presents grave problems for imagining what development in old age could ever mean.

Any interpretation of the self—"I am (or will be) this kind of person, and not that"—constitutes a limit, a refusal of other possible interpretations. The absence of limits is simply the failure of interpretation, the evasion of choice, and so the absence of any possibility of development. Limit and development are correlative ideas. There is never one without the other. It is this idea of development, finally, that constitutes the "hermeneutic circle" of life-span development. Development is what makes emancipation possible, and emancipatory knowledge alone is what makes it possible to enunciate criteria for what will count as adult development in the first place: for example, what counts as "wisdom" or "creativity" or "self-actualization" in the last stage of life.

My argument has been that some such concept of freedom—of emancipatory discourse—must stand at the center of our theories of aging and life-span development. It is this universal human interest that gives rise to the demand for an emancipatory praxis in opposition to those social structures—of work, sex roles, age stereotypes, or the political order—that circumscribe human possibilities and therefore cut short human development, whether in childhood or in the later stages of life.

Opposition to limits is not the same as opposition to social structures of domination—here lies the failure of the antinomian culture of advanced industrialized societies today. Our modern or postmodern culture seems decidedly inhospitable to any concept of meaning or limits that would give a positive content to the last stage of life (Cole, 1985; Gruman, 1978). On the contrary, what is called for is a definition of *valid* limits on the self—for example, limits such as commitment or faith—that make emancipatory knowledge at all possible.

It is striking to note the gap between our public policy—dominated by instrumental reason in the service of the welfare state—and the rich texture of the life-world revealed in humanistic accounts of old age, in historical study, in biography and autobiography, in reflective philosophical thought concerning death and dying. Our current social policies in industry, education, and human services reflect a shrunken and fragmented view of what the human life course might be (Moody, 1987a). But the state and the marketplace do not succeed in altogether "absorbing" the uses of time in old age. Late life can become an opening through which those dominating forces can be seen for what they are.

This is not merely a theoretical point. It is confirmed by the testimony of old people themselves when reflecting on their earlier life experience or their current prospects. Indeed, candid conversation will often reveal that many old people experience their lives precisely as an awakening from domination. Detached, sometimes disillusioned, they may see deeper than younger people who are utterly absorbed by conventional institutions and contemporary values (Kuypers, 1977). It would not be the first time that those who are marginal, those at the periphery, can tell us something important that those at the center are unable to see. Without romanticizing or sentimentalizing old age, it may be possible for some at that stage to recover dimensions of life—

such as contemplation—that the dominant values of modernity have rejected (Moody, 1986b).

THE LIMITS OF INSTRUMENTAL REASON

The limits of our present theories of aging are linked to the limits of dominant views of the life course and the relationship between theory and practice in academic and scientific discourse. Habermas's version of Critical Theory seeks to challenge those dominant forms of rationality that are widespread in advanced industrial society, in theories of aging as in other areas of life.

The basic problem is that limited forms of instrumental-technical rationality have spread beyond technology into domains where they conceal value commitments and hidden modes of domination. We have seen the rise of instrumental-technical rationality, as exemplified in medicine and also in the planning and control systems engendered by the social sciences. The spread of instrumental reason poses special problems for the aged because of the need for autonomy and personal meaning at a period of life when dependency and vulnerability loom larger.

The way out of the crisis will come only with an explicit recognition of the problem of values. Gerontology pretends to be *both* a value-free form of science *and also* a discipline that aims at enhancing the well-being of the elderly. This peculiar mixture of science and advocacy, knowledge and ideology, demands a far-reaching critique (Cole, 1983). The ideological structure of this explanatory system—the "scientific study of aging"—is directly relevant to problems of service delivery and the politics of aging in a period of fiscal crisis of the state. The hegemony of value-free social science, linked to instrumental reason, paves the way for managerial control in new systems of domination.

A Critical Gerontology would entail a critique of this hegemony of instrumental reason within the social scientific structure of gerontology. First, instead of "objectifying" old age, Critical Gerontology would seek to thematize the subjective and interpretive dimensions of human aging. Second, gerontology would be based no longer on technology but on the primacy of praxis. Not "tools" of reason but acts of mutual deliberation and dialogue become the new model. Third, Critical Gerontology would entail new relationships between theory and practice, between the academic world and the world of practitioners. Finally, a Critical Gerontology is an emancipatory enterprise. It would aspire toward liberation from the system of domination in our historical past and from a depreciation of the meaning of old age inculcated by the spirit of modern culture. It would hold out a definition of liberation, of tangible human freedom, freedom grounded not in utopianism (e.g., an "age-irrelevant society") but in the concrete praxis of those who struggle to interpret their own life experience and to create collective conditions for self-development.

CONCLUSION

The humanities are neither nostalgic remnants of a vanished past nor sentimental projections of an imaginary future. Rather, the disciplines of history, literature, and philosophy are best understood as collective human acts of self-interpretation and self-development, symbolic expressions of our enduring human interest in technical, practical, and emancipatory goals. So understood, the humanities represent the self-reflexive voice of aging, the voice we hear when we listen to the speaker along with what is said. The fundamental categories of time, narrative, and development finally represent not separate or discrete categories but successive moments of our own self-consciousness of what it means to grow old—to move through time, to have a personal history, to disclose unsuspected possibilities for self-development in the future. Instead of old age as an "object" of study, the process of aging becomes constitutive of who-I-am at every point in the life course: a being rooted in history but open to my own future as part of an uncompleted narrative whose further unfolding depends on my own actions.

To achieve this understanding does not require the scholarly study of the humanities, no more than the achievement of practical wisdom demands the study of philosophy. Taken by themselves, the humanities disciplines cannot simply be juxtaposed with concepts of social gerontology to achieve a better balance. Serious deformations of self-understanding affect the academic disciplines of the humanities as well as those of the social sciences. Mystification and dehumanized discourse are to be found in the humanities no less than in the social sciences. Without critical reflection on theory and practice, on the relationship between discursive knowledge and lived experience, we will look in vain for the humanities to "humanize" us.

Nonetheless, recent scholarly work in the humanities contains rich implications for gerontology: for example, in autobiography, in social ethics, in the history of the human life course, and the meaning of the stages of life. This body of work can make an indispensable contribution to theories of aging and can play an important and vital role in the social sciences. But, ultimately, the humanities' greatest heuristic and critical contribution to theory construction will require a closer kind of collaboration; not multidisciplinary coexistence but a deeper form of discourse, reminding us of the experience of time and aging in our own lives.

REFERENCES

Alexander, J. (1985). Review essay. Habermas's new critical theory: Its promise and problems. *American Journal of Sociology, 91*(2), 400–425.

Bauman, Z. (1978). *Hermeneutics and social science: Approaches to understanding.* London: Hutchinson.

Bengtson, V. L., Cutler, N. E., Mangen, D. J., & Marshall, V. W. (1985). Generations, cohorts, and relations between age groups. In R. Binstock & E. Shanas (Eds.), *Handbook of aging and the social sciences*. New York: Van Nostrand Reinhold.

Bernstein, R. (1983). *Beyond objectivism and relativism: Science, hermeneutics, and praxis*. Philadelphia: University of Pennsylvania Press.

Bleicher, J. (1982). *The hermeneutic imagination: Outline of a positive critique of scientism and sociology*. London: Methuen.

Bruner, J. (1986). *Actual minds, possible worlds*. Cambridge, MA: Harvard University Press.

Bubner, R. (1982). Habermas's concept of critical theory. In J. Thompson & D. Held (Eds.), *Habermas: Critical debates*. Cambridge, MA: MIT Press.

Cole, T. (1983). The "enlightened" view of aging: Victorian morality in a new key. *Hastings Center Report, 13*(3), 34–40.

Cole, T. (1985). Aging and meaning: Our culture provides no compelling answers. *Generations, 10*(2), 49–52.

Cole, T., & Gadow, S. (Eds.). (1986). *What does it mean to grow old? Views from the humanities*. Durham, NC: Duke University Press.

Commission on the Humanities. (1980). *The humanities in American life*. Berkeley, CA: University of California Press.

Dannefer, D. (1984). Adult development and social theory: A paradigmatic reappraisal. *American Sociological Review, 49*, 100–116.

De Beauvoir, S. (1972). *Coming of age*. New York: Putnam.

Erikson, J. (1963). *Childhood and society*. New York: W. W. Norton.

Freeman, M. (1984). History, narrative and life-span developmental knowledge. *Human Development, 27*, 1–19.

Furth, H. (1983). A developmental perspective on the societal theory of Habermas. *Human Development, 16*, 181–197.

Furth, H. (1984). A developmental interpretation of Habermas' concept of communicative action. *Human Development, 17*, 183–187.

Gadamer, H. G. (1975a). Hermeneutics and social science. *Cultural Hermeneutics, 2*, 307–316.

Gadamer, H. G. (1975b). *Truth and method* (Garrett Barden & John Cumming, Trans.). New York: Seabury Press.

Gadamer, H. G. (1976). *Philosophical hermeneutics* (David E. Linge, Trans.). Berkeley, CA: University of California Press.

Giddens, A. (1976). *New rules of sociological method: A positive critique of interpretive sociologies*. New York: Basic Books.

Giddens, A. (1977). Habermas's critique of hermeneutics. In A. Giddens (Ed.), *Studies in social and political theory*. London: Hutchinson.

Giddens, A. (1984). *The constitution of society: Outline of the theory of structuration*. Berkeley, CA: University of California Press.

Graebner, W. (1980). *A history of retirement: The meanings and function of an American institution, 1885–1978*. New Haven, CT: Yale University Press.

Gruman, G. (1978). Modernization of the life cycle. In S. Spicker, K. Woodward, & B. Van Tassel (Eds.), *Aging and the elderly: Humanistic perspectives on gerontology* (pp. 359–387). Atlantic Highlands, NJ: Humanities Press.

Gurvitch, G. (1962). *Dialectique et Sociologie*. Paris: Flammarion.

Haan, N., et al. (Eds.). (1983). *Social science as moral inquiry*. New York: Columbia University Press.

Habermas, J. (1979). *Communication and the evolution of society* (T. McCarthy, Trans.). Boston: Beacon Press.

Habermas, J. (1971). *Knowledge and human interests* (Jeremy J. Shapiro, Trans.). Boston: Beacon Press.

Hegel, G. W. S. (1979). *Phenomenology of spirit* (A. V. Miller, Trans.). New York: Oxford University Press.

Hempel, C. (1970). *Aspects of scientific explanation*. New York: Free Press.

Horkheimer, M. (1972). Traditional and critical theory. In *Critical theory*, (M. J. O'Connell, Trans.). New York: Herder & Herder.

Horkheimer, M., & Adorno, T. (1972; orig. 1944). *Dialectic of enlightenment*. New York: Herder & Herder.

Jaques, E. (1982). *The form of time*. London: Crane Russak.

Kastenbaum, R. (1965). Theories of human aging: The search for a conceptual framework. *Journal of Social Issues, 21*, 13–37.

Kastenbaum, R. (1978). Gerontology's search for understanding. *The Gerontologist, 18*, 59–63.

Kenyon, G. (1985). *A philosophical analysis of scientific meanings of aging in psychosocial gerontology*. Unpublished doctoral dissertation, University of British Columbia.

Klineberg, S. (1978). The role of the humanities in gerontological research. *The Gerontologist, 18*(6), 574–576.

Kohlberg, L. (1981). *Essays in moral development*. New York: Harper & Row.

Kohli, M. (1984). Social organization and the subjective construction of the life course. In A. B. Sorensen, et al., *Human development: Interdisciplinary perspectives*. Hillsdale, NJ: Erlbaum.

Kuhn, T. S. (1970). *The structure of scientific revolutions*. Chicago: University of Chicago Press.

Kuypers, J. (1977, Fall). Aging: Potentials of personal liberation. *Humanities*.

Levi, A. W. (1970). *The humanities today*. Bloomington, IN: University of Indiana Press.

Levinson, D. (1978). *The seasons of a man's life*. New York: Knopf.

McCarthy, T. (1978). *The critical theory of Jurgen Habermas*. Cambridge, MA: MIT Press.

McKee, P. L. (1982). *Philosophical foundations of gerontology*. New York: Human Sciences Press.

Mendelsohn, J. (1979). The Habermas–Gadamer debate. *New German Critique, 18*, 44–73.

Moody, H. R. (1986). The meaning of life and the meaning of old age. In T. Cole & S. Gadow (Eds.), *What does it mean to grow old? Views of the humanities*. Durham, NC: Duke University Press.

Moody, H. R. (1988). *The abundance of life: Human development policies for an aging society*. New York: Columbia University Press.

Neugarten, B. (1984). Interpretive social science and research on aging. In A. Rossi (Ed.), *Gender and the life course*. Chicago: Aldine.

Overend, T. (1978). Enquiry and ideology: Habermas' trichotomous conception of science. *Philosophy of the Social Sciences, 8*, 1–13.

Philibert, M. (1968). *L'Echelle des ages*. Paris: Le Seuil.

Popper, K. R. (1972). *Conjectures and refutations: The growth of scientific knowledge* (4th ed.). London: Routledge & Kegan Paul.

Prado, C. G. (1983). Aging and narrative. *International Journal of Applied Philosophy, 1*, 1–14.

Reichenbach, M., & Mathern, A. (1959). The place of time and aging in the natural sciences and scientific philosophy. In J. Birren (Ed.), *Handbook of aging and the individual: Psychological and biological aspects*. Chicago: University of Chicago Press.

Ricoeur, P. (1981). Hermeneutics and the critique of ideology. In J. Thompson (Ed.), *Hermeneutics and the human sciences* (pp. 63–100). Cambridge: Cambridge University Press.

Riegel, K. F. (1972). Time and change in the development of the individual and society. In H. W. Reese (Ed.), *Advances in child development and behavior*. New York: Academic Press.

Riegel, K. F. (1975). Toward a dialectical theory of development. *Human Development, 18*, 50–64.

Riegel, K. F. (1976). The dialectics of human development. *American Psychologist, 31*, 689–700.

Roderick, R. (1986). *Habermas and the possibility of critical theory*. New York: St. Martin's Press.

Rosenmayr, L. (1981). Objective and subjective perspectives of life span research. *Aging and Society, 1*, 1.

Sabia, D. R., & Wallulis, J. (Eds.). (1983). *Changing social science: Critical theory and other critical perspectives*. Albany, NY: SUNY Press.

Shapiro, G., & Sica, A. (Eds.). (1984). *Hermeneutics*. Amherst, MA: University of Massachusetts Press.

Skinner, Q. (1985). *The return of grand theory in the human sciences*. Cambridge: Cambridge University Press.

Spicker, S., Woodward, K., & Van Tassel, B. (1978). *Aging and the elderly: Humanistic perspectives on gerontology*. Atlantic Highlands, NJ: Humanities Press.

Staude, J. R. (1981). *Wisdom and age*. Berkeley, CA: Ross Books.

Taylor, C. (1979). Interpretation and the sciences of man. In R. Rabinow & W. Sullivan (Eds.), *Interpretation in the social sciences*. New York: Springer Publishing Co.

Van Tassel, D. (Ed.) (1979). *Aging, death and the completion of being*. Philadelphia: University of Pennsylvania Press.

Vaughan, C. E. (1982, March). Some contributions which humanists can make to social gerontology. *Convergence in Aging*, pp. 127–133.

Warren, S. (1984). *The emergence of dialectical theory: Philosophy and political inquiry*. Chicago: University of Chicago Press.

Wershow, H. J. (1981). *Controversial issues in gerontology*. New York: Springer Publishing Co.

3

The Impact of Research Methodology on Theory Building in the Developmental Sciences*

K. Warner Schaie

It is well recognized that theory building in science will often proceed inductively by observations of empirical phenomena that suggest sufficiently orderly patterns or sequences. These then permit construction of a schematic that allows predictions regarding the patterns that should be found in other related phenomena or data as yet unobserved. Inductive theories are essentially efforts to organize empirical observations in such a way that possibly isolated phenomena can be assigned to a more comprehensive supraordinate and overarching schema. Such schemas then allow a better understanding of each of the singular and infraordinate observations. By contrast, a deductively adduced theory begins with the elucidation of central assumptions and corollaries. The theory is then tested by investigating data sets that might fit the a priori theoretical propositions.

Many developmentalists, moreover, subscribe to a dialectic view of scientific inquiry. This view specifies the dynamic interplay of empirically derived inductive models, which are then expanded or differentiated deductively and

*Preparation of this chapter was supported in part by research grant AG-04770 from the National Institute on Aging.

applied to new data sets. Revised models are then once again generated in an inductive fashion. An implicit assumption of this process is the notion that the dialectic interplay is informed primarily by substantive empirical observations and the search for data sets that could provide substantive tests of theory (cf. Riegel, 1976).

The purpose of this chapter is to explore how theory building in the developmental sciences is informed and impacted by advances in research methodology (cf. Baltes & Willis, 1977). I will begin this exploration with some brief remarks on how methodological innovation leads to different views of extant data bases and the subsequent revision of theoretical models and developmental theory. To provide concrete illustration of this process I will then exercise the reader through two rather different examples illustrating the impact of methodology upon theory construction and theory testing. My first example involves primarily the impact of research-design issues related to the age-period-cohort problem upon the formulation of models for the study of development. The second example considers how the availability of a new method of analysis, confirmatory factor analysis, has impacted theorizing in work on adult development.

METHODOLOGICAL INNOVATION AND THEORY CONSTRUCTION

Important recent innovations in research methodology in the developmental sciences have been essentially of three varieties: advances in (1) instrumentation, (2) research design, and (3) techniques of analysis. The first involves the level of instrumentation and sophistication of measurement devices or scales. For example, introduction of computer-assisted tomography and direct measurements of blood flow have led to the obsolescence of earlier indirect approaches to the assessment of the integrity of cortical structures. Given the availability of these methods, it becomes increasingly implausible to formulate theories of neuropsychological aging that make assumptions about neural structures that can now be examined noninvasively. Likewise, moving from a strictly descriptive electroencephalographic description of the resting brain to an analysis of evoked potentials must lead to a paradigmatic shift in conceptualizing the role of the cortex and its structures as they interact with an active environment.

Advances in instrumentation may also involve a shift from mere categorical description of the presence or absence of a phenomenon to the development of scales that have ordinal or interval properties. An advance of this kind was represented by the realization that psychological scales could be developed for subjective properties, as evidenced, for example, by the method of comparative judgment and the more modern techniques of multidimensional scaling (Cliff,

1982). Given the scalability of subjective phenomena, it then becomes possible to specify theories that in addition to directly observed antecedents may include mediator variables based upon experiential evidence.

A second class of methodological innovations that may impact both theory building and the manner in which theory is tested concerns the specification of novel schemas for collecting data and for evaluating the validity of theoretical constructs. For example, specifications for determining the internal and external validity of experiments and quasi-experiments (Campbell & Stanley, 1963; Cook & Campbell, 1979) and the application of these concepts to developmental studies (Schaie, 1977, 1978) require the theorist to explicate the additional corollaries needed for existent theories to denote the side conditions under which propositions derived from theory can be expected to hold. Methodological discussions that specify alternate models for the structuring of developmental data collections (cf. Schaie, 1965), moreover, will impact theory by specifying the required properties of the data set to be explained by the theory or to be employed for testing the theory.

Methodological innovations in methods of analysis, finally, will lead to the possibility of performing tests of theory that were previously not feasible (e.g., the estimation of complex causal models à la Jöreskog, 1979), as well as to major paradigmatic shifts. An example of the latter impact would be the shift from theories that relate directly observable variables to theories that account relationships among latent (unobserved) variables. This shift occurred as a consequence of the general acceptance of confirmatory factor analysis and canonical correlation approaches as state-of-the-art techniques in the behavioral and social sciences.

In each of the above instances, the introduction of methodological advances has at a minimum permitted the testing of theoretical propositions that were previously not amenable to empirical study. Beyond that, however, the discovery of constraints identified by the methodological information requires expansion of theoretical formulations, and new models must be derived that can explain and include the attributes of the phenomena that methodological innovations have uncovered. There probably is no uniform path in which this intersection of methodological innovation and modification of theoretical thinking operates in every instance. To obtain a better understanding, it seems necessary then to examine some relatively detailed examples. These will be provided in the remaining sections of this chapter.

RESEARCH DESIGN AND THEORY: THE CASE OF THE AGE-COHORT-PERIOD PROBLEM

One of the more prominent examples of the impact of research methodology on theory formation and testing in studies of adult development has been the controversy engendered by the debate about appropriate methodologies involved in the study of change over time, commonly referred to as the age-cohort-period problem (cf. Mason, Mason, Winsborough, & Poole, 1973; Palmore, 1978; Ryder, 1965; Schaie, 1965, 1973, 1977, 1984, 1986). It presents a ready illustration of the dialectic interaction between puzzling data sets, the examination of the appropriateness of standard research design, and the specification of alternate designs leading to the collection of new data sets that would fit the new paradigms. Of equal importance, for our present purposes, is the impact that the resulting methodological innovations have had with respect to theories of how adult aging might best be conceptualized.

Some Historical Context

The work to be referred to here began with the realization that data on the adult development of mental abilities showed wide discrepancies between cross-sectional and longitudinal data collected on the same subject population over a wide age range. In particular, it became evident that for some dependent variables substantial age differences obtained in cross-sectional studies could not be replicated in the longitudinal data, while for other dependent variables longitudinal age changes reflected more profound decrement than was shown in the comparable cross-sectional age difference patterns (Schaie & Strother, 1968).

In an inductive effort to explain these discrepancies a general model for the study of developmental change was developed that explicated the relationship between the cross-sectional and longitudinal methods (Schaie, 1965).[1] From this model it became possible to show that cross-sectional data involve the description of age differences at a single point in time; that they represented a separate samples design à la Campbell and Stanley (1963). Designs of this type suffer from the problem that maturational change (age) is confounded with cohort acting as a selection factor (Schaie, 1984). Longitudinal data, by contrast, involve a time series assessing the same individuals at two or more points in time. Here maturational change (age) is confounded with historical (secular) trends. Specification of the general model in a deductive manner then allowed the specification of a third approach to the collection of developmental data, for which the term "time-lag" was coined (see also Palmore, 1978). This latter approach involves the comparison of two samples at the same chronological age but at different calendar times, as would be the case, for example, in the comparison of SAT scores for successive classes of high school graduates. In this design, cohort differences are confounded with historical trends. Consideration was then given to the possibility of deducing more complex designs, termed "sequential methods," that proposed to permit estimates of the magnitude of specific components of developmental change by controlling for the confounds mentioned above (Schaie, 1965).

The sequential designs were applied to empirical data sets obtained as part of the Seattle Longitudinal Study (Schaie, 1983). From these applications it soon became apparent that there are specific patterns of data acquisition that lend themselves most readily to optimal utilization of the sequential analysis strategies (Schaie & Willis, 1986a). It also became apparent that different sequential designs are appropriate for different developmental questions (Schaie, 1973) and that there is a need to specify design complications that allow for the control of some of the validity threats specified by Campbell and Stanley (1963). Design variations were therefore explicated that permit controls for reactivity, practice, and experimental mortality (Schaie, 1977).

Implications for Theory Building

Three different aspects of the design considerations as they have implications for theory building will now be considered. First, we will indicate how the manner in which different designs confound sources of individual-difference variances may influence theories about the normative course of aging. Second, implications for the structuring of theory-guided data collection will be noted; and third, we will discuss implications for the explanation of phenomena involving change over time and age.

Implications for Aging Theories

Many theories of aging, whether involving wear and tear, cumulations of waste products, or successive loss of neurons, implicitly or explicitly include the assumption of irreversible decrement. The design specifications resulting from the general developmental model, however, clearly indicate that in behavioral data irreversible decrement would represent only one of a number of observable patterns of aging. The plausibility of the irreversible decrement model, like that of any other model, can be tested only under certain conditions; a multicohort longitudinal study would be needed to protect against the possibility that adverse historical effects could either inflate or suppress maturationally determined change. As part of the specifications of the theoretical model, it would therefore seem necessary to indicate under what conditions the predicted age effects could validly be observed (cf. Baltes, Cornelius, & Nesselroade, 1979).

Consideration of the design confounds involving developmental data suggests that alternative models of aging should be considered and tested. For example, the recognition that positive secular trends may indeed suppress observable aging effects over some portion of the life span would lead us to give more serious considerations to models that posit stability across most of adulthood and involve decrement with compensation, positive age trends, or even recursive or cyclical phenomena (cf. Schaie, 1973).

The availability of designs that allow the modeling of theories that imbed multidimensional forms of the aging process also can be fruitful in extending existing theoretical systems into considerations of adulthood and aging. I have done so, for example, in proposing an outline for a stage theory of cognitive aging that is essentially an extension of Piagetian thinking (cf. Schaie, 1977/ 1978). The essential basis of this theorizing was the design-guided data acquisition that showed the need to posit life stages representing growth, stability, and decremental change for different cognitive traits. In another extension, I was able to show how developmental designs introduced in aging studies might be useful in disaggregating environmental and genetic factors that influence development (Schaie, 1975).

In examining the contributions of aging research methodology it is important to distinguish between models that serve to help interpret the results of data acquisitions from models that explicitly specify how data should be acquired (cf. Schaie & Baltes, 1975). This is obviously the distinction between explanation and description to which we will next turn.

Implications for Models of Data Collection

If alternative models of aging are to be tested, it becomes necessary to embed theory into data-acquisition plans. Given the confounds described above, few theory-based questions are likely to be answerable by studying a single cross-sectional data set or even a single sample followed longitudinally over time. A logical consequence then is to conceptualize data-collection plans so that extensions of the initial acquisition can be suitably added. This involves data acquisitions that are structured as cross-sectional or longitudinal sequences (cf. Baltes, 1968; Schaie & Baltes, 1975).

One important derivative from the theoretical analysis of the general developmental model has been the specification of recommendations for an optimal data-collection approach that permits flexible application of sequential data-analysis strategies, as well as the provision of controls to protect against major threats to the internal validity of developmental studies. Noting the fact that all longitudinal studies must begin somewhere with a single first-measurement occasion, I have long been convinced that it is always prudent to commence with an age-comparative cross-sectional design. However, in those instances where such a design cannot answer the questions of interest, it would prove reasonable to collect additional data across time.

A hypothetical data collection of this kind, which I have previously identified as the "most efficient design," requires the identification of a population frame that provides a reasonable representation of the full range of dependent variables to be studied (Schaie, 1965; Schaie & Willis, 1986a). Optimally, the population frame should be a natural one, such as a school system, a health plan, a broadly based membership organization, or the like. If the population frame is reasonably large, it is then possible to assume that members leaving the population will on average be replaced by other members with similar characteristics (sampling with replacement). An age range of interest is defined at Time 1 and is sampled randomly at intervals that are optimally identical with the time chosen to elapse between successive times of measurement. At Time 2, previous participants are retrieved and restudied, providing short-term longitudinal studies of as many cohorts as there were age intervals at Time 1. At the same time, a new random sample is drawn from the population frame over the same age intervals as in the Time 1 sampling, with one additional sample at the age level currently attained by the oldest subsample assessed at Time 1. The whole process can be repeated again and again with retesting of old subjects (adding to the longitudinal data) and initial testing of new samples (adding to the cross-sectional data). Three assessment points provide maximum design benefits, although one or two additional measurement points allow additional design refinement.

The second data collection converts the original cross-sectional study into a series of C (number of cohorts studied at T_1) longitudinal studies, and the additional cross-section provides a cross-sectional sequence over two occasions. A series of C time-lag comparisons is also available. In addition, it is now possible to examine the repeated measurement data as a cohort × time matrix allowing cross-sequential analyses. The cross-sectional sequence can be further examined as an age × time matrix (time-sequential strategy) or as an independent measures cohort × time matrix (cross-sequential strategy). A cross-sectional experimental mortality analysis can be done by comparing T_1 data for those individuals who were successfully reexamined and those who were not retrieved at T_2 (cf. Costa et al., 1987, for a recent application of this design).

The third data collection, in addition to replicating longitudinal findings upon the samples first tested at T_2, permits the analysis of age × cohort data matrices for $C - 1$ data sets for both repeated measurements on the same subjects or independent samples from the cross-sectional sequence. In addition, age × time and cohort × time matrices can be analyzed for a $3 \times C$ data matrix. Experimental mortality analyses, classifying dropout to occur after both the first and second occasion, can now be conducted, using either an age × time × dropout model or a cohort × time × dropout model. Alternatively, it is possible to estimate effects of practice for either an age × time × practice level design or a cohort × time × practice level design (cf. Schaie & Parham, 1974).

All of the sequential paradigms can be estimated by three measurement occasions, but there are some additional options available if further extensions of the data collection are possible. A fourth measurement occasion permits three replications of longitudinal data over one time segment, two replications over two time segments, and an estimate of longitudinal change over three time segments. The study of experimental mortality data can then be extended to an age × cohort × dropout model, and it would be possible to cross experimental mortality and practice effects within an age × time × practice × dropout paradigm or a cohort × time × practice × dropout paradigm. A fifth measurement occasion, finally, allows estimating an age × cohort × practice × dropout model, in addition to allowing four replications of longitudinal data over one time segment, three replications over two time segments, two replications over three time segments, and an estimate of change over four time segments (cf. Schaie, 1977).

Implications for the Study of Age and Time

More recent analyses of the age-cohort-period problem have also provided a better understanding of what needs to be done if the dependency of chronological age upon calendar time is to be broken in a meaningful manner. Models that contain parameters, one of which is wholly determined by the others, are well known in science (e.g., the attributes of volume, pressure, and temperature in physics). Just as in the case of confounded physical parameters, there are many reasons why one would want to examine the relative contributions of any of the three possible sets of two developmental parameters. The recent literature on the analysis of sequential data matrices, moreover, would finesse the problem of invalid parametric assumptions by promoting regression models that estimate simultaneously the effects of age, period, and cohort under an additivity assumption that allows for no interaction among the factors (e.g., Buss, 1979/1980; George, Siegler, & Okun, 1981; Horn & McArdle, 1980; Mason et al., 1973; Winsborough, Duncan, & Read, 1983). Regression models for the study of sequential data sets do represent a step forward in the modeling of average developmental functions by employing sophisticated applications of the general linear model. They are prone to errors of inference, nevertheless, whenever the assumption of additivity, or other parametric assumptions needed to identify the model, are violated (Glenn, 1976, 1981). None of these efforts, however, satisfied the original objective of providing unambiguous estimates of the variance accounted for by each of the individual components of developmental change. This observation leads to the conclusion that there is no purely statistical solution (Schaie & Hertzog, 1982).

An alternative approach may be suggested, however, that can reorient our thinking and offer a possible way out of what has become a methodological impasse. The concern with methodologies designed to separate age, cohort, and period effects arose in essence from our preoccupation with the role of age as the independent variable of prime interest to students of development (Featherman, 1985; Slife, 1981). It can be shown, however, that cohort and period may have more interesting explanatory properties than age. This is done by conceptually separating cohort effects and historical time from calendar time. *Cohort* then becomes a selection variable (Nesselroade, 1983) that characterizes the common point of entry for a group of individuals into a given environment, and *period* becomes a measure of event density (for further elaboration see Schaie, 1984, 1986). Similarly, *chronological age* is reconceptualized as a functional age dimension. Given such reconceptualizations it is then possible to reformulate the general developmental model, utilizing indicators that have been freed from the calendar restrictions that have thus far been accepted as virtually immutable. In this approach, chronological age, or other age functions related to calendar time, rather than serving as explanatory concepts, emerge as useful scalers that measure the amount of time elapsed within the lives of individuals, over which developmental phenomena have occurred. The dependencies implicit in the age-cohort model, moreover, can be shown to have been resolved, and all three effects can be directly estimated, whenever one of the dimensions is redefined in terms other than calendar time.[2]

METHODOLOGICAL INNOVATIONS THAT INFORM THEORY: THE CASE OF CONFIRMATORY FACTOR ANALYSIS

Some Historical Context

Most direct observations conducted by psychologists are of interest only to the extent that such observations represent reliably measured markers of latent (unobserved) psychological constructs. Theory-guided research requires the specification of the psychological constructs of interest, as well as the observations that will be used to estimate the constructs. Notable examples of theoretical models (inductively derived) that specify the relationship between latent constructs and observable measures are the structure of human ability models developed by Thurstone (1938) and by Guilford (1967).

More early concerns in the study of aging were related to the estimation of development as a function of change in performance level on directly observable measures (cf. Dixon, Kramer, & Baltes, 1985). More recent work has extended these concerns to the comparison of structure (i.e., the regression of observables upon latent constructs) across different age groups and within cohorts over time (Cunningham, 1980, 1981; Cunningham & Birren, 1980; Hertzog & Schaie, 1986; Schaie & Hertzog, 1985, 1986; Schaie, Willis, Hertzog, & Schulenberg, 1987). This work was made possible as a direct consequence of the methodological developments in restricted factor analysis most notably represented by the work of K. G. Jöreskog and his associates. Jöreskog (1971) and other methodologists such as Bock and Bargmann (1966) and Bentler (1980) demonstrated that hypotheses about the relationships among latent constructs that underlie empirically observed variables can be formulated as structural models. They furthermore showed that maximum-likelihood methods can be used to test the plausibility of such structural models and to estimate the parameters of the linear model. Further extensions of this work allow the testing of alternative, hierarchically nested models as well as contrast the fit of empirical data to a model of theoretical interest with that attained for its falsification.

The original objective of confirmatory factor analysis was to permit the fitting of data to specific measurement models depicting the relationship between latent constructs and observed variables. It soon became apparent, however, that confirmatory factor analysis could also be used to test the equivalence of factor structure across and within groups (Jöreskog, 1979). In addition to the estimation of measurement models, it was also shown that covariance structures representing the relationships between two or more sets of latent constructs could be formulated as structural models.

Implications for Theory Building

An important role of confirmatory factor analysis in theory-guided research, and one that requires attention by those who do cross-sectional or longitudinal work, is the applicability of structural equation models to the demonstration of measurement equivalence (Hertzog, 1986; Schaie & Hertzog, 1985). Structural equation models may also be of particular utility in aging studies because the unidirectionality of time permits sounder guides for the specification of causal paths than is possible in studies using single observation points only. Longitudinal factor analysis may be a particularly useful approach to the modeling of individual differences in intraindividual change, the central focus of any individual-differences approach to aging (cf. Hertzog & Schaie, 1986; Jöreskog, 1979; Jöreskog & Sörbom, 1977). Finally, confirmatory factor analysis turns out to be the method of choice to test the stability of latent constructs under conditions of serendipitous or planned interventions in the aging process (cf. Schaie & Willis, 1986b).

Equivalence of Psychological Constructs Across Time

Utilization of the same questionnaire or test apparatus does not guarantee measurement equivalence over time or different subject populations. Indeed, in the developmental sciences the broad dilemma must be faced that no two individuals, or groups of individuals, have identical characteristics at the same point in time, nor does a group of individuals retain identical characteristics over different points in time. Two fundamentally different aspects are at issue. The first includes the traditional problem of reliability of measures across occasion and regression to the mean when using fallible measures (cf. Nesselroade, Stigler, & Baltes, 1980). The second issue concerns the fact that measurement equivalence would not be guaranteed, even if only perfectly reliable measures were used, because of systematic but nonuniform changes occurring among individuals over time.

In cross-sectional studies it is legitimate to ask whether a task that may be a good estimate of one construct in young adulthood remains so in late life or if it in fact becomes a measure of some other construct. What must be demonstrated then is the invariance of factor structure across multiple groups or subpopulations (cf. Alwin & Jackson, 1981). Similar issues occur when samples are followed longitudinally. Here, of course, we are concerned with demonstrating factorial invariance for the same individuals measured longitudinally. Structural equation analysis seems to be the approach of choice to assess measurement equivalence issues involving multiple groups and occasions (cf. Rock, Werts, & Flaugher, 1978; Schaie & Hertzog, 1985).

Availability of explicit statistical models for testing construct equivalence has profound effects for theory building and testing in aging research. For example, any discussion of a model that argues for the successive differentiation and dedifferentiation of human abilities (cf. Reinert, 1970) must not only specify the constructs that are involved in such a process but also must specify hypotheses on the manner in which the constructs may be represented by different abilities (or the same abilities weighted differentially) at different life stages. The issue of equivalence of constructs is also likely to impact future work in experimental gerontology. The experimental literature on age differences (cf. Salthouse, 1982) is largely an account of manipulations of single observable measures in the laboratory context. In order for such data to become meaningful in understanding age-related behavior in real-life contexts, it will certainly be necessary to formulate more complex structural models and to attempt manipulations at the latent-variable level. Recent discussions of the role of experience (Salthouse, 1987) and the relationship between cognition and everyday behaviors (Willis, 1985; Willis & Schaie, 1986) clearly indicate that methodological advances are beginning to transform our behavior in theory building and theory testing.

The Structuring of Causal Models in Aging Research

Age-comparative experimental research can at best test whether a given manipulation has a differential effect on samples of different age composition. If the age-by-treatment interaction is significant, if the main effect for age favors the younger group, and if the treatment is more effective for the older group, it may then be argued that the manipulation indeed accounts for the age difference. The investigation of structural causal models involving longitudinal data, by contrast, directly addresses the question of whether particular antecedent conditions that may represent multiple levels of causation significantly impact consequent behavior. In this approach it is possible to model correlations observed across time as indications of the direct influence of one latent variable upon another, as an indirect influence mediated through other variables, or as a causally spurious correlation (cf. Schaie & Hertzog, 1985).

Whenever a theoretical model can be represented as a path diagram that indicates the direction of causal influences, it then becomes possible to test variations of that model which allow for different mediators, make more or less stringent assumptions, or represent falsifications à la Popper. Causal models have been used in aging research to study the relationships among environmental influences, health status, and cognitive change, and in particular to evaluate the validity of the differentiation-dedifferentiation hypothesis (cf. Gilewski, 1982; Hertzog & Schaie, 1986; Stone, 1981).

Equivalence of Constructs in Age Simulation or Intervention Models

Theory construction designed to model the aging process frequently involves making assumptions about unobserved change processes (cf. Baltes & Nesselroade, 1973). To provide a reasonably coherent theoretical proposition it may often be necessary to assume age changes at the latent-construct level that have not reached levels critical enough to lead to change in observed behaviors. Likewise, changes in one behavioral marker of a major theoretical construct may well compensated for by another, and it consequently becomes reasonable to specify behavioral stability at the construct level, albeit requiring change at the observable level. Again confirmatory factor analysis has provided us with the necessary tools to provide explicit formulation of the theoretical model in quantitative terms that allow tests of the model by examining relevant empirical data bases (cf. Hertzog & Schaie, 1986; Schaie & Hertzog, 1985).

Confirmatory factor analysis methods also make it possible to formulate and test theoretical propositions about construct equivalence in intervention studies that involve multivariate effect models (cf. Schaie & Willis, 1986b). Much of the controversy regarding reversal of age decrement, whether by serendipitous environmental changes or by planned intervention, is concerned with the question of whether the intervention might result in changing the construct that is to be modified. For example, it has been argued that certain training paradigms might change the nature of fluid abilities to crystallized abilities (Donaldson, 1981). Any research design that incorporates both observed and latent constructs, of course, must be theory-guided (cf. Baltes & Willis, 1982). That is, the observable latent-construct relationship must arise from a theoretical model of the variable structure. It is then possible, however, to express such theoretical models by confirmatory factor analysis paradigms and to derive additional hypotheses that would test certain corollaries which must follow if latent constructs remain stable across interventions or are indeed perturbed by the training effort. Specifically, it is possible to determine empirically whether structural change has been caused by intervention. The exact nature of such change, if any, can be tested for further by imposing suitable constraints regarding the structural equivalence of experimental and control groups prior and subsequent to intervention (cf. Schaie et al., 1987). Conclusions drawn from such studies, once again, will inform us on the plausibility of theoretical formulations regarding the aging process and can guide future theory building.

SOME CONCLUDING THOUGHTS

The purpose of this chapter has been to examine a number of ways in which developments in research methodology impact theory building in the aging-research community. Methodological innovations can require major changes in the way in which theories are tested, or can demand the addition of new corollaries and boundary conditions to retain the viability of existent theories. Other methodological innovations can directly produce paradigm shifts either by permitting the direct investigation of phenomena that were not previously specifiable by a theoretical model or by providing methods that allow investigation at different levels of conceptual specification.

There does not seem to be a single model, however, that would clearly specify how shifts in research methodology lead to modification of theory. Nevertheless, it is not difficult to provide substantive examples where shifts in methods have impacted theory. Such links between methodology and theory can be seen most clearly in cases where investigators have been forced to abandon previous methods of measuring, designing, or analyzing data in favor of conceptually superior innovations. We therefore proceeded to examine two distinct series of methodological developments that have had particular impact upon the thinking of gerontological researchers: the age-period-cohort model in research design, and confirmatory factor analysis in model testing.

The most immediate effect of methodological developments upon theory is the likely increase in effective ways of expressing theoretical thinking in explicitly testable terms. Theories of aging, in the past at least, have frequently not been well articulated, have lacked full specification of assumptions and corollaries, and thus have had little impact in guiding research. Methodological advances introduced via the wide acceptance of the age-cohort-period model, for example, have required the incorporation of formal specifications of assumptions regarding internal and external validity in many research plans. Explicit operationalization of theoretical models, moreover, including their measurement assumptions, become necessary when methodologies such as confirmatory factor analysis or linear structural analysis are utilized. Finally, introduction of new methodologies lead to paradigm shifts, whether by moving from theoretical models relating observables to systems specifying the relationship among constructs, or by introducing new constructs such as cohort or functional age. In conclusion, I would like to suggest that theory building that influences and guides the research enterprise will inevitably follow upon the incorporation of sound methodological innovation in any science. It is hoped that the examples provided in this chapter demonstrate the validity of this argument for theory development in the field of human aging.

NOTES

[1]Surfacing of these issues certainly represented the *zeitgeist*, as concurrent and quite independent discussions may be found in the sociological literature by Ryder (1965).

[2]Empirical examples of data sets that would allow direct estimation of age, cohort, and period effects, given the proposed reformulation of the general developmental model, are provided in Schaie (1986).

REFERENCES

Alwin, D. F., & Jackson, D. J. (1981). Applications of simultaneous factor analysis to issues of factorial invariance. In D. J. Jackson & E. F. Borgatta (Eds.), *Factor analysis and measurement* (pp. 249–278). London: Sage.

Baltes, P. B. (1968). Longitudinal and cross-sectional sequences in the study of age and generation effects. *Human Development, 11*, 145–171.

Baltes, P. B., Cornelius, S. W., & Nesselroade, J. R. (1979). Cohort effects in developmental psychology. In J. R. Nesselroade & P. B. Baltes (Eds.), *Longitudinal research in the study of behavior and development* (pp. 61–87). New York: Academic Press.

Baltes, P. B., & Nesselroade, J. R. (1973). The developmental analysis of individual differences on multiple measures. In J. R. Nesselroade & H. W. Reese (Eds.), *Lifespan developmental psychology: Methodological issues* (pp. 219–252). New York: Academic Press.

Baltes, P. B., & Willis S. L. (1977). Toward psychological theories of aging and development. In J. E. Birren & K. W. Schaie (Eds.), *Handbook of the psychology of aging* (pp. 128–154). New York: Van Nostrand Reinhold.

Baltes, P. B., & Willis, S. L. (1982). Enhancement (plasticity) of intellectual functioning in old age: Penn State's Adult Development and Enrichment Project (ADEPT). In F. I. M. Craik & S. E. Trehub (Eds.), *Aging and cognitive processes* (pp. 353–389). New York: Plenum Press.

Bentler, P. M. (1980). Multivariate analysis with latent variables: Causal modeling. *Annual Review of Psychology, 31*, 332–456.

Bock, R. D., & Bargmann, R. E. (1966). Analyses of covariance structure. *Psychometrika, 31*, 507–534.

Buss, A. R. (1979/1980). Methodological issues in life-span developmental psychology from a dialectical perspective. *Journal of Aging and Human Development, 10*, 121–163.

Campbell, D. T., & Stanley, J. C. (1963). Experimental and quasi-experimental designs for research in teaching. In N. L. Gage (Ed.), *Handbook of research on teaching* (pp. 171–246). Chicago: Rand-McNally.

Cliff, N. (1982). What is and isn't measurement. In G. Keren (Ed.), *Statistical and methodological issues in psychology and social science research*. Hillsdale, NJ: Erlbaum.

Cook, T. C., & Campbell, D. T. (1979). *Quasi-experimentation: Design and analysis issues for field settings*. Chicago: Rand-McNally.

Costa, P. T., Jr., Zonderman, A. B., McCrae, R. R., Cornoni-Huntley, J., Locke, B. Z., & Barbano, H. E. (1987). Longitudinal analyses of psychological well-being in a national sample: Stability of means. *Journal of Gerontology, 42*, 50–55.

Cunningham, W. R. (1980). Age comparative factor analysis of ability variables in adulthood and old age. *Intelligence, 4*, 133–149.

Cunningham, W. R. (1981). Ability factor structure differences in adulthood and old age. *Multivariate Behavioral Research, 16*, 3–22.

Cunningham, W. R., & Birren, J. E. (1980). Age changes in the factor structure of intellectual abilities in adulthood and old age. *Educational and Psychological Measurement, 40*, 271–290.

Dixon, R. A., Kramer, D. A., & Baltes, P. B. (1985). Intelligence: A life-span development perspective. In B. B. Wolman (Ed.), *Handbook of intelligence: Theories, measurements, and applications* (pp. 301–350). New York: Wiley.

Donaldson, G. (1981). Letter to the editor. *Journal of Gerontology, 36*, 634–636.

Featherman, D. L. (1985). Individual development and aging as a population process. In J. R. Nesselroade & A. von Eye (Eds.), *Individual development and social change: Explanatory analysis*. New York: Academic Press.

George, L. K., Siegler, I. C., & Okun, M. A. (1981). Separating age, cohort, and time of measurement: Analysis of variance and multiple regression. *Experimental Aging Research, 7*, 297–314.

Gilewski, M. (1982). *Self-assessed memory function in young-old age: Structural models of explanatory factors*. Unpublished doctoral dissertation, University of Southern California, Los Angeles.

Glenn, N. D. (1976). Cohort analysts' futile quest: Statistical attempts to separate age, period and cohort effects. *American Sociological Review, 41*, 900–904.

Glenn, N. D. (1981). Age, birth cohort, and drinking: An illustration of the hazards of inferring effects from cohort data. *Journal of Gerontology, 36*, 362–369.

Guilford, J. P. (1967). *The nature of human intelligence*. New York: McGraw-Hill.

Hertzog, C. (1986). On the utility of structural regression models for developmental research. In P. B. Baltes, D. Featherman, & R. M. Lerner (Eds.), *Life-span development and behavior* (Vol. 8). Hillsdale, NJ: Erlbaum.

Hertzog, C., & Schaie, K. W. (1986). Stability and change in adult intelligence: I. Analysis of longitudinal covariance structures. *Psychology and Aging, 1*, 159–171.

Horn, J. L., & McArdle, J. J. (1980). Perspectives on mathematical-statistical model building (MASMOB) in research on aging. In L. F. Poon (Ed.), *Aging in the 1980s* (pp. 503–541). Washington, DC: American Psychological Association.

Jöreskog, K. G. (1971). Simultaneous factor analysis in several populations. *Psychometrika, 36*, 409–426.

Jöreskog, K. G. (1979). Statistical estimation of structural models in longitudinal developmental investigations. In J. R. Nesselroade & P. B. Baltes (Eds.), *Longitudi-*

nal research in the study of behavior and development (pp. 303–351). New York: Academic Press.

Jöreskog, K. G., & Sörbom, D. (1977). Statistical models and methods for analysis of longitudinal data. In D. J. Aigner & A. S. Goldberger (Eds.), *Latent variables in socioeconomic models* (pp. 285–325). Amsterdam: North Holland.

Mason, K. G., Mason, W. H., Winsborough, H. H., & Poole, W. K. (1973). Some methodological problems in cohort analyses of archival data. *American Sociological Review, 38*, 242–258.

Nesselroade, J. R. (1983). Temporal selection and factor invariance in the study of development and change. In P. B. Baltes & O. G. Brim, Jr. (Eds.), *Life-span development and behavior* (Vol. 5, pp. 60–87). New York: Academic Press.

Nesselroade, J. R., Stigler, S. M., & Baltes, P. B. (1980). Regression towards the mean and the study of change. *Psychological Bulletin, 88*, 622–637.

Palmore, E. B. (1978). When can age, period, and cohort be separated? *Social Forces, 57*, 282–295.

Reinert, G. (1970). Comparative factor analytic studies of intelligence throughout the human life-span. In L. R. Goulet & P. B. Baltes (Eds.), *Life-span developmental psychology: Research and theory* (pp. 467–484). New York: Academic Press.

Riegel, K. F. (1976). *Psychology of development and history.* New York: Plenum.

Rock, D. A., Werts, C. E., & Flaugher, R. L. (1978). The use of analysis of covariance structures for comparing the psychometric properties of multiple variables across populations. *Multivariate Behavioral Research, 13*, 403–418.

Ryder, N. B. (1965). The cohort as a concept in the study of social change. *American Review of Sociology, 30*, 843–861.

Salthouse, T. A. (1982). *Adult cognition: An experimental psychology of human aging.* New York: Springer-Verlag.

Salthouse, T. A. (1987). The role of experience in adult cognitive behavior. In K. W. Schaie (Ed.), *Annual review of gerontology and geriatrics* (Vol. 7) (pp. 135–158). New York: Springer Publishing Co.

Schaie, K. W. (1965). A general model for the study of developmental problems. *Psychological Bulletin, 64*, 91–107.

Schaie, K. W. (1973). Methodological problems in descriptive developmental research on adulthood and aging. In J. R. Nesselroade & H. W. Reese (Eds.), *Life-span developmental psychology: Methodological issues* (pp. 253–280). New York: Academic Press.

Schaie, K. W. (1975). Research strategy in developmental human behavior genetics. In K. W. Schaie, E. V. Anderson, G. E. McClearn, & J. Money (Eds.), *Developmental human behavior genetics* (pp. 205–220). Lexington, MA: D. C. Heath.

Schaie, K. W. (1977). Quasi-experimental designs in the psychology of aging. In J. E. Birren & K. W. Schaie (Eds.), *Handbook of the psychology of aging* (pp. 39–58). New York: Van Nostrand Reinhold.

Schaie, K. W. (1977/1978). Toward a stage theory of adult cognitive development. *Aging and Human Development, 8*, 129–138.

Schaie, K. W. (1978). External validity in the assessment of intellectual development in adulthood. *Journal of Gerontology, 33*, 695–701.

Schaie, K. W. (1983). The Seattle Longitudinal Study: A twenty-one year exploration of psychometric intelligence in adulthood. In K. W. Schaie (Ed.), *Longitudinal studies of adult psychological development* (pp. 64–135). New York: Guilford Press.

Schaie, K. W. (1984). Historical time and cohort effects. In K. A. McCloskey & H. W. Reese (Eds.), *Life-span developmental psychology: Historical and generational effects* (pp. 1–15). New York: Academic Press.

Schaie, K. W. (1986). Beyond calendar definitions of age, time and cohort: The general developmental model revisited. *Developmental Review, 6,* 252–277.

Schaie, K. W., & Baltes, P. B. (1975). On sequential strategies in developmental research: Description or explanation? *Human Development, 18,* 384–390.

Schaie, K. W., & Hertzog, C. (1982). Longitudinal methods. In B. B. Woman (Ed.), *Handbook of developmental psychology* (pp. 91–115). Englewood Cliffs, NJ: Prentice-Hall.

Schaie, K. W., & Hertzog, C. (1985). Measurement in the psychology of adulthood and aging. In J. E. Birren & K. W. Schaie (Eds.), *Handbook of the psychology of aging* (2nd ed., pp. 61–92). New York: Van Nostrand Reinhold.

Schaie, K. W., & Hertzog, C. (1986). Toward a comprehensive model of adult intellectual development: Contributions of the Seattle Longitudinal Study. In R. J. Sternberg (Ed.), *Advances in human intelligence* (Vol. 3, pp. 79–118). New York: Academic Press.

Schaie, K. W., & Parham, I. A. (1974). Social responsibility in adulthood: Ontogenetic and sociocultural change. *Journal of Personality and Social Psychology, 30,* 483–492.

Schaie, K. W., & Strother, C. R. (1968). The cross-sequential study of age changes in cognitive behavior. *Psychological Bulletin, 70,* 671–680.

Schaie, K. W., & Willis, S. L. (1986a). *Adult development and aging* (2nd ed.). Boston: Little, Brown.

Schaie, K. W., & Willis, S. L. (1986b). Can intellectual decline in the elderly be reversed? *Developmental Psychology, 22,* 223–232.

Schaie, K. W., Willis, S. L., Hertzog, C., & Schulenberg, J. E. (1987). Effects of cognitive training upon primary mental ability structure. *Psychology and Aging, 2,* 233–242.

Slife, B. D. (1981). Psychology's reliance on linear time: A reformulation. *Journal of Mind and Behavior, 2,* 27–46.

Stone, V. (1980). *Structural modeling of the relations among environmental variables, health status and intelligence in adulthood.* Unpublished doctoral dissertation, University of Southern California, Los Angeles.

Thurstone, L. L. (1938). *The primary mental abilities.* Chicago: University of Chicago Press.

Thurstone, L. L., & Thurstone, T. G. (1941). *Factorial studies of intelligence.* Chicago: University of Chicago Press.

Willis, S. L. (1985). Towards an educational psychology of the adult learner: Cognitive and intellectual bases. In J. E. Birren & K. W. Schaie (Eds.), *Handbook of the psychology of aging* (2nd ed., pp. 818–847). New York: Van Nostrand Reinhold.

Willis, S. L., & Schaie, K. W. (1986). Practical intelligence in later adulthood. In R. J. Sternberg & R. K. Wagner (Eds.), *Practical intelligence: Origins of competence in the everyday world* (pp. 236–268). New York: Cambridge University Press.

Winsborough, H. H., Duncan, O. D., & Read, P. B. (1983). *Cohort analysis in social research.* New York: Academic Press.

4

Settings and Sequences: The Heuristics of Aging Research

Richard T. Campbell
Angela M. O'Rand

Aging is an area of research on which diverse—and occasionally competing—research traditions have converged. As such, the phenomenon has exerted centripetal force on research programs across several disciplines, a kind of force that has been observed infrequently in the history of the sciences. The convergence of disparate fields, ranging from neuroendocrinology to cognitive psychology to sociology, offers the basis for both optimism and pessimism about the possibility and utility of a unified metatheory of aging. Pessimism stems from the uneasy communication across fields, making aging research a virtual Tower of Babel conceptually and methodologically. Paradoxically, however, optimism grows from the increased potential for cross-fertilization and scientific innovation afforded by cross-disciplinary exchange. Many examples of the progressive effects of such exchanges in the history of the sciences can be found. The origins of molecular biology (Mullins, 1972) and radio astronomy (Edge & Mulkay, 1976), for example, were founded on the cross-disciplinary transfer of people, ideas or methods. Successful theory construction and validation in aging will require unprecedented cooperation between the biological and social sciences. In the remainder of this chapter these issues will be explored from the perspective of the sociology of science.

Nearly 40 years ago Robert K. Merton (1967) wrote a classic essay, "The Bearing of Empirical Research on Sociological Theory." In it he argued that the relationship between data and theory is necessarily dialectic. He proposed several ways in which data and empirical research affect the process of theory construction and validation, including the serendipitous pattern in which unanticipated results influence theory and the cumulative processes by which new data and procedures lead to the recasting of theory, the refocusing of interests, and the clarification of concepts. All of these apply to research on aging over the past two decades. But we will emphasize that in the case of aging research methods have assumed a stronger role in theory change than even Merton's highest expectations.

In many ways, the field of aging is still in its formative stages and just beginning to collect data of the kind that will permit theory construction. In other ways, however, the availability of substantial amounts of new data and the appearance of new strategies for analysis have led to unexpected results, which have already refocused our interests and redefined our problems. In this chapter, we extend the Merton argument in two ways, both of which reflect cumulative developments in the technical capacities of the social sciences since Merton wrote his essay.

THE IMPACT OF DATA AND MODELS
ON THEORY CONSTRUCTION

First, we will argue that data, particularly the kind of multidisciplinary and multivariate longitudinal materials we are now accumulating, must be understood within the context of mathematical/statistical models applied to them. These models "engage" the data, but they differ radically in their assumptions and in the way they lead us to conceptualize problems and processes. Technical developments in data analysis have affected our conceptualizations of aging and human development in ways that Merton could not have anticipated exactly but which are certainly foreshadowed in his essay. When Merton wrote, data analysis in sociology was relatively primitive. Most data analysis involved the visual inspection of simple cross-tabulations and partitioned variable relationships. The emergence of whole batteries of quantitative techniques since 1949 has introduced an intermediary in the linkage between data and theory, with strong influences on the definition of both. Quantitative methods have come to exert an independent influence on theory by introducing new and subtle links between data and theory and by making new demands of the data themselves. As such, techniques have assumed an "ontological" importance in generating ideas, which transcends their traditional "heuristic" role as operational extensions of conceptual frameworks. They have also assumed a determinant role in defining the empirical domain. This ascendance of method has grown more and more evident in interdisciplinary fields such as research on aging, where different empirical traditions converge on a common problem. The exchange of techniques or procedures is often more easily accomplished than the exchange of core concepts and organizing theoretical frameworks. Yet the techniques ultimately influence ideas and can redefine the problem domain (empirical world) to which they apply.

Our second proposition is that research on aging has undergone a problem shift in response to technical innovations. This redefinition of the problem has introduced time and social structure as necessary considerations for the study of aging. This is hardly a radical position. Indeed, in some ways it has been received as wisdom among those identified with the "life course perspective in aging."

Ryder's (1965) seminal essay, written more than 20 years ago, on the role of cohort flow in social change focused the attention of sociologists and demographers on the importance of cohort analysis. Shaie's (1965) equally important discussion of the age-period-cohort issue, written in the same year, drew psychologists' attention to many of the same issues. Despite these papers, we would argue that relatively little systematic attention has been paid to the implications of the life-course perspective for data collection, and vice versa. We are only just beginning to realize that single-cohort, single-time period studies yield essentially descriptive data, and that even in this simple case, "descriptive" refers to particular conceptualizations of aging and human development which themselves are subject to revision in light of data collected on new cohorts at different points in time. To use one well-known example, to which we will return: Much of our knowledge of the retirement process is derived from studies of men who were born in the first 20 years of this century. As a cohort, they faced particular sequences of historical events and encountered social structures, technological resources, and economic forces uniquely specific to their historical category. The data collected on their specific experiences cannot form the basis of a "theory of retirement." They offer little variation.[1] If we wish to understand how variation in social structure leads to variation in human behavior (and in turn how human behavior affects social structure), then the data we have available must permit such variation. The data we have available, in almost any area of interest to students of gerontology, fail to do so.[2]

Thus, in the remainder of this chapter, we argue that to understand the future of research and theory on aging one must appreciate the nature of a problem domain, its research traditions and heuristics (its ways of formulating and solving problems), and the data it has available. We also argue that all of these are in rapid flux. The fundamental heuristic for research on aging will eventually consist of a cross-temporal, cross-cultural data base and a set of mathematical/statistical techniques for exploring it.[3]

SOME EXAMPLES FROM OTHER DISCIPLINES

Examples of the interdependence of disciplinary traditions, problem definitions, and research tools (heuristics) are numerous in the sciences, particularly in the biomedical sciences. Studer and Chubin's (1980) study of the confluence of three research traditions—virology, bacteriology, and molecular biology—on the problem domain of cancer provides two strategic illustrations. The histories of virology and molecular biology during the middle of the 20th century reveal how tools can influence scientific (theoretical) development. In the case of virology, the persistent dependence on one orthodox and discipline-bound technique limited the advancement of theory on the viral bases of cancer for several decades. The failure to ask questions beyond the limits of current orthodox methodology constrained scientific progress. In effect, it neither disconfirmed old theories nor generated alternative new hypotheses.

In molecular biology, however, the opposite was true. Molecular biology was born of cross-disciplinary interaction (among physics, chemistry, and biology) and developed primarily with the introduction of new techniques. Electrophoresis, ultracentrifugation, paper chromatography, and ultraviolet spectroscopy—borrowed from physical chemistry—led more to the discovery of DNA than did existing conceptual interests and indeed ultimately replaced the nucleoprotein theory of the gene with the molecular theory. Studer and Chubin (1980) discuss these developments in detail arguing that

> In marked contrast to our presentation of the key events in the development of oncogenic virus research, research into the biochemistry of the transformation process is replete with references to new methodologies. The virus research which has been described could be called the Waring-Blender-Berkefeld filter tradition. But developments in cell transformation are virtually synonymous with the introduction of new methods in physical chemistry. (p. 33)

Thus, techniques served to retard one discipline's progress in research relevant to cancer but to accelerate another's progress almost without the aid of theory.[4]

The recent history of research in aging and gerontology exhibits the effects of substantial multidisciplinary cross-fertilization. Indeed, in some ways, the very nature of the field is changing. Not only is a new problem definition emerging, but new ways of dealing with aging phenomena in terms of mathematical modeling are rapidly finding their way into the field. At the same time, new data resources are forcing students of aging to pay attention to phenomena that were once beyond their ken. These processes are interrelated, of course, and we now turn our attention to showing these relationships.

SETTINGS AND SEQUENCES: A NEW SYNTHESIS

Life Course Analysis as an Emerging Problem Definition

Within recent years, social gerontologists have been faced with the emergence of a new paradigm for the study of aging in the form of life-course analysis. Advocates of the life-course approach are clearly interested in traditional social gerontology, but only as it is encompassed in a broader and more dynamic view of the life course. In many respects, those who have been long interested in social gerontology have tended to ignore the life-course approach; this is reflected in the relatively little attention paid to the approach in the recently published second edition of the *Handbook of Aging and the Social Sciences* (Binstock & Shanas, 1985).

The reasons for the limited adoption of life-course concepts and methods by traditional social gerontology are both intellectual and social. Intellectually, the traditional concerns of this field have been social-problem–oriented with a strong operational prescription to study age-related patterns of behavior and their determinants in the older population. The characterization of the aged has been the object of research. A good deal of the theoretical work has been oriented to either providing conceptual bases for understanding age differences or providing integrating mechanisms for seemingly disparate phenomena. For example, role theory has been called into service to deal with issues in the study of retirement.[5]

Socially, gerontology has developed self-consciously as a highly specialized, multidisciplinary "discipline," with separate journals, research schools, and societies. This has created a "social distance" between this field and other social science fields. Accordingly, other social science approaches to age and aging, as they have developed following other theoretical orientations, have not fallen automatically into the social gerontologists' tool kit of concepts and methods.

However, the problem of aging has emerged as an important object of research in several of the social sciences, particularly social history (Demos & Boocock, 1978; Fisher, 1978), anthropology (Kertzer & Keith, 1984), economics (Easterlin, 1980), and sociology (Featherman & Sorensen, 1983; O'Rand & Henretta, 1982; Riley, 1986; Riley, Johnson, & Foner, 1972). This work has tended to ignore or at least downplay previous work in social gerontology, treating the study of aging as a topic area within the particular discipline, rather than a discipline in its own right. Concomitantly, the behavioral sciences—particularly cognitive and developmental psychologies—have moved more into adulthood and aging studies after a long tradition of studying development in infancy and childhood (Baltes, 1968; Schaie, 1983).[6] The confluence of these traditions on the problem of aging has expanded the domain of study traditionally attached to gerontology beyond old age to the life course (or life span) studied within historical and cultural contexts.

Stated simply, the problem definition (object of research) has shifted from the "aged" to "aging." The theoretical agenda attached to the problem shift, consequently, has turned to more general concerns about the processes and patterns of aging over time and place, and away from specific theories of age status. And the methodological agenda has turned to dynamic, historical analysis strategies with new data requirements.

Development as Duration Dependence

A recent paper by Featherman and Lerner (1985) provides a particularly striking exemplar of this change in orientation in that it shows both the influence of dynamic approaches to model formulation and data analysis and the importance of a data base that permits new conceptualization.[7] While ostensibly writing on the topic of socialization, they actually consider issues pertinent to almost any aspect of the life course. Featherman and Lerner deal with two major issues: (1) the definition of development and (2) an elaboration of the relationship between social structure on the one hand and the individual life course on the other. They discuss a particular orientation to data and models, derived from work in a variety of fields, which has the potential for significantly changing our conceptualization of aging and human development. After briefly reviewing the paper and discussing its implications we will provide two examples of the new approach. We will then be in a position to elaborate our argument that this approach carries with it strong operational prescriptions (i.e., heuristics) for research, on which it is built and without which it is not empirically testable.

Featherman and Lerner (1985) begin by noting that both biological and social scientists find it difficult to define what is meant by development and how development is affected by environment and social structure. These two issues are intimately related; definitions of development determine, in large part, the extent to which environment can play a role. Some definitions of development and theoretical orientations toward it are so biologically circumscribed that environmental effects are moot. Other definitions are so imbued with a social and environmental perspective as to assume that the organismic basis of development is completely plastic in its response to environment. Featherman and Lerner argue for an "ontological pluralism" and see development "as a multidimensional but inherently social process at all its levels of manifestation including the biological."

This point of view, however, begs the essential question: What *is* development? To deal with this, they begin with the traditional definition of development as consisting of "sequential, time-dependent change in behavior and capacity" (Featherman & Lerner, 1985, p. 667), to which they add an additional requirement. Change of any kind will be considered developmental, they argue, only if it can be shown that there is *duration dependence* in the *rate of change*. Thus, change can occur at random with respect to duration in state and not be "developmental." The notion of duration dependence means that for any individual the probability of change or transition at any given instant depends on how long the individual has already been in the state. It is important to note that duration can be defined with respect to any baseline. Birth, which defines the baseline for age, offers only one basis for measuring duration dependence. Duration can also be measured with respect to some event specific to an individual (e.g., years of marriage until loss of spouse or years of labor force participation until loss of employment) or events that are common to all members of a given population (e.g., economic fluctuations, wars, changes in social policy).

This definition of development has important and profound implications for research on human development and aging. It affects the way we collect data, the way we think about aging and the aged, and, equally important, our ability to communicate with other researchers, since the duration-dependence perspective requires approaches to quantitative methods somewhat different from those most researchers have used in the past.

Origins of the New Perspective in Statistical Models

Many research questions in human development basically concern the rate at which some event or transition occurs with respect to time. However, most of the available analytic tools that psychologists, sociologists, and others are taught (principally, least-squares methods) deal with time only tangentially, if at all. Thus we ask: "What is the subject's status at time t," an inherently static approach, rather than framing the question dynamically (and developmentally) as: "What is the rate of change with respect to time and what are the determinants of variation therein?" Indeed, the standard panel survey that forms the backbone of much research on aging is largely oriented to a static rather than a dynamic conceptualization of development.

In recent years a number of investigators in very diverse fields have attempted to deal with this problem by introducing a new mode of analysis for longitudinal data. The approach draws on statistical developments in biometry, epidemiology, quality control and reliability (failure) analysis, demography, and several other fields. Within sociology, the approach is known as *event history analysis*; however, there are several other terms in common use, including *hazard models, survival models*, and others. While Hannon and Tuma (1979) are primarily responsible for introducing these ideas into sociology in the late 1970s, the notion of an event history model has diverse origins and goes back many years. Like many other statistical developments, the model was relatively unknown until increased computer power made it feasible.[8]

The basic idea in event history analysis is rather straightforward. Given some baseline, we are often interested in how much time ensues before an event occurs. We might also be interested in the rate at which the event occurs with respect to time, whether the rate changes with time, and whether different subgroups of a population might show variation in relationship of the rate to time.[9] Examples include childbirth following marriage or onset of intercourse, retirement following disability, and so on. Dynamic models are most easily discussed in the case of discrete transitions such as retirement; however, the ideas apply to continuous change (such as morale) as well. In the discrete case, we form a statistical model that relates the rate of transition to time and, potentially, to other variables. If the risk does not vary over time, then in the Featherman-Lerner definition the transition does not represent development. For example, if the risk of mortality were constant with respect to time, then mortality would not have a developmental component. On the other hand, if one found that the risk of a serious illness increased after experiencing the loss of a spouse, then this process would be developmental, but with respect to a baseline other than birth. Note that the risk of widowhood itself is developmental, since its risk does increase with age.

Dealing with duration dependence in the case of discrete transitions requires us to have information on the exact timing of transitions. Unfortunately, we often lack exactly this information. Sometimes this is due to design. For example, in the classic panel study, we only know if the transition has taken place up to the nth wave of measurement. In effect, the data for many panel surveys consist of a series of snapshots portraying the subject at the time of data collection. For example, we know if a subject is widowed at time t, $t+1$, $t+2$, and so on. More important, regardless of the data-collection plan, observations will almost always be censored, meaning that no matter how long we wait, it is likely that some persons will undergo the transition after we stop observing them. For example, if we recruit a cohort of subjects at risk for retirement and follow them over time, some subjects will remain in the labor force long after the study ends, and we will not observe the transition. Conventional approaches to this problem—for example, regression models that treat time-till-transition as the dependent variable—lead to biased results with censored observations. The event history approach deals with this problem by forming a model for the *rate* of transition with respect to time. The mathematics are worked out in such a way that each subject contributes to the estimation of a model for the rate proportionally to the time that he or she is actually observed, and it is possible to compute unbiased estimates of the rate of transition using some fairly complicated but tractable statistical computations. Estimates of the rate model are obtainable under a wide variety of assumptions regarding the form of duration dependence in the data. There is a great deal of flexibility permitted in the treatment of time, which can be dealt with continuously or in discrete intervals. Moreover, and most important, we need not assume that the rate is the same for all persons in the population. On the contrary, we can include variables in the model that account for heterogeneity in the rate. Thus, although rates describe populations, we can assume heterogeneous populations that can be described in terms of varying rates.[10]

Models of this kind are at the heart of the Featherman-Lerner definition of development. Indeed, it is unlikely that they would have arrived at that definition had models for rates of transitions not been available. Here is a clear case of essentially technical developments that had been spurred by the need for usable models in somewhat unrelated fields having an impact in a very different field. The interplay of statistical and theoretical development is by no means unique to this particular case. On the contrary, statistical models provide a fundamental heuristic device in many social science disciplines. Thus, the development and elaboration of a particular technique stems in large part from the inadequacies of a particular approach to data collection and analysis. But, importantly, the technique feeds back to recast theory and refocus conceptual interest in the way that Merton originally described in 1949. The Fisherian approach to analysis of variance provides the basic concepts for experimental design in psychology and related disciplines. The path diagram provides a fundamental conceptual tool for the sociologist. In effect, these statistical techniques allow the analyst to conceptualize (indeed visualize in the case of path analysis) alternative designs and analyses quickly and almost without thinking of them. To the psychologist, notions of blocking factors, split plots, and random versus fixed effects are building blocks, as are concepts like direct and indirect effect to the sociologist. The often-repeated charge that we are faddish and unthinking in our willingness to adopt ever newer methods ignores the extent to which new quantitative methods permit new conceptualizations.

The value of the duration-dependence perspective, in our opinion, is that it encompasses a wide range of alternative models for the data. It directs attention away from fruitless attempts to define development in terms of end points or direction, and ties development to time in state. Indeed, it is irrelevant whether one accepts duration dependence as a necessary condition for change to be categorized as developmental; it only matters that one distinguish change that is duration-dependent from change that is not. We do not wish to argue that all problems are solved by the duration-dependence approach, or even that it will become dominant in the field; however, we do think it provides a good example of how theory and technique interrelate.

Social Structure and Duration Dependence

Concomitant with their definition of development as duration-dependent rates of change, Featherman and Lerner (1985) argue that it is necessary to see development as a "person-population process." By this they mean that development on the one hand and social structure on the other are products of the interaction between individual and social structure across specific sociohistorical circumstances. Social institutions and social structure set limits on the range of behavior and adaptation that can flow from a particular genetic potential (population). In turn, the particular patterns of development seen at a given time affect further development and change the context in which younger cohorts develop. Although Featherman and Lerner do not emphasize the reciprocity and dialectic of individual and social change, this point of view is well articulated by Riley, Johnson, & Foner, (1972) and by Hernes (1976).

The model is synergistic, built on interaction across levels of analysis over time and is a clear departure from immutable *life stage* approaches of the past.

Featherman and Lerner (1985) describe their point of view as *developmental contextualism*, a term that has fairly self-evident meaning. As they note, this idea has appeared in many forms over a long period of time in the social science literature. The idea has its more current antecedents in the work of life-course researchers. Elder's (1974) influential *Children of the Great Depression* is perhaps the best known of the works that take this point of view. Although Elder deals with the effect of the Depression on the form and rate of development of the birth cohorts affected by it, it is also clearly the case that the "Depression generation" brought about changes in social structure in the form of a much stronger version of the welfare state, which in turn affected the developmental context of younger cohorts. Although it is important to note that Elder's work really cannot disentangle the effects of the Depression from many other influences—that is, that age, period, and cohort are confounded—it nevertheless anticipates the Featherman-Lerner position. As Elder would be the first to note, it is only when one is able to compare other cohorts that have gone through other social upheavals that one is able to get a good theoretical purchase on the problem. Elder's (1986) more recent work on the effects of military service is a case in point.

Unlike the idea of duration dependence, in which it is possible to point to a line of development in statistics that had a clear influence on further conceptualization, the sources and implications of developmental contextualism are less clear-cut. Although the idea of cohort comparison has taken hold in a rather formal way, in the sense that one can statistically compare coefficients, there is not a rigorous method for linking macro-level social structural phenomena to micro-level developmental concepts. This is true both conceptually and on a more technical level.

There are at least three reasons why effective macro-micro analysis remains a future goal rather than a realized opportunity. First, as noted, data with sufficient variation in time are difficult to come by. In the United States the various public-use samples of the census go back to 1940, with manuscript versions available for the previous century, but it is fair to say that the data base for research is limited relative to the broad historical sweep in which we are inclined to think.[11] The micro-survey data base, especially with reference to older adults, is basically nonexistent prior to 1950 and very scattered until about 1960.

Second, we are, in a sense, at the mercy of history when it comes to understanding the importance of existing data. This is particularly true when one thinks in cohort-comparative terms. For example, U.S. birth cohorts born in the mid-1940s through the early 1950s were called upon to fight a war that was highly unpopular. As such, these cohorts are unique in American history.[12] Our understanding of their development must take that experience into account, just as we must take the Depression into account for other cohorts. Yet our understanding of the Vietnam effect will be contingent on events yet to come, just as our understanding of the Depression cohorts must be seen in the light of World War II. Although the possibility of U.S. involvement in future "wars of national liberation" in Latin America is the most salient example, developments in the economy, particularly in terms of the position of the United States vis-à-vis other industrial societies, are equally important. Although all of this is perfectly obvious perhaps, we would argue that it is not completely obvious how one goes about devising a rational program of data collection that permits effective analysis. *Children of the Great Depression* was possible because of the largely accidental conjunction of a unique set of data and an investigator with ideas and tenacity. We will not always be so lucky. We will return to this issue below.

Finally, conceptual tools for thinking about how to model the effects of social structure are primitive relative to the rather elegant methods we have discussed above. In order to deal with the task of linking social structure and development it will be necessary first to show that duration-dependence models in fact differ across cohorts known to have experienced different historical sequences, and then to more formally model the multilevel effects. Multilevel analysis is just coming into its own in sociology and is not well known in other disciplines (Mason, Wong, & Entwhistle, 1983). Moreover, as noted above, successful analyses will require abundant variation in social-structure parameters. Short-run data collections are likely to be dominated totally by simple linear effects in time and thus unlikely to permit more than descriptive analyses. In summary, although the idea of linking development to social structure is seductive and in a sense "obvious," neither the data nor the analytic techniques are sufficiently developed to permit much more than interesting speculation. On the other hand, as we discuss in more detail below, the data base is expanding at a rapid rate and, as was the case with Elder's work on the Depression, data generate their own energy.

Some Examples

One can argue that concepts of duration dependence and contextualism are not that unique, and indeed, we have gone to some length to show that they depend on particular developments in statistical methods and data collection. On the other hand, Featherman and Lerner (1985) present an agenda that makes sense to us and that is at least in part applicable to real problems faced by those who seek to understand aging. As such, it represents a confluence of research interests across a number of disciplines, yielding a consensus among scholars about the appropriate goals for a social science of human development and aging. It is also inspired by technical resources now available that have assisted in redefining these goals. In order to demonstrate the usefulness of these concepts we shall discuss two examples of life-course events, one focusing on a discrete transition and the other on a continuous process.

A Discrete Transition – Retirement

Retirement is among the last major transitions in the life course, over which individuals' economic statuses decline and their economic roles qualitatively change. The quantifiable decline in economic status is observable as income drops, often so precipitously as to represent a qualitative change. The economic role change is indicated by movement out of the paid labor force and by the shift in the primary source of income from earnings to assets (primarily retirement savings in the form of pension benefits) and transfer payments.

But while retirement is age-related, it is a transition the timing of which is embedded in history and biography. Historically, the trend toward early retirement has come about as a result of multiple factors. The expansion of pensions and related retirement support systems in health have provided the opportunity structure for retirement from work to subgroups of the labor force (Barfield & Morgan, 1969). Paralleling this development, the economic shift from manufacturing to service occupations has encouraged the retirement of selected worker cohorts in declining industries and their replacement in the workforce by other workers in different industries. Retirement-age men 55 years and older have been influenced overwhelmingly by both of these trends to retire early (Pampel & Weiss, 1983). These cohorts have been replaced by younger workers, and particularly by women, across age groups selected to work in the most rapidly growing economic sectors (DeViney & O'Rand, 1987).

Long-term patterns in population fertility and the extension of life expectancy over time have also affected age-specific rates of retirement. The remarkable growth of early retirement that became apparent by the late 1960s and early 1970s was conditioned by the distinctive age structure of the population, characterized then by a large baby-boom cohort flooding the workplace, as older cohorts born during the first decade of the 20th century began to retire. This older group was also a vanguard in the extension of life expectancy. They retired, on average, into longer (though not necessarily healthier) post-work lives. And they revealed the widening gender difference in life expectancy that has continued to the present time (O'Rand, 1984).

Biographically, the transition to retirement is the culmination of an event-graded sequence over the life courses of individuals that is not immutably tied to specific ages. This sequence is a heterogeneous, time-organized process by which subgroups of individuals become workers who, in turn, are differentially able to sustain their work attachments over time in order to save for retirement and to tie retirement to pension benefit eligibility. As such, retirement can be viewed as the final transition in the pension (retirement income) acquisition process, when pension changes from a savings to an income.

The pension acquisition process is time-organized because it is related to participation schedules regulated by the pension structure (O'Rand & Mac-Lean, 1986) and by historical circumstances that influence pension policies. The process can be portrayed as an event sequence, beginning with (1) selection into the labor force and followed by (2) employment in firms with pension coverage, (3) participation in the firm pension plan, (4) final vesting or eligibility for a pension, and (5) pension benefit receipt upon retirement. The sequence can be conceived as a narrowing opportunity structure for pension income at retirement, beginning with worker status and ending with benefit receipt. The process produces heterogeneity in the population over time and shapes the individual's career of retirement saving. At each event in the sequence, segments of the worker population are at risk for exclusion as a result of individual, firm-related, industrial, and social policy factors.

The transition rate from one state in the sequence to another is duration-dependent. The duration of pension participation affects the rate of pension vesting (O'Rand, 1985). In turn, pension eligibility influences the timing of retirement (Henretta & O'Rand, 1983; O'Rand & Henretta, 1982). The rate of retirement can thus be modeled as a function of duration of pension participation and a set of explanatory variables, such as health, marital status, occupation, and earnings in addition to age.

Historical events, episodically and unpredictably, can influence the process at each point in the sequence. Periods of high inflation, plant closings, and governmental legislation can operate either to limit or to extend the pension acquisition process. Periods of high inflation, for example, can delay the timing of retirement even if a worker is eligible for a pension, that is, has been participating long enough to be vested. Plant closings can dramatically terminate the pension acquisition process. And government legislation can strongly influence pension rights and pension provision policies. The Employee Retirement Income Security Act of 1974 (ERISA) significantly intervened in the pension acquisition process by standardizing and rationalizing participation criteria, which up to that time varied enormously and, at times, quite arbitrarily. In the same vein, the 1983 amendments to the Social Security Act redefined spouses' rights to pension benefits after divorce by tying these rights to the duration of the marriage (10 years).

In short, the discrete transition to retirement is both biographically embedded and historically conditioned. It cannot be understood outside the contexts of time and social structure. Thinking of retirement in terms of rates of transitions has several advantages. First, it emphasizes the dynamic nature of the process. Second, it allows us to treat the rate as a characteristic of a population, asking how it differs across subgroups and changes over time. Gender and cohort encounter social structure differently. Finally, it permits us to model the retirement process with respect to multiple baselines, of which birth is only one example.

A Continuous Transition – Morale

The study of morale and well-being has been a staple of social gerontology. Most such studies have looked at the determinants of morale and rarely at the determinants of changes in morale. Indeed, most studies have either looked at morale at some specific point in the life course, such as age 65 or 1 year after widowhood, or have been cross-sectional. The subjects for such studies have been old, of course, but most samples show substantial variability in age and other characteristics. Indeed, in many cross-sectional studies, age has been treated as one of the predictors of morale.

What does the notion of duration dependence have to teach us about the study of morale? First, we realize that we have to be concerned about changes over time with respect to some baseline. The baseline might well be birth, but it could be other events as well, for example, widowhood. Second, it is possible to model duration dependence for continuous variables just as it is for discrete transitions.[13] We can ask how the rate of change in morale varies with respect to time, and we can include other variables in the model. Thus, we might ask how duration dependence differs for men and women by including a dummy variable for gender. By framing the question in terms of duration and change we place the study of morale in a dynamic context, just as in the case where we ask how the rate of leaving the labor force differs as a function of time since labor force entry and other variables. If we are willing to extend the definition of "morale" to include the concept of "engaged/disengaged," we can see that arguments about whether disengagement is part of the normal life course can be reformulated. Rather than ask whether people do or do not disengage, we can ask whether *the rate of change* in engagement differs over time, across social groups, or whatever. With appropriate data this is an answerable question and permits the issue to be posed in a theoretically tractable way.

The study of morale also provides an opportunity to examine the notion of the person-population perspective. Easterlin (1980) argues that many aspects of psychological and social well-being are a function of cohort size. In brief, he argues that large cohorts suffer from two difficulties. First, they must compete for scarce resources throughout their lives. Second, it will almost always be the case that large cohorts will find themselves economically disadvantaged relative to their parents. This occurs because the parents of large birth cohorts tend to come from small cohorts, and small cohorts enjoy relative economic advantage as a result of the economic leverage they bring to the labor market. Small cohorts, in light of their economic well-being, have large numbers of children, who subsequently find themselves economically disadvantaged. In response, they have fewer children, in part because wives enter and stay in the labor force, and the cycle repeats itself.

Easterlin's work has focused primarily on the young. He deals with crime and delinquency rates, unemployment, divorce, and to a very limited extent with psychological well-being. There is no reason why his analysis should not be extended to late life, however. His work would suggest, of course, that members of large cohorts should enter old age in worse financial shape than other cohorts. This would be true because the large cohorts would not have been able to save as much. If morale is related to economic well-being, as there is every reason to believe that it is, then we would expect the gradient of decline in morale following retirement to be steeper for economically disadvantaged cohorts.

There are many reasons why this prediction might not be true in practice. The elderly in general, and large cohorts of elderly in particular, are not without political power. They may well be able to bring about a relocation of resources, as argued by Preston (1984). In effect, such political activity means that groups of individuals are affecting their own development. In order to understand such a phenomenon, it would be essential to have information on successive cohorts.

THE HEURISTICS OF THE NEW SYNTHESIS

The examples of retirement and morale as life-course transitions illustrate the relationship between theory and method in life-course analysis. The problem-definition shift from the aged to aging has come about as the result of the confluence of disciplinary interests in the study of age outside gerontology. The notion of duration dependence provides a basis for the synthesis of age stratification theory with developmental psychology. And, more important, the synthesis is directly inspired by a method—event history analysis—borrowed from still another tradition. This method-driven theory has inherent operational requirements or heuristics for research that have long-term theoretical implications for the study of aging, which cannot be completely envisioned but which encourage speculation.

For sociologists and social gerontologists, the preeminent research tool has been the social survey, particularly the longitudinal survey. Any standard exposition of research methods in aging argues for the importance of the longitudinal design. And although there is great dispute within the social sciences about the desirability of quantitative methods and an approach to social science that models itself on the physical sciences (for examples, see Neugarten, 1985, and Lieberson, 1985), even the most hostile critics see some value in survey approaches if only for descriptive purposes. Within the past 20 years, a number of important longitudinal surveys of the elderly have been carried out. Campbell, Abolafia, and Maddox (1985) review a number of these. Prominent examples are the Social Security Administration's Retirement History Survey (Irelan, 1972) and the National Longitudinal Surveys of Labor Market Experience (Parnes, 1975), both of which provide repeated measures on respondents over at least a decade.

Despite the availability of a rather sophisticated data base, the number of published analyses that take full advantage of the longitudinal character of the data has been small. In part this reflects the lack of expertise in quantitative approaches to longitudinal analysis on the part of many investigators, but it also reflects a more fundamental problem. The classic panel design draws on two disparate traditions. The first stems from studies of child development and emphasizes repeated measures of subjects at frequent and precise intervals. The subjects share a common baseline (birth), and attention is focused on their pattern and rate of development with respect to that baseline. The second tradition underlying the standard panel design draws on the work of Paul Lazarsfeld and the Columbia school. Studies of voting behavior carried out there in the 1940s also emphasized repeated measures, but the focus was not on development from a common baseline but rather on change from initial to later measurement when the researchers knew in advance that a particular event (an election campaign) would intervene between the waves of measurement.

While current longitudinal surveys generally consist of repeated measures on individuals and relatively fixed intervals, they lack both of the features described above. The samples do not share a common baseline. Instead, they tend to be heterogeneous with respect to age. Moreover, the events that occur between waves of measurement vary across subjects, are not under the investigator's control, and do not occur either in a fixed order or at the same time. Thus, some subjects lose a spouse, some become seriously ill, some leave the labor force, and so on. Given this lack of coherence in design, it is no wonder that researchers have found it difficult to carry out effective analyses of the data.

As Featherman and Petersen (1986) argue, the lack of effective analysis stems in part from attempts to force what should be dynamic concepts on data collected from a static point of view. Taking advantage of duration concepts will require changes in how we go about collecting data. There are two forms of data for event history analysis. What might be called the *strong form* requires exact dates of transitions and states. The *weak form*, as noted above, requires information on whether or not a transition has taken place by time t. The former is far superior to the latter. Thus, if the full force of the duration-dependence approach is to be realized, it will be necessary to collect data in such a way that we have the exact timing of transitions. Moreover, it is obviously necessary to repeat studies on successive cohorts if the full value of the person-population perspective is to be realized. "Snapshot" approaches to data collection will have to be abandoned.[14] In other words, if we are to study development using the duration-dependence model, we need a sequence of longitudinal studies across a wide range of birth cohorts in which we collect detailed information on the timing, pattern, sequence, etc., of many specific biological and social transitions, as well as detailed data on rates of change in continuous variables. Further, all of this information must be coordinated in some way with data on macro–social structure. Ideally, of course, all of this should be comparative.

This may seem like an impossible order, fantastically expensive, and beyond the ability of even the most talented and tenacious researchers. But in a sense, the data are already being collected. The availability of machine-readable information on aging and human development is increasing at a very high rate. With regard to the United States, in 1980 we had reasonably complete information on cohorts entering late adulthood who were born roughly between 1890 and 1910. Prior to that date, the survey data base was scattered and unreliable. By the turn of this century we will have data on about 40 or 50 birth cohorts as they have entered late adulthood. Those cohorts will have been born under and experienced very diverse historical circumstances. The spontaneously occurring variation will allow us to understand a great deal about aging as we look at cohorts who experienced economic hardship versus those who were affluent, at those who went to war versus those who did not, at women who worked and those who did not, and so on. There is now emerging a rich archive of data from many other nations as well, although our appreciation of it is still limited.

But if data are already being collected, it seems fair to say that the process is unplanned, accidental, and somewhat chaotic. Campbell et al. (1985), for example, briefly describe more than 20 national surveys devoted to the study of health, noting large and important gaps in cohort and topic coverage. Other surveys (e.g., Americans View their Mental Health, carried out in 1957 and 1976) would be of immensely more value if regularly replicated. In large part perhaps, it is simply not possible to rationalize data collection over an extended period of time. The cost of data collection is so high that it is unlikely that anyone but the federal government will fund it, and the government responds to economic and political factors that are simply beyond our control. On the other hand, the emergence of a particular theoretical model, such as that of duration dependence, provides a template for survey design and analysis that is quite different, and perhaps better, than we have had in the past. The difficult task is to ensure that theory plays its reciprocal role in collection, and that task is made easier if we work harder to understand the interrelatedness of data, method, and theory.

A POSTSCRIPT

We began this essay with Merton's early observations on the relationship between research and theory. His insights, despite the more conventional textbook view of the secondary roles of methods and techniques in theory building, are more relevant today in the social sciences than ever. In rapidly developing problem domains, like aging, techniques and designs feedback strongly on theory—often so much so as to redefine the problem under study. Indeed, these domains can often come to be method- rather than theory-driven over the course of their development.

Merton understood this point at a general level 40 years ago. We are not convinced, however, that modern social scientists have yet come to terms with his point. Research on aging has become increasingly quantitative and formally technical. Statistical modeling is the most obvious aspect of the technology. In addition, however, data resources have come to play an equally important but less completely understood role. These technologies have assumed primary roles in theory development and theory change. Theorizing without the recognition of the technical bases of our knowledge is precarious, at best, and foolhardy, at worst. As Merton noted, not only must research and theory "exchange solemn vows—they must know how to carry on from there."

NOTES

[1] The term *social structure* is subject to many definitions. The foregoing example should clarify our use of the term. We use it to refer to institutionalized constraints on the life course, such as factors that select individuals into the work force (e.g., technical and economic, gender and family role, etc.), factors that determine access to desired outcomes (e.g., firm size, labor markets, and other factors that determine access to pensions), the effects of cohort size, and other social and institutional factors.

[2] Many researchers attempt to deal with this by doing comparative research. Certainly such research is invaluable, but the assumption that phylogeny recapitulates ontogeny is dubious at best.

[3] Our application of the concepts of problem domain, research tradition, and the heuristics of research programs is in keeping with post-Kuhnian efforts in the philosophy, history, and sociology of the sciences to link intellectual and social developments in the study of scientific change. Where Kuhn (1970) proposed a sociological critique of the logical positivism inherited from earlier 20th century philosophy of science, the period since Kuhn has produced a "rationalist critique" of oversocialized conceptions of the sciences. Exponents of this point of view call for a more careful study of (1) the multidimensional aspects of cognitive and social factors and (2) the reciprocal interdependence of intellectual and technical features of the scientific enterprise (i.e., theory, method, instrumentation) and the social and cultural factors (i.e., specialty formation, disciplinary resistance to change, etc.). Those architects of the post-Kuhnian project who are especially related to our approach include the philosophers Lakatos (1978)

and Laudan (1977), the biologist Fleck (1979), and the sociologists Studer and Chubin (1980) and Edge and Mulkay (1976). Problem domains are research areas with cross-disciplinary relevance. Aging, cancer, and crime are three examples of problem domains. They are not defined by a single body of theory. Instead, they represent "sociocognitive regions" of problem solving that different disciplines come to share. The common problem domain comes to exert an influence of its own on problem solving across disciplines. However, disparate empirical traditions nevertheless approach the common problem with different conceptual and method-ological tools. Scientific developments in this context can emerge quite unpredictably from the (1) engagement of the object of study with the different research traditions and (2) confluence of multiple traditions on the common problem (Studer & Chubin, 1980).

[4]Studer and Chubin (1980) also documented the influence of "external" factors on the progress of research on cancer. They show, in particular, the impact of govern-ment initiatives (e.g., The National Cancer Institute) on the course of scientific change. The National Institute on Aging has had a similar influence on the study of gerontology, both by bringing new resources to the field and by fostering greater integration of the social and biological sciences.

[5]See the chapter by Passuth and Bengtson in this volume for extended examples.

[6]For earlier and somewhat more synoptic reviews of the emerging literature on the life-course perspective, see Featherman (1981) and Riley (1985).

[7]A more technical presentation of some of the ideas to be discussed here can be found in Featherman and Petersen (1986). They provide a thorough introduction to the notion of dynamic models. Featherman (1985) also discusses many of these ideas in a more demographically oriented perspective. Although work by Featherman and his various collaborators has been among the most visible in this area, we do not mean to imply that he is solely responsible for the introduction of dynamic models into aging and life-course research. A comprehensive review, for example, would include work by Tuma et al. (1979), who used dynamic models in an analysis of the effects of income maintenance programs on marital stability. However, Featherman has certain-ly emerged as the most prominent advocate of the use of dynamic models in research on aging.

[8]Tuma and Hannan (1984) provide a thorough exposition of these ideas. Allison (1985) contains a short but excellent overview. Both of these volumes contain refer-ences to the more technical literature.

[9]The term *rate* is used loosely here. Strictly speaking, we are modeling the instanta-neous rate of change with respect to time. Some authors prefer to talk about models for the risk of a transition in the next instant of time.

[10]Some readers will recognize the notion of a Markov process in this discussion. The usual Markovian assumptions require homogeneity (transition probabilities do not differ across persons) and stability (transition rates are constant over time). The models under discussion here relax both of these assumptions while dealing with transitions in continuous time as well.

[11]The 1940 and 1950 data have become available so recently that their impact has not yet been realized, but it will be immense.

[12]While unique in recent American history, they are by no means unique in terms of recent world history. One thinks immediately in terms of France in both Algeria

and Vietnam. It is not too fanciful to imagine that someday social scientists in the USSR will face a similar opportunity with respect to Afghanistan.

[13]Note that a model for the rate of change in morale is basically a differential equation. That is, once we are dealing with models for rates of change in continuous variables, we need to consider the second derivative (i.e., change in the rate of change) of the level of morale with respect to time. See Blalock (1969, Appendix B) for a brief exposition of these ideas. Coleman (1964) discusses the topic at length as do Tuma and Hannan (1984).

[14]These ideas are elaborated in Campbell (1986, 1988).

REFERENCES

Allison, P. D. (1985). *Event history analysis*. Beverly Hills, CA: Sage.

Baltes, P. B. (1968). Longitudinal and cross-sectional sequences in the study of age and generation effects. *Human Development, 11*, 145–171.

Barfield, R. E., & Morgan, J. N. (1969). *Early retirement: The decision and the experience*. Ann Arbor, MI: University of Michigan Press.

Binstock, R. H., & Shanas, E. (Eds.). (1985). *Handbook of aging and the social sciences*. New York: Van Nostrand Reinhold.

Blalock, H. B., Jr. (1969). *Theory construction*. Englewood Cliffs, NJ: Prentice-Hall.

Campbell, R. T. (1986). Design issues in panel studies of the lifecourse. Presented at International Symposium on Panel Surveys, Washington, D.C., November, 1986.

Campbell, R. T. (1988). Integrating conceptualization, design and analysis in panel studies of the life course. In K. W. Schaie, R. T. Campbell, W. Meridith, & S. Rawlings (Eds.), *Methodological issues in aging research*. New York: Springer Publishing Co.

Campbell, R. T., Abolafia, J., & Maddox, G. L. (1985). Life course analysis in social gerontology: Using replicated social surveys to study cohort differences. In A. S. Rossi (Ed.), *Gender and the life course* (pp. 301–318). New York: Aldine.

Coleman, J. S. (1964). *Mathematical sociology*. New York: The Free Press.

Demos, J., & Boocock, S. S. (Eds.). (1978). *Turning points: Historical and sociological essays on the family*. Chicago: University of Chicago Press.

DeViney, S., & O'Rand, A. M. (1987). Retirement policy, economic change and labor force participation among older men and women, 1951–1979. Unpublished manuscript. Duke University, Durham, NC.

Easterlin, R. A. (1980). *Birth and fortune*. New York: Basic Books.

Edge, D. O., & Mulkay, M. J. (1976). *Astronomy transformed: The emergence of radio astronomy in Britain*. New York: Wiley.

Elder, G. H., Jr. (1974). *Children of the Great Depression*. Chicago: University of Chicago Press.

Elder, G. H., Jr. (1986). Military time and turning points in men's lives. *Developmental Psychology, 22*, 233–245.

Featherman, D. L. (1981). The life span perspective. In *The 5-year outlook on science and technology, 2*; 621–648. Washington: U.S. Government Printing Office.

Featherman, D. L. (1985). Individual development and aging. In J. R. Nesselroade & A. von Eye (Eds.), *Individual development and social change*. New York: Academic Press.

Featherman, D. L., & Lerner, R. M. (1985). Ontogenesis and sociogenesis: Problematics for theory and research about development and socialization across the lifespan. *American Sociological Review, 50, 659–676.*

Featherman, D. L., & Petersen, T. (1986). Markers of aging: Modeling the clocks that time us. *Research on Aging, 8, 339–365.*

Featherman, D. L., & Sorensen, A. B. (1983). Societal transformation in Norway and change in the life course transitions into adulthood. *Acta Sociologica.*

Fisher, D. H. (1978). *Growing old in America*. New York: Oxford University Press.

Fleck, L. (1979). *Genesis and development of a scientific fact*. Chicago: University of Chicago Press.

Hannan, M. T., & Tuma, N. B. (1979). Methods for temporal analysis. *Annual Review of Sociology, 5, 303–328.*

Henretta, J. C., & O'Rand, A. M. (1983). Joint retirement in the dual worker family. *Social Forces, 62, 504–520.*

Hernes, G. (1976). Structural change in social processes. *American Journal of Sociology, 82, 513–547.*

Irelan, L. M. (1972). Retirement history study: Introduction. *Social Security Bulletin, 35, 3–8.*

Kertzer, D. I., & Keith, J. (Eds.). (1984). *Age and anthropological theory*. Ithaca, NY: Cornell University Press.

Kuhn, T. S. (1970). *The structure of scientific revolutions*. Princeton, NJ: Princeton University Press.

Lakatos, I. (1978). The methodology of scientific research programs. *Philosophical Papers* (Vol. 1). Cambridge: Cambridge University Press.

Laudan, L. (1977). *Progress and its problems: Towards a theory of scientific growth*. Berkeley, CA: University of California Press.

Lieberson, S. A. (1985). *Making it count*. Berkeley, CA: University of California Press.

Mason, W. M., Wong, G. Y., & Entwisle, B. (1983). Contextual analysis through the multilevel linear model. In S. Leinhart (Ed.), *Sociological methodology 1983–1984* (pp. 72–103). San Francisco: Jossey Bass.

Merton, R. K. (1967). The bearing of empirical research on sociological theory. In R. K. Merton (Ed.), *On theoretical sociology: Five essays old and new* (pp. 156–172). New York: Free Press.

Mullins, N. C. (1972). The development of a scientific specialty: The phage group and the origins of molecular biology. *Minerva, 10, 51–82.*

Neugarten, B. L. (1985). Interpretive social science and research on aging. In A. S. Rossi (Ed.), *Gender and the life course* (pp. 291–300). New York: Aldine.

O'Rand, A. M., (1984). Women. In E. Palmore (Ed.), *Handbook of the aged in the United States* (pp. 125–142). New York: Greenwood Press.

O'Rand, A. M. (1985). *Age, job attachment and pension acquisition*. Paper presented at the 80th Annual Meeting of the American Sociological Association, Washington, DC., August, 1985.

O'Rand, A. M. & Henretta, J. C. (1982). Delayed career entry, industrial pension structure and early retirement in a cohort of unmarried women. *American Sociological Review, 47*, 365–373.

O'Rand, A. M., & Mac Lean, V. M. (1986). Labor markets, pension rule structure and retirement benefit promise for long-term employees. *Social Forces, 65*, 134–141.

Pampel, F. C., & Weiss, J. A. (1983). Economic development, pension policies, and the labor force participation of aged males: A cross-national, longitudinal approach. *American Journal of Sociology, 89*, 350–372.

Parnes, H. S. (1975). The national longitudinal surveys: New vistas for labor market research. *American Economic Review, 65*, 224–249.

Preston, S. H. (1984). Children and the elderly: Divergent paths for America's dependents. *Demography, 21*, 431–438.

Riley, M. W. (1985). Age strata in social systems. In R. H. Binstock & E. Shanas (Eds.), *Handbook of aging and the social sciences* (pp. 369–414). New York: Van Nostrand Reinhold.

Riley, M. W., Johnson, M., & Foner, A. (1972). Elements in a model of age stratification. In M. W. Riley & A. Foner (Eds.), *Aging and society* (Vol. 3, pp. 3–26). New York: Russell Sage.

Ryder, N. B. (1965). The cohort as a concept in the study of social change. *American Sociological Review, 30*, 843–861.

Schaie, K. W. (1965). A general model for the study of developmental problems. *Psychological Bulletin, 64*, 92–107.

Schaie, K. W. (Ed.). (1983). *Longitudinal studies of adult psychological development*. New York: Guilford Press.

Studer, K. E., & Chubin, D. E. (1980). *The cancer mission: Social contexts of biomedical research*. Beverly Hills, CA: Sage.

Tuma, N. B., & Hannan, M. T. (1984). *Social dynamics*. New York: Academic Press.

Tuma, N. B., Hannan, M. T., & Groeneveld, L. P. (1979). Dynamic analysis of event histories. *American Journal of Sociology, 84*, 820–854.

PART II
Biological Theories in Aging: Implications for the Behavioral and Social Sciences

5

Disease Models of Aging: Brain and Behavior Considerations

Gene D. Cohen

Sometimes a good rhetorical technique is to exaggerate a point in order to make the point. In the process, various relationships not previously recognized become more apparent. Disease can effect a similar result; by disrupting various underlying physiological pathways or emotional tendencies, disease can lead to the identification of pathways or tendencies not previously apparent. Hence, attention to diseases of the brain and mind in later life may provide new windows to the influence of the brain on normal aging. New views on behavioral theories of aging also might emerge. To the extent that the diseases of the brain being studied alter behavior in the elderly, a better understanding of these disease states may offer us a better understanding of the broader interaction of brain and behavior in aging *per se* (Cohen, 1985; Cohen, in press).

From a different perspective, disease models where brain changes alter behavior in later life focus our attention on the potential modifiability of behavior in general with aging. Granted, change is in the direction of dysfunction with disease, as opposed to adaptability that is commonly associated with health or normality. But the specter of generic modifiability is raised, and with it the search for underlying mechanisms and influences on these mechanisms that can effect positive change with aging. In the process, the borderline between normal aging and disease states in later life can also become better defined, as suggested in the chapter by Henry (this volume).

This is a phenomenological approach to theory building, not unlike phenomenological approaches followed in other chapters, such as that of Passuth
and Bengtson examining social phenomena and that of Reker and Wong
studying what growing old "means" to those experiencing it. Here, efforts are
made to derive further understanding about brain/behavior relationships in
normal aging from apparent magnifications of brain/behavior interactions
seen in certain diseases. The disease models presented have been selected
because they seem to provide examples of such magnification.

Alzheimer's disease in particular is informative, for two reasons. First, it was
long viewed as an accelerated version if not the inevitable outcome of the
aging process; second, so many of its clinical manifestations for so much of its
natural history are behavioral.

ALZHEIMER'S DISEASE: A PARADIGM FOR STUDYING
RELATIONSHIPS BETWEEN THE BRAIN AND BEHAVIOR

One of the truly extraordinary aspects of Alzheimer's disease is that although
it is a devastating brain disorder, most of its major symptoms well into the
course of the illness are of a behavioral nature. More striking physical problems, such as incontinence, typically do not occur until the late stage of the
disorder. Even incontinence, when it first occurs in Alzheimer's disease, is
often more a factor of poor concentration on the part of the patient rather
than somatic insufficiency. Although pathologic neuroanatomical and neurochemical changes have been identified in the brains of those with Alzheimer's
disease, physical manifestations may not be evident over much of the clinical
course of the disorder (Reisberg, 1983). This explains in part why Alzheimer's
disease is so difficult to diagnose clinically.

Unlike a stroke, where one can observe nerve, motor, and muscular deficits,
somatic manifestations are typically absent in Alzheimer's disease. Instead, one
witnesses cognitive, psychological, and behavioral problems. Accordingly, one
can appreciate how the early stage of Alzheimer's disease could easily be
confused with depression—or how depression could be confused with Alzheimer's disease—since both can alter functioning along cognitive, psychological, and behavioral axes. Cognitive problems are those of memory and intellectual impairment; psychological problems can include depression and
delusions; behavior problems are commonly those of wandering and agitation.
As a result of this constellation of changes, interpersonal relationships and
psychosocial functioning become significantly impaired in patients with Alzheimer's disease. The point relevant to this discussion is that brain changes can
be unapparent but have profound consequences on how one thinks, feels,
behaves, and interacts with other people. Indeed, as in the case of Alzheimer's
disease, brain changes can be quite marked and still be missed. Whereas we

recognize that external environmental factors can affect motivation, attitudes, emotions, the approach to tasks, the orientation to new experiences, and the nature of social involvement in later life, we have looked less at the role of internal influences within the aging brain. Such influences are, of course, more difficult to observe and demand considerably greater study.

BEHAVIOR AND BRAIN PLASTICITY

When brain changes in general are considered, an association of unmodifiability commonly accompanies such attention. In other words, a general expectation exists that once brain changes occur they are difficult if not impossible to either modify or reverse—even more so in the elderly. Findings from brain research, however, have given us new insights about the potential for brain plasticity (modifiability)—including plasticity of the normal aging brain (Diamond, Rosenzweig, Bennett, Lidner, & Lyon, 1972). Results, for example, from experiments studying the impact of challenging and stimulating environments on the brains of rats are revealing. Following such stimulation, the cerebral cortices, or the thinking part of the brains of these rats were found to have thickened, to have increased in weight, and to have contained greater activity of the enzyme acetylcholinesterase. That enzyme affects the metabolism of the neurotransmitter acetylcholine, viewed as being involved in memory and intellectual function. These studies also found an increase in the glial cells of the rat brains. Glial cells are believed to carry out a number of auxiliary metabolic functions to aid neurons (the primary cells of the cerebral cortex). Glial cells are thought to be involved in the transport of important substances between capillaries and neurons, in the formation of the fatty sheath that insulates the neuron's axon, and in influencing various enzymatic activities that affect neuronal functions.

Subsequent studies in this area focused more intensively on age by attempting to replicate results with young rats in studies of aging ones (Diamond, 1983). Diamond examined the terminal dendrites of neurons in rats placed in enriched environments. Dendrites permit one neuron to communicate with many other neurons. Diamond's research showed that the neurons of older rats exposed to more challenging stimuli had significantly longer dendrites than neurons of aged rats receiving less stimulation. The alteration in dendritic architecture raised the idea that improved communication had resulted among existing neurons, and that the capacity for these changes did not cease with aging. From a different vantage point, these studies illustrated that behavioral stimulation influenced not only neurochemical enzymatic changes but neuroanatomical alterations as well. Behavior influenced brain structure, including the structure of *aging* brains. Those who have advised "use it or lose it" in later life, in referring to the aging brain as analogous to muscle, have taken notice of these findings.

Research on brain plasticity suggests possible connections between biological and behavioral modifiability, and provides us with new information for challenging or constructing theoretical formulations about psychosocial phenomena in later life. To the extent that behavioral or environmental stimulation can effect changes in brain cell chemistry and anatomy, then a brain/behavior feedback loop might be postulated. Whereas Alzheimer's disease illustrates how brain changes can profoundly affect behavior, the enriched-environment research points to the reverse—the influence of behavior on brain changes. One might then postulate a potential cycle that could occur if these sequences were to connect in the normal aging brain. Specifically, a theory could be offered in which sustained psychosocial stimulation could be viewed as influencing the neuroanatomy and neurophysiology of the aging brain; in turn, these structural and physiological brain changes would then function in feedback fashion to exert influence on behavior in the older adult. Such speculative changes, for example, might influence the level or ease of behavioral responsiveness. By applying these considerations to the *Activity Theory* versus *Disengagement Theory* debate, further perspective is added to the potential role of social activity in helping to better facilitate inherent brain plasticity that accompanies the aging process—and, in turn, behavioral plasticity.

BEHAVIORAL DISORDER AND BRAIN CHANGES

Whereas research has shown various effects of positive environmental stimulation on brain changes, studies also have pointed to effects of adverse environmental stimuli on brain cell anatomy and chemistry. Kandel's (1983) research on the *Aplysia* (a giant marine snail) has been looked at in this light. Kandel has attempted to study the effects of stress on brain neurons. From his work, a search at the molecular level has raised the possibility that certain structural changes linked to chronic anxiety occur within brain cells. Since nerve cells communicate with one another via the release of neurotransmitters, anxiety may be associated with the increased release of certain specific chemical communicators. Chronic anxiety may result from a structural alteration in the number or size of vesicles on neurons that store and release these neurotransmitters. Stimuli affecting vesicle status could come from either internal (e.g., genetic expression) or external (e.g., environmental stress) sources, or a combination of these and other factors. Applying these considerations to certain perceived negative behaviors in later life, one might hypothesize that prolonged adverse psychosocial conditions from earlier life might influence specific brain changes which could then play a part in limiting behavioral plasticity with aging. Such a hypothesis would provide yet another illustration of the many changes that can occur in later life as a factor of underlying illness, as opposed to generic or inevitable effects of aging alone.

On the other hand, brain changes associated with aging itself may influence in a positive way some of the behavioral disorders that occur in later life. The course of schizophrenia in later life is a case in point. Neurochemically, an excess of dopamine in the brain has been associated with schizophrenic disorder (Weiner, 1985). Supporting this theory is the fact that many of the drugs used to treat schizophrenia have mechanisms of action that block the neurotransmission of dopamine. But with advancing years, it has been estimated that 30 to 40% of schizophrenics experience a gradual reduction (often referred to as burnout) of the intensity of their symptoms, even in the absence of drug therapy. One hypothesis for this phenomenon holds that based on the dopamine-excess view of schizophrenia, symptomatic individuals who had relatively high dopamine levels, due to the loss of dopamine-producing neurons that can accompany the aging process, gradually would return to a more normal state of functioning (Finch, 1985). Certain commonly occurring (normal?) aging brain changes, in other words, may serve to ameliorate one of the major disorders of humankind that characteristically has its onset in younger adulthood.

NEW INFORMATION FOR BEHAVIORAL AND PSYCHOSOCIAL THEORIES OF AGING

What the above discussion in general suggests is that potentially new insights into behavioral and psychosocial theories of aging could come from a better understanding of the interaction of the brain and behavior in later life. Again, looking at disease states in the elderly may help separate the forest from the trees in recognizing or interpreting normal behavioral changes with aging. Hence, just as normal aging brain changes have been implicated in mitigating the symptomatology of many schizophrenics as they grow old, one theoretical question might be: Do normal aging brain changes influence some of the behavioral manifestations that have been suggested as reflecting developmental changes with advancing years? For example, could it be that neurotransmitter changes with aging play a part in altering impulses in such a way as to influence one's perspective of the world, and thereby one's behavior in society in later life?

Consider, for example, discussions of wisdom—a phenomenon often suggested as a candidate for what might be considered behavior more likely to occur with aging (Baltes & Willis, 1977; Birren, this volume). The dynamics of wisdom are complex and explanations of it vary. Part of wisdom may be a behavioral dynamic of being able to stand back from a situation to gain perspective, fostering better judgment. Impulsivity could interfere with judgment; dispassion might promote it. Too much dispassion could slip into apathy, which itself could grow to pathological proportions, as can be seen in various cases of depression and Alzheimer's disease. Depression can also accompany Alzheimer's disease, compounding the degree of dysfunction in that disorder. When antidepressant medications are given in both depression and the subtype of Alzheimer's disease with depression, apathy in both cases may be lifted (Fann & Wheless, 1981). The drug response further reflects the underlying influence on behavior of neurotransmitters upon which psychoactive agents are postulated to exert their effects (Schildkraut, 1978). This brings us back to the initial question: Could neurotransmitter changes in the aging brain set the stage for postulated later-life behavior such as wisdom?

Again, a later-life disease model (Alzheimer's disease) serves to magnify the potential influence of brain phenomena on behavioral phenomena and to attract our attention in the search to recognize or understand possible normal, age-related behavioral phenomena. A better understanding of brain changes and their effects on behavior in later life would only add to our ability to theorize about distinctive patterns or tendencies in social interactions influenced by the aging process.

REFERENCES

Baltes, P. B., & Willis, S. L. (1977). Toward psychological theories of aging and development. In J. E. Birren & K. W. Schaie (Eds.), *Handbook of the psychology of aging* (pp. 128–154). New York: Van Nostrand Reinhold.

Cohen, G. D. (1985). Toward an interface of mental and physical health phenomena in geriatrics. In C. M. Gaitz & T. Samorajski (Eds.), *Aging 2000: Our health care destiny* (pp. 284–290). New York: Springer-Verlag.

Cohen, G. D. (in press). *The brain in human aging*. New York: Springer Publishing Co.

Diamond, M. C., Rosenzweig, M. R., Bennett, E. L., Lindner, B., & Lyon, L. (1972). Effects of environmental enrichment and impoverishment on rat cerebral cortex. *Journal of Neurology, 3*, 47–64.

Diamond, M. C. (1983). The aging rat forebrain: Male–female left–right; environment and lipofuscin. In D. Samuel, S. Algeri, S. Gershon, V. E. Grimm, & G. Toffano (Eds.), *Aging of the brain* (pp. 93–98). New York: Raven Press.

Fann, W. E., & Wheless, J. C. (1981). Treatment and amelioration of psychopathologic affective states in the dementias of late life. In N. E. Miller and G. D. Cohen (Eds.), *Clinical aspects of Alzheimer's disease and senile dementia* (pp. 161–185). New York: Raven Press.

Finch, C. E. (1985). A progress report on neurochemical and neuroendocrine regulation in normal and pathologic aging. In C. M. Gaitz and T. Samorajski (Eds.), *Aging 2000: Our health care destiny* (pp. 79–90). New York: Springer-Verlag.

Kandel, E. R. (1983). From metapsychology to molecular biology: Explorations into the nature of anxiety. *American Journal of Psychiatry, 140*, 1277–1293.

Reisberg, B. (Ed.). (1983). *Alzheimer's disease*. New York: The Free Press.

Schildkraut, J. J. (1978). Current status of the catecholamine hypothesis of affective disorders. In M. A. Lipton, A. DiMascio, & K. F. Killam (Eds.), *Psychopharmacology: A generation of progress* (pp. 1223–1234). New York: Raven Press.

Weiner, H. (1985). Schizophrenia: Etiology. In H. I. Kaplan & B. J. Sadock (Eds.), *Comprehensive textbook of psychiatry/IV (Volume 1, 4th ed.)* (pp. 650–680). Baltimore, MD: Williams & Wilkins.

6

The Dynamics of
Aging and Time:
How Physical Action Implies
Social Action

F. Eugene Yates

BACKGROUND

At our body size our median life span ought to be only 27 years (Calder, 1984); we live three times as long as we should, according to allometric scaling arguments for other mammals (Yates & Kugler, 1986). Nevertheless, aging and mortality stand out among the concerns of most human adults, inviting cheerful or resigned acceptance, or denial, according to one's temperament and philosophy of life.

In spite of their dramatic presence in human life, aging and senescence are not ubiquitous in the biosphere—some transformed cells go on reproducing in the laboratory as long as you feed them, having escaped the "Hayflick limit" that applies to many normal mammalian cells. Single-cell organisms do not usually last long in the wild, often getting eaten or done in by circumstances; but having the option of dividing without mating, or mating and then dividing, they assure that some of their genes will appear in new organisms before they themselves become old or destroyed. Let them enjoy their eternal youthfulness—my purpose here is to take the anthropocentric view and theorize about human aging and the immutable death rate of one per person.

Theory in Gerontology

Sacher (1980) classified theories of aging and did not like what he saw: "The manifold aspects of the phenomenology of aging make it possible for investigators with different disciplinary backgrounds to perceive many diverse growing points for the development of theories about the aspects of aging that are most apposite to their own research interests" (p. 3). He went on to list "the program theory of aging," "the mutation theory of aging," "the autoimmune theory of aging," and "physiological theories of aging" among many others, and noted:

> This reasoning process, whereby a part becomes equated to the whole, so that each aspect-theory pretends to be a comprehensive theory competing with all others, is detrimental to the healthy growth of gerontology in both its experimental and theoretical aspects, and tends to diminish the stature of gerontology in the eyes of scientists from other disciplines.

Sacher then pointed out that one of the detrimental consequences of pluralism in theory building is that it takes attention away from the need to develop a *comprehensive theoretical structure for gerontology* that might integrate several aspect-theories into a more coherent whole. He concluded by saying: "There is an evident need for a competent, professional approach to gerontological theory-building in its own right."

In this chapter I suggest a physical foundation for a general gerontological theory. In so doing I have to select a thematic content for the theory that I shall propose (Holton, 1973): My choice is to address the question of how aging relates to thermodynamics of irreversible processes and nonlinear mechanics. According to Sacher's classification of gerontological theories, mine belongs in the category called "evolutionary." The elements with which I shall work are the First and Second laws of thermodynamics, qualitative dynamics viewed as the geometry (topology) of behavior, and the concepts of fluctuations, variability, adaptability, and stability. Overall, my approach will be through dynamics—the physical science of motion and change. Classical dynamics has two subdivisions: *kinetics* (when forces are accounted for) and *kinematics* (when motions are examined without specifying causal forces). I shall draw upon both.

My purpose is not to prove a theorem but to provide a sketch painted with a broad brush; a narrative in a very discursive style, gaining, I hope, in useful imagery what it lacks in rigor. For background and more technical detail about thermodynamics and biology I recommend Mercer (1981), Atkins (1984), Conrad (1983), Morris (1984), Yates (1981, 1982a,b, 1984), Yates, Marsh, and Iberall (1972), and Yates and Iberall (1982). Accounts of differing *concepts of time* as they appear in physics can be found in Morris (1984), Boxenbaum

(1986), Fischer (1967), Landes (1983), and Mehlberg (1980). For those wanting an authoritative but popular account of space-time manifolds, see Gardner (1976). Finally, a view of topological dynamics has been given in a very colorful manner, without equations, by Abraham and Shaw (1982–1984). Some of the ideas that I shall develop can be found also in Kugler and Turvey (1986).

Physics versus Biology: Dynamics versus Information

Physics is about all the beings and becomings, states and rates in the universe. It addresses two questions: (1) What is the universe made of? (2) What are the rules that govern motion and change within it? Most physicists make the Assumption of Simplicity, which supposes that surface complexities always arise out of deep simplicity, that, at bottom, nature is simple (Weinberg, 1985). Physics seeks laws that are (nearly) exact, universal, inexorable, and invariant under coordinate transformations. It is powerful and parsimonious in its explanations and reductionistic in outlook. A favorite topic is the transformation of energy in reversible, conservative, linear, nondissipative processes. Even though thermodynamics (including classical, reversible equilibrium thermostatics and near-equilibrium, linear, irreversible statistical thermodynamics) are parts of physics, it is not unusual to find physicists who actively dislike the thermodynamic outlook, with its interest in entropy production and bookkeeping. Normal physics prefers energy over entropy, or even better, it chooses the vacuum and quantumstuff. Physics is *not* about information, and "information" is not a fundamental, technical term in physics; though, of course, it is in some branches of engineering.

In contrast, biology concerns self-organizing, dissipative, nonlinear, irreversible, complex processes that might be described as having a (relative) surface simplicity arising out of deep complexity. Above all, the biosphere shows variety and diversity beyond anything normally addressed by physics. Furthermore, the gulf between physics and biology is widened by the habits of biologists who insist on using an information-theoretic jargon to describe their favorite topics. To somewhat oversimplify but dramatize the difference, we can say that physics is about dynamics (motion and change), while biology claims to be about information (Yates, 1985, 1987a,b). The relationship of biology to physics has been very thoughtfully discussed by Rosen (1986).[1]

If the above contrasts are roughly correct, then it is going to be an uphill task to provide a physical theory for human aging and senescence. It will be necessary to attenuate the view that DNA is information-rich, serving to provide *codes* and *programs* that *direct* biological processes, and to take instead the view that DNA is a structural constraint on chemical kinetic networks as part of a dynamic system. Of course, no biologist denies that DNA is structure, but to emphasize its form as a constraint on kinetics, rather than as a code or a message or a commander or a director or otherwise "smart" molecule, is to go against the grain of his closet vitalism.

Sacher (1980) has made a similar point, although he is more comfortable using the term *information* than I am. He remarked that the accepted concept of the relationship of genotype to phenotype (one with which he and I disagree) is that a given genotype precisely determines a particular phenotype, in the absence of environmental variation, so that any within-group variation in an isogenic population must be due to environmental variation. Sacher correctly complained that this approach fails to take into account the informational cost entailed in specifying that the genetically determined character must lie within some vanishingly small range. It also neglects the possibly important role of internal fluctuations. Large though the information content of the mammalian genome is, it is nevertheless finite. It can specify (with some error) perhaps 100,000 proteins. It cannot directly specify spatial coordinates of the phenotype at all, nor program timing in a clocklike fashion. It is a changeable constraint in an execution-driven, self-organizing, energy-transforming, dissipative process. No more "information" is involved in the shaping of such processes than is requisite for sustained performance in the present environment, including the characteristic level of internal and external environmental fluctuations and noise.

For a *formal system* (e.g., a program running in a computer) to simulate such a biophysical process requires discrete, serial operations and an *explicit representation* of every aspect of the process. In actual biophysical realizations the operations are mainly those of parallel and coordinated dynamics, and many changes need no explicit description because they are taken care of by the dynamical laws involving real space, time, and energy (Kugler, Kelso, & Turvey, 1980). The most dramatic demonstration that DNA is a constraint on chemical kinetics is seen when it is copied—here it acts as a template for itself in an ordinary chemical sense but does not contain a description of itself. In that fashion it meets the now famous von Neumann criterion for escaping an infinite regress in designing a self-constructing system: A living system encapsulates a description of itself but it avoids the paradox seemingly inherent in so doing by not trying to include a description *of* the description *in* the description (see Poundstone, 1985). The point is that when DNA is constraining a mapping from genes to protein structure, the same kinds of making, breaking, and exchanging of chemical bonds are involved as in the copying. We *arbitrarily* call the copying process "dynamic," the mapping process "informational," and DNA a "description" for convenience of discussion and for insights about which segments of DNA structure constrain which amino acid linkings; but similar chemical kinetic principles underlie transcription, translation, and copying.

The reason I bring the dynamics on stage is to get at scientific issues of stability and instability; then we can hope to rationalize aging as a problem of time-varying constraints leading to progressive instability. I am confident that the scientific explanation of aging will ultimately be based on the fundamental dynamic style of description, rather than on the higher-level, metaphorical, informational style of description. (Hans Bremmerman has humorously remarked that "physics-envy is the curse of biology!" To me the issue is: Can we strengthen biology through epistemological reductions to physics? I see no chance for expunging intellectually pernicious or vapid vitalism, entelechy, élan vital, and "Just So stories" from biology unless we strive for that reduction, at least in principle.)

Biological Processes Are Not Program-Driven

It is almost impossible to talk about or even think about the genome, the immune system, the endocrine system (hormones and their receptors), and the nervous system without anthropomorphizing by injecting smart, linguistically competent elements into the account. But there is little hope of joining biology and physics while we do that. Elsewhere I have argued in more detail (Yates, 1987a) that computer metaphors and information science can be inimical to clear thinking about "problem-solving" processes in biology, whether at the organism level or at the species level.

It is true that symbol strings and syntactic production rules can adequately account for the classical indicational and injunctional aspects of information used by human beings. These categories include the Shannon-Weaver information of the selective kind and also much descriptive information such as resolution of a measurement. Selective information tells us, among other things, how surprised we should be if a symbol or symbol string occurred twice in succession; injunctional information directs or commands states of affairs ("Stop!"). Kugler and Turvey and their colleagues have emphasized that indicational and injunctional information for human beings requires also a companion *specificational* sense of *information* (a concept introduced by Gibson that is distinct from the other orthodox sense of the term *information*). Gibsonian specificational information is a physical variable that can be associated with some low-dimensional macroscopic properties of low-energy or low-mass physical fields (i.e., kinematic fields) lawfully generated by physical properties of system and surround. Optical flow fields provide a convenient example; their physical singularities charge the situation with "information" without involving internal representations, codes, messages, or privileged content (Carello, Turvey, Kugler, & Shaw, 1984; Turvey & Kugler, 1984; Yates & Kugler, 1984).

We can stop a car at an intersection because we can read a symbol string or recognize a sign of the type "Slow down" or "Stop" that is intended to direct the dynamics of traffic flow. But complying with these injunctions is possible only if there is a continuously available information flow specific to the retarding of forward motion and enough time to contact with the place where the velocity is to go to zero. This information arises from the pseudomotion of fixed objects in the surround as we move through a textured scene. The rate of dilation of the visual solid angle to the point of observation is a singularity created and self-organized in a kinematic field. It specifies continuously time and place of stop (or collision). Without information in this kinematic (dynamic) specificational sense, symbolic information in the indicational/injunctional sense is impotent.

Freeman and Skarda (1985), taking a similar stand against smart elements in biology, have argued that the notion that an internal "representation" of "external" reality, whether it appears in the field of artificial intelligence or psychology, is destructive of clear thinking about adaptive behavior in living systems. The existence of such representations is unprovable and, in any case, the concept is unnecessary. The root of the difficulties is that the referents, contexts, and meanings of representations are invariably in the brain of the observer and not in that of the observed. Freeman and Skarda then present striking experimental evidence that animals detect and classify odors through dynamics, not through classical "information."

Much of what we tend to think of as informational in biological systems has very strong dynamic aspects (Yates, 1985, 1987a,b). During animal development, as daughter cells of the same parent cell differentiate, we see different kinds of offspring arising from the same genetic message. In that process the genome participates as an interacting component in a large dynamic array involving activators and inhibitors and fluctuations in chemical fields. (See Higgins, 1967, for a purely chemical view of such events.) The genome is not just sitting as a static linear array bearing a code. By the time chromosomal operations take place, the mix of information and dynamics is overwhelming.

In contrast, the perfect embodiment of formal computing is a machine that is transparent to the user in the sense that its dynamics (lags, delays, switching transients, and mechanical-electrical failures) never reach his or her attention. The dynamics of computers are suppressed. But the genotype-phenotype relationship not only expresses dynamics, it bends the dynamics back toward the genome. Although we are not likely to let go of words like *repressor, enhancer,* or *promoter*, the more general and less loaded terms *activation* and *inhibition* better describe what is physically involved in gene expression. Viewed that way, genetic chemistry comes closer to being real chemistry, in which we can regard a developmental trajectory as being execution-driven rather than program-driven.

The events and stages of the unfolding of a self-organizing process in biology are not clocked nor driven by a program—they are shaped by the dynamical accomplishments of the preceding stages of the processes, in which some genes serve as modifiable constraints on cooperative kinetics that generate new structures as new constraints at the next stage. It makes no more sense to say that "genes direct development" than it does to say "balloons rise by levity."

Of course, in some narrow sense almost every computer program also seems execution-driven because the state of some switches may be determined by the outcome of a preceding operation. However, I use the term *execution-driven* more precisely to mean that the execution of one stage of processing leads to a change in the master program itself, if there is a program, or in the hardware available for subsequent stages. Program-driven simulations in digital computers can imitate (model) many execution-driven processes in the material world through subroutines, intermittent calling-up of peripheral devices, and so on. But in such cases everything must be on hand in advance, contrary to the conditions of truly execution-driven processes, which are *self-organizing* (Yates, 1987a). Kugler et al. (1980) have also emphasized the importance of appreciating DNA as a dynamic constraint rather than as a message. They remark (omitting the internal references):

> It becomes more apparent that the conditions for a biological process are not to be found invested in any single part or any special subset of parts but in the total organization. . . . The tendency to explain a phenomenon . . . by investing the phenomenon in an independent device (say, the sequence of instructions in the DNA program) is in keeping with the style of scientific inquiry that has been dubbed "self-actional" by Dewey and Bentley. The extreme consequence of this style of inquiry is a semantic regress—each distinguishable phenomenon has an independent device as its source. The main general consequence is that many phenomena . . . are conceived as unique and fundamental and not explainable through an appeal to other principles. But . . . a very different style of inquiry, dubbed transactional by Dewey and Bentley and coalitional by Shaw and Turvey, is consonant with the approach taken when a dynamic rather than a machine stance is adopted. Roughly, this style of inquiry looks at the system in full, emphasizes the mutuality of its "components" and tries to understand phenomena as system properties. The claim on which we are converging is that the order in biological and physiological processes is primarily owing to dynamics and that the constraints that arise, both anatomical and functional, serve only to channel and guide dynamics; it is not that actions are caused by constraints—it is, rather, that some actions are excluded by them. (pp. 8–9)

The point here is that the concepts and language of classical dynamics are sufficient to account for activation and inhibition in chemical networks and can help anchor our discussions of biological development and senescence in established principles of physics and chemistry, thus driving the residual vitalism out of the assertions of molecular biologists when they discuss causality in their systems.

Finally, consider the remark by the inventive topologist René Thom (1986), developer of modern Catastrophe Theory:

The almost simultaneous appearance, in the middle of the twentieth century, of computers and molecular biology developed the idea that genetic material, DNA, was the analogue of a computer program for the development of an adult organism from an egg. This interpretation offered a new, important breakthrough: previously the mechanical analogy had constantly raised the problem of biological finality. How could all these organs, so beautifully adapted to their function and of such a huge efficiency, be formed, apparently by themselves, during embryological development? Was it not necessary to postulate the assistance of a "genius," a demiurge who had to direct and control the whole process of epigenesis? The proposition that the complete structure of the organism might be encoded in the genomic nucleotide sequence of DNA solved the problem: one had only to admit that DNA, playing the role of the demiurge, directed the full development of the embryo, exactly as an engineer dictates orders to his or her subordinates in a manufacturing plant. . . . But, in the initial case of metazoan embryonic development, the situation is entirely different: one has to understand how the genetic information supposedly included in the DNA can render itself in the 3-dimensional organic structure of the embryo and later of the adult. . . . As a result, all modern biological thought has been trapped in the fallacious homonym associated with the phrase "genetic code," and this abuse of language has resulted in a state of conceptual sterility, out from which there is little hope of escape. To achieve some progress in solving this difficulty, only a major theoretical jump will be any help. . . . All the regulatory properties of an organic structure rely on some geometric properties of a "figure of regulation" which lies in some abstract space of metabolic activities. A function is then a regulatory apparatus of a formal, dynamic nature insuring homeostasis of some physiologically important character or parameter, such as chemical energy content, oxygen content, etc. . . . When all these functions perform correctly they insure canalization of the metabolic state of the system around a specific attractor (the figure of regulation). The aim of theoretical biology is to describe (with the utmost accuracy possible) this geometric object.

To which I can add only: "Hear! Hear!"

PHYSICAL SENESCENCE

I have taken some pains (admittedly arguing ex cathedra and polemically—but see the references for some substantiating details) to wring the toxic juices of "information" or "computation" out of molecular biology in order to close the gap between biology and physics so that we can make some progress toward a comprehensive scientific theory of the aging of biological systems. In that physical theory aging will be seen as a progressive loss of dynamical stability dependent on changing constraints. That alteration of constraints is the touch of the Second Law in biochemical networks. The theory will also require the concept that there are two kinds of time for biological organisms.

External and Intrinsic Times in Biological Dynamics: Quantized Action

Living systems are embedded in physical and social environments for which an "external" time is one of the four dimensions of a space-time manifold. The Special Theory of Relativity invoked a "flat" Minkowski four-dimensional space-time that had no curvature, being in that respect like the two- and three-dimensional spaces defined by the axioms of Euclid. The General Theory enlarged the scope and introduced the concept of a four-dimensional space-time world that is not flat but curved. The curvature of this world is generated by matter and energy: near a large amount of matter the curvature of the four-dimensional world is large; far away from matter it is close to zero. Through its field equations the theory provided the exact relationship between curvature (now a physical variable instead of a parameter) of space-time on the one hand, and matter and energy on the other. Even so, in spite of this achievement, Einstein's theories leave the nature of physical time still unclear, and deep confusions, contradictions, or paradoxes remain unresolved (Mehlberg, 1980; Thom, 1983).

In the following discussion I take the simplest view consistent with Einsteinian locality, which I accept as an absolute postulate concerning the physics of ordinary macroscopic human experiences, including that of aging. [For discussions of the necessity for and difficulties attending the assumption of Einsteinian locality as an absolute postulate, see Thom (1983), Challifour (1985), and Herbert (1985).]

At terrestrial scales the external physical space and time for the biosphere are those of Special Relativity (flat space-time). The *external time* is causal with respect to the biosphere, both deterministically through the structure of time in periodic geophysical processes such as the rising and setting of the sun, the ebb and flow of tides, and so on, and randomly, through external fluctuations. External geophysical time gives us the clock time by which we scale chronological age, but *it does not necessarily give us intrinsic human age*, which may be determined by internal process time, as described below.

Intrinsic time is created by biological processes as an emergent property of their nonlinear dissipative dynamics, leading to the result, as Richardson and Rosen (1979) point out, that the intrinsic biological significance of a unit of external time cannot itself be constant but must change with chronological age. For instance, if we rescale time so that two extrinsic time intervals are similar in that the probability of death of an organism (intrinsically determined) is the same for each of them, then the length of extrinsic time intervals so matched progressively shrinks as the organism ages.

External time and intrinsic time for an individual are coupled through circadian (and perhaps other) endogenous rhythms that can be entrained by geophysical and social rhythms. This, I believe, is the chief function of many of the so-called biological clocks—to connect intrinsic and extrinsic times. (But not all intrinsic time is entrainable by periodic processes in external time.)

Quantized Action

The origin of intrinsic time is quantized action. The cyclic integral in Bohr's first version of quantum theory: $\oint p\ dq = nh$ (where p is momentum of a particle, q is position, and n is any integer; h is Planck's constant and represents the quantum of action) points the way for the quantization of macroscopic phenomena as well. *Action is the fundamental physical quantity for which "atomicity" is assured at all scales.* The time scaling of internal metabolic processes arises out of the discretization of action, and that in turn arises out of the general dynamics of complex systems (Richardson & Rosen, 1979; Yates, 1982a). For every sustained or persistent process there is a time intrinsic to its operation, rising out of the process itself. This concept sounds tautological, but it is not. If a process involves changes over time, it is not empty to assert that there will be some parameter t_0 that is a characteristic time for the completed change. (The mean relaxation time in statistical mechanics, the half-life of a drug in a pharmacokinetic process, or the period of an oscillation are examples.) Similarly, every process will have a characteristic spatial dimension (analogous to the mean free path in statistical mechanics). These space-time characteristic parameters emerge from the combination of natural law under constraints and energy throughput. The parameters are functions of the constraints.

The Second Law of Thermodynamics can be interpreted as stating (informally) "Constraints shall not last!" and so all process constraints are ultimately time-varying. In persistent systems they vary according to another set of processes with other, longer characteristic times. A thermodynamic process (i.e., a natural process that can be modeled using transport and reaction rate coefficients that are functions only of thermodynamic potentials—such as temperature or pressure—and *not* of time, over the period of measurement) in an open system with characteristic time t_1 will have its constraints modified by processes with longer characteristic times, t_2 and so on.

Persistence and Cycles

To the above notions we need to add one additional postulate—that to achieve *persistence* in open thermodynamic systems that can exchange matter and energy at their boundaries and organize space and time, there must be *internal recurrent processes*. The element of temporal organization is the *cycle*. There are only three possible outcomes for the flow of energy-matter through an open thermodynamic system: (1) the system will be *broken*, torn down or degraded (these are the common wear-and-tear, relaxational phenomena); (2) the system will have its form and function *sustained* (these are the thermodynamic engine *cycles* from molecular to geophysical scale); or (3) the system may self-organize and show stages of construction, *growth, and development*. An account of irreversible thermodynamics aimed at explaining these varieties of processes can be found in Iberall (1977–1978). The cyclic sustaining processes are self-scaling in time and space through the effects of constraints. If anything happens on another time scale to change the constraints, the intrinsic process periods may also change.

Up to this point I have attempted to introduce the following notions, which I shall require in order to proceed further: (1) biological systems are open thermodynamic systems; (2) exchanges of matter and energy at their boundaries drive (a) cyclic sustaining, (b) relaxational-degradative, and (c) developmental processes within them; (3) every energetic internal process has a characteristic intrinsic time as an emergent property of the quantization of action by the process itself; (4) some, but not all, internal recurrent processes are entrainable by environmental (including social) near-periodic processes; (5) biological systems are part of the world of physical dynamics—their "informational" attributes have been exaggerated by biologists and their dynamics have been underappreciated; (6) aging and senescence are a problem in dynamics and not in information—they are a manifestation of time-variation in constraints according to the Second Law of Thermodynamics.

Energy Flows and the Creation and Destruction of Form

We are indebted to Prigogine and his colleagues for putting irreversible thermodynamics and self-organizing processes near the top of the scientific theoretical agenda during the last 30 years (Prigogine, 1967, 1969, 1976, 1978; Prigogine & Nicolis, 1971; Prigogine, Nicolis, & Babloyantz, 1972; Prigogine, Nicolis, Herman, & Lamb, 1975; Prigogine & Wiame, 1946). The resulting Dissipative Structure Theory has been described for biologists by Kugler, Kelso, and Turvey (1982), Mercer (1981, pp. 139–156), and Atkins (1984, pp. 157–177). The ideas have also been summarized by Prigogine (1980) in a splendid technical book, but the reader should be cautioned that to get the ideas from the more popular version he did in collaboration with Stengers (Prigogine & Stengers, 1984) would be unwise without reading some balancing commentary from physicists. [See, for example, the severe criticism of this book by Pagels (1985).]

Today, as a result of these developments and the popular and technical attention focused on the problem, we can all agree with Prigogine (1980): "Classical thermodynamics was associated . . . with the forgetting of initial conditions and the destruction of structures. We have seen, however, that there is another *macroscopic* region in which, within the framework of thermo-dynamics, structures may spontaneously appear" (p. 150). In open thermody-namic systems *local decreases in entropy* are natural coupled processes. The forms they create can act as constraints on subsequent dynamics, giving new shape to old processes—or to new processes, leading to still newer forms. That, as suggested by René Thom (1975), may be the basis of biological growth and development, with its succession of stages, described by Thom through the concept of mathematical catastrophes. (See Thom, 1983, for an imaginative and updated view of principles of morphogenesis.)

However, there is a catch. For energy flow to construct a system and create a local reduction of entropy, there must be a degree of freedom or a dynamical mode or dimension not already macroscopically occupied within the system. In filling out the new mode, degree of freedom, or dimension, coherence can appear. The new form then freezes out a degree of freedom, thereby con-straining future possibilities but enriching present possibilities. Dynamics are paradoxically enriched at the same time they are restricted (Medawar, 1975).

The constructive process stops when the energy flows have led through execution-driven successions of bifurcations into new forms and motions, into a situation in which the *action* (energy × time product or integral) is now finally *scaled* to the environmental sources of supply and most of the internal, macroscopic degrees of freedom previously available for structure formation are filled out. At this scaling all mammals appear to turn over about 200 kcal/g of metabolizing tissue per lifetime (Rubner, 1908). However, on closer examination, as Sacher (1980) points out, it is lifetime *action* (not energy) that has the least variance (among 85 mammalian species analyzed) of any function of metabolic rate or life span.

The Beginning of Senescence

Once the macroscopic dynamic modes and degrees of freedom have been filled out, a new situation arises. Senescence begins. Energy throughput in a mature, open, dissipative system [e.g., an "organism" that degrades Gibbs free energy and produces entropy (S)] now enters a near-stationary state. In the notation for a near steady-state system:

$$\left(\frac{dS}{dt}\right)_{sys} = \left(\frac{d_e S}{dt}\right)_{sys} + \left(\frac{d_i S}{dt}\right)_{sys} \cong 0 \tag{1}$$

where the subscripts e and i refer to the external and internal processes that contribute to the system's entropy. Using the dissipative system itself as refer-ence frame (subscript sys), then it must be the case, because of the Second Law for a dissipative system, that

$$\left(\frac{d_i S}{dt}\right)_{sys} > 0 \qquad\qquad (2)$$

and so, from Equations (1) and (2), the entropic contribution from the environment to the system must be negative in the steady state:

$$\left(\frac{d_e S}{dt}\right)_{sys} < 0 \qquad\qquad (3)$$

That is, to sustain an internal steady state there must thus be some steady acquisition of "negentropy" or an "exportation" of entropy.[2] The positive value of the term in Equation (2) must be compensated for by work performed on the system from the outside, by absorption of light or high grade chemical energy, or by the "export" of "high entropy" chemicals. In living systems the important compensatory processes [Equation (3)] are the absorption of light and high grade chemical energy, with concomitant export of heat, sometimes light, and low-grade chemical energy (high entropy materials).

However, the internal thermodynamic engine cycles are not perfect, being themselves subject to the Second Law—the constraints on their processes are altered by the very processes they constrain as well as by surrounding processes. The result is that

$$|d_i S/dt|_{sys} > |d_e S/dt|_{sys}$$

The discrepancy between the two values represents an *entropy accumulation rate* that drives senescence. This entropy accumulation shrinks the viability reserves of the organism and renders it more susceptible to the action of fluctuations. [Fries & Crapo (1981) have expressed this idea very clearly.] These are the consequences of the alterations of constraints by energy flows, and they provide the transition to frequency-dependent probabilities of failure as modeled by Strehler and Mildvan (1960).

This hypothesis also takes account of the aspect-theory of aging provided by Cutler (e.g., Cutler, 1983). Cutler views the aging process as largely one of dysdifferentiation, the slow progression of cells away from their proper state of differentiation. Longevity of a species is then determined by processes acting to stabilize the cells' proper state of differentiation against the destabilizing effects of by-products of energy metabolism. Among these threatening by-products are toxic free radicals arising from oxygen metabolism. To Cutler it appears as if a species' aging rate is proportional to its specific metabolic rate. This notion is supported by demonstrations that under laboratory conditions food restrictions may slow the aging process in rats (Masoro, 1984).

Effects of Entropy Accumulation on Means, Variances, and Limits

At maturity, healthy human beings exhibit both homeostatic and homeodynamic aspects of the overall dynamic stability that comprises health. *Homeostasis* refers to the relaxational tendency of a physiological variable to recover a regulated mean operating point after perturbation away from that point. The transient elevation of blood sugar during a glucose tolerance test is a familiar clinical example of a homeostatic response. *Homeodynamics* refers to the tendency of a physiological variable engaged in a sustaining thermodynamic process to regain a near-periodic, orbital trajectory after a perturbation. The transients in the circadian rhythm organization of core temperature, or in sleep/wakefulness alternations, accompanying the jet lag phenomenon are familiar examples. In other words, *homeostasis refers to point stability* (point attractors); *homeodynamics refers to orbital stability* (limit-cycle-like attractors). Variations around homeostatic operating points may be systematic (as in respiratory perturbations of heart rate) or random (as in emotional effects on heart rate). Variations around homeodynamic mean operating points always have a periodic component, onto which random or systematic contaminating influences may be impressed (in additive or multiplicative couplings).

The traces of entropy accumulation that always attend the constellation of physiological processes comprising metabolism, can, by altering constraints, affect (1) the mean operating points of homeostatic or homeodynamic variables, (2) the magnitude or structure of their variances, or (3) their limits. There is no general rule regarding these changes—they depend upon which constraints have been entropically altered. For example, with increasing age (after age 30) maximum achievable heart rate decreases roughly according to the linear function

$$HR_{max} \text{ (in beats per minute)} = 220 - age \text{ (in years)},$$

mean glomerular filtration rate decreases, and systolic blood pressure (sometimes) increases.

As β-adrenergic receptors are lost from the heart with increasing age, heart rate variability (variance) decreases in some individuals (this change is one example of restricted variability sometimes called homeostenosis); but in other individuals replacement of the conducting cells of the His-Purkinje system with fat and collagen leads to erratic heart beats and a variety of cardiac dysrhythmias, and therefore to an increased heart rate variability. These two effects can coexist, leading to a change in either direction of heart rate variance or to no change. It follows from these uncertainties that accompany entropy accumulation within an aging *individual* that the *population variance* for a physiological variable tends to *increase* as birth cohorts age.

Fluctuations and Order

Most of biological information is structure acting as constraint on dynamic processes that create and maintain structure. As energy flows through open thermodynamic systems, new structures, as products of a process, appear as new constraints on the next stage because dynamics can "memorize" fluctuations and lock them up as structures if they occur at critical bifurcation points (often created as a by-product of earlier forms precipitating out of ongoing dynamics). The concept that order can arise from fluctuations is a major mathematical discovery and empirical observation in the field of nonlinear, qualitative dynamics. I cannot go into details here, but the interested reader may consult Prigogine (1980, pp. 89–94, 131–150), Thom (1983), Diener (1984), Abraham and Shaw (1982–1984). Before these discoveries, in most models of systems small fluctuations tended to have no persistent effect, whereas large fluctuations could destroy the system. According to the new formulation, some fluctuations can *construct* the system.

As long as macroscopic dynamical modes or degrees of freedom are still open to a system, further energy transformations and fluctuations may lead to new forms and shapes of processes. When the time and space scaling match the energy throughput, the possibilities for novelty are exhausted and the system enters a mature steady state that scales action similarly for many species of mammals, according to environmental potentials. From then on, energy throughput leads to slow alteration of constraints, with a loss of dynamical range and richness and an increase of population variances for regulated processes. Under those conditions, even moderate internal or external fluctuations can become lethal, as described in Sacher's fluctuation view of physiological mortality (Sacher & Trucco, 1962) and by Strehler and Mildvan (1960).

This new thermodynamic picture of aging that invokes catastrophes, fluctuations, bifurcation theory, and nonlinear mechanics gathers together many different older aspect-theories, including caloric theory, rate-of-living theories, free-radical theories, and even genetic loss-of-information theories. In that sense it has satisfactory scope, but as with many theories of great scope, it lacks precision in that it cannot state in advance which constraints will alter fastest or most significantly in any particular individual organism. The decay of constraints is partly an aleatory phenomenon, but there is no doubt that certain subsystems are more susceptible than others to changes in their ongoing constraints. The cardiovascular system seems particularly vulnerable in human beings.

The theoretical sketch I have provided comes down in favor of the gradualist view of senescence. And it is uniformitarian. It argues that the *rate of age change is constant* once physical action is scaled at maturity, and so the fundamental events in senescence occur at an essentially uniform rate throughout life. (It rejects the opposing position that senescence begins late in life and then follows a rapid and devastating course.)

Summary: Living Systems as Physical Systems

Below are some conclusions I think follow when one takes a physical view of biological systems. They are repeated from the essay "Physics of Self-Organization" (Yates, 1987c).

Physics dominates the sciences through the generality, parsimony, and implied causality of its explanations. With only a few general forces (not more than three, perhaps only one), a few principles (e.g., conservation, invariance, symmetry — these three even being interrelated), a few "natural" constants (e.g., C, b, k, G), the logical equivalences of mathematics, and a small number of general theories and concepts, the physicist attempts to explain all of the beings and becomings of the universe. Yet there is a peculiarity: in practice, physicists seem to do better in illuminating processes very much faster (e.g., at Planck time, 10^{-43} sec; propagation of light at 3×10^{10} cm/sec) or very much slower (e.g., the unfolding of the cosmos for perhaps 2×10^{10} years) than those at the scale of individual humans (10^{-10} to 10^2 years). They theorize better concerning spatial or mass domains very much smaller (quarks) or very much larger (supragalactic clusters) than humans, or temperatures very much colder (a few tenths of a degree K) or very much hotter (10^{15} GeV; 10^{31}°K) than those of the human condition (near 300°K).

The frontier work of physicists prospers at the above extremes, but why do we not have a more fully developed physics of life or humans? The difficulty is not that ordinary dynamics are poorly defined at the space-time dimensions of humans. On the contrary, the detailed processes that we find in humans pose no particular mystery after we uncover them. Of course, there are currently interesting physical investigations at terrestrial scales (e.g., acoustical properties of the nonlinear media of earth, atmosphere, and oceans, electromagnetic properties of amorphous substances), but the problem seems to be that a human operates as a system whose degrees of freedom and interactions are mostly internal and whose responses are dominated by action (energy × time) rather than by momentum (mass × velocity). As a result, the human system is slow and "soft" in the sense of being characterized by numerous transports and transformations only loosely coupled, with greatly delayed internal processing. The transports are predominantly diffusive and convective; only a few are wave-propagative. The transformations are weak exchanges of chemical bonds of no more than a few electron volts per exchange. Given the soft couplings, it becomes difficult to ascribe sharply defined macroscopic output behaviors to any particular set of macroscopic inputs, present or past. Stimulus and response are joined by numerous, delayed internal couplings.

Today we have a more interesting picture of the physical status of biological systems than we have ever drawn before. There are strong reasons for believing that terrestrial life has the following physical characteristics:

1. Life obeys all of the known laws of physics, with their universal constants (both dimensional and dimensionless) and conservations, that are applicable to its scales of time and space. No new fundamental postulates are required to explain the dynamics of life.

2. Life operates lawfully in the domain of applicability of near-to-equilibrium, irreversible thermodynamics. Atomistic interactions and constraints below imply a limited set of possibilities for "governors" and "bureaucracies" above. Similarly, neighbors, other species, and local features of the lithosphere, atmosphere, and hydrosphere constrain the biosphere from above. (See the last section of this chapter for discussion of the "sandwich" character of constraints acting on a complex system.)

3. Life has historical, evolutionary (time-irreversible), and "informational" features that are not ordinarily considered as aspects of standard physics. We must either accept these features as being in some sense extraphysical or else, as argued here, we must extend normal physics to rationalize these attributes of the biosphere (Blumenfeld, 1981, p. 18).

4. The dynamics of organisms are nonlinear in the couplings and operate thermodynamically close-to-equilibrium in the relaxations.

5. Life does not possess any unusual "antientropic" tendencies. (It is entertaining but gratuitous to claim that life feeds on "negentropy" for its survival.) Life has no more order by entropic measures than does a rock (Blumenfeld, 1981, pp. 8–14). It is the quality, the specialness of the order, not its quantity, that is remarkable.

6. The genetic code is arbitrary—a frozen accident. The nucleotide sequences of prebiological macromolecules were very likely chemically arbitrary or only slightly biased by chemical constraints. However, after a first two-stranded molecule arose by a random process of low probability, such that on one strand matrix synthesis had time to be completed before the spontaneous polymer hydrolysis, then, as Blumenfeld comments (1981):

> . . . the situation changed abruptly. The nucleotide sequence existing in such long-living two-strand polymers is now meaningful. This meaning is quite obvious: in a stable two-strand molecule capable of reduplication this sequence exists, but other, in principle allowed sequences, do not. Due to specific properties of the two-strand structure (diminished hydrolytic rate, matrix synthesis) the concentration of unistrand polymer molecules, having this, now specific, sequence, will increase. These unistrand polynucleotides are now in dynamic equilibrium not only with monomers, but also with stable two-strand structures having the same nucleotide sequence. The two-strand polymer concentration will increase on account of monomers due to the reduplication process. . . .

Thus, owing to *the memorizing of the random choice* . . . a meaningful ordering has arisen, a system capable of creating meaningful information has been made. . . . The physical properties of polymer molecules having this sequence may not differ from those of other polymers. This sequence has a meaning just because a self-reproducing polymer system with this sequence has accidentally arisen. The meaning of ordering is, thus, a biological category, i.e., it is determined by all the history of the formation of a system, by its evolution. It does not mean that the concept of "meaning" is somewhat mystical and does not obey the laws of physics. All properties of meaningful objects can be logically derived from their physical characteristics, provided we know their history, their evolution. . . . For biological systems with a meaningful ordering it is the quality and not the quantity of information that is most important. (pp. 16–18)

7. Biological systems are dissipative structures of the first kind in that they are maintained off but near equilibrium by dissipation of energy that enters from the outside. They are stabilized mainly by kinetic means: transition to the equilibrium state would involve destruction of the already existing structure and so require that a potential barrier be overcome. Living systems are *not* dissipative structures of the second kind, those whose deviations from equilibrium are extremely great. Such structures may not be stable.

If these views are correct, then life does not lie far from the reach of standard physical models, and we can be optimistic about the possibilities for generalizations of existing physics to provide a basis for comprehending life and aging in their extraordinary variety. We now need to decide what aspects of standard physics to keep for this job (surely symmetries, conservations, invariances) and what to discard (perhaps the classical–mechanical initial and boundary conditions).

It is my hope that by beginning with this physical foundation we can define senescence so as to avoid Murphy's complaint (1982): "Biology is full of notions like senescence . . . that are not facts at all. At present, they scarcely rise to the dignity of being ideas. I know of no nontrivial predictions from them that are not merely tautologous rearrangements of the facts out of which they are constructed in the first place."

SOME IMPLICATIONS FOR HEALTH: A HYPOTHESIS ABOUT DANGERS OF DESUETUDE

If senescence is progressive instability that arises from a slow and continuing change of constraints as a by-product of energy throughput and action, we would expect to find many different manifestations of dynamic instability. We do in fact see the following: cancers as failures of the regulation of cellular growth and metabolism, hypertension as a failure of the constraints that gate ionized calcium in arteriolar smooth muscle, coronary artery disease as a failure of the constraints that mobilize lipids from cells to liver, dementias as a failure to sustain dendritic growth processes, and the replacement of more differentiated tissues (e.g., skeletal muscle) with less differentiated cells of connective tissue.

As the (external time) years go by, our genetic characteristics become more revealed in the phenotypic dynamics. If we have survived the accidents of nature in the earlier years of our lives, then the slow decay of the genetically shaped constraints over time become manifest. The rate of aging, which by hypothesis here is independent of age within an individual, nevertheless differs between individuals because they have different macromolecules (genes) as initial conditions upon which the Second Law can play. Point, clustered, or cumulative mutational effects or chemical alterations of the gene or of gene products lead to very different results if their manifestations occur in collagen or in hemoglobin, in their genes or in mRNAs. We could not predict how aging will manifest itself in a particular individual without having a complete and comprehensive dynamical theory of nucleic acids as constraints and initial conditions. It is useless to hope for that. In any event, social policy has to be aimed at populations and not at individuals, and so I seek guidelines from this physical theoretic that can have beneficial population effects. What might such guidelines be?

I do not feel that we should try to extend the maximum life-span potential for Homo sapiens, even though it might be doable. The molecular initial conditions most responsible for shaping life-span action may comprise no more than 0.6% of the genome (Cutler, 1975; Sacher, 1975). Rather, we should look after the secular factors susceptible to changes by acceptable social policy. Insofar as inheritance, sex, and chronological age influence the trajectory of one's life, there is nothing to be done that we would want to do, given current knowledge. In the matters of life-style that include quasi-elective risk factors (dietary mix, smoking, motorcycle riding, daily exercise, and stress level) it is worthwhile to reexamine the conventional wisdom.

Current wisdom says that no more than 30% and perhaps only 10 to 15% of our total caloric intake should be from fats; we should not smoke; we should drink only moderately; we should add about 2,000 kcal per week to our energy turnover through exercise spread out over the week; we should learn the relaxation response or meditation; we should look on life humorously, keep pets, love our children, see our friends, have someone close living with us regularly, be successful, and not be poor. Oh yes, and skip the junk food, upping the fiber intake whether we like it or not. Now each of these recommendations can be tested empirically, without theory, and presumably most of them arose out of empirical interpretations of actuarial or demographic data. In the absence of imperatives derivable from a theoretical construct, we are stuck with having to draw conclusions from partial data that may be of low quality.

A Dynamical Imperative

There is one *dynamical and theoretically based imperative* that might be drawn from the physical construct I have offered here – "*Act so as to explore the full spectrum of human action modes.*" Human action partitions into about 20 discrete behavioral modes, about 15 of which I estimate are recurrent in a near-periodic fashion (Yates et al., 1972). Some of the action modes are inescapable (eating, drinking, voiding, sleeping); these are the housekeeping modes. About the others, we each have presumably a natural spectrum defining our personality type according to the frequency with which we enter the recurring modes. Being sexual is one such mode.

In the case of being sexual, the original Kinsey report suggested that the frequency of entry into the mode declines with the years, but whether that is a result of extrinsic factors (habituation to or loss of interested partner) or intrinsic factors (e.g., falling free-testosterone levels in the male) is not yet clear. One way to find out is to keep the extrinsic factors spectrally rich for the elderly, thereby letting the internal processes of the aged person establish the range of his or her possible responses. There is a strong assumption here – that constraints that operate on action modes decay faster (or that at constant rate of decay they have more grievous consequences) if any action mode is not entered. Behind this assumption lies a hypothesis about the consequences of disuse of a physiological function.

If a system has the capability of responding to the spectrum of environmental fluctuations with a repertoire of 20 different action modes, and (for whatever reason) its behavior is biased away from some subset of those modes so that they are not visited, then, I hypothesize, there will be a loss of dynamic range and adaptive capacity that will threaten the remaining modes. In other words, there is a dynamical basis for the "street smarts" that you should "use it or lose it" – and I'm not referring just to being sexual. I could as well be referring to deep reflection and creative thinking. Below I express these hunches in a semiformal fashion.

According to the Second Law, the *total* internal entropy change brought about by the metabolism of a mature organism is always positive [Equation (2)]. However, with respect to a *particular* behavioral mode, or internal physiological function, F, consisting of a process p and its structural constraints,

Autodynamics of F		Couplings between F and q	

$$\left(\frac{d_i S}{dt}\right)_F = \left(\frac{d_{pc}S}{dt}\right) + \left(\frac{d_{pa}S}{dt}\right) \quad + \quad \left(\frac{d_{qc}S}{dt}\right) + \left(\frac{d_{qa}S}{dt}\right)$$

(4)

>0	<0	>0	<0
self-destruction	self-repair	F-destructive effects of q	F-repairing or maintaining effects of q

Any internal process p is invariably coupled to some other process, q, and the running of p and q is always associated with some catabolic (c, entropy increase of F) effects. But there can also be anabolic (a, entropy decrease of F) effects. Equation (4) shows that any particular $(d_iS/dt)_F$ can be $+$, $-$ or 0 (subject to the restriction of Equation [2] that the aggregate of *all* physiological functions leads to $d_iS/dt > 0$). Furthermore, because $d_{qc}S/dt$ and $d_{qa}S/dt$ each could consist of a spontaneous component and a p-provoked component acting through couplings of p to q, it follows that if $|d_{qa}S/dt|_p$ is large, then $(d_iS/dt)_F$ will be smaller when p is running than when it is not. That is, the running of p preserves the potential for running p better than does having p be idle or "resting." Of course, Equation (4) is just a bookkeeping statement, not a formal theory. I do not yet have a developed dynamical model for this concept.

In the framework of the scheme of Equation (4), I hypothesize that natural selection leads to large values of $|d_{qa}S/dt|_p$ for the major physiological action modes (those that obligate appreciable energy throughput). An evolutionary optimum for persistence of an organism is achieved by negentropic couplings (i.e., large, negative value of $d_{qa}S/dt$) that largely offset the thermodynamic costs of maintaining fundamental behavioral modes, F, and so allow complex behaviors to occur close to global equilibrium conditions.

Adaptation and Adaptive Value

If a fundamental mode is threatened by circumstance, the dynamics may adapt. Adaptation is the discovery of or creation of a new "basin of attraction" (in a topological sense) (Yates, 1984) that represents a marginally stable dynamic regime that can replace a lost regime and its attractor when they have been annihilated by decaying or changing constraints. Because of the many nonlinear couplings and cooperative phenomena within the complex biological organism, the loss of some constraints might lead to creation of new ones, providing that energy is channeled into the new behavioral mode, and assuming that the *local* constructive aspects of dynamics dominant in youth but enfeebled with time can always operate to some extent, even though the *global* dynamics are undergoing decline in regulation through changes of constraints.

To the above ideas, I add a generalization of Demetrius's (1984) concept of "adaptive value" to complete my picture of the physics of human aging. His formalism is based upon a statistical mechanical model of self-organization in certain macromolecular systems making the transition from a random assembly of interactng oligomers to a system of stable heteropolymers. It describes the correlation between environmental variability and the variability in replication and mutation rates of the interacting oligomers. Environments can have both activating and inhibiting influences. He proves that the structure of the final equilibrium state clearly depends on the environmental noise as well as the detailed chemistry of the macromolecules.

Substitute human beings for the macromolecules, and Demetrius's model might still hold in general outline—especially in its demonstration that environmental factors are crucial elements in organizing stable states. In noise-free environments (an idealization in which all thermodynamic potentials in the environment are constant and nonfluctuating), interactions of a very special kind are required to generate multiple stable states. In noisy, variable environments with fluctuations in potentials, multiple stable states can arise. The analysis in this model revolves around a potential function that depends upon a single parameter (adaptive value) and thus corresponds to a mean-field theory in statistical mechanics. I do not think it is too big a jump from these statistical mechanical arguments to social policies (see following section) because societies are also statistical thermodynamic, physical entities (see, for example, Iberall, 1987; Iberall & Soodak, 1987; Soodak & Iberall, 1987).

The implied result of the *dynamic imperative* I derived from my physical view of aging (*"At all stages of life keep options open and the social and physical environments richly varied!"*) is that behavioral richness of individuals will be preserved over longer epochs, as will higher levels of their internal dynamic stability (i.e., of health). The physical construct offered here and an analysis of risks (Urquhart & Heilmann, 1984) suggest that those varied environments should *not minimize risk*. For stability, the optimum for risk lies somewhere between minimum and maximum. It is fortunate that this is so because then the optimal environmental spectrum for our stable dynamics as we age will not bore us to death.

TOP-DOWN AND BOTTOM-UP (SANDWICH) CONSTRAINTS: THE BASIS FOR SOCIAL ACTION

Complex systems are hierarchical, and even though the concept of "level" can be fuzzy (not all hierarchies are strong hierarchies in which a system component is unambiguously at some level and does not appear at another) we cannot escape the need for a "sandwich" view of such systems if we are to understand their motions and changes (Iberall & Soodak, 1978). Physical analysis of any complex system, to be comprehensive, must always address some level "below" the chosen system and also some level "above" that in which the system is embedded, in order to obtain all of the constraints that govern the dynamics. Structures and functions at levels above and below a system of interest together restrict the possibilities for the dynamics of that referent system (Yates, 1982a). Thus, the dynamics of an individual human being, which include aging processes, are inevitably shaped by his or her social and physical environments, as much as by biochemical networks internally. A single-level view is bound to fail to account for the physics of such a complex phenomenon.

Modern biology, being methodologically reductionistic in the image of physics, tries to explain the phenomena of life mainly through the bottom-up approach. In a dramatic and now classical case, sickle cell anemia (a macroscopic disease that inconveniences or even kills the whole human being even while protecting against malaria) can be "explained" by propagation upward of consequences arising from the molecular genetic level following a single point mutation. This is a seemingly satisfying bottom-up story. Similarly, single strands of RNA are thought to be the basis for acquired immune deficiency syndrome (AIDS). But smoking (a macroscopic behavior) is as much the cause of cancer of the lung as are the microscopic, molecular carcinogens in volatilized tobacco. Causality can also be a top-down chain of influences. Other examples of top-down causality abound: Political systems can create or ameliorate starvation; a person can commit suicide.

Even though a comprehensive physical account of the phenomenon of human aging requires both bottom-up and top-down descriptions, *from the point of view of interventions top-down approaches are currently more plausible.* We do not know how to intervene at the molecular level to close the approximate seven-year gap between median life spans of men and women in the United States, but we can try to give serious attention to secular factors such as life-style changes for the individual and social policies as means to affect dynamical constraints on a top-down basis—to increase median life spans and well-being for both sexes.

The top-down approach to minimizing the undesirable aspects of aging, especially that of increasing dependency, should include meeting the dynamic imperative described in the preceding section—at all stages of life keep options open and the social and physical environments richly varied. However, because it is not often practical to launch the old-old (those 85 years and older) on world tours to the antipodes to obtain climatic and geophysical variety, we must tap another great and more immediate source of environmental variation for human beings—viz., other human beings. (Images of other human beings in movies or television are not satisfactory surrogates, nor are pets.) To keep their health—that is, to keep the dynamic state space fully explored within the limits of the current status of the constraints—human beings must be exposed more than casually to other human beings to whom they have not habituated to the point of unresponsiveness. As we consider designs for new "built environments" for the aged we can make strong top-down gains through assuring small-scale group memberships (family size to tribal size; i.e., groups from 2 to 200 members).

A very noticeable by-product of ambulatory monitoring of physiological variables is that *social* variables can drive some endogenous physiological responses (like blood pressure) through their full dynamic ranges. Even exercise may not be more potent (L. A. Benton & F. E. Yates, unpublished observations on human heart rate and blood pressure for 24 hours, from ages 18 to 95; see also, Yates & Benton, 1987). Social policies that lead to group membership at family or tribal scales on the part of aged citizens are good physics, according to what we understand of the dynamics of complex systems. In physical models the isolated system usually has much less varied behavior than does the system open at its boundaries to matter, energy, and information. Here is a handle on the problems associated with aging that has perhaps even greater leverage than does education with respect to personal habits such as smoking, exercise, or dietary adjustments. Meaningful group membership (again, at family or tribal scales) is a key to providing the dynamical constraints from top down that can help to optimize health for the individual. It is an intervention that can become a plausible design variable in social planning, whereas drugs and other molecular approaches remain ethically controversial. [Some people strongly believe that we are overdosing the elderly with medications (Burns & Phillipson, 1986).]

In conclusion, the top-down physical analysis of human physiological dynamics indicates that we should bring to bear a social force for variety to attenuate the aging processes. We have met that force—and it is us. I do not think I need to apologize for invoking physics of complexity to arrive at a prescription that we all intuitively sensed and sought anyway, without drawing upon physical theory. Psychologists and social scientists have had long experience with these aspects of aging (see Birren & Schaie, 1985, Parts 2, 3, and 6; also Binstock & Shanas, 1985). It is not trivial to anchor social policy in deeper physical principles and to show that it is a matter of dynamic optimization that we should design a rich environmental spectrum (including diverse social and physical components) to sustain the physical well-being of the old. That we need detailing for such designs has come to the attention of the Institute of Medicine (see "America's Aging—Health in an Older Society—1985 Report of the Committee on an Aging Society of the IOM; National Academy Press, Washington, D.C.; and the second report from the same committee entitled "Report on a Symposium on a Social and Built Environment in an Aging Society," now in press). But it is a political matter whether or not a society wants to expend resources on sustaining the health of its elderly.

NOTES

[1]Robert Rosen has recently sent me preprints of three excellent papers extending his views on this subject, without indicating where they will ultimately appear. The interested reader should ask Rosen for them at the Department of Physiology and Biophysics, Dalhousie University, Halifax, Nova Scotia, Canada B3H 4H7. The titles are "Biology and Physics—an Essay in Natural History," "On the Scope of Syntactics in

Mathematics and Science—the Machine Metaphor," and "Effective Processes and Natural Law."

[2]Any language that invokes "transport" of entropy has the same flaw as did the old caloric theory of heat. Physically, entropy is usually regarded as being a statistical property of an ensemble of interacting, atomistic entities in a field. It cannot be transported itself, but its value can be affected by energy shuffling or altering processes, including transports (e.g., momentum, energy, or mass diffusivities) and chemical reactivities.

REFERENCES

Abraham, R. H., & Shaw, C. D. (1982–1984). *Dynamics: The geometry of behavior*: Part 1. Periodic behavior. Part 2. Chaotic behavior. Part 3. Global behavior. Santa Cruz, CA: Ariel Press.

Atkins, P. W. (1984). *The second law*. New York: Scientific American Books.

Binstock, R. H., & Shanas, E. (Eds.). (1985). *Handbook of aging and the social sciences* (2nd ed.). New York: Van Nostrand Reinhold.

Birren, J. E., & Schaie, K. W. (Eds.). (1985). *Handbook of the psychology of aging* (2nd ed.). New York: Van Nostrand Reinhold.

Blumenfeld, L. A. (1981). *Problems of biological physics*. Berlin: Springer-Verlag.

Boxenbaum, H. (1986). Time concepts in physics, biology and pharmacokinetics. *Journal of Pharmaceutical Sciences, 75*, 1053–1062.

Burns, B. & Phillipson, C. (1986). *Drugs, ageing and society*. London: Croom Helm.

Calder, W. A., III (1984). *Size, function and life history*. Cambridge, MA: Harvard University Press.

Carello, C., Turvey, M. T., Kugler, P. N., & Shaw, R. (1984). Inadequacies of the computer metaphor. In M. S. Gazzaniga (Ed.), *Handbook of cognitive neurosciences* (pp. 229–248). New York: Plenum Press.

Challifour, J. L. (1985). Review of *Quantum Fluctuations* by Edward Nelson. *Science, 229*, 645–646.

Conrad, M. (1983). *Adaptability: The significance of variability from molecule to ecosystem*. New York: Plenum Press.

Cutler, R. G. (1975). Evolution of human longevity and the genetic complexity governing aging rate. *Proceedings of the National Academy of Sciences of the United States of America, 72*, 4664–4670.

Cutler, R. G. (1983). Species probes, longevity and aging. In W. Regelson & F. M. Sinex (Eds.), *Intervention in the aging process: Part B—Basic research and preclinical screening: Vol. 3B. Modern Aging Research* (pp. 69–144). New York: Allan R. Liss.

Demetrius, L. (1984). Self-organization in macromolecular systems: The notion of adaptive value. *Proceedings of the National Academy of Sciences of the United States of America, 81*, 6068–6072.

Diener, M. (1984). The canard unchained or how fast/slow dynamical systems bifurcate. *Mathematical Intelligencer, 6*, 38–49.

Fischer, R. (Ed.). (1967). Interdisciplinary perspectives of time. *Annals of the New York Academy of Sciences, 138*, 367–915.

Freeman, W. J., & Skarda, C. A. (1985). Spatial EEG patterns, non-linear dynamics and perception: The neo-Sherringtonian view. *Brain Research Reviews, 10,* 147–175.

Fries, J. F., & Crapo, L. M. (1981). *Vitality and aging.* San Francisco: W. H. Freeman.

Gardner, M. (1976). *The relativity explosion* (2nd ed.). New York: Vintage Books, Random House.

Herbert, N. (1985). *Quantum reality: Beyond the new physics.* Garden City, NY: Anchor Press/Doubleday.

Higgins, J. (1967). The theory of oscillating reactions. *Journal of Industrial and Engineering Chemistry, 59,* 18–62.

Holton, G. (1973). *Thematic origins of scientific thought: Kepler to Einstein.* Cambridge, MA: Harvard University Press.

Iberall, A. S. (1977–1978). A field and circuit thermodynamics for integrative physiology: I. Introduction to the general notions. II. Power and communicational spectroscopy in biology. III. Keeping the books—a general experimental method. *American Journal of Physiology/Regulatory Integrative Comparative, 2,* R171–180; *3,* R3–R19; *3,* R85–R97.

Iberall, A. S. (1987). A physics for studies of civilizations. In F. E. Yates (Ed.), *Self-organizing systems: The emergence of order* (Chap. 28). New York: Plenum Press.

Iberall, A., & Soodak, H. (1978). Physical basis for complex systems. Some propositions relating to levels of organization. *Collective Phenomena, 3,* 9–24.

Iberall, A. S., & Soodak, H. (1987). A physics for complex systems. In F. E. Yates (Ed.), *Self-organizing systems: The emergence of order* (Chap. 28). New York: Plenum Press.

Kugler, P. N., Kelso, J. A. S., & Turvey, M. T. (1980). On the concept of coordinating structures as dissipative structures: I. Theoretical lines of convergence. In G. E. Stelmach & J. Requin (Eds.), *Tutorials in motor behavior* (pp. 3–47). Amsterdam: North-Holland.

Kugler, P. N., Kelso, J. A. S., & Turvey, M. T. (1982). On the control and coordination of naturally developing systems. In J. A. S. Kelso & J. E. Clark (Eds.), *The development of movement control and co-ordination* (pp. 5–78). New York: John Wiley.

Kugler, P. N., & Turvey, M. T. (1987). *Information, natural law and the self-organization of rhythmic movements: A study in the similitude of natural law.* Hillsdale, NJ: Erlbaum.

Landes, D. S. (1983). *Revolution in time: Clocks and the making of the modern world.* Cambridge, MA: Harvard University Press.

Masoro, E. J. (1984). Food restrictions and the aging process. *Journal of the American Geriatric Society, 32,* 296–302.

Medawar, P. (1975). A geometric model of reduction and emergence. In F. J. Ayala & C. H. Waddington (Eds.), *Studies in the philosophy of biology* (pp. 57–64). Berkeley, CA: University of California Press.

Mehlberg, H. (1980). *Time, causality, and the quantum theory: Vol. 1. Essay on the causal theory of time; Vol. 2. Time in a quantized universe.* Boston Studies in the Philosophy of Science, Vol. 19. Boston: D. Reidel.

Mercer, E. H. (1981). *The foundations of biological theory.* New York: Wiley.

Morris, R. (1984). *Time's arrows: Scientific attitudes toward time.* New York: Simon and Schuster.

Murphy, E. A. (1982). Muddling, meddling, and modeling. In V. E. Anderson, W. A. Hauser, J. K. Penry, & C. F. Sing (Eds.), *Genetic basis of epilepsy* (pp. 333–348). New York: Raven Press.

Pagels, H. R. (1985). Is the irreversibility we see a fundamental property of nature? (Review of *Order Out of Chaos* by I. Prigogine & I. Stengers—Bantam Books, New York, 1984). *Physics Today, 38*, 97–99.

Poundstone, W. (1985). *The recursive universe: Cosmic complexity and the limits of scientific knowledge.* New York: William Morrow.

Prigogine, I. (1967). *Introduction to thermodynamics of irreversible processes* (3rd ed.). New York: Wiley-Interscience.

Prigogine, I. (1969). Structure, dissipation and life. In M. Marois (Ed.), *Theoretical physics and biology* (pp. 23–32). Amsterdam: North-Holland.

Prigogine, I. (1976). Order through fluctuation: Self-organization and social systems. In E. Jantsch & C. H. Waddington (Eds.), *Evolution and consciousness: Human systems in transition* (pp. 93–126). Reading, MA: Addison-Wesley.

Prigogine, I. (1978). Time, structure and fluctuations. *Science, 201,* 435–438.

Prigogine, I. (1980). *From being to becoming: Time and complexity in the physical sciences.* San Francisco: W. H. Freeman.

Prigogine, I., & Nicolis, G. (1971). Biological order, structure and instabilities. *Quarterly Reviews of Biophysics, 4,* 107–148.

Prigogine, I., Nicolis, G. & Babloyantz, A. (1972). Thermodynamics of evolution. *Physics Today, 25,* 11–12.

Prigogine, I., Nicolis, G., Herman, R., & Lamb, T. (1975). Stability, fluctuations and complexity. *Collective Phenomena, 2,* 103–109.

Prigogine, I., & Stengers, I. (1984). *Order out of chaos.* New York: Bantam Books.

Prigogine, I., & Wiame, J. (1946). Minimum entropy production principle as evolutionary goal—biology and thermodynamics of irreversible phenomena. *Experientia, 2,* 451–453.

Richardson, I. W., & Rosen, R. (1979). Aging and the metrics of time. *Journal of Theoretical Biology, 79,* 415–423.

Rosen, R. (1986). Some epistemological issues in physics and biology. In B. J. Hiley & F. T. Peat (Eds.), *Quantum theory and beyond.* Oxfordshire, England: Routledge & Kegan Paul.

Rubner, M. (1908). Probleme des Wachstums und der Lebensdauer. *Gesellchaft für Innere Medizin und Kinderheilkunde, 7,* 58–81.

Sacher, G. A. (1975). Maturation and longevity in relation to cranial capacity in homonid evolution. In R. Truttle, (Ed.), *Antecedents of man and other primates: Functional morphology and evolution* (Vol. 1, p. 417). The Hague: Mouton.

Sacher, G. A. (1980). Theory in gerontology: Part I. *Annual Review of Gerontology and Geriatrics, 1,* 3–25.

Sacher, G. A., & Trucco, E. (1962). The stochastic theory of mortality. *Annals of the New York Academy of Sciences, 96,* 895–1007.

Soodak, H., & Iberall, A. S. (1987). Thermodynamics and complex systems. In F. E. Yates (Ed.), *Self-organizing systems: The emergence of order* (Chap. 2). New York: Plenum Press.

Strehler, B. L., & Mildvan, A. S. (1960). A general theory of mortality and aging. *Science, 132,* 14–21.

Thom, R. (1975). *Structural stability and morphogenesis.* (D. H. Fowler, Trans.). New York: W. A. Benjamin.

Thom, R. (1983). *Mathematical models of morphogenesis.* New York: Halsted Press (Wiley).

Thom, R. (1986). Organs and tools: A common theory of morphogenesis. In J. Casti (Ed.), *Complexity, language and life: Mathematical approaches.* IASA, Luxembourg: Springer-Verlag.

Turvey, M. T., & Kugler, P. N. (1984). A comment on equating information with symbol strings. *American Journal of Physiology/Regulatory Integrative Comparative,* R925–927.

Urquhart, J., & Heilmann, K. (1984). *Risk watch: The odds of life.* New York: Facts on File.

Weinberg, S. (1985). Origins. *Science, 230,* 15–18.

Yates, F. E. (1981). Temporal organization of metabolic processes: A biospectroscopic approach. In R. N. Bergman & C. Cobelli (Eds.), *Carbohydrate metabolism: Quantitative physiology and mathematical modeling* (pp. 389–417). New York: Wiley.

Yates, F. E. (1982a). Outline of a physical theory of physiological systems. *Canadian Journal of Physiology and Pharmacology, 60*(3), 217–248.

Yates, F. E. (1982b). Systems analysis of hormone action: Principles and strategies. In R. F. Goldberger & K. R. Yamamoto (Eds.), *Biological regulation and development: Vol 3A. Hormone action* (pp. 25–97). New York: Plenum Press.

Yates, F. E. (1984). The dynamics of adaptation in living systems. In O. G. Selfridge, E. L. Rissland, & M. A. Arbib (Eds.), *Adaptive control of ill-defined systems* (pp. 89–113). New York: Plenum Press.

Yates, F. E. (1985). Semiotics as a bridge between information (biology) and dynamics (physics). *Recherches Semiotiques/Semiotic Inquiry, 5,* 347–360.

Yates, F. E. (1987a). Evolutionary computing by dynamics in living organisms. In M. Kochen & H. M. Hastings (Eds.), *Advances in cognition – steps toward convergence.* AAAS Selected Symposia Series. Boulder, CO: Westview Press.

Yates, F. E. (1987b). Quantumstuff and biostuff. In F. E. Yates (Ed.), *Self-organizing systems: The emergence of order* (pp. 615–644). New York: Plenum Press.

Yates, F. E. (Ed.) (1987c). *Self-organizing systems: The emergence of order.* New York: Plenum Press.

Yates, F. E. & Benton, L. A. (1987). Ultradian oscillations in human blood pressure: Effects of age. In L. Rensing, V. an der Herden, & M. C. Mackey (Eds.), *Temporal disorder in human oscillatory systems* (pp. 141–149). New York: Springer-Verlag.

Yates, F. E. & Iberall, A. S. (1982). A skeleton of physical ideas for the dynamics of complex systems. *Mathematics and Computers in Simulation, 24,* 430–436.

Yates, F. E., & Kugler, P. N. (1984). Signs, singularities and significance: A physical model for semiotics. *Semiotica, 52,* 49–77.

Yates, F. E., & Kugler, P. N. (1986). Similarity principles and intrinsic geometries: Contrasting approaches to interspecies scaling. *Journal of Pharmaceutical Sciences, 75*(11), 1019–1027.

Yates, F. E., Marsh, D. J., & Iberall, A. S. (1972). Integration of the whole organism: A foundation for a theoretical biology. In J. A. Behnke (Ed.), *Challenging biological problems: Directions toward their solution* (pp. 110–132). London: Oxford Press.

7

An Overview of the Theories of Biological Aging*

Vincent J. Cristofalo

Aging is a nearly universal phenomenon in biology which has intrigued scientists throughout recorded history. Despite this interest, very little is known about the biology of aging. Historically, and even in the modern era, gerontology has attracted more than its share of investigators of questionable talent, motives, and integrity. As a result, outstanding scientists who have been interested in aging have shied away from research in this important area. The absence of a large number of scientists working in this field is not the only reason for the lack of real progress in gerontology. The problem itself is intrinsically difficult. The myriad of different aging scenarios has thoroughly obscured any unifying principles. For example, some, but not all, protozoa can be considered to age. Aging in the lower metazoa is confusing, and discussions tend to focus on semantics rather than facts. A good general definition of biological aging is not available. From an evolutionary point of view, it is difficult to envision why aging has evolved (for one discussion of this, see Birren, this volume). If one assumes that it is longevity that has evolved, even then the evolution of postproductive longevity remains unexplained. Furthermore, most animals in the wild never achieve anything near their maximum life span because of death due to predators and other accidental causes. Finally, there is the confusion surrounding aging versus mortality and aging versus

*Substantial portions of this draft have been published elsewhere: *Atherogenesis*, Springer-Verlag, 1986. This work was supported in part by U.S. Public Health Service grant AG-00378.

disease. Mortality is usually considered the end point of aging, yet it is a very poor end point. Death is an accidental event that may or may not occur from causes related to aging. Vulnerability to certain diseases seems to be age-associated, and some of these diseases cause death. The relationship of the disease process to aging and the basis of the vulnerability to disease that aging brings remain obscure.

Clearly, a comparison of various populations with widely differing degrees of sophistication in health care reveals major differences in average life span (Comfort, 1979). These differences are due primarily to a reduction in infant mortality and in deaths of young individuals. Thus, life expectancy can be modified by controlling disease and other life-threatening events. However, the maximum human life span appears to have remained constant at about 110 years throughout recorded history.

Three of the formal, general questions that gerontology asks are (1) What is the mechanism(s) by which life span is determined? (2) How is the process of aging regulated? (3) What are the changes underlying the increased vulnerability to certain diseases with aging? This chapter is an attempt to present an overview of the field of biological gerontology rather than a detailed review. The purpose is to provide a framework of fundamentals that I hope will be useful to the reader in interpreting from a biological perspective more detailed information presented elsewhere in this volume (for example, see chapters by Finch, Perlmutter, and Yates.)

CHARACTERISTICS OF AGING

I will begin with a review of some of the salient general characteristics of aging:

1. There is an increased mortality with age (Strehler, 1977).
2. There are changes in the chemical composition of the body with age. This has been studied mostly in higher vertebrates and includes, for example, a decrease in lean body mass and an increase in fat. Also characteristic are increases in lipofuscin pigment in certain tissues and increased cross-linking in matrix molecules (Strehler, 1977).
3. There is a broad spectrum of progressive deteriorative changes (Shock, 1985).
4. Perhaps the hallmark of aging is the reduced ability of the older individual to respond adaptively to environmental change (Adelman, 1980). Thus, for example, it is not the resting pulse rate or the fasting serum glucose that changes so much with aging, but rather the ability of the pulse rate and the serum glucose to return to normal after exercise or a meal high in carbohydrates.

5. There is a well-documented but poorly understood increased vulnerability to disease with age (Shock, 1985).

There is a catalog available of changes in human functional capacity with age (Shock, 1985). Such things as glomerular filtration rate, vital capacity, and other measures of system functional capacity decline linearly from about age 30 years on. Mortality from various diseases, however, increases exponentially with age over the same time period. This exponential increase appears to occur from a large number of diseases, so that if one does not die in old age from the most common cause of death for his or her age group, one will die shortly thereafter from the second, third, or fourth most common cause of death for that age group. From these data, demographers have calculated that if all atherosclerosis and neoplasia were eliminated as causes of death in the population, this would add only about 10 years to the average life span. This emphasizes the point that there are changes in cells and tissues which underlie the increased vulnerability to disease and mortality.

THEORIES OF AGING

Despite the large number of aging changes that have been cataloged for humans and other species, there is as yet no adequate theory of biological aging. There is insufficient fundamental information to allow formulation of the principles of this subscience within biology. On the other hand, there is certainly no shortage of theories. One of the problems in gerontology is the ease and frequency with which new theories have appeared. Rather than delineating each theory, it seems more useful to discuss the two major classes of aging theories and several examples of each. The reader should be aware that this classification is not precise and that the theories are not mutually exclusive.

Stochastic Theories

The first class is composed of the stochastic theories of aging, which depend on the accumulation of environmental insults that eventually reaches a level incompatible with life. An example of this class of theory is the somatic mutation theory (Failla, 1958), which had its greatest impetus in the years following World War II and the flurry of research in radiation biology (see Birren, this volume). This theory states that mutations (genetic damage presumably resulting from background radiation of various types) will produce functional failure eventually resulting in death. The major experimental support for this theory derived from the well-documented observation that exposure to ionizing radiation shortens life span. It must be remembered, however, that there is no information whatsoever that relates radiation-induced life-span shortening to the normal process of aging. There is little, if any, evidence in support of this theory other than some limited studies by Curtis and Miller (1971) that showed an increase in chromosome abnormalities in mouse liver as a function of age. On the other hand, there are experiments that argue directly against this theory. For example, if the theory were correct, inbred animals would have a longer life span than outbred ones because they are homozygous at most genetic loci. In fact, the reverse is true. Second, the calculated mutation rate is much too low to produce the overall changes associated with aging. Most compelling, however, are studies on the wasp *Habrobracon* (Clark & Rubin, 1961). These animals can be maintained in the haploid or diploid condition. One would expect haploid animals to be significantly more radiation-sensitive than diploid animals because they have two copies of the genetic information at each locus. Experimentally, this is true. However, unirradiated animals, haploid or diploid, have the same life span. This observation is very difficult to reconcile with the somatic-mutation theory of aging.

A second example of a stochastic theory is the error theory (Orgel, 1963), which states that protein molecules containing errors will eventually be turned over and replaced by correct copies. Thus, error-containing molecules do not accumulate. However, if an erroneously synthesized protein is a protein involved in the synthesis of the genetic apparatus, then this original error will produce faulty molecules in the genetic apparatus, which will then produce more error-containing proteins. Orgel envisioned an eventual "error catastrophe" that would cause the death of the individual. This has been a very appealing theory, especially because of its testability. Although aberrant proteins are found with increased frequency in old cells and tissues, these are probably due to variations in the rate or extent of post-translational modifications. There is, as yet, no documented example of erroneously synthesized proteins accumulating in old tissues and certainly no evidence for an error catastrophe (Sharma & Rothstein, 1980).

Developmental-Genetic Theories

This class of theories considers the process of aging as a continuum with the process of development, genetically controlled and perhaps programmed. There are many variations of this general approach, four of which are considered below.

The first are the neuroendocrine theories (Finch & Landfield, 1985). These include theories in which aging is viewed as the result of functional decrements in neurons and their associated hormones. An important version of this depends on the hypothalamic-pituitary axis being the master timekeeper of the body. Functional changes in this important system are accompanied by a decline in functional capacity in all systems. This is a very popular approach to aging, and an enormous amount of data has accumulated relating aging of the organism to loss of responsiveness of the neuroendocrine tissue to various signals. In some cases, there is a loss of receptors, while in other cases the changes seem to be post-receptor modifications.

The neuroendocrine approach to the study of aging seems tenable in higher vertebrates, where a good case can be made for the importance of the neuroendocrine system as a super-timekeeper. However, it is unlikely that this theory is universally applicable, since obviously not all organisms that undergo aging have highly developed neuroendocrine systems. Also, as with other theories, the formal possibility exists that the differences we observe are effects of aging rather than causes. Of course, this is true for all of the theories discussed here.

A second theory in this class that bears mentioning is referred to as intrinsic mutagenesis. This was first proposed by Burnet (1974) and is an attempt to reconcile stochastic theories with the obvious genetic regulation of maximum life span. Burnet suggests that each species is endowed with a specific genetic constitution which regulates the fidelity of the genetic material and its replication. The degree of fidelity regulates the rate of appearance of mutation or errors and thus the life span. Alternatively, one can envision a case in which new fidelity regulators appear at different stages in the life history. These have diminished capacity, thus allowing an increase in mutational events. Although there is no substantial evidence to support this theory, it is attractive, and various methods of mutation analysis are being used to test its validity.

There is some controversial evidence for increases in DNA excision repair with species maximal life span (Hart & Setlow, 1974). There is also evidence that the fidelity of DNA polymerase may diminish with age (Linn, Karus, & Holliday, 1976; Murray & Holliday, 1981), but this too is, at present, controversial.

A third developmental-genetic theory is the immunological theory of aging. This theory, as proposed by Walford (1969), is based on two observations: (1) that the functional capacity of the immune system declines with age, as is seen in T cell function and is most evident in the decline of resistance to infectious disease in older individuals, and (2) that the fidelity of the immune system declines with age, as evidenced by the striking age-associated increase in autoimmune disease. Walford has related these immune system changes to the major histocompatability complex of genes in rats and mice. Congenic animals that differ only at the major histocompatability locus appear to have different maximal life spans, suggesting that life span is regulated (at least in part) by this locus. Interestingly, this locus also regulates superoxide dismutase and mixed-function oxidase levels, a finding that relates the immunologic theory of aging to the free-radical theory of aging (see below). As with the neuroendocrine theory, the immunologic theory is very attractive but lacks universality, since many organisms that lack a complex immune system show age-related changes very similar to those of higher animals. Further research will help to interpret the significance of this theory.

The fourth example is the free-radical theory of aging. This theory, usually attributed to Harman (1981), proposes that most aging changes are due to free-radical damage. Free radicals are highly chemically reactive species that are generated in single-electron-transfer reactions in metabolism. These free radicals are rapidly destroyed by protective enzyme systems. Presumably, however, there is enough leakage of these molecules to allow damage from them to occur and accumulate. This theory might properly be included under the general rubric of stochastic theories. I have included it here, however, because aspects of the free-radical theory relate to various genetic and developmental processes. For example, the German physiologist Rubner (1908) determined that for a series of mammals, the bigger the animal, the lower its metabolic rate. The adaptive significance of this is that as animals get larger, there is a disproportionate change in their surface-to-volume ratio, which results in a reduction in the animal's ability to dissipate the heat produced in metabolic reactions. Thus, a high metabolic rate could cause serious overheating in a large animal.

Sacher and Duffy (1979) and others later observed that, for a limited group of mammals, life span is more or less a direct function of body size. (Actually, the relationship is most precise if body size is modified by a factor for brain size.) Bigger homoiotherms, by and large, live longer, suggesting an inverse relationship between metabolic rate and life span. Thus, investigators have speculated that each species is endowed for its lifetime with a given number of calories to burn. Those species that burn them rapidly live a short time; for those that burn them more slowly, life span is extended. This notion, as stated, is unlikely to be correct, since it implies that active individuals would have a shorter life span than sedentary ones. There is no evidence to support this. However, since metabolic rate is related directly to free-radical generation and inversely to life span, it is reasonable to suggest that the rate of free-radical production is in some way related to life-span determination. Evidence to support this view is only circumstantial. For example, superoxide dismutase-specific activity in the liver appears to be directly proportional to species maximum life span (Tolmasoff, Ono, and Cutler, 1980). Similarly, proponents point to the observation made for several species that caloric restriction can increase mean and maximal life span by approximately 50%. This remains the only method known for extending the life span of warm-blooded animals and has evoked a great deal of interest. On the other hand, Masoro (1985) has recently shown that the specific metabolic rate of calorically restricted rats appears to be the same as those fed ad libitum. Of course, this does not diminish the significance of the observation but only complicates its interpretation. This area of investigation remains a promising one for gerontology.

RESEARCH ON FUNDAMENTAL ISSUES IN AGING

I would like to conclude this chapter with a discussion of two of the fundamental issues addressed by current aging research.

The first is whether aging is regulated intrinsically or by environmental
factors. There is no question that environmental factors can regulate or modify mortality rates. In some cases, environmental factors are recognized to
modify the process of aging as well. For example, the rate of skin aging (as we
understand it) is clearly accelerated by sun exposure. Overall, however, most
gerontologists would agree that life span is regulated intrinsically. The major
evidence in support of this view is that maximum life span is a species
characteristic. Variability in life span within a species is much less than among
different species. This implies genetic determination of maximum life span and
thus overall intrinsic control. Also there are genetically regulated diseases of
precocious aging such as Hutchinson-Guilford syndrome, Werner's syndrome,
Down's syndrome, and others. In individuals with these syndromes, many of
the commonly recognized aging changes occur at an accelerated rate.

Accepting as a reasonable working hypothesis that genetic mechanisms do
operate in the aging process, one can then ask the second question, whether
aging is characteristic of individual cells or only of the integrated functioning
among cells. To examine this question, we must go back in history. The 19th-
century embryologist Weissman, for example, appears to be the first biologist
to emphasize the distinction between somatic cells, which senesce, and germ
cells, which do not. He proposed that aging was the price cells paid for their
specialized function. He was also probably the first to suggest that the failure
of somatic cells to replicate indefinitely limited the life span of the individual.
This view was brought into serious question by the experiments of Alexis
Carrel and his co-workers at Rockefeller University, who, beginning with
experiments in 1911, were able to keep chick heart cells proliferating continuously in culture until 1945, when Carrel retired and terminated the experiment (Carrel, 1912, 1914; Carrel & Burrows, 1911). Since 34 years is longer
than the life span of the chicken, this was considered compelling evidence that
individual cells were immortal. This work and the concepts emanating from it
dominated biology in general, and especially gerontology, for the first half of
this century. This view was that aging was not a characteristic of cells and that
isolated cells were immortal; it was the tissues that were involved in the aging
process.

In the late 1950s and 1960s, Hayflick and Moorhead were developing
methods to detect latent human tumor viruses. Their approach required that
normal human cells be grown in tissue culture. During the course of this
work, they noticed that a period of rapid and vigorous cellular proliferation
was consistently followed by a decline in proliferative activity, during which
the cells acquired characteristics reminiscent of senescent cells in vivo, and
finally the death of the cultures. Swim and Parker (1957) and perhaps others

had made this same observation previously, but Hayflick and Moorhead had the extraordinary insight to recognize it as a process of senescence in culture. Thus, they proposed a new view, namely, that aging was a cellular as well as an organismic phenomenon and that perhaps the loss in functional capacity of the aging individual reflected the summation of the loss of critical functional capacities of the individual cells. This interpretation has changed our understanding of the process of aging and the direction and interpretation of aging research (Hayflick, 1965; Hayflick & Moorhead, 1961).

Repeated attempts to replicate and verify the early experiments of Carrel have been uniformly unsuccessful (Gey et al., 1974), and there is no documented explanation for his finding. Generally, the opinion among scientists is that there was artifactual introduction of fresh young cells into the culture at regular intervals.

In other experiments on human cells, Hayflick and Moorhead (1961) were able to show that a deteriorative change in the cells was not dependent on environmental influences; rather, it was intrinsic to the cells. Hayflick (1965) also addressed the generality of this phenomenon and pointed out that unless transformation occurred at some point in the life history of the cells, senescence always resulted. Transformation can occur at any point in the life history; and if transformation occurs, the cells acquire a constellation of abnormal characteristics, including chromosomal abnormalities and an indefinite life span—properties of tumor cells.

Finally, we might examine the relationship between the cellular aging phenomenon in culture and aging of the individual. No simple relationship is apparent. Clearly, there is no reason to believe that the life span of humans is limited directly by the replicative capacity of mesenchymal cells that grow in culture. However, it is not life span but rather the process of aging that is being studied. By any definition of aging, normal cells in culture age. There is a major failure in functional capacity—in this case, proliferative capacity—and the cells show changes similar to changes in vivo. Further evidence of the relationship is the fact that the replicative life span of cells in culture is inversely related to the age of the donor (Martin, Spargue, & Epstein, 1970; Schneider & Mitsui, 1976) and directly related to the maximum life span of the species (Röhme, 1981). Similarly, cells from individuals with genetic diseases of precocious aging often have a much reduced replicative life span in culture (Epstein et al., 1966). Clearly, aging changes in vivo are expressed in cell culture, and the mechanisms underlying the deteriorative changes can be studied under controlled environmental conditions. This observation of cellular aging under controlled environmental conditions and in the absence of tissue- and cell-type interactions has profound implications for the theories of biological aging mentioned above. The results suggest that underlying environmental effects, including the effects of various proposed "master timekeeping" systems, cells contain individual "clocks" that ultimately limit their life span. The concept is a complicated one because studies of the life spans of individual clones and subclones of human cells suggest that genetic death in a population is a stochastic event. One way to envision the organism's aging scenario is that each cell and tissue type has its own aging trajectory. Death occurs when homeostasis in one of the more rapidly aging components of the organism falls beyond the point necessary to maintain the organism. This causes death and terminates the aging trajectory of other, larger-level subsets of cells within the organism. If this is so, then the reductionist approach, that is, cell type by cell type, will probably be the best approach to understanding the aging process.

A great deal of research is being done now on cellular and molecular aspects of aging. Careful dissection of changes that occur at this level will be important to our understanding of aging. I believe this approach will result in very exciting developments and will provide insight into the control of both the quality of life and life span.

REFERENCES

Adelman, R. C. (1980). Hormone interaction during aging. In R. T. Schimke (Ed.), *Biological mechanism in aging* (p. 686). Washington, DC: U.S. Department of Health and Human Services.

Burnet, M. (1974). *Intrinsic mutagenesis: A genetic approach for aging*. New York: Wiley.

Carrel, A. (1912). On the permanent life of tissues outside the organism. *Journal of Experimental Medicine, 15*, 516–528.

Carrel, A. (1914). Present condition of a strain of connective tissue twenty-eight months old. *Journal of Experimental Medicine, 20*, 1–2.

Carrel, A. & Burrows, M. T. (1911). On the physiochemical regulation of the growth of tissues. *Journal of Experimental Medicine, 13*, 562–570.

Clark, A. M., & Rubin, M. A. (1961). The modification by X-irradiation of the life span of haploid and diploid *Habrolracon. Radiation Research, 15*, 244–253.

Comfort, A. (1979). *The biology of senescence* (3rd ed.). New York: Elsevier.

Curtis, H. F., & Miller, K. (1971). Chromosome aberrations in lower cells of guinea pigs. *Journal of Gerontology, 26*, 292–293.

Epstein, C. J., Martin, G. M., Schaltz, A. L. & Motulsky, A. G. (1966). Werner's syndrome—a review of its symptomology, natural history, pathologic features, genetics and relationship to the natural aging process. *Medicine, 45*, 177–221.

Failla, G. (1958). The aging process and carcinogenesis. *Annals of the New York Academy of Sciences, 71*, 1124–1135.

Finch, C. E., & Landfield, P. W. (1985). Neuroendocrine and automatic functions in aging mammals. In C. E. Finch and E. L. Schneider (Eds.), *Handbook of the biology of aging* (p. 567–594). New York: Van Nostrand Reinhold.

Gey, G. O., Svotelis, M., Foard, M. & Bang, F. R. (1974). Long-term growth of chicken fibroblasts on a collagen substrate. *Experimental Cell Research, 84*, 63–71.

Harman, D. (1981). The aging process. *Proceedings of the National Academy of Sciences of the United States of America, 78*, 7124–7128.

Hart, R. W., & Setlow, R. B. (1974). Correlation between DNA excision repair and life span in a number of mammalian species. *Proceedings of the National Academy of Sciences of the United States of America, 71*, 2169–2173.

Hayflick, L. (1965). The limited in vitro lifetime of human diploid cell strains. *Experimental Cell Research, 37*, 614–636.

Hayflick, L., & Moorhead, P. S. (1961). The serial cultivation of human diploid cell strains. *Experimental Cell Research, 25*, 585–621.

Linn, S., Karus, M. & Holliday, R. (1976). Decreased fidelity of DNA polymerase activity isolated from aging human fibroblasts. *Proceedings of the National Academy of Sciences of the United States of America, 13*, 2818–2822.

Martin, G. M., Spargue, C. A. & Epstein, C. J. (1970). Replication lifespan of cultivated human cells: Effects of damage, tissue, and genotype. *Laboratory Investigation, 23*, 86–92.

Masoro, E. J. (1985). Metabolism. In C. E. Finch and E. L. Schneider (Eds.), *Handbook of the biology of aging* (pp. 540–556). New York: Van Nostrand Reinhold.

Murray, V., & Holliday, R. (1981). Increased error frequency of DNA polymerases from senescent human fibroblasts. *Journal of Molecular Biology, 146*, 55–76.

Orgel, L. E. (1963). The maintenance of the accuracy of protein synthesis and its relevance to aging. *Proceedings of the National Academy of Sciences of the United States of America, 49*, 517–521.

Röhme, D. (1981). Evidence for a relationship between longevity of mammalian species and lifespan of normal fibroblasts in vitro and erythrocytes in vivo. *Proceedings of the National Academy of Sciences of the United States of America, 78*, 3584–3588.

Rubner, M. (1908). *Das Problem der Lebensdaver und seine Beziehungen zum Wachstum und Ernährung.* Munich: Oldenbourg.

Sacher, G. A., & Duffy, P. H. (1979). Genetic relation of life span to metabolic rate for inbred mouse strains and their hybrids. *Federation Proceedings, 38*, 184–188.

Schneider, E. L., & Mitsui, Y. (1976). The relationship between in vitro cellular aging and in vivo human age. *Proceedings of the National Academy of Sciences of the United States of America, 73*, 3584–3588.

Sharma, H. K., & Rothstein, M. (1980). Altered enolase in aged *Turbatrix aceti* results from conformational changes in the enzyme. *Proceedings of the National Academy of Sciences of the United States of America, 77*, 5865–5868.

Shock, N. W. (1985). Longitudinal studies of aging in humans. In C. E. Finch & E. L. Schneider (Eds.), *Handbook of the biology of aging* (p. 721–743). New York: Van Nostrand Reinhold.

Strehler, B. L. (1977). *Time, cells and aging* (2nd ed.). New York: Academic Press.

Swim, H. E., & Parker, R. F. (1957). Culture characteristics of human fibroblasts propagated serially. *American Journal of Hygiene, 66*, 235–243.

Szilard, L. (1959). On the nature of the aging process. *Proceedings of the National Academy of Sciences of the United States of America, 45*, 30–45.

Tolmasoff, J. M., Ono, T., & Cutler, R. G. (1980). Superoxide dismotase: Correlation with life span and specific metabolic rate in primate species. *Proceedings of the National Academy of Sciences of the United States of America, 77*, 2777–2781.

Walford, R. (1969). *The immunologic theory of aging.* Copenhagen: Munksgaard.

8

Aging in the Female Reproductive System: A Model System for Analysis of Complex Interactions during Aging*

Caleb E. Finch

This chapter describes changes in the female reproductive system that may be useful as a model for analyzing other complex physiological and biochemical changes that also influence brain function. In turn, many aspects of behavior and social dynamics can be traced to physiologic functions of the brain. Even if human behaviors are less sensitive to gonadal hormone fluctuations than those of most lower mammals (Beach, 1961; Money & Ehrhard, 1972), the changes of reproductive functions in women during aging surely modify their behaviors and their social roles.

Most biologists might agree that aging processes in humans and other mammals are very complicated. The characteristics of individuals at birth that have been determined by parental genes are then subject to many influences throughout the life span, as individuals follow their trajectories over the hills and valleys of their life courses. Even inbred mice, with >99% identical sets of genes, manifest remarkable differences between individuals in the timing and severity of age changes. Thus, the mortality of inbred mice distributes with a variance similar to that of humans (Finch & Witten, in preparation).

*This research was supported by grants from the NIA to CEF (AG00117) and by an NIA training grant to the Gerontology Center (5T32 AG 00037).

Individual differences are now known to include the cellular level (e.g., the number of ovarian oocytes) and the physiological level (e.g., the patterns of female reproductive aging), both as described below. To penetrate this network of complex individual differences, I have found it useful to focus on interactions between the cellular and physiological level, which can serve to model even more complex interactions within the brain and immunological systems that determine age changes and their individual differences.

The loss of fertility in females during midlife is characteristic of aging in most mammals. In contrast, males of most species retain some degree of fertility throughout the life span (Finch & Gosden, 1986; Harman & Talbert, 1985). For example, paternity is documented to at least 94 years in humans (Seymour, Duffy, & Koerner, 1935). Analysis of female reproductive age changes in humans and laboratory rodents indicates changes at many levels of function, including loss of oocyte and follicles in the ovary, decreased peripheral sex steroids and increased hypothalamic secretion of LHRH, and reproductive behavior. The study of aging in the reproductive system promises valuable insights for analysis of other complex age changes involving humoral and neuroendocrine interactions, such as in alterations of the immune responses, glucose regulation, and control of blood pressure. See recent reviews for more comprehensive discussions of reproductive aging (Aschheim, 1976; Finch & Gosden, 1986; Finch et al., 1980, 1984; Harman & Talbert, 1985; Wise, 1983).

ANALYSIS OF FEMALE REPRODUCTIVE SENESCENCE

The Ovary

The ovary ages irreversibly because the production of primary germ cells ceases by birth in nearly all mammals (Zuckerman & Baker, 1977). Most of the maturing follicles are subsequently lost through atresia. And, by puberty, rodents (Faddy, Gosden & Edwards, 1983) and humans have lost more than 50% of their original stock (Figure 8-1). After puberty, the loss of growing follicles by atresia appears to decrease (Faddy et al., 1983). Despite a massive loss of primary follicles, the number of ova produced at each cycle remains remarkably constant in aging rodents, until just before complete exhaustion of the follicular reserve. This striking example of compensation for deficits during aging (an aspect of homeostasis) results from an increased rescue of growing follicles from atresia (Gosden, Liang, Felicio, Nelson, & Finch, 1983).

According to a current hypothesis, the mechanism of increased rescue of follicles from atresia results from increased plasma FSH, which is one of the earliest age changes in rodents even before cycles lengthen (DePaolo & Chappel, 1986). FSH secretion increases as the ovarian follicular output of inhibin decreases with a smaller mass of growing follicles (Sherman, West, & Korenman, 1976). Plasma FSH increases become prominent during the approaching

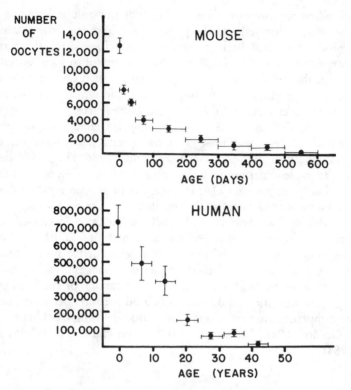

FIGURE 8-1. Populations of ovarian oocytes during postnatal life in mice (*top*) and humans (*bottom*). Data redrawn from Jones and Krohn (1961) and Block (1952). (Reprinted from Finch et al., 1984, © by the Endocrine Society.)

failure of ovulatory cycles in mice (Parkening, Collins, & Smith, 1982) and humans (Sherman et al., 1976). After ovarian exhaustion, as plasma estradiol approaches castrate levels, plasma LH becomes elevated in mice (Gee, Flurkey, & Finch, 1983; Parkening et al., 1982), rhesus monkeys and humans (Chakravarti, Collins, Newton, Oram, & Studd, 1977). A similar process may be found in the rapid increases of FSH and reduction of atresia that follow unilateral ovariectomy in rodents, thereby doubling the yield of ova from the remaining ovary by the next proestrus (Butcher, 1977).

Patterns of Cycle Change with Aging

Deviations in ovulatory cycle regularity and length precede the loss of ovulatory cycles. Longitudinal studies of mice and women show strikingly similar increases during aging in the mean length and variance of ovulatory cycles

(Figure 8-2). Nonetheless, some cycles of normal length are interspersed within strings of longer cycles throughout these changes (Nelson, Felicio, Randall, Simms, & Finch, 1982; Flurkey & Finch, in preparation). The increased instability of biorhythms may be a fundamental property of aging in mammals (Samis & Zajac-Batell, 1983), and will be discussed below for its possible relation to the homeostatic limit and mortality.

Extensive variations in reproductive aging between individuals of the same population occur in humans and in mice (Figure 8-3). These variations in mice are intriguing. Because the inbred C57BL/6J strain was established by 1936, more than 100 generations ago, C57BL/6J mice had achieved their asymptotic approach to the limits of homozygosity from 20 generations of brother-sister matings (Green & Doolittle, 1963). Moreover, the mice charted in Figure 8-3 are from the same birth cohort. One cause of the variability in reproductive senescence is individual differences in the numbers of ovarian oocytes, which at 5 months of age can range from 1,000 to 5,000 oocytes/ ovary (Gosden et al., 1983). Another possible influence on oocyte number or neuroendocrine development is the sex of the neighboring fetus in utero: Female mice flanked by two males have an earlier loss of fertility than females flanked by one or more females (vom Saal & Moyer, 1985) and show more aggressive behavior as adults (vom Saal & Bronson, 1980; vom Saal, 1981). Although the male-flanked females have higher plasma steroids in utero during late gestation (vom Saal & Bronson, 1980), the role of uterine vasculature in these striking phenomena is unclear. The higher estradiol in the male-flanked female fetuses might partially masculinize the neuroendocrine system, by analogy with the delayed anovulatory syndrome. The delayed anovulatory syndrome is induced in rats (Gorski, 1968; Harlan & Gorski, 1977, 1978) and mice (Mobbs, Kannegieter, & Finch, 1985) by small doses of estradiol or other aromatizable steroids during the critical postnatal period for sexual differentiation; after puberty, normal ovulatory cycles begin, but then cease prematurely, with neuroendocrine impairments that resemble aging in many regards (Mobbs et al., 1985). Nongenetic influences on preimplantation zygotes of inbred mice were also implied from the larger individual differences in postnatal growth rate of litter mates versus experimentally induced quadruplets (Gartner & Bauneck, 1981). Whatever the mechanisms of prenatal influences on reproductive aging, these phenomena illustrate important epigenetic influences on aging that would be difficult to resolve in outbred populations.

During the lengthening of cycles in mice, the timing of elevations in plasma estradiol is also delayed (Figure 8-4). We hypothesize that the numbers of growing follicles may fluctuate as the primary follicle pool dwindles; a smaller mass of growing follicles in a given cycle would produce less estradiol, in turn requiring longer to achieve the critical threshold for plasma estradiol to trigger the preovulatory surges of LH and FSH from the hypothalamus and pituitary (Felicio, Nelson, & Finch, 1986; Nelson, Felicio, Osterburg, & Finch, 1981).

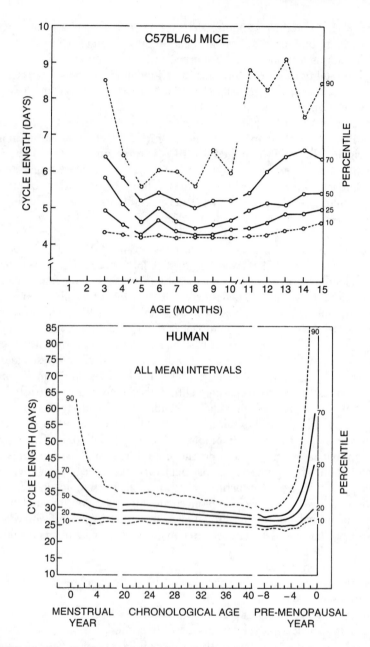

FIGURE 8-2. The distribution of ovulatory cycle lengths in mice (*top*) and women (*bottom*) as determined from longitudinal studies. Data are redrawn from Nelson et al. (1982) and Treolar, Boynton, Behn, & Brown, (1967). (Reprinted from Finch et al., 1984, © by the Endocrine Society.)

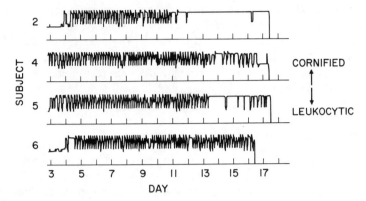

FIGURE 8-3. Longitudinal profile of daily vaginal smear patterns. (Reprinted from Finch et al., 1980.)

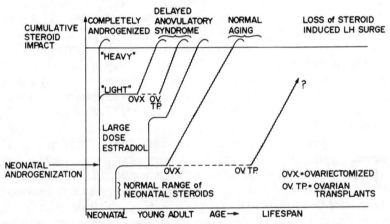

Q: Does neonatal exposure to steroids set specific extra-ovarian limits on the number of estrous cycles.

Q: Does postpubertal exposure to steroids act on the same locus as in the neonate.

FIGURE 8-4. A continuum concept of ovary and steroid-dependent neuroendocrine aging, which posits a cumulative impact of ovarian steroids during development and adulthood. If rodents are given "heavy" doses of aromatizable steroids as neonates, they never can cycle as adults; if neonates are given "light" doses followed by ovariectomy, the replacement of ovaries in adults or further steroid implants appears to reactivate the process of steroid accumulation, again leading to precocious cessation of cycles (Arai, 1971; Harlan & Gorski, 1978). Replacement of ovaries at middle age in long-term ovariectomized mice (not treated as neonates) leads to almost the same number of cycles as in young control transplants (Felicio, Nelson, Gosden, & Finch, 1983). (Reprinted from Finch, et al., 1980.)

The threshold E2 dose appears to include requirements for suppressing plasma gonadotropins to low levels (priming phase) as well as a short-term estradiol elevation (surge-inducing phase) (Bronson, 1981; Gee, Flurkey, Mobbs, Sinha, & Finch, 1984). In rodents and humans, the dose of estradiol required for induction of the LH surge has strength-duration (commutative) properties (Karsch et al., 1973; Krey & Parsons, 1982).

Fertility, Fetal Abnormalities, and Aging

During the approach of acyclicity in humans and rodents, fertility drops strikingly (Harman & Talbert, 1985). The decrease of fertility results mainly from postimplantation embryo loss, through fetal resorptions or spontaneous abortions. The aging rodent generally maintains normal-size clutches of ova, despite impending ovarian depletion (Gosden et al., 1983). The incidence of successful matings is also largely unaffected, as determined by the frequency of seminal plugs and the frequency of implantation sites up to 10 days of gestation (Holinka & Finch, 1981; Holinka, Tseng, & Finch, 1979). After gestation day 10, there is a striking increase of fetal resorptions in aging mice; at least some of the fetuses have abnormal morphology or karyotypes (Fabrikant & Schneider, 1978; Harman & Talbert, 1985). The increase of Down's syndrome (trisomy of chromosome 21) with maternal age is well known in humans. The high incidence of aneuploidy in spontaneous human abortuses suggests that aneuploidy involving many different chromosomes increases with maternal age (reviewed in Butcher & Page, 1981; Finch & Gosden, 1986; Kram & Schneider, 1978).

Several mechanisms have been proposed. In the "production-line theory" of oogenesis, the time of oocyte formation during embryogenesis could influence their properties later; or because chiasma frequency after fertilization decreases with maternal age in mice, the oocytes formed later in maternal development are postulated to be ovulated last and to have fewer chiasmata (Henderson & Edwards, 1968). Other hypotheses link disturbances in timing of ovulation to oocyte aneuploidy, through delayed ovulation (Butcher & Fugo, 1967; Crowley, Gulati, Hayden, Lopez, & Dyer, 1979). Many studies show that experimentally induced delays of ovulation in young rodents cause increased fetal aneuploidy and fetal absorptions (reviewed in Butcher & Page, 1981); the correlation of reduced resorptions in aging rodents mated after a normal short (4- to 5-day) cycle, compared with longer cycles, supports cycle length as a strong influence on developmental success and diminishes the possibility that intrinsic factors of aging in the oocyte itself account for the increase of fetal abnormalities with maternal age. Thus, the diminishing follicular pool ultimately may be linked to fetal aneuploidy because of the increased cycle lengthening associated with smaller numbers of growing follicles. The fetal aneuploidy that is associated with cycle lengthening and delayed ovulation may be provisionally viewed as the result of a cascade originating in the ovary, proceeding to the hypothalamus-pituitary, returning to the ovary, and thence to the fetus.

Neuroendocrine Functions

The involvement of hypothalamic-pituitary age changes in reproductive senescence is an area of much current interest. Rodents, apparently unlike primates, depend on increased secretion of LHRH by the hypothalamus for the surges of LH and FSH at proestrus (Fink, 1979; Goodman & Knobil, 1981; Ramirez, Feder, & Swayer, 1984). During the phase of aging when cycles lengthen, the preovulatory LH surges become progressively smaller; smaller LH surges are also observed in rodents that are ovariectomized and treated with steroids to induce an LH surge (Cooper, Conn, & Walker, 1980; Finch et al., 1980; Mobbs et al., 1984). The decreased size of the preovulatory surge is convincingly correlated with loss of cyclicity, since longitudinal studies show that rats with the smallest surges become acyclic before those with larger surges (Nass et al., 1984a). Despite the smaller gonadotropin surges, normal-size clutches of ova are usually produced, since ≤ 10% of the normal-size LH peak suffices for full ovulation (Turgeon, 1979). However, the smaller LH and FSH surges could influence follicular recruitment, thereby affecting successive cycles. Tonic (basal) gonadotropin levels may influence follicular growth (Richards, Jonassen, & Kersey, 1980), but remain to be characterized in aging rodents.

A prevalent view holds that the pituitary remains competent to respond to LHRH in aging rodents, although impaired pituitary responses are observed in some hormonal states (Smith, Cooper, & Conn, 1982). The pulsatile pattern of LH release is impaired in aging female rats (Estes & Simpkins, 1982); striking impairments in LH secretion are also seen in male mice (Coquelin & Desjardins, 1982). Thus, the impaired release of LH in aging rodents appears to be consequent to an impaired secretion of LHRH; however, evidence for this is indirect so far. The hypothalamic content of LHRH, however, is not decreased in old acyclic rodents (Wise, 1983), nor is there any decrease in the number of neurons that contain LHRH in aging mice (Hoffman & Finch, 1986). In old rats, immunocytochemical reactivity of LHRH cell bodies is more intense (Merchanthaler, Lengvari, Horvath, & Setalo, 1980), suggesting a greater retention of LHRH in the cell body, which is consistent with reduced LHRH release (Rubin, King, & Bridges, 1984).

Other evidence suggests neurochemical and morphological age-correlated changes in the hypothalamus. The release of LHRH is thought to be closely controlled by noradrenergic terminals in the hypothalamus. The acceleration of norepinephrine turnover just before the LH surge is well documented; a variety of experimental treatments by drugs or hormones that block the LH surge also block the preceding acceleration of norepinephrine turnover (Barraclough & Wise, 1982). The smaller increases of norepinephrine turnover (Wise, 1983) and dopamine-B-hydroxylase (Banerji, Parkening, & Collins, 1982) in middle-age rodents with impaired LH surges thus suggests impairments in the control of hypothalamic norepinephrine turnover by estradiol. Small, age-correlated decreases in basal catecholamine levels and turnover occur in female rats (Demarest, Moore, & Riegle, 1982). In 2-year-old male rodents, there is also a slowed turnover of hypothalamic norepinephrine (Demarest et al., 1982; Osterburg, Donahue, Severson, & Finch, 1981) and reduced dopamine content in hypophyseal portal blood (Reymond & Porter, 1981). These alterations occur at later ages than the loss of cycling in females; no changes in hypothalamic catecholamines were found during the early stages of acyclicity in C57BL/6J mice (Telford, Mobbs, Sinha, & Finch, 1986), although hypothalamic serotonin metabolism may also be impaired with age (Simpkins, Mueller, Huang, & Meites, 1977; Telford et al., 1986; Walker & Timiras, 1980). Although the role of serotonin in the LH surge is less clear than for norepinephrine, the serotonin-rich suprachiasmatic nucleus appears to have a key role in timing the LH surge (Moore, 1978; Moore-Ede & Sulzman, 1978). Several circadian rhythms are disrupted or become more variable in aging female rats, including the timing of the LH surge (Cooper et al., 1980), and spontaneous running and drinking (Mosko, Erickson, & Moore, 1980) occur.

Morphologic changes accompanying reproductive senescence are seen at several loci. Changes in LHRH neurons are described above. The increased activity of microglia and astrocytes in the arcuate nucleus regions of aging mice and rats (Schipper, Brawer, Nelson, Felicio, & Finch, 1981) implies degeneration of neuronal processes, but so far no gross neuronal loss has been proved. These morphologic correlates of reproductive senescence do not establish their role in dysfunction, although the beginnings of a serious argument in favor of the significance of the glial changes can be made (as described below).

Ovary-Dependent Neuroendocrine Aging

The concept that some neuroendocrine aging processes are under ovarian influence arises from studies on the performance of ovarian grafts. Nearly 20 years ago, Pierre Aschheim (1965) reported that young ovarian grafts given to 2-year-old noncycling rats failed to reactivate regular estrous cycles, unless the old hosts were ovariectomized when young and allowed to age without ovarian influences (see also Aschheim, 1976). Subsequent studies from this laboratory extended Aschheim's key finding: Ovulatory cycles can be reinitiated by young ovaries in very old mice if ovariectomized when young (Felicio et al., 1983; Nelson, Felicio, & Finch, 1980); moreover, middle-aged long-term ovariectomized mice with young ovaries can support nearly as many (80%) regular cycles as are supported in young control transplants (Felicio et al., 1983).

Other neuroendocrine age changes that are substantially attenuated by postpubertal ovariectomy are the maintenance of the estradiol-induced LH surge, the elevation of LH after castration, hypothalamic gliosis, and the incidence of lactotrophic pituitary tumors (Table 8-1). These ovary-dependent hypothalamic-pituitary dysfunctions illustrate a neuroendocrine cascade of aging (Finch, 1976; Finch et al., 1984), which is triggered by factors extrinsic to the brain (ovarian steroids). Ovarian-dependent aging could involve a cumulative impact of ovarian steroids on the brain and pituitary (Figure 8-4). This speculative model is consistent with the summation of steroid impact acquired during development, with further steroid impact during adult life, as discussed above for the delayed anovulatory syndrome and the effects of the sex of neighboring fetuses on adult reproduction. Nonetheless, the pacemaker in this cascade is clearly the ovary, since grafting of young ovaries to middle-aged

TABLE 8-1. Manipulations of Reproductive Aging in Rodents

Markers of reproductive aging	Chronic ovariectomy delays	Chronic-E2 treatment accelerates
Ovarian cycles lost	[a]	[b]
Smaller LH surge	[c]	[b]
Smaller postovariectomy LH rise	[d]	[e]
Glial hyperactivity in arcuate nucleus	[f]	[g]
Lactotrophe adenomas (a late effect)	[b]	[i]

[a]Capacity for cycles assayed with ovarian grafts: Aschheim (1976); Nelson et al. (1980); Felicio et al. (1983).

[b]Kawashima (1960); Brown-Grant (1975); Brawer, Naftolin, Martin, & Sonnenschein (1978); Mobbs, Gee, & Finch (1984b).

[c]LH surge induced by estradiol implants. Mobbs et al. (1984a).

[d]Gee et al. (1983).

[e]Mobbs et al. (1984b).

[f]Schipper et al. (1981).

[g]Brawer et al. (1978).

[b]Nelson, Felicio, Sinha, & Finch (1980); Mobbs et al. (1985).

[i]Brawer & Sonnenschein (1975); Casanueva et al. (1982).

hosts before cycles cease then nearly doubles the numbers of cycles (Felicio, Nelson, & Finch, 1986).

There is an underlying progression toward neuroendocrine impairments even in the chronic absence of the ovary, since the capacity to sustain regular estrous cycles with young ovary grafts ultimately diminishes with age (Felicio et al., 1983), as does the estradiol-induced LH surge (Mobbs, Gee, & Finch, 1984). The role of ovary-independent neuroendocrine impairments during the early stages of reproductive senescence remains to be identified, but includes the transition from 4-day to 5-day cycles (Felicio et al., 1986).

The ovarian factor in ovary-dependent aging may be estradiol. During aging, as cycles lengthen and cease, the ratio of plasma estradiol to progesterone increases gradually at first and then sharply (Nelson et al., 1981). The increased ratio may be related to the smaller numbers of growing follicles as ovarian exhaustion becomes imminent (Gosden et al., 1983). The high ratio of estradiol to progesterone may produce a situation of "unopposed estrogen" since progesterone is an antagonist of estradiol. For example, in the uterus, progesterone causes rapid release of the nuclear bound estradiol receptor (Okulicz, Evans, & Leavitt, 1981). Antagonism of estradiol by progesterone also occurs in neuroendocrine loci (reviewed in Nelson et al., 1981). Although such antagonistic effects of estradiol and progesterone in the hypothalamus and pituitary are not well established in humans, it is well known that abnormally sustained estrogenic stimulation in the uterus is associated with metaplasia and increased risk of malignancy (MacDonald & Siiteri, 1974; reviewed in Finch & Flurkey, 1977). These considerations suggest that age changes should be precociously induced in young rodents by experimental elevations of plasma estradiol. This prediction is strongly supported by studies showing that relatively short-term (1–3 months) elevations of plasma estradiol can induce most neuroendocrine impairments found in rodents at later ages (Mobbs et al., 1985) (Table 8-1). Sheep also develop some neuroendocrine impairments and sterility (clover disease) if grazed on clover that contains phytoestrogens (Adams, 1976, 1977). Thus, a wide range of adult mammals may be susceptible to long-lasting effects from unremitting stimulation by estradiol. Several future decades of careful observation may be required to rule out adverse consequences of steroid-based contraceptives and postmenopausal steroid replacements on neuroendocrine functions in humans (Finch, 1986).

Taken together, these manipulations of reproductive senescence by ovarian steroids argue powerfully that aging in this system can be described in terms of known physiological factors and processes. Thus far, it has not been necessary to invoke any new biological mechanisms in aging beyond those already well documented in development and differentiation, which include cell death and changes in cell functions through inducers and other regulatory factors. Although the molecular (subcellular) basis for ovary-dependent effects on neuroendocrine functions is still unknown, these studies clearly show a major role in these phenomena for physiological and reciprocating interactions. Cascading interactions between neural and endocrine systems are proposed as a major phenomenon in mammalian aging (Finch, 1976; Finch et al., 1984), and they may also involve pituitary-thyroid interactions (Denckla, 1974), adrenal steroid–hippocampal interactions (Finch & Landfield, 1985; Landfield, Sundberg, Smith, Eldridge, & Morris, 1980; Sapolsky, Krey, & McEwen, 1985), and thymus-neuroendocrine interactions (Fabris, 1982; Pierpaoli & Besedovsky, 1975). In some cases, hormone target cells may undergo age-related loss of sensitivity because of interactions with their afferent stimuli (Finch et al., 1984).

FLUCTUATIONS AND HOMEOSTASIS

The approach of ovarian exhaustion illustrates that some phenomena observed as compensatory (homeostatic) mechanisms respond near their limit. As the pool of growing ovarian follicles diminishes, the variability of ovulatory cycle length increases strikingly (Figures 8-2, 8-3). An increased variance of functions as the compensatory limit is approached could be particularly important for homeostatic systems in which severe fluctuations are life-threatening, for example, in blood pressure (transient ischemia), blood glucose, blood electrolytes, or body temperature. The phenomenon of female senescence provides insight for understanding age changes in other systems in which key units are subject to irreversible losses with age, including neurons and nephrons (Hiramoto, Bernecky, & Jurand, 1962; Potter & Osathandoth, 1966); the thymus may also be considered here because of the progressive loss of the thymus-dependent maturation of B lymphocytes with donor age (Szewczuk, Dekruyff, Goidl, Weksler, & Siskind, 1980). A future area of research could emerge from the study of fluctuations during aging in relation to the loss of cells in specific systems.

It is already clear that neural systems differ greatly in their ability to compensate for cell loss. For example, the dopaminergic nigrostriatal system has a huge compensatory ability, which sustains normal motor functions even with > 90% loss of neurons (Bernheimer, Birkmayer, Hornykiewicz, Jellinger, & Seitelberger, 1973; Ranje and Ungerstedt, 1977). In contrast, the A2 catecholaminergic nucleus of the brain stem has very little compensatory ability, and even a 10% cell loss causes a permanent increase of blood pressure fluctuations (Talman, Snyder, & Reis, 1980) (Figure 8-5). If blood pressure is not regulated by drug treatment, the animal will die. Assessment of a wide range of neural and other systems according to their reserve and compensatory ability could help to identify systems in which a relatively small loss of cells could have major consequences during aging.

The homeostatic limit can be described as an envelope that demarcates the

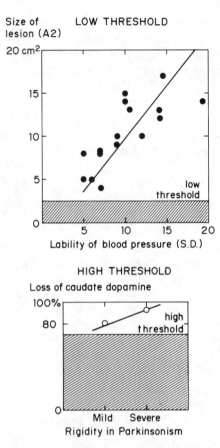

FIGURE 8-5. The response of different brain basal functions to lesions of varying size in catecholaminergic loci showing a *low* threshold in the brain stem A2 nucleus (*top*, redrawn from Talman et al., 1980) and the *high* threshold in the nigrostriatal system (*bottom*, redrawn from Bernheimer et al., 1973). (Reprinted from Finch, 1982.)

viable range of variations of physiological parameters* (Figure 8-6). Body temperature, for example, varies around a characteristic value close to 37°C, which may differ between individuals. Fluctuations of internal temperature much above or below 37°C, which approach the confines of the envelope, will trigger well-known homeostatic responses, including sweating, drinking, shivering, and eating. Blood osmolality, which has a functional relationship to thermoregulatory sweating, is also represented in this hypothetical case as a

---

*The development of these views was greatly stimulated by discussions with Arthur Iberall (UCLA), Charles Mobbs (USC), and Eugene Yates (UCLA). See Yates (1987) for further aspects.

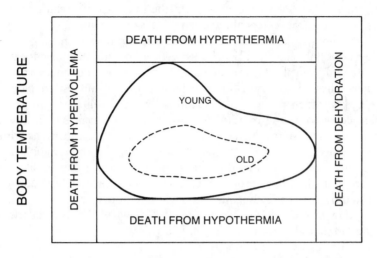

FIGURE 8-6. The homeostatic envelope for variations in body temperature and blood osmolality in young and old individuals. Data are not available for this hypothetical example, but it seems plausible that hypo-osmolality might give marginal, initial protection against hyperthermia by providing an extra source for sweat production.

second variable. However, if the variations exceed some limit (outside the homeostatic envelope), then the organism may not be able to regulate temperature or blood osmolality, leading to death.

The greater mortality of the elderly during heat waves (Shattuck & Hilferty, 1932) or during cold (Finch, Foster, & Mirsky, 1969) suggests that the homeostatic envelope becomes progressively smaller with age (Figure 8-6). Impaired autonomic and neuroendocrine responses are probably important in the diminished temperature regulation of elderly mammals. There is a subgroup of elderly who are particularly susceptible to accidental hypothermia: Despite large loss of core temperature during controlled studies of hypothermia, their shivering was less intense than in other elderly (Collins, Easton, & Exton-Smith, 1981; Collins, Exton-Smith, & Dore, 1981; Collins, Exton-Smith, James, & Oliver, 1980). Febrile responses are also impaired with age (Clark, Gean, & Lipton, 1980; Wollner & Spaulding, 1978) and represent another facet of impaired thermogenesis. On the other hand, sweating during exposure to heat is impaired in the elderly (Foster, Ellis, Dore, Exton-Smith, & Weiner, 1976). The origins of these and other impairments with age (Finch & Landfield, 1985) is unknown, but may include changes in the autonomic nervous system (Finch & Landfield, 1985; Hervonen, Vaalast, Partanen, Kanerva, &

Hervonen, 1978), as well as changes in the hypothalamus and elsewhere in physiologic control centers of the brain (Shimazu, 1980).

As the homeostatic envelope becomes smaller with increasing age, then endogenous fluctuations or signal noise even within normal range for younger adults could be fatal. One example might be the rupture of aneurysms during ordinary physical activity. Other variables of obvious interest are blood pressure and secretion patterns of hormones such as insulin, growth hormone, renin, aldosterone, and catecholamines; few data are available on how aging affects their short-term fluctuations. Disturbances in sleep patterns with age, especially sleep apnea, are also likely to be correlated with mortality risk.

Another case may be found in the spontaneous ventricular fibrillation that can occur in the absence of infarcts and is often fatal. Fibrillation can be mediated by aberrant sympathetic controls and potentiated by hypothalamic lesions (Lown et al., 1976; Verrier, Calvert, & Lown, 1975). The effects of age on the threshold for fibrillation are unknown.

Thus, one category of mortality in old age might result from "lethal physiologic noise." Perhaps this would constitute a true "senile death," as distinct from death due to specific diseases such as cancer. Clinicians recognize a subgroup of "frail elderly," who have high mortality risk (Isaacs, Gun, McKechan, McMillan, & Neville, 1971; Rowe, 1985) for which lethal physiologic noise may be pertinent. The topological analysis of sudden cardiac death from ventricular fibrillation proposed by Winfree (1983) suggests the possibility of constructing quantitative models for various types of lethal events involving fluctuations and entrainment.

The speed of physiologic fluctuations is also intuitively important and should be distinguishable from effects of amplitude. Yates (1987) hypothesized that high frequency fluctuations may be most dangerous; that is, the homeostatic envelope may shrink with age most for responses involving rapidly fluctuating parameters. Rapid blood pressure fluctuations and transient ischemic accidents may represent such phenomena. However, long-lasting fluctuations could also be important because of the larger number of homeostatic responses that may be brought toward their limit of compensation. For example, brief elevations in diastolic pressure might be less risky than prolonged elevations, which could alter the cellular and mechanical properties of the vasculature and induce compensatory hemodynamic responses. Similar considerations can be developed for the different effects of sporadic versus sustained hyperglycemia.

Decreases in the signal to noise ratio for key physiological parameters could be directly related to mortality risk. Each individual might be considered to have a mortality risk trajectory, which is a function of genotype, diet, drug and alcohol use, and social and professional activities. Descriptions of age changes in physiologic fluctuations in a neutral (unstressful) environment are not generally available on a detailed time course for most parameters; acquisition of such data could be a valuable step toward the development of quantitative models that bridge the important gap between biochemical-physiological changes with age and the exponential increases of mortality.

SUMMARY

This chapter traced a line of reasoning that began by considering events of reproductive aging in females and then considered a number of equally or more complex phenomena within the context of homeostasis and fluctuations. Yet no overarching theory was proposed that would account for or even rationalize the age-related changes in mammals—let alone worms, flies, or redwoods! In conclusion, various species of organisms differ so greatly in their physiological organization as to defy strong theory building about aging at the present. Such views are not pessimistic. Rather, they are warmly optimistic because we now have, for the first time in biological studies of aging, a wide range of well-defined aging processes that can be analyzed for particular mechanisms of aging. A similar reductionalism in scope has been widely adopted in approaching the cellular basis of development and cell differentiation (Davidson, 1986). The author views our present state of research as focusing on *micro*gerontologic hypothesis and theories. Strong *macro*gerontologic theories may be possible at some time in the future, pending deeper understandings of evolution and development in higher animals and plants.

REFERENCES

Adams, N. R. (1976). Pathological changes in the tissue of infertile ewes with clover disease. *Journal of Comparative Pathology, 86*, 29–35.

Adams, N. R. (1977). Morphological changes in the organs of ewes grazing on oestrogenic subterranean clover. *Research in Veterinary Science, 22*, 216–221.

Arai, Y. (1971). Possible process of the secondary sterilization delayed anovulation syndrome. *Experientia, 27*, 463–464.

Aschheim, P. (1965). Resultats fournis per la greffe heterchrone des ovarie dans l'etude de la regulation hypothalamus-hypophyso-ovarienne de la ratte senile. *Gerontologia, 10*, 65–75.

Aschheim P. (1976). Aging in the hypothalamic-hypophyseal-ovarian axis in the rat. In A. V. Everitt & J. A. Burgess (Eds.), *Hypothalamus, pituitary and aging* (pp. 376–416). Springfield, IL: Thomas.

Banergi, T. K., Parkening, T. A., & Collins, T. J. (1982). Effects of aging on the activity of hypothalamic dopamine-beta-hydroxylase during various stages of the estrous cycle in C57BL/6J mice. *Neuroendocrinology, 34*, 14–19.

Barraclough, C. A., & Wise, P. M. (1982). The role of catecholamines in the regulation of pituitary luteinizing hormone and follicle stimulating hormone secretion. *Endocrine Reviews, 3*, 91–119.

Beach, F. A. (1961). *Hormones and behavior*. New York: Cooper Square.

Bernheimer, H., Birkmayer, W., Hornykiewicz, O., Jellinger, K., & Seitelberger, F. (1973). Brain dopamine and the syndrome of Parkinson and Huntington. Clinical, morphological and neurochemical correlations. *Journal of the Neurological Sciences, 20*, 415–455.

Block, E. (1962). Quantitative morphological investigations of the follicular system in women: Variations at different ages. *Acta Anatomica, 14*, 108–123.

Brawer, J. R., & Sonnenschein, C. (1975). Cytopathological effects of estradiol on the arcuate nucleus of the female rat. A possible mechanism for pituitary tumorigenesis. *American Journal of Anatomy, 144*, 57–58.

Brawer, J. R., Naftolin, F., Martin, J., & Sonnenschein, C. (1978). Effects of a single injection of estradiol valerate on the hypothalamic arcuate nucleus and on reproductive function in the female rat. *Endocrinology, 103*, 501.

Bronson, F. H. (1981). The regulation of luteinizing hormone secretion by estrogen: Relationships among negative feedback, surge potential, and male stimulation in juvenile, peripubertal, and adult female mice. *Endocrinology, 108*, 506–516.

Brown-Grant, K. (1975). On "critical periods" during the postnatal development of the rat. International Symposium on Sexual Endocrinology of the Perinatal Period. *INSERM, 32*, 357–376.

Butcher, R. L. (1977). Changes in gonadotropins and steroids associated with unilateral ovariectomy of the rat. *Endocrinology, 101*, 830–840.

Butcher, R. L., & Fugo, M. W. (1967). Overripeness and the mammalian ova: II. Delayed ovulation and chromosome anomalies. *Fertility and Sterility, 18*, 297–302.

Butcher, R. L., & Page, R. D. (1981). Role of the aging ovary in cessation of reproduction. In N. B. Schwartz & M. Hunzicker-Dunn (Eds.), *Dynamics of ovarian function* (pp. 253–271). New York: Raven Press.

Casaneuva, F., Cocchi, D., Locatelli, V., Flauto, C., Zambotti, F., Bestetti, G., Rossi, G. L., & Muller, E. (1982). Defective central nervous system dopaminergic function in rats with estrogen-induced pituitary tumors, as assessed by plasma prolactin concentration. *Endocrinology, 110*, 590–599.

Chakravarti, S., Collins, W. P., Newton, J. R., Oram, D. H., & Studd, J. W. W. (1977). Endocrine changes and symptomatology after oophorectomy in premenopausal women. *British Journal of Obstetrics and Gynaecology, 84*, 768–775.

Clark, S. M., Gean, J. T., & Lipton, J. M. (1980). Reduced febrile responses to peripheral and central administration of pyrogen in aged squirrel monkeys. *Neurobiology of Aging, 1*, 175–180.

Collins, K. J., Easton, J. C., & Exton-Smith, A. N. (1981). Shivering thermogenesis and vasomotor responses with convective cooling in the elderly. *Journal of Physiology, 32*, 76P.

Collins, K. J., Exton-Smith, A. N., & Dore, C. (1981). Urban hypothermia: Preferred temperature and thermal perception in old age. *British Medical Journal, 282*, 275–277.

Collins, K. J., Exton-Smith, A. N., James, M. H., & Oliver, D. J. (1980). Functional changes in automatic nervous responses with aging. *Age and Aging, 9*, 17–24.

Cooper, R. L., Conn, P. M., & Walker, R. F. (1980). Characterization of the LH surge in middle-aged female rats. *Biology of Reproduction, 23*, 611–615.

Coquelin, A., & Desjardins, C. (1982). Luteinizing hormone and testosterone secretion in young and old mice. *American Journal of Physiology, 243*, E257–263.

Crowley, P. H., Gulati, D. K., Hayden, T. L., Lopez, P., & Dyer, R. (1979). A chiasma-hormonal hypothesis relating Down's syndrome and maternal age. *Nature, 280*, 417–419.

Davidson, E. H. (1986). *Gene activity in early development* (3rd ed.). New York: Academic Press.

Demarest, K. T., Moore, K. E., & Riegle, G. D. (1982). Dopaminergic neuronal function, anterior pituitary dopamine content and serum concentrations of prolactin, luteinizing hormone and progesterone in the aged female rat. *Brain Research, 247*, 347–354.

Denckla, W. D. (1974). Role of the pituitary and thyroid glands in the decline of minimal O_2 consumption with age. *Journal of Clinical Investigation, 53*, 572–581.

DePaolo, L. V., & Chappel, S. C. (1986). Alterations in the secretion and production of follicle-stimulating hormone precede age-related lengthening of estrous cycles in rats. *Endocrinology, 118*, 1127–1133.

Estes, K. S., & Simpkins, J. S. (1982). Resumption of pulsatile luteinizing hormone release after α-adrenergic stimulation in aging constant estrous rats. *Endocrinology, 111*, 1778–1784.

Fabrikant, J. D., & Schneider, E. L. (1978). Studies of the genetic and immunologic component of the maternal age defect. *Developmental Biology, 66*, 337–343.

Fabris, N. (1982). Neuroendocrine-immune network in aging. *Developmental immunology: Clinical problems and aging.* New York: Academic Press.

Faddy, M. J., Gosden, R. G., & Edwards, R. G. (1983). Ovarian follicle dynamics in mice: A comprehensive study of three inbred strains and a F1 hybrid. *Journal of Endocrinology, 96*, 23–33.

Felicio, L. S., Nelson, J. F., & Finch, C. E. (1986). Prolongation and cessation of estrous cycles in aging C57BL/6J mice are differentially regulated events. *Biology of Reproduction, 34*, 849–858.

Felicio, L. S., Nelson, J. F., Gosden, R. G., & Finch, C. E. (1983). Restoration of ovulatory cycles by young ovarian grafts in aging mice: Potentiation by long-term ovariectomy decreases with age. *Proceedings of the National Academy of Sciences of the United States of America, 80*, 6076–6080.

Finch, C. E. (1976). The regulation of physiological changes during mammalian aging. *Quarterly Review of Biology, 51*, 49–83.

Finch, C. E. (1982). Rodent models for Alzheimer's processes in the human brain. In S. Corkin et al. (Eds.), *Aging: Volume 19, Alzheimer's disease: A report of progress in research.* New York: Raven Press.

Finch, C. E. (1986). New questions about steroids. *Journal of the American Geriatric Society, 34*, 393–394.

Finch, C. E. (1987). Neural and endocrine determinants of senescence: Investigation of causality and reversibility of laboratory and clinical interventions. In H. Warner (Ed.), *Modern biological theories of aging.* New York: Raven Press.

Finch, C. E., Felicio, L. S., Flurkey, K., Gee, D. M., Mobbs, C. V., Nelson, J. F., & Osterburg, H. H. (1980). Studies on ovarian-hypothalamic-pituitary interactions during reproductive aging in C57BL/6J mice. In D. E. Scott & J. R. Sladek (Eds.),

Brain-endocrine interactions: IV. Neuropeptides in development and aging. Fayetteville, NY: ANKHO International, Inc.; and *Peptides, 1*(Suppl. 1), 163–175.

Finch, C. E., Felicio, L. S., Mobbs, C. V., & Nelson, J. F. (1984). Ovarian and steroidal influences on neuroendocrine aging processes in female rodents. *Endocrine Reviews, 5*, 467–497.

Finch, C. E., & Flurkey, K. (1977). The molecular biology of estrogen replacement therapy. *Contemporary Obstetrics and Gynecology, 9*, 97–107.

Finch, C. E., Foster, J. R., & Mirsky, A. E. (1969). Aging and the regulation of cell activities during exposure to cold. *Journal of General Physiology, 54*, 690–712.

Finch, C. E., & Gosden, R. G. (1984). Animal models for the human menopause. In L. Mastroianni & C. A. Paulsen (Eds.), *Aging, reproduction and the climacteric.* New York: Plenum Press (pp. 3–34).

Finch, C. E., & Landfield, P. W. (1985). Neuroendocrinology of aging. In C. E. Finch & E. L. Schneider (Eds.), *Handbook of the biology of aging* (2nd ed., pp. 79–90). New York: Van Nostrand Reinhold.

Fink, G. (1979). Feedback actions of target hormones on hypothalamus and pituitary with special reference to gonadal steroids. *Annual Review of Physiology, 41*, 571–585.

Foster, K. G., Ellis, F. P., Dore, C., Exton-Smith, A. N., & Weiner, J. S. (1976). Sweat responses in the aged. *Age and Aging, 5*, 91–101.

Gartner, K., & Bauneck, E. (1981). Is the similarity of monozygotic twins due to genetic factors alone? *Nature, 292*, 646–647.

Gee, D. M., Flurkey, K., & Finch, C. E. (1983). Aging and the regulation of luteinizing and spontaneous elevations at advanced ages. *Biology of Reproduction, 28*, 598–607.

Gee, D. M., Flurkey, K., Mobbs, C. V., Sinha, Y. N., & Finch, C. E (1984). The regulation of luteinizing hormone and prolactin in C57BL/6J mice: Effects of estradiol implant size, duration of ovariectomy, and aging. *Endocrinology, 114*, 685–693.

Goodman, R. L., & Knobil, E. (1981). The sites of action of ovarian steroids in the regulation of LH secretion. *Neuroendocrinolgy, 32*, 57–68.

Gorski, R. A. (1968). Influence of age on the response to paranatal administration of a low dose of androgen. *Endocrinology, 82*, 1001–1004.

Gosden, R. G., Liang, S. C., Felicio, L. S., Nelson, J. F., & Finch, C. E. (1983). Imminent oocyte exhaustion and reduced follicular recruitment mark the climacteric in aging mice. *Biology of Reproduction, 28*, 255–267.

Green, E. L., & Doolittle, D. P. (1963). Methods for testing linkage. In W. J. Burdette (Ed.), *Methodology in mammalian genetics* (pp. 56–82). San Francisco: Holden-Day.

Harlan, R. E., & Gorski, R. A. (1977). Correlations between ovarian sensitivity, vaginal cyclicity and luteinizing hormone and prolactin secretion in lightly androgenized rats. *Endocrinology, 101*, 750–759.

Harlan, R. E., & Gorski, R. A. (1978). Effects of postpubertal ovarian steroids on reproductive function and sexual differentiation of lightly androgenized rats. *Endocrinology, 102*, 1716–1724.

Harman, S. M., & Talbert, G. B. (1985). Reproductive aging. In C. E. Finch & E. L. Schneider (Eds.), *Handbook of the biology of aging* (2nd ed, pp. 457–510). New York: Van Nostrand Reinhold.

Henderson, S. A., & Edwards, R. G. (1968). Chiasma frequency and maternal age in mammals. *Nature, 218*, 22–28.

Hervonen, A., Vaalast, A., Partanen, M., Kanerva, L., & Hervonen, H. (1978). Effects of aging in the histochemically demonstrable catecholamines of human sympathetic ganglia. *Journal of Neurocytology, 7*, 11–23.

Hiramoto, R., Bernecky, J., & Jurand, J. (1962). Immunochemical studies of kidney hypertrophy in the rat. *Proceedings of the Society for Experimental Biology and Medicine, 111*, 648–651.

Hoffman, G. E., & Finch, C. E. (1986). LHRH neurons in the female C57BL/6J mice: No loss up to middle-age. *Neurobiology of Aging, 7*, 45–48.

Holinka, C. F., & Finch, C. E. (1981). Efficiency of mating in C57BL/6J female mice as a function of age and previous parity. *Experimental Gerontology, 16*, 393–398.

Holinka, C. F., Tseng, Y. -C., & Finch, C. E. (1979). Reproductive aging in C57BL/6J mice: Plasma progesterone, viable embryos, and resorption frequency throughout pregnancy. *Biology of Reproduction, 20*, 1201–1212.

Isaacs, B., Gun, J., McKechan A., McMillan I., & Neville, Y. (1971). The concept of pre-death. *Lancet, 1*, 1115–1118.

Jones, E. C., & Krohn, P. L. (1961). The relationships between age, numbers of oocytes, and fertility in virgin and multiparous mice. *Journal of Endocrinology, 21*, 469–496.

Karsch, F. J., Weick, R. F., Butler, W. R., Dierschke, D. J., Krey, L. C., Weiss, G., Hotchkiss, J., Yamaji, T., & Knobil, E. (1973). Induced LH surges in the rhesus monkey: Strength-duration characteristics of the estrogen stimulus. *Endocrinology, 92*, 1740–1747.

Kawashima, S. (1960). Influence of continued injections of sex steroids on the estrous cycle in the adult rat. *Annat. Zool. Japan, 33*, 266–282.

Kram, D., & Schneider, E. L., (1978). An effect of reproductive aging: Increased risk of genetically abnormal offspring. In E. L. Schneider (Ed.), *Aging and reproduction* (pp. 237–270). New York: Raven Press.

Krey, L. C., & Parsons, B. (1982). Characterization of estrogen stimuli sufficient to initiate cyclic luteinizing hormone release in acutely ovariectomized rats. *Neuroendocrinology, 34*, 315–322.

Landfield, P. W., Sundberg, D. K., Smith, M. S., Eldridge, J. C., & Morris, M. (1980). Mammalian aging: Theoretical implications of changes in brain and endocrine systems during mid and later life. *Peptides, 1* (Suppl. 1), 185–196.

Lown, B., Tempte, J. V., Reich, P., Gaughan, C., Regestein, Q., & Hai, H. (1976). Basis for recurring ventricular fibrillation in the absence of coronary heart disease and its management. *New England Journal of Medicine, 294*, 623–629.

MacDonald, P. C., & Siiteri, P. K. (1974). The relationship between the extraglandular production of estrogen and the occurrence of endometrial neoplasia. *Gynecologic Oncology, 2*, 259–263.

Merchanthaler, I., Lengvari, I., Horvath, J., & Setalo, G. (1980). Immunocytochemical study of the LHRH-synthesizing neurone system of aged female rats. *Cell Tissue Research, 209*, 497–503.

Mobbs, C. V., Flurkey, K., Gee, D. M., Yamamoto, K., Sinha, Y. N., & Finch, C. E. (1984). Estradiol-induced adult anovulatory syndrome in female C57BL/6J mice:

Age-like neuroendocrine, but not ovarian, impairments. *Biology of Reproduction,* *30,* 556–563.

Mobbs, C. G., Gee, D. M., & Finch C. E. (1984). A reproductive senescence in female C57BL/6J mice: Ovarian impairments and neuroendocrine impairments that are partially reversible and delayable by ovariectomy. *Endocrinology, 115,* 1653–1662.

Mobbs, C. V., Kannegieter, L. S., & Finch, C. E. (1985). Delayed anovulatory syndrome induced by estradiol in female C57BL/6J mice: Age-like neuroendocrine, but not ovarian, impairments *Biology of Reproduction, 32,* 1010–1017.

Money, J., & Ehrhard, A. (1972). *Man & woman, boy & girl.* Baltimore: Johns Hopkins.

Moore, R. Y. (1978). Central neural control of circadian rhythms. In W. F. Ganong & L. Martini (Eds.), *Frontiers in neuroendocrinology* (Vol. 5, pp. 185–206). New York: Raven Press.

Moore-Ede, M. C., & Sulzman, F. M. (1978). The physiological basis of circadian timekeeping in primates. *Federation Proceedings,* 17–25.

Mosko, S. S., Erickson, G. F., & Moore, R. Y. (1980). Dampened circadian rhythms in reproductively senescent female rats. *Behavioral and Neural Biology, 28,* 1–14.

Nass, T. E., LaPolt, P. S., Judd, H. L., & Lu, J. H. K. (1984a). Alterations in ovarian steroid and gonadotropin secretion predicting the cessation of regular oestrous cycles in aging female rats. *Journal of Endocrinology, 100,* 43–50.

Nass, T. E., Matt, D. W., Judd, H. L., & Lu. J. H. K. (1984b). Prepubertal treatment with estrogen of testosterone precipitates the loss of regular estrous cyclicity and normal gonadotropin secretion in adult female rats. *Biology and Reproduction, 31,* 723–731.

Nelson, J. F. & Felicio, L. S. (1985). Reproductive aging in the female: An etiological perspective. In M. Rothstein (Ed.), *Review of biological research in aging: Volume 2.* New York: Raven Press. (pp. 251–314).

Nelson, J. F., Felicio, L. S., & Finch, C. E. (1980). Ovarian hormones and the etiology of reproductive aging in mice. In A. A. Dietz (Ed.), *Aging—its chemistry* (pp. 64–81). Washington, DC: American Association of Clinical Chemists.

Nelson, J. F., Felicio, L. S., Osterburg, H. H., & Finch, C. E. (1981). Altered profiles of estradiol and progesterone associated with prolonged estrous cycles and persistent vaginal cornification in aging C57BL/6J mice. *Biology of Reproduction, 24,* 784–794.

Nelson, J. F., Felicio, L. S., Randall, P. K., Simms, C., & Finch, C. E. (1982). A longitudinal study of estrous cyclicity in aging C57BL/6J mice: I. Cycle frequency, length, and vaginal cytology. *Biology of Reproduction, 27,* 327–339.

Nelson, J. F., Felicio, L. S., Sinha, Y. N., & Finch, C. E. (1980). An ovarian role in the spontaneous pituitary tumorigenesis and hyperprolactinemia of aging female mice. *Gerontologist, 20,* 171.

Okulicz, W. C., Evans, R. W., & Leavitt, W. W. (1981). Progesterone regulation of the nuclear estrogen receptor. *Science, 213,* 1503–1505.

Osterburg, H. H., Donahue H. G., Severson, J. A., & Finch, C. E. (1981). Catecholamine levels and turnover during aging in brain regions of male C57BL/6J mice. *Brain Research, 224,* 337–352.

Parkening, T. A., Collins, T. J., & Smith, E. R. (1982). Plasma and pituitary concentrations of LH, FSH, and prolactin in aging C57BL/6J mice at various times in the estrous cycle. *Neurobiology of Aging, 3*, 31–36.

Pierpaoli, W., & Besedovsky, H. O. (1975). Role of the thymus in programming of neuroendocrine functions. *Clinical and Experimental Immunology, 20*, 323–338.

Potter, E. L., & Osathandoth, V. (1966). Normal and abnormal development of the kidney. In F. K. Mostofi & D. E. Smith (Eds.), *The kidney* (pp. 1–16). Baltimore: Williams & Wilkins.

Ramirez, V. D., Feder, H. H., & Swayer, C. H. (1984). The role of brain catecholamines in the regulation of LH secretion: A critical inquiry. In L. Martini & W. F. Ganong (Eds.), *Frontiers in neuroendocrinology* (pp. 27–84). New York: Raven Press.

Ranje, C., & Ungerstedt, U. (1977). High correlations between number of dopamine cells and motor performance. *Brain Research, 134*, 83–93.

Reymond, M. J., & Porter, J. C. (1981). Secretion of hypothalamic dopamine into pituitary stalk blood of aged female rats. *Brain Research Bulletin, 7*, 69–73.

Richards, J. S., Jonassen, J. A., & Kersey, K. S. (1980). Evidence that changes in tonic luteinizing hormone secretion determine the growth of preovulatory follicles in the rat. *Endocrinology, 107*, 641–648.

Rowe, J. W. (1985). Geriatric medicine. In C. E. Finch & E. L. Schneider (Eds.), *Handbook of the biology of aging* (2nd ed.). New York: Van Nostrand Reinhold.

Rubin, B. S., King, J. C., & Bridges, R. S. (1984). Immunoreactive forms of LHRH in the brains of aging rats exhibiting persistent vaginal estrus. *Biology of Reproduction, 31*, 343–351.

Samis, H. V., & Zajac-Batell, L. (1983). Aging and temporal organization. In R. F. Walker (Ed.), *Experimental and clinical interactions in aging* (pp. 397–419). New York: Dekker.

Sapolsky, R. M., Krey, L. C., & McEwen, B. S. (1985). Prolonged glucocorticoid exposure reduces hippocampal neuron number: Implications for aging. *Journal of Neuroscience, 5*, 1222–1227.

Schipper, H., Brawer, J. R., Nelson, J. F., Felicio, L. S., & Finch, C. E. (1981). The role of gonads in the histologic aging of the hypothalamic arcuate nucleus. *Biology of Reproduction, 25*, 413–419.

Seymour, F. I., Duffy, C., & Koerner, A. (1935). A case of authenticated fertility in a man of 94. *Journal of the American Medical Association, 105*, 1423–1424.

Shattuck, G. C., & Hilferty, M. M. (1932). Sunstroke and allied conditions in the United States. *American Journal of Tropical Medicine and Hygiene, 12*, 223–245.

Sherman, B. M., West, J. H., & Korenman, S. G. (1976). The menopausal transition: Analysis of LH, FSH, estradiol and progesterone concentrations during menstrual cycles of older women. *Journal of Clinical Endocrinology and Metabolism, 42*, 629–636.

Shimazu, T. (1980). Changes in neural regulation of liver metabolism during aging. In R. C. Adelman, J. Roberts, G. T. Baker, S. I. Baskin, & V. J Cristofolo (Eds.), *Neural regulatory mechanisms during aging* (pp. 159–185). New York: Liss.

Simpkins, J. W., Meuller, G. P., Huang, H. H., & Meites, J. (1977). Evidence for depressed catecholamine and enhanced serotonin metabolism in aging male rats: Possible relation to gonadotropin secretion. *Endocrinology, 100,* 1672–1678.

Smith, W. A., Cooper, R. L., & Conn, M. P. (1982). Altered pituitary responsiveness to gonadotropin-releasing hormone in middle-aged rats with 4-day estrous cycles. *Endocrinology, 111,* 1843–1848.

Szewczuk, M. R., Dekruyff, R. H., Goidl, E. A., Weksler, M. E., & Siskind, G. W. (1980). Ontology of B lymphocyte function: VIII. Failure of thymus cells from aged donors to induce the functional atration of B lymphocytes from immature donors. *European Journal of Immunology, 10,* 918–923.

Talman, W. T., Snyder, D., & Reis, D. J. (1980). Chronic lability of arterial pressure produced by destruction of A2 catecholamine neurons in brainstem. *Circulation Research, 46,* 842–853.

Telford, N., Mobbs, C. V., Sinha, Y. N., & Finch, C. E. (1986). The increase of anterior pituitary dopamine in aging C57BL/6J female mice is caused by ovarian steroids, not intrinsic pituitary aging. *Neuroendocrinology, 43,* 135–142.

Treolar, A. E., Boynton, R. E., Behn, B. G., & Brown, B. W. (1967). Variation of the human menstrual cycle through reproductive life. *International Journal of Fertility, 12,* 77–126.

Turgeon, J. L. (1979). Estradiol-luteinizing hormone relationship during the proestrous gonadotropin surge. *Endocrinology, 105,* 731–736.

Verrier, R. L., Calvert, A., & Lown, B. (1975). Effect of posterior hypothalamic stimulation on ventricular fibrillation threshold. *American Journal of Physiology, 223,* 923–927.

vom Saal, F. S. (1981). Variation in phenotype due to random intrauterine positioning of male and female fetuses in rodents. *Journal of Reproduction and Fertility, 62,* 633–650.

vom Saal, F. S., & Bronson, F. H. (1980). In utero proximity of female mouse fetuses to males: Effect on reproductive performance during later life. *Biology and Reproduction, 22,* 777–780.

vom Saal, F. S., & Moyer, C. L. (1985). Prenatal effects in reproductive capacity during aging in female mice. *Biology and Reproduction, 32,* 1116–1126.

Walker, K. F., & Timiras, P. S. (1980). Loss of serotonin circadian rhythms in the pineal gland of androgenized female rats. *Neuroendocrinology, 31,* 265–269.

Winfree, A. T. (1983). Sudden cardiac death: A problem in topology. *Scientific American, 248,* 144–161.

Wise, P. M. (1983). Aging of the female reproductive tract. *Review of Biological Research in Aging, 1,* 195–222.

Wollner, L., & Spalding, J. M. K. (1978). The autonomic nervous system. In J. E. Brocklehurst (Ed.), *Textbook of geriatric medicine and gerontology* (pp. 245–267). Edinburgh: Churchill Livingstone.

Yates, F. E. (1987). Senescence from the aspect of physical stability. In preparation.

Zuckerman, S., & Baker, T. G. (1977). The development of the ovary and the process of oogenesis. In S. Zuckerman & B. J. Weir (Eds.), *The ovary, Vol. 1: General aspects.* (pp. 41–67). New York: Academic Press.

PART III
Psychological Concepts and Theories of Aging

9

A Contribution to the Theory of the Psychology of Aging: As a Counterpart of Development

James E. Birren

The intent of this chapter is to make a contribution to more explicit psychological theorizing about human aging and to present a view of aging as a counterpart of development. Since psychologists differ greatly in their topics of interest, it is necessary to be explicit in defining what it is that we are trying to explain when we discuss aging. Some psychological theories of aging address broad characteristics such as personality, while others may explore particular facets of perception or memory. In any case, the purpose of the psychology of adult development and aging is to explain how behavior is organized over the adult years and the circumstances under which it becomes optimum or disorganized. In developing a theory, the researcher adopts an orientation that fits the level of complexity of the phenomenon that is to be explained.

There are few topics that have greater implications than aging. Aging is not only an area of scientific interest but also a heavily value laden area of personal and social concern (Pifer & Bronte, 1986). There are many scientific concepts and metaphors used at present that are carryovers from previous eras. These outdated metaphors of aging often represent stereotypes that slow the process of adaptation and retard the development of choices of individuals and societies.

The scientific era in thought about aging essentially began in the last century and still faces the legacy of these deeply entrenched beliefs about aging (Gruman, 1966). For example, one of the underlying thoughts still evident in contemporary medicine is that only disease produces the degradation observed with age, that one never dies from old age per se. In this view, one attains adulthood but unfortunately is beset by outside forces that lead to disability and death. This point of view was enlarged upon during the post-World War II period through an analogy to radiation damage that provided a transiently credible model for aging. In this theory, the cell incurs "hits" with time, and when sufficient damage has accumulated to the DNA of a cell, it dies (Szilard, 1959). Essentially, this is a random-accident model of aging; the deteriorative changes are viewed not as organized but as random in time. It provides the latent optimism that if individuals could be shielded from "accidents" they would be immortal.

Beneath the surface of most scientific views of human aging there has been a tenacious presence of this hope that we have the potential for immortality. However, even though as individuals we may wish for infinite plasticity in our capacity to change, realism suggests that we have limitations with age. Although death may be viewed as an accident, it is an accident to which the individual becomes increasingly susceptible with the passage of life time. Like a table that has been well used and beaten upon by daily hammerings, the organism may collapse after many years, apparently from a light blow. The final blow may be less important in the collapse than the readiness or vulnerability of the organism itself. The final environmental stressors that precipitate the end of a long life may be less important in explaining the event than the vulnerability or readiness for a disproportionately great response to what was earlier a trivial stimulus. Thus, molecules, cells, organisms, institutions, and societies may become vulnerable with time, and our explanations of why they become disorganized or disintegrate must increasingly be expressed in terms that satisfy the 20th-century mind and replace ancient beliefs that protect against the fears of the unknown.

This chapter attempts to provide such explanation, presenting a theory of aging as a *counterpart* of development (Birren, 1960). First, an attempt is made to gain insight into the organization of behavior over the adult life, to identify the variables under study, and to define concepts essential to a counterpart theory of aging. Next, age is examined in relation to time as a natural phenomenon; here, the point is made that the direction of time is important in building a cogent theory of adult development and aging. This leads to a discussion of aging as an evolutionary phenomenon, and late-life behavior as a counterpart of traits selected for earlier in development. Finally, humankind is examined as a species of strategic animals, able to interact with the genetic and environmental forces that shape the life course and, to an extent, able to control the outcomes.

THEORY DEVELOPMENT: TOWARD A DEFINITION OF AGING

In order to develop cogent theory in aging, a number of properties that help to define the process should first be discussed. It is important to determine at what level of organization and under which conditions this process takes place.

Aging and Complexity

Most researchers tend to view aging as a property of living things. Inorganic objects—stones, for example—might erode or degrade with time, but there is no known property in such objects that is responsible for the organization of change. There does not appear to be a "clock" within the stone in the same sense that there is in a living form that struggles to survive and reproduce. Earlier, Gerard (1959) raised the question: At which level of organization does aging as a phenomenon first appear? Although the question appears more relevant to the concerns of the molecular biologist than to those of the behavioral scientist, the point should be noted that phenomena of aging may vary as a function of the level of complexity of the object or system that is observed, whether it be a molecule, cell, organism, or population.

One hypothesis about the development of behavior in the individual is that it proceeds from a global, less differentiated state to increasing differentiation with age. In this view, complexity itself increases with age. The mature adult, in comparison with the child, is capable of more behaviors and more complex behaviors, and is capable of adapting to more demands of environmental circumstance. Late in life, it is believed by some, there occurs a dedifferentiation of behavior, whereby the individual shows a constricting repertory of behavior dominated by general needs and functional capacities. Thus, the very ill elderly may demonstrate a trend toward dedifferentiation if not disorganization of behavior. As yet there is no clear distinction between the disorganization or entropy of an aging biological system and such dedifferentiation of behavior.

Methods of observation vary, and to date there have been no longitudinal observations of the full range of human behaviors over the life course. What exists are observations at different levels of complexity within limited time periods. The resulting picture of the psychology of aging is one of scattered islands of more or less densely packed information. Put in other words, the psychology of aging at present is data-rich and theory-poor.

Universals

Science is concerned with the general. Therefore, theories of aging should provide us with explanations of patterns of change over the adult years that appear in all or most individuals. Whereas a chance explanation of aging would have all late-life change resulting from random events, evolution would seem to have resulted in organisms with driven or proactive patterns of change. Although it is unreasonable to expect that *all* late-life change rests upon evolved biological programs, the relative fixity of the species with regard to their maximum length of life precludes dismissal of *some* universal phenomena of aging resting upon an evolutionary basis.

Evolution may have provided a partial program in the human genome for late-life change, but its interaction over time with social and cultural environments may have led to other patterns of change. In this regard, one must distinguish the universal phenomena that arise from the genome, the active organism, from those that arise reactively with our environmental structure.

Individual Differences

In contrast to biological and social theories of aging, psychological theories should attend to explaining individual differences, since there appear to be wide differences in many behavioral characteristics with age (Birren & Schaie, 1985). The sources of influence that give rise to individual differences presumably involve different explanations than do the universal behaviors that all humans will show over wide ranges of environmental differences. The evolution of a large brain appears to carry with it the capacity to intervene in the way in which we age. To be discussed more fully later is the relevance of the evolution of human capacity to plan and develop strategies. Without an active organism, however, such strategies are equivalent to the software of a computer programmed to control events. The active organism uses these strategies to put an imprint on change as it strives to maintain a dynamic equilibrium with its environment.

Dependent and Independent Variables in Aging

As one proceeds to develop a behavioral theory of aging, it is necessary to define the dependent and independent variables that make up the process. The variables we choose will guide the research questions and determine the level of complexity we are able to explain. Table 9-1 is a simplified list of dependent and independent variables to illustrate the point. Although this list does not include all possible variables or explanations, it represents a sampling of key factors necessary to understanding psychological, biological, and social aging.

Because of the present data-rich, theory-poor state of the psychology of

TABLE 9-1. Variables in Theories of Aging

Dependent variables (to be explained)	Independent variables (variables invoked in explanations)
Interspecies longevity	Heredity
Intraspecies longevity	Pleiotropy; brain/body weight ratio
Physical health	Age-dependent disease – adventitious disease
Physiological well-being	Disuse/activity & exercise
Mental health	Stress and accumulation
Productivity	Chance
Adaptive capacities	Ecological specialization
Psychological & social competence	Historical period
Wisdom	Socialization

aging, it may be desirable to use some broad characteristics of individuals to gain insight into the organization of behavior over adult life. *Longevity, or length of life*, is the simplest broad organizing variable but it is usually eschewed by psychologists because it appears to be exclusively biological in character. However, the interaction between the environmental circumstances of life and length of life may provide a fertile territory to explore and uncover relationships between and within the biobehavioral and sociobehavioral domains.

A second variable of a broad type is *productivity*. Its measurement, unlike that of length of life, is more complex because human products range so widely in character. Individuals, through their mental or physical efforts, yield a range of products (objects, processes, ideas, relationships) of use to society or to themselves. The suggestion is offered that the products of human activity over a life span can be studied in relation to the characteristics of the producers and their environments. Presumably, productivity varies with length of life, perhaps mediated by variables such as vigor and health if not by strategies and styles of life. In this area, attempts have been made to characterize productivity in scholarly and scientific pursuits over the life span (Dennis, 1956; Hall, 1922; Lehman, 1953). Of interest is the age of peak qualitative and quantitative productivity as well as the sum over the life span, that is, total productivity. In reference to the measurement of productivity, Yates (1982) has suggested that human behaviors be examined in terms of the changes in the spectrum of activities over the life span. This is somewhat analogous to the detailed observations of a single child or an adult throughout a day, such as that carried out by Barker and Barker (1968). The question is, how many behaviors as well as what types of behaviors are emitted by individuals who vary by age, sex, and other characteristics? Underlying the analyses of the observed data would be the intent to identify patterns of changes in behavior with age.

A third broad or overarching variable to be observed or measured over the life span is *adaptive capacity*. The events of life evoke responses that are designed to reestablish an equilibrium between the environment and the internal milieu. For example, changes in the environment may include temperature changes that require the organism to make self-regulatory adjustments to survive. At a social level, there may be political upheavals involving war and massive immigration. Adjustments of attitudes and behaviors are required when political refugees are settled in a new homeland with different religions, physical environment, and customs. These changes can be examined with regard to the adaptive capacities of individuals to the destruction of a long-standing previous way of life. The question of what are the strengths and weaknesses in adaptive capacities with advancing age easily leads to the further question: What are the strengths or latent qualities that may emerge to aid the survival of individuals and groups? Both the expected and unexpected events of our lives — depressions, wars, hurricanes, bereavements — challenge and evoke adaptive responses. The basic query is, how do our adaptive capacities change with age and experience?

Another broad dependent variable for studying the life span is the *meaning* that an individual places on his or her life. Kierkegaard has said that one lives life forward but understands it backward. This captures the essence of our subjective lives, and the question arises as to how the meanings we attach to our lives influence our choices of behavior as well as our survival when we are challenged (see Reker and Wong, this volume).

Yet another way of looking at the organism, the most common one adopted by psychologists, is via measurement of *cognitive capacity*. Cognitive capacity can be defined as our capacity for knowing; this includes intelligence, which has been much studied in relation to age. Although this topic has been the most active area of research for psychologists interested in the course of life, it leaves open many issues of competence shown by the active organism. Cognitive capacity by itself may touch on only the most manifest areas of adult potential, missing areas of the potential for novel adaptations. The present author favors the use of the Greek trilogy of *cognition, affect*, and *conation* to capture the major dimensions of the organization of behavior: knowing, feeling, and acting. Although many other approaches are viable, the above-noted variables are highly relevant to any discussion of psychological aging.

The foregoing suggests that behavior should be studied in broad scope over the life span both in terms of causes and in terms of consequences. Further, it indicates that important patterns are to be found. An alternative point of view is that aging is a process of random change in an organism that is programmed for development but not for adult life. In this view, aging would be the random transformation of an organism reasonably well perfected for life at early maturity or about the age of optimum reproductive capacity. At this point it seems desirable to introduce some definitions and concepts en route to describing "a counterpart theory of aging."

Determinants of Aging

Aging is defined here as the transformation of the human organism after the age of physical maturity—that is, optimum age of reproduction—so that the probability of survival constantly decreases and there are regular transformations in appearance, behavior, experience, and social roles. One of the earlier students of aging, Cowdry (1952), pointed out that "almost all living organisms pass through a sequence of changes, characterized by growth, development, maturation, and finally senescence" (p. 15). He also pointed out that "there can be no doubt that in all animals, from the single-celled protozoa through the invertebrates to man, the length of life is largely determined by inheritance" (p. 56). There seems little to dispute the fundamental idea that genetic inheritance is a major factor in setting the usual length of life of a species. While environmental variations—for example, variations in temperature and diet—are important in modifying the species life span, the various species appear to hold positions relative to one another with dramatic fixity (Sacher, 1977). The mouse, rat, cat, dog, horse, whale, and man, as well as other animals, maintain their characteristic lengths of life. In fact, we are surprised if a family pet dog lives beyond 17 years.

These expectations not only surround other animals but are built into many features of our culture, and they determine the accepted ideas about how long we as humans usually live. Further, we act on these beliefs, often constructing our own future. It is in this point that one finds the basis for the interaction of the biological characteristics of our species with the socially collected knowledge and attitudes we call *culture*. Culture may be described as the "DNA of society," the collection of prescribed roles, beliefs, and behaviors typical of society that are passed on. As noted above, genetically controlled characteristics of humans interact with the physical and social environments. Our culture has within it customs surrounding our coming of age as well as the biological features of reproductive behavior, eating, sleeping, and also growing old. Were our usual genetically determined length of life to change dramatically, there would have to be major alterations in our culture and the institutions we have created to allow for this change.

It is therefore frivolous to contend that "aging is all a matter of heredity" or that it is all a matter of the environments in which we find ourselves. Since our biological histories are much longer than our cultural transmission of written history, it seems expedient to begin with a consideration of genetic control over aging and how it may relate to a counterpart point of view.

There are many positions or hypotheses a psychologist may take in explaining aging. The most common hypotheses define aging as (1) a result of disuse of previous skills or capacities, (2) a consequence of random wear and tear, (3) a consequence of selective reinforcement by the environment leading to decrements or increments in adaptive capacity, and (4) loss of resources. Insofar as the psychologist is also a biological scientist, aging is often viewed as (5) a consequence of genetic control over later-life characteristics. Finally, most psychologists will add (6) aging as a consequence of individual choice and creation of new problem-solving solutions that may never have been seen by the species.

Aging in this sense refers to an orderly or regular transformation with time of representative organisms living under representative environments. Strains or individual animals that have a genetically based defect may not be typical of their species and do not lend themselves to a characterization of normal aging. Thus, the typicalness of the genetic backgrounds of individuals and their environments enters into the considerations of psychologists in attempting to characterize and explain the usual patterns of change seen over the life span.

The course of behavior over the life span is assumed to have three influences: (1) genetic influences, (2) environmental influences, and (3) individual choice and adaptations. Birren and Schroots (1984) proposed three dynamic processes associated with these forces: *senescence*, the process of increasing probability of dying with age; *eldering*, the process of acquiring social roles and behaviors appropriate to our age group; and *geronting*, the self-regulation we exercise. Since the manner of our aging is presumed to be a product of these three forces, the psychologist must be at the same time a biologist and social scientist and must incorporate thinking from the "islands of dense information" explored by these different areas. Further, since our biological existence is a prior condition to either our culture or individual identity, it is a prerequisite to explore the origins of control over our aging, or our *senescing*.

AGE AND THE ORGANIZATION OF NATURAL PHENOMENA: TIME DIRECTION AND AGING

"Time is the messenger of the gods that passes without restraint through space, matter, and minds" (Birren & Cunningham, 1985). This metaphorical statement is intended to emphasize the importance and the pervasiveness of time in all phenomena. To the above statement we might add that time also passes without restraint through societies. The placing of events in a time sequence is basic to our concepts of causality. A cause cannot occur after or during the effect that it is believed to have brought about; it must occur before. *Before* and *after* are fundamental ideas in our explanations of the organization of our natural world.

Our concepts of time are particularly important to the development of a cogent theory of the psychology of aging. Any organization that is said to *age* must have direction in time (Reichenbach & Mathers, 1959). It is therefore surprising how few scholars have focused on the issues of the dynamic processes that provide the basis for time direction in biological, psychological, and social systems (Baltes & Willis, 1977; Lowenthal, 1977; Shock, 1977).

To change with time, and therefore to age, an organism must have at least two properties. It must have a force that supplies motion to the system and a mechanism that prevents the system from returning to its original position or state. If time did not flow in one direction, life might be lived in such a way that one could "degrow" and change from an adult to a child. Intuition suggests that time flows in one direction for the physical world, the biological world, and in some sense, the psychological and social worlds as well. What gives time its direction is a question that is pursued through research on different systems, from cells to institutions.

In a mechanical clock, the ratchet and cog prevent time from flowing backward; they also prevent it from going forward all at once. Likewise, for the universe it is easy to assume that time has one direction, which is determined by its continual expansion. If the universe were to reach a point of maximum expansion and begin to contract, it would presumably result in a reversal of time direction. Time, then, is closely linked to the direction of events, which lead either to increased disorder (entropy) or to the opposite, increased order (negentropy).

There is also time direction toward increased order in the fertilized human egg, which takes from its environment the molecules it requires to construct an organization, the individual organism. The genetic material of the cell exercises an influence such that the system moves from *less* to *more* organization. It may be said that there is a purpose of the fertilized egg, to create an organization that will become increasingly self-regulating, that is, less influenced by the environmental perturbations. This is readily appreciated in the infant who proceeds to grow up and become more biologically, psychologically, and socially self-regulating.

What then is aging? Is there a phase in life where the organism begins to lose its capacity for self-organization, a phase in which it moves from order to disorder, toward increased entropy and away from negentropy? Such a simple view might fit single-cell organisms but hardly complex organisms such as humans.

Although during the later adult years of life the probability of dying increases as a consequence of the organism's lowering biological capacity for self-regulation, one can observe an orderly maturation of the individual in which early biological capacity for self-regulation is followed by achieving social and psychological self-regulation. Thus, when additional energy and information must be added to the individual to support its survival, often it is provided in the form of psychological or social systems.

One of the international scientists concerned with direction of time is Stephen Hawking. As a consequence of a degenerating disease of the nervous system he has been confined to a wheelchair. In 1986 he gave a speech, but no longer being able to speak, he typed his address into a computer mounted on his wheelchair. From this, the speech was delivered from a synthesizer as an artificial voice. Here, we clearly see support systems providing increased energy and information to maintain him in the face of biological decrement, while at another level he was attempting to supply negentropy through his thoughts about the direction of time in the universe.

This example illustrates the fact that there is a loose coupling between biological time and psychological time; and perhaps, up to a point, the arrows of time—the thermodynamic arrow and the psychological arrow—may move in different directions. Of note in the example of Hawking's behavior is that he was generating information at one level while he was losing information at another.

The biological view of age changes as being fundamentally thermodynamic or chemical is an incomplete picture of the aging of individuals, since humans learn as a result of experience and change psychologically and socially with age as a consequence of accumulated learning. Changes with age noted in the organization of experience are not directly explained by considerations of energy in the nervous system but by its properties as an information system. The necessary and sufficient condition for explaining the organization of behavior with age is not therefore the energy consumed by particular cells of the nervous system but their pattern of activity or information content as a result of experience. It is obvious that whether we learn English, Chinese, or Spanish does not depend upon the energetic characteristics of the nervous system; nor are our thoughts about the nature of aging itself explained by the chemistry of aging.

The forward direction of time in a behavioral sense is a result of the cumulation of experience, the "traces" of past events that become the elements for further learning. It is proposed that time direction in a psychological sense derives from memory, the storage of the past. It is memory in the active organism that enables humankind to be strategic, to extend dramatically the possibilities for successful adaptions to personal limitation and for interaction between the way we grow old biologically and the social environments in which we live.

It should be noted that technological change has brought about some new mechanisms in social organizations that may strengthen time direction. In primitive societies the elders had an important role because their memories of earlier events and processes were important to the survival of the tribe and family. Currently, the existence of libraries reduces the value of the stored experience of elders. Also, computer access to information is fast, and increasingly we can access useful information in an impersonal system. In the contemporary era, we can know exactly when a new product or process was introduced, in contrast to the uncertainties, for instance, of how and when early man came to North America and how the cultural transmissions of tool discovery took place. The postindustrial age, with its emphasis on storage and retrieval of masses of information, contributes to humankind's increasing self-consciousness about its position in the flow of events.

At present there is a movement toward incorporating information from scientific research in our newspapers, television programming, and novels. This emphasis reduces the time lag between new understanding and the capacity of language to render a subject discoursable in a contemporary sense. In relation to science, there is a positive value placed by present society on the incorporation of new terms and concepts into the media. In this case, *older* or *aging* applied to society might refer to the rate of uptake of new information or rate of movement from a less differentiated state of knowledge to a more differentiated state. This would be somewhat parallel to our notions of the development of individuals who move rapidly from infancy through child-hood, from *less* to *more* differentiation.

Time Direction and Memory: Psychological Aging

The minimum statement that might be made about time direction for an organism is that time flows in one direction because of the accumulation of consequences of events. This creates the need to specify the mechanism that results in the irreversible accumulation of consequences. For subjective time flow, memory may be the mechanism that provides a forward direction to time. Like the ratchet and cogwheel of a clock, memory can provide us with a basis of "before and after." Thus, the psychological arrow of time travels forward from beginning to end, from early to late life. At a minimum, Chronos must have a memory.

It should be noted in the above that memory might be the mechanism of time direction in behavior, but experiences themselves could be random over time. Memory, as such, does not seem to contain any explanatory potential for complex phenomena of aging beyond irreversibility and cumulation. Without other properties, the organism appears passive in aging, having only the potential to react. If memory were the only mechanism operating, the socialization of an individual would impart sequence to the behaviors that were encouraged, but the individual would be passive in the way he or she was transformed with time.

Observations of old persons suggest that there is a pattern to the changes that occur over time, that such changes are not merely the consequences of happenstance or chance. In short, there seems to be an active organism that interacts with its history and the environment. Positing an active organism brings purpose and intent back into the picture. It suggests that there are goals to which the organism is directing itself.

The change of the organism toward adulthood and reproduction clearly seems goal-driven from within the organism. Less clear is the trend toward death in later life. Some theories posit a goal-driven developing organism with later chance degradation of the adult through the slings and arrows of existence, for example, the random-accident models discussed earlier in this chapter. However, also as noted earlier, the relatively fixed length of life of different species of organisms suggests that there must be some control over adult life change, albeit with much environmental interaction. The emphasis here is to point out that theory of adult development and aging must attend to matters of the goals of the organism, and presumably the goal of increasing self-regulation persists into late life.

THE EVOLUTION OF AGING: A COUNTERPART THEORY

The existence of a persisting goal of self-regulation through time, as evidenced by increasing psychological capacity (see Perlmutter, this volume) in the face of biological decrement, raises the question of whether longevity has been selected for by evolution. However, one of the roadblocks to accepting the idea of the evolution of aging has been the difficulty in conceiving how longevity could be selected, since the trait does not appear until long after the age of reproduction is past. It is much easier to accept the fact that animals whose development has placed them in an optimum position to reproduce will contribute to the development of the species. That is, animals who have survived to the age of reproduction have evolved characteristics that favor them during reproduction, and these characteristics will determine the future course of the species. This selection produces a concentration of optimum features at the age of reproduction and, to a lesser extent, toward the end of parenting, and then a gradient of decline toward the end of life. The assumption is that negative characteristics expressed in late life can not be removed by selection. Put metaphorically, nature has interest only in seeing that the "best" reproduce and has a declining interest in individual animals after their reproductive and parenting life is finished. Nature is thus a "passive bystander" observing the collection of negative traits that appear toward the end of the life span. The result would be a random degradation of late-life organisms who were as near perfect as selection could bring their development around the time of reproduction.

From the foregoing logic, some scientists conclude that aging is beyond evolutionary explanation, at best representing a wide-ranging collection of independent processes. However, the evidence for some genetic control is growing. In addition to the characteristic species life span, evidence clearly demonstrates a trait of familial longevity in humans that accounts for an appreciable amount of individual difference in how long individuals live (Jarvik, Blum, & Varma, 1972). Also, studies of length of life in identical twins show more similarity in length of life than in other siblings. Thus, at birth there exists some control over the likely length of life to be lived by the individual; it cannot be solely the product of environmental circumstance. The question now becomes not whether there is genetic control over late-life phenomena but how it evolved and how it exercises its effects. Research must now account for the evolution of genetic control over both positive and negative characteristics of late life.

The Counterpart Pathway to Genetic Control over Late Life

One pathway to late-life change appears to be derivative of early development. Specialization at the time of reproduction may have late-life indirect consequences. For example, young animals that can rapidly mobilize for a high energy expenditure may show an increase in blood pressure in old age. Thus, genes that do one thing in early life may express a different control in late life; that is, genetic loci on the DNA may predispose for more than one trait. This phenomenon, called pleiotropism or pleiotropy, is the property of a gene expressing itself in several ways (McClearn & Foch, 1985).

In addition to the advantage of such selected traits as activity, appearance, and stamina at age of reproduction, there are behaviors that can lead to selective breeding. For example, the ability to learn, solve problems, and communicate presumably has been the result of selective pressures. It is easy to appreciate the selective advantage of such behaviors at the early end of life, but how could positive late-life behaviors be selected? Although variations in longevity do not appear until long after reproduction has been completed, intelligent, long-lived parents are able to provide an environment favorable for their young to survive. For example, in hunting-gathering societies, intelligent long-lived parents could more likely provide their young with food and protection. Furthermore, individuals who showed great capacity for learning, retention of information, and wisdom in late life would not only provide a selective advantage for their offspring's survival but also for their tribe's or clan's. Particularly in preliterate society, the chances of survival would increase if there were long-lived elderly or leaders. The issue is that natural selection for longevity may have been coupled with selected favorable behavioral characteristics appearing in late life. This line of reasoning suggests the possibility of indirect selection for positive late-life characteristics that embrace a wide range of complex biological and behavioral characteristics—for example, wisdom and potential for a long life—as well as a recession of negative traits.

Potential for Senescence

Were there not systematic changes in organic molecules, it would be impossible to date bones of long dead persons and ascribe to them not only a period in which they lived but individual ages as well. Racemization refers to the process whereby molecules that exist in two optical forms, only one of which is biologically active, are catalyzed into the alternative optical form. The important point is that there are universal changes that occur in organic molecules with the passage of time, and these changes continue long after age of reproduction.

The fact that thickening of collagen fibers occurs in tissues of rats with advancing age is significant in regard to the above, since these animals rarely obtain physical maturity in the wild. Such animals must have a *potential* for senescent changes even though in the wild state they rarely have the opportunity to express them. Reproducing and showing high mortality during physical development when they are still growing in size suggests that the universal late-life pattern of change in connective tissue must be a consequence of selection of early developmental processes. The point of logic is that there is a *potential for senescence* shared by all animals in a species, even though the pattern may not be directly subject to selective pressure. Its origin is thus postulated as being *counterpart* or derivative of selection for patterns of development and pleiotropism. Genes and behavior thus can play different roles in development than in senescence.

Control over Longevity

Sacher (1977) points out that there are two parameters governing longevity, *rate of aging* and *vulnerability*. The latter refers to the vulnerability to disease that is shown long before the onset of aging. In human populations the lowest level of vulnerability is between 10 and 12 years, when the mortality rate is at a minimum. "It is, therefore, related to the genetically determined vigor of the genotype" (p. 586). Much biological research is directed toward the factors that affect the rate of aging. For example, the Gompertz equation shows the relationship between the death rate and age in the following form:

$$q_x = q_0 e^{ax}$$

In this equation, q_0 is the vulnerability factor and is the parameter controlling the rate of aging; a is the rate of aging factor. The term x represents age.

As the standard of living has improved in the population, the minimum death rate, q_0, has consistently improved, that is, declined. However, the doubling time for the death rate at advanced ages has been remarkably constant, suggesting a fixed character of the determinants of the death rate in contrast to circumstantial influences on the vulnerability factor. Thus, the fact that animals in the wild and in captivity show similar Gompertz curves, albeit with different levels, that is, q_0, suggests the rate of aging governing the Gompertz curve is the outcome of natural selection of the species.

Longevity of animals is related to their body size. However, for behavioral scientists it is of great importance that longevity is correlated with brain size and with the brain weight/body weight ratio. *Encephalization* is the key factor in length of life. That brain weight is coupled with longevity suggests that there has been selection of mammalian species toward relatively large brain sizes, representing an evolutionary commitment to brain control over the organism. In turn, this appears to have an advantage in longevity.

The contribution to longevity and the pattern of aging of the species by encephalization is viewed here as a counterpart, just as pleiotropy was discussed earlier; that is, the course of natural selection that has led to specialization in development has also led by counterpart to specialization in aging. The long life of neurons, the cells that are specialized to store experience, is of great significance for late-life behavior as a counterpart of encephalization. In comparison with other animals, because of encephalization the fixed cells (neurons) provide humans with a greater portion of their behavior controlled as a result of experience or learning, in contrast to controls exercised by dividing cells of other organs.

The suggestion is made that natural selection has provided humankind with a brain that is relatively large compared with the rest of the body. Neurons, however, lose their capacity for mitotic division and do not multiply after the fetal period, though the support cells of the brain, the glia, may continue to divide. The fixed postmitotic neurons appear to comprise the great archival system of the body. Thus, relatively more functions of the human organism are organized on the basis of the experience of the organism in contrast to the more rigid phylogenetic expression of control seen, for example, in insects. Not only is the nervous system essential in the development of organization of behavior in humans, the nervous system is as vital as the key organ systems in regulating the physiology of the organism (Frolkis, 1982). Recent progress in the neurosciences indeed suggests that the nervous system is pervasive in its influence in the regulation of endocrine glands, metabolism, and, in fact, all of the vegetative or somatic processes of the organism. As the major integrating organ system of the body as well as its archive, the nervous system is in a key position to disseminate influences to other organs. It is precisely at this point in the discussion that the implications of the term *counterpart* become apparent. That is, the elaborated nervous system of the human organism, as a result of evolution, makes it possible to a considerable extent to regulate the organism on the basis of that experience rather than upon the details of the genome or our genetic program. Thus, human aging has evolved to be a complex joint product of evolution and our specialization in accumulating the consequences of experience.

How we age is therefore viewed not as a direct expression of evolution but as a counterpart of evolution and its effect on development and accumulation of experience. The mixture of genetically programmed and acquired behavior has always been paradoxical in interpreting human development in the early years of life. Related to aging is the new issue that late-life controls are an indirect counterpart of early developmental selection. Evolution has provided us with a mixed pattern and level of genomic and acquired characteristics. Within the human species there is not only an expression of phylogenetic universals with age but also acquired individual characteristics, influencing how long we live, how we live, and how well we live.

Questions about adult development can degenerate into simple nature/ nurture controversies with overattribution of causality either to the environment or to genetic influences. Many such disputes arose in conjunction with child development, and it is not unexpected that similar claims of overdetermination from a limited class of forces can be expected in the field of aging. The counterpart position is that the outcomes of historical determinants, both phylogenetic and environmental, interact in present situations. But the outcomes are indirect effects, not direct expressions. Hence, the word *counterpart* is used to soften any implied directness of the linkage of the outcomes of current circumstances with genetic and acquired programming of the past. Counterpart is meant to suggest that development and aging are linked as complements so that the outcomes are translations rather than products of direct expression.

Six classes of forces contributing to outcomes in aging are considered in relation to a counterpart orientation: (1) genetic, (2) selective reinforcement and experiential history, (3) resources and characteristics of the current situation, (4) the new behaviors generated by the individual, for example, through reasoning and creativity, (5) disuse, and (6) wear and tear. Included in generation of new behavior are factors of the state of the organism (e.g., mood) at the time of events. The organization of behavior is viewed as comprised by processes of cognition, conation, affect, and the special properties of awareness or consciousness.

Order or pattern in lives is presumably due to the cumulation of the outcomes of sequences of the person × situation interaction. Runyan (1984) favors the use of the term *transaction* rather than *interaction* to give emphasis to the idea that the behavior of the individual changes *the situation*. Thus, one is looking at the outcomes of long sequences of person × behavior × situation transactions. In this vein three processes are identified: (1) situation-determining processes, (2) person-determining processes, and (3) behavior-determining processes (interactions of persons and situations). These processes are not unlike those posed by Birren and Schroots (1984) to describe the processes of adult development and aging: eldering (situation-determining), senescing (biological-determining), and geronting (behavior-determining).

This amplifies the point that the counterpart theory of aging (transformations of forces) assumes that the organism is active and goal-driven and makes choices of behavior in situational interactions according to the state of the individual and awareness at the time of the interaction. As mentioned earlier, developmental psychology, and indeed much of all psychology, has eschewed use of the teleological concepts of purposes, goals, and directedness of behavior; however, it seems obvious that the genome functions as though it has purpose. It programs organisms to grow up and become effective in self-regulation so that the probability of survival increases as development proceeds. Following this assumption of the organism's purpose in attaining self-regulation, it is suggested that the person × situation interactions of older adults are also purposeful in that individuals seek to maintain or maximize self-regulation in ways consistent with biological and behavioral past history (Buhler & Massarik, 1968; Vaillant, 1977).

Thus, the biological capacities for self-regulation are the necessary but not the sufficient conditions for survival. Similarly, our capacities for social self-regulation, whether we are team hunters or otherwise, are necessary but not sufficient for survival. It is when we consider *strategies* which are generated by the individual through his or her own awareness, wisdom, that we enter into a discussion of the significant domain of the executive nervous system and its role in aging. Decisions can be made that carry influences over long spans of time and can override the principles of biological and social self-regulation.

WISDOM AND HUMANS: CONTROL OVER LONGEVITY

All organisms have devices to facilitate their survival, as seen in the evolution in humans of the capacity for learning from experience and for generating novel strategies to aid in survival by gaining information and energy. The complex nervous system that has evolved has the capacity for devising ad hoc strategies that can facilitate biological self-regulation as well as increase the conditions that will lead to advantageous environmental conditions for the organism. Humankind appears also to have evolved the capacity to create the metastrategies for expanding information.

Over a lifetime, the individual develops a repertory of tactics or coping devices for meeting environmental demands and for the management of bodily needs. These tactics vary from person to person in their efficiency to foster survival and other long-term goals. The term *wisdom* suggests that individuals can maximize the outcomes of complex relationships and can contribute to a state of greater organization concurrent with an increase in biological entropy (Clayton & Birren, 1980). This is not meant to imply that the time directions of the metastrategic "mind" and its capacities can run totally opposite to the thermodynamic arrow. It is meant to suggest that the wise individual, over wide ranges of variation in biological capacity for self-regulation, may have a relative independence in effectiveness in generating information. It may only be near a limiting condition of biological disorganization (terminal decline) that the thermodynamic and psychological arrows are coupled in a parallel flight in one direction.

It is difficult to derive a functional view of later life in which some processes for self-regulation may decline, others may stay the same, and some may improve. However, given human capacity for long-range memory, as well as short-term memory and learning, we can develop strategies that for some persons seem to extend over a lifetime and influence their ability to adapt and survive.

Humankind has a great capacity for adapting to environmental circumstances and events. This appears to be more than merely showing passive *plastic adaptability*, such as the reptile displays by reducing metabolism activity in cold weather; it involves *strategic adaptability*. Unlike the capacity for adaptation that has been built into species by selective pressures and expressed through DNA, our nervous system permits the self-generation of novel adaptations as well.

The nervous system has the potential to intrude its influence into somatic processes, and indeed, it can override them through "executive" decisions. On a winter's hike we might make a strategic error and decide to take a shortcut that overextends our capacities, and we might succumb to overexposure and hypothermia. However, we can also use strategies to anticipate cold and build a campfire early in the evening, thus overcoming our limited capacity to adapt to the cold.

An older individual may show a restricted range of adaptability to the environment because the capacity for biological self-regulation may diminish and because, as an accompaniment of advanced age, the individual may have a reduction in the social support networks of earlier years. Yet this individual may continue to obviate such limitations by effective strategies. It is at this point that the concept of wisdom is introduced—that quality of an individual that appears to take into account his or her physical limitations and social circumstances and yet gives rise to a superordinating control that extends the capacity for self-regulation beyond its previous bounds. This underlies the frustrations of the empirical scientist, who attempts to extrapolate from experimental studies predictions of the competence of an individual who, in everyday life, is expanding effectiveness and capacity for self-regulation, even in the presence of decreasing internal and external resources.

Wisdom and Impulsivity

The combination of increased experience with advancing age and a lower drive to act impulsively is relevant to the idea of a late-life state of wisdom. One senses that a complex trait of wisdom could have led to selective survival of families and tribes by having elders present who were reflective, experienced, and not prone to impulsive acts. It is here that the reasoning of a counterpart theory would suggest that biological, experiential, and environmental forces may result in some proportion of the population having a pattern or balance of behavioral characteristics not found in the young, which promotes the attributed state of wisdom and which may be found in organisms that are increasingly biologically vulnerable.

It would be facetious to argue that evolution is destined to make us wise if we live long enough or that wisdom results solely from living in wisdom-inducing environments. Earlier it was posed that person × behavior × situation relationships produce outcomes that can best be characterized as transactions. It is in such circumstances that counterpart is meant to provide an orientation that adult development and aging are complex outcomes of biological, social, and individual forces.

Novel Strategies

An extension of the implications of self-generating strategies would include those persons who are not merely reactive to the environment but who create the environment by novel means. These could be described as proactive older adults whose wisdom embraces far more than just adaptation to the present. The evolution of modern science brings with it an enlarged capacity for strategies whereby we can supersede our earlier limits for biological self-regulation and be that which we were not—for example, a species that has the capacity for overcoming toxic effects of viruses the species has never met during the course of evolution. We have also exposed ourselves to environments that the species has never met before, such as the weightless state in space, which points to the strategic and creative overrides on biological and social limitations.

One of the areas in which we can exercise creativity and strategic override is in our attitudes toward ourselves. How do we regard ourselves in relation to age? What is our self-concept—our self-esteem and related aspirations? These influence how we deploy ourselves. In brief, some strategies involve the maintenance and expansion of the concept of self that is correlated with good mental health and survival, as well as matters of social productivity and life satisfaction (Tyler, 1978).

For example, one strategy would be to deemphasize the concept of aging as a disease, accentuating aging as a natural, intrinsic, and *normal part of life* that requires some preparation to be fully enjoyed. Another strategy would be to extend the view that aging, in addition to being a normal part of life, has some meaning of its own, which is most clearly expressed as having *open-ended hope* or *transcendence* as a fundamental characteristic inherent to the aging process.

In a biological sense, the human species became committed to the drive for transcendence as the brain evolved to its current complexity. However, it seems too simplistic to restrict the concept of transcendence to only the overcoming of biological barriers; psychological and social obstacles also have to be overcome.

Because the topic of aging reminds us of our mortality, it is an area for dialogue between the sciences and the humanities. Through such dialogue we may encourage societies that not only have intelligent and wise individuals within them, but also are wise, intelligent societies that build humane as well as technologically advanced cultures.

Care of dependent older persons and the circumstances under which lives are ended influence the above attitudes. Human groups are noted for their tendency to develop rituals surrounding the dying and the dead. Some people believe that if they fail to take care of the dying and the dead appropriately, the spirits of the departed may blight their future lives. Clearly, by personal projection, the dying and the dead are part of us, and we are treating a part of us in our care and rituals. Robert Anderson (1970), toward the end of his play *I Never Sang for My Father*, made the point that death ends a life but it does not end a relationship. The relationships we have had with others do continue to influence our lives. It is not surprising, therefore, that a certain mystique has developed about the care of the very old and the circumstances of death. It is not easy to neglect the care of the elderly without neglecting our self-concept at the same time, and it is not easy to wish for the death of another without at the same time wishing for a part-death in oneself. This is another area where the term *counterpart* seems useful, that is, our self-regard is a by-product of psychological projection, of the regard for others.

Aging is a major aspect of life onto which our metaphors project our uncertainties, fantasies, fears, and unresolved ambitions (Birren & Renner, 1980). It is not unreasonable that an empirical science of aging impacts upon religious tenets about the aged and death. Religious institutions have a role in managing and expressing our thoughts about aging, the care of the aged, and the dying. Humanistic enlightenment has not lessened our need for creativity in the development of systems of faith. Wagar (1971) said, "Man . . . suddenly found himself living in a post ideological, anti-utopian, demythologized world in which the will to believe had withered and failed" (p. 196). One of the issues needing attention is whether an empirical ideology can suffice to maintain the self-respect and productivity of individuals and societies as they grow old. Again, aging is too important to leave to the scientists, but also, it is too important to leave to the theologians and humanists. From all of their knowledge and our experiences can come the creative metastrategies that will enable society to develop the condition in which there will be more wise and productive older persons.

SUMMARY AND CONCLUSIONS

This chapter represents an orientation toward theory in the psychology of aging. It pointed out elements that should be considered in any theory of aging and more particularly in psychological theory. One might pose the question of the essential differences between a psychological theory and a biological or social one. The difference lies in what one is attempting to explain. A psychological theory should deal primarily with the organization of behavior in the adult years of life, if not over the whole life span, with interests in explaining differences that appear among children, young adults, middle-age adults, the old, and the very old.

Students of aging are beginning to recognize that our state of knowledge can be characterized as islands of densely packed information with few bridges. Knowledge within those islands of information is mostly organized by microtheory. In the present state of the science of aging, adaptations are made by analogies from theories in other areas. In the future it is possible that theories of aging—being both more basic and more complex, in a hierarchical sense, than most things we attempt to explain—will provide the patterns of thought for other areas of inquiry. At present we try to explain aging in terms of things we know more about, but we will begin to explain other phenomena as analogous to it.

There is little doubt that the task of a psychological theory of aging is a complex one. Adding to the complexity is the fact that psychology lies between the biological and social sciences. It is at the same time a product of scientific patterns of thinking and explanation as well as of its own traditions. Biology uses genetics and evolution as concepts for organizing forces, whereas the social sciences use concepts of culture, social structure, and socialization to refer to the organization of social phenomena. Clearly, the individual is a product of both domains. It is in this sense that a psychological theory, in order to be robust in its implications, should have an ecological perspective— that is, individual organisms grow up and grow old as a consequence of their heredity and their environments. In the present chapter the term *counterpart* has been used to refer to this interactive quality in aging. To the biological and social forces must be added the contribution made by the choices of behavior. The human organism is not a passive product of biological and social influences. Humankind is also strategic and can alter environments, and it is on the verge of manipulating its own genetic material.

For the human species the expression of aging is thus not only a matter of genetics and environments but of strategic planfulness. This links aging to the evolved complex nervous system as an expression of the importance of the brain in aging, which is shown in the high correlation of species longevity with the ratio of brain weight to body weight. There must have been some survival advantage for the human species in having such a large brain in relation to body size. This evolved large brain now is the primary integrative organ of the body, and it regulates not only behavior but the whole internal physiological milieu. Not only is it programmed on the basis of the species evolution, it is also programmed on the basis of experience; it learns and develops strategies and might even be described as self-programming. It is in this sense that the human as a metastrategic animal can in part age the way it wants to age, as well as the way it has to age as a counterpart of many influences. Without a parallel psychological perspective on human aging, the biological and social sciences by themselves would not give much weight to the complex and puzzling influence of the nervous system as a cause as well as a consequence of aging.

The thesis of this essay on a psychological theory of aging is that our aging is a counterpart of many complex forces. Our wisdom and our metastrategies bear directly on the issue of how we want to grow old. Therefore, theory development in the behavioral sciences must include these many factors in considering the process of aging, and it should define carefully the variables being examined and the metaphors of the theorist. Only through such examination and multidisciplinary interchange can psychological theory in aging progress.

REFERENCES

Anderson, R. (1970). *I never sang for my father*. New York: Signet.

Baltes, P. B., & Willis, S. L. (1977). Toward psychological theories of aging and development. In J. E. Birren & K. W. Schaie (Eds.), *Handbook of the psychology of aging* (pp. 128–154). New York: Van Nostrand Reinhold.

Barker, R. G., & Barker, L. S. (1968). The psychological ecology of old people in Midwest, Kansas and Yoredale, Yorkshire. In B. Neugarten (Ed.), *Middle age and aging* (pp. 453–460).

Birren, J. E. (1960). Behavioral theories of aging. In N. W. Shock (Ed.), *Aging: Some social and biological aspects* (pp. 305–332). Washington, DC: American Association for the Advancement of Science.

Birren, J. E., & Cunningham, W. R. (1985). Research on the psychology of aging. In J. E. Birren & K. W. Schaie (Eds.), *Handbook of the psychology of aging* (pp. 3–34). New York: Van Nostrand Reinhold.

Birren, J. E., & Renner, V. J. (1980). Concepts and issues of mental health and aging. In J. E. Birren & R. B. Sloane (Eds.), *Handbook of mental health and aging* (pp. 3–33). Englewood Cliffs, NJ: Prentice-Hall.

Birren, J. E. & Schaie, K. W. (1985). *Handbook of the psychology of aging* (2nd ed.). New York: Van Nostrand Reinhold.

Birren, J. E., & Schroots, J. F. (1984). Steps to an ontogenetic psychology. *Academic Psychology Bulletin, 6*, 177–190.

Buhler, C., & Massarik, F. (Eds.). (1968). *The course of human life*. New York: Springer Publishing Co.

Clayton, V., & Birren, J. E. (1980). The development of wisdom across the lifespan. A re-examination of an ancient topic. *Life span development and behavior, 3*, 103–135.

Cowdry, E. V. (1952). Aging of individual cells. In A. I. Lansing (Ed.), *Problems of aging* (pp. 50–88). Baltimore, MD: Williams & Wilkins.

Dennis, W. (1956). Age and achievement: A critique. *Journal of Gerontology, 2*, 331–337.

Frolkis, V. V. (1982). *Aging and life–prolonging processes*. New York: Springer Verlag.

Gerard, R. W. (1959). Aging and organization. In J. E. Birren (Ed.), *Handbook of aging and the individual* (pp. 264–275). Chicago: University of Chicago Press.

Gruman, G. J. (1966). *A history of ideas about the prolongation of life: The evolution of prolongevity hypotheses to 1800*. Philadelphia: American Philosophical Society.

Hall, G. S. (1922). *Senescence*. New York: Appleton Century.

Jarvik, L. F., Blum, J. E., & Varma, A. O. (1972). Genetic components and intellectual functioning during senescence: A 20-year study of aging twins. *Behavioral Genetics, 2*, 159–171.

Lehman, H. D. (1953). *Age and achievement*. Princeton, NJ: Princeton University Press.

Lowenthal, M. F. (1977). Toward a sociopsychological theory of change in adulthood and old age. In J. E. Birren & K. W. Schaie, (Eds.), *Handbook of the psychology of aging* (pp. 116–127). New York: Van Nostrand Reinhold.

McClearn, G. & Foch, T. T. (1985). Behavioral genetics. In J. E. Birren & K. W. Schaie (Eds.), *Handbook of the psychology of aging* (pp. 113–143). New York: Van Nostrand Reinhold.

Pifer, A., & Bronte, L. (1986). *Our aging society*. New York: W. W. Norton.

Reichenbach, M., & Mathers, R. A. (1959). The place of time and aging in the natural sciences and scientific philosophy. In J. E. Birren (Ed.), *Handbook of aging and the individual* (pp. 43–80). Chicago: University of Chicago Press.

Runyan, W. M. (1984). *Life histories and psychobiography*. New York: Oxford University Press.

Sacher, G. E. (1977). Life table modification and life prolongation. In C. E. Finch & L. Hayflick (Eds.), *Handbook of the biology of aging* (pp. 582–638). New York: Van Nostrand Reinhold.

Shock, N. W. (1977). Systems integration. In C. E. Finch & L. Hayflick (Eds.), *Handbook of the biology of aging* (pp. 639–665). New York: Van Nostrand Reinhold.

Szilard, L. (1959). On the nature of the aging process. *Proceedings of the National Academy of Sciences, 45*, 30–45.

Tyler, L. E. (1978). *Individuality: Human possibility and personal choice in the psychological development of men and women*. San Francisco: Jossey-Bass.

Wagar, W. W. (1971). Religion, ideology, and the idea of mankind in contemporary history. In W. W. Wagar (Ed.), *History and the idea of mankind* (pp. 196–221). Albuquerque, NM: University of New Mexico Press.

Vaillant, G. E. (1977). *Adaptation to life*. Boston: Little, Brown.

Yates, F. W. (1982). Outline of a physical theory of physiological systems. *Canadian Journal of Physiology and Pharmacology, 60*, 217–248.

10

Language and Aging:
Competence versus Performance*

Leah L. Light

Until fairly recently it was widely argued that language functions are spared from the deterioration typically observed in other areas of cognition in the elderly. There are three reasons for this belief. First, the results from psychometric studies of aging suggest that verbal abilities are well preserved in old age. For instance, performance on vocabulary tests is stable across the adult years (Salthouse, in press). Also, scores on the Verbal subtests of the Wechsler Adult Intelligence Scale show much less change in adulthood than scores on the Performance subtests, a pattern that Botwinick (1985) calls the "classic aging pattern." The pervasiveness of this view is indicated by Salthouse's (1982) analysis of classification of intellectual abilities that hold across the adult years and those that do not. Although only three of the eleven dichotomies listed explicitly use the terms *language* or *verbal* in referring to abilities that are preserved, the general tenor of the classificatory schemes is that ability to acquire new information suffers in old age while ability to use old information does not. Thus, it is claimed that because language skills are largely acquired in childhood, there is no reason to expect any change in language in old age.

Second, this belief in the immunity of language from the effects of aging is fostered by results of neuropsychological studies. Although age differences

*Deborah Burke and Elizabeth Zelinski made helpful comments on earlier versions of this chapter which sharpened my thinking on several theoretical points. I am grateful for the many discussions of these issues we have had over the years.

favoring young adults are sometimes found on test batteries used to assess language deficits in aphasia, the apparent negative relationship between age and performance on these tests can be explained by the presence of confounding factors such as hearing loss in the elderly (Goldstein & Shelly, 1984) or cohort differences in education (Borod, Goodglass, & Kaplan, 1980; Duffy, Keith, Shane, & Podraza, 1976; Goodglass & Kaplan, 1983).[1]

Third, as pointed out by Kemper (in press), systematic comparisons of language comprehension and production across the adult years have been undertaken only recently, probably because of a belief that once the child has mastered sentence structure and learned about social constraints of language use there is little or nothing left of interest to study from a developmental perspective. As Riegel (1973) put it, "language functions remain highly stable and do not reveal any dramatic or 'interesting' changes in development" (p. 479).

In this chapter, evidence is reviewed that suggests that the view that language is unchanging across the adult years is partially, but not entirely, correct. In particular, we argue that there are no changes in linguistic *competence* in old age but that there are *performance* factors that set limits on older adults' ability to understand and produce language.

THE NATURE OF PERFORMANCE LIMITATIONS

The distinction between competence and performance was first introduced by Chomsky (1965) to distinguish between "the speaker-hearer's knowledge of the language" and "the actual use of language in concrete situations" (p. 4). Performance, unlike competence, is affected by such factors as memory limitations, distractions, and attentional lapses. Thus, the argument made here is that young and older adults do not differ in their knowledge of the language but that performance factors affect comprehension and production of language in old age.[2]

Although the major restriction on performance postulated by linguists is that of memory (Chomsky, 1965; Church, 1980; Frazier & Fodor, 1978; Kimball, 1973), we consider performance limitations more generally within a processing-resource framework (e.g., Kahneman, 1973; Navon, 1984; Navon & Gopher, 1979). According to processing-resource theorists, mental operations require varying amounts of cognitive resources for their execution. Further, cognitive resources are a limited commodity, with individuals varying in the amount of cognitive resources available to them at any moment in time as well as in their maximum allotment. An additional assumption necessary for making predictions with regard to cognition and aging is that, on average, the amount of processing resources declines with increasing age in adulthood.

Salthouse (1985b) has pointed out that there are at least three ways to conceptualize resource limitations on performance in old age. First, and most common, is the idea that there is limited short-term memory capacity; that is, in old age there is less mental space available for the storage of information. Second, the total amount of mental energy or attention available for the execution of operations may be reduced in old age. A third view of performance limitations in old age arises out of the observation that older people are slower in carrying out many activities and that slowing may underlie deterioration in cognition (Birren, Woods, & Williams, 1980; Salthouse, 1982, 1985a, b). The working-memory-capacity approach taken by many cognitive psychologists (e.g., Baddeley, 1986; Baddeley & Hitch, 1974; Daneman & Carpenter, 1980; Kintsch & van Dijk, 1978; Levelt, 1983; Sanford & Garrod, 1981) is a hybrid of the first two approaches, which are based on spatial and energy metaphors, respectively; in this view, both storage and manipulation of information must compete for the same limited supply of attentional resources. Because performance decrements may arise from limitations in any of these resources and because predictions from the three versions of the limited-resources hypothesis are often indistinguishable, we will use spatial, energy, and temporal metaphors interchangeably in our discussion of language in old age.

The processing-resource approach is compatible with what we know about cognition and aging. There is considerable evidence that older adults perform less well than young adults on tasks requiring simultaneous storage and manipulation of information (e.g, Craik, 1977; Parkinson, Lindholm, & Urell, 1980; Wright, 1981). Although it has been argued that age differences on traditional memory-span tasks that tap short-term memory capacity are negligible (Craik, 1977; Eysenck, 1977), findings of smaller digit spans, letter spans, word spans, and sentence spans are the norm rather than the exception (Burke & Light, 1981; Light & Anderson, 1985). Such findings have led many investigators to conceptualize age-related declines in intelligence, memory, problem solving, and reasoning in terms of deficits in processing resources (e.g., Baddeley, 1986; Craik, 1977, 1985; Craik & Byrd, 1982; Craik & Rabinowitz, 1984; Hartley, 1986; Hasher & Zacks, 1979; Horn, 1982; Light & Anderson, 1985; Perlmutter & Mitchell, 1982; Rabbitt, 1977).

In this chapter, the processing-resource approach is extended to the domain of language and aging. There are two points that need to be made at this juncture. First, we have used the term *processing-resource approach* advisedly. The processing-resource approach to cognition and aging does not constitute a formal theory from which precise predictions can be made, and indeed we do not believe there are any formal theories of cognition and aging. Rather, the processing-resource approach is a loose set of organizing principles that guide the selection of research questions and the interpretation of experimental and naturalistic observations. Further, there is no single processing-resource theory within cognitive psychology. As noted above, several different metaphors are currently used to capture the meaning of the term *processing resources*, and these concepts are embodied in a variety of models and operationalized in different ways in different experimental paradigms. Hence the goal here is not to formulate or to evaluate *a* processing resource theory of language and aging but rather to organize the existing literature with respect to language and aging and to assess the extent to which findings are consistent with the processing-resource approach, broadly conceived. Some difficulties inherent in this strategy are taken up in the final sections of the chapter.

Second, it is important to be clear about the logic of our analysis. Because all of the research reviewed here deals with behavior, it could be argued that we are always examining performance and can make no inferences with respect to underlying competence. However, to the extent that age constancy in behavior is observed, constancy in competence can be assumed. Whenever variables sensitive to variations in processing resources are manipulated and interactions of age with these variables are observed, such that age differences are greatest under conditions demanding more processing resources, we infer performance limitations in the success of older adults to understand or produce language.

We begin our discussion with a review of findings suggesting that linguistic competence as assessed in studies of the organization of knowledge in semantic memory is unaffected by normal aging but that reduced processing resources in old age may affect knowledge utilization. We then consider performance limitations on language comprehension and production in old age. Finally, we address the question of whether the processing-resource approach can explain all interesting aspects of language in old age.

THE ORGANIZATION OF KNOWLEDGE
IN SEMANTIC MEMORY

The term *semantic memory* refers to an individual's knowledge of the meanings of words as well as general world knowledge (Tulving, 1972). One way to evaluate the effects of aging on linguistic competence is to determine whether the representation of knowledge in semantic memory is the same in young and older adults, as would be expected if there were no age differences in knowledge of the language. Several aspects of the organization of semantic information in adulthood have been studied, including word associations, the structure of categories, and knowledge about scripted activities. These tasks are usually untimed and do not place heavy burdens on processing resources because little manipulation of information is required. Hence, even if older adults have reduced processing resources, large age differences in performance on these tasks would not be expected, and our review suggests they are not to be found. However, as we will see, access to and utilization of semantic information are not always age-invariant but, at least in some situations, are negatively affected by reduced processing resources in old age.

Word Associations

In word association tasks, people are asked to produce the first word that comes to mind when a stimulus word is presented. If people are following the instructions and are not operating under a set to produce novel or interesting responses, then the words they generate should reveal the organization of semantic memory. The reasoning behind this claim is that concepts in semantic memory are organized in networks based on semantic similarity and that when a stimulus term is presented, there is an automatic spread of activation to related concepts. The word sharing the most attributes with the stimulus term should receive the greatest activation and should be produced. Automatic processes, such as spreading activation, are believed not to involve the expenditure of processing resources. Thus, to the extent that young and older adults have similar conceptual organization, they should produce similar word associations (Burke & Peters, 1986).

Early research in this area suggested that young and older adults might differ in semantic organization. Riegel and Riegel (1964) found that people aged 17 to 65 years were most likely to give responses in the same form class as the stimulus (paradigmatic responses). However, older adults were less likely to do so than young adults and also were more likely to give syntagmatic responses, that is, words that might appear near each other in a sentence (e.g., responding with "town" to the stimulus "walk"). In addition, the responses of older adults were more variable on two measures: older adults gave a greater number of different responses, and they gave more unique responses. There was also a nonsignificant tendency for the old to be less likely to produce the primary response (the most frequent one) to a given stimulus. Perlmutter (1979) found that 18- to 29-year-olds and 59- to 70-year-olds produced about the same percentage of associates that were the most common responses to their stimulus terms in published word association norms (though there was a marginally reliable difference favoring the young), but older adults were less consistent in their responses on repeated testing.

However, the above findings, which suggest that the organization of word meanings differs across the adult years and is less stable in later adulthood, have not held up in subsequent work. Lovelace and Cooley (1982) found that vocabulary scores, but not age or education, predicted both paradigmatic word associations and commonality of associations. The importance of vocabulary rather than age as a predictor of paradigmatic responding and response variability has been confirmed by Burke and Peters (1986).

Finally, later research has not supported the existence of greater response variability in the elderly. Neither Perlmutter and Mitchell (1982) nor Burke and Peters (1986) found evidence for age differences in the proportion of responses that were repeated on a retest. These contrary findings may arise from differences in methodology across various studies. Perlmutter's (1979) subjects gave repeated responses on four occasions within a single test session, and it is possible that older subjects may have adopted the strategy of giving different responses if they incorrectly assumed that the task was intended to measure creativity. Such a response set would be unlikely to affect associates given on two occasions several months apart as in the Burke and Peters study. Also, Perlmutter and Mitchell (1982) found that people in their twenties and sixties were equally good at generating either the same or different responses on two occasions when requested to do so, providing further evidence for similar processing in the word association task. Apparent age differences in the likelihood of generating the most common associate to a stimulus word may also be due to cohort differences in associations (Bowles, Williams, & Poon, 1983).

Taken together, these results suggest that any observed differences in word associations across the adult years may be best attributed to differences in verbal ability across ages, cohort differences in most frequent responses, and strategic variables operating in the test situation, rather than to aging.

Representation of Categorical Information

Rosch (1973) has pointed out that members of natural categories are not all equally good examples of those categories. Good or typical exemplars of categories tend to be produced more often when people are asked to list instances that belong to particular categories. In addition, in speeded classification tasks, in which people are asked to judge whether instances belong to particular categories, typical exemplars produce faster response times than do atypical exemplars.

There is considerable evidence for stable organization of the representation of categories across the adult years. Howard (1980) asked young, middle-age, and older adults to generate members of taxonomic categories (e.g., TREE, FURNITURE, SPORT). The correlations among the frequencies with which category members were produced as responses were highly reliable for all pairs of age groups. Older adults were no more variable than young adults on any of several measures. Using a different approach, Howard (1983) asked adults in each decade from the twenties to the seventies to rate all possible pairs of 16 animal names for similarity. Multidimensional scaling solutions of the similarity judgments suggested that adults of all ages base their judgments on the same two dimensions, predativity (ferocity) and size.

Additional evidence for structural similarity in the representation of categories comes from the speeded classification task; the relative increase in time to classify atypical rather than typical exemplars is the same for young and older adults, indicating that categories are represented in the same way across ages (Byrd, 1984; Mueller, Kausler, Faherty, & Olivieri, 1980; Petros, Zehr, & Chabot, 1983).

Scripted Activities

There is evidence that our knowledge of routine activities is represented in memory in the form of scripts that specify conventional roles, props, action sequences, reasons for engaging in an activity, and expected outcomes for ordinary activities (Schank & Abelson, 1977). For instance, we expect to find waiters and menus in restaurants, we go to restaurants because we are hungry, we eat, and then we leave after paying the bill. Scripts play an important role in comprehension and memory for particular instances of conventional activities (Bower, Black, & Turner, 1979). Details that are omitted from a particular instantiation of a script are inferred on the basis of the stereotypic sequence that defines a well-known situation. Hence, comprehension problems could easily arise if young and older adults do not share the same scripts for common activities. However, the representation of scripted activities in semantic memory seems to be constant across adulthood. Light and Anderson (1983) asked young and older adults to generate a list of common actions or events for six routine activities (e.g., writing a letter to a friend, going to the doctor). The frequencies with which each action was generated correlated highly for the two age groups, and there was no age difference in the proportion of unique actions generated for any of the six scripts. In addition, there were very few age differences in ratings of how typical or necessary each action was for completion of any activity. Hess (1985) has obtained similar results.

Summary

The evidence with respect to organization of semantic memory suggests that there are no differences in conceptual organization across the adult years that are due to aging. Therefore, it may be concluded that in terms of competence, there are no important age differences in this area. We next consider the possibility of performance factors having differential effects across ages on retrieval or utilization of information from semantic memory.

UTILIZATION OF SEMANTIC INFORMATION

Here we are concerned with access to and use of semantic information in tasks that stress speed or in other ways require expenditure of processing resources. We focus on tasks that involve retrieval of individual words and their meanings. Factors that affect comprehension of larger units of discourse are taken up in the section that follows. In this section, we discuss priming in semantic memory, particularization of word meanings, solution of verbal analogies, and verbal fluency. In each case, the prediction from the processing-resource framework is that young and older adults should not differ in performance when the task does not require allocation of processing resources, but that older adults should demonstrate performance decrements whenever mental operations draw heavily on such resources.

Priming in Semantic Memory

When words are encountered, relevant semantic information in long-term memory is activated and becomes available. In addition, activation spreads to related concepts, priming them so that they are more readily accessed (e.g., Anderson, 1983; Collins & Loftus, 1975). Activation processes play a crucial role in language comprehension (Anderson, 1983) so that age differences in activation, if present, could cause comprehension problems in old age.

Both automatic and attentional processes are thought to be involved in semantic priming (e.g., Neely, 1977; Posner, 1978; Stanovich & West, 1983). The spreading of activation from a concept just processed to semantically related concepts is automatic, inasmuch as it is rapidly recruited, cannot be influenced by interpretation strategies or expectations, and involves the expenditure of little if any attentional resources. Attentional processes, on the other hand, are slower to begin, are subject to the effects of expectation, and require attentional capacity to be allocated. On this analysis, young and older adults should show no difference in semantic priming when only automatic processes are involved but might show differences when attentional mechanisms are implicated.

Most studies of semantic activation across adulthood have used the lexical decision task. In this task, strings of letters are presented, and the subject indicates whether each is an acceptable English word. This priming effect is attributed to the spread of activation from the prime word to the target, making the target more available. A number of investigators have attempted to separate automatic from effortful processes in lexical decision by including a neutral condition against which to evaluate benefits from related targets and costs from unrelated targets (Bowles & Poon, 1985; Chiarello, Church, & Hoyer, 1985; Howard, Shaw, & Heisey, 1986). Benefits are believed to arise from both automatic and attentional processes, whereas costs reflect only attentional processes. The results from these studies indicated age constancy in benefits, with the exception of the finding of Howard et al. that facilitation was unreliable for older adults when the prime-target interval was very short, suggesting that recruitment of automatic activation may be slower in old age.

However, neither Bowles and Poon nor Howard et al. observed any inhibitory effects, and inhibitory effects were transitory in the Chiarello et al. study, making it difficult to conclude anything about attentional effects in these studies.

Burke, White, and Diaz (1987) used a different technique to isolate attentional processes in lexical decision. They told their subjects to expect certain relations between prime and target. In one condition, the word targets were members of the category named by the prime 80% of the time (the Same condition), and in another they were members of a different category 80% of the time (the Different condition). On the remaining 20% of the trials in the Same condition, the target belonged to a different and unexpected category; whereas on the remaining trials in the Different condition, the target was a member of the category named by the prime. Stimulus-onset asynchronies were either 410 or 1,550 ms. At the shorter interval, Same category targets had faster latencies than Different category targets but not at the longer interval, implicating automatic processes that have rapid recruitment as well as rapid decay. Expected targets had shorter latencies than unexpected targets for both stimulus-onset asynchronies, but the effect was larger for the longer interval; this result is to be expected because attentional processes take longer. There were no interactions of either target-prime relatedness or expectation with age. Thus, there was no evidence for age differences in either automatic or attentional processes in semantic priming. Further evidence for age constancy in the automatic component of spreading activation comes from studies by Burke and Yee (1984) and Howard, Lasaga, and McAndrews (1980).

In sum, the results suggest that neither automatic nor attentional components of activation are affected by aging. These results are somewhat anomalous from the perspective of processing resource accounts of cognitive aging, which predicts age differences when attentional processes that require expenditure of cognitive resources are involved.

Particularization of Word Meanings

The contexts in which words appear determine the particular aspects of their meanings that are activated (e.g., Anderson & Ortony, 1975; Onifer & Swinney, 1981; Tabossi & Johnson-Laird, 1980). For instance, sentence or discourse contexts specify salient properties of nouns, appropriate instantiations of general terms, and antecedents of referentially ambiguous pronouns. It has been suggested that because of reductions in processing resources, older adults do not use context to specify meanings to the same degree that young adults do, but rather encode meanings "in the same old way" from situation to situation (e.g., Craik & Byrd, 1982; Hess, 1984; Rabinowitz, Craik, & Ackerman, 1982; Simon, 1979). This conclusion is based on findings from studies involving retention. Studies that tap comprehension as it occurs do not, however, obtain differences in the use of linguistic context across ages. Two illustrative studies will be described. We should note in advance that in both cases the absence of age differences provides additional grounds for believing that young and older adults share the same underlying knowledge of the language, and raises problems for resource limitation hypotheses.

Burke and Harrold (in press) presented subjects with sentences that suggested particular properties of nouns, such as "The oranges fell off the uneven table" or "The oranges satisfied the thirst of the hot children." After reading each sentence subjects were asked to determine whether a property ("round" or "juicy") was true of a target noun (in this case, "orange"). Both young and older adults were quicker to make such decisions after reading sentences that biased the relevant property. Thus, older adults seem to be aware of implications of sentences that depend on understanding linguistic context, and on-line comprehension shows highly specific analysis of word meanings.

Using a different approach to this issue, Light and Capps (1983) capitalized on a subtle property of verbs known as implicit causality (Garvey & Caramazza, 1974). Young and older adults completed sentence fragments, such as "John apologized to Bill because he . . ." and "John blamed Bill because he . . . ," with reasons or motives appropriate to the action in the first part of the sentence. The pronouns in these sentences are referentially ambiguous. However, the semantics of the verbs lead us to expect continuations, which in the case of "apologize" assign the pronoun to John—that is, to the first noun mentioned—and to Bill, the second noun, in the case of "blame," although continuations that assign the pronoun differently are certainly possible. If older adults are not sensitive to presuppositions about human interactions underlying the use of verbs such as these, we might expect to find age differences in strategies of pronoun assignment in the sentence completion task. Yet, contrary to the predictions from processing-resource theory, no age differences were obtained.

Solution of Verbal Analogies

Solution of verbal analogies such as "GRANARY is related to CORN as STABLE is related to: FIELD, COWS, GRAIN, COTTAGE, FARMER" requires the detection of a relation between the first two terms and generalization of this relation from the third to a fourth term, either present (as in our example) or absent. Such activities presumably tax working memory capacity because the relation extracted from the first two terms must be held in working memory while the relation between the third and potential fourth terms is computed. Hence, age differences on this task would be expected by our analysis, and indeed Riegel (1959) found that older adults were less able to solve verbal analogies than young adults. Similar results were obtained by Farmer, McLean, Sparks, and O'Connell (1978) in a task in which alternatives were not presented and people had to generate their own answers. However, interpretation of their findings is clouded by the fact that the young subjects were graduate students or colleagues of the first author, whereas the older adults were residents of nursing homes, raising the possibility that the observed age differences were produced by education or health differences across age.

Ability to solve analogies is important because it has been argued that comprehension of figurative language (e.g., proverbs or metaphors) may rely on the same mental operations needed for analogy solution (Miller, 1979). Thus, one might expect to find age differences in comprehension of figurative language. Although published evidence on this matter is sparse, Bromley (1957) has reported that older adults are impaired on interpreting proverbs, both when asked for explanations and when alternatives were given on a multiple choice test. Since much of our language is figurative (Lakoff & Johnson, 1980), difficulties in understanding figurative language could result in serious comprehension problems in old age.

Verbal Fluency

Although the evidence suggests that the vocabularies of older adults are at least as large as those of younger adults and although semantic priming seems to be unaffected by aging, older adults perform more poorly than do young adults on tasks measuring verbal fluency. That is, older adults produce fewer responses when asked to generate as many words as they can that begin with a specified letter or that are members of a particular category (e.g., Birren, 1955; Birren, Riegel, & Robbin, 1962; Howard, 1980; Obler & Albert, 1985; Schaie & Parham, 1977; Stones, 1978). Word-fluency tasks are timed, and, at least with written responding, the reduced output of older adults may be attributed in part to motor slowing. In the case of oral responding, it is not clear whether the smaller number of words produced by older people is due to slower speaking rates (see Walker, Hardiman, Hedrick, and Holbrook, 1981, for a review) or to other age-related cognitive changes. Birren et al. (1962) suggest that reduced verbal fluency is due to difficulties that older adults have in rejecting inappropriate associations to words they produce. One limitation of research in this area is that fluency tests are generally administered as part of a psychometric battery. There has been relatively little effort to analyze the results in terms of a model of underlying cognitive operations (e.g., Gronlund & Shiffrin, 1986). Hence, conclusions in this area await more systematic investigations.

Summary

The literature on semantic memory and aging offers no evidence for age-related changes in the organization of semantic information or in ability to access that information which could be interpreted as changes in linguistic competence. Further, both automatic and attentional components of semantic activation appear to be constant across age. The finding that attentional components of activation show no age impairment is perhaps surprising, and it poses a problem for models that predict age-related changes in any activity requiring allocation of attentional capacity. A similar problem arises when we consider the results of studies of particularization of word meaning. To the extent that interpretation of sentence context involves attention (see Carroll, 1986, for a discussion of this issue), older adults should show decreased use of linguistic context to specify meaning. However, there do not appear to be any age differences in this area. It is possible that the amount of attention that is required for successful performance of these operations is very small; and we have seen that the solving of analogies and performance on verbal fluency tasks, both of which arguably involve more complex mental operations, do suffer in old age. There does not, however, appear to be an easy way for processing resource approaches to explain age-related deficits in another aspect of utilization of semantic information, that is, word finding. A cautionary note here is that there has been no independent assessment of the attentional demands of these tasks, so such explanations run the risk of being either vacuous or circular.

PERFORMANCE LIMITATIONS ON COMPREHENSION

This section reviews research on age-related differences in comprehension of sentences and longer discourses. The focus is on studies which have manipulated variables that permit inferences to be made about performance limitations on comprehension, in particular on variables that are believed to affect working-memory capacity. However, evaluating the effects of resource limitations on comprehension is complicated by the fact that older adults may also be data-limited. That is, older adults have impaired vision and impaired hearing, which affect the quality of the information available to them for processing. Thus, it is important to know whether particular comprehension problems in old age arise from data limitations or from resource limitations (Norman & Bobrow, 1975). For this reason, we first take up studies of speech perception across the life span. We next consider studies from the neuropsychological and experimental literature that suggest that older adults have deficits in understanding sentences which have complex syntax. Finally, research dealing with integrative processes in discourse comprehension is examined.

Speech Perception

Presbycusis, or pure-tone hearing loss, constitutes a major sensory decrement in old age (Butler & Lewis, 1982). The elderly also have impaired perception for words and sentences that is not always well predicted by hearing loss as measured by pure-tone audiometry (e.g., Dubno, Dirks, & Morgan, 1984; Duquesnoy, 1983; Jerger, 1973; Jerger & Hayes, 1977; Plomp & Minden, 1979). Further, speech discrimination (as measured by the percentage of words or sentences correctly identified at a given loudness level) may be worse for sentences than for isolated words in the elderly (Jerger & Hayes, 1977). Finally, older adults show relatively greater impairment than do younger adults when speech perception is measured under adverse listening conditions, such as when speech is presented in noise (e.g., Bergman, 1981; Bergman et al., 1980; Dubno et al., 1984; Marston & Goetzinger, 1972) or when speech is time-compressed by periodic deletions of small segments (e.g., Bergman, 1981; Bergman et al., 1976; Konkle, Beasley, & Bess, 1977; Sticht & Gray, 1969; Wingfield, Poon, Lombardi, & Lowe, 1985).

It is unclear whether age-related decrements in speech perception are due to changes in peripheral aspects of the auditory nervous system (see Olsho, Harkins, & Lenhardt, 1985, for a review) or to more central factors, such as reduced speed in integration of information, or both (Corso, 1977, 1981). A number of findings are consistent with the hypothesis that central factors such as reduced working-memory capacity or reduced speed of processing play an important role in impaired speech perception in the elderly. Several studies of time-compressed speech have reported age-by-compression rate interactions, with the performance of the old impaired disproportionately by more speeded presentation rates (e.g., Calearo & Lazzaroni, 1957; Konkle et al., 1977; Sticht & Gray, 1969; Wingfield et al., 1985). However, this effect appears to be mediated by the nature of the speech materials used. For instance, Wingfield et al. presented young and older adults with 5- and 8-letter strings that were either normal sentences, syntactically correct strings that were semantically anomalous, or random sequences. Strings were presented at four rates varying from 275 to 425 words per minute. There were age and rate effects with all types of material, as well as an interaction of these two factors, which suggests that the old suffered more from reduced processing time at the faster rates. Performance for both age groups was over 90% accurate for the normal sentences for all presentation rates, with the elderly showing relatively worse performance than the young at faster rates, as first semantic redundancy and then syntactic redundancy were stripped away in the syntactic string and random string conditions. The use of linguistic context to mitigate the effects of reduced processing speed argues for a central locus of the effects in this study.

Cohen and Faulkner (1983) also reported contextual effects in speech perception. Their young and old subjects identified target words presented in isolation or in sentence contexts at three signal-to-noise ratios. Both age groups showed contextual facilitation, with the older group actually benefiting more from context than the young. In the word condition, the young scored higher than the old at all three noise levels, but with sentence contexts the age difference was reliable only for the highest noise level. Cohen and Faulkner suggest that older adults use linguistic context to compensate for hearing loss unless the noise level is high enough to prevent even the context from being understood. Beneficial effects of context for old and young have also been reported by Bergman (1981) and by Obler, Nicholas, Albert, and Woodward (1985).

One other finding in the speech perception literature deserves mention here. We have noted that sentence identification is relatively worse than word identification in old age. There are at least two factors that may contribute to this problem. First, as pointed out by Olsho et al. (1985), individual words in speech perception tasks are carefully enunciated; whereas in normal conversational speech, sounds are often lost or modified when combined with each other (e.g., "Great Britain" may be uttered as "Grape Britain"). The less precise pronunciation, when combined with high-frequency hearing loss, may render the signal highly degraded. Rabbitt (1968) has shown that if part of a message is presented in noise, other parts are less well retained even when presented without noise. The suggestion here is that older adults' attempts to interpret a degraded speech signal may result in allocation of attention to that part of a message at the expense of other processing necessary for comprehension of the message.

Second, it is important to note that tests of word and sentence perception are actually tests of short-term memory. Subjects are typically required to repeat aloud the material they have heard. Thus, tests of word perception involve memory for single items while tests of sentence perception involve memory for longer strings. Given age-related declines in memory span, it is not at all mysterious that memory for sentences should decline more precipitously than memory for single words.

Sentence Comprehension

The concept of performance limitations was introduced by Chomsky (1965) to account for the fact that people have difficulty in understanding certain well-formed but complex syntactic structures. To the extent that greater demands on processing resources are made when more complex sentences are to be understood, we would expect to see interactions of age with sentence complexity. Evidence on this matter comes from both neuropsychological and experimental studies. For instance, neuropsychologists have examined the effects of age on performance on the Token Test, in which a series of commands of increasing syntactic and semantic complexity are given for manipulating a set of small pieces of plastic varying in size, shape, and color. Lesser (1976) has found that scores on the Token Test correlate negatively with age and with measures of short-term memory, suggesting that age declines on the Token Test are the consequence of reduced working-memory capacity in old age. Similar findings of lower scores on the Token Test in older adults were obtained by Bergman (1981) and by Emery (1985).

However, there have also been claims that age is unrelated to Token Test scores (DeRenzi & Faglioni, 1978; Orgass & Poeck, 1966; Swisher & Sarno, 1969). The discrepancies in these results may stem from age differences in the samples tested by different researchers. The mean age of Orgass and Poeck's oldest group was 64.4 years and Swisher and Sarno's subjects were aged 70 and under, whereas the youngest older adult tested by Emery was 75. Thus, it may be that the Token Test is indeed sensitive to age but only for very elderly adults. Unfortunately, neither DeRenzi and Faglioni nor Bergman report the ages of their samples, and Emery tested no one between 40 and 74; so this hypothesis must remain in the realm of speculation for the present.

In experimental studies of the effect of syntactic complexity on comprehension in adulthood, subjects have typically been asked to respond either by manipulating objects (Emery, 1985; Feier & Gerstman, 1980) or by repeating sentences presented auditorily (Bergman, 1980; Emery, 1985; Kemper, in press). Hence, these studies involve working memory, and we would expect to see not only age differences but also the interaction of age with syntactic complexity.

Feier and Gerstman (1980) presented subjects aged 18 to 25, 52 to 58, 63 to 69, and 74 to 80 years with 27 sentences and asked them to act out the sentences by manipulating small human or animal figures. The sentences were either compound or contained relative clauses. Although there were reliable age differences, with the oldest group scoring lower, there was no effect of sentence complexity and no interaction of complexity with age. Failure to observe complexity effects here is surprising because they have been obtained in other studies. For instance, Bergman (1980) presented young and older Israelis with three types of Hebrew sentences against a background babble to reduce ceiling effects: (1) simple sentences ("The scientist began to teach the young dolphin in the laboratory"), (2) sentences containing right-branching relative clauses ("In the laboratory the scientist taught the dolphin who played with little children"), and (3) sentences containing center-embedded relative clauses ("The dolphin, whom the scientist taught in the laboratory, played with little children"). Center-embedded clauses impose greater memory loads than simple or right-branching sentences because of the greater separation of subject and predicate terms that belong together, and, as expected, older adults were relatively more impaired in gist memory for the center-embedded sentences. Bergman suggests that people "temporarily disregard the relative clause until they have the main idea in mind, but then forget that clause" (p. 113) and attributes the aging deficit to limitations in short-term memory.

Kemper (in press) tested adults between the ages of 50 and 89 on their ability to imitate right-branching and left-branching constructions of increasing length, thereby obtaining estimates of their memory spans for these constructions. Comprehension of left-branching constructions places greater burdens on working memory, and hence, the processing-resource approach would predict greater age differences on left- than on right-branching sentences. The left-branching sentences ranged from "Running impresses me" to "How John's running long distances every week has helped his mental concentration improve impresses me"; right-branching versions of these ranged from "I like running" to "I like how John's running long distances every week has helped his mental concentration improve." Age was reliably correlated with ability to imitate both right-and left-branching sentences, although only the age difference for left-branching sentences was reliable. In addition, Wechsler Adult Intelligence Scale digit spans (forward and backward), which also correlate with age, were good predictors of left-but not right-branching spans, further implicating the role of working-memory limitations here.

Emery (1985) found that pre-middle-aged (32–40) high school graduates scored higher than old (75 and over) adults on an extensive battery of sentence comprehension tasks, some of which tapped knowledge of fairly complex syntactic constructions. Working-memory capacity is heavily implicated in understanding many of the constructions used, and some of them also required reasoning. For instance, in "John runs faster than George but slower than Humphrey," the subject must construct a three-term series by figuring out that Humphrey is faster than George, a feat that requires not inconsiderable mental gymnastics. This sentence is also more complex syntactically than the sentence "John and Mary ran to the hospital really fast," which is of the same length. Thus, it is not surprising that the relative deficit in comprehension for the old was greater on sentences like those in the first example.

The results reviewed in this section are consistent with the view that reduced processing resources limit comprehension of complex syntactic structures in old age. Note, however, that as in the case of speech perception, studies of sentence comprehension have generally required people to remember the material that has been presented and thus are really tests of short-term memory. Our conclusion could thus just as easily have been couched in terms of the effects of resource limitations on memory.

Integration of Information in Discourse

It has been proposed that one consequence of reduced attentional capacity for natural language understanding in old age is less efficient integration of information in a discourse. Cohen (1979, 1981, in press) has argued that older adults may process surface aspects of discourse without full comprehension of meaning due to reduced processing resources. The result of this more superficial processing of information is that older adults may be less likely to draw inferences from what they hear or read, either because they fail to detect the relationship between two or more pieces of information presented in a discourse or because they are less able to integrate new information with previously stored general world knowledge. In this section, we summarize evidence that suggests that older adults draw inferences as well as younger adults when working-memory capacity is not strained and hence have unimpaired knowledge of the rules for drawing inferences. When working memory is burdened, however, older adults exhibit difficulty in drawing inferences, which is due either to forgetting information essential for making the inference or to problems in working memory.

Age differences in both logical and pragmatic implication have been studied. We speak of logical implication when an utterance necessarily implies some information and of pragmatic implication (or invited inference) when an utterance leads the hearer or reader to expect something that is neither explicitly stated nor logically implied but which nevertheless seems likely on the basis of prior experience or general world knowledge (Geis & Zwicky, 1971; Harris & Monaco, 1978). Pragmatic implication is fundamental to discourse comprehension. Readers and listeners generally assume that they share the same world knowledge as writers or speakers and expect to be able to interpret what they read or hear in the light of this knowledge (Clark & Marshall, 1981). Therefore, problems in the use of general world knowledge in older adults would be expected to lead to difficulties in comprehension.

A number of investigators have reported that older adults have difficulty in drawing both logical and pragmatic inferences from discourse. Thus, Cohen (1981, Experiment 1) and Light, Zelinski, and Moore (1982) have found that older adults are less likely to draw logical inferences than are young adults when integration of information from several sources is required, especially when memory load is high, because the information necessary for making the inference must be retrieved from memory and/or because the order in which information is presented is not optimal for integration.

Results from studies of pragmatic implication have been mixed. The studies that have reported age-related differences in pragmatic implication by and large have measured retention rather than comprehension (Cohen, 1979, 1981; Till, 1985; Till & Walsh, 1980). These studies leave open the possibility that older adults' apparent problems in making pragmatic inferences arise from failure to remember explicitly stated information relevant to the inference rather than from problems in accessing or using pragmatic information in semantic memory (Light & Albertson, in press).

When comprehension is examined more directly, the evidence suggests that age differences in ability to use pragmatic information are negligible. Thus,

Belmore (1981) found no age differences in accuracy of answers to questions requiring integration of new information with previously stored general world knowledge when prose passages had just been viewed; however, older adults were less able than young ones to answer such questions correctly after a delay. Burke and Yee (1984) observed similar priming effects for young and older adults in a lexical decision task when the target was pragmatically implied by the preceding sentence context. In a related vein, although memory rather than comprehension was studied, neither Light and Anderson (1983) nor Hess (1985) found evidence of age-related differences in reliance on knowledge of routine stereotypical action sequences, or scripts, in remembering stories about daily activities. Taken together, these results suggest that reasoning based on pragmatic information proceeds in the same way regardless of age.

Understanding anaphoric devices, such as pronouns or noun phrases that refer to concepts introduced earlier in a discourse, is crucial for establishing discourse coherence—that is, for determining how what was said before is connected to what is being said currently. Difficulties in determining co-reference could thus lead to comprehension failure and lack of integration of material. The evidence suggests that older adults do have problems in determining the antecedents of anaphors, but only when working memory is taxed so that antecedent information is forgotten. In a series of studies conducted by Light and Capps (1986), young and older adults listened to a series of short passages such as the following:

John stood watching while Henry jumped across a ravine.
The ground was so rocky and uneven that only goats used this path.
There were no flowers but a few weeds grew here and there.
He fell in the river.

Assigning an antecedent to the pronoun *he* in the last sentence requires an inference based on general world knowledge because both people named in the first sentence are masculine and singular. It is necessary to call up information that those who jump across ravines are more likely to have accidents than those who only stand and watch. Young and older adults were equally likely to assign the pronoun *he* to Henry in this example when only the first and last sentences were presented. When there were two intervening sentences, older adults were more apt to forget the content of the first sentence than young adults and, when forgetting occurred, people of all ages were less able to use general world knowledge to assign the pronoun. Light and Albertson (in press) also compared young and older adults in a task that tapped on-line comprehension of noun-phrase anaphors during the reading of short paragraphs and found no evidence of impaired integration processes in older adults.

Thus, integrative processes dependent on the drawing of inferences appear to proceed on similar lines in young and old. Our review of the literature suggests that older adults are not deficient in making logical or pragmatic inferences necessary for discourse integration except under conditions where memory load is high.

Summary

The findings discussed in this section implicate performance limitations on language comprehension in old age and are readily interpreted in terms of processing-resource models. As expected, older adults are more impaired relative to younger ones in speech perception when material is presented under speeded conditions. Older adults perform less well than young adults on tests of sentence comprehension involving complex syntactic structures. And finally, age differences in integrating information in discourse are not seen unless working memory is taxed.

PERFORMANCE LIMITATIONS ON PRODUCTION OF SPOKEN AND WRITTEN DISCOURSE

As we have seen, there has been a great deal of research relevant to the issue of performance limitations on natural language understanding. In contrast, there are very few studies that bear directly on whether there are performance limitations on spoken and written discourse in old age. This is unfortunate because working memory is believed to play an important role in speech production (e.g., Bock, 1982; Ford & Holmes, 1978; Laver, 1980; Levelt, 1983), and one would therefore expect to find evidence for differences in language production paralleling those observed in language comprehension. This section reviews those few studies we have found that are germane to this question.

One clear prediction is that reduced working-memory capacity in old age should be accompanied by production of shorter and less syntactically complex speech and writing. However, the evidence on this point is not consistent. For instance, Obler (1980) reported two studies of written descriptions of the cookie-theft picture from the Boston Diagnostic Aphasia Examination that suggested that older adults use more elaborate language. However, in a more naturalistic study of diaries kept by the same people over several decades, Kemper (in press) observed reliable declines in syntactic complexity, with older adults using fewer clauses per sentence. Their diary entries showed reductions in the frequency of a number of clause types, including relative clauses, subordinates, gerunds, and double and triple embeddings. Similar results were also obtained in a cross-sectional diary study. These reductions in sentence complexity with age cannot be attributed to older adults simply producing shorter sentences because, in fact, sentence length did not decline with increasing age. Since Kemper's analysis is based on long entries (150–1,300 words) sampled at five-year intervals, her results argue persuasively for age-related declines in complexity of written sentences.

With respect to speech, the data are also somewhat equivocal. Walker, Hardiman, Hedrick, and Holbrook (1981) computed the number of words in a T-unit (a main clause and any subordinate clauses attached to or embedded in it) for young and older adults and found reliably shorter productions for the older group. Although the young also had slightly more words per clause and clauses per T-unit, these differences were not reliable. Ulatowska, Cannito, Hayashi, and Fleming (1985) compared the discourse of middle-aged and older nuns and found that the syntactic complexity of expressions used to refer to entities within the discourse did not vary significantly across age groups. On the other hand, Kynette and Kemper (1986) studied the spontaneous speech of 50- to 90-year-olds, and while mean length of utterance did not vary across age, the younger subjects in their sample were more likely to use a variety of complex syntactic structures and to use them correctly. In particular, people in their seventies and eighties were less likely to use left-branching constructions, which tax working memory, and many of their grammatical errors were associated with attempts to use such structures. We conclude from these studies that, as predicted by the working-memory-capacity hypothesis, older adults use less complex syntax in their written and spoken language although the length of their sentences may not vary much over the years.

The speech of older adults may also be marked by an increase in dysfluencies such as interjections, repetitions, and revisions of incomplete phrases (Walker et al., 1981; Yairi & Clifton, 1972). However, young and old do not seem to differ much in the proportion of speech that is constituted by pauses (Walker et al., 1981). Dysfluencies and pauses in speech may occur for a variety of reasons, including the need to plan what one is going to say next (Boomer, 1965; Butterworth, 1980; Goldman-Eisler, 1968; Maclay & Osgood, 1958) or to revise what has already been said. They may also stem from word-finding difficulties. Speech errors may result from attentional lapses, and inattention may cause them to go undetected and uncorrected. Our hypothesis that older adults have reduced attentional resources predicts increases in planning time, increases in speech errors, and reduced error correction in the elderly. At present there are no published data that permit us to test these hypotheses.

As indicated above, speech dysfluencies may stem from word-finding problems. There is evidence from a number of sources that such problems are more prevalent in old age. Older adults report more forgetting of names than do younger adults (Cavanaugh, Grady, & Perlmutter, 1983) and score lower on tests of object or action naming (Goodglass, 1980; Obler & Albert, 1985). They also give fewer synonyms as responses on the WAIS Vocabulary subtest (Botwinick, West, & Storandt, 1975). Bowles and Poon (1985) found that older adults were less able than young adults to produce words when given their synonyms, despite the fact that the two age groups did not differ in WAIS Vocabulary subtest scores (indicating that the old had no difficulty in getting from a word to its meaning and could give adequate definitions) or in amount of priming in lexical decision. The latter result suggests that activation of semantic information is the same across age. Bowles and Poon's results thus point to a specific problem in accessing lexical information about the phonological realization of a word given conceptual information, that is, a problem in getting to a word from its meaning.

Burke and Harrold (in press) found in a diary study that older adults reported more frequent tip-of-the-tongue experiences during everyday activities. In the tip-of-the-tongue state one is unable to think of a word that one is certain he or she knows perfectly well (Brown & McNeill, 1966). In Burke and Harold's study, older adults always were ultimately able to recover the desired words, suggesting that the necessary connections between meaning and lexical entry were intact but momentarily inactive. Word-finding problems are also manifest in conversations elicited in the laboratory. Ulatowska et al. (1985) found that, relative to middle-age adults, the speech of older adults contained more ambiguous references, more use of general nouns, fewer proper nouns, and less lexical variety of nouns; these results are consistent with greater problems in getting from meanings to specific lexical entries.

It is not clear that these word-finding results can be handled within a processing-resource framework. The specific pattern of deficits does not seem to be readily predictable by postulating reduced attention or reduced working-memory capacity in the elderly. Additional mechanisms appear to be necessary to account for these findings.

Summary

Studies of language production in old age are less plentiful than studies of comprehension. They are, in addition, somewhat equivocal in their support for processing-resource approaches to language and aging. Although some studies report decreased syntactic complexity in written and spoken language, others do not. Further, the increased word-finding problems of older adults seem to require the postulation of retrieval mechanisms that are not readily formulated in terms of processing-resource models. Finally, the available data do not allow us to test several interesting hypotheses about possible age-related performance limitations in language production. This is clearly an area in need of additional research.

IMPLICATIONS FOR FUTURE RESEARCH

We have presented evidence that there are no age differences in linguistic competence but that older adults exhibit a pattern of impairment in language comprehension and production which, on the whole, is consistent with performance decrements due to reduced processing resources. Studies of the organization of semantic memory find no systematic age differences and suggest that the representation of knowledge is similar across ages. Access to and utilization of word meanings is also resistant to age-related declines unless particular tasks make demands on processing resources. With respect to language comprehension, older adults are less successful in dealing with complex syntactic structures but show age-related declines in tasks requiring integration of information only when demands on processing resources are high. And the few published studies on language production in old age suggest that the processing-resource hypothesis will provide at least a partial account of age-related changes in this area of cognition.

This does not mean, however, that all aspects of language in old age can be readily interpreted in these terms or that there are no unanswered questions in this domain. In this final section, we address four issues. First, we review some findings that appear to pose problems for processing-resource explanations of age-related declines in language. Second, we discuss the relation between language and memory in old age. Third, we explore the relevance of the processing-resource approach to the study of language use in social situations. Finally, we take up briefly some general issues associated with the processing-resource approach to cognitive aging.

Problematic Findings

Although the processing-resource approach can explain much of what is known about language and aging, there are a number of findings that it does not readily accommodate. These tend to be concentrated in the area of access to and utilization of words and their meanings. For instance, older adults experience increased difficulty in word finding, that is, in retrieving a word from the internal lexicon when conceptual information is available, even when it can be demonstrated that they know the word in question. In discussing naming difficulties in aphasia, Butterworth, Howard, and McLaughlin (1984) suggest that the problem lies in reduced reliability of the association between meaning and name. It is unclear whether the tip-of-the-tongue phenomenon will prove amenable to analysis within the framework of a resource-deficit performance model or whether other types of performance factors will need to be postulated.

The need for greater specification of the processing-resource framework as applied to the study of language and aging is also apparent when we consider the literature on priming in semantic memory. As discussed earlier, the finding that automatic components of priming do not differ in young and older adults is consistent with processing-resource models, but the absence of processing-rate differences in attentional components of priming tasks is problematic. It is possible that the tasks used to measure priming are insensitive to small age differences (Salthouse, 1985b) or that processes labeled automatic are not "free" in terms of their processing-resource requirements but rather are simply so "cheap" that age differences are negligible (Navon, 1984).

Further, studies of speech perception and particularization of word meanings demonstrate context effects in older adults of equal or greater magnitude to those observed in young adults, a theoretically important finding. It argues against Rabbitt's (1979) claim that older adults are less able to take advantage of redundancy. However, it also poses something of a challenge to positions that older adults should show impairments when attentional processes are brought to bear on a task. Understanding linguistic context, that is, computation of sentence meaning, is believed not to be automatic but to require attentional capacity (Carroll, 1986). Nevertheless, older adults are, if anything, more likely to make use of available syntactic and semantic information than are young adults. It may be that, as suggested by Light and Anderson (1983), language comprehension is a high priority for older adults and that more attention is allocated to ongoing comprehension activities at the expense of other possible operations, such as storing information for later retrieval. It is also possible that the attentional demands of sentence comprehension are very minimal and are for this reason unaffected by age. The problem with this line of thought is that current resource-deficit models are so underspecified that it is not possible to determine before the fact how much attentional capacity a particular mental operation requires. This results in a certain amount of circularity and may ultimately render the theory untestable.

The Relation Between Language and Memory in Old Age

As noted earlier, our approach is similar to that of investigators of age-related deficits in memory who have explained the memory problems of the aged in terms of reduced processing resources. In the domains of both language and memory, reductions in working-memory capacity have been credited with producing age-related decrements in performance. In particular, it has been suggested that age decrements in language comprehension are the cause of memory problems in the elderly. Thus, older adults have been said to have deficits in extracting meaning from words or sentences and to encode information in a more general, less contextually specific manner; and it has been claimed that these deficits underlie their memory problems (e.g., Craik, 1977; Eysnck, 1974; Rabinowitz et al., 1982). However, as we have seen, older adults rely on linguistic context to determine the precise meanings of words at least as much as do young adults, and studies of comprehension that do not depend on memory measures show little evidence of age-related declines in semantic processing. Hence, although we subscribe to the view that both language and memory deficits in old age can be traced to deficits in resources, we do not believe that there are semantic deficits that can account for memory impairment.

Rather, we believe that apparent problems in comprehension in the elderly arise in two situations. First, when working memory is taxed by the presence of large amounts of material or by the need to perform complex mental operations (Light & Albertson, in press; Light & Anderson, 1985; Light et al., 1982), the demands of information storage and manipulation may exceed the available capacity, with a resulting breakdown in comprehension. Second, the elderly may be more prone to forget earlier parts of a discourse, so these are unavailable to serve as background information against which to interpret new information (e.g., Light & Anderson, 1985; Light & Capps, 1986), and development of a coherent representation of the discourse is less probable. At this level, problems in subsequent memory may indeed be caused by earlier interpretive failures, since it is easier to remember what one has understood (Bransford & Johnson, 1972). However, the root of the problem is not deficient semantic processing per se. Instead, one memory failure leads to another downstream.

Our analysis may raise more problems than it solves, because it assigns the locus of comprehension problems to deficiencies in memory, and we have no adequate explanation for forgetting in old age. It is, of course, possible that the difficulty lies in encoding rather than in comprehension. Older adults may not have problems with semantic processing during comprehension but may lay down less well elaborated traces, which are less durable (Craik & Rabinowitz, 1984). The difficulty with this approach is that there are no theoretical grounds for separating comprehension and encoding. It is precisely the sorts of operations that are involved in comprehension that are thought to underlie encoding. The explanation we have just outlined suggests that after successfully understanding something older adults engage in less satisfactory subsidiary encoding strategies. Why they should do so is unclear. Further, the point at which comprehension processes end and encoding processes begin has never been articulated, and we believe that under most circumstances these processes are not separable (Light & Albertson, in press). We need more precise theoretical treatment of the relationship between language comprehension and memory if we are to understand the interplay between language and memory in old age.

Social Psychological Aspects of Language and Aging

The research we have reviewed in this chapter has come primarily from the experimental psychology of aging, with some contributions from the psychometric and neuropsychological literature. The research, with the exception of a few studies concerned with speech production in interviews, has been conducted in laboratory settings in which the performance of single individuals has been measured. As pointed out by Ryan, Giles, Bartolucci, and Henwood (1986), almost nothing is known about "the interactional dimension in communication that is of most direct relevance for the elderly themselves and to those who care about them and for them" (p. 1).

Although the processing-resource framework as currently formulated does not deal directly with interactional aspects of language, both the actual and the perceived cognitive abilities of older adults may have an impact on communications directed toward them. Based on her research, Cohen (1979) recommended that "in practical terms . . . information should be presented to old people in such a way that relevant facts are made completely explicit and not left for the listener to infer; key facts or gist need to be stressed and not left for the listener to extract himself; and speech should be slow and messages short" (p. 428). Similarly, Blazer (1978) suggested that physicians speak to their elderly patients slowly, clearly, and in simple sentences.

There is evidence that speech addressed to elderly adults may in fact differ from speech addressed to young adults. Older adults are perceived as less cognitively able, and the communications directed toward them may be less complex. For instance, Rubin and Brown (1975) asked undergraduates to explain a game to a listener represented by a picture of a person who was said to be "noninstitutionalized, middle-class, and of average intelligence." The mean number of words per utterance, which may be taken as an index of complexity, was lower for elderly listeners than for middle-age ones, suggesting that people modify their speech to accommodate to their stereotypes of their listeners.

This phenomenon is not restricted to young speakers. Molfese, Hoffman, and Yuen (1981–1982) asked old speakers to give directions on a map-reading task to either a similar-age or a young partner. Communications to the peer were longer and more utterances were used. There were also more exact repetitions and more frequent instances of starting over when the partner was elderly. It is hard to tell whether these results stem from the elderly sharing a negative stereotype of old age or from the behavior of the partners because the older partners had more trouble understanding the task and requested more clarification. It is also unclear why the utterances were longer to the elderly in this study but shorter to the elderly in the Rubin and Brown study. However, these results do suggest that both old and young accommodate their speech to the perceived abilities of their listeners.

Parents speak to their young children in baby talk, a special speech register that simplifies and clarifies their messages and conveys affection. Similar speech is also used for other audiences deemed less cognitively able—for example, the hard of hearing, the mentally retarded, foreigners, household pets, and even plants (Brown, 1977; Ferguson, 1977). Caporael (1981) studied the speech of caregivers in a health facility for residents who did not need extensive nursing care but did need help with daily living activities. Of the total sentences recorded from caregivers over a month during lunch, 22% constituted baby talk to care receivers. When tapes of the speech of caregivers and student aids at a nursery school to two-year-olds were filtered so that content was not available, baby talk addressed to the elderly could not be distinguished from that addressed to young children by undergraduates. Baby talk is more likely to be used in speaking to elderly in nursing facilities for the less functionally able and less healthy (Caporael & Culbertson, 1986). In addition, Caporael, Lukaszewski, and Culbertson (1983) found that the expectations of caregivers about the functional abilities of their elderly residents were related to their predictions of how much care receivers would like baby talk and to their belief that adult speech would not be effective in interacting with residents. Residents' lower functional ability was associated with greater liking for baby talk. Although older people who are functioning well find baby talk demeaning and offensive (Ryan et al., 1986), those who are cognitively impaired may experience it as supportive and sympathetic. Certain aspects of baby talk, in particular its exaggerated intonation patterns, may also have cognitive benefits. One intriguing observation by Cohen and Faulkner (1986) bears this out. They found that healthy noninstitutional older adults remembered more names and made more inferences after hearing stories with increased stress on focal words.

Although such findings make sense given what we know about cognition in old age, they are certainly not explicitly predicted by the assumptions of the processing-resource framework as laid out in the introduction to this chapter. It is also likely that certain aspects of language in old age will prove resistant to simplistic interpretation in terms of processing resources alone. For instance, Boden and Bielby (1986) report that older adults manage the flow of topics within a conversation in an elegant manner but that the content of their conversations centers around events in their past, something not seen in the conversations of young adults. One could hypothesize that the reason for this choice of topics is that, in talking about one's own life history, retrieval problems are minimized and processing resources are less taxed. Such an approach, however, does not seem to capture the richness and complexity of conversational interaction. Without an integrated approach that takes into account both cognitive and social psychological factors, our knowledge of language in old age is destined to be impoverished.

Some General Concerns about the Processing-Resource Approach

Resource deficit models have proved to be useful in understanding age-related declines in intelligence, memory, problem solving, and reasoning. In the present chapter, we have reviewed evidence that the resource-deficit approach can also serve as a heuristic for conceptualizing age-related changes in language. Thus, the processing-resource approach shows promise as a general account of cognitive declines in old age. However, for this promise to be realized, we believe that proponents of this approach will need to face up to certain challenges. Although the points we make here arise out of an examination of the language and aging research, we believe that they are relevant for all research on cognitive aging conducted within the resource-deficit framework (see Light, in press, for more detailed discussion of some of these issues).

As we have noted, several different metaphors (space, time, and energy) are used in conceptualizing processing resources, and we have not discriminated among these in reviewing the literature. Some workers have expressed clear preferences for one metaphor over another. For instance, Salthouse (1985b) has argued forcefully that all cognitive declines in old age can be explained in terms of reduced speed of mental operations but has not applied this analysis to language. Baddeley (1986) has suggested that normal aging is associated with a drop in overall processing capacity. Zacks and Hasher (in press) develop a model of inference generation based on reduced storage capacity in working memory. Given the diversity of approaches within the processing-resource framework, it is important that predictions be developed for different experimental paradigms using each of the metaphors and the models in which they are embodied. Such an exercise could determine whether in fact the different metaphors lead to equivalent predictions, whether there are situations in which one metaphor is to be preferred, or whether some tasks are totally resistant to analysis in terms of one or more metaphors. It would also be propaedeutic to delimiting the scope of processing-resource approaches; that is, there may be phenomena (e.g., word-finding problems) that are not amenable to analysis in terms of resource deficits but require additional theoretical machinery for their explanation.

There are additional problems associated with operationalizing processing-resource concepts in particular experimental situations. It is not always possible to determine in advance how demanding of cognitive resources a given mental operation will be. The difficulty arises in part because it is not always clear theoretically which aspects of a task are automatic and which tax capacity (Jonides, Naveh-Benjamin, & Palmer, 1985; Kahneman & Treisman, 1984) and in part because independent assessment of resource demands is rarely undertaken. Without further advances in these areas, reasonable interpretation of studies of cognitive aging carried out within the resource-deficit framework will become increasingly difficult.

Finally, although this situation is changing fairly rapidly, the focus in studies of cognitive aging has been on group differences rather than on individual differences. The processing-resource approach assumes that individuals differ in their allotment of cognitive resources. It is a natural extension of this view to assume that there are also individual differences in loss of processing resources with advancing age. There have been a few studies in memory (e.g., Hartley, 1986; Light & Anderson, 1985) and language (e.g., Kemper, in press) that investigate individual differences in processing resources; but more concerted efforts, such as those of Salthouse (1985b), will be needed if we are to understand individual differences in rate of cognitive aging.

CONCLUSION

Viewing language within the framework of resource-deficit models provides a useful guide for organizing extant findings. Our survey of the literature offers support for the view that language competence is preserved in old age but that decreased processing resources limit performance as measured in studies of language comprehension and production, thus extending the range of phenomena to which resource-deficit analyses of cognitive aging can be successfully applied. However, we do have some recommendations for future research and theorizing about language and aging, and more generally about cognition and aging. First, greater specification of the processing-resource framework is needed to render predictions about aging more precise. Second, the relationship between language and other aspects of cognition needs more detailed analysis. Third, research in more natural settings incorporating methodology from social psychology and sociolinguistics will enhance our understanding of cognition in old age. And last, greater attention to individual differences in processing resources will help us to understand why people vary in the extent to which they show cognitive declines in old age.

NOTES

[1]Possible cohort effects are not treated at length in this chapter. Although early researchers frequently did not control for variables such as educational level and sometimes did not report relevant information about such variables that might affect language use, later studies have generally been sensitive to the importance of potential cohort effects. We believe that the results discussed in this chapter represent genuine aging effects.

[2]Cognitive gerontologists have used this distinction more broadly to characterize behavior limited by extraneous factors such as familiarity of text materials, motivation, and amount of recency of practice (e.g., Baltes & Willis, 1982; Reese & Rodeheaver, 1985; Salthouse, 1985b). We construe the competence-performance dichotomy more narrowly to refer to the difference between the underlying knowledge of one's language and the demonstration of that knowledge in understanding or producing language.

REFERENCES

Anderson, J. A. (1983). A spreading activation theory of memory. *Journal of Verbal Learning and Verbal Behavior, 22,* 261–295.

Anderson, R. C., & Ortony, A. (1975). On putting apples into bottles – A problem of polysemy. *Cognitive Psychology, 7,* 167–180.

Baddeley, A. (1986). *Working memory.* Oxford: Clarendon Press.

Baddeley, A. D., & Hitch, G. (1974). Working memory. In G. H. Bower (Ed.), *The psychology of learning and motivation* (Vol. 8, pp. 47–89). New York: Academic Press.

Baltes, P. B., & Willis, S. L. (1982). Plasticity and enhancement of intellectual functioning in old age: Penn State's Adult Development and Enrichment Project (ADEPT). In F. I. M. Craik & S. Trehub (Eds.), *Aging and cognitive processes* (pp. 353–389). New York: Plenum Press.

Belmore, S. M. (1981). Age-related changes in processing explicit and implicit language. *Journal of Gerontology, 36,* 316–322.

Bergman, M. (1980). *Aging and the perception of speech.* Baltimore: University Park Press.

Bergman, M., Blumenfeld, V. G., Cascardo, D., Dash, B., Levitt, H., & Margulies, M. K. (1976). Age-related decrement in hearing for speech. *Journal of Gerontology, 31,* 533–538.

Birren, J. E. (1955). Age changes in speed of simple responses and perception and their significance for complex behaviour. In International Association of Gerontology (Ed.), *Old age in the modern world: Report of the Third Congress of the International Association of Gerontology, London 1954.* Edinburgh: E. & S. Livingston.

Birren, J. E., Riegel, K. F., & Robbin, J. S. (1962). Age differences in continuous word associations measured by speech recordings. *Journal of Gerontology, 17,* 95–96.

Birren, J. E., Woods, A. M., & Williams, M. V. (1980). Behavioral slowing with age: Causes, organization, and consequences. In L. W. Poon (Ed.), *Aging in the 1980's: Psychological issues* (pp. 293–308). Washington, DC: American Psychological Association.

Blazer, D. (1978). Techniques for communicating with your elderly patient. *Geriatrics, 33,* 79–84.

Bock, J. K. (1982). Toward a cognitive theory of syntax: Information processing contributions to sentence formulation. *Psychological Review, 89,* 1–47.

Boden, D., & Bielby, D. D. (1986). The way it was: Topical organization in elderly conversation. *Language & Communication, 6,* 73–89.

Boomer, D. S. (1965). Hesitation and grammatical encoding. *Language and Speech, 8,* 148–158.

Borod, J. C., Goodglass, H., & Kaplan, E. (1980). Normative data on the Boston Diagnostic Aphasia Examination, Parietal Lobe Battery, and the Boston Naming Test. *Journal of Clinical Neuropsychology, 2,* 209–215.

Botwinick, J. (1985). *Aging and behavior* (3rd ed.). New York: Springer Publishing Co.

Botwinick, J., West, R., & Storandt, M. (1975). Qualitative vocabulary test responses and age. *Journal of Gerontology, 30,* 574–577.

Bower, G. H., Black, J. B., & Turner, T. J. (1979). Scripts in memory for text. *Cognitive Psychology, 11*, 177–220.

Bowles, N. L., & Poon, L. W. (1985). Aging and retrieval of words in semantic memory. *Journal of Gerontology, 40*, 71–77.

Bowles, N. L., Williams, D., & Poon, L. W. (1983). On the use of word association norms in aging research. *Experimental Aging Research, 9*, 175–177.

Bransford, J. D., & Johnson, M. K. (1972). Contextual prerequisites for understanding: Some investigations of comprehension and recall. *Journal of Verbal Learning and Verbal Behavior, 11*, 717–726.

Bromley, D. B. (1957). Some effects of age on the quality of intellectual output. *Journal of Gerontology, 12*, 318–323.

Brown, R. (1977). Introduction. In C. E. Snow & C. A. Ferguson (Eds.), *Talking to children: Language input and acquisition* (pp. 1–27). New York: Cambridge University Press.

Brown, R., & McNeill, D. (1966). The "tip of the tongue" phenomenon. *Journal of Verbal Learning and Verbal Behavior, 5*, 325–337.

Burke, D. M., & Harrold, R. M. (in press). Approaches to the study of language and memory in old age. In L. L. Light & D. M. Burke (Eds.), *Language, memory and aging*. New York: Cambridge University Press.

Burke, D. M., & Light, L. L. (1981). Memory and aging: The role of retrieval processes. *Psychological Bulletin, 90*, 513–546.

Burke, D. M., & Peters, L. (1986). Word associations in old age: Evidence for consistency in semantic encoding during adulthood. *Psychology and Aging, 1*, 283–292.

Burke, D. M., White, H., & Diaz, D. L. (1987). Semantic priming in young and older adults: Evidence for age-constancy in automatic and attentional processes. *Journal of Experimental Psychology: Human Perception and Performance, 13*, 79–88.

Burke, D. M., & Yee, P. L. (1984). Semantic priming during sentence processing by young and older adults. *Developmental Psychology, 20*, 903–910.

Butler, R. N., & Lewis, M. I. (1982). *Aging & mental health: Positive psychosocial and biomedical approaches* (3rd ed.). St. Louis: C. V. Mosby.

Butterworth, B. (1980). Evidence from pauses in speech. In B. Butterworth (Ed.), *Language production: Vol. 1. Speech and talk* (pp. 155–176). New York: Academic Press.

Butterworth, B., Howard, D., & McLoughlin, P. (1984). The semantic deficit in aphasia: The relationship between semantic errors in auditory comprehension and picture naming. *Neuropsychologia, 22*, 409–426.

Byrd, M. (1984). Age differences in the retrieval of information from semantic memory. *Experimental Aging Research, 10*, 29–33.

Calearo, C., & Lazzaroni, A. (1957). Speech intelligibility in relation to the speed of the message. *Laryngoscope, 67*, 410–419.

Caporael, L. R. (1981). The paralanguage of caregiving: Baby talk to the institutionalized aged. *Journal of Personality and Social Psychology, 40*, 876–884.

Caporael, L. R., & Culbertson, G. H. (1986). Verbal response modes of baby talk and other speech at institutions for the aged. *Language & Communication, 6*, 99–112.

Caporael, L. R., Lukaszewski, M. P., & Culbertson, G. H. (1983). Secondary baby talk: Judgments by institutionalized elderly and their caregivers. *Journal of Personality and Social Psychology, 44,* 746–754.

Carroll, D. W. (1986). *Psychology of language.* Monterey, CA: Brooks/Cole.

Cavanaugh, J. C., Grady, J. G., & Perlmutter, M. (1983). Forgetting and use of memory aids in 20 to 70 year olds everyday life. *International Journal of Aging and Human Development, 17,* 113–122.

Chiarello, C., Church, K. L., & Hoyer, W. J. (1985). Automatic and controlled semantic priming: Accuracy, response bias, and aging. *Journal of Gerontology, 40,* 593–600.

Chomsky, N. (1965). *Aspects of the theory of syntax.* Cambridge, MA: MIT Press.

Church, K. W. (1980). *On memory limitations in natural language processing.* Bloomington, IN: Indiana University Linguistics Club.

Clark, H. H., & Marshall, C. R. (1981). Definite reference and mutual knowledge. In A. K. Joshi, B. L. Webber, & I. A. Sag (Eds.), *Elements of discourse understanding* (pp. 10–63). New York: Cambridge University Press.

Cohen, G. (1979). Language comprehension in old age. *Cognitive Psychology, 11,* 412–429.

Cohen, G. (1981). Inferential reasoning in old age. *Cognition, 9,* 59–72.

Cohen, G. (in press). Age differences in memory for texts: Production deficiency or processing limitations? In L. L. Light & D. M. Burke (Eds.), *Language, memory, and aging.* New York: Cambridge University Press.

Cohen, G., & Faulkner, D. (1983). Word recognition: Age differences in contextual facilitation effects. *British Journal of Psychology, 74,* 239–251.

Cohen, G., & Faulkner, D. (1986). Does "Elderspeak" work? The effect of intonation and stress on comprehension and recall of spoken discourse in old age. *Language & Communication, 6,* 91–98.

Collins, A. M., & Loftus, E. F. (1975). A spreading-activation theory of semantic processing. *Psychological Review, 82,* 407–428.

Corso, J. F. (1977). Auditory perception and communication. In J. E. Birren & K. W. Schaie (Eds.), *Handbook of the psychology of aging* (pp. 535–553). New York: Van Nostrand Reinhold.

Corso, J. F. (1981). *Aging sensory systems and perception.* New York: Praeger.

Craik, F. I. M. (1977). Age differences in human memory. In J. E. Birren & K. W. Schaie (Eds.), *Handbook of the psychology of aging* (pp. 384–420). New York: Van Nostrand Reinhold.

Craik, F. I. M. (1985). Paradigms in human memory research. In L.-G. Nilsson & T. Archer (Eds.), *Perspectives on learning and memory* (pp. 197–221). Hillsdale, NJ: Erlbaum.

Craik, F. I. M., & Byrd, M. (1982). Aging and cognitive deficits: The role of attentional resources. In F. I. M. Craik & S. Trehub (Eds.), *Aging and cognitive processes* (pp. 191–211). New York: Plenum Press.

Craik, F. I. M., & Rabinowitz, J. C. (1984). Age differences in the acquisition and use of verbal information: A tutorial review. In H. Bouma & D. G. Bouwhuis (Eds.), *Attention and performance: X. Control of language processes* (pp. 471–499). Hillsdale, NJ: Erlbaum.

Daneman, M., & Carpenter, P. A. (1980). Individual differences in working memory and reading. *Journal of Verbal Learning and Verbal Behavior, 19,* 450–466.

DeRenzi, E., & Faglioni, P. (1978). Normative data and screening power of a shortened version of the Token Test. *Cortex, 14,* 41–49.

Dubno, J. R., Dirks, D. D., & Morgan, D. E. (1984). Effects of age and mild hearing loss on speech recognition in noise. *Journal of the Acoustical Society of America, 76,* 87–96.

Duffy, J. R., Keith, R. L., Shane, H., & Podraza, B. L. (1976). Performance of normal (non-brain injured) adults on the Porch Index of Communicative Ability. In B. H. Brookshire (Ed.), *Clinical aphasiology: Proceedings of the conference 1976* (pp. 32–42). Minneapolis: BRK.

Duquesnoy, A. J. (1983). The intelligibility of sentences in quiet and in noise in aged listeners. *Journal of the Acoustical Society of America, 74,* 1136–1144.

Emery, O. B. (1985). Language and aging. *Experimental Aging Research, 11,* 3–60.

Eysenck, M. W. (1974). Age differences in incidental learning. *Developmental Psychology, 10,* 936–941.

Eysenck, M. W. (1977). *Human memory: Theory, research, and individual differences.* Oxford: Pergamon.

Farmer, A., McLean, S., Sparks, R., & O'Connell, P. F. (1978). Young adult, geriatric and aphasic group responses to simple analogies. *Journal of the American Geriatrics Society, 26,* 320–323.

Feier, C. D., & Gerstman, L. J. (1980). Sentence comprehension abilities throughout the adult life span. *Journal of Gerontology, 35,* 722–728.

Ferguson, C. A. (1977). Baby talk as a simplified register. In C. E. Snow & C. A. Ferguson (Eds.), *Talking to children: Language input and acquisition* (pp. 209–235). New York: Cambridge University Press.

Ford, M., & Holmes, V. M. (1978). Planning units and syntax in sentence production. *Cognition, 6,* 35–53.

Frazier, L., & Fodor, J. D. (1978). The sausage machine: A new two-stage parsing model. *Cognition, 6,* 291–325.

Garvey, C., & Caramazza, A. (1974). Implicit causality in verbs. *Linguistic Inquiry, 5,* 459–464.

Geis, M. L., & Zwicky, A. M. (1971). On invited inferences. *Linguistic Inquiry, 2,* 561–566.

Goldman-Eisler, F. (1968). *Psycholinguistics: Experiments in spontaneous speech.* New York: Academic Press.

Goldstein, G., & Shelly, C. (1984). Relationships between language skills as assessed by the Halstead-Reitan battery and the Luria-Nebraska language-related factor scales in a nonaphasic patient population. *Journal of Clinical Neuropsychology, 6,* 143–156.

Goodglass, H. (1980). Naming disorders in aphasia and aging. In L. K. Obler & M. L. Albert (Eds.), *Language and communication in the elderly* (pp. 37–45). Lexington, MA: Lexington Books.

Goodglass, H., & Kaplan, E. (1983). *The assessment of aphasia and related disorders* (2nd ed.). Philadelphia: Lea & Febiger.

Gronlund, S. O., & Shiffrin, R. M. (1986). Retrieval strategies in recall of natural categories and categorized lists. *Journal of Experimental Psychology: Learning, Memory, and Cognition, 12*, 550–561.

Harris, R. J., & Monaco, G. E. (1978). Psychology of pragmatic implication: Information processing between the lines. *Journal of Experimental Psychology: General, 107*, 1–22.

Hartley, J. T. (1986). Reader and text variables as determinants of discourse memory in adulthood. *Psychology and Aging, 1*, 150–158.

Hasher, L., & Zacks, R. T. (1979). Automatic and effortful processes in memory. *Journal of Experimental Psychology: General, 108*, 356–388.

Hess, T. M. (1984). Efforts of semantically related and unrelated contexts on recognition memory of different-aged adults. *Journal of Gerontology, 39*, 441–451.

Hess, T. M. (1985). Aging and context influences on recognition memory for typical and atypical script actions. *Developmental Psychology, 21*, 1139–1151.

Horn, J. L. (1982). The theory of fluid and crystallized intelligence in relation to concepts of cognitive psychology and aging in adulthood. In F. I. M. Craik & S. Trehub (Eds.), *Aging and cognitive processes* (pp. 237–278). New York: Plenum.

Howard, D. V. (1980). Category norms: A comparison of the Battig and Montague (1969) norms with the responses of adults between the ages of 20 and 80. *Journal of Gerontology, 35*, 225–231.

Howard, D. V. (1983). A multidimensional scaling analysis of aging and the semantic structure of animal names. *Experimental Aging Research, 9*, 27–30.

Howard, D. V., Lasaga, M. I., & McAndrews, M. P. (1980). Semantic activation during memory encoding across the adult life span. *Journal of Gerontology, 35*, 884–890.

Howard, D. V., Shaw, R. J., & Heisey, J. G. (1986). Aging and the time course of semantic activation. *Journal of Gerontology, 41*, 195–203.

Jerger, J. (1973). Audiological findings in aging. *Advances in Otorhinolaryngology, 20*, 115–124.

Jerger, J., & Hayes, D. (1977). Diagnostic speech audiometry. *Archives of Otolaryngology, 103*, 216–222.

Jonides, J., Naveh-Benjamin, M., & Palmer, J. (1985). Assessing automaticity. *Acta Psychologica, 60*, 157–171.

Kahneman, D. (1973). *Attention and effort*. Englewood Cliffs, NJ: Prentice-Hall.

Kahneman, D., & Treisman, A. (1984). Changing views of attention and automaticity. In R. Parasuraman & D. R. Davies (Eds.), *Varieties of attention* (pp. 29–61). Orlando, FL: Academic Press.

Kemper, S. (in press). Geriatric psycholinguistics. In L. L. Light & D. M. Burke (Eds.), *Language, memory, and aging*. New York: Cambridge University Press.

Kimball, J. (1973). Seven principles of surface structure parsing in natural language. *Cognition, 2*, 15–47.

Kintsch, W., & van Dijk, T. A. (1978). Toward a model of text comprehension and production. *Psychology Review, 85*, 363–394.

Konkle, D. F., Beasley, D. S., & Bess, F. H. (1977). Intelligibility of time-altered speech in relation to chronological aging. *Journal of Speech and Hearing Research, 20*, 108–115.

Kynette, D., & Kemper, S. (1986). Aging and the loss of grammatical forms: A cross-sectional study of language performance. *Language & Communication, 6*, 65–72.

Lakoff, G., & Johnson, M. (1980). *Metaphors we live by*. Chicago: University of Chicago Press.

Laver, J. (1980). Monitoring systems in the neurolinguistic control of speech production. In V. A. Fromkin (Ed.), *Errors in linguistic performance: Slips of the tongue, ear, pen, and hand* (pp. 287–305). New York: Academic Press.

Lesser, R. (1976). Verbal and non-verbal memory components in the Token Test. *Neuropsychologia, 14*, 79–85.

Levelt, W. J. M. (1983). Monitoring and self-repair in speech. *Cognition, 14*, 41–104.

Light, L. L. (1987). [Review of *A theory of cognitive aging*]. *American Journal of Psychology, 100*, 125–132.

Light, L. L., & Albertson, S. (in press). Comprehension of pragmatic implications in young and older adults. In L. L. Light & D. M. Burke (Eds.), *Language, memory, and aging*. New York: Cambridge University Press.

Light, L. L., & Anderson, P. A. (1983). Memory for scripts in young and older adults. *Memory & Cognition, 11*, 435–444.

Light, L. L., & Anderson, P. A. (1985). Working-memory capacity, age, and memory for discourse. *Journal of Gerontology, 40*, 737–747.

Light, L. L., & Capps, J. L. (1983). *Comprehension of implicit causality in young and older adults*. Unpublished manuscript, Pitzer College, Claremont, CA.

Light, L. L., & Capps, J. L. (1986). Comprehension of pronouns in young and older adults. *Developmental Psychology, 22*, 580–585.

Light, L. L., Zelinski, E. M., & Moore, M. (1982). Adult age differences in reasoning from new information. *Journal of Experimental Psychology: Learning, Memory, and Cognition, 8*, 435–447.

Lovelace, E. A., & Cooley, S. (1982). Free associations of older adults to single words and conceptually related word triads. *Journal of Gerontology, 37*, 432–437.

Maclay, H., & Osgood, C. E. (1959). Hesitation phenomena in spontaneous English speech. *Word, 14*, 19–44.

Marston, L. E., & Goetzinger, C. P. (1972). A comparison of sensitized words and sentences for distinguishing nonperipheral auditory changes as a function of aging. *Cortex, 8*, 213–223.

Miller, G. A. (1979). Images and models, similes and metaphors. In A. Ortony (Ed.), *Metaphor and thought* (pp. 202–250). Cambridge: Cambridge University Press.

Molfese, V. J., Hoffman, S., & Yuen, R. (1981–1982). The influence of setting and task partner on the performance of adults over age 65 on a communication task. *International Journal of Aging and Human Development, 14*, 45–53.

Mueller, J. H., Kausler, D. H., Faherty, A., & Olivieri, M. (1980). Reaction time as a function of age, anxiety, and typicality. *Bulletin of the Psychonomic Society, 16*, 473–476.

Navon, D. (1984). Resources—A theoretical soup stone? *Psychological Review, 91*, 216–234.

Navon, D., & Gopher, D. (1979). On the economy of the human-processing system. *Psychological Review, 86*, 214–255.

Neely, J. H. (1977). Semantic priming and retrieval from lexical memory: Roles of inhibitionless spreading activation and limited-capacity attention. *Journal of Experimental Psychology: General, 106*, 226–254.

Norman, D. A., & Bobrow, D. G. (1975). On data-limited and resource-limited processes. *Cognitive Psychology, 7*, 44–64.

Obler, L. K. (1980). Narrative discourse style in the elderly. In L. K. Obler & M. L. Albert (Eds.), *Language and communication in the elderly* (pp. 75–90). Lexington, MA: D. C. Heath.

Obler, L. K., & Albert, M. L. (1985). Language skills across adulthood. In J. E. Birren & K. W. Schaie (Eds.), *Handbook of the psychology of aging* (pp. 463–473). New York: Van Nostrand Reinhold.

Obler, L. K., Nicholas, M., Albert, M. L., & Woodward, S. (1985). On comprehension across the adult life span. *Cortex, 21*, 273–280.

Olsho, L. W., Harkins, S. W., & Lenhardt, M. L. (1985). Aging and the auditory system. In J. E. Birren & K. W. Schaie (Eds.), *Handbook of the psychology of aging* (pp. 332–377). New York: Van Nostrand Reinhold.

Onifer, W., & Swinney, D. A. (1981). Accessing lexical ambiguities during sentence comprehension: Effects of frequency of meaning and contextual bias. *Memory & Cognition, 9*, 225–236.

Orgass, B., & Poeck, K. (1966). Clinical validation of a new test for aphasia: An experimental study of the Token Test. *Cortex, 2*, 222–243.

Parkinson, S. R., Lindholm, J. M., & Urell, T. (1980). Aging, dichotic memory and digit span. *Journal of Gerontology, 35*, 87–95.

Perlmutter, M. (1979). Age differences in the consistency of adults' associative responses. *Experimental Aging Research, 5*, 549–553.

Perlmutter, M., & Mitchell, D. B. (1982). The appearance and disappearance of age differences in adult memory. In F. I. M. Craik & S. Trehub (Eds.), *Aging and cognitive processes* (pp. 127–144). New York: Plenum Press.

Petros, T. V., Zehr, H. D., & Chabot, R. J. (1983). Adult age differences in accessing and retrieving information from long-term memory. *Journal of Gerontology, 38*, 589–592.

Plomp, R., & Minden, A. M. (1979). Speech-reception threshold for sentences as a function of age and noise level. *Journal of Acoustical Society of America, 66*, 1333–1342.

Posner, M. (1978). *Chronometric explorations of mind*. Hillsdale, NJ: Erlbaum.

Rabbitt, P. M. A. (1968). Channel-capacity intelligibility and immediate memory. *Quarterly Journal of Experimental Psychology, 20*, 241–248.

Rabbitt, P. (1977). Changes in problem solving ability in old age. In J. E. Birren & K. W. Schaie (Eds.), *Handbook of the psychology of aging* (pp. 606–625). New York: Van Nostrand Reinhold.

Rabbitt, P. M. A. (1979). Some experiments and a model for changes in attentional selectivity with old age. In F. Hoffmeister & C. Muller (Eds.), *Brain function in old age* (pp. 82–94). Berlin: Springer-Verlag.

Rabinowitz, J. C., Craik, F. I. M., & Ackerman, B. P. (1982). A processing resource account of age differences in recall. *Canadian Journal of Psychology, 36*, 325–344.

Reese, H. W., & Rodeheaver, D. (1985). Problem solving and complex decision making. In J. E. Birren & K. W. Schaie (Eds.), *Handbook of the psychology of aging* (pp. 474–499). New York: Van Nostrand Reinhold.

Riegel, K. F. (1959). A study of verbal achievements of older persons. *Journal of Gerontology, 14*, 453–456.

Riegel, K. F. (1973). Language and cognition: Some life-span developmental issues. _Gerontologist, 13_, 478–482.

Riegel, K. F., & Riegel, R. M. (1964). Changes in associative behavior during later years of life: A cross-sectional analysis. _Vita Humana, 7_, 1–32.

Rosch, E. H. (1973). On the internal structure of perceptual and semantic categories. In T. E. Moore (Ed.), _Cognitive development and the acquisition of language_ (pp. 111–144). New York: Academic Press.

Rubin, K. H., & Brown, I. D. R. (1975). A life-span look at person perception and its relationship to communicative interaction. _Journal of Gerontology, 30_, 461–468.

Ryan, E. B., Giles, E., Bartolucci, G., & Henwood, K. (1986). Psycholinguistic and social psychological components of communication by and with the elderly. _Language & Communication, 6_, 1–24.

Salthouse, T. A. (1982). _Adult cognition: An experimental psychology of human aging_. New York: Springer Verlag.

Salthouse, T. A. (1985a). Speed of behavior and its implications for cognition. In J. E. Birren & K. W. Schaie (Eds.), _Handbook of the psychology of aging_ (pp. 400–426). New York: Van Nostrand Reinhold.

Salthouse, T. A. (1985b). _A theory of cognitive aging_. Amersterdam: North-Holland.

Salthouse, T. A. (in press). Effects of aging on verbal abilities: Examination of the psychometric literature. In L. L. Light & D. Burke (Eds.), _Language, memory, and aging_. New York: Cambridge University Press.

Sanford, A. J., & Garrod, S. C. (1981). _Understanding written language: Explorations of comprehension beyond the sentence_. Chichester, England: John Wiley.

Schaie, K. W., & Parham, I. A. (1977). Cohort-sequential analyses of adult intellectual development. _Developmental Psychology, 13_, 649–653.

Schank, R. C., & Abelson, R. P. (1977). _Scripts, plans, goals, and understanding_. Hillsdale, NJ: Erlbaum.

Simon, E. (1979). Depth and elaboration of processing in relation to age. _Journal of Experimental Psychology: Human Learning and Memory, 5_, 115–124.

Stanovich, K. E., & West, R. F. (1983). On priming by a sentence context. _Journal of Experimental Psychology: General, 112_, 1–36.

Sticht, T. G., & Gray, B. B. (1969). The intelligibility of time compressed words as a function of age and hearing loss. _Journal of Speech and Hearing Research, 12_, 443–448.

Stones, M. J. (1978). Aging and semantic memory: Structural age differences. _Experimental Aging Research, 4_, 125–132.

Swisher, L. P., & Sarno, M. T. (1969). Token Test scores of three matched patient groups: Left brain-damaged with aphasia; right brain-damaged without aphasia; non-brain-damaged. _Cortex, 5_, 264–273.

Tabossi, P., & Johnson-Laird, P. N. (1980). Linguistic context and the priming of semantic information. _Quarterly Journal of Experimental Psychology, 32_, 595–603.

Till, R. E. (1985). Verbatim and inferential memory in young and elderly adults. _Journal of Gerontology, 40_, 316–323.

Till, R. E., & Walsh, D. A. (1980). Encoding and retrieval factors in adult memory for implicational sentences. _Journal of Verbal Learning and Verbal Behavior, 19_, 1–16.

Tulving, E. (1972). Episodic and semantic memory. In E. Tulving & W. Donaldson (Eds.), _Organization of memory_ (pp. 382–403). New York: Academic Press.

Ulatowska, H. K., Cannito, M. P., Hayashi, M. M., & Fleming, S. G. (1985). Language abilities in the elderly. In H. K. Ulatowska (Ed.), *The aging brain: Communication in the elderly* (pp. 125–139). San Diego, CA: College-Hill Press.

Walker, V. G., Hardiman, C. J., Hedrick, D. L., & Holbrook, A. (1981). Speech and language characteristics of an aging population. In N. J. Lass (Ed.), *Speech and language: Advances in basic research and practice* (Vol. 6, pp. 143–202). New York: Academic Press.

Wingfield, A., Poon, L. W., Lombardi, L., & Lowe, D. (1985). Speed of processing in normal aging: Effects of speech rate, linguistic structure, and processing time. *Journal of Gerontology, 40*, 579–585.

Wright, R. E. (1981). Aging, divided attention, and processing capacity. *Journal of Gerontology, 36*, 605–614.

Yairi, E., & Clifton, N. F. (1972). Disfluent speech behavior of preschool children, high school seniors, and geriatric persons. *Journal of Speech and Hearing Research, 15*, 714–719.

Zacks, R. T., & Hasher, L. (in press). Capacity theory and the processing of inferences. In L. L. Light & D. M. Burke (Eds.), *Language, memory, and aging*. New York: Cambridge University Press.

11

Aging as an Individual Process: Toward a Theory of Personal Meaning*

Gary T. Reker
Paul T. P. Wong

The exponential increase in research activity on aging in the past two decades has prompted this review of the state of theory and search for direction toward future theory building. The ontogenic or maturational perspective has come under critical scrutiny as attempts to extend it to the entire life span (e.g., Neugarten, 1969) did not lend itself to high-level predictability. The usefulness of the mechanistic and organismic metamodels of life-span development was also questioned, precipitating a crisis with respect to the aims of traditional scientific research to explain, predict, and control human behavior (Gergen, 1980).

The emerging crisis has been intensified by an increasing emphasis on the capacity of the human organism to influence the environment in significant ways, as opposed to merely reacting to it. Such a view makes precise prediction and control problematic. This has led Gergen (1980) to suggest that the major function of theory ought to be "not as that of enhancing prediction and control, but as a means of rendering intelligible and communicable one's

*This research was supported by a Leave Fellowship (451-85-0040) from the Social Sciences and Humanities Research Council of Canada to the first author, and in part by a Strategic Research Grant (Population Aging) from the SSHRC to both authors.

experiences of the world" (p. 32). In a similar vein, Neugarten (1984) calls attention to a different philosophy of science, an interpretive social science, as a way of diversifying our means of comprehension and our methods and techniques of study. According to Neugarten (1984), the goal of interpretive social science is "to explicate contexts and thereby to achieve new insights and new understandings" (p. 292). Kenyon (1985; this volume) and Moody (this volume) exhort social scientists to move beyond a restricted traditional view of aging toward a more expansive, comprehensive personal existence perspective.

An example of this new interpretive perspective is the resurgence of research on the whole person through biographical studies, historical narrative, and the life-span construct approach (Birren & Hedlund, 1987; Freeman, 1984; Mc-Adams, 1985; Starr, 1982–1983; Whitbourne, 1985). There is also a revival of Murray's (1938) personology in current works of personality theorists (e.g., Atwood & Tomkins, 1976; Carlson, 1982; Runyan, 1982); developmental psychologists (e.g., Levinson, 1978); and sociologists (e.g., Bertaux, 1981). The appearance in 1978 of the first volume of *Biography*, a new journal which focuses on biography as a form of art and science, adds an interdisciplinary flavor to the current trends of interpretive research.

The general populace, too, seems to have become increasingly receptive to reading biographies and autobiographies. Freeman (1985) noted that, all across the continental United States, there exists an enormous reading appetite for people's lives, historical and contemporary. For example, in 1971, 944 biographies and autobiographies were published; by 1983, the number of original works had risen to over 2,000.

How is one to account for what appears to be a widespread interest by social scientists and the general public in the study of whole persons and how they live their lives? Biographies may tell a completed story—a life with a beginning, a middle, and an end. By learning more about how other people have lived their lives, one gains some understanding of how to live one's own life. Cole (1984), a cultural historian, has pointed out that the spectacular gains in longevity through scientific and technological progress have been accompanied by "widespread spiritual malaise . . . and confusion over the meaning and purpose of human life—particularly in old age" (p. 329). Perhaps biographies and autobiographies provide useful insights on the meanings that attribute to human existence.

The purpose of this chapter is to incorporate certain aspects of the interpretive social science approach in formulating a view of personal meaning with respect to aging. We will first discuss the interpretive social science perspective and present the case that this new approach qualifies as science. In the second section, we will elaborate on the nature of personal meaning as conceptualized by Frankl (1963) and Maddi (1970). We will propose a personal meaning system that is closely tied to societal and personal values. This will be followed by a description of the development of personal meaning. In the third section, we will examine how personal meanings are constructed and reconstructed across the life span and how notions of time perspective, religiosity, and death attitudes provide continuity and give meaning to life. In the fourth section, we will present a number of measurement approaches deemed suitable to the explication of contexts within an interpretive world view. In the final section, we will consider the implications of our view of aging for research, allied disciplines, and public policy.

THE INTERPRETIVE SCIENCE PERSPECTIVE

In the last twenty years, a number of investigators from psychology and sociology have contributed to the development of what may be termed interpretive science (Rabinow & Sullivan, 1979). Regardless of whether it is called "symbolic interactionism" (Blumer, 1969), "phenomenology" (Keen, 1975; Kelly, 1955), or "humanistic science" (Chein, 1972), proponents of this new approach share at least two common premises.

First, humans are regarded as conscious, active, purposive, self-reflecting organisms capable of symbolization and symbol manipulation. Symbolization enables the human organism to *represent* the environment, not merely to respond to it (Kelly, 1955). The internal representation may or may not map objective reality. However, only internal representation is considered to be effective reality in that it directs subsequent behavior (Kelly, 1955; Thomae, 1970).

Self-constructions are as real to the individual as the environment itself. They are not epiphenomena. What is construed may not exist, as in the case of a highly developed delusional system, but the perception does.

The ability of humans to represent their experience symbolically has given them the power to transcend time boundaries of past, present, and future; to reminisce; to anticipate; to give meaning to existence. As a result, the individual has acquired tremendous flexibility *in the interpretation* of all life events. Gergen (1980) states the implication of this most eloquently:

> In particular, the possibility for multiple symbolic translations of the same experiential conditions, and for singular translations of multiple and varying conditions, enable the individual to move in any number of directions at any time (or conversely to remain stable over a variety of seemingly diverse circumstances). (p. 43)

As the individual passes through time, he or she constructs and reconstructs "reality." Self-construction individualizes the aging process, giving the person the power to accommodate and transcend both personal and societal limitations (Birren & Hedlund, 1987). Within an interpretive perspective, aging may be viewed as a process of change in personal constructions over time, resulting from the reciprocal interplay between the biological and psychological processes of the organism and the social, cultural, and historical contexts in which the individual is embedded.

Second, personal meanings attached to objects and events are more significant realities for investigation than the physical attributes of the natural world. "The meaning that things have for human beings are central in their own right. To ignore the meaning of the things toward which people act is seen as falsifying the behavior under study" (Blumer, 1969, p. 3).

Meanings are both subjective and intersubjective in that they derive from interactions and one's interpretations of these interactions. Personal meanings constitute a reality that is self-evident to both the individual and others who share the same reality of everyday life and with whom one communicates and interacts (Berger & Luckman, 1966).

In short, interpretive science no longer recognizes the physical world as the only reality for scientific investigations and acknowledges the existence of several realities. The symbolic reality of meanings, images, and feelings is far more important than physical reality because symbols have a much more direct and pervasive influence on human behavior.

In this chapter the term *meaning* has broad implications. It includes the value that individuals place upon the events and flow of life. Meaning also embraces the connotations and denotations of what is conveyed when individuals speak of their lives and the significance they attach to their existence.

Guardians of orthodox views of science may question the legitimacy of both the premises and the methods of interpretive science. However, a case may be made that the new science has many of the same ingredients of traditional approaches.

Traditional versus Interpretive Science

It is generally acknowledged that traditional science deals with empirical knowledge. Scientific inquiry presupposes the existence of phenomena that are observable and describable. Inferences made about such phenomena are tested against the "real world" by scientific methods, which typically involve observation, prediction, and control.

In the traditional scientific enterprise, observation consists of describing singular events in physical terms. Events are accepted as facts only when they meet the criteria of intersubjective testability and intersubjective agreeability. That is, events must be open to public inquiry and must be observable and describable by more than one person. Second, there must be a high degree of agreement among different people to ensure that what is being described or measured is objective and reliable.

Prediction is based on the discovery of scientific laws and formulation of scientific theories. Laws are summary statements of regularities in terms of general characteristics of a class of events and relationships between classes of events. Theories consist of a set of constructs that are operationally defined and propositions that are testable by empirical means. Theories enable us to understand the nature or underlying processes of empirical laws. Deductions can be made from these theories to make predictions about new situations.

Control implies the isolation and manipulation of variables to produce certain predicted results. In experimentation, control typically requires eliminating aspects of nature unrelated to the variables under investigation, and the use of control groups to eliminate confound and rival hypotheses. Thus, "reality" in the traditional scientific perspective is limited to what can be observed and described in physical terms, found regularly or consistently, and verified through observation and experimentation.

From the perspective of interpretive science, we maintain that facts of empirical science exist not only in the physical world of nature but also in the phenomenological symbolic world of consciousness. For example, the presence or absence of meaning can be regarded as an empirical fact because it meets the criteria of intersubjective agreement and testability. When one describes the emptiness of a life without meaning, such a description is readily understood by others who share a common language and culture. Lack of meaning is communicated through symbols and metaphors, yet it can have as high a degree of intersubjective agreement as descriptions of physical entities. The absence of meaning in an individual also meets the criterion of intersubjective testability because different people, through interacting with this person, can come to the same conclusion that the person lacks meaning in his or her life.

Therefore, facts include phenomenological experiences that can be communicated in terms of symbols, images, and feelings, and their existence does not necessarily depend on the use of operational definitions. As long as subjective experiences are communicated in a way that can be understood by others, they have the status of empirical facts. Self-reports of the pain of jealousy or rejection are just as objective and empirical as self-report of pain due to electric shock or lesion. In short, the interpretive science perspective broadens the scope of experiences and events that are admitted as facts for scientific investigations.

In terms of scientific laws, the new approach departs from the traditional science in several significant ways. First of all, certain laws are considered self-evident truths—they cannot be contradicted by data, and their truthfulness or verity rests on common human experiences. For example, certain human rights, such as the right to pursue freedom and happiness, are accepted as self-evident truths in Western democratic societies because they accord with our own experiences and the fundamental conception of human beings as autonomously functioning individuals. A challenging task, from the perspective of interpretive science, is to discover from the vast literature of human experiences those verities that are rooted in human nature and are compellingly self-evident.

Second, empirical laws can be studied in qualitative terms or typologies. Since laws refer to regularities, then the existence of certain patterns or types has the status of empirical laws. In our recent investigation of reminiscence, we have discovered different types of reminiscence. For example, integrative reminiscence refers to reconciling past conflicts, resolving discrepancies between achievements and aspirations, and achieving a sense of continuity among past, present, and future. Obsessive reminiscence refers to preoccupations with failures, shame, and guilt. Different people examining the contents of reminiscence can readily identify these two types of reminiscent orientations.

Third, empirical laws can include relationships between classes of phenomenological events. Our preliminary evidence that links integrative reminiscence with personal meaning in life is a case in point. Such a relationship, where established by empirical means, qualifies as an empirical law.

Fourth, empirical laws can be idiographic. If we can establish the patterns and relationships of various classes of events pertaining to one individual, as in the case of clinical observations, then we have discovered the empirical laws that govern the behavior and psychological reactions of this particular individual. Here the empirical laws do not necessarily have to deal with universals as in traditional science. However, when many similar cases are observed, idiographic laws have the potential to become nomothetic laws.

With regard to theorizing, the interpretive-science perspective again adopts a less rigid stance. The hypotheticodeductive model is no longer regarded as the only or the best way to theory building. Conceptual frameworks may be constructed in terms of images and metaphors to provide insights into human behavior and guidelines for empirical investigations. In the traditional scientific approach, issues that are uniquely human or significantly relevant to everyday living are often lost in various machine and animal models of human behavior. Furthermore, low-level mini-theories that are characteristic of contemporary psychological theorizing tend to be limited to a restrictive domain and based on a limited data set. We propose that the total image of personhood, the qualities of a life that confer individuality, are more likely to emerge when we paint with bigger brushes on a larger canvas.

The interpretive-science approach also encourages greater latitude in methods. It no longer accepts the doctrinaire views on the rules of science. Detailed descriptions of subjective life experiences become just as important as experimental control in a laboratory. Qualitative analysis is no longer treated as inferior to quantitative analysis. Personal documents, such as the life history narrative (Freeman, 1984), the life review (Butler, 1963), and guided autobiography (Birren & Hedlund, 1987), are accepted as legitimate sources of data.

Qualitative analyses in terms of life drawing techniques (Whitbourne & Dannefer, 1985–1986) and typological analyses are also considered valid methods.

In sum, the interpretive-science perspective has the essential ingredients of traditional science and yet takes a much more liberal approach with respect to the rules of scientific conduct. This liberated view enables us to explore the inner recesses of subjective experiences that are declared out of bounds by the traditional sciences (Neugarten, 1984).

THE NATURE OF PERSONAL MEANING

Conceptual Issues

Personal meaning, as distinct from definitional meaning, is concerned with the meaning in life. It is related to such constructs as value, purpose, coherence, and belief system. When we ask, "What is the meaning in life?", we are asking; "What is worth living for? What is the purpose in life?" Such questions call for value judgments and cannot be answered apart from one's belief system or world view.

Perhaps one way to clarify the concept of personal meaning is to recognize that it is a multidimensional construct with at least three related components: cognitive, motivational, and affective.

The *cognitive component* has to do with making sense of one's experiences in life. We postulate that each individual constructs a belief system, a world view, to address a number of existential concerns such as: "Is there an ultimate purpose in human existence? Is there order and purpose in the universe? What is the total meaning in life?"

The belief system deals with not only "cosmic meaning" (Yalom, 1980) but also existential understanding of specific life events. In this respect, the individual seeks to understand the value and purpose of various encounters. Thus, from the cognitive perspective, meaning is an explanation or interpretation of one's life (Weisskopf-Joelson, 1968).

According to Frank (1977), belief systems are essentially a moral and cognitive map of the universe, which helps individuals "select from and make sense of the welter of their experiences" (p. 555). Another major function of belief systems is to provide an antidote to ontological anxiety, "the prospect of disappearing into nothingness, which all humans must face" (p. 557).

The *motivational component* of personal meaning refers to the value system constructed by each individual. Values are essentially guides for living, dictating what goals we pursue and how we live our lives. Values are determined by our needs, beliefs, and society. Both the process of pursuing selected goals and the eventual attainment give a sense of purpose and meaning to one's existence. It is the worthwhile ends one cherishes that keep one going in spite of the obstacles and setbacks.

Finally, there is the *affective component*. Although the pursuit of individual happiness may not result in meaningfulness, the realization of personal meaning is always accompanied by feelings of satisfaction and fulfillment. Whatever is meaningful must also provide satisfaction to the pursuer. "Without subjective satisfaction, meaning is incomplete" (Baird, 1985, p. 119).

Thus, personal meaning may be defined as the cognizance of order, coherence, and purpose in one's existence, the pursuit and attainment of worthwhile goals, and an accompanying sense of fulfillment. This view of personal meaning may be represented by a triangle, as shown in Figure 11-1, which indicates the hypothesized structure of personal meaning with the cognitive component as the cornerstone.

A proper understanding of personal meaning requires both a bottom-up (elemental) view and a top-down (holistic) view of life. Hocking (1957) puts it this way:

> In the one direction, meaning ascends from the parts to the whole: life has meaning if it contains a goodly number of these satisfying spots — their worth colours the frame in which they are set. In the other direction, meaning descends from the whole to the parts: human life has meaning if (and only if) there is total meaning in the world in which it can participate. (p. 112)

According to the elemental view, it is not meaningful to talk about life as a whole as having meaning; life only *contains* meanings — a series of meaningful activities, quests, and goals. However, such a view may be an inadequate antidote to ontological anxiety. One also needs a vision, no matter how dim, of some ultimate purpose or total meaning. To achieve an enduring type of personal meaning, specific activities need to be integrated into a larger and higher purpose. Our definition of personal meaning incorporates both the elemental and holistic views of meaning.

Theoretical Perspectives

The importance of personal meaning in life has been stressed in the writings of a number of theorists (e.g., Frankl, 1963, 1978; Klinger, 1977; Maddi, 1970; Yalom, 1980) and researchers (e.g., Battista & Almond, 1973; Fisk, 1980; Reker & Peacock, 1981; Reker, Peacock, & Wong, 1987). Notable among the theorists are the seminal contributions of Frankl and Maddi.

Frankl (1963) asserts that the "will to meaning" is a significant and universal human motive. Loss of meaning leads to "noogenic neurosis," characterized by boredom, hopelessness, depression, and the loss of the will to live. For Frankl, an ultimate meaning and purpose already exists in the world, but it must be personally discovered. Through the exercise of responsibility, commitment to self and others, and the acceptance of future potentialities, the individual

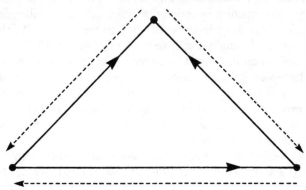

FIGURE 11-1. The structure of personal meaning. Solid arrows represent the direction of influence; dashed arrows represent feedback.

moves toward a self-transcendent state and the discovery of a deeper sense of meaning and purpose.

Maddi (1970) describes the failure in the search for meaning in life in terms of *existential sickness*, the extreme form of which has the cognitive, affective, and conative properties of meaninglessness, apathy, and aimlessness. Unlike Frankl, however, Maddi does not envision an ultimate meaning. Rather, individuals create their own meanings through the mental processes of symbolization, imagination, and judgment. Klinger (1977) perceives these characteristics as components of inner experience, the integration of which provides a sense of meaning.

Our approach is to fuse aspects of Frankl's and Maddi's conceptualizations of personal meaning with the cognitive approach of Kelly (1955). Our *fundamental postulate* is that every individual is motivated to seek and find personal meaning in existence. In fact, "part of what it means to be human is to wonder about what it means to be human" (Baird, 1985, p. 117). To search for meaning implies that there is some kind of meaning "out there" to be discovered. Thus, we agree with Frankl that there is some ultimate purpose or meaning that is obtainable by individuals who are willing to pay the price to search for it.

To postulate that ultimate meaning can be discovered does not necessarily negate Maddi's (1970) view that meaning can be created. Individuals discover meaning from the givens, such as the existence of the universe, the existence of life. Individuals also create meaning through making choices, taking actions, and entering into relationships. For example, Baird (1985) has pointed out that "part of what it means, then, to be fully human is to create meaning by establishing depth relationships, by committing ourselves to projects, that give order and purpose to our days, and by placing our lives in the context of meaning-creating stories" (p. 123). Thus, meaning is created in commitments, achievements, and relationships.

From the Kellian perspective, personal constructs provide the internal structure of personal meanings. More specifically, one's belief system and value system dictate what goals are to be pursued and what relationships are to be established. For example, if one does not believe in immortality and eternal values, then all of one's strivings will be restricted to the temporal sphere. Beliefs, together with one's need states, determine one's value system which, in turn, provides a guide for one's pursuits and commitments.

According to our analysis, personal meaning functions as a cognitive mediating variable (see Reker, 1985) that provides an interpretation of life experiences and integrates the contradictions, conflicts, and absurdities of human existence. At the same time, personal meaning functions as an intervening motivational variable that guides, directs, and invigorates behavior.

The scientist is motivated by the postulate that there is order in the universe that can be discovered through systematic observation and experimentation. Similarly, we postulate that there is purpose and meaning in human existence, which can be discovered, not by traditional scientific methods, but by individual experiences, religious or philosophical insights, and perhaps a different level of consciousness.

Sources of Personal Meaning

Our definition suggests that both beliefs and value systems give rise to meaning. In this section, we want to develop a taxonomy of personal meaning through a detailed analysis of values and beliefs.

Academic psychology has been dominated by mechanism and ethical naturalism. However, recently, there is increasing realization of the importance of values in research and psychotherapy (Bergin, 1980; Braginsky & Braginsky, 1974; Feinstein, 1979; Frank, 1977). For example, Bergin (1980) has pointed out that "not only do theories, techniques and criteria reveal pervasive value judgements, but outcome data comparing the effects of diverse techniques show that non-technical value-laden factors pervade professional change processes" (p. 97). The same may be said about other domains of human activities. Values have been defined as constructs that transcend specific situations and that are personally and socially preferable (Rokeach, 1973). Values incorporate modes of conduct (instrumental values) and goals in life (terminal values), and impel one to action. As stated earlier, values function as important guiding principles in life. Values may also be conceptualized as "incentives" (Klinger, 1977).

Values are related to personal needs. For example, bread has no value to someone who is not hungry, and water becomes more valuable than gold to someone dying of thirst. The various levels of needs postulated by Maslow (1968) give rise to a parallel set of values. Thus, physiological needs are related to survival values, and self-esteem needs are linked to achievement-oriented values.

Beliefs also contribute to the development of values. The value of self-reliance and hard work (i.e., the Protestant work ethic) has been linked to Protestant beliefs (Weber, 1905). By the same token, spiritual values are based on religious beliefs. One values worship and prayer only when one believes that there is a God worthy of praise. Conversely, the lack of religious beliefs also has an impact on values. If one does not believe in the existence of God and an eternal scheme of things, one's values will be confined to the earthly realm.

Since values determine one's objectives and aspirations, the study of values will be very informative regarding sources of personal meaning. Conversely, values are reflected in the answers individuals provide when questioned about sources of personal meaning.

Bengtson (1975) investigated the global value orientations of humanism/materialism and collectivism/individualism across grandparent-parent-youth lineages and within families. He found generational differences in collectivism/individualism but not in humanism/materialism. Grandchildren endorsed values of individualism (skill, an exciting life, personal freedom, sense of accomplishment); grandparents endorsed greater collectivism (religious participation, loyalty, patriotism, friendship). However, large within-generation variation was also found, obscuring clear interpretation of between-generation differences. When value orientations were examined within families, some evidence of family transmission emerged on the collectivism/individualism dimension, but the effect was minimal.

Of particular interest to us is the substantial degree of individual differences in value orientations and the apparent source of such heterogeneity. Bengtson (1975) suggests that global value orientations "may be more reflective of the individual's unique personal biography, or of his or her response to sociohistorical events, than to effects attributable either to family or generational factors" (p. 369). Such an interpretation is consistent with our view that self-definitions may emerge from the social definitions of values.

Allport, Vernon, and Lindzey (1951) developed a scale to measure six types of values and motives. The *theoretical* person emphasizes the discovery of truth. The chief aim in life is to acquire and systematize knowledge. The *economic* person is concerned with utilities and profits. The *aesthetic* person considers beauty and charm as the highest value. The *social* type values altruism. The *political* person is mainly interested in the pursuit and exercise of power. The *religious* person tends to be mystical and transcendental.

Allport et al. recognize that their study of values does not allow for "baser" values, such as hedonic, sensuous value. Nevertheless, the six types of values have been recognized as primary by a number of other investigators.

For Frankl (1963), meaning stems from three broad sources: (1) creative, or what one accomplishes in terms of creative work, or art, or scholarly endeavor; (2) experiential, or what one derives from beauty, truth, or love; and (3) attitudinal, or what one derives from reflections on negative aspects of life such as pain and suffering.

Based on case studies, Yalom (1980) identified five general values: altruism, dedication to a cause, creativity, hedonism, and self-actualization. In a study investigating sources of meaning in life among undergraduate students, DeVogler and Ebersole (1980, 1983) identified eight categories: relationships, service, personal growth, beliefs, hedonism, expression, obtaining, and understanding. Hedlund and Birren (1984) analyzed the autobiographical essays of women between the ages of 22 and 78. They found that relationships, service, personal growth, and beliefs accounted for most of the responses.

Thurnher (1975) examined the value orientations of a cross-sectional sample of adults and identified seven sources of meaning: personal achievement, marriage and family, humanitarian-moral concerns, coping with the givens of life (e.g., earning a living, adjusting), happiness, religious life, and leaving a legacy. Klinger (1977) asked undergraduates to describe what made their life meaningful. He generated 14 different categories of activities, such as friendships, leisure time, vocational plans, religion, etc. Many, if not all, of his activities, however, overlap with the sources of meaning already described.

On the basis of prior studies of values and meaning, there seem to be a few major sources of meaning, namely: personal relationships, personal growth, success (achievements), altruism (service to others), hedonism, creativity, religion, and legacy. These are by no means exhaustive. For example, one may add that being alive or life itself is a source of meaning; cultural heritage, which gives one a sense of identity and continuity, may be an important source of meaning for ethnic minorities. Thus, several sources can contribute to an overall sense of personal meaning. Degree of personal meaning in life is defined as the total amount of meaning derived from all available sources.

On the dual premise that an individual derives meaning from several valued sources and that a greater variety of values contribute to a greater sense of meaning, we offer the *breadth* postulate: An individual's degree of personal meaning will increase in direct proportion to his or her diversification of sources of meaning.

Having stated the above postulate, we hasten to add that some of the values may be conflicting. For example, hedonistic values may conflict with the achievement of important life goals that require dedication and hard work.

The breadth postulate holds only when the individual has managed to reconcile conflicting values.

Levels of Personal Meaning

Frankl (1963) is of the conviction that the full meaning of life can be achieved only by transcending self-interests. The individual must value something beyond himself or herself. Explicit in Rokeach's (1973) system is the hierarchical nature of values in which certain values hold greater significance than others. Both of these positions suggest the need for postulating levels of personal meaning.

At the lowest level, we see self-preoccupation with hedonistic pleasure and comfort. At the second level, the person devotes time and energy to the realization of his or her potential. Personal growth, creativity, and self-actualization are examples. At the third level, the individual moves beyond the realm of self-interests into areas that involve service to others and dedication to a larger societal or political cause. At the fourth level, the individual entertains values that transcend individuals and encompass cosmic meaning and ultimate purpose.

Based on the theoretical views of Frankl and Rokeach, we formulate the following *depth* postulate: An individual's degree of personal meaning will increase in direct proportion to his or her commitment to higher levels of meaning.

Personal Meaning System Complexity

One of the hallmarks of positive mental health is the ability of the individual to cope with a variety of stressful situations, to reconcile contradictions, to incorporate personal limitations into his or her identity, and to adapt to changing conditions. Based on the cognitive complexity literature (e.g., Bieri, 1961; Reker, 1974), we assert that a highly differentiated and integrated personal meaning system is necessary to promote optimal adaptation. A complex meaning system is a flexible one; it facilitates divergent thinking and thereby alternative constructions of reality.

Our breadth and depth postulates, in combination, provide the basis for the development of a complex meaning system. Since the complexity of the personal meaning system is influenced, in part, by the range and quality of experiences encountered, we propose the following *meaning system* postulate: The personal meaning system of an individual who has available a variety of sources of meaning and who strives for higher levels of personal meaning will be highly differentiated and integrated.

The structure of the personal meaning system can be revealed through the "implication ladder" (Bannister & Mair, 1968). The degree of complexity of the system can also be determined through operational measures of differentiation and integration (Reker, 1974). These procedures will be taken up in more detail in the measurement section. Having described the basis of the structure, we now turn our attention to the personal meaning context.

Personal Meaning Contexts

Phenomenologists often talk about "horizons" as the background against which experience can be described (Keen, 1975). In describing the development of personal meaning, we refer to horizons as meaning-producing contexts. We propose two kinds of meaning-producing contexts: social definitions and self-definitions.

Social Definitions

It is important to point out that how the social context is perceived by the individual is more important than the actual context itself. Interpretation of reality begins at the individual level and becomes social reality when shared with others. Widely shared social reality (i.e., across generations) forms the basis of accepted social definitions. Overgeneralized social definitions lead to social stereotypes (Hickey, 1980). In short, collective perceptions are the emergent properties of individual processes.

The individual is born into an a priori set of societal values and expectations. These are passed on through socialization from the beginning of life and provide the context for a social definition of personal meaning. They tell the individual "what is" and "what ought to be." Human development transpires within the constraints of social expectations, cultural traditions, and historical episodes. Society provides prohibitions and sanctions to establish norms for acceptable behavior. Societal institutions (e.g., family, schools) enforce these expectations through socialization practices in order to make collective existence possible. The "expectation" boundaries, however, are fairly broad, allowing for considerable latitude in individual behavior. As a member of a pre-established social order, the individual becomes a bearer of collective experiences (culture bearer), while simultaneously retaining a unique birth, death, and life course, and a personal history not shared by anyone. The implication of this is that the individual remains free, within the limits of cultural prescriptions, to choose his or her destiny.

Individuals who choose to abide by societal expectations and who incorporate the concomitant labels find meaning in shared values. They stick close to the norm and act according to what is expected of their age. They become the "foreclosed" (adoption of parental standards) identity-status young adults (Côté & Reker, 1979) or *conformists* who perceive very little choice and who find meaning through serving the dictates of society (Maddi, 1970).

Social definitions in varying degrees shape the aspirations and values of individual members of a given community. Values vary from culture to culture, primarily because of social definitions. Thus, it is not possible to have a complete understanding of personal meaning apart from cultural contexts.

Self-Definitions

Self-definitions address the intentional and reflective capacity of the human organism. It is the ability of the individual to self-reflect, to introspect, to self-examine that gives existence to this meaning-producing context. The Socratic imperative "know thyself" provides the essential backdrop (McAdams, 1985).

Some individuals who extract meaning from self-definitions find meaning in private or idiosyncratic values. Such individuals often transcend the boundaries of societal expectations by ignoring or refusing to accept them. They can emancipate themselves from their past and discover themselves anew (McAdams, 1985). They are the achievement-status young adults (Côté & Reker, 1979), or *individualists* who perceive a great deal of choice and personal control over their lives (Maddi, 1970).

In our conceptualization, meaning-producing contexts form a continuum, anchored by social definitions and self-definitions. The individual can choose any position on the continuum, stabilize at one position, or move back and forth toward either extreme. The position taken up at any given time is the one that maintains individual equilibrium.

From this we generate our *choice* postulate: An individual chooses for himself or herself a position on the meaning-producing continuum for the construction of his or her personal meaning system.

On the premise that having both more choices and control over one's life is tantamount to increasing the range and quality of experiences, we offer our *individuality* hypothesis: The personal meaning system of an individualist will be more differentiated and integrated compared to that of a conformist.

PERSONAL MEANING ACROSS THE LIFE SPAN

We take the position that the incorporation of values precedes the formation of a meaning system in life-span development. We offer two arguments in support of this view. First, the individual is born into a preestablished value system. Second, the meaning system requires the manipulation of symbols and the ability of self-reflection. Although Frankl, Maddi, and Kelly do not discuss the early development of meaning and the meaning system, it is our view that an effective personal meaning system cannot be established until the individual has acquired the basics of language. Chronologically, this means by about the third year of life. A 3-or 4-year-old may not be able to articulate his or her meaning system when conventional research methods are used. However, this should not lead to the conclusion that it does not exist. It simply means that we need to tailor our methods to suit the individual's level of cognitive development.

The fundamental postulate holds that all individuals, even at a very young age, are motivated to seek and to find personal meaning in human existence. Since values, shared and private, are the sources of personal meanings, once values have been incorporated by the young person, they give birth to meaning. Similarly, beliefs acquired and constructed by the individual also give rise to personal meaning. As one's belief system evolves and values change across the life span, one's personal meaning undergoes transformation as well. In fact, the only continuity or sameness is the fact of *change*. The important life-span developmental questions "are not how people *respond* to life change or *proceed through* stages, but how they negotiate and generate the reality and meaning of change, stages, and development" (Gubrium & Buckholdt, 1977, pp. 8–9).

The importance of studying an individual's perception of life changes was echoed by Neugarten (1977) in her review of personality and aging:

> . . . psychologists will probably gain enormously by focusing more attention upon the issues that are of major concern to the individual—what the person selects as important in his past and his present, what he hopes to do in the future, what he predicts will occur, what strategies he elects, and what *meanings he attaches to time, life, and death*. (pp. 639–640, emphasis added)

Personal Meaning and Time Perspective

An individual's temporal perspective, or the way he or she internally represents and partitions time into past, present, and future, has a powerful influence on a wide range of psychological processes (e.g., motivation, expectations, problem-solving). At any given moment, the individual can reminisce about the past, reflect on current concerns, or anticipate the future (Lewin, 1948; Rakowski, 1979; Reker & Wong, 1985).

Time orientation (Nuttin, 1985), or the amount of time engaged in the processes of reminiscence, current reflection, and anticipation, is affected by values, shared or private. For example, in a society that values ancestor worship, the past may be of primary concern. Eskimos, whose survival depends on the daily hunt, have a keen sense of the present. Western society, with emphasis on profits, life insurance, and savings banks, is dominated by a sense of future (Gonzalez & Zimbardo, 1985).

On an individual level, the perception of continuity of past, present, and future provides a sense of self that is stable through time. An individual who perceives the future as a continuation of the present and the past displays a high degree of temporal integration. An individual with a high degree of time integration may be described as time-competent (Nuttin, 1985; Shostrom, 1968).

The relative importance of past, present, and future can shift over the course of a life. When an individual is young, a future orientation may predominate (Reker, Peacock, & Wong, 1987). For an aging individual, the past plays an important role in adjusting to the present as well as to the future (Birren & Hedlund, 1987; Butler, 1963; Kaminsky, 1984; Rakowski, 1979). Birren and Hateley and Butler contend that one's present and future meaning depends on a review and evaluation of one's past life.

Personal Meaning and Time Continuity

Given that one's life is irrevocably bound to the temporal dimension, we feel that a complete understanding of personal meaning is not possible without taking into account the flow of time.

Meaning from the past is discovered primarily through life review or reminiscence. Significant others in the past (e.g., parents, teachers), past achievements, major events or branching points, cultural heritage, and family roots are all fertile grounds for finding personal meaning.

Present meaning is primarily based on commitments, activities, and pursuits. The zest and vitality of goal-directed activities, the sweat of hard work and the joy of success, the excitement and satisfaction of engaging in intimate relationships, and the many personal experiences that give color, texture, and richness to the tapestry of life are the raw materials for present meaning. We create meaning through choices and actions as we move through life, but we also discover meaning from many "happenings" that come our way each day.

As we are occupied with the day-to-day business of living, we also derive energy and inspiration from what lies ahead. The basis for future meaning is optimism—the anticipation of desired events, achievements, and attainment of important life goals. For the transcendental mystics, their optimism extends beyond earthly existence and reaches out into eternity.

Thus, reminiscence, commitment, and optimism provide a constant flow of meaning that sustains and enlivens an otherwise mundane and often painful existence. The amount of contribution from these three sources will vary according to the stage of one's life cycle.

A Matter of Life and Death

Personal meaning is a matter of how a life has been lived, is lived, and will be lived. Because each individual can transcend time boundaries, he or she can construct for himself or herself a meaningful "personal timetable for living" (Hickey, 1980, p. 84). An individual timetable may or may not coincide with that of other individuals or with the societal timetable of education, marriage, parenthood, work, and retirement. Whether it does or does not depends to a large extent on where the individual locates himself or herself on the meaning-producing continuum.

Our choice postulate advocates that an individual can shift positions over the course of a life. Through socialization, societal values and expectations may impact significantly on the early development of the personal meaning system.

What factors might prompt a move along the meaning-producing continuum? We assert that changes in personal and societal values provide the catalyst for shifting positions. If an individual's physical, psychological, and social resources become depleted with advancing age, long-cherished personal values may become dysfunctional and some reorientation must take place (Thurnher, 1975). In addition, the older person may be less likely to be influenced by societal values and expectations and become more inner-directed (Markson, 1973). When societal values are threatened by the erosion of traditional values and rapid social changes, or when culturally supported ideals of old age are nonexistent (Cole, 1984; Gutmann, 1981), the "de-cultured" individual looks toward self-generated meaning. Thurnher (1975) cites evidence for different value shifts for men and women across four life stages in terms of content and timing. In broad terms, the value curve begins with educational, occupational, and material concerns, turns toward marriage and family responsibilities, and ends with contentment and withdrawal from goal strivings.

Major value changes have implications for the structure of the personal meaning system. The system may undergo reconstruction in order to accommodate the change. The meaning system becomes temporarily suspended as stipulated by our *reconstruction* postulate: The personal meaning system of an individual who faces major value changes will become temporarily dis-integrated.

A number of life-span psychologists have theorized about the development of changing values and meanings over the life course. Most notable is Erikson (1963), who linked societal values with developmental tasks to be accomplished. Meanings for the adolescent, young, and middle-aged adult are centered on establishing a stable identity, forming intimate relationships, and being productive and creative. The task of late life is to develop a sense of integrity, an appreciation of why and how one has lived.

Buhler (1959) identified four developmental phases that emphasize changes in goal setting (personal values): expansion, consolidation, evaluation, and integration. Meaning is derived at each phase through satisfying one or more of four basic tendencies (need-satisfying, adaptive, creative, inner order). In the early phases, successes and failures in life are evaluated, and new directions for the course of one's life are contemplated. During the later years, integration becomes the primary goal.

Jung (1971) theorized about a changing set of values over the life span. The first half of life is spent in preparation for living; primary emphasis is on materialistic or instrumental values. The second half is spent in preparation for old age and death, with more emphasis on spiritual or transcendent values. Meaning in the later years is derived through an examination of the "inner" part of life, through contemplation, reflection, and self-evaluation. A large-scale series of studies, known as the Kansas City Studies of Adult Life, provide some evidence for this claim (Neugarten, 1977).

The common thread of these positions is that as the individual ages, the developmental task is directed toward integrating and transcending the experiences of a lifetime. Integration becomes a meaning-producing process. Such a theoretical view has also been advanced by others, particularly by Butler (1963), who focused on the process of life review, and Birren (1964), who focused on the processes of reconciliation and integration through guided autobiography (Birren & Hedlund, 1987). Buhler and Massarik's (1968) analysis of biographies and the cross-sectional investigations of personality (Neugarten & Associates, 1964) and life transitions (Thurnher, 1975) offer empirical support for the important role of integration in the quest for meaning by the elderly.

These observations suggest the following *developmental* hypothesis: The personal meaning system of an individual will become increasingly more integrated as a function of age.

Death, Meaning, and Religion

As one enters into the final stage of life, and the prospect of personal death looms larger, many existential questions press for an answer: Do I have a reason for living when I am confined to a nursing home or a hospital bed? Has my life been worthwhile? Is there ultimate meaning when I disappear from the face of the earth?

According to Erikson (1963), the elderly person faces the developmental crisis of integrity versus despair, attempts to assert that life has meaning and purpose, and prepares himself or herself for the inevitable end. This crisis triggers the life review process (Butler, 1963), in which the individual reevaluates the past and attempts to integrate the entire life into a meaningful whole. However, life review does not always achieve integrity. When past conflicts remain unresolved, and discrepancies in life remain unreconciled, feelings of guilt and despair may set in. In such cases, the person would have difficulties finding personal meaning, and accepting death, unless he or she has some other means of achieving integration, such as religion.

Since many of the existential issues in the last development crisis are related to religious concerns (i.e., ultimate meaning, personal destiny, and so on), religion provides both direction and support for the elderly to put life and death into perspective (Achenbaum, 1985). For example, religious beliefs that incorporate immortality, the existence of heaven, and ultimate meaning, are effective antidotes to death anxiety. In fact, a number of studies have shown that religious elderly are less fearful of death than are their nonreligious counterparts (Faunce & Fulton, 1958; Jeffers, Nichols, & Eisdorfer, 1961; Jeffers & Verwoerdt, 1969).

There is a vast literature on the important role of religion in the discovery of personal meaning. Space will not permit a thorough review of this literature. We would quote from a few authorities to illustrate the scope of religious influence on personal meaning.

Jung (1938): "No matter what the world thinks about religious experiences, the one who has it possesses the great treasure . . . that provides him with some of life's meaning and beauty" (p. 113). William James (1902): "When we see all things in God, and refer all things to Him, we read in common matters superior expressions of meaning" (p. 475). Allport (1960): "Religious strivings . . . often originate in the desires of the body, in the pursuit of meanings beyond the range of our intellectual capacity, and in the longing that value be conserved" (pp. 107–108). Frankl (1963, 1969) also emphasizes a person's spiritual (noetic) nature and the importance of spiritual commitment as a basis for discovering personal meaning.

The weight of evidence seems to support the above views in that religion tends to be positively correlated with life satisfaction (Blazer & Palmore, 1976; Hendricks & Hendricks, 1977) and with meaning in life. Paloutzian (1981), for example, found religious converts to score significantly higher on the Purpose in Life (PIL) test (Crumbaugh & Maholick, 1969) compared to nonconverts. Crandall and Rasmussen (1975) found the religious value of salvation to be associated with higher meaning in life. Soderstrom and Wright (1977) report data associating an intrinsic religious orientation to high PIL scores.

We have shown that the shadow of death prompts the quest for meaning in life through life review and religious beliefs. There is yet another way death contributes to meaning. According to Frankl (1971), the prospect of death motivates individuals to respond to opportunities and to assume personal responsibilities. In other words, one can reduce existential despair by transforming

> . . . a given reality into a possibility, into a potentiality for accomplishing something. An apparent obstacle or a limitation in life may become a source for new personal meaning and self-realization. Thus, for Frankl, death is not the end but rather the beginning of the birth of meaning in human living. (Kovacs, 1982, p. 202)

While religious beliefs in an afterlife promote an approach-oriented acceptance in which the individual regards death as a passage to a more blessed existence (Gesser, Wong, & Reker, 1987–1988), Frankl's emphasis on commitment and responsibility promotes a neutral type of acceptance in which the individual accepts death as an inevitable aspect of life, and accepts the challenge of making the most of life's opportunities. These two types of death acceptance need not be mutually exclusive; in fact, they can be complementary to each other.

Our analysis has revealed that there are at least three channels whereby an individual can find meaning in the face of death: review of the past, commitment to the present, and belief in immortality and ultimate meaning. These three channels may work in concert to transform death into a meaningful reality. This conceptual analysis once again illustrates the importance of time perspective in the development of personal meaning.

MEASUREMENT APPROACHES

A viable, useful theoretical system requires appropriate procedures by which the concepts can be transported into the empirical arena. We will identify existing procedures and offer additional tailor-made measures for testing some of our postulates and hypotheses. Emphasis on individual processes allows us to study the characteristics of a single person in a specific situation or to aggregate over homogeneous subgroups in broader environmental contexts. The strength of this approach lies in the use of quantitative and qualitative measurements and multiple research methods (e.g., open-ended questionnaires, structured interviews, personal documents, life journals, self-report scales, in-depth observations). The merit of this approach has been demonstrated in a series of studies by Ryff (1986). Working within a phenomenological and interpretive framework, Ryff employed structured self-report inventories to explore people's personal experiences of change in values and personality as they age. This approach provides a deeper and broader understanding of the aging process.

Currently, personal documents such as the life history narrative (Freeman, 1984), life review (Butler, 1963), biographies (Buhler, 1959), guided autobiography (Birren & Hedlund, 1987), and the life-drawing technique (Whitbourne, 1985; Whitbourne & Dannefer, 1985–1986), are enjoying a revival as acceptable sources of information in understanding human behavior and development. The guided autobiographical approach, in particular, appears to be a very promising technique for investigating the development of personal meaning in life (Birren & Hedlund, 1987). An autobiographical statement is a retrospective personal account of how an individual perceives the course of his or her life. Important information is obtained on how the individual interprets and attaches meaning to the experiences of a lifetime. An individual who constructs his or her own "story" is able to look back over the flow of past events, to relate them to the present, and to project them into the future. As such, guided autobiography can be used as a powerful tool in restoring lost meaning and in facilitating the reconstruction of the personal meaning system.

Whitbourne's (1985) life-drawing technique is a measure based on the premise "that it is the individual's cognitive and emotional construction of the life span that will ultimately determine how the individual will develop through the experiences of a lifetime" (p. 615). The life drawing, an open-ended technique, asks the respondent to draw his or her life on a blank sheet of paper that contains only a horizontal line labeled "age and/or year." Through the drawing, an individual's temporal orientation and integration of past, present, and future can be profiled. Much like guided autobiography, the life-drawing technique can trigger the life-review process, reveal changes in identity, and index sources of personal meaning through the identification of values.

Ebersole and DeVogler-Ebersole (1985) use the personal-document approach in their assessment of *types* and *depth* of meaning in life. Scripts obtained through biographical sources or provided by respondents are content-analyzed for sources of meaning. Unfortunately, these researchers do not provide a conceptual definition of meaning in life, nor is their approach guided by theory.

Self-report scales of meaning and purpose in life have also been constructed. The most frequently cited is the Purpose in Life (PIL) test, a scale designed to measure the *degree* to which an individual experiences a sense of meaning and purpose in life (Crumbaugh & Maholick, 1969). However, item heterogeneity and susceptibility to socially desirable responding have been cited as weaknesses inherent in the scale (Battista & Almond, 1973; Ebersole & DeVogler-Ebersole, 1985; Yalom, 1980).

Battista and Almond (1973) developed the Life Regard Index, a 28-item, 5-point scale designed to measure "an individual's belief that he is fulfilling a life-framework or life-goal that provides him with a highly valued understanding of his life" (p. 410). Their scale is based on the concept of positive life regard, which, conceptually, may be related more to the concept of self-esteem than to the construct of "meaningful life."

The need for additional tailor-made measures for testing our postulates and hypotheses is apparent. We have developed, or are in the process of developing, a number of suitable scales and techniques, including the Sources of Meaning Profile, the implication ladder, meaning system complexity, the life and death attitude profiles, and the Personal Meaning in Time Perspective Scale.

Sources of Meaning Profile

We have developed a scale to measure the sources and degree of personal meaning in one's life — the Sources of Meaning Profile (SOMP). The SOMP is primarily a measure of present meaning. The individual is asked to rate 13 sources of meaning (pleasurable or leisure activities, meeting basic needs, creative abilities, personal relationships, personal achievement, personal growth, religious beliefs and activities, social or political causes, service to others or altruism, acceptance and recognition by others, enduring values and ideals, traditions and culture, and legacy) in terms of the amount of meaning derived from each source. Subjects respond to 7-point Likert scales anchored by "none" (1) and "a great deal" (7). These sources of meaning can be grouped a priori into our four levels of personal meaning, and indices of variety in meaning sources can be derived. Thus, the SOMP offers a way to test the depth, breadth, and meaning system postulates.

Implication Ladder

The implication ladder can reveal the structure of the personal meaning system. In this approach, the individual is asked to identify a source of meaning and to indicate what it is about the source that makes it meaningful. This generally elicits another construct dimension, and the individual is asked once again why that construct is meaningful. For example, suppose an individual finds meaning in *personal relationships*. When asked why, he or she responds with the positive pole of a new construct, namely, *commitment to others*. When asked why for the second time, he or she responds, *affectionate bond*. When asked why for the third time, he or she says, *security*. A series of subordinate constructs are thus revealed, and the process is repeated until at least 10 constructs are elicited. If 10 constructs cannot be elicited from one source of meaning, another source is identified. The resultant ladder of implications describes the structure of the person's meaning system (Bannister & Mair, 1968).

Meaning System Complexity

The complexity (differentiation and integration) of the personal meaning system elicited by way of the implication ladder can also be measured. For each of the 10 constructs, the individual is asked to provide the opposite pole (e.g., security–*insecurity*). A 7-point scale is constructed for each construct; the positive pole is always assigned the value 7, the negative pole, the value 1. Each of the 13 sources of meaning in the SOMP are rated on the 10 constructs. The ratings can be cast into a 13×10 matrix. Alternatively, personal meaning constructs can be provided. These constructs should reflect the components of personal meaning (e.g., meaningful–meaningless, order–chaos, valuable–

worthless, significant–insignificant, fulfilling–empty, desirable–undesirable). Indices of differentiation and integration can be obtained by methods described by Reker (1974).

Life and Death Attitude Scales

The *degree* and *strength* of motivation to find personal meaning in life can be measured by the self-report attitude scale constructed by Reker and Peacock (1981). The Life Attitude Profile (LAP) is a multidimensional measure based on Frankl's (1963) meaning theory. It consists of seven dimensions: Life Purpose, Existential Vacuum, Life Control, Death Acceptance, Will to Meaning, Goal Seeking, and Future Meaning. The LAP is a psychometrically sound instrument that has been used in life-span research (Reker, Peacock, & Wong, 1987).

A complementary instrument to the LAP is the Death Attitude Profile (DAP) constructed by Gesser, Wong, and Reker (1987–88). The DAP is a multidimensional scale of the entire range of death attitudes, including Fear of Death/Dying, Neutral Acceptance, Approach-Oriented Acceptance, and Escape-Oriented Acceptance. The DAP has also been shown to be psychometrically sound. The different dimensions are sensitive to age differences and have different correlates with various personality characteristics (e.g., happiness, hopelessness, suicidal tendencies).

Personal Meaning in Time Perspective (PMIT)

Throughout this chapter, we have stressed the importance of time perspective in personal meaning. We have reiterated the conviction that at any point in time an individual derives meaning from past, present, and future. We are now in the process of developing an instrument that takes into account the temporal dimension of personal meaning.

Our strategy is to focus on reminiscence for past meaning, commitment for present meaning, and optimism for future meaning. For example, in the case of past meaning, the individual will be asked to review his or her past life as a whole; to examine major domains of life, such as achievement, relationships, and life event change; and to decide to what extent these past experiences provide meaning for his or her present existence.

Regarding present meaning, the individual will be asked to indicate the amount of meaning he or she derives from a number of present commitments, such as achievement and relationships. The measurement of present meaning will focus on both the process of pursuing and the actual realization of worthwhile objectives.

With respect to future meaning, the individual is asked to indicate the amount of meaning he or she derives from anticipation of achieving future goals, as well as from beliefs in afterlife.

The purpose of the PMIT is to determine the amount of contribution from past, present, and future to personal meaning, and the qualitative difference in meaning structure in these three time orientations. Such an instrument will be extremely useful in studying personal meaning from a life-span perspective.

IMPLICATIONS

In her review of personality and aging, Neugarten (1977) encouraged researchers to combine the phenomenological and the objective perspectives as a way of diversifying the comprehension and the methods of studying phenomena. Gergen (1980) cautioned theorists not to become committed to only one view of science, but to remain open to alternative conceptualizations. Our approach incorporates these views and provides new building blocks for theory construction and data collection with implications for research, allied disciplines, and public policy.

Implications for Research

Throughout the chapter, we have proposed a number of personal meaning postulates and related hypotheses, namely:

Fundamental postulate: Every individual is motivated to seek and to find personal meaning in human existence.

Breadth postulate: An individual's degree of personal meaning will increase in direct proportion to his or her diversification of sources of meaning.

Depth postulate: An individual's degree of personal meaning will increase in direct proportion to his or her commitment to higher levels of meaning.

Meaning system postulate: The personal meaning system of an individual who has available a variety of sources of meaning and who strives for higher levels of personal meaning will be highly differentiated and integrated.

Choice postulate: An individual chooses for himself or herself a position on the meaning-producing continuum for the construction of his or her personal meaning system.

Reconstruction postulate: The personal meaning system of an individual who faces major value changes will become temporarily dis-integrated.

Developmental hypothesis: The personal meaning system of an individual will become increasingly more integrated as a function of age.

Individuality hypothesis: The personal meaning system of an individualist will be more differentiated and integrated compared to that of a conformist.

In addition, we provide a number of appropriate measuring instruments and suggest different research methods. The retrospective methods of biography, autobiography, and the historical narrative may encourage more longitudinal studies. Personal documents are relatively inexpensive and yet provide important information on an individual's passage through life. Our six postulates and two hypotheses and the means for systematic measurement should pave the way for future theory construction and research concerning aging as an individual process.

Implication for Allied Disciplines

We began with the hope that our individualistic perspective would encourage "real" interdisciplinary collaboration. From a psychological perspective, personal meanings yield insight into an individual's perception of himself or herself as changing or unchanging over the life span. From a sociological perspective, personal meanings reveal the individual's valuation of social norms at successive life stages. We strongly believe that the derivation of personal meaning in life is a key process in successful aging that can have positive psychological, social, economic, and medical implications. Individuals are not victims of their own age. They possess personal resources and competencies. They can be active and independent and take advantage of opportunities for continued growth. In short, there is tremendous potential for intrapersonal development.

Furthermore, the information obtained by exploring the sources of meaning in individual lives can be shared with others, thus optimizing individuals' welfare and that of society. The direct benefits to society may be at the level of reducing mounting health care costs. In the medical field, the emphasis on personal meaning as a resource will help focus attention on prevention as opposed to treatment strategies. Prevention can have the dual effect of promoting a sense of high-level wellness in adequately functioning individuals and in developing the potential of individuals at risk for loss of meaning.

Personal Meaning and the Brain

Studies of personal meaning also have implications for neuroscience. If we accept the dualism premise that every subjective conscious process has its parallel counterpart in objective processes within the brain, then the personal meaning system must have its anatomical substrates within the brain. Since no one has explicitly investigated the relationship between personal meaning and brain structures, we can be only speculative.

In the case of definitional meaning of a verbal symbol or signal learning in Pavlovian conditioning, sensory input is essential. Miller (1981) postulates that this type of cognitive learning involves diffusely connected neural networks in which every neuron has the potentiality of influencing every other neuron. Miller also hypothesizes that omniconnected networks are located in the cerebral neocortex.

Personal meaning is further removed from sensory experiences than definitional meaning. Personal meaning involves reflections on symbolic representations of events and definitional meanings. Following Miller's reasoning, we can also hypothesize that the neocortex is involved in the construction of personal meaning.

We can also make some tentative statements about hemisphere differences in existential beliefs and meaning. Frank (1977) proposes that transcendental experiences and beliefs are mediated primarily by the right hemisphere, whereas analytic and verbal reasoning are primarily associated with the left hemisphere. Mandell (1980), on the other hand, believes that both hemispheres, as well as the limbic system are involved in transcendental experiences. Henry (1986; this volume) talks about the symbol system of myths or archetypes as being derived from neuroendocrine patterns of instinctual response. "They form the link between the emotions of our genetic inheritance and the abstract decisions of science and reason" (Henry, 1986, p. 51).

Since personal meanings are related to values and needs, brain structures involved in various physiological needs also play a part in the construction of personal meaning. The meaning assigned to existence may be related to genetically determined survival need (Clark, 1982).

Perhaps one way to clarify the relationship between meaning and brain structures is to investigate changes in personal meaning following lesions in various parts of the brain. It seems to us that meaning changes following brain damage may have more profound effects on personality and behavior than do lesion-produced memory deficits.

Implication for Public Policy

Our society is facing a future in which a larger number of aging individuals are living 20 or 30 years beyond retirement. Unless steps are taken to provide aging with a sense of meaning, the personal resources (e.g., wisdom, competence, experience) of our elderly will be lost to society. In addition, many members may become increasingly at risk for mental and physical health problems. What is needed is a "culturally viable ideal of old age [that] legitimates norms and roles appropriate to the last stage of life" (Cole, 1984, p. 329). Our society continues to be hung up on viewing the elderly as unproductive recipients of society's benevolence and mere products of historical forces. Public policy must be directed toward *increasing the options* available to the elderly in the areas of work, education, personal development, and so on (i.e., sources of meaning). Public policy needs to marshal individual meanings into a collective and in so doing give birth to renewed social meanings. The nurturing of renewed social meanings by the social system will help provide a "new opium for the aging population."

SUMMARY AND CONCLUSION

The aim of this chapter was to generate a theory not *about* aging but about what growing old *means* to those who are experiencing it. We began by documenting the emerging trend toward an individualistic perspective, espoused by a new breed of social scientists and ordinary people.

In the first section, we introduced the interpretive paradigm as a promising approach understanding the conscious experiences of an individual. We stressed the importance of viewing the individual as an active, self-constructing, self-reflecting agent, embedded in social, cultural, and historical contexts.

In the second section, we defined personal meaning and elaborated on its nature, drawing specifically on the seminal theoretical contributions of Frankl (1963), Maddi (1970), and Kelly (1955). The search for personal meaning was offered as our fundamental postulate. We proposed a personal meaning system, closely tied to shared and personal values. We identified sources and levels of personal meaning and offered the breadth, depth, and meaning system postulates.

In the same section, we advocated two broad meaning-producing contexts, social definitions and self-definitions, and introduced the choice postulate. The choice postulate is considered the key component of our conceptualization of aging as an individual process. We argued that while the individual lives out his or her life within societal constraints, he or she has a certain amount of freedom to choose how life is to be lived. Such freedom increases choices that influence the structure of the meaning system. We offered the individuality hypothesis to test this linkage.

In the third section, we concentrated on the development of personal meaning across the life span. We argued that personal meaning is built on the foundation of experiences, values, and beliefs. We also focused on the meaning of psychological time, the life timetable, religiosity, and death, the transcendence of which provides continuity and gives meaning to existence. We noted that changing values create shifts on the social/self continuum and influence the structure of the personal meaning system in ways stipulated by the reconstruction postulate.

In the fourth section, we briefly outlined a number of measures and methods most appropriate to our theoretical position and emphasized the importance of taking into account time perspectives. These were offered to give researchers a vehicle for testing our postulates and hypotheses.

Finally, we drew attention to a number of implications of our theoretical view for allied disciplines concerned with human development, research, and public policy. The primary goal of this chapter was to provide a conceptual analysis of personal meaning from the interpretive perspective, and to highlight the importance of meaning in providing fulfillment within the constraints of aging and dying.

REFERENCES

Achenbaum, W. A. (1985). Religion in the lives of the elderly: Contemporary and historical perspectives. In G. Lesnoff-Caravaglia (Ed.), *Values, ethics and aging* (pp. 98–116). New York: Human Sciences Press.

Allport, G. W. (1960). *The individual and his religion.* New York: Macmillan.

Allport, G. W., Vernon, P. E., & Lindzey, G. (1951). *Study of values: A scale for measuring the dominant interests in personality.* Boston: Houghton-Mifflin.

Atwood, G. E., & Tomkins, S. S. (1976). On the subjectivity of personality theory. *Journal of the History of the Behavioral Sciences, 12,* 166–177.

Baird, R. M. (1985). Meaning in life: Discovered or created? *Journal of Religion and Health, 24,* 117–124.

Bannister, D., & Mair, J. M. M. (1968). *The evaluation of personal constructs.* New York: Academic Press.

Battista, J., & Almond, R. (1973). The development of meaning in life. *Psychiatry, 36,* 409–427.

Bengtson, V. L. (1975). Generation and family effects in value socialization. *American Sociological Review, 40,* 358–371.

Berger, P. L., & Luckman, T. (1966). *The social construction of reality: A treatise in the sociology of knowledge.* Garden City, NY: Doubleday.

Bergin, A. E. (1980). Psychotherapy and religious values. *Journal of Consulting and Clinical Psychology, 48,* 95–105.

Bertaux, D. (Ed.). (1981). *Biography and society: The life history approach in the social sciences.* Beverly Hills, CA: Sage Publications

Bieri, J. (1961). Complexity-simplicity as a personality variable in cognitive and preferential behavior. In D. W. Fiske & S. Maddi (Eds.), *Functions of varied experience* (pp. 355–379). New York: Dorsey.

Birren, J. E. (1964). *The psychology of aging.* Englewood Cliffs, NJ: Prentice-Hall.

Birren, J. E., & Hedlund, B. (1987). Contributions of autobiography to developmental psychology. In N. Isenberg (Ed.), *Contemporary topics in developmental psychology.* New York: Wiley.

Blazer, D., & Palmore, E. (1976). Religion and aging in a longitudinal panel. *Gerontologist, 16,* 82–85.

Blumer, H. (1969). *Symbolic interactionism: Perspective and method.* Englewood Cliffs, NJ: Prentice-Hall.

Braginsky, D., & Braginsky, B. (1974). *Mainstream psychology: A critique.* New York: Holt, Rinehart & Winston.

Buhler, C. (1959). Theoretical observations about life's basic tendencies. *American Journal of Psychotherapy, 13,* 561–581.

Buhler, C., & Massarik, F. (Eds.). (1968). *The course of human life*. New York: Springer Publishing Co.

Butler, R. (1963). The life review: An interpretation of reminiscence in the aged. *Psychiatry, 4*, 1–18.

Carlson, R. (1982). Personology lives! *Contemporary Psychology, 27*, 7–8.

Chein, I. (1972). *The science of behavior and the image of man*. New York: Basic Books.

Clark, S. R. L. (1982). *The nature of the beast: Are animals moral?* Oxford: Oxford University Press.

Cole, T. R. (1984). Aging, meaning, and well-being: Musings of a cultural historian. *International Journal of Aging and Human Development, 19*, 329–336.

Côté, E. J., & Reker, G. T. (1979). Cognitive complexity and ego identity formation: A synthesis of cognitive and ego psychology. *Social Behavior and Personality, 7*, 107–112.

Crandall, J. E., & Rasmussen, R. D. (1975). Purpose in life as related to specific values. *Journal of Clinical Psychology, 31*, 483–485.

Crumbaugh, J. C., & Maholick, L. T. (1969). *Manual of instruction for the Purpose in Life Test*. Munster, IN: Psychometric Affiliates.

DeVogler, K. L., & Ebersole, P. (1980). Categorization of college students' meaning in life. *Journal of Psychology, 46*, 387–390.

DeVogler, K. L., & Ebersole, P. (1983). Young adolescents' meaning in life. *Psychological Reports, 52*, 427–431.

Ebersole, P., & DeVogler-Ebersole, K. (1985). Meaning in life of the eminent and the average. *Journal of Social Behavior and Personality, 1*, 83–94.

Erikson, E. H. (1963). *Childhood and society*. New York: Norton.

Faunce, W. A., & Fulton, R. L. (1958). The sociology of death: A neglected area of research. *Social Forces, 36*, 205–209.

Feinstein, A. D. (1979). Personal mythology as a paradigm for a holistic psychology. *American Journal of Orthopsychiatry, 49*, 198–217.

Fisk, R. C. (1980). The effect of loss of meaning on the mental and physical well-being of the aged. *Dissertation Abstracts International, 40*, 3925-B.

Frank, J. D. (1977). Nature and function of belief systems: Humanism and transcendental religion. *American Psychologist, 32*, 555–559.

Frankl, V. E. (1963). *Man's search for meaning*. New York: Washington Square Press.

Frankl, V. E. (1969). *The will to meaning*. New York: New American Library.

Frankl, V. E. (1971). *The doctor and the soul* (2nd ed.) New York: Bantam Books.

Frankl, V. E. (1978). *The unheard cry for meaning: Psychotherapy and humanism*. New York: Simon & Schuster.

Freeman, J. (1985, May). Everybody is reading biographies. *Los Angeles Herald Examiner*. Sunday, May 26, 1985, Section F, pp. 1–2.

Freeman, M. (1984). History, narrative, and life-span developmental knowledge. *Human Development, 27*, 1–19.

Gergen, K. J. (1980). The emerging crisis in life-span developmental theory. In P. B. Baltes & O. G. Brim (Eds.), *Life-span development and behavior* (Vol. 3, pp. 31–63). New York: Academic Press.

Gesser, G., Wong, P. T. P., & Reker, G. T. (1987–88). Death attitudes across the life-span: The development and validation of the Death Attitude Profile (DAP). *Omega, 18*, 113–128.

Gonzalez, A., & Zimbardo, P. G. (1985, March). Time in perspective. *Psychology Today*, pp. 21–26.

Gubrium, J., & Buckholdt, D. (1977). *Toward maturity*. San Francisco: Jossey-Bass.

Gutmann, D. (1981). Observations on culture and mental health in later life. In J. E. Birren & R. B. Sloane (Eds.), *Handbook of mental health and aging* (pp. 429–447). Englewood Cliffs, NJ: Prentice-Hall.

Hedlund, B., & Birren, J. E. (1984). *Distribution of types of meaning in life across women*. Paper presented at the Gerontological Society of America, San Antonio, Texas, November, 1984.

Hendricks, J., & Hendricks, C. D. (1977). *Aging in mass society: Myths and realities*. Cambridge, MA: Winthrop.

Henry, J. P. (1986). Religious experience, archetypes, and the neurophysiology of emotions. *Zygon, 21*, 47–74.

Hickey, T. (1980). *Health and aging*. Monterey, CA: Brooks/Cole.

Hocking, W. E. (1957). *The meaning of immortality in human experience*. New York: Harper & Brothers.

James, W. (1902). *The varieties of religious experience*. Garden City, NY: Doubleday.

Jeffers, F., Nichols, C., & Eisdorfer, C. (1961). Attitudes of older persons toward death. *Journal of Gerontology, 16*, 53–56.

Jeffers, F. C., & Verwoerdt, A. (1969). How the old face death. In W. E. Busse & E. Pfeiffer (Eds.), *Behavior and adaptation in late life* (pp. 163–181). Boston: Little, Brown.

Jung, C. G. (1938). *Psychology and religion*. New Haven, CT: Yale University Press.

Jung, C. G. (1971). The stages of life. In J. Campbell (Ed.), *The portable Jung* (pp. 3–22). New York: Viking Press.

Kaminsky, M. (1984). *The uses of reminiscence: New ways of working with older adults*. New York: Haworth Press.

Keen, E. (1975). *A primer in phenomenological psychology*. New York: Holt, Rinehart & Winston.

Kelly, G. A. (1955). *The psychology of personal constructs*. New York: W. W. Norton.

Kenyon, G. (1985). The meaning of aging: Vital existence vs. personal existence. *Human Values and Aging Newsletter, 8*, 4–6.

Klinger, E. (1977). *Meaning and void*. Minneapolis: University of Minnesota Press.

Kovacs, G. (1982). The philosophy of death in Viktor E. Frankl. *Journal of Phenomenological Psychology, 13*, 197–209.

Levinson, D. J. (1978). *The seasons of a man's life*. New York: Alfred A. Knopf.

Lewin, K. (1948). Time perspective and morale. In K. Lewin (Ed.), *Resolving social conflicts* (pp. 103–124). New York: Harper and Row.

Maddi, S. R. (1970). The search for meaning. In A. Williams & M. Page (Eds.), *The Nebraska Symposium on Motivation* (pp. 134–183). Lincoln, NE: University of Nebraska Press.

Mandell, A. J. (1980). Toward a psychobiology of transcendence: God in the brain. In J. M. Davidson & P. J. Davidson (Eds.), *The psychobiology of consciousness* (pp. 379–464). New York: Plenum Press.

Markson, E. W. (1973). Readjustment to time in old age: A life cycle approach. *Psychiatry, 36*, 37–48.

Maslow, A. H. (1968). *Toward a psychology of being*. New York: D. Van Nostrand.

McAdams, D. P. (1985). *Power, intimacy, and the life story: Personological inquiries into identity*. Homewood, IL: Dorsey Press.

Miller, R. (1981). *Meaning and purpose in the intact brain*. Oxford: Clarendon Press.

Murray, H. A. (1938). *Explorations in personality*. New York: Oxford University Press.

Neugarten, B. L. (1969). Continuities and discontinuities of psychological issues into adult life. *Human Development, 12*, 121–130.

Neugarten, B. L. (1977). Personality and aging. In J. E. Birren & K. W. Schaie (Eds.), *Handbook of the psychology of aging* (pp. 626–649). New York: Van Nostrand Reinhold.

Neugarten, B. L. (1984). Interpretive social science and research on aging. In A. Rossi (Ed.), *Gender and the life course* (pp. 291–300). New York: Aldine.

Neugarten, B. L., & Associates. (1964). *Personality in middle and late life*. New York: Atherton.

Nuttin, J. (1985). *Future time perspective and motivation*. Hillsdale, NJ: Erlbaum.

Paloutzian, R. F. (1981). Purpose in life and value changes following conversion. *Journal of Personality and Social Psychology, 41*, 1153–1160.

Rabinow, P., & Sullivan, W. M. (Eds.). (1979). *Interpretive social science: A reader*. Berkeley, CA.: University of California Press.

Rakowski, W. (1979). Future time perspective in later adulthood: Review and research directions. *Experimental Aging Research, 5*, 43–88.

Reker, G. T. (1974). Interpersonal conceptual structures of emotionally disturbed and normal boys. *Journal of Abnormal Psychology, 83*, 380–386.

Reker, G. T. (1985). Toward a holistic model of health, behavior, and aging. In J. E. Birren & J. Livingston (Eds.), *Cognition, stress, and aging* (pp. 47–71). Englewood Cliffs, NJ: Prentice-Hall.

Reker, G. T., & Peacock, E. J. (1981). The Life Attitude Profile (LAP): A multidimensional instrument for assessing attitudes toward life. *Canadian Journal of Behavioural Science, 13*, 264–273.

Reker, G. T., Peacock, E. J., & Wong, P. T. P. (1987). Meaning and purpose in life and well-being: A life-span perspective. *Journal of Gerontology, 42*, 44–49.

Reker, G. T., & Wong, P. T. P. (1985). Personal optimism, physical and mental health: The triumph of successful aging. In J. E. Birren & J. Livingston (Eds.), *Cognition, stress, and aging* (pp. 134–173). Englewood Cliffs, NJ: Prentice-Hall.

Rokeach, M. (1973). *The nature of human values*. New York: Free Press.

Runyan, J. W. (1982). *Life histories and psychobiography*. New York: Oxford University Press.

Ryff, C. D. (1986). The subjective construction of self and society: An agenda for life-span research. In V. W. Marshall (Ed.), *Later life: The social psychology of aging* (pp. 33–74). Beverly Hills, CA: Sage Publications.

Shostrom, E. L. (1968). Time as an integrating factor. In C. Buhler & F. Massarik (Eds.), *The course of human life* (pp. 351–359). New York: Springer Publishing Co.

Soderstrom, D., & Wright, W. E. (1977). Religious orientation and meaning in life. *Journal of Clinical Psychology, 33*, 65–68.

Starr, J. M. (1982–1983). Toward a social phenomenology of aging: Studying the self-process in biographical work. *International Journal of Aging and Human Development, 16*, 255–270.

Thomae, H. (1970). Theory of aging and cognitive theory of personality. *Human Development, 13*, 1–16.

Thurnher, M. (1975). Continuities and discontinuities in value orientation. In M. F. Lowenthal, M. Thurnher, D. Chiriboga, & Associates (Eds.), *Four stages of life: A comparative study of women and men facing transitions* (pp. 176–200). San Francisco: Jossey-Bass.

Weber, M. (1905). *The Protestant ethic and the spirit of capitalism*. New York: Scribners.

Weisskopf-Joelson, E. (1968). Meaning as an integrating factor. In C. Buhler & F. Massarik (Eds.), *The course of human life: A study of goals in the humanistic perspective* (pp. 359–383). New York: Springer Publishing Co.

Whitbourne, S. (1985). The psychological construction of the life span. In J. E. Birren & K. W. Schaie (Eds.), *Handbook of the psychology of aging* (pp. 594–618). New York: Van Nostrand Reinhold.

Whitbourne, S., & Dannefer, W. D. (1985–1986). The "life drawing" as a measure of time perspective in adulthood. *International Journal of Aging and Human Development, 22*, 147–155.

Yalom, I. D. (1980). *Existential psychotherapy*. New York: Basic Books.

12

Cognitive Potential Throughout Life*

Marion Perlmutter

Different terms have been used to describe age-related changes that occur at particular points in the life span. Often these terms carry positive or negative connotations. For example, age change from birth to maturity often is referred to as *development* and assumed to be positive, whereas age change prior to death is referred to as *aging* and assumed to be negative. It is important to note, however, that virtually all psychological processes are the manifestation of a host of underlying factors, each of which may increase, decrease, or remain stable throughout any given portion of life. The present chapter argues that our society has inappropriately focused on decline when describing age change in late life. Although there is, no doubt, some decline in late life, there is also evidence of maintenance or improvement of some functions. Research, therefore, should focus on variables that can maintain or increase performance throughout life. Findings from this perspective could positively impact the quality of life of older adults, as well as allow society to take better advantage of a significant resource, its older population. Moreover, findings from such research could provide understanding about life-span development that goes beyond present theoretical conceptualizations.

*This chapter was written while the author was a fellow at the Institute for Advanced Study at the Andrus Gerontology Center of the University of Southern California. Thanks are extended to the staff and fellows of the Institute, who contributed to an extremely stimulating, productive, and enjoyable time; as well as to the Brookdale Foundation, whose National Fellowship Award made this opportunity possible.

PERSPECTIVES ON DEVELOPMENT AND AGING

All things change through time. When considered from the perspective of the beginning, this change is referred to as *development*; and when considered from the perspective of the end, this change is referred to as *aging*. Age-related changes may be viewed as two distinct phenomenon or as different vantage points in a multiprocess phenomenon.

According to a *dual-phenomenon conception of age change*, two opposite forces direct two separate kinds of age change. Development is driven by processes that move things away from their beginning state, and aging is driven by processes that move things toward their end state. From this perspective, development is assumed to reflect growth, and aging to reflect deterioration; that is, describing change as development or aging connotes a specific directionality as well as a specific quality of change.

For contrast, according to a *multiprocess conception of age change*, separate, opposing forces are not the underlying factors in age change. Throughout life, age-related change is multicausal and multidirectional. *Development* and *aging* simply describe changes that occur with the accumulation or diminution of time. Development accrues with an increase in time from beginning, and aging accrues with a reduction of time until ending. From this more neutral perspective, development and aging do not reflect different phenomena. That is, the difference in labels refers only to differences in vantage points.

The appropriateness of viewing development and aging as different perspectives on a single, multiprocess age-change phenomenon that operates throughout life, versus viewing them as two separate opposing phenomena that predominate at particular portions of the life span, depends upon whether there are distinct teleologic forces operating at early and later life to drive things away from their beginning and toward their ending. Thus, it depends upon whether there is only age-specified growth and decline or multidirectional, multicausal age change throughout life.

At a biological level, current thinking favors the dual-phenomenon conception. One process results in physical growth that expands organisms beyond their beginning state (conception) in early life, and another process results in physical deterioration that retracts biological systems toward their death state in late life. However, this view of aging is rapidly changing. Increasingly, many of the age-related biological changes that had been assumed to be attributable to programmed aging are now known to be caused by health or environmental factors. Still, most biologists currently subscribe to the view that at least part of the decline that is evidenced toward the end of life is caused by a biologically programmed process that moves organisms toward death (see Cristofalo, this volume; Finch, this volume). Thus, in observing age change in biological functions it is appropriate to expect eventual decline, and in building biological theories it is appropriate to include separate dynamic processes of development (growth) and aging (deterioration).

At a psychological level, however, it is probably unnecessary, or even inappropriate, to assume distinct phenomena of development and aging. Throughout life, age change is multidirectional and multicausal. Moreover, there appears to be no age-based dynamism that moves humans toward psychological death. Even the "death wish," which some believe is part of human nature, is not analogous to the time-based biological process of programmed aging. Since no death-directed psychological process seems to underlie psychological change in healthy humans, it may be misguided to posit separate processes of development and aging in psychological theory. Rather, it seems preferable to view *psychological development and aging as different vantage points on a multiprocess phenomenon*, referred to here as life-span development.

The purpose of this chapter is to develop the case that psychological aging should be viewed in this more neutral way. *The view that late life is dominated by an aging process that produces decline, while perhaps reasonable for characterizing biological functions, is rejected for describing psychological functions*. The argument developed here should not be taken as a claim against the reality of some decline with age, nor even of programmed decline with age. Hair grays, movements slow, and bodies become frail. The point is that these changes reflect physical health and/or biological aging. Whereas some biological aging undoubtedly limits psychological function, there appears to be no separate inevitable decline in the psychological underpinnings of behavior. For example, in healthy individuals there appears to be no age-related deterioration of the knowledge base that supports thinking and action, nor is it likely that there is age-related fragmentation of the emotional system or structure of personality.

Mounting evidence justifies rejection of the view of psychological aging as movement toward psychological death. Moreover, rejection of a decline view of psychological aging may be quite productive. First, it might lead to a reemphasis on biology for conquering the deterioration that presently is associated with increasing age. Perhaps more important, it provides a radically new image of potential in late life, an image that demands the reexamination of present age structuring in society. If there is psychological growth throughout life, it behooves society to include the presumably most psychologically developed oldest segment of the population in important roles, regardless of possible physical frailness and slowing.

In this chapter the case for rejecting a decline model of psychological aging will be developed for only a single domain, cognition. It is hypothesized, however, that the case is more general. That is, the notion of aging in the distinct phenomenon sense of movement toward death should be rejected in other psychological domains as well. For example, it is likely that healthy adults are capable of emotional and personality development that is driven by a process of growth or expansion or improvement throughout life (see Birren, this volume).

The present discussion starts with an overview of the topic of cognition.

Then evidence against universal decline and for continued potential in adult cognition is reviewed. This review is followed by presentation of a new model of cognition that effectively integrates findings about age change and lifelong potentials into a multidisciplinary perspective. Then, practical, theoretical, and research implications of accepting a continued potential view of later life are considered. Finally, main points and conclusion are highlighted.

OVERVIEW OF THE STUDY OF COGNITIVE DEVELOPMENT

Cognition is defined here as the psychological ability that accounts for all of mental life. It includes perception, memory, intelligence, reasoning, judgment, and decision making. It permits humans to represent and think about the world, to conceptualize experience, fantasize beyond experience, maintain a sense of self, and communicate with others. It expands individual competence and allows us to solve and circumvent problems. Memory, for example, keeps track of events that have occurred in different times and distant places. Intellectual skills enable us to reflect upon experiences and attach meaning and significance to them. As individuals, this ability gives us the power to anticipate and plan for the future, to develop strategies, hypothesize alternatives, and evaluate consequences. In addition, we can share our perceptions, thoughts, hunches, and interpretations with other people. As a species, this ability gives us the power to profit from a wide variety of skills and a great diversity of experiences. Cognition, then, is extremely important. It underlies all personal adaptation and all societal progress.

For some time now, cognitive psychologists have been attempting to understand the ways in which the cognitive system operates and changes with age. Presently, most scholars considering cognitive development work only loosely within any particular theoretical perspective. In general, the assumptions they hold and the overriding issues they attempt to address are at best vaguely specified. Still, those working even loosely within a given perspective tend to view cognition and development in particular ways.

The *organismic approach* is represented by the work of scholars such as Chomsky (1986), Kohlberg (1969), Piaget (1983), and Werner (1948). They view humans as active constructors of knowledge, but also consider biological constraints central in determining both the nature of cognition and the nature of cognitive development. For organismically oriented theorists, human cognition at all ages functions in the same invariant manner as all other biological activity, that is, with the complementary processes of assimilation and accommodation. The basic units of cognition are assumed to be holistic structures that cannot be reduced to constituent parts. These structures of thought are assumed to change systematically across phylogeny and ontogeny. Thus, humans are assumed to move through biologically specified universal stages of cognitive organization. Cognitive development is conceived of as an ordered sequence of intrinsically guided qualitative transitions in the level of organization of cognitive structures.

The *mechanistic approach* is represented by the work of researchers such as Bandura (1977), Bijou and Baer (1961, 1965), Kendler (1963), and Siegler (1983). Strictly speaking, this approach views humans as basically reactive and assumes that knowledge directly reflects the external environment. However, at present mechanistically oriented researchers view humans as reasonably active in their knowing of the world. The mechanistic approach considers the basic units of cognition to be elemental components that can be conceptually decomposed and experimentally isolated. Through time, humans are assumed to experience essentially age-irrelevant and entirely open changes in cognition. Thus, cognitive development is conceived of as environmentally determined quantitative change in the cognitive system.

The work of researchers such as Baltes, Dittman-Kohli, and Dixon (1984), Charlesworth (1976), and Vygotsky (1978) is characteristic of the *contextual approach*. This approach represents an important departure from the other perspectives, particularly in regard to its focus on inputs to development. An important assumption of the contextual approach is that development is a reciprocal or bidirectional process between organism and context. Moreover, social context is given more emphasis in the contextualist perspective than it is afforded in other approaches. Openness in the system is stressed, and diversity, in both the nature of cognition and the trajectories of cognitive development, is considered of theoretical interest.

The *psychometric approach* is represented by the work of researchers such as Cattell (1963), Guilford (1967), and Horn (1982). It originated as a largely atheoretical approach. Few assumptions about the nature of cognition or the nature of development were made. Rather, large differential studies of cognitive performance were carried out. These studies have provided considerable empirical information about the nature of cognitive performance across the life span. For example, they have indicated that different aspects of cognition follow different trajectories of age change. Such findings should be considered central in thinking about lifelong cognitive change.

EVIDENCE AGAINST UNIVERSAL DECLINE IN ADULT COGNITION

Until recently, views about cognition and cognitive development have been at least loosely tied to knowledge about the biological system that is assumed to support cognition. Therefore, it generally has been assumed that cognition is a universal aplastic system that has a biologically programmed age change trajectory. When investigating age-related changes in children's cognition, researchers have searched for cognitive growth that is assumed to parallel physical growth in childhood; and when investigating age-related changes in adult cognition, researchers have searched for cognitive decline, assumed to correspond to physical decline in later adulthood. These patterns of growth in childhood and decline in adulthood were thought to be veridical and inevitable. Moreover, when characterizing development and aging, researchers have attended almost exclusively to patterns of cognition that are general across individuals. In addition, age most often has been viewed as a causative variable, instead of simply as correlated to other important factors.

Several lines of evidence argue for a reevaluation of the assumption that cognition inevitably and universally declines with age, or that the cognitive system is essentially a determined, aplastic system. In addition, several kinds of data pose the possibility of continued improvement of existing cognitive skills and the acquisition of compensatory and new cognitive skills throughout life. Research supporting these ideas is summarized below.

Absence of Cognitive Decline

One kind of evidence that points to the inadequacy of a universal-decline view of adult cognition comes from the numerous individuals who have made important contributions at very old ages. Sigmund Freud, Jean Piaget, Michelangelo, Grandma Moses, Pablo Picasso, Marc Chagall, Oliver Wendell Holmes, and Frank Lloyd Wright are but a few of the better-known such individuals from the past. Claude Pepper, Vladimir Horowitz, B. F. Skinner, George Burns, and Ronald Reagan are some of the more visible examples of late vitality today. These examples of continued productivity and accomplishment in old age should no longer be ignored.

Extensive information about productivity in later life is contained in a book in which Simonton (1983) provides a histrometric analysis of genius, creativity, and leadership. He suggests that productivity probably peaks in the forties but that the age curve is relatively immune from the impact of extrinsic events, such as physical vigor and social reinforcers. Rather, he argues that it is the internal waning of enthusiasm that accounts for the observed age trend in productivity. Perhaps more interestingly, his analysis supports a model of constant probability of success. According to this view, the proportion of top-quality products varies across individuals but stays relatively constant throughout a career. Thus, historical data suggest that although there tends to be a decline in quantity of productive activity in later life, there probably is potential for stability or increase in the amount of production throughout life. Moreover, there appears to be stability in the quality of cognitive products throughout life.

Further evidence against a universal-decline view of adult cognitive change comes from studies of job performance. Waldman and Alvolio (1983) recently reviewed more than a dozen studies of adult performance in the work place and found little support for deterioration of performance with increasing age. Indeed, many objective measures of job performance showed improvement with age, especially for workers' performance as in professional jobs. Nevertheless, supervisors rated older workers slightly worse than younger workers. The reasons for the discrepancy between objective measures of job performance and superiors' subjective ratings is unclear, but may be related to stereotypes of decline in ability in later adulthood.

Support for the absence of age-related decline in cognition also comes from questionnaire studies. Perlmutter and Kaplan (1986) asked 20-, 40-, 60-, and 80-year-olds to rate themselves on each of 45 aspects of cognition. In addition, they asked the two younger groups to indicate the level they expected to be at on these skills when they became old, and the two older groups were asked to indicate their levels when they were young. A factor analysis of the items yielded seven factors. Whereas the younger subjects expected to decline on all but one of these (wisdom), the older subjects believed they had improved on all but one (wisdom). The discrepancy in expectations of the young and the self-perceptions of the old is especially provocative and provides some reason to question stereotypes about aging.

Many ordinary, vital older adults are, in fact, forcing society-wide reassessment of stereotypes about intellectual potential in old age. For example, syndicated columnist Bob Greene (1985) reported that numerous 60-, 70-, 80-, and 90-year-olds had written how they feel about being old in America. "Over and over again, older people said that they were feeling at the peak of their intellectual powers when they were forced to retire . . . they feel they have much to offer American society." Yet it remains for both the elder citizenry and the scientific community to articulate adequately the important and possibly unique contributions that could come from the older population.

Plasticity of Cognitive Function

Compelling evidence about the plasticity of the human cognitive system comes from demonstrations of historical and cultural effects on adult intelligence (e.g., Baltes et al., 1984; Cunningham, 1986; Schaie, 1965). Although early cross-sectional studies of psychometric test performances indicated extended and extensive intellectual decline in adulthood, more recent longitudinal studies indicate later onset of and less pervasive cognitive decline in old age. This discrepancy turns out to be very informative. Whereas in cross-sectional studies developmental change is inferred from age differences in different individuals, in longitudinal studies age change is assessed by testing the same individuals at different times in their lives. Thus, longitudinal studies are more appropriate for determining true developmental change.

Available longitudinal studies portray a relatively optimistic view of adult cognitive potential. Still, cross-sectional data indicate true age differences in the population. Since such age differences cannot be attributed primarily to age change, it can be concluded that there are historical time differences in intelligence. In particular, it appears that the general level of intellectual functioning of the population has improved in recent cohorts. This generational change suggests that intelligence is not as predetermined as previously thought, but rather is susceptible to cultural influences.

A number of intervention and training studies also indicate that there is considerable plasticity or malleability in cognitive function. For example, Baltes and Willis (1982) and Willis and Schaie (1984) have found that rather limited training of older adults' intellectual skills produces substantial and sustained improvement in intelligence test performance. In addition, Baltes and Kliegel (1984) have been able to train older adults to perform memory-span tasks at a level well beyond that typically observed in untrained young adults. The ease with which older adults' cognitive performance can be improved through training suggests that some of the advantage typically observed in younger adults' cognitive performance may be related to the cognitive demands that their life activities require of them every day, and/or that older adults' poor cognitive performance may be at least partially attributable to the cognitively unchallenging situations and undemanding routines in which many of them find themselves. Since younger subjects typically are college students who are used to the types of tasks employed in research on cognition, and older subjects often are retirees who have relatively few externally imposed achievement demands placed on them, these explanations of observed cognitive differences are especially viable.

EVIDENCE FOR CONTINUED POTENTIAL IN ADULT COGNITION

Improvement of Existing Skills

A number of cognitive abilities are known to remain fairly stable or even increase throughout life for most healthy adults. These have been labeled crystallized abilities (Horn, 1979), the prototype being vocabulary. Throughout life, vocabulary has the potential to increase. Furthermore, there is no evidence that early vocabulary is lost with age, unless an individual encounters particularly severe health problems.

Although other cognitive abilities have been shown to decline with age, they do so only in some individuals, and they appear to be maintained or even to improve with age in other individuals. For example, Schaie and Willis's (1986) longitudinal study suggests that different subgroups of adults show stability, decline, and improvement on spatial tasks and block design tasks. The important question of what accounts for these individual differences in the pattern of age change remains to be examined, although Schaie's (1984) data provide preliminary hints that life-style and attitude may be relevant.

Another kind of cognitive skill that seems to have the potential to develop and improve throughout life is expertise, that is, the skills underlying an activity that is especially well mastered, perhaps because of one's occupation or hobbies. Although most research in the area of expertise is nondevelopmental, it is relevant to cognitive growth in adulthood. In studies of expertise the knowledge base and performance characteristics of experts and novices typically are compared. When age has been held relatively constant (e.g., Chi, 1984; Glaser, 1984), it has been found that professional experience can lead to interesting domain-specific refinements in cognition. An expert's knowledge base in his or her area of expertise is not only quantitatively larger than a novice's, it also is more organized and operative. Likewise, an expert's performance of his or her skill tends to be exceptional in its speed, endurance, power, and precision. Perhaps most important, an expert's performance is likely to be strategic. Over a lifetime of work and leisure all individuals undoubtedly acquire a number of specific areas of expertise. In addition, in some sense, older individuals may be universal experts, with advanced organizations of knowledge and general strategies of operation.

Acquisition of Compensatory Skills

A number of studies have shown that in some domains older adults acquire compensatory skills that enable them to perform complex tasks as well as younger adults, even though they have experienced some deterioration in component skills required for performance of the complex task. For example, Salthouse (1982) carried out an extensive study of typists of various ages. He found that although basic reaction time of older typists generally was slower than that of younger typists, older typists were able to maintain comparable typing speed. The older typists apparently looked further ahead than the younger typists. When the number of characters that the typists were allowed to view was limited, older, but not younger, typists' performance was hampered. In similar research, Charness (1985) examined chess and bridge players of various ages. When asked to bid a bridge hand or choose a chess move, the older players were slower. Nevertheless, the older players' bids and moves were as good as the younger players. Apparently, older players developed some skills that compensated for the speed they had lost. Such evidence of acquisition of compensatory skills by older adults indicates that there is continued cognitive potential even in late life.

Similar compensatory skills are common in athletes. For example, tennis players become slower with age, and sometimes less powerful, although power usually can be retained reasonably well if an adequate training routine is followed. Despite the loss of speed, older tennis players frequently outplay younger, faster opponents. Strategy improves long after speed is lost, and this improvement can be quite advantageous. It is likely that analogous strategies develop for cognitive tasks. Moreover, because most cognitive tasks are not nearly as dependent on speed and strength as are athletics, in the cognitive domain strategies might be even more relevant.

Acquisition of New Skills

Research on post-formal reasoning, wisdom, metacognition, and emotional development all promise to contribute to understanding about new potentials for cognitive growth in later adulthood. Although the nature of the optimally developed older cognitive system is not yet specified, it almost surely includes an experientially based control system that ever more adaptively reviews, plans, and manages activity. Such a control system is likely to reflect increased awareness, mediation, and integration of emotion and thought. Moreover, it is likely to reflect a more stable and refined hierarchy of values and priorities. Such a system may lead to improved evaluation and judgment and perhaps account for the as yet vague quality of wisdom. In addition, an understanding of the optimally developed older cognitive system will require an integrated perspective that includes life context. For example, it will need to account for the ways in which individual differences in life activity may be related to individual differences in developmental patterns. Growth is expected to be characteristic of only some individuals in only some domains. Nevertheless, the potential for extension of growth seems likely.

INTEGRATION OF KNOWLEDGE ABOUT COGNITION ACROSS THE LIFE SPAN

Thus far, some of the important assumptions inherent in various approaches to cognition were outlined, and representative research pointing to the lack of universal decline and potential for continued growth of adult cognition was summarized. Here, research findings are integrated into a model of cognition that incorporates these diverse data. The model is then framed within a multidisciplinary perspective that should aid further research on development.

A three-tier conception of cognition is portrayed in Figure 12-1 (see also Perlmutter, in press, for more extensive discussion of this model). The first tier is assumed to be available at birth, the second tier to emerge postnatally, and the third tier probably not to be in place until even later in development. The first tier is a *fairly closed biological system* in which there is little ontogenetic change; the second tier is a *somewhat open psychological system* in which there is potential for some ontogenetic growth throughout life; and the third tier is an

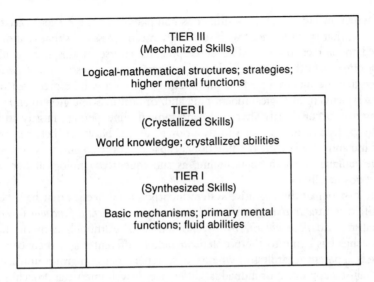

FIGURE 12-1. Three-tier model of cognition.

extremely open psychological system in which very substantial ontogenetic change can occur.

Each overlay tier gives the cognitive system impressive new power. This power is gained as cognition gets filtered through layers that are added postnatally and rooted in experience. That is, starting fairly soon after birth, cognition moves from being simply a biological process programmed into the organism to a psychological process constructed by the organism. Cognition no longer represents a basic biological structure that is unencumbered by history. Rather, with the accumulation of experience and memory, cognition becomes a system that has been ontogenetically fine-tuned to the subtleties of the environment. Previous modes of operation are not abandoned, but with the addition of environmentally based tiers, the cognitive system can become more effective and more efficient. In addition, with the overlay of new layers, considerable slippage in more primitive layers is tolerated. Minor perturbations in lower operations become relatively unimportant in the overall functioning of the ever more powerful system. Still, at some threshold, breakdowns in foundation layers may disrupt effective cognition.

As implied above, the first tier of the cognitive system is assumed to be the most primitive layer and to reflect an essentially biological process. Its general structure and function are assumed to be established at a species level. However, individual genetic differences result in some diversity in members of the population. This tier is operable early in life and subsequently gets called into play when an individual faces situations comparable to those experienced in early life, that is, when faced with seemingly meaningless tasks that cannot be related to past encounters. The developmental course of this tier parallels development of other largely biological systems. Thus, assessments of performance that are mainly based on this level of cognition will be predicted well by assessments of biological functioning and/or health. Some growth and fine tuning may occur shortly after birth, and some decline, perhaps largely attributable to disease, may occur shortly prior to death. However, between very early life and very late life the functional capacity of the cognitive system as a whole remains open throughout life, as subsequent psychological tiers are added postnatally.

The first tier of the cognitive system incorporates processes that have been identified as *basic mechanisms* by mechanists, *primary mental functions* by contextualists, and *fluid abilities* by psychometricians. Although each of these approaches has come to the problem in rather different ways, their convergence is apparent regardless of whether researchers focus on group similarities (mechanistic approach) or individual differences (psychometric approach).

A second tier of the cognitive system incorporates what has been identified as *world knowledge* by mechanists and *crystallized abilities* by psychometricians. At this tier, external experiences are recorded rather passively, resulting in habituation to unimportant events and anticipation of important novel events. Thus, the system is given the power to operate in an ever more environmentally responsive and adaptive manner. Since many experiences are common to all individuals in a population, much of this second cognitive layer is shared by all individuals in the population. However, because some experiences are unique to an individual, part of this second cognitive layer also is unique. It may not be surprising, therefore, that this aspect of cognition has been identified in both normative (mechanistic) and differential (psychometric) studies. Likewise, because this tier derives from external experience, it should not be surprising that it begins to emerge only after life begins, or that it slows in its rate of growth as newness of experience diminishes. Moreover, because this layer is assumed to be a psychological addition to the biological layer, independent measures of biological functioning or health are not expected to be good predictors of performance involving this level of cognition, except in situations where severe biological breakdowns limit psychological activity.

Although evidence for a third tier of the cognitive system is less clear, there is some support for its inclusion. Such a tier may reflect what has been identified by mechanists as *strategies* and by contextualists as *higher mental functions*. It gives humans extensive potential for adaptive modification, which presumably could increase throughout life. The unique aspect of this tier may be that it derives from internal experiences of the cognitive system. That is, it is a layer of the cognitive system that emerges from the system's own activity.

This tier is believed to be especially valuable because it allows the cognitive system to adapt in a way that is not only responsive to the external world but also responsive to its own apparatus (e.g., the first tier). According to this view, while the addition of the second tier primes the cognitive system to operate in an ever more environmentally adaptive manner, the addition of the third tier gives the cognitive system the capacity to actually adjust its modus operandum in a way that can optimize attainment of a specified goal. This tier also is assumed to be relatively immune to the biological fluctuations that may be related to state or age.

Whereas the second tier seems to emerge out of the organism's activity in the environment, the third tier seems to emerge out of the organism's cognition about its own cognitive activity. The idea here is that if cognition becomes an object of itself, it has the power to construct further layers. This process seems similar to what Piaget (1983) described as *reflective abstraction* and what Flavell (1977) articulated as *metacognition*. Although Piaget suggested that the development of this aspect of cognition is primarily driven by internal mechanisms, Vygotsky (1978) argued that development of higher mental functions is directed by social interaction. Further research should clarify the contribution of both of these factors.

Although the present view postulates only three tiers, it is possible to speculate even further and envision a fourth or possibly fifth cognitive layer. Such layers might derive from the cognitive system's cognition about emotional and biological experience. What is implied here is that as emotional and biological activity are cognitively reflected upon, new cognitive layers could emerge that would result in more adaptive regulation or control of the emotional and biological systems. Indeed, there is some evidence of better integration of affect and cognition in later adulthood (e.g., Labouvie-Vief, 1985). In addition, there is substantial evidence of the potential for at least partial cognitive regulation of physiological processes through biofeedback techniques (e.g., Miller, 1971); as well as suggestive evidence of a potential for some control over biochemical factors that mediate health (e.g., Henry, this volume).

In summary, it appears that presently identified cognitive abilities can be incorporated into a three-tier conception of cognition. This novel way of viewing cognition is believed to be more powerful than previous conceptions because it incorporates important developmental phenomena. A first biological tier is relatively closed, in place at birth, and susceptible to deterioration associated with programmed biological aging and health problems. A second external-environmentally based psychological tier is somewhat more open, emerges postnatally, and is relatively immune from deterioration associated with programmed biological aging and health problems. At least one additional infinitely open psychological tier, which is internal-experientially based, seems to be added during subsequent development. This tier also is relatively immune from the deterioration associated with programmed biological aging and health problems.

A multidisciplinary framework that can facilitate inquiry about causes of age change is illustrated in Figure 12-2. As is indicated, both endogenous and exogenous factors relate to the cognitive system and, most likely, contribute to development of it. Biological factors impact Tier I; environmental factors, from both the physical and social worlds, impact Tier II; and the cognitive system itself is the main impetus for development of Tier III, although the social world may also provide important input. The main advantage of framing the cognitive system in such a multidisciplinary perspective is that it highlights the diversity of factors that impinge upon cognitive development, and hopefully encourages cross-disciplinary inquiry into causes of age change. As independent variables from each of these spheres are investigated, it is possible that additional aspects of cognition will be illuminated.

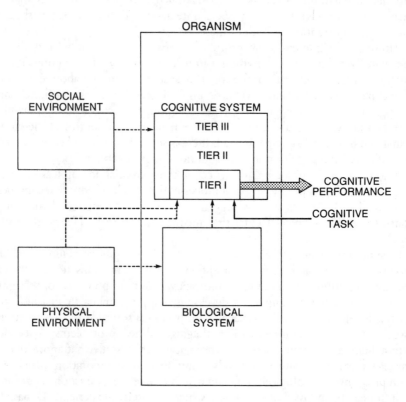

FIGURE 12-2. Multidisciplinary framework for considering development.

IMPLICATIONS OF THE CONTINUED-POTENTIAL VIEW OF ADULTHOOD

It appears that a childhood growth/adulthood decline view of age change may well portray the biological system that supports cognition and thus may characterize performance of some basic cognitive processes. However, the cognitive system seems also to be a malleable, experientially based system that incorporates the past in structuring experience and guiding activity. Thus, with age the cognitive system becomes increasingly adapted to the environmental circumstances it regularly encounters. With age the adult may operate with a slightly slower or less effective biologically based processing system. However, the past experience that is incorporated in thought and decision may compensate for processing limitations. Indeed, for many tasks, older adults' experientially rich cognitive systems should give them a cognitive advantage over the more agile but less adapted cognitive systems of younger adults. Incredibly, laboratory research on cognition has all but ignored such tasks. Thus, very little presently is known about how adult cognition may improve with age.

Nevertheless, there is good scientific reason to dispel the societal stereotype of feebleminded, unproductive old age. As indicated above, it already is clear that such a view of older adults is far from accurate. Very old, vital individuals can no longer be considered rare deviants. They are becoming quite familiar. Furthermore, they should serve as valuable resources from whom the capabilities that can develop from a lifetime of experiences, as well as the factors that may be the precursors of late-life vitality, can be discovered. A number of the practical, theoretical, and research implications of adopting this new perspective are discussed below.

Practical Implications

First, rejection of past views of universal, inevitable decline in later life could actually reduce the prevalence of age-related deterioration. The view of universal inevitable decline is not only inaccurate but probably leads to expectations about later life that are unnecessarily frightening and may themselves contribute to decline in old age. We already know, for example, that expectations about achievement can affect performance in early (Rosenthal & Jacobson, 1968) and middle life (Kanter, 1972). It is likely, too, that expectations about decline in later life can set into motion environmental and social contingencies that diminish challenges for older adults, and in so doing limit the quality of their lives as well as the potential for their contribution. A new perspective on change is needed. Although research should not ignore the declines that can occur with age, particularly in the unhealthy, it also should not ignore the lifelong growth that is possible.

If some aspects of an individual's cognitive skill continue to improve throughout life, then very old age could be a time of great contribution. For example, if throughout life an artist's appreciation increases, a historian's expertise broadens, or a scientist's understanding deepens, then the very old artist, historian, and scientist may have wisdom and insights that should be valued and nurtured. Some individuals have produced great works well into their eighties and nineties. Other important contributions should be expected from the increasing numbers of very old individuals in the population. Perhaps more important, it is possible that a better understanding of potential in later life could lead to a change in present negative expectations about old age, and thereby improve both the quality of life of the very old and their potential role in society. Reduced societal significance (see Uhlenberg, this volume) is not inevitable and no longer should be tolerated for later stages of life. Rather, it may be appropriate to give the oldest segment of the healthy population roles of increased power and impact.

Theoretical Implications

From a theoretical perspective, the continued-potential view implies that the oldest portion of the population represents a uniquely important subject sample. Such individuals should provide data about performance potentials and performance limits that are only possible to obtain from extreme age groups. For example, to the degree that any process is hypothesized to improve or decline with age, change should be most evident in extreme age groups. At the extreme end of the age continuum the contributions of both species-generalized development and unique individualized experience should culminate in a highly developed and individuated population.

Moreover, developmental patterns of stability, improvement, and deterioration of various cognitive abilities could provide new understanding about the nature of cognition. Consider, for example, distinguishing cognitive abilities in terms of the directions of their developmental trajectories. Mechanized processes (Tier I) might be operationalized as processes that decline in later life, crystallized processes (Tier II) as skills that remain stable in later life, and synthesized processes (Tier III) as abilities that improve or first emerge in later life. The similarity in developmental history of cognitive processes may provide clues to more important distinctions. For example, the adaptive potentials and liabilities of cognitive skills might be evident in the orchestration of growth and decline, and the optimal conditions to foster growth or maintenance of cognitive skills might become distinguished from developmental patterns. To the degree that such a perspective is fruitful, information about very old adults should be especially important. At extreme ages, growth (synthesized) and decline (mechanized) processes should be most differentiated and should be easiest to classify and characterize.

The continued-potential view also focuses attention on factors that mediate change in functioning. Traditional models have tended to consider age change to be fairly fixed and time-dependent. The new model assumes that age change is relatively plastic or malleable and regulated by factors such as health, social roles, personality, attitudes, and life-style. Rather than age itself being hypothesized to be a direct regulator of function, these other variables are assumed to mediate function. Some of these variables, such as health and certain social roles, tend to be age-correlated, and therefore they lead to age-stereotyped functioning. However, others of these variables, such as personality, attitudes, and life-style, tend to be relatively independent of age, and therefore they contribute to individual differences that are observed across age. Although chronological age is sometimes a good indicator of functioning, it is imperfect. Thus, age can no longer be utilized as a major theoretical explanation of performance.

Moreover, because the mediating effects of factors such as personality, attitudes, and life-style accumulate across time, chronological age should be least useful as an index of functional level for the very old. In contrast, the impact of mediating factors should be most apparent in that age group. For example, if a life of cognitive challenge enhances cognitive function, cognitively challenged and unchallenged individuals should appear increasingly different with age. The individual who maintains a life habit of extensive reading may enter old age with an exceptionally intact cognitive system, and the emeritus professor who continues active research and teaching past retirement may stay mentally sharp to his or her last days.

Research Implications

At least three features should be incorporated into future research in order to help overcome some of the shortcomings of present knowledge about cognitive aging. First, a *mediating-factors approach* should be used. Variables besides age should be considered as possible mediating factors of observed age differences. As discussed above, a mediated-factors view of aging assumes that individual differences in functioning are systematically related to health, personality, social roles, attitudes, and life-style. This view is quite novel, and to date little systematic research has focused on factors that mediate cognitive performance. Therefore, research in which mediating factors are analyzed for their possible relationship to cognitive performance should be fruitful. It is expected that these variables will predict cognitive performance above and beyond age differences. Moreover, because the effects of these mediating factors are assumed to accumulate across time, it is hypothesized that the strength of such relationships will increase with age.

Second, a *comprehensive eclectic approach* should be taken to the conceptualization and measurement of cognition; that is, cognitive functioning should be evaluated more extensively and from a broader range of perspectives than is typical. This broadening of approach is especially called for in work on adult cognitive change. Although the basic processing components of cognition that have been the focus of psychometric and experimental studies appear to decline somewhat during adulthood, these functions are probably closely tied to biological function and, ultimately, do not limit everyday cognitive function except in extreme situations. The pragmatics of cognition that are the focus of more ecological studies appear to remain stable or even to improve during adulthood. Although these pragmatic abilities have not been included in standard tests of intelligence, they are incorporated in a number of promising new conceptualizations of intelligence. For example, Gardner (1983) has proposed that academic abilities represent one of at least seven kinds of human intelligence. The seven that he identifies are linguistic, musical, logical-mathematical, spatial, bodily-kinesthetic, personal, and interpersonal intelligence. In a compatible and complementary theory, Sternberg (1984) has proposed that three aspects of intelligence are necessary for understanding cognition in humans. In particular, he argues that intelligent behavior depends upon context, experience, and component processes. All of these factors must be investigated in future work on cognitive development.

Moreover, because it is possible that new forms of cognition metamorphize in late life, truly novel and extensive explorations of older adults' cognition are needed. It may be that the most advanced forms of thinking have not yet been incorporated into conceptions or investigations of intelligence because adequate examination of the range of older adults' skills have not been considered. If the study of butterflies focused only on the structure and activity of its earlier form (i.e., caterpillars), the butterfly surely would be underappreciated.

Third, an *optimal-performance approach* should be taken. Extreme age groups should be included; some individuals who are assumed to be at the extreme of the population in terms of their levels of functioning should be studied; and some task domains that represent subjects' areas of specialization should be investigated. As discussed above, the peak potentials of cognitive performance are expected to emerge on a select set of cognitive abilities, here labeled synthesized cognition. Moreover, these peaks of performance are expected to be most evident in one's area of specialization, that is, in areas most practiced. Finally, these peaks of performance are expected to be most evident in the healthy very old who have had the greatest number of years of growth, and in particular, in the very select individuals who have had lifelong habits conducive to peak functioning.

SUMMARY AND CONCLUSIONS

Two conceptions of age change were articulated in the present chapter. First, according to a dual-phenomenon conception, two separate kinds of age change are driven by two separate processes. Development predominates in early life and is driven by a force that moves things away from their beginning state. Aging predominates in later life and is driven by a force that moves things toward their ending state. In contrast, according to the multiprocess-phenomenon conception, two dominant opposing processes do not drive age change. Rather, multiple change forces operate throughout life. Development and aging simply reflect multidirectional and multicausal lifelong age change. The separate terms describe change that accrues with the accumulation or diminution of time; that is, they refer to different vantage points on a set of processes, not to distinct processes. It was argued that although a dual-phenomenon conception may be valid for biological (hardware) age change, it probably is inappropriate for psychological (software) age change. Although it appears that there may be a programmed force driving living organisms toward biological death, no analogous process seems to drive humans toward psychological death. Thus, all age-related psychological change might simply be referred to as life-span development. Moreover, theory about the psychology of aging should be indiscriminable from theory about the psychology of development. Both must explain the dynamics of growth and decline that occur throughout life.

The case for this perspective was developed by examining age-related change in adult cognition. It was indicated that although decline is evident in some basic cognitive processes, this decline probably is not nearly as universal nor inevitable as previously had been assumed. Moreover, the declines that are observed appear to be closely tied to the biological system. Furthermore, they do not seem to be critical for the accomplishment of many impressive cognitive feats. Only in the case of relatively extreme breakdowns of the biological underpinnings of cognition are there important deficits in more advanced cognitive abilities. Finally, it was indicated that some lifelong cognitive skills may continue to improve throughout life, and some new cognitive abilities may emerge in later life, as long as adequate health is maintained.

A number of implications of this perspective of continued potential were discussed. Most important perhaps, it was suggested that while biologists continue to address the deterioration that presently is associated with increasing age, a new image of the psychological capabilities of the older adult is called for. Indeed, according to this perspective, humans are psychologically at their most highly developed state when they are very old. If this is true, a reexamination of the present age structuring of society is needed. Even if the old are physically frail or slow, they should be called upon to fill important roles.

Although the case for rejection of a decline view of psychological aging already appears reasonably strong, there is reason to believe that it is only the tip of the iceberg. First, little effort has been placed on identifying the possibly unique ways of understanding that may emerge in later adulthood. With an appreciation of this possibility, new discoveries are likely to accumulate. In addition, with increases in life span and improvements in childhood education and adulthood health, further opportunity for increased psychological growth throughout life is likely. Finally, because psychological processes tend to be relatively malleable and mold to expectation, it is likely that rejection of past images of inevitable late-life decline and acceptance of new images of continued potential throughout life will facilitate the actualization of greater potential in late life. Butterflies should fly.

REFERENCES

Baltes, P. B., Dittman-Kohli, F., & Dixon, R. A. (1984). New perspectives on the development of intelligence in adulthood: Toward a dual-process conception and a model of selective optimization with compensation. In P. B. Baltes & O. G. Brim, Jr. (Eds.), *Life-span development and behavior* (Vol. 6, pp. 34–76). New York: Academic Press.

Baltes, P. B. & Kliegel, R. (1984). *Training of expert memory to limits of functioning.* Unpublished manuscript.

Baltes, P. B., & Willis, S. (1982). Plasticity and enhancement of intellectual functioning. In F. I. M. Craik & S. Trehub (Eds.), *Aging and cognitive processes.* New York: Plenum Press. (pp. 353–389).

Bandura, A. (1977). *Social learning theory.* Englewood Cliffs, NJ: Prentice-Hall.

Bijou, S. W. & Baer, D. M. (1961). *Child development I: A systematic and empirical theory.* New York: Meredith.

Bijou, S. W. & Baer, D. M. (1965). *Child development II: Universal stage of infancy.* New York: Meredith.

Cattell, R. B. (1963). Theory of fluid and crystallized intelligence: A critical experiment. *Journal of Educational Psychology, 54,* 1–22.

Charlesworth, W. (1976). Human intelligence as adaptation: An ethological approach. In L. B. Resnick (Ed.), *The nature of intelligence.* Hillsdale, NJ: Erlbaum. (pp. 147–169).

Charness, R. (1985). Aging and problem solving performance. In R. Charness (Ed.), *Aging and human performance.* Chichester, UK: Wiley. (pp. 225–260).

Chi, M. (1984, December). *Expert knowledge development in children.* Discussion at the Social Science Research Council Conference on Expertise, New York, NY.

Chomsky, N. (1986). *Knowledge of language: Its nature, origins, and use.* New York: Praeger.

Cunningham, W. (1980). *Historical and cultural effects on aging.* Paper presented at a convocation entitled *The Power of Years,* University of Southern California, Los Angeles, June, 1980.

Flavell, J. H. (1977). *Cognitive development.* Englewood Cliffs, NJ: Prentice-Hall.

Gardner, H. (1983). *Frames of mind: The theory of multiple intelligences.* New York: Basic Books.

Glaser, R. (1984, December). *Overview of expertise.* Discussion at the Social Science Research Council Conference of Expertise, New York, NY.

Greene, B. (1985, November 11). Lesson of the ages taught by elderly. *The Chicago Tribune*, pp. 14–15.

Guilford, J. P. (1967). *The nature of human intelligence*. New York: McGraw-Hill.

Horn, J. L. (1979). Organization of data on life-span development of human abilities. In L. R. Goulet & P. B. Baltes (Eds.), *Life-span development psychology* (pp. 424–466). New York: Academic Press.

Horn, J. L. (1982). The theory of fluid and crystallized intelligence in relation to concepts of cognitive psychology and aging in adulthood. In F. I. M. Craik & E. E. Trehub (Eds.), *Aging and cognitive processes* (pp. 237–278). New York: Plenum Press.

Kanter, R. M. (1972). *Commitment and community: Communes and utopias in sociological perspectives*. Cambridge, MA: Harvard University Press.

Kendler, T. S. (1963). Development of mediating responses in children. In N. C. Wright & J. Kagen (Eds.), *Basic cognitive processes in children. Monographs of the Society for Research in Child Development, 28*(2), 33–51.

Kohlberg, L. (1969). Stage and sequence: The cognitive developmental approach to socialization. In D. A. Goslin (Ed.), *Handbook of socialization theory and research*. New York: Rand-McNally. (pp. 347–480).

Labouvie-Vief, G. (1985). Object knowledge, personal knowledge, and processes of equilibration in adult cognition. *Human Development, 28*, 25–39.

Miller, N. E. (1971). *Selected papers*. Chicago: Aldine Atherton.

Perlmutter, M. (in press). Cognitive development in life span perspective: From description of differences to explanation of changes. In M. Hetherington, R. Lerner, & M. Perlmutter (Eds.), *Child development in life span perspectives*. Hillsdale, NJ: Erlbaum.

Perlmutter, M., & Kaplan, M. (1986). *Self-perceptions and implicit theories of one's own cognitive development*. Unpublished manuscript.

Piaget, J. (1983). Piaget's theory. In P. H. Mussen (Ed.), *Handbook of child psychology* (Vol. 1, pp. 103–128). New York: Wiley.

Rosenthal, R., & Jacobson, L. (1968). *Pygmalion in the classroom: Teacher expectations and pupils' intellectual development*. New York: Praeger.

Salthouse, T. A. (1982). *Adult cognition*. New York: Springer-Verlag.

Schaie, K. W. (1965). A general model for the study of developmental change. *Psychological Bulletin, 64*, 92–107.

Schaie, K. W. (1984). Midlife influences upon intellectual functioning in old age. *International Journal of Behavioral Development, 7*, 463–478.

Schaie, K. W. & Willis, S. (1986, May). *Can decline in adult intellectual functioning be reversed?* Paper presented at the Aging Conference, University of Southern California, Los Angeles.

Siegler, R. S. (1983). Information processing approaches to development. In P. H. Mussen (Ed.), *Handbook of child psychology* (Vol. 1, pp. 103–128). New York: Wiley.

Simonton, D. K. (1983). Age, skill, and management. *International Journal of Aging and Human Development, 17*, 15–18.

Sternberg, R. J. (1984). Higher-order reasoning in postformal operational thought. In M. L. Commons, F. A. Richards, & C. Armon (Eds.), *Beyond formal operations: Late adolescent and adult development* (pp. 74–91). New York: Praeger.

Vygotsky, L. S. (1978). *Mind in society*. Boston: Cambridge University Press.

Waldman, D. A., & Avolio, B. S. (1983). *Enjoy old age*. New York: Norton.

Werner, H. (1948). *Comparative psychology of mental development*. New York: International Universities Press.

Willis, S. L. & Schaie, K. W. (1984). *Training intellectual performance in older adults*. Unpublished manuscript.

13

The Archetypes of Power
and Intimacy

James P. Henry

In their "Human Aging: Usual and Successful," featured in a recent issue of *Science*, Rowe and Kahan (1987) draw attention to the growing realization that it is wrong to attribute age-related deficits of thinking and physical capacities to the aging process itself. They decry the tendency to regard such changes as inevitable. It is true that there are many persons who have deteriorated as they have aged but the question arises as to whether these changes could have been prevented. It might be that the nature of the diet of such persons and the exercise they engaged in was critical. Indeed their personal habits and a number of psychosocial factors connected with the culture may have been of critical importance. Thus a distinction can be made between successful aging and the more typical prospective deterioration. An example of the latter is the rise of the blood pressure by a millimeter for every year over the age of twenty, with the result that by the time the person reaches sixty, treatment for high blood pressure is needed. In those aging in this way, body weight will have increased excessively while maximum cardiac output and kidney function will have significantly decreased. The result is that such a person reaches retirement in a mentally and physically handicapped condition. By contrast, in successful aging the extrinsic social factors, including the habits of drinking, smoking, and diet, have played a neutral or even a positive role. In those aging successfully there has been little physiological or psychological impairment of function and, in their final decades, these individuals enjoy remarkable psychosocial effectiveness and often undiminished creativity.

The present work proposes that successful development is not limited to the first half of life, but that human evolution has determined that *some individuals will survive to progress in the second half of life*, developing special leadership skills that are vital for the welfare of the social group.

In this regard, Perlmutter (this volume) has extended Light's observations (also presented in this book) of the remarkable retention of verbal skills by the aged. Rejecting the decline view of psychological aging, she presents the case for continued cognitive potential throughout life. Using the metamorphosis of the insect from the larval to the flight form as an analogy, Perlmutter proposes that in later life there may be advanced and presumably valuable forms of thinking. Here, we suggest that these forms represent an integration of the instinctually determined patterns of power and intimacy and propose that the development of this integration is a vital key to longevity and productivity in the later years of life.

In their recent review of the Interpersonal Circle as a structural model for the integration of personality studies, Wiggins and Broughton (1985) synthesize the last thirty years of work in this area. As described by Kiesler (1983), "the circular array represents a two-dimensional Euclidian space reflecting the joint interaction of two basic interpersonal dimensions or motivations almost universally designated as Control and Affiliation." As Figure 13-1 indicates, these dimensions define respectively the vertical and horizontal axes of a circle. A large body of research convincingly demonstrates that interpersonal behavior represents the joint expression of these two underlying dimensions, which in this chapter are termed *power* and *intimacy*. The extent to which each dimen-

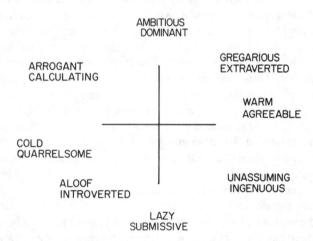

FIGURE 13-1. Basic vectors of interpersonal behavior, the Interpersonal Circle. (From Wiggins & Holzmuller, 1981, *Journal of Research in Personality*, Academic Press. Used by permission.)

sion is involved reflects the assumption that when people interact they are in essence determining their mutual position in an ethological dominance hierarchy. They are at the same time deciding how friendly or hostile they will be— that is, how closely they are affiliated. Thus, their responses will reflect shades of the primary emotions associated with control (power) and affiliation (intimacy).

This approach recently has been used fruitfully by the social psychologist Dan McAdams (1985b). He has expanded on his mentor David McClelland's (1975, 1979) seminal studies of the schema or archetype of power and achievement by focusing on the affiliative aspects of personality (McAdams, 1985a). His recent quantitative study of *Power, Intimacy and the Life Story* (McAdams, 1985b) is particularly relevant to the question of the relation between aging and control and attachment behavior. During the past 20 years the control of access to desiderata (i.e., power) has been shown to be a crucial mechanism motivating animal behavior (Miller, 1980). Over the past three decades, the equally critical importance of attachment behavior (i.e., intimacy) has been demonstrated, not only for the parental-infant tie in primates (Hinde, 1974) but for social bonding in human society (Bowlby, 1970) as well. The present chapter will explore how these instinctually determined patterns of behavior affect the life span of individuals.

The Survival Curve

The progressive "rectangularization" of the survival curve (see Figure 13-2) is an expression of the fact that the health of the most carefully nurtured animal, including humans, will eventually collapse as the end of the life span is approached. As a result of recently revised life-style practices and advances in medicine, many more individuals reach their eighties. However, they do so only to experience a collapse in health as the intrinsic biological limits for the species are reached (Fries & Crapo, 1981). Demographers Myers and Manton (1984) have challenged this view, stating that "there is no evidence that rectangularization has had a significant effect on population or mortality dynamics of the elderly." However, Fries (1984) has recently rebutted their observations, vigorously defending the theory that the age of onset of significant disability can be moved upward more rapidly than life expectancy. He posits that by postponing chronic illness and by improving vitality through increased physical, psychological, and social exercise, mortality can indeed be compressed into a shorter period at the end of life.

The present work accepts this concept of the rectangularization of the survival curve and examines the possible causes underlying it. In this regard, evidence will be presented that humans have instinctually determined patterns of behavior, arguing that although we are creatures of our learned culture, the organism must first biologically be prepared to acquire this learning rapidly. Further, it is proposed that frustration of basic inherited patterns is a major

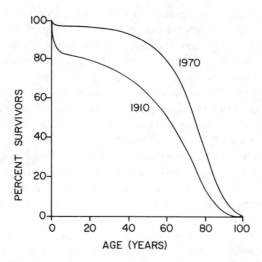

FIGURE 13-2. The rectangular curve. Survival curves for 1910 and 1970 are calculated from deaths/year/1,000 individuals. Curve for 1970 has become rectangularized due to lower infant mortality and increased survival at older ages. (From James F. Fries and Lawrence M. Crapo, *Vitality and aging.* © by W. H. Freeman. Used by permission.)

source of anxiety, fear, anger, and grief, which fuel the chronic illnesses that cause disability and the eventual collapse of those who are aging. This type of evolutionary perspective on human social behavior is supported by the research of Ohman and Dimberg (1984), who argue that our behavioral tendencies have evolved in a social being that has been shaped into an integrated whole by evolution. The extent to which any particular social system denies these tendencies in later life will determine the rate of the physical and mental impairment that results.

THE INHERITANCE OF BEHAVIORAL PROGRAMS

Power and Intimacy as Conflicting Drives

Behavioral and psychosomatic medicine propose that much of the deterioration of the health of those living in the modern technocratic state is due not to infection or malnutrition but to chronic emotional disturbance. The precise nature of the problem and indeed the emotions involved are a matter for vigorous debate. The present approach will follow up on physiological clues that have pointed to the basis of this decline, the arousing effect on the organism of frustration of the instinct for control over satisfaction of needs, and the failure of society to provide a sufficiently nurturant milieu to permit a relaxed satisfaction of the instinct for attachment.

The imago or schemata or archetypes of power and intimacy, found to be so basic by McClelland (1975, 1979) and McAdams (1985b) appear to be none other than the psychophysiologists' drives for control and attachment. These fundamental unlearned components of our personality are often in conflict with the demands of our society and our culture. As noted above, the ensuing chronic emotional arousal triggers the deterioration of health that so often passes for the aging process (Henry, 1985; Henry & Stephens, 1977).

The drive for power or control is described as feeling strong, having an impact on one's environment. Measurement of this control is subjective: It may be experienced vicariously through others who hold power, may involve "doing one's duty" and offering help to others, or may entail making the material and social worlds conform to one's own image of what they should be. Intimacy (communion or attachment behavior), on the other hand, may be defined as joy and mutual delight, mutual dialogue, openness, contact, union, perceived harmony, concern for the well-being of the other, or surrender of manipulative control and of the desire to master while relating to another. McAdams (1985b) argues that, in keeping with Erikson's (1959) theme of generativity and Jung's (1954) concept of individuation (Goldbrunner, 1964), the often conflicting power and intimacy motifs need to be reconciled in the later stages of the life course. Indeed, he concludes that an "interesting positive relationship" was obtained in his quantitative studies "between Erikson's generativity ratings and the combination of power and intimacy motivation." Earlier in the same passage he recognizes this as an aspect of the midlife "crisis" rather than something to do with the identity problems of the young. Thus, he identifies the integration of power with intimacy as a pressing concern of those who have reached "the second half of life."

A number of other researchers have pointed to similar dichotomous personality traits. McAdams (1985b) uses *power* and *intimacy* as the words that most adequately describe the nature of long-familiar basic aspects of personality; however, he recognizes that Bakan's (1966) *agency* and *communion* describe the same concepts. Likewise, Wiggins and Broughton (1985) and Kiesler (1983) pay tribute to a number of personality psychologists who over the last 30 years have identified these same two orthogonal coordinates of the interpersonal circle, which they identify as *control* and *affiliation*. In keeping with past work, control is defined here as deriving from the physiologists' defense response; and affiliation, as the ancient mammalian mother/infant attachment response (Henry, 1986a) also referred to by Bowlby (1970) as attachment.

Neuroendocrine Responses Involved in Power and Intimacy

Various complex mechanisms are beginning to be recognized by which changes in neuroendocrine patterns, and thus in health, develop as a result of emotions and their disturbance (Ohman & Dimberg, 1984; Henry, 1986a;

Henry & Stephens, 1977). Dimensions of power (drive to control) and intimacy (affiliation) are fundamental aspects of the personality. They are, in fact, closely related to the basic neuroendocrine patterns of response involved in the activation of the sympathetic adrenal medullary and the pituitary adrenal cortical system, respectively.

These hormonal systems form the vital link between the emotional state of the individual and his or her bodily responses. Current work shows the extent to which, even in the face of active denial and complete unawareness, these responses occur. Often, frustration will gradually inflict the damaging changes in the body that are associated with high blood pressure or the autoimmune processes of diseases such as arthritis (Lynch, 1985; Locke & Colligan, 1986).

For example, in the work sphere, Karasek, Schwartz, and Theorell (1982) describe the deleterious effects of jobs with high demand and low control. These are jobs involving much sympathetic arousal in the effort to control, and little opportunity for the relaxed affiliative behavior that is associated with low cortisol levels. They can be contrasted with the less noxious effects of jobs with effective control and low demands that satisfy these needs (see Figure 13-3).

The same problem of satisfying the need for a sense of control and reasonable demands can be identified at home in the nuclear family. The self confidence of the male who is still in the first half of life, can be affected when he perceives his wife's work role as challenging his adequacy (i.e., control) as provider. Likewise, the young husband perceiving himself as failing to successfully support his wife appears to be more vulnerable to coronary disease (Eaker, Haynes, & Feinleib, 1983). Hence, the recent, only semifacetious title, "Is an educated wife hazardous to your health?" (Suarez & Barrett-Conner, 1984). The other side to this coin—that is, the perception that the wife is not supportive and lacking in intimacy—has been shown to result in symptoms associated with coronary heart disease, such as angina (Medalie & Goldbourt, 1976). In past cultures, especially those in which traditional religion prescribes a separation of roles within the family, the emphasis has been on control or power for the male and intimacy for the woman. Feminism, with its rising levels of self-awareness, and the more complex relationships of the two-income family have challenged traditional patterns with increasing need for the demonstration of a balance between power and intimacy in both partners (Eaker et al., 1983; Staines et al., 1986).

Recent work also demonstrates the harmful effects of perceived lack of social support, as represented in actual rates of disease such as depression, cancer, and heart attacks (Berkman & Syme, 1979). Brown, Bhrolchain, and Harris (1975) have shown that women who lack a confidante or intimacy are vulnerable to depression. Thus, an uncaring, insensitive alcoholic or workaholic husband will increase this risk (Brown et al., 1975). Berkman and Syme's (1979) classic study of San Francisco area men and women also showed higher mortality rates in those perceiving lower levels of social support.

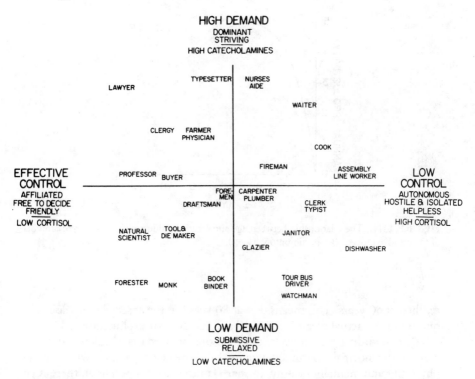

FIGURE 13-3. Mean job characteristics scores by 1970 Census Occupational Codes and U.S. Quality of Working Life Surveys. Abscissa: work load (i.e., demands); ordinate: extent of control (i.e., decision latitude). Jobs that are in the high-control quadrant (*lower left*) are associated with lower rates of cardiovascular disease than those in the upper right quadrant, which are associated with high demand and low control. Note the modern tendency for demand to become higher and control less as in the production lines of technocracy. In contrast, the arts and crafts have changed little over the centuries: lower demand and more control. (From Henry, 1986d.)

Social Effects on the Potential for Continued Productivity

Simonton (1984) has traced the quality and quantity of productive output during the careers of distinguished psychologists: persons who have been successful and on the whole well treated and valued by the society of which they are members. He reports an observed constant probability for success. For example, they produce well-accepted articles throughout their entire careers even though they extend into the seventh or eighth decade. In this regard, in his discussion of age and achievement, he plots the curve (see Figure 13-4) of an equation relating age and productivity, which shows the expected peak performance at 40 years, as well as an unexpected, long half-life of 35 years. Thus, for scholars, if the career begins at 25 years of age, midpoint is

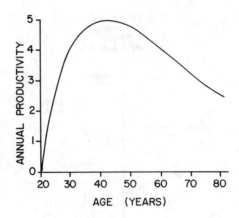

FIGURE 13-4. The relationship between age and creative productivity according to a model of the creative process. (From Simonton, 1984.)

reached at 60 years. This means that at 80 years, in the absence of disease, one quarter of the actual creative potential still remains for exploitation.

The extraordinary performances of various octogenarian leaders are examples of the normal continued vitality of those aged persons who remain physically and mentally healthy. In sharp contrast to this potential, there is an unfortunate and enormous waste of highly skilled and potentially creative persons in current society (see Uhlenberg, this volume). Much of this loss can be attributed to social practices. Not yet clear is to what extent early, forced retirement and self-destructive attitudes conveyed by the culture, resulting in retirement from the socially significant tasks of the worker, lead to chronic states of emotional disturbance and hence to chronic disease.

Thus, healthy individuals retain cognitive potential well into the eighties. However, if society persists in regarding them as having lost their capacity to contribute, they will be vulnerable to depression and a resulting loss of brain function. This loss is demonstrated in studies from behavioral medicine suggesting that, in chronically disturbed emotional states, there is an inhibition of integration of the right hemisphere's drive to intimacy with that of the left hemisphere for control (Gazzaniga, M., 1985; Henry, 1986b,c). The ensuing loss of competence results in frustration and persistent anxiety and anger, which increase vulnerability to chronic disease states. If they progress and become severe, these disease states may eventually eliminate the possibility of working due to irreversible physical and mental deterioration (Henry, 1986b; Henry & Stephens, 1977).

A decrement can also develop due to emotional disturbance in the more intimate sphere of interaction with family and friends. Kornhaber's (1985) article "Grandparenthood and the New Social Contract," together with Gutmann's (1985) "Deculturation and the American Grandparent," raise questions as to the vulnerability of depressed alienated persons to chronic drug abuse and to the deleterious effects of loss of meaning on mental and physical health. The question therefore arises: What is the degree of openness of these various innate behaviors to the deleterious effects of social situations?

Closed and Open Genetic Programs for Behavior

In his discussion of behavioral programs and evolutionary strategies, Mayr (1974) draws an important distinction concerning the perennial question of nature versus nurture, that is, of the acquired versus the innate behavioral pattern. Some genetic programs, notably in insects, do not allow modification during translation from one generation to the next. They are "closed" to experience. On the other hand, the mammal's "open" genetic programs allow new information to be inserted as they are translated into bodily mechanisms during the lifetime of the organism.

Even the most open program is by no means a clean slate, or tabula rasa. Certain types of information are more easily incorporated than others. For example, in the case of the human capacity for language, Chomsky (1972) cites evidence that inherited brain structures determine the syntax by which the young child develops speech. Children will use pronouns correctly in spite of hearing grammatical errors made by their parents. Eimas (1985) has recently presented data supporting this view. In studies of the speech perception of infants, children were found to be richly endowed with "innate perceptual mechanisms well-adapted to the characteristics of human language that prepare them for the linguistic world."

It is now clear that an infant is born with many of the neurological underpinnings of later speech perception and comprehension. In addition to the specialized anatomy of the larynx and vocal tract, and Broca's and Wernicke's speech centers in the left neocortex, as yet unidentified brain mechanisms may contribute to the child's innate perceptual capacities, capacities that evolved specifically for the perception and comprehension of speech. Their effectiveness is "reflected in the swiftness with which the child joins the community of language" (Eimas, 1985). Thus, even the relatively open genetic program of language, to which the child must be exposed for years in order to learn the particular linguistic code employed by the group to which he or she belongs, has genetically determined characteristics that are closed. Yet despite these inherited aspects, speech is not a faculty we share with other primates—it evolved in the very recent evolutionary past as the hominids developed a means of communicating in the new social groups; in other words, in reaction to the environmental demands.

Ohman and Dimberg (1984) comment that phobias are examples of biologically prepared, learned responses. We as primates have a biological readiness to associate fear with situations that threatened the well-being of our primate ancestors; thus, innate tendencies can develop over evolution in response to experiential demands. A series of sophisticated studies (as cited by Ohman and Dimberg) show that monkeys reared in laboratories do not have a spontaneous fear of snakes. However, experiments show the gene pool equips the monkey with a capacity to develop such a fear with greater ease than to develop fear of more neutral objects. Once this fear is developed, it is very hard to extinguish. The presence of a significant individual, such as the mother, who shows fear of the snake will greatly enhance the naive animal's speed of learning (Ohman & Dimberg, 1984). The importance of the social aspect of the response can be seen in opposite reactions of monkeys trained to fear a light because it signals a shock. They evince no fear when in a familiar group whose members are not so trained. They therefore ignore the light. The investigators showed that in the latter case, the animal's adrenal cortical secretion, a good measure of emotional distress, remains normal. In contrast, when alone with the shock and without social support, the animal shows distress and has increased cortical secretion (Stanton, Patterson, & Levine, 1985).

A number of characteristics of human society appear to be homologous to those of mammalian groups in general. Greater personal space is given a dominant animal, and there is a grooming cluster around the leader of a pack, be it human, baboon, or wolf. In human society, respect for the dominant also is seen in the submissive's bared and bowed head and in the deference for private property and the desk of the superior (Henry & Stephens, 1977; Maclay & Knipe, 1972). The penetrating unself-conscious gaze of the dominant compares with the shifty gaze of the fearful subordinate. Almost like humans, dominant chimpanzees threaten by fixating with wide open, staring eyes, frowning brow, and narrow slit mouths with the corners turned down. Unlike subordinates, dominants are not frightened by seeing a threatening display and merely intensify their own posture.

Much behavior directed toward other conspecific individuals, such as that cited above, consists of formal signals (Mayr, 1974; Ohman & Dimberg, 1984). There is a high selective premium for these signals to be unmistakable. As a result, the essential components of this signaling behavior must show low variability, and hence must be largely controlled genetically. Although those aspects of culture that are based on learning and that rely heavily on language often do not use genetically programmed signals, there are many aspects of our face-to-face contacts that are based primarily on closed genetic programs. Ekman (1972) and his associates have disentangled the role of culture in this communication system. They note that an important fraction of the many anatomically possible facial muscular configurations are universal expressions (i.e., found all over the world). They further note that these are vital in that they convey the basic emotions. Regardless of language or culture, emotional expressions of happiness, sadness, anger, fear, disgust, and surprise all elicit their own peculiar facial expressions (Henry & Stephens, 1977). For example, recently discovered tribes in New Guinea, with no prior contact with our culture, make the same facial expressions of fear and grief as we do. Furthermore, individuals who are born blind, and even those born blind and deaf, display these same standard emotional facial expressions (Ekman, 1972). Facial expressions are ubiquitous in the social life of all primates as a means of controlling social interaction. Comparative studies suggest that these facial displays have a common evolutionary origin and are homologous to human facial expressions. Thus, the human smile and laughter is seen as a combination of displays of submissiveness and playfulness (Henry & Stephens, 1977; Ohman & Dimberg, 1984).

This evidence that facial expressions depend on closed genetic programs permits further conclusions, since fear and anger relate to pain mechanisms and aversion, whereas happy expressions are the reverse. In a series of experiments, Ohman and Dimberg (1984) were able to show that although facial displays elicit reflex responses in observers, the inhibitory effect of a happy expression superimposed on painful (i.e., aversive) conditioning was offset by having the display (i.e., the face) directed away during the conditioning process. This shows that even the most clearly closed (i.e., inherited) genetic programs of facial expressions must be determined by the appropriate behavior of those engaged in the communication.

The mother responding to her newly born infant during the first hours after birth will follow a schema or archetypical pattern that urges her to lie *en face*, placing her face so that her eyes and those of the infant are directly opposite each other. Not only does she greet her baby with universal face-to-face smiles, but she also displays universal behavior as she lifts her head with bobbing movements, raises her eyebrows briefly, and then lowers her head toward the baby—smiling and talking. This entire pattern is repeated rhythmically (Henry, 1986a; Henry & Stephens, 1977). Although this pattern can be changed by an act of conscious will or lost in abnormal states such as depression, this ritual "dance" is universal and depends on relatively closed genetic programs. It is accompanied by strong emotions and is one of the mechanisms by which the normal mother and infant establish their permanent attachment.

The above supports the theme of this chapter: The interpersonal expressions of universally accepted motivations toward control and affiliation are inherited and not learned characteristics; so are other aspects of interpersonal behavior that result from various combinations of these primary behavioral patterns (see Figure 13-5.) As in the case of a depressed mother who does not display traditional interaction with her child, it is true that gross disturbances of behavior, representing psychosocial pathology, can alter these otherwise universal tendencies. Nevertheless, the human animal responds to emotional and social states by a remarkable set of closed genetic programs of behavior.

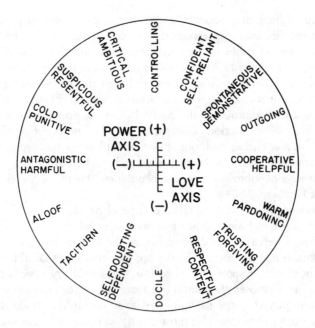

FIGURE 13-5. The 1982 Interpersonal Circle of Kiesler has been redrawn to present various aspects of interpersonal behavior and the opposites (located at the segment directly across the circle). The items chosen are Kiesler's mild to moderate social expression of the various subsets of the basic "power" (dominant–submissive) and "love" (affiliative–hostile) axes. (From Kiesler, D. J., The 1982 interpersonal circle: A taxonomy for complimentarity in human interaction. *Psychological Review, 98.* © 1983 by the American Psychological Association. Reprinted by permission.)

Closed Genetic Programs of Posture

Posture also plays an important role in the closed, genetically programmed nonverbal communication system. Recent work has shown that, as early as in nursery school, 2- to 3-year-olds exert leadership not by aggressive behavior but by pacifying, attractive behavior. Behaviorist Montagner has used ethological methods to establish their common repertoire of gestures (Pines, 1986). They include extending the hand as though begging, or taking the other child's chin in the hand and/or cocking the head over the shoulder. This programmed behavior differs sharply from the threatening fight gestures of clenching teeth or fists and leaning the trunk or head forward. It also differs from the flight component of the fight-flight response. Running away is accompanied by averted eyes and a backward gesture of the head or whole body. The isolation of depression is seen in the child who stands or sits apart or lies curled up in the fetal position and/or crying. In the adult these same inborn gestures persist.

There are many of these nonverbal messages: for example, the arrogant strut of the dominant monkey and of the movie gunslinger (Henry & Stephens, 1977); the military bearing with erect posture reflecting optimum confidence and assertion; and the defeated and depressed slouch. These behaviors are genetically programmed, and they represent responses similar to those found in rodents and in carnivora as well as in primates (Henry & Stephens, 1977; Maclay & Knipe, 1972). Further, they serve the social system and preserve the individual.

The dominance hierarchy is an important device that controls potential conflict between the social needs and individual motives of group members. By defining the roles of various group members that are in mutual competition for resources, group cohesion is increased and the group functions better as a social unit. Because in the wild state predators and other dangers abound, it is safer to stay in the group (Henry & Stephens, 1977). Low rankers with low self-assertion do so; and as long as food and harborage are sufficient, they survive. However, if conditions worsen, they are forced to leave the group and are then the first to die. This occurs in part because of their unfavorable neuroendocrine set leading to timid subordinate behavior.

The systems sketched in Figure 13-6 are flexible and subject to various overriding controls in the mammal. Despite the fact that dominant and subordinate behavior represent unlearned (innate) programs, in primates—and especially in humans—they can be as overridden by more firmly genetically determined behaviors, such as eating, drinking, and sexual responses. Further, even these behaviors are subject to change by the culture.

The recent epidemic of anorexia and bulimia in college students shows how a change in the set of the higher centers can override the basic hunger drive (Steiner & Litt, 1985). Indeed, self-starvation, which can lead to death, is a weapon used by strong-willed prisoners. Likewise, the history of celibate social systems such as the Catholic priesthood and nuns is further evidence of the feasibility of controlling genetic programs with cultural dictates. Yet the existence of such overrides does not mean that many of our learned responses are not biologically prepared. They are prewired so that given the right inputs and the right occasion we will respond quite predictably.

Just as grammar is concerned with the rules or patterns underlying communication by speech, so the terms *biogrammar* and *prepared learning* can be used to refer to the patterns underlying flexible behaviors that mammals use to attain desiderata such as food or mate. Our grammar does not determine the specifics of what we say, nor does *prepared learning* or a *biogrammar* precisely dictate behavior, but it does tell us the forms that are likely to be taken (Henry & Stephens, 1977).

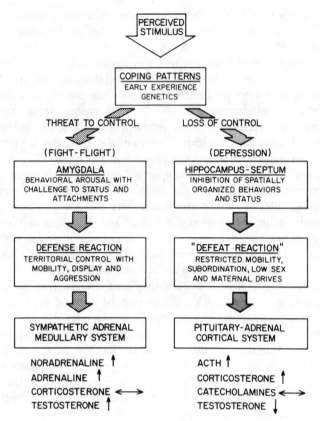

FIGURE 13-6. The defense response and the sympathoadrenal system are activated when the organism is challenged in its control of the environment. By contrast, when there is loss of territorial control and failure to meet expectations, the adrenocortical system becomes more involved as the defeat reaction takes over. The physiological consequences of these two response patterns differ as shown. (From Henry & Stephens, 1977.)

Archetypes, Imagos, and Inherited Programs

The terms *archetype*, or *emotional aptitude* (Jung, 1966), and *imago* (McAdams, 1985a,b) are expressions of the concept discussed above, as is the term *instinct*. Martindale (1980) discusses *sub-selves* — that is, internal representations of situations and personal dispositions — and presents evidence of the existence of intermediate "chunking units" in semantic memory strongly connected to the emotional systems. He perceives them as the same thing as Jung's archetypes and refers to them as deep-level person prototypes. As evidence he cites various types of dissociative states, hypnotic states, hysterical conversion states, multiple personality, and even the self-perception of creative individuals. For example, the novelist Dickens said that his characters "spoke" to him. One way of accounting for such phenomena would be to attribute them to the activity of the subselves in a brain that is made up of multiple subsystems (Gazzaniga, 1985).

Markus and Sentis (1982) use the term *schemata* to describe memory structures of conceptually related elements guiding information processing. These schemata are used to categorize and interpret social events and, by representing the self to the self as being of a certain type, they can generate choices and guide actions. The dominant individual thus has a different self-perception from one who is thoroughly defeated.

In their recent work on explanatory style and depression, Peterson and Seligman (1987) present evidence that the negative style characteristic of helplessness and defeat is associated with impaired health and life expectancy. Those suffering from this style as a lifelong trait, which commenced with childhood difficulties, are at a disadvantage because there is a robust relationship between depression and the subordinated attitude. The neuroendocrine basis for these differences and the way in which the hormones affect behavior are the subject of an overwhelming body of experimental evidence (Henry, 1986a). Figure 13-6 points to the hormonal differences between dominants and subordinates. The effect of testosterone in increasing persistence and the rise in level of this hormone in those who perceive an improvement in status as a result of winning a contest is another example of the interaction of a hormone and a pattern of behavior (Henry, 1986; Mazur & Lamb, 1980). Like Jung many decades before, Markus and Sentis (1982) propose masculine and feminine schematas: imagos or archetypes (i.e., self-schemata) the interactions of which can lead to states of androgyny or masculine/feminine behavior patterns. Thus, the combination of hormonal and emotional psychological influences affect the open, genetically determined patterns that characterize the behavior of primates, particularly highly socialized and recently evolved humankind (Mazur & Lamb, 1980).

Wiggins and Holzmuller (1981) report that the dominant and nurturant vectors of the interpersonal circle (see Figure 13-1) accurately reflect masculinity and femininity in a study of Canadian college students. The importance of testosterone for the capacity to achieve control (Mazur & Lamb, 1980) and of the female sex hormones for appropriate mother-infant behavior in mammals suggests that the interpersonal circle reflects important brain mechanisms. Despite cultural reinforcement according to assigned gender identity, the driving mechanisms are relatively closed programs and not learned behavior purely determined by the culture (Henry, 1985, 1986a).

Humankind's huge cortex, recently acquired in evolution, has a primary function of memory storage, analysis, and integration. It is divided into a logical, analytic left hemisphere, dominated by speech and involved in explaining the causes of things (Gazzaniga, 1985), and a right hemisphere, dominant in spatial sense and in the decoding and encoding of affective behavior (Ross, 1984). The vital, emotionally active subcortical limbic systems largely located in the two temporal lobes have been shown to be strongly connected to the cortex and are now believed to have been important factors in the evolution of the human brain. Vilensky, Van Hoesen, and Damasio (1982) have pointed to the higher level of development of this system in humans compared with the other primates and suggest that the limbic system's evolution was critical for humankind's capacity for symbolic representation. Thus, prime responsibility for our advanced social and communicative behavior may be not so much the development of the associational neocortex but rather of these subcortical structures.

It is true that the brain, especially the associational neocortex, has aspects of a clean slate on which anything can be written. However, as the preceding evidence indicates, the genetic programming of various aspects of social communications shows that there are also innate aspects to our behavior. The important discoveries of contemporary neurobiology force us to recognize that the revision of medieval Christian and ancient concepts of human nature by the philosophers of the Enlightenment may itself require revision. As Sperry's former associate Gazzaniga (1985, p. 86) puts it: "Civilized, educated twentieth century humans believe they are freely acting agents. Even habitual behaviors are viewed as freely willed." However,

> . . . basic cognitive phenomena such as acquiring and holding social beliefs are just as much a product of human brain organization as our desires to eat, sleep, and have sex. These special human properties of the mind are the result of brain organization and as such reveal that many of the surface differences in cultural beliefs are the inevitable product of how the brain interprets the many milieus of this world. (p. 7)

Neurobiology forces us to recognize that the philosophical foundations on which our culture rests may not fit the findings of biological science.

Summary

To summarize, the human brain does contain systems that are extraordinarily open and correspond to Locke's tabula rasa. However, there are regions that operate on much more closed genetic programs. Contemporary personality research and psychiatry as well as neurobiology are now aware of these biologically prepared systems that are already programmed. Perhaps the most eloquent description of evolutionary biological aspects of human social behavior is the chapter by Ohman and Dimberg (1984) in Waid's (1984) *Sociophysiology*. They conclude that compelling arguments can be advanced for the thesis that both closed and open genetic programs play a part in the control of behavior. Humans operate with three levels: the gene pool, individual experiences or learned engrams stored in the central nervous systems of individuals, and a cultural pool of information built up by the totality of shared experience.

Affiliation and control are genetically programmed behaviors that greatly impact on well-being in the later years. Frustration of these drives can result in disease processes that are often confused with normal aging. One of the tasks of the later years is the integration of these drives. An innate movement toward integration helps us to adapt to the cultural changes that accompany increasing age. Integration alleviates some of the frustration that results from the loss of ability to perform like a youth. Thereby it fosters a tolerance of the growing deficiencies of healthy aging.

The second half of this chapter will explore how this movement toward integration is not only a programmed behavior but supported by the social systems of some societies. This is not so much the case in the modern industrialized society. Changes have occurred that inhibit the expression of these genetically programmed behaviors. The result is a high prevalence of diseases such as hypertension, triggered in part by failure to integrate the warrior drive for power with more subtle and peaceful joys of intimacy.

SPONTANEOUS DEVELOPMENT OF THE IMAGO-ARCHETYPE IN LATER LIFE

Conspicuous Signals of Healthy Aging

We will now turn to the aging individual and see what evidence there is that the affectively toned subsystems that have been called imagos (McAdams, 1985b) or archetypes (Jung, 1966) change with age and differ in their characteristics in the second half of life. Quite apart from the effects of progressive disease, in the normal healthy individual significant developmental psychological changes accompany the neuroendocrine shifts of the aging process. Perlmutter (this volume), in her discussion of the possibilities of continued cognitive potential, supports the idea that these psychological changes may not always involve deterioration: Progression to a further socially significant phase in the development of a long-lived social animal may occur, a phase that is needed for important functions in the social context in which it evolved. The problem is whether this is adequately appreciated in contemporary technocracy.

In his description of the working of a healthy primate social order, Eaton (1976) describes the dominance hierarchy in a troop of Japanese macaque monkeys living under close observation. The complexity of the social system is as striking as its stability. In the context of aging, it is interesting that the bonds between mother and daughters remain strong throughout their lives.

They spend much time grooming each other (an activity that in humans is perhaps taken over in part by conversation), and it is not uncommon to see two or three fully grown sisters "deftly picking through their mother's fur as their own offspring play beside them." Thus, their relationships persist into the third generation, and in the female primate, grandparenting would appear to be built into the behavioral heritage.

Wynne-Edwards (1962), a pioneer student of inherited aspects of social behavior, points to the conspicuous physical changes of the middle-age human. He argues that like those at puberty, these changes signal a new stage in life and are not expressions of organic failure. There is a whitening of the hair, which includes the male's beard, and, in the Nordic races especially, there is a tendency for the men to grow bald on the crown. By contrast, the eyelashes retain their pigmentation indefinitely, and baldness is extremely localized and confined to only a few races of human males. Other parts, such as the eyebrows, grow more vigorously at this time of life than before. Wynne-Edwards argues that these changes are highly developed in man because they are of great social significance. They indicate that individuals have reached an age at which their experience and wisdom can be of value to the social group. This is especially true in nonliterate communities, where memories of rarely used resources, such as routes to little-used water holes or food, can be critical for group survival. Since the baldness is very localized and does not affect the protective eyebrows, he argues that they are positive and adaptive changes (see Figure 13-7).

Status in man is not simply a product of fighting ability; nor is it just reproductive performance based simply on sexual vigor. Rather, it includes providing for family welfare, correct decision making based on experience, and continuing to reproduce through later years. Perhaps in early societies and surely today, elders have high positions not only because of accumulated information and experience but also as a result of longer periods to collect the

FIGURE 13-7. A continuum of human physical status signals can be expressed along the age gradient in humans from puberty to old age. A number of such signal combinations are portrayed here: for example, changes in size of neck, nose, beard, and eyebrows, degree of balding, graying, and wrinkling. The signs of age do not exclude high status; indeed, deference is paid to their possessors. (From Guthrie, 1976.)

various items that symbolize status and hence privilege (Guthrie, 1976). Seniority systems and forms of gerontocracy stretch well back into our proto-hominid ancestry. Physical changes may reinforce a social position that is based directly or indirectly on seniority. Thus, having visible symbols of age past maturity may increase the total effect of status, improving one's likelihood of maintaining a dominant position and an increase in life span. A longer life would in turn increase the likelihood of a greater genetic contribution to the next generation.

The possibility of retaining vigor and creativity after the menopause has always been recognized. Wynne-Edwards (1962) reports that among the Australian aborigines there was a formal rite of passage of much importance, at the time when the oldest child of a couple was declared marriageable. To some extent, it was comparable to the earlier initiation ceremonies but symbolized entry into the third degree of seniority. Such valuing of the vigorous aged is also found in small, traditionalist folk societies. Gutmann (1980) describes it as participatory gerontocracy. The older individuals acquire special powers and privileges partially based on the mere successful accomplishment of surviving until old age in a difficult environment, which implies a measure of competence. In such societies, aging individuals do not permanently disengage from social behavior, as has been described as a pattern of Western technocracy by Cumming and Henry (1961). Instead, in the traditional groups the older individual has an active role in maintaining the various norms of the society. As he or she switches from involvement in the everyday work of production, he or she may disengage, but, according to Gutmann, it is a temporary phase and "a prelude to new beginnings rather than the beginning of the end."

Traditional Roles of the Aged in Society

Gutmann (1980) suggests that permanent disengagement represents a disturbance of the natural sequence of changes in motivation and function of the imago-archetype complexes as the individual ages. He blames it on the absence of a ritual appropriate for later life re-engagement, which is missing in rapidly changing secular industrial and postindustrial societies. Gutmann's view is that loss and disengagement are an expression of culture and not a universal, genetically determined program. This view is compatible with current understanding of the development of chronic disease. As long as individuals can escape the deterioration of chronic arthritis, chronic cardiovascular disease, and emotional disorders such as depression, there is good reason to anticipate vigorous activity without serious loss of professional skills well into the seventh and eighth decades (Fries, 1984; Fries & Crapo, 1981).

Gutmann's (1985) discussion of deculturation and the American grandparent has expanded on the above views. He argues that secular industrialized society in its current mode has rejected gerontocracy. In part, this is due to the reaction against the "old country" by the immigrants who had fled its stultifying influences. Kornhaber (1985) has presented data indicating that intimacy or attachment, which McAdams (1985a,b) sees as a necessary balance to power, is rejected by the American grandparent in part because of this society's perceptions of the teachings of egalitarianism. This philosophy teaches that regardless of race, country, or social standing, anyone can better his lot with strenuous application and labor; and by the same token the most exalted can lose in the struggle. Knowledge is power, and the pursuit of self-interest in social conditions of liberty and toleration is a goal within reach. So much for today's popularization of the proposals by philosophers of the Enlightenment like John Locke. As a Christian, Locke had added the caveat that egalitarianism, with its skepticism and mistrust of authority, was to be tempered by the recognition that power must be combined with intimacy in order to avoid a rapacious egotism (Wood, 1983). Thus, as a result of their religious traditions the Enlightenment philosophers accepted a balancing emphasis on affiliative behavior that avoided the secularist's narcissistic obsession with power and control.

Gutmann (1980, 1985) sees a clash between the traditional society's ethos of familialism and a new ethos of ascendant individuality. Separation from the secure intimacy of a social system that promotes affiliative behavior may lead to unchecked hedonism instead of stopping with the achievement of self-sufficiency. Thus, it is feared that with power-oriented secularism there is loss of the cultural imperatives that characterized the traditional systems promoting affiliative behavior. Gutmann further argues that value formation has been made relative, so the various members of our culture no longer share the same ideals and myths. Yet without myths held in common by a shared culture, the individual will not endure the deprivations necessary to maintain and raise the next generation in a stable society. It may well be that in periods of rapid change, as in today's industrial and postindustrial societies, a temporary anomie and loss of standards develops. Fortunately for humankind, however, there is a bright side to this picture. Because the myths are an expression of closed inherited behavior patterns, they are continually being rediscovered by healthy social systems, and eventually a new culture and a new mythology develop that incorporates them (Henry & Stephens, 1977).

Aging, Androgyny, and Individuation

Gutmann (1980) sees the elderly in a preindustrial, stable society as wardens of the culture, a role he sees as slipping away as the rapidly changing contemporary industrial societies lose contact with the discredited myths and traditions. He argues that by observing aging in only a single culture you cannot disentangle the relatively closed genetic programs from the pressures of social conditions. His transcultural studies of the Maya of Mexico, the Navajo of the

United States, and the Druze of Israel, together with reports of societies in Asia, the Middle East, and Africa, have led him to conclude that universals (i.e., the biogrammar that forms the inner imagos or archetypes) push people into different behavioral patterns at various stages in life.

For example, in contrast to younger men, older men are more interested in community and in giving and receiving love than in agency or acquiring power. They see power as lodged outside themselves in a capricious secular or supernatural authority. Thus, it can be controlled only through prayer or other forms of accommodation. Younger men tend to be businesslike. They do not go out of their way to seek pleasure nor do they avoid work-related discomfort. Gutmann (1980) says that even their pleasure is bound up with work. Their chief pleasure is to achieve control over the resources on which their security and that of their dependents is based. They look at the world as an arena for competition and action. Older men derive some incidental bonus and aesthetic pleasure from their daily routine. In this way they form a valuable counterpoise to the drive for control. Guttman states that women age psychologically in the reverse direction, and even in normally patriarchal societies they become more androgenic and prepared to manage and enter political life. Unlike older men's trend to become more easygoing, women become more agentic (Gutmann, 1980) and interested in seeing that access to desiderata is properly controlled, especially from the viewpoint of giving a "fair chance" rather than abstract "justice" (Gilligan, 1982). Thus, the data indicate that during the postparental years, each sex becomes something of what the other used to be, and the normal androgyny of later life is ushered in.

Although the mechanisms of these changes that Gutmann (1980) describes so eloquently remain to be determined, it is likely that they involve effects of hormones on subcortical regions. The perception by the young father and mother of the children's needs involves an arousal by the sex hormones of "masculine" (controlling) and "feminine" (nurturing) behavior, respectively. At this stage in life, there is cultural emphasis on a team role, with the man practicing control over resources and the woman over the family nurturance and intimacy—roles for which, at that age, each is best equipped by their genetic programs, including their neuroendocrine (testosterone and estrogen) differences.

By contrast, in later life it is helpful to have collective representations that will quite openly and consciously carry imago-archetype representations differing from those of the prime of life. The traditional religions of the nonindustrialized societies, with their collective rituals, bound their members to the all-powerful, all-including gods. As Gutmann (1980) says, "Under these circumstances death loses its personal sting. For what becomes important is not the persistence of self but the persistence of the gods and the proper life ways that reflect their mythic nature." The fact that skills do not deteriorate in the normal, healthy, aging individual (Light, this volume; Perlmutter, this volume) means that it is possible to maintain one's social identity, or *persona*, unchanged from youth into late life (Stein, 1982). Thus, identity (persona), or the compromise between the individual and society as to the individual's significance as a working role-player, can stay intact into the 60- to 80-year period. It is proposed that this is the state of affairs in the pretechnocratic traditional society: To use Jung's terms, both the culturally determined persona and the inherited archetypal value systems protect against chronic emotional disturbances. This may explain why the incidence of chronic disease such as hypertension or coronary heart disease is less in such societies than in today's industrialized societies, whose rapidly changing, fluid state has led to abandonment of the traditional myths (Henry, 1986d).

Gutmann (1980) suggests that the changes that occur in the personality with age are normal expressions of activity of "deep structures" in the human psyche. This is compatible with the observations cited above that there are accompanying physical and neuroendocrine changes, such as the whitening of the hair and the menopause, that have no connection with the classic chronic diseases of aging.

Recent work suggests that the denial of intimacy, that is, of loving attachment, and an exaggerated need for control are at the root of what is termed narcissism (Lowen, 1983). It appears connected with an emphasis on power and emergency responses and can, as part of the posttraumatic stress syndrome, be triggered by severe emotional trauma, for example, warfare, prison camps, and various crises and catastrophes (Henry, 1986b,c). The mechanism of the resulting emotional disturbance is not known, but there is evidence of an alexithymic failure to communicate and experience nuances of emotion. This may be due to some block between the analytic-verbal "controlling" left hemisphere and the right hemisphere, which is critical for the decoding and encoding of affective behavior and the expression of intimacy (Henry, 1986b; Ross, 1984).

The resulting challenge facing our society is summarized in the last sentence of Gutmann's 1985 paper: "We will have to enlist the elders who have traditionally been the wardens of culture to help us and even guide us in this vital process of reversing deculturation and crafting the new myths on which reculturation can be based" (p.181). However, Passuth and Bengtson (this volume) have reviewed recent trends in the social psychology of family life and aging, and the evidence does not support the foregoing thesis insofar as it postulates a decline in intergenerational family contacts. He finds that most elderly parents are contacted weekly by their offspring, most grandparents have regular contact with their grandchildren, and in divorce the failing parent/child tie is often compensated for by the older generation. The care of the demented aged by family members is still the major support they receive.

In explaining this familial maintenance of nurturant behavior one can call on the ethological concept of the instincts involving bonding, that is, attachment behavior. The relationships between mother and child and among grandmother, mother, and child are based on a bonding that depends on permanent changes in the brain mechanisms responsible for instinctual behavior. The process is not dependent on learning the culture. It involves closed, genetically determined programs. Studies of children brought up in the Israeli kibbutzim have shown that marriages do not take place between members that have belonged to the same group and shared the same nursery as preschoolers. As adults they show great attachment for each other, but as in any other normal family that is raised together, erotic attachment behavior is tempered by an incest prohibition that works spontaneously without having to be taught (Sheper, 1971). In other work Spiro (1979) has recanted on his previous explanation of culturally learned female behavior in the kibbutz. The past 25 years have seen a steadily increasing emphasis on an elaborate wedding ceremony, a demand for more elaborate private family housing, and the opportunity for the expression of individual attachment behavior such as each mother putting her own children to bed at night. Spiro now attributes these trends to "precultural" motivational dispositions, that is, to innate programs that have overridden the conscious culture and learned values of the kibbutz.

The attachment between family members and across the generations that develops even in the secularized postindustrial societies is probably not an expression of learned but of inherited behavior. The roles of father and grandfather, mother and grandmother, brothers and sisters appear to involve elements of closed-genetic programs or imagos and archetypes. It would account for Passuth and Bengtson's (this volume) observations of the persistence of the behavior despite failure of our pluralistic culture to provide strong guidelines (Kornhaber, 1985). On the other hand, the marriage bond, insofar as it is based on a social contract, will not be so tenacious. Hence, our vulnerability to divorce.

If there is genetic programming for intimate familial behavior, this would imply a natural bias toward sustaining relationships that help to preserve the family and recreate the myth. This would occur in spite of the loss of myths and increasing secularization during the intense social changes of two centuries of industrial and postindustrial development. In normal persons not suffering from the brain damage of psychic trauma (Henry, 1986b) there is a bias toward intimacy and affection between those whom family membership has bonded. Thus, inherited patterns of behavior will support the bias of the normal aged to respect the intimate ties of "blood" relationships and to craft the new myths that will power the needed reculturation. The corresponding biological ties of marriage depend on the mechanisms of romantic love and the psychiatrists' "transference phenomenon" (Stein, 1982). Their biological importance is hinted at by the superior survival statistics of the married (Henry, 1985). That the bonding induced between men and women should be stable is as critical for group survival as are the ties of "blood" and the stable attachment between parents and children.

In his recent paper on this bonding or love, which he entitles "Some Reflections on the Two Psychologies of Love," McClelland (1986) has made a cogent analysis of the determinants of affiliative behavior. He cites experimental evidence that it does not depend only on the conscious values of the self-report (presumably, he says, mediated more by the left brain). Rather, people are more likely to behave in an affiliative way when their social skills are supported by the (presumably more right-brain) unconscious evaluations of feeling and fantasy (or in Jung's terms, by *archetypal symbols*). In Jung's (1954) *Psychology of the Transference*, he comments as follows:

> The transference phenomenon is without doubt one of the most important syndromes in the process of individuation; its wealth of meaning goes far beyond mere personal likes and dislikes. By virtue of its collective contents and symbols it transcends the individual personality and extends into the social sphere. . . . The symbols of the circle and quaternity, the hallmarks of the individuation process, fall back on the one hand to the original and primitive order of human society and forward on the other to an inner order of the psyche. It is as though the psyche were the indispensable instrument in the reorganization of a civilized community. (p. 321)

SUMMARY

In their introduction to the recent *Handbook of Mental Health and Aging*, Birren and Renner (1980) define aging as the regular changes that occur in mature, genetically representative organisms living under representative environmental conditions as they advance in chronological age. It is now recognized that these underlying changes with aging are not only degenerative. There can also be positive progression of personal and social characteristics involving roles and the exercise of the instincts for power and for intimacy associated with them: complex skills can increase with age.

Shock's (1960) famous biological data from the 1960s show a steady decline of various physiological functions with age; particularly of cardiac output, renal blood flow, and maximum breathing capacity. This well-established decrement of vital biological parameters may be the basis for the belief that performance at the psychological and social level also falls off progressively with age. However, it is now realized that silent, asymptomatic chronic disease, such as arteriosclerosis, contributes part of the deterioration of Shock's supposedly normal subjects.

In 1984 Rodeheffer et al. (1984) published in *Circulation* a study of cardiac output, at rest and during exercise, in healthy active men and women of ages ranging up to 79 years. Their title summed up matters with the statement,

"Exercise: Cardiac output is maintained with advancing age in healthy human subjects: Cardiac dilatation and increased stroke volume compensate for a diminished heart rate." They attributed their results to the deliberate exclusion of persons with coronary heart disease and suggest that disease may have accounted for the age-related decline in cardiac performance that has previously been observed.

The following year Lindeman, Toben, and Shock (1985) reported on longitudinal studies on the rate of decline of renal function with age. Shock's original 1960 report had described a decline in these vital functions with age. Twenty-five years later, after excluding all subjects with possible renal or urinary tract disease, the group left had a very modest mean annual decrease in clearance. Further analysis showed that one-third of these had no absolute decrease in renal function with age. As in the case of the recent work with cardiac output, the new study arrived at the conclusion that renal changes do not necessarily occur with age in those fortunate enough to escape subclinical pathology. For a long time a rise of blood pressure was regarded in our society as a normal accompaniment of aging. It is only recently that it has been recognized as a preventable disease (Henry, Stephens, & Ely, 1986). Current students of aging perceive that, especially in those free from disease and despite progressive changes, gross physiological deterioration does not necessarily occur and the performance of some social roles may remain stable or even improve.

Bengtson and Treas (1980) suggest that aging can be viewed as a career that involves the successful negotiation of changes in social positions. This chapter presents evidence that changes in social performance do not occur only in response to cultural demand. They are also expressions of genetically determined, instinct-driven programs. The passage from one generation to the next, from mother and father to grandmother and grandfather, is accompanied by positive changes leading to the integration of basic parenting dimensions. In the older generation the previously separate drive to control the environment in the attempt to secure desiderata becomes integrated with the exercise of affiliative behavior in family and group situations. Power and intimacy—agentic (masculine) and nurturant (female) behavior—are related descriptors. With the passage from one generation to the next, there is a trend for these two functions and related personality characteristics to become less typical of the "father" and of the "mother." In the aging individual, males become more nurturant and females more agentic.

It is proposed that the evolution of humanity has involved this genetically determined integration of the personality characteristics of power and intimacy, an integration that is typical of healthy, successful individuals. It has survival value not only for the individual but also for the social group, which uses the balanced knowledge and wisdom of such individuals to educate, lead, and counsel. Grandparenthood is a natural biological event that is timed to coincide with this effective fusion of major personality dimensions.

The integrated personality has been recognized and cultivated by major religious systems. This mind-set has been identified as individuation by Jung (1933) and as generativity by Erikson (1959). It is found in those who are creative and whose effect on others tends to be positive. Antonovsky's (1979, 1987) capacity to perceive the world as coherent and Maddi and Kobasa's (1984) hardiness may be related. Both have been shown to be associated with maturity and to be important in controlling the intensity of the anxiety, anger, fear, and grief that fosters chronic disease and faulty decision making.

As Rowe and Kahan (1987) point out, an increasing number of the aged successfully avoid the usual severe deterioration of the biological support systems due to chronic disease states and their health is far better than is generally realized. Such successfully aging persons maintain performance by flexibility and continued learning. The present approach proposes in addition that the genetically controlled sequencing of the behavioral characteristics that develop during maturation continues into later life. It results in the appearance in some persons of a particularly effective combination of the different systems. This is not only acquired (i.e., learned) behavior. It represents an inherited response to the demands imposed by natural selection on the newly evolved human societies. It helped in the solution of their growing and increasingly complex problems by synthesizing the emotional and intellectual capacities' lifetime exercise of the drive for power with the social skills of intimacy.

REFERENCES

Antonovsky, A. (1979). *Health, stress and coping: New perspectives on mental and physical well-being*. San Francisco: Jossey-Bass.

Antonovsky, A. (1987). *Unraveling the mystery of health: How people manage stress and stay well*. San Francisco: Jossey-Bass.

Bakan, D. (1966). Agency and communion in human sexuality. In D. Bakan (Ed.), *The duality of human existence: An essay on psychology and religion* (pp. 102–153). Skokie, IL: Rand-McNally.

Bengtson, V. L., & Treas J. (1980). The changing family context of mental health and aging. In J. E. Birren (Ed.), *Handbook of mental health and aging* (pp. 400–428). Englewood Cliffs, NJ: Prentice-Hall.

Berkman, L., & Syme, S. (1979). Social networks resistance and mortality: A nine year follow-up of Alameda county residents. *American Journal of Epidemiology, 190*, 186–204.

Birren, J. E., & Renner, J. (1980). Concepts and issues of mental health and aging. In J. E. Birren (Ed.), *Handbook of mental health and aging* (pp. 3–33). Englewood Cliffs, NJ: Prentice-Hall.

Bowlby, J. (1970). *Attachment and loss* (Vol. 1). London: Hogarth Press.

Brown, G. W., Bhrolchain, M. N., & Harris, T. (1975). Social class and psychiatric disturbance among women in an urban population. *Sociology, 9*, 225–254.

Chomsky, N. (1972). *Language and mind*. New York: Harcourt Brace Jovanovich.

Cumming, E., & Henry, W. E. (1961). *Growing old: The process of disengagement*. New York: Basic Books.

Eaker, E. D., Haynes, S. G., & Feinleib, M. (1983). Spouse behavior and coronary heart disease in men: Prospective results from the Framingham Study II. *American Journal of Epidemiology, 118*, 156–169.

Eaton, G. G. (1976). The social order of Japanese macaques. *Scientific American, 235*, 97–106.

Eimas, P. D. (1985). The perception of speech in early infancy. *Scientific American, 252*, 46–52.

Ekman, P. (1972). Universal and cultural differences in facial expressions of emotion. In J. K. Cole (Ed.), *Nebraska Symposium on Motivation* (pp. 207–283). Lincoln, NE: University of Nebraska Press.

Erikson, E. J. (1959). Identity and the life cycle: Selected papers. *Psychological Issues, 1*, 5–165.

Fries, J. F. (1984). The compression of morbidity: Miscellaneous comments about a theme. *The Gerontologist, 24*, 354–359.

Fries, J. F., & Crapo, L. M. (1981). *Vitality and aging: Implications of the rectangular curve*. San Francisco: W. H. Freeman.

Gazzaniga, M. (1985). *The social brain: Discovering the networks of the mind* (pp. 6–7). New York: Basic Books.

Gilligan, C. (1982). *In a different voice: Psychological theory and women's development*. Cambridge, MA: Harvard University Press.

Goldbrunner, J. (1964). Individuation: A study of the depth psychology of Carl Gustav Jung. Indiana: University of Notre Dame Press.

Guthrie, R. D. (1976). *Body hot spots: The anatomy of human social organs and behavior*. New York: Van Nostrand Reinhold.

Gutmann, D. L. (1980). The post-parental years: Clinical problems and developmental possibilities. In W. H. Norman & T. J. Scaramella (Eds.), *Mid-life: Developmental and clinical issues* (pp. 38–52). New York: Brunner/Mazel.

Gutmann, D. L. (1985). Deculturation and the American grandparent. In V. L. Bengtson & J. E. Robertson (Eds.), *Grandparenthood* (pp. 173–181). Beverly Hills: Sage.

Henry, J. P. (1985). Psychosocial factors in disease and aging. In J. E. Birren & J. Livingston (Eds.), *Cognition, stress and aging* (pp. 21–44). Englewood Cliffs, NJ: Prentice-Hall.

Henry, J. P. (1986a). Neuroendocrine patterns of emotional response. In R. Plutchik & H. Kellerman (Eds.), *Emotion: Theory, research and experience: Vol. 3. Biological foundations of emotion*. Orlando, FL: Academic Press.

Henry, J. P. (1986b). Relation of psychosocial factors to the senile dementias. In M. L. M. Gilhooly, S. H. Zarit, & J. E. Birren (Eds.), *The dementias: Policy and management* (pp. 38–65). Englewood Cliffs, NJ: Prentice-Hall.

Henry, J. P. (1986c). Religious experience, archetypes and the neurophysiology of emotions. *Zygon 21*, 47–74.

Henry, J. P. (1986d). Education, lifestyle and the health of the aging. In J. E. Birren, J. E. Thornton, & D. A. Peterson (Eds.), *Education and aging*. (pp. 149–184). Englewood Cliffs, NJ: Prentice Hall.

Henry, J. P., & Stephens, P. M. (1977). *Stress, health and the social environment: A sociobiologic approach to medicine*. New York: Springer-Verlag.

Henry, J. P., Stephens, P. M., & Ely, D. L. (1986). Psychosocial hypertension and the defense and defeat reactions. *Journal of Hypertension, 4*, 687–697.

Hinde, R. A. (1974). *Biological bases of human social behavior*. New York: McGraw-Hill.

Jung, C. G. (1933). Psychological types or the psychology of individuation. New York: Harcourt, Brace.

Jung, C. G. (1954). Psychology of the transference. In C. G. Jung (Ed.), *Collected works: Vol. 16. The practice of psychotherapy* (pp. 163–341). New York: Routledge, Kegan Paul.

Jung, C. G. (1966). *Two essays on analytical psychology*. Princeton, NJ: Princeton University Press.

Karasek, R., Schwartz, J., & Theorell, T. (1982). Job characteristics, occupation and coronary heart disease. *Final Report to the National Institute of Occupational Safety and Health*. Mimeo. Department of Industrial and Systems Engineering, University of Southern California.

Kiesler, D. J. (1983). The 1982 interpersonal circle: A taxonomy for complementarity in human transactions. *Psychological Review, 90*, 185–214.

Kornhaber, A. (1985). Grandparenthood and the "new social contract." In V. L. Bengtson & J. E. Robertson (Eds.), *Grandparenthood* (pp. 159–171). Beverly Hills, CA: Sage.

Lindeman, R. D., Tobin, J., & Shock, N. W. (1985). Longitudinal studies on the rate of decline in renal function with age. *Journal of American Geriatrics, 33*, 278–285.

Locke, S., & Colligan, D. (1986). *The healer within: The new medicine of mind and body*. New York: Dutton.

Lowen, A. (1983). *Narcissism: Denial of the true self*. New York: Macmillan.

Lynch, J. J. (1985). *The language of the heart: The body's response to human dialogue*. New York: Basic Books.

Maclay, R., & Knipe, H. (1972). *The dominant man: The pecking order in human society*. New York: Delacorte Press.

Maddi, S. R., & Kobasa, S. C. (1984). *The hardy executive: Health under stress*. Homewood, IL: Dow Jones Review.

Markus, H., & Sentis, K. (1982). The self in social information processing. In J. Suis (Ed.), *Psychological perspectives on the self* (Vol. 1). (pp. 41–71). London: Erlbaum.

Martindale, C. (1980). Subselves: The internal representation of situation and personal dispositions. In L. Wheeler (Ed.), *Review of personality and social psychology* (Vol 1, pp. 193–218). Beverly Hills, CA: Sage.

Mayr, E. (1974). Behavior programs and evolutionary strategies. *American Scientist, 62*, 650–659.

Mazur, A., & Lamb, T. A. (1980). Testosterone, status and mood in human males. *Hormonal Behavior, 14*, 236–246.

McAdams, D. P. (1985a). The "imago": A key narrative component of identity. In P. Shaver (Ed.), *Self, situations, and social behavior* (pp. 115–142). Beverly Hills: Sage.

McAdams, D. P. (1985b). *Power, intimacy, and the life story: Personological inquiries into identity*. Homewood, IL: Dorsey Press.

McClelland, D. C. (1975). *Power: The inner experience*. New York: Irvington.

McClelland, D. C. (1979). Inhibited power motivation and high blood pressure in men. *Journal of Abnormal Psychology, 88*, 182–190.

McClelland, D. C. (1986). Some reflections on the two psychologies of love. *Journal of Personality, 54,* 334–353.

Medalie, J. H., & Goldbourt, U. (1976). Angina pectoris among 10,000 men. Psychosocial and other risk factors as evidenced by a multivariate analysis of a five-year incidence study. *American Journal of Medicine, 60,* 910–921.

Miller, N. E. (1980). Effects of learning on physical symptoms produced by psychological stress. In *Selye's guide to stress research* (pp. 131–167). New York: Van Nostrand Reinhold.

Myers, G. C., & Manton, K. G. (1984). Compression of mortality: Myth or reality? *The Gerontologist, 24,* 346–353.

Ohman, A., & Dimberg, U. (1984). An evolutionary perspective on human social behavior. In W. M. Waid (Ed.), *Sociophysiology* (pp. 47–86). New York: Springer-Verlag.

Peterson, C., & Seligman, M. E. P. (1987). Explanatory style and illness. *Journal of Personality, 55,* 237–266.

Pines, M. (1986). Children's winning ways. *Psychology Today, 18,* 59–65.

Rodeheffer, R., Gorstenbleth, E., Becker, L. C., Fleg, J. L., Weisfelt, M., & Lakatta, E. G. (1984). Exercise cardiac output is maintained with advancing age in healthy human subjects. *Circulation, 69,* 203–213.

Ross, E. D. (1984). Right hemisphere's role in language, affective behavior and emotion. *Trends in Neurosciences, 7,* 342–346.

Shaper, J. (1971). Mate selection among second generation Kibbutz adolescents and adults: Incest avoidance and negative imprinting. *Archives of Sex Behavior, 1,* 293–307.

Shock, N. W. (1960). Discussion of mortality and measurement in aging. In B. L. Strehler, S. D. Ebert, H. B. Glass, & N. W. Shock, (Eds.), *The biology of aging: A symposium* (pp. 141–162). Washington, DC: American Institute of Biological Science.

Simonton, D. K. (1984). *Genius, creativity, and leadership, historiometric inquiries.* Cambridge, MA: Harvard University Press.

Simonton, D. K. (1985). Quality, quantity, and age: The careers of ten distinguished psychologists. *International Journal of Aging and Development, 21,* 241–254.

Spiro, M. E. (1979). *Gender and culture: Kibbutz women revisited.* Durham, NC: Duke University Press.

Stanton, M. E., Patterson, J. M., & Levine, S. (1985). Social influences on conditioned cortisol secretion in the squirrel monkey. *Psychoneuroendocrinology, 10(2),* 125–134.

Stein, M. (1982). *Jungian analysis.* London: Open Court.

Steiner, H., & Litt, I. F. (1985). Anorexia nervosa and bulimia: Stress syndromes? In P. Pichot, P. Bessier, R. Wolf, & K. Thau (Eds.), *Psychiatry: State of the art. Vol 2: Biological psychiatry* (pp. 798–800). New York: Plenum Press.

Suarez, L., & Barrett-Conner, E. (1984). Is an educated wife hazardous to your health? *American Journal of Epidemiology, 119,* 244–249.

Vilensky, J. A., Van Hoesen, G. W., & Damasio, A. R. (1982). The limbic system and human evolution. *Journal of Human Evolution, 11,* 447–460.

Waid, W. M. (1984). *Sociophysiology.* New York: Springer-Verlag.

Wiggins, J. S., & Broughton, R. (1985). The interpersonal circle: A structural model for the integration of personality research. *Perspectives in Personality, 1*, 1–47.

Wiggins, J. S., & Holzmuller, A. (1981). Further evidence on androgyny and interpersonal flexibility. *Journal of Research in Personality, 15*, 67–80.

Wood, N. (1983). *The politics of Locke's philosophy: A social study of "An essay concerning human understanding."* Berkeley, CA: University of California Press.

Wynne-Edwards, V. C. (1962). *Animal dispersion in relation to social behavior.* Edinburgh: Oliver & Boyd.

14

On Growing, Formative Change, and Aging

Johannes J. F. Schroots

FORMATIVE CHANGE

The title of this chapter refers to D'Arcy Thompson's (1961) *On Growth and Form*, first published in 1917 and later edited and abridged by Bonner. This chapter is not only intended as a homage to the outstanding literary and scientific qualities of Thompson's masterpiece, but also as a commentary on the subtle differences of opinion in the natural, behavioral, and social sciences, which appeared since Thompson's publication. These differences will provide an opportunity to elaborate on some prolegomena to earlier articles on *ontogenetic psychology* (Birren & Schroots, 1984; Schroots, 1982b).

The purpose of this chapter is to advance theory and research on the study of the organization of behavior over the course of an individual's life, often divided into a developing phase and an aging phase. An important difference should be pointed out between the two terms, *growth* and *growing*. This difference parallels the more general distinctions made between substantive and gerund, static and dynamic, product and process, space and time, being and becoming. It reflects the change during the past century in the research questions psychologists ask themselves. Research in the early days of psychology focused, appropriately, on the question: How *is* behavior organized?," e.g., D. O. Hebb's (1949) famous book, *On the Organization of Behavior*. As research was undertaken into studies of growth, development, and, much later, into aging, a second question was implicitly asked: How does behavior *become* organized? (Birren & Schroots, 1983).

Although in early developmental studies time was not completely neglected—concepts of age norms, age stratification, and time of measurement, for instance, have a history nearly as long as psychology itself—almost no attention was paid to the passage of time. It is not surprising, therefore, that space and spatial metaphors predominated psychologists' earlier models of the mind (Gentner & Grudin, 1985). Time is of utmost relevance for the study of aging. Because of the many kinds of time, however, a warning is warranted in combining space and time into spatiotemporal metaphors. This combination will not automatically result in improved scientific metaphors for the description and explanation of behavioral changes over the course of the individual's life. For example, chronological age, which is expressed in terms of calendar or clock time (i.e., linear-physical time), seems to lose much of its descriptive and explanatory power when people grow older. For this reason, some problems related to different scientific metaphors of life will be discussed from a morphogenetic perspective in the next section.

Noteworthy is the complete absence of the term *aging* in Thompson's title and in his book as well. In fact, any reference to more or less equivalent terms, such as *senescence*, *growing older*, and *old age*, is completely lacking. The reason for this becomes clear in Thompson's own explanation of the title of his book:

> I have called this book a study of *Growth and Form*, because in the most familiar illustrations of organic form, as in our own bodies for example, these two factors are inseparably associated, and because we are here justified in thinking of form as the direct resultant and consequence of growth: of growth, whose varying rate in one direction or another has produced, by its gradual and unequal increments, the successive stages of development and the final configuration of the whole material structure. (pp. 36–37)

In other words, growth is a matter of incremental change and form, the final result. It is clear, then, according to Thompson, that decremental changes do not belong in the book, if they exist at all. Organic forms, having reached their final configuration, stop changing eventually. This concept no longer holds because people do change during their lives in many respects, although changes in form and size are slow after adolescence. These so-called *formative changes* in adulthood will be discussed in the sections that follow entitled "Growing" and "Aging." In those sections a survey will be given of recent theories, which can contribute to descriptions and/or explanations of growing and aging from a morphogenetic perspective.

Formative change is the third and final of the concepts outlined above. As noted earlier, Thompson promotes the concept of form as a static product, rather than as a dynamic process. However, one does not necessarily have to attribute static qualities to form. As Rose (1980) so eloquently demonstrates:

> In *Art as Experience*, Dewey (1934) emphasizes that "form is the moving integration of an experience" (p. 184). It selects and intensifies the temporal and spatial features of perception, thus drawing conscious attention to the characteristics underlying an integrated, complete experience. Form makes these qualities manifest for their own sake. In clarifying the process of organizing space and time in any developing life-experience, form elicits the quality of experience more energetically than does ordinary life itself. (p. 1)

To avoid any entanglement and to emphasize the changing qualities of form, the term *formative change*, or *morphogenesis*, will be used in the present chapter. *Formative change is taken to include not only the changes in shape of the outer surface or boundary of an organism but also its internal structure.*

Finally, in the last section of this chapter, entitled "Ontogenetic Psychology," an attempt will be made to discuss, integrate, and summarize the findings regarding growing and aging from a morphogenetic perspective.

SCIENTIFIC METAPHORS AND THE DESCRIPTION OF BEHAVIOR

Every explanation of behavior must start with a description of that behavior. Before ontogenetic psychology can begin to answer the question of the organization of behavior over time, a description of an individual human life must first be presented. However, a precise description is impossible because it would be impossible to replicate literally the individual life in one way or another and because science and scientific description characteristically employ metaphors and are, in an essential way, themselves metaphorical (Leatherdale, 1974; Ortony, 1979; Schroots, 1982a). Therefore, for the purpose of clarity, we must first define the metaphors inherent in the study of ontogenesis.

The Branching Tree

One of the oldest metaphors of life is that of a *tree of life*, situated in the center of the earthly paradise, a symbol of the immortality of humanity. In earlier days, this tree was often depicted above the entrance of a human settlement. In the literature one can find numerous analogies between the annual cycle of growing, budding, blooming, shedding leaves, and dying, on the one hand, and the individual life cycle on the other hand. A recent example of this cyclical nature is given in Erickson's *The Life Cycle Completed* (1982). But the tree has not only been used for centuries as a metaphor for human ontogenesis; it has also been used as a *genealogical tree* or a tree diagram of phylogenesis, for the repetitive branching of a tree aptly describes the relationship of the past, present, and future of various genus, species, generations, and families. Knipscheer's diagram of a multigenerational family (this volume) is a fine example of this.

At the turn of the century psychology used this botanical metaphor for the description of mental processes (Vygotsky, 1978). Gesell (1928), for example, described child development in terms of plant growth, which should be well kept by a gardener or teacher; hence, the concept of kindergarten. Since that time the tree metaphor has found many applications in psychology. Well known in modern cognitive psychology is the so-called *decision tree*, which represents the potential and/or actual choices a person makes or might make to reach a decision. Another example is the essay that students write for Birren's Guided Autobiography seminar (Birren & Hateley, 1985), in which one of the theme assignments concerns the "history of the major branching points in life." Students are asked to think of their lives as *branching trees*, with the branching points defined as events, experiences, and happenings that have significantly affected the direction of their lives.

Finally, Hofstadter (1979) showed that some geometrical structures have a treelike form, which can be generated by some simple mathematical formula developed by Fibonacci in 1202 A.D. This formula, then, could be the starting point for a tentative mathematical description of the successive turning points of the individual life.

Canalized Pathways of Change

Although the tree as a metaphor of life is very powerful, there is one serious flaw: The tree is basically a spatial metaphor that only vaguely suggests some kind of temporality (cf. Gentner & Grudin, 1985; Lakoff & Johnson, 1980). Therefore, the *flowing river* is a more useful metaphor of life, because flowing implies time as well as change. In fact, the combination of the spatial tree metaphor with the temporal river results in an even more powerful spatiotemporal metaphor of life as a flowing and branching river, which has its source or origin at the very moment of conception, flows in one direction only, and ends eventually in the ocean at the moment of death. This metaphor has some interesting implications with regard to the cognitive-informational and energetic-entropic aspects of the individual's life course; these will be discussed in later sections on growing and aging.

Waddington (1957) has given some scientific prestige to the spatiotemporal metaphor of life by introducing the concept of *chreode* (the pathway of desire or necessity), or *canalized pathway of change*. This concept refers to the developmental trajectory of a living system as it crosses the metaphoric *epigenetic landscape*. In this metaphor the path followed by the developing organism as it rolls downward corresponds to the developmental history of the organism. As development proceeds, there is a branching series of alternative paths represented by valleys. These correspond to the potential pathways of development of the organism. Genetic changes or environmental perturbations may push the course of development away from the valley bottom and up the neighboring hillside; but unless the organism is pushed above the threshold into another valley, the process of development will find its way back. It will not return to the point from which it started but to some later position on the canalized pathway of change.

Waddington's metaphoric chreode and landscape can be applied not only to living systems and developing organisms but also to subsystems or parts of the organism, for example, organs, cells, tissues. Thus, in the course of the developing organism, the three-dimensional landscape changes to a multidimensional landscape of increasing complexity, traversed by a branching series of canalized pathways of change. This spatiotemporal metaphor of life corresponds with the modern understanding of development, which states that intra- and interindividual differences tend to increase over the life span (Birren, Kinney, Schaie, & Woodruff, 1981). The resulting differentiation with age from the simple to the complex is the combined product of one's genetic makeup, developmental "noise" (chance events during development), the (social) environment and — for human beings at least — individual choices over the life span (Dannefer, this volume; Lewontin, 1982).

It follows that individual morphogenesis or formative behavioral change over the life span might best be described in terms of branching, multidimensional development, during which the initially homomorphic organization of behavior changes into an increasingly heteromorphic complexity with age. In other words, as the number of canalized pathways of change increases with age, the number of dimensions, parameters, or variables necessary for an adequate description of the developing organism also increases. However, this conception refers only to the spatial organization of behavioral development in linear time (chronological age). An exact description of the developing organism becomes more complicated when one takes into account that development, generally speaking, proceeds nonlinearly over the life span. That is to say, formative change does not take place at the same rate in each age interval; also, it may vary in rate from one canalized pathway to another, that is, polychronic change (cf. Hall, 1983). The resulting temporal variability is low at younger ages and increases as development proceeds and as the number of pathways increases with age. From this it follows that as development proceeds the organization of behavior becomes increasingly complex, not only spatially but also temporally. Thus, the once homomorphic, synchronic behavioral organization gradually changes into a heteromorphic, asynchronic complexity with age.

In summary, a number of conclusions emerge. First, Waddington's approach is essentially descriptive because no explanation is given for the morphogenesis of a living system. Therefore, the metaphoric concepts of chreodes and *N*-dimensional, epigenetic landscapes are just descriptive conveniences (Waddington, 1969). Second, the metaphor of branching, polychronic development for life and morphogenesis makes abundantly clear that linear models of behavioral development with their stages, phases, transitions, seasons, and passages (Erickson, 1963; Gould, 1978; Levinson, 1978; Lowenthal, Thurnher, & Chiriboga, 1975; Maas & Kuypers, 1974; Sheehy, 1977) are inadequate descriptions of the human life span. As the branches, with their varying rates of development, grow in number with age, it will become increasingly difficult to find a single spatiotemporal denominator for the developing and/or aging organism. This increasing spatiotemporal variability with (calendar) age also explains why a single variable, such as biological age (Birren & Cunningham, 1985), is an inadequate predictor of aging.

GROWING

Almost thirty years ago, Harris (1957a) edited *The Concept of Development*. In this almost classical reference book the protean concept of development was discussed from a biological, psychological, and sociocultural perspective. The result of this discussion was summarized by Harris (1957b) in five points:

> Discussions of development commonly include as essential the ideas of (1) organism conceived as living system; (2) time; (3) movement over time toward complexity of organization; (4) "hierarchization," or the comprehension of parts or part-systems into larger units or "wholes;" and (5) an end-state of organization which is maintained with some stability or self-regulation.
>
> These last ideas inevitably bring up the troublesome issue of "purpose," so easy to dispose of in simple mechanical systems, but so difficult to avoid in one guise or another in discussions of biological systems.
>
> These elements, essential for describing the growth and organization of the biological individual, have been applied to processes of organization of phenomena in other fields. By analogy, the concept of development has been applied to psychological, sociological, economic, political, and even artistic and esthetic events. (pp. 3–4)

The concept of development as described by Harris (1957b) has changed little. Currently, in point (3), *movement over time* might be replaced by the term *change*, and in point (5) the idea of an *end-state of organization* would be challenged on the basis that according to modern opinion development does not stop with adulthood but goes on till death. These two marginal notes, however, only emphasize the protean nature of the concept of development as "some indication of change over the life span." At least, the dubious advantage of this definition of development is that the issue of *purpose* disappears from opinion almost completely.

Also important was Harris's (1957b) allusion to the biological origin of development in terms of growth and organization of the biological individual—in brief, *growing*. Its biological origin not only explains the metaphoric character of the concept of *psychological development* but also, and even more interesting, its primarily morphological nature (Flavell & Wohlwill, 1969). From this point of view it would be more suitable to define psychological development as *metamorphosis* (fr. Greek), *transformation* (fr. Latin), or *formative change* of individual behavior over the life span, rather than as simple *change*. Of course, the term *growing* would be an even better replacement for the concept of psychological development—not only because growing implies formative change, which was earlier defined as the change in internal and external (shape of the outer surface or boundary) structure of an organism from beginning to end, but also because growing reflects the process of increasing branching or differentiation of an organism over time. Thus, although we continue to use the term *development* for reasons of convention, it must be understood here as the process of differentiation or formative change of an organism toward increasing complexity.

Beyond the use of the particular scientific metaphors, the question arises: What theories can explain the phenomenon of growing or increasing differentiation from a morphogenetic perspective? Three theoretical approaches have been brought forward in recent years that may contain some useful explanatory principles: (a) general systems theory, (b) catastrophe theory, and (c) formative causation theory.

General Systems Theory

In the same introduction in which Harris (1957b) describes the problems of formulating a scientific concept of development, he also sets forth a hardly noticed plea for the then-new systems-theoretical approach to explaining the transformation principles of growing. In doing so, he refers to general systems theory. This theory is generally attributed to Ludwig Von Bertalanffy (1968); over the years it has been further explored by many other scientists (e.g., Boulding, 1956; Buckley, 1967; Laborit, 1977; Miller, 1978; Wilden, 1980). According to the proponents of general systems theory, the individual is a living system made up of the same elements as inanimate matter. It follows, therefore, that the elements themselves are not the basic characteristics of life but merely contribute to its structure. That is to say, the structure is the whole set of relationships existing among the elements of a set.

According to the systems-theoretical viewpoint, humans are regarded primarily as living systems, hierarchically organized from many subsystems, such as cells, cell tissues, organs, and so on, according to levels of complexity. As a system, humans can be conceived as part of an even more complex, larger system—for example, the social environment. From a thermodynamic or energetic point of view, a living system of any sort is *open*. That is to say, a current of energy passes through the hierarchically organized (sub) systems in a chain of reactions. This flow of energy starts with the sun as solar energy and gets transformed into chemical energy via plants and animals, which are our food. Metabolism introduces further *transformations*, in which food with a relatively high energy level is converted into waste products, such as carbon dioxide and water, with low energy levels.

According to the Second Law of Thermodynamics, there is an increase of *entropy* in energetic systems; entropy is defined here as the degree to which relationships between the components of any aggregate or system are mixed up, undifferentiated, or random. According to this law, one may say that each living system (e.g., human organism) moves toward maximum disorder (entropy) or *minimal differentiation*—in short, toward death. This tendency can be counterbalanced by the release of entropy to the environment. In other words, the tendency to maximum disorder can be prevented by the tendency toward a maximum energy level in the system, which corresponds with a tendency toward order—*maximum differentiation*. This order is often called negative entropy (negentropy) or *information*. Thus, the growing of living systems, that is, the process of increasing differentiation, is explained in terms of absorbing information and the free and continuous exchange of information at each level of the hierarchical organization of open subsystems.

At first sight, the physical and mathematical formalism of general systems theory, which includes information theory and cybernetics, appears to give a plausible explanation of growing. However, twenty five years have passed since Harris's plea, and one wonders why Sameroff (1982) emphasized again the need for a systems approach in developmental studies. Apparently, not much empirical work on this concept has been successfully conducted during this period, at least not in developmental psychology.

It should be pointed out that growing systems are open systems that proceed toward increasing complexity of form and organization. The concepts of entropy and information, on the other hand, were developed within the framework of *closed* systems, which ruled out an increase in information and entropy during morphogenesis. In conclusion, then, it might be said that although general systems theory cannot offer a scientifically rigid explanation of growth, it does nevertheless provide us with the conceptual framework for an advance in understanding of basic, natural processes, at least in metaphorical terms (cf. Birren & Schroots, 1984).

Catastrophe Theory

As early as 1917, D'Arcy Thompson demonstrated that the shape of a fish or of an animal's skull, drawn on a rectilinear grid, can be altered by a continuous, smooth transformation to that of a related fish or to the animal's evolutionary predecessor. It proved impossible to develop quantitative mathematics for this remarkable visual relationship, but Thompson's (1961) *On Growth and Form* has had a pervasive influence on Waddington's concepts of chreode and epigenetic landscape. Both scientists in turn inspired René Thom (1975) to develop the so-called *catastrophe theory*, which is partly developed by Zeeman (1977) and forms part of topology, a branch of qualitative mathematics that deals with *qualitatively distinct forms* and their *transformations*.

According to Zeeman (1976), catastrophe theory can be applied with particular effectiveness in those situations where gradually changing forces or motivations lead to abrupt changes in behavior (thus the term *catastrophe theory*). Applications are to be found especially in the biological, behavioral, and social sciences, where *discontinuous* and divergent phenomena are ubiquitous. Many people have wondered, for example, at the similarity of branching patterns in a tree, a river system, a nerve cell, and an epigenetic landscape. How does this qualitative similarity emerge from four very different sets of circumstances? Is it coincidence or an indication of a common principle at work? These are some of the questions that catastrophe theory tries to answer.

Briefly summarized, catastrophe theory assumes that recurrent identifiable elements—like the characteristic shape of branching patterns or the characteristic process of metamorphosis that turns a caterpillar into a butterfly—have the property of *structural stability*. That is to say, their qualitative features are recurrent, even though the circumstances giving rise to those features are never exactly the same in quantitative terms. Because of the persistent recurrence of similar forms, it is also assumed that there is only a limited number of archetypal structures, topological stable unfoldings, or *elementary catastrophes*, as they are called alternatively. Thom (1975) has shown this to be correct. For a very wide range of formative changes, only seven stable unfoldings—seven elementary catastrophes—are possible. The rather exotic names of these unfoldings are suggested by visual features of the graph that depicts them: fold, cusp, swallowtail, butterfly, and so on.

The unfoldings are called catastrophes because each of them has regions in which a dynamic system can jump suddenly from one state to another, although the factors (independent variables) controlling the process (dependent variable) change continuously. Each of the seven catastrophes represents a pattern of behavior determined only by the *number* of control factors (maximum of four factors), not by their nature or by the interior mechanisms that connect them to the system's behavior. Therefore, the elementary catastrophes can be models for a wide variety of processes, even those in which we know little about the quantitative laws involved.

Woodcock and Davis (1978) present a comprehensive overview of the many applications of catastrophe theory in the physical, biological, behavioral, and social sciences. In psychology, for instance, they model such diverse behaviors as learned helplessness, reactive and process schizophrenia, anorexia nervosa, and auditory illusions in terms of a variety of elementary catastrophes. No example, however, is given with regard to development or growing, although Freedle (1977) made a serious attempt in modeling development as a sequence of topological catastrophes that increased (or decreased) systematically in complexity over time.

The lack of examples in regard to development will not come as a surprise to anyone who holds the pessimistic view that even the simplest biological form, let alone *change* of form, involves so many different factors that the elementary catastrophes (limited to four control factors) cannot possibly be applied. However, it was Thom's (1975) final objective to produce topological models that correspond as closely as possible to growing and formative change. In our opinion he reached this objective insofar as he succeeded in giving a formal description and the beginning of an explanation of some archetypal transformations. Thus, in this point of view, elementary catastrophes can be conceived of as providing the root metaphors of formative change.

Formative Causation Theory

In science the key to the problems of growing, differentiation, and development, about which very little is known, is situated in the understanding of genetic control of the organism within a specific environment. The genetic program, the repository of instructions encoded in the DNA and selected for by the capacity to generate organisms that show morphogenetic change and adaptive behavior patterns, seems to be the answer. In brief, DNA is conceived of as an extraordinarily complex computer, equipped with instructions for all kinds of biological, psychological, and social behavior and gifted with cognitive, affective, and conative qualities as well.

However, no one has yet defined exactly how the genetic program is supposed to generate organisms of specific form and behavior. What it can do is control the production of specific molecules and macromolecules in particular parts of the organism at particular times in its development. The assembly of large molecules into the characteristic structures of cells, and these into organisms of specific form and behavior, is generally assumed to follow either from the known laws of physics and chemistry or from yet-to-be discovered extensions of these. In other words, DNA, as the very promising key to the fundamental problems of growing and formative change, has as yet the status of metaphor, albeit a useful scientific one.

While acknowledging that physical and chemical principles impose constraints on formative change, Sheldrake (1981b) offers a radically distinct metaphor in his book, *A New Science of Life: The Hypothesis of Formative Causation*. His metaphor, molded in the *formative causation* hypothesis, proposes that the characteristic forms taken up by each level of a *hierarchically organized* system of molecules, crystals, cells, tissues, organs, organisms, and organismic behaviors are regulated not only by known energy and material factors but also by nonenergetic, invisible organizing matrices, termed *morphogenetic fields*. Morphogenetic fields do not themselves consist of matter and energy, but they can order it into spatial and temporal patterns and so select and stabilize growing and morphogenetic change. The structures of these fields are derived from the morphogenetic fields associated with previous similar systems; that is, the morphogenetic fields of past systems influence subsequent similar systems by a process called *morphic resonance*. Thus, this hypothesis proposes that the characteristic temporal and spatial organization of systems depends on influences that lead to a repetition of the forms and patterns of previous systems. In other words, the effect of morphic resonance is to stabilize forms and formative change in developing organisms similar to those that exist or have existed elsewhere.

Sheldrake's theory allows an alternative explanation of the inheritance of growing and morphogenetic change in animals, plants, and human organisms. By introducing both the concept of a hierarchy of morphogenetic fields and morphic resonance, and by extending these concepts to the spatial and temporal organization of probabilistic events within the nervous system, Sheldrake (1981b) interprets the inheritance of instinctive, archetypal, and learned patterns of behavior in terms of *morphogenetic, teleological causation*, rather than mechanistic, causal DNA programs.

The explanatory concepts that Sheldrake (1981b) introduces are not new. The hierarchical organization of morphogenetic fields, for instance, reminds one of general systems theory; and the morphogenetic fields themselves bear closely on Waddington's chreodes and epigenetic landscape and, to a lesser extent, also on Thom's topological surfaces and elementary catastrophes. The trouble, however, is that no one has ever been able to define these fields or explain how they work; most theoretical biologists consider them to be a mere descriptive convenience, a sort of shorthand for complicated sets of conventional physical and chemical interactions, the details of which remain unknown (cf. Sheldrake, 1981a, pp. 766–767). By contrast, the hypothesis of formative causation enables biological, behavioral, and social scientists to interpret these fields as a new type of physical field, which acts without attenuation over both space and time by morphic resonance, so that organisms can influence the formative change of other (related) organisms despite separation in space and time.

Since Sheldrake makes specific predictions about the outcome of clearly defined experiments, formative causation theory must be understood as a scientific theory, of which the experimental consequences are spelled out much more clearly than those dependent on a genetic program. However, most scientists are reluctant to share this view (cf. letters in *New Scientist*, June, July, and August, 1981; *Nature*, 24 September 1981), not only because of the proposed dualism of energetic and nonenergetic fields but also because the proposed experiments seem to be inconclusive in the sense that it will always be possible to postulate another morphogenetic field to account for some result. Indeed, the broad explanatory power of Sheldrake's theory is perhaps too much of a good thing, although nothing much is said about the origin of morphogenetic fields as such.

Nevertheless, a few scientists are actively studying the theory's implications. Keutzer (1982), for instance, drew a parallel between Jung's archetypes (cf. Henry, this volume) as the primary contents of the collective unconscious on the one hand and Sheldrake's conception of a morphogenetic field on the other hand. Furthermore, in *The Journal of Mind and Behavior*, Keutzer (1983) successfully demonstrated the intrinsic compatibility of the formative-causation hypothesis with Popper and Eccles's (1977) "three worlds" theory, Pribram-Bohm's "holographic model of the universe" (Pribram, 1979, 1986), and Prigogine's (1979) "nonequilibrium systems theory," which will be discussed in the next section on aging. In conclusion, it might be said that Sheldrake's theory of formative causation has the potential of deserving the same scientific metaphoric status as the DNA-computer metaphor for the explanation of growing and formative change.

AGING

It may appear at first that there is no fundamental difference between growing and aging, that the term *aging* is in fact a synonym for *growing* or *development*. Indeed, the concepts of growing and aging can be conceived as a tautology of formative change over the life span; and aging—understood as a series of transformations in time—also can be described or explained in terms of a general systems theory, catastrophe theory, or formative causation theory. The question therefore arises as to whether the two fundamental processes of formative change—growing and aging—can be distinguished in morphogenesis.

Typically, growing and aging are viewed as two successive processes in time. The transition point is located around the end of maturity or the beginning of adulthood, when the end-state of organization—that is, adult form—has been reached (Harris, 1957b). This point of view is largely held by Anderson (1964/1980) in what is likely one of the few books that explicitly addresses the *Relations of Development and Aging* (Birren, 1964/1980).

> The psychologist who studies development from birth to maturity and the psychologist who studies aging in later life have common interests. . . . Development and aging alike are not a series of random, unprogrammed events but are a series of orderly changes of many types. . . . The life cycle begins with conception and ends with death. There is rapid upward change in infancy and childhood, slower upward change in youth, a long stable period of adult life, and

downward changes in later adult life. . . . Although the terms development and aging may be used for all age changes, in this paper *development* is used for the upward and *aging* for the downward changes. (pp. 11–12)

This conception of aging is consistent in many works. For example, Birren and Renner (1977) offered the following general definition of aging for the behavioral sciences: "Aging refers to the regular changes that occur in *mature* genetically representative organisms living under representative environmental conditions" (p. 4, emphasis added). However, in a more recent work Birren and Cunningham (1985) took a broader view: "Ontogenetic psychology is divided into an early phase – the developmental psychology of childhood, adolescence and young adulthood – and a second phase – middle and old age" (p. 4). They further contradicted the more traditional view of aging decline theoretically when they stated that "the formal properties of definitions of aging involve one or more independent variables whose influence is thought to bring about the changes in the nature of frequency of the dependent variable over the *life span* of the individual organism" (p. 5, emphasis added). Thus, *length of life* from conception to death was proposed to be the primary dependent variable (see also Strehler, 1977).

This position corresponds with the long-held view in the biological sciences that there is an ontogenetic basis for senescence (cf. Konigsberg, 1960). Waddington (1966) explicitly supports this position when he states that "the study of aging should really be looked upon as a part of embryology, but it is a somewhat separate field, as is the study of growth" (p. 107). On the other hand, the conception of aging as a lifelong process raises the question of whether there is any distinction between growing and aging, apart from practical considerations. In reviewing the evidence, Strehler (1977) eventually arrived at the following:

> In summary, then, current opinion maintains that there is no demonstrable causal relationship between development and senescence except for the obvious fact that *the development of an ordered structure is a necessary prerequisite to its disintegration*. The progressive decrease in growth rate during the maturation of animals of finite body size may or may not be a cause of the aging process. It is certainly feasible for a great many, but perhaps not all (particularly DNA), subcellular structures to be replaced on a regular schedule without interfering seriously with the function of the cells.
>
> On the other hand, differentiation, depending on the mechanism of its achievement and on the factors which stabilize a differentiated cell, may indeed give rise to cells which go through an optimum with respect to their chemical constituents. (p. 305)

From this it might be concluded that the fertilized egg is the ordered structure, subject to two distinct processes of formative change from the very beginning: growing and aging. Of course, the question now arises as to what theories can explain this distinct phenomenon of aging from conception to death in morphogenetic perspective. In the previous section on growing, three different theories were suggested implicitly. In the following sections, these theories will be examined again from the perspective of the psychology of aging. Further, we will build on these theories utilizing Prigogine's nonequilibrium systems theory and Birren's counterpart theory. Finally, an attempt will be made to integrate these findings from a morphogenetic perspective.

Nonequilibrium Systems Theory

As has been discussed in the section on general systems theory, each living system shows two opposing tendencies: on the one hand, the tendency to maximum entropy, chaos, minimum differentiation, maximum disorganization, or death; and on the other hand, the tendency to maximum negentropy, order, differentiation, organization, or life. The tendency to increasing differentiation of a human organism has been termed *growing*, a process of formative change explained in terms of absorbing *information*. Implicitly, it was assumed that aging related to increasing entropy, since differentiation is the opposite of entropy. Thus, according to general systems theory, *aging* is explained in terms of increasing entropy, or *disorganization*. However, this conception of two basic processes of formative change, growing and aging, raises some serious questions.

The first question has been dealt with already. Both concepts of information and entropy were developed within the framework of closed systems and therefore may be used only in metaphoric extension. The second question, however, poses a more serious problem, as it directs the relationship between information and entropy, or between order and disorder. The Second Law of Thermodynamics teaches that there is an increase of entropy in energetic systems. In other words, a living system evolves from order to disorder. Thus, development toward increasing order is highly improbable. Growing, however, implies increasing differentiation and complexity. How is this possible? After all, the concept of information, or negentropy, as the negative equivalent of entropy offers hardly a sufficient explanation: Apart from the minus sign, both concepts have exactly the same explanatory power.

Recently Prigogine (1979; Prigogine & Stengers, 1984) pointed out that a variety of living systems do not follow the classical model of equilibrium thermodynamics developed during the 19th century. This model led to the introduction of thermodynamic concepts like entropy, dealing with processes near equilibrium for closed systems only. However, living systems (like the human organism) are open systems, exchanging matter or energy (and information) with their environment. This suggests that open systems are continuously fluctuating, and therefore equilibrium thermodynamics would not be the best model for such systems. To solve this problem Prigogine and his co-workers developed the *nonequilibrium systems theory*, or the *theory of dissipative structures*.

This theory postulates that a single fluctuation or a combination of them may become so powerful—as a result of *positive feedback*—that it passes a critical level and shatters the preexisting form or pattern of organization. At this moment—termed the *bifurcation point*—it is inherently impossible to determine in advance which direction formative change will take: whether the system will disintegrate into *chaos* or leap to a new, more differentiated *order*, that is, a dissipative structure. However, the more complex the form, pattern, or structure is, the more energy it must dissipate or disperse in order to sustain its complexity. Thus, Prigogine's solution of the paradox of two opposing tendencies is that order emerges because of, and not despite, entropy or disorder. Order, form, or pattern of organization can actually arise spontaneously out of disorder and chaos through a process of *self-organization*.

In a series of experiments for which he was awarded the Nobel Prize in chemistry (1977), Prigogine furnished proof of an ordering principle in entropy itself. With this he demonstrated clearly that entropy is not merely a downward slide toward disorganization; under nonequilibrium conditions certain systems run down while other systems simultaneously evolve and grow more coherent. By implication this means that *in terms of nonequilibrium systems theory aging is a process of formative change or a series of transformations toward an increasing disorderly and orderly form, pattern, or structure*.

Perhaps it is useful at this point to draw a parallel between Prigogine's theory and some of Laborit's conceptions (cf. Birren & Schroots, 1984). In *Decoding the Human Message*, Laborit (1977) makes a distinction between entropy on the one hand and two types of information on the other hand: circulating information and information structure. Furthermore, he introduces cybernetic concepts, such as positive and negative feedback, open and closed regulated systems, and servomechanisms, in his theorizing about human organisms as living systems. Although the parallel may not be clear immediately and a discussion of Laborit's concepts is well beyond the scope of this chapter, it should be noted that the concept of *information structure* corresponds with Prigogine's *order* out of chaos, or entropy, and that the above-mentioned cybernetic concepts parallel the processes of positive feedback, self-regulation, and self-organization in living systems.

In conclusion I want to call attention to the supportive evidence from general systems theory, nonequilibrium systems theory, and Laborit's conceptions for a preliminary definition of aging at a largely psychological level. This type of aging, termed *geronting*, can now be defined as the processes of self-regulation in the individual behavioral organization, which may occur in the presence of increasing behavioral disorganization with age.

Counterpart Theory

In the preceding subsection it has been suggested that the two basic types of formative change, growing and aging, are related *synchronically*; for certain systems run down or age under nonequilibrium conditions while other systems *simultaneously* evolve and grow more coherent. Birren (1960) addressed the same question with regard to the relations of growing and aging from a *diachronic* point of view.

He noticed that natural selection is not very obvious in the case of aging since some of the traits of old organisms do not appear until long after the age of reproduction has passed. For example, rodents in the wild do not usually survive the growth phase because predators kill them before they reach maturity. Thus, rodents reproduce while still growing physically to the adult size. However, if rodents are placed in the favorable conditions of a laboratory colony, they will live several times longer in an artificial environment than they do in the wild, and a *pattern of aging* will appear that would never have had an opportunity for expression in the natural or wild environment. Thus, animals show a potential for senescence that presumably they never had the opportunity to express in their natural environments and that was never directly subject to the pressures of selection. The issue is how the potential for senescence could arise through evolution if its manifestations were never directly subject to pressures of selection (cf. Birren, this volume).

The answer was given in terms of a *counterpart theory*, which states that "any biologically based order in late-life characteristics must arise in association from counterpart characteristics of development which were subject to pressures of selection" (Birren, 1960, p. 309). In other words, the counterpart theory views *ordered* formative changes in the postreproductive organism as the expression of counterpart characteristics of earlier ontogenesis, which suggests a diachronic relationship. As Birren (this volume) has repeatedly emphasized, however, counterpart theory does not hold that all traits or characteristics of the postreproductive organism arise by counterpart of earlier ontogenesis. It suggests a *pathway* through which some order has been introduced into later-life changes. In the final analysis, however, counterpart theory finds its raison d'être in the *genes* of the organism.

It is interesting to note that Birren uses the term *pathway* as a metaphor for the diachronic relationship between growing and aging. This suggests that there is some kind of relationship but not a very strict or direct one, as one might expect on the basis of a genetic program of aging. For instance, in discussing the deleterious effects of increasing blood pressure with age, Birren and Schroots (1983) came to the conclusion that specialization in early ontogenesis, for example, rise in blood pressure as adaptive mechanism, will have consequences for the manner in which the organism ages, for example, later-life hypertension; but the expression of the early adaptation in the old organism is *not* a direct path.

In a previous section we introduced Waddington's concept of *chreode*, which was defined as *canalized pathway of change* and depicted as a chreodic valley in the epigenetic landscape. Birren's pathway and Waddington's chreode show a remarkable similarity with regard to formative changes in later life as consequences of early specialization. Translated in Waddington's theoretical framework, Birren's pathway would be represented by a chreodic valley which starts early in the epigenetic landscape and soon becomes deeper, narrower, and steeper-walled as a result of specialization or canalization. The consequence of this early canalization is, of course, that formative change at older age becomes increasingly difficult because the narrower and the deeper the chreodic valley, the less influence genetic and/or environmental forces can exert toward formative change in later life.

Whereas counterpart theory stresses an explanation of certain patterns of aging in terms of natural selection and genetic programs, formative causation theory offers a supplementary explanation of aging and formative change in terms of morphogenetic fields and morphic resonance. As discussed earlier, morphogenetic fields are a result of morphic resonance from previous similar systems. The detailed structure of an organism and the patterns of oscillatory activity (morphic resonance) within its nervous system will generally resemble *itself* more closely than any other organism. Thus, the most specific morphic resonance acting upon it will be that from its own past. The next most specific resonance will come from genetically similar organisms that lived in the same environment, and the least specific from organisms of other races living in different environments. Thus, once a particular organism shows specialized behavior in early life, its subsequent behavior in later life will tend to be canalized primarily by morphic resonance from its own past states, and secondarily by morphic resonance from genetically similar, but older organisms that lived in the same environment. Of course, the more often specialized behavior is repeated, the stronger will this canalization become. Such characteristic formative changes in later life, or "patterns of aging," are thus the consequences of past "learning" by morphic resonance, primarily within individuals and only secondarily within similar older organisms (Sheldrake, 1981b, p. 170).

FORMATIVE CHANGE AND AGING

In the second edition of the *Handbook of the Psychology of Aging*, Birren and Cunningham (1985, p. 4) observe that many articles and books are written about aging without any reference to its definition. They note a hierarchy in the sciences, in which biologists most often provide definitions of aging, psychologists rarely, and social scientists almost never. It should be added that when psychologists do define aging, they often use concepts and phrases descended from the natural sciences.

Levinson (1978, p. 327), for example, discusses phases in the human life cycle from a biological perspective on growing and senescence (Bidder, 1932), which describes the growth sequence as follows. First, the organism goes through a process of *positive growth* until it reaches an optimal size. A *regulating mechanism* is needed to limit growth when the optimal size is reached. This regulator produces a phase of *non-growth*, which maintains the optimal state for a while, and then a phase of increasing *negative growth* for which death is a normal outcome. Thus, Levinson (1978) conceives aging on a psychological level as a matter of growing *plus* some regulating mechanism. Translated into modern, cybernetic terms, the latter is a *feedback* mechanism.

Levinson (1978) does not define *growing*, although it may be concluded from his book that growing implies increase of some undefined parameter that has a positive value conotation, like the exchangeable term *development*, for instance. In other words, Levinson conceives the human life cycle as an undefined "something" — presumably behavior — under the influence of positive (growth) and/or negative (senescence) feedback. These regulating mechanisms and feedback loops are important insofar as they emphasize not only the processing of information in living organisms but also the *temporal mechanisms* involved. When the emphasis is on the temporal nature of a regulating mechanism, aging is discussed in terms of clocks, clockshop, and increasing desynchronization (cf. Schroots, 1986).

Until recently not much attention has been paid in the behavioral sciences to the energetic basis of growing and aging in terms of entropy. In all probability this neglect has been caused by the emphasis in psychology on cognitive information processing rather than on the processes of increasing entropy in living systems. After all, the explanatory power of entropy is small, given the fact that the mathematical expressions of information and entropy are each other's opposite. Prigogine and Stengers (1984), however, have made it clear in their nonequilibrium systems theory that there is something more to the concept of entropy. This added value is worded very eloquently by Campbell (1982) when he observes that producing an orderly process is unreasonably expensive:

> Economists are fond of saying that there is "no free lunch"; everything must be paid its value so that price and value always balance out, the economist Nicholas Georgescu-Roegen has written. The entropy law teaches us that mankind lives under a harsher commandment: *in entropy terms*, the cost of a lunch is greater than its price. . . . Order is improbable and hard to create. Time is its enemy, because entropy tends to increase with time. Orderly energy can do

work, but in the very process of working, it decays into disorderly energy. As a matter of fact, it creates more disorder than order in the end. (pp. 41–42)

A faint echo of this new insight is reflected in Sameroff's (1982) conception that adaptive self-stabilization in the face of environmental challenge calls for increases in complexity of organization and that such complexity carries a price: The more complex the adaptive process, the less stable the system and the more energy it must dissipate or disperse in order to stabilize and maintain its complexity.

Before defining aging from this morphogenetic perspective, it is necessary to understand how aging as formative change fits into Thom's catastrophe theory with its emphasis on structural stability, as well as how this theory relates to concepts of bifurcation points and chreodes. Prigogine and Stengers (1984) have made some very interesting remarks in this regard:

> The concept of chreod is part of the qualitative description of embryological development Waddington proposed more than twenty years ago. It is truly a *bifurcating* evolution: a progressive exploration along which the embryo grows in an "epigenetic landscape" where coexist stable segments and segments where a choice among several developmental paths is possible. . . . C. H. Waddington's chreods are also a central reference in René Thom's biological thought. They could thus become a meeting point for two approaches: the one we are presenting, starting from local mechanisms and exploring the spectrum of collective behaviors they can generate; and Thom's, starting from global mathematical entities and connecting the qualitatively distinct forms and transformations they imply with the phenomenological description of morphogenesis. (pp. 326–327)

As discussed before, Thom's catastrophe theory provides us with the root metaphors of formative change—catastrophes—whether these changes relate to processes of growing, aging, or just transformations.

Furthermore, Thom's theory is a timeless, atemporal theory, proposing no final catastrophe, or death, since infinite energy is taken for granted. As such, Thom's conceptions about living systems correspond closely with the often implicit assumptions of life-span (developmental) psychology, which imply that human ontogenesis is merely a matter of growing, unfolding, or development.

Prigogine, on the other hand, bases his theory of nonequilibrium systems on a new interpretation of the Second Law of Thermodynamics with its concept of increasing entropy in organisms, from which disorder and order emerge. An increasing trend toward more disorder than order results, in the end, in death. Therefore, Prigogine's theory relates to a finite series of transformations of formative behavior in an organism toward a behavioral organization pattern of increasing uniqueness, which is termed *individuation*, a term originally developed by C. G. Jung. By means of this very process of individuation, which starts right at the beginning of conception, the individual creates his or her own time. As Prigogine and Pahaut (1984) would say, each living system has an *internal age*, which is not measured in terms of external parameters—calendar time, for instance—but *depends* on the number of transformations, intrinsic to the dynamics of the system; in brief: time, age, and aging as dependent variables.

The question, of course, arises as to how to measure these transformations from the very beginning. Hershey and Wang (1980) tried to answer this question by developing *A New Age-Scale for Humans*, based on an entropic analysis of living human systems in which the energy metabolism is measured. However, this analysis only partially takes into account the order that emerges from disorganization under certain disequilibrium circumstances. Therefore, to measure internal age, additional information must be collected with regard to the order of the human system by transformation. In the next section, on ontogenetic psychology, an attempt will be made to point to the direction research should take in this respect.

Summary

In conclusion, it seems useful to summarize the main points of the theories of formative change, growing, and aging, presented in the last three sections. A summary of these theories is provided in Table 14-1.

As is indicated in Table 14-1, the morphogenetic theories discussed are characterized in terms of their descriptive and explanatory nature (indicated by D or E) on the one hand and in terms of independent and dependent variables on the other hand. As can be seen in the column headed "Aging," nonequilibrium systems theory is the only theory with order (form, pattern), disorder (chaos, randomness), and time (internal age) as dependent variables. As a result, nonequilibrium systems theory, proceeding from the concepts of entropy, feedback, and age as independent variables, can explain not only disorderly formative change over the individual's life span but also orderly change, both types of changes resulting in increasing unique spatiotemporal structures of aging, termed individuation. *Aging from a morphogenetic perspective thus refers to the finite series of transformations in an organism toward increasing individuation so that each transformation modulates the potential life span of the organism cumulatively and nonlinearly, with death as the final transformation.*

ONTOGENETIC PSYCHOLOGY

The increasing awareness of psychologists of the limitations of radical behaviorism—epitomized in the research question, How *is* behavior organized?—makes it more significant to look at human life and its course as a whole. This

TABLE 14-1. Summary of Theories of Formative Change, Growing, and Aging

Descriptive (D) and/or explanatory (E) theories	Independent variables	Dependent variables		
		Formative change	Growing	Aging
D – Epigenetic landscape	Age	Chreode/canalized pathway of change		–
E/D – General systems	Information processing (feedback)	–	Differentiation	–
	Entropy (age)	–	–	Disorder
D/E – Catastrophe	Control factors	Elementary catastrophes	–	–
E – Formative causation	Morphogenetic fields/morphic resonance	Repetition of forms and patterns of behavior		
E – Counterpart	Genetic program (age)	Pathway of change	Pathway of change	Pattern
E – Nonequilibrium systems	Information processing (positive feedback) Entropy (age)	Complexity	Differentiation	Individuation (order, disorder, internal age)

view is reflected in ontogenetic psychology, which studies the organization of behavior over the course of an individual's life and therefore focuses on a different research question: How does behavior *become* organized? This onto-genetic view also stimulates the awareness that individuals are purposive and self-constructing (Jantsch, 1980; Pot, 1980). In terms of systems theory one might say that self-organizing systems like human organisms are directed toward a goal, that is to say, "they strive to fulfill their form." In this respect Campbell (1982) quotes Aristotle: "The end and aim of all *becoming* is the development of potentiality to actuality, the incorporation of form in matter" (p. 269, emphasis added). With these words, not only mechanistic or *efficient* causes are proposed as being responsible for bringing about change in this world, but also causes of *matter*, without which nothing would happen at all; causes of *form*, implicit in the things that change; and causes of *purpose*, which a thing naturally tends to approach when it changes.

Earlier in this chapter, the purposive (teleological) and formative (morpho-genetic) nature of human ontogenesis was pointed out implicitly. Two tenden-cies can be distinguished from a morphogenetic perspective: growing (increas-ing *differentiation*) and aging (increasing *individuation*). These two tendencies can be combined into a third, overall tendency of formative change or morphogenesis: the increasing *complexity* of the living system. The question now arises as to how this increasing complexity can be described from an ontogenetic-psychological point of view.

In discussing the steps in a hierarchy of more and more complex behavior, Anderson (1964/1980) provides us with the key to the question above. He observes that these steps perhaps are better viewed as:

> *Choice points*, a term used to designate a phenomenon in time which changes the direction or shape of the living organism and creates a "tree" in the topological sense, which differs from the "tree" that would have appeared had another choice been made. If we view the living person, whether young or old, as an open-end system of irreversible relations both within the living system itself and in its personal and social relations with the surrounding field of forces, we can think of a choice point, whether the decision be made by the person or forced upon him by outside circumstances, as a new orientation of the person. However, it should be clear that the choice point cannot be defined in terms of the immediate moment but in terms of the consequences which follow subsequently over a period of time. It may also be preceded by antecedents which also occur over a period of time. (p. 15, emphasis added)

In a roundabout way we return to the discussion of scientific metaphors of life and morphogenesis. However, a description and analysis of the branching tree should be less problematical by now in light of the discussions concerning branching points, turning points, chreodes, catastrophes, bifurcations, choice points, and transformations. Indeed, human morphogenesis might best be understood as a bifurcation evolution from the simple to the complex with the *tree diagram* as a metaphor (Schroots, 1985a). Of course, the question arises immediately how this metaphor can be developed more explicitly.

Generally speaking, there are a number of ways to approach the problem of giving concrete form to the tree of life. For instance, one might consider operationalizing the branching points, bifurcations, or transformations of an individual life at a purely biological, psychological, or social level. Given a psychological level of analysis, one further might try to operationalize the organization of behavior over the life span from a purely cognitive, affective, or conative perspective (Schroots, 1985b). Although this approach will result undoubtedly in distinct tree diagrams at diverse levels for different dimensions, it seems more fruitful for the time being to discuss some general principles of a branching tree.

Branching Tree: General Principles

It is first important to emphasize that branching points are the transformations of a system in the sense of Prigogine's bifurcation points. That is to say, in the absence of fluctuations the system maintains a dynamic equilibrium and moves through time in a straight line until emerging fluctuations change the direction and form of the system. The phenomenon is termed *transformation* or, metaphorically speaking, branching point. Formative change of a human system, then, consists of a series of transformations or branching points over the life span.

At the beginning of the life course—with conception—the individual is awaiting an as yet unknown but finite number of transformations. As the individual moves through time and transformations occur, a branching pattern emerges that looks very much like a real tree (see Figure 14-1). The question arises: Is this an accident or not?

In exploring spatial patterns, Stevens (1974) discovered that many different systems—for instance, human lungs, cows' livers, economic market areas, streams, arteries, electrical discharges, and trees—branch in a similar fashion. That is to say, their branching patterns correspond with simple rules. For example,

1. Branches of each order are three to five times as numerous as the branches of the next higher order with bifurcation ratios of 3 to 5 (first-order branch defined as end point; second-order branch originates at the junction of two first-order branches, and so forth).
2. Branches of lower order are shorter and more numerous than branches of higher order (branching patterns fan out at the periphery; thus, a hierarchy of branches develops in which the small ones always outnumber the large ones).

Conception   Death

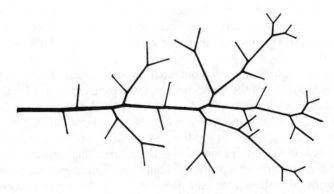

FIGURE 14-1. Diagram of a branching tree from conception to death. (Adapted from Stevens, 1974, p. 130.)

3. The smaller the branch, the closer to 90 degrees will be its angle of divergence from the trunk (based on the principle of "least effort").
4. Small branches make large angles with the trunk and deflect it a small amount; large branches make small angles with the trunk but deflect it greatly.
5. The Fibonacci number series 1, 1, 2, 3, 5, 8 . . . , in which each term is the sum of the two preceding terms, provides in quite a few cases an adequate description of the geometric progression of branching patterns.

In general, then, it might be said that the variations of proportion of a bifurcating branched structure and the successive repetition of that structure will lead to a branching tree of distinct form (Lord & Wilson, 1984).

Although the tree diagram in Figure 14-1 is only a two-dimensional model of reality, it nevertheless shows some topologically interesting characteristics of growing, aging, and formative change over the life span of an individual. Growing, for instance, is expressed in the increasing number of branching points with age, that is, increasing differentiation. Aging, on the other hand, is expressed in the emergent branching pattern of increasing uniqueness, that is, increasing individuation. Formative change, finally, is reflected in the combination of increasing differentiation and individuation, that is, increasing complexity with age.

Internal Age

The previous subsection requires some clarification. First, aging was generally typified before as a matter of increasing entropy with age. Hershey and Wang (1980) demonstrated that the entropy accumulation of human subjects increases rapidly until the age of about 20 years and decreases slowly afterward till death, entropy production being measured in terms of basal metabolism. In Figure 14-2 the plot of standard basal metabolic rate versus age is shown.

From this figure it is only one step back to Figure 14-1, by projecting mentally the trunk of the branching tree (as depicted in Figure 14-1) on top of the X-axis (age) in Figure 14-2. The result of this mental projection is a remarkable similarity between the rate of basal metabolism, which reflects entropy accumulation with age (i.e., *entropic age*), on the one hand, and the rate of geometric progression of the tree's branching pattern on the other hand. Of course, the demonstrated similarity is not complete, but the difference might be explained, at least partially, by the difference in entropy accumulation of plants and humans.

In this regard it is interesting to note that the tree of Figure 14-1, generated by a simple rule, is similar to the trees generated by random numbers. In the

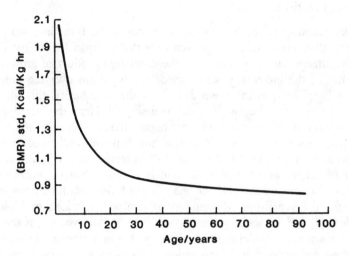

FIGURE 14-2. Plot of standard basal metabolic rate versus age. (Adapted from Hershey & Wang, 1980, p. 97.)

words of Stevens (1974), "Profoundly different models can portray the same phenomena equally well. Randomness can appear regular and regularity random" (p. 130). That is to say, entropy accumulation is basically a matter of increasing disorder, chaos, or randomness, and consequently, the increasing number of transformations or branching points of the tree in Figure 14-1 is the spatiotemporal reflection of an entropic process, which was earlier identified with aging. However, this view is only one side of the coin. The other side is that the concept of transformation—that is, Prigogine's bifurcation point—has been defined earlier as the moment at which it is inherently impossible to determine in advance which direction formative change will take: whether the system will disintegrate into chaos (i.e., randomness) or leap to a new, more differentiated order. That is to say, under nonequilibrium conditions certain systems run down, whereas other systems simultaneously evolve and grow more coherent. By implication this means that some transformations or branching points reflect the entropic process, resulting in an entropic age of the organism, and other transformations represent new order. The combination of both types of transformation is indicative of the organism's *internal age.*

Thus, each transformation modulates the potential life span of the organism in terms of its internal age. Therefore, since transformations are the result of fluctuations at a biological, psychological, or social level, studies of aging should be directed toward tracing the determinants of fluctuations at each level of the human organism, in order to reconstruct patterns of aging retrospectively and to prevent negative patterns of aging prospectively.

Self-Organization

Generally speaking, formative change can be conceived as the increasing number of transformations of the organism over the life span. More specifically, formative change can be described as the combined product of growing and aging, that is, the increasing *complexity* of the organism over the individual course of life. The question arises as to how this complexity, this combined product of growing and aging, best can be described. Here, the branching tree may be a good model from a diachronic perspective; it does not need to be so from a *synchronic* point of view. In fact, although many synchronic "trees" can be found in nature—take, for example, a cross-section of the brain—they are never used, as far as we know, as models of individual organisms, social systems, or the organization of behavior. Instead, *networks* have been used as models for the synchronic description of complex relations in biological, psychological, and/or social systems. Well known, for instance, is the information network as a model of the nervous system in biology and psychology, just as the social network has a reputation in sociology (cf. Knipscheer, 1980). Parallel to the social network, an attachment network has been hypothesized as model of the affective relations of an individual (Kahn & Antonucci, 1980), but it has been difficult to give concrete form to this type of network because of the complexity of affective structures (Schroots, 1984).

Recent developments in geometry, however, also permit the use of branching trees as models of complex structures, patterns, or forms from both a diachronic and synchronic perspective (Mandelbrot, 1982). An example of such a branching tree is given in Figure 14-3.

Essentially this tree is a two-dimensional cross-section of an *N*-dimensional branching tree with a recursive structure; that is to say, the bifurcating branched structure (or transformation) is repeated more and more at the periphery of the tree so that the complexity of the structure increases synchronically and diachronically and the outer and inner shapes of the tree fade away. The irregularity or complexity of this form cannot be described in classical, geometric terms like line (one-dimensional) or surface (two-dimensional). A new geometrical concept therefore was developed—the *fractal*—which is a model of complex structures arising from order and randomness, with a dimensionality between one and two (Nicholis, 1984). Although lack of space does not allow us to develop this line of thought further, fractal geometry might well be the new tool for the description and analysis of complex morphological problems.

SUMMARY

In the foregoing, a number of methods and theories were discussed with regard to the basic question of ontogenetic psychology: How does behavior become organized? From a morphogenetic or formative change perspective, an even more fundamental question—How does behavior become increasingly

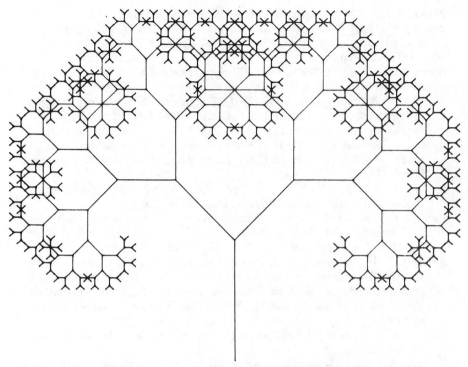

FIGURE 14-3. Diagram of a two-dimensional cross-section of an *N*-dimensional branching tree. (Adapted from Ernst, 1985, p. 85.)

more complex over time?—now can be answered. For the popular version of the three main laws of thermodynamics—(1) you can't win, (2) you are sure to lose, (3) you can't get out of the game—makes it highly improbable that individual lives show more complex organizational structures and functions over time; in brief, show *self-organization from the simple to the complex*. The answer was given in terms of Prigogine's nonequilibrium systems theory based on the premise that there is an ordering principle in entropy itself. On the basis of this theory a model was developed, the branching tree for the description and analysis of growing, aging, and formative change over the individual's life span. The concept of transformation or branching point was then described as an essential element of this model.

REFERENCES

Anderson, J. E. (1964; 1980 reprint). Developmental principles in childhood and maturity. In J. E. Birren (Ed.), *Relations of development and aging*. New York: Arno Press. (pp. 11–28).

Bidder, G. P. (1932). Senescence. *British Medical Journal, 2*, 5831.

Birren, J. E. (1960). Behavioral theories of aging. In N. W. Shock (Ed.), *Aging: Some social and biological aspects* (pp. 305–332). Washington, DC: American Association for the Advancement of Science.

Birren, J. E. (Ed.), (1964; 1980 reprint). *Relations of development and aging*. New York: Arno Press.

Birren, J. E., & Cunningham, W. R. (1985). Research on the psychology of aging: Principles, concepts and theory. In J. E. Birren & K. W. Schaie (Eds.), *Handbook of the psychology of aging* (2nd ed., pp. 3–34) New York: Van Nostrand Reinhold.

Birren, J. E., & Hateley, B. J. (1985). Guided autobiography: A special method of life review. In R. Blum & G. Simon (Eds.), *The art of life and family writing*. American Lives Endowment. (pp. 20–40).

Birren, J. E., Kinney, D. K., Schaie, K. W., & Woodruff, D. S. (1981). *Developmental psychology: A lifespan approach*. Boston: Houghton Mifflin.

Birren, J. E., & Renner, V. J. (1977). Research on the psychology of aging: Principles and experimentation. In J. E. Birren & K. W. Schaie (Eds.), *Handbook of the psychology of aging* (pp. 3–38). New York: Van Nostrand Reinhold.

Birren, J. E., & Schroots, J. J. F. (1983). Eine psychologische Theorie von der Verhaltensorganisation im Alter. In H. Löwe, U. Lehr, & J. E. Birren (Eds.), *Psychologische Probleme des Erwachsenenalters: Theoretische Positionen und empirische Untersuchungsergebnisse* (pp. 24–33). Berlin: VEB Deutscher Verlag der Wissenschafter.

Birren, J. E., & Schroots, J. J. F. (1984). Steps to an ontogenetic psychology. *Academic Psychology Bulletin, 6*, 177–190.

Boulding, K. (1956). *The image*. Ann Arbor, MI: University of Michigan Press.

Buckley, W. (1967). *Sociology and modern systems theory*. Englewood Cliffs, NJ: Prentice-Hall.

Campbell, J. (1982). *Grammatical man: Information, entropy, language, and life*. New York: Simon & Schuster.

Dewey, J. (1934). *Art as experience*. New York: Minton, Balch.

Erickson, E. H. (1963). *Childhood and society* (2nd ed.). New York: Norton.

Erickson, E. H. (1982). *The life cycle completed*. New York: Norton.

Ernst, B. (1985). *Bomen van Pythagoras: Variaties van Jos de Mey*. Amsterdam: Aramith.

Flavell, J. H., & Wohlwill, J. F. (1969). Formal and functional aspects of cognitive development. In D. Elkind & J. H. Flavell (Eds.), *Studies in cognitive growth: Essays in honor of Jean Piaget*. New York: Oxford University Press.

Freedle, R. (1977). Psychology, Thomian topologies, deviant logics, and human development. In N. Datan & H. W. Reese (Eds.), *Life-span developmental psychology: Dialectical perspectives on experimental research* (pp. 317–341). New York: Academic Press.

Gentner, D., & Grudin, J. (1985). The evolution of mental metaphors in psychology: A 90-year retrospective. *American Psychologist, 40*, 181–192.

Gesell, A. (1928). *Infancy and human growth*. New York: Macmillan.

Gould, R. L. (1978). *Transformations: Growth and change in adult life*. New York: Simon & Schuster.

Hall, E. T. (1983). *The dance of life: The other dimension of time*. New York: Anchor Press/Doubleday.

Harris, D. B. (Ed.). (1957a). *The concept of development*. Minneapolis: University of Minnesota Press.

Harris, D. B. (1957b). Problems in formulating a scientific concept of development. In D. B. Harris (Ed.), *The concept of development* (pp. 3–14). Minneapolis: University of Minnesota Press.

Hebb, D. O. (1949). *The organization of behavior*. New York: Wiley.

Hershey, D., & Wang, H. H. (1980). *A new age scale for humans*. Toronto: Lexington Books.

Hofstadter, D. R. (1979). *Gödel, Escher, Bach: An eternal golden braid*. New York: Basic Books.

Jantsch, E. (1980). *The self-organizing universe*. Oxford: Pergamon Press.

Kahn, R. L., & Antonucci, T. C. (1980). Convoys over the life course: Attachment, roles, and social support. In P. B. Baltes & O. G. Brim, Jr. (Eds.), *Life-span development and behavior* (Vol. 3, pp. 253–286). New York: Academic Press.

Keutzer, C. S. (1982). Archetypes, synchronicity, and the theory of formative causation. *Journal of Analytical Psychology, 27*, 255–262.

Keutzer, C. S. (1983). The theory of "formative causation" and its implications for archetypes, parallel inventions, and the "hundredth monkey phenomenon." *The Journal of Mind and Behavior, 4*, 353–367.

Knipscheer, C. P. M. (1980). *Oude mensen en hun sociale omgeving: Een studie van het primaire sociale netwerk*. The Hague: VUGA-Boekerij.

Konigsberg, I. R. (1960). On the relationship between development and aging. *Newsletter of the Gerontological Society, 7*, 33–34.

Laborit, H. (1977). *Decoding the human message*. London: Allison & Busby.

Lakoff, G., & Johnson, M. (1980). *Metaphors we live by*. Chicago: University of Chicago Press.

Leatherdale, W. H. (1974). *The role of analogy, model and metaphor in science*. Amsterdam: North-Holland.

Levinson, D. J. (1978). *The seasons of a man's life*. New York: Knopf.

Lewontin, R. (1982). *Human diversity*. New York: Scientific American Library.

Lord, E. A., & Wilson, C. B. (1984). *The mathematical description of shape and form*. New York: Wiley.

Lowenthal, M. F., Thurnher, M., & Chiriboga, D. (1975). *Four stages of life: A comparative study of women and men facing transitions*. San Francisco: Jossey Bass.

Maas, H. S., & Kuypers, J. A. (1974). *From thirty to seventy*. San Francisco: Jossey Bass.

Mandelbrot, B. B. (1982). *The fractal geometry of nature*. New York: Freeman.

Miller, J. G. (1978). *Living systems*. New York: McGraw-Hill.

Nicholis, G. (1984). Symmetriebreuken en waarneming der vormen. In M. Baudson (Ed.), *Tijd, de vierde dimensie in de kunst*. Brussels: Vereniging van Tentoonstellingen van het Paleis voor Schone Kunsten. (pp. 35–41).

Ortony, A. (Ed.). (1979). *Metaphor and thought*. Cambridge: Cambridge University Press.

Popper, K., & Eccles, J. (1977). *The self and its brain*. Berlin: Springer International.

Pot, J. S. (1980). *Scientific relevance and the rehabilitation of the goal concept.* Groningen, The Netherlands: Stabo/Allround.

Pribram, K. H. (1979). Behaviorism, phenomenology and holism in psychology: A scientific analysis. *Journal of Social and Biological Structures, 2,* 65–72.

Pribram, K. H. (1986). The cognitive revolution and mind/brain issues. *American Psychologist, 41,* 507–520.

Prigogine, I. (1979). *From being to becoming.* San Francisco: W. H. Freeman.

Prigogine, I., & Pahaut, S. (1984). De tijd herontdekken. In M. Baudson (Ed.), *Tijd, de vierde dimensie in de kunst.* Brussels: Vereniging van Tentoonstellingen van het Paleis voor Schone Kunsten. (pp. 23–33.)

Prigogine, I., & Stengers, I. (1984). *Order out of chaos: Man's new dialogue with nature.* Toronto: Bantam.

Rose, G. J. (1980). *The power of form.* New York: International Universities Press.

Sameroff, A. J. (1982). Development and the dialectic: The need for a systems approach. In W. A. Collins (Ed.), *The concept of development* (pp. 83–103). Hillsdale, New Jersey: Erlbaum.

Schroots, J. J. F. (1982a, June). *Metaphors of aging: An overview of their nature and implications.* Paper presented at the Invitational Research Symposium, Metaphors in the Study of Aging, University of British Columbia, Vancouver.

Schroots, J. J. F. (1982b). Ontogenetische psychologie, een eerste kennismaking. *De Psycholoog, 17,* 68–81.

Schroots, J. J. F. (1984). The affective consequences of technological change for older persons. In P. K. Robinson, J. Livingston, & J. E. Birren (Eds.), *Aging and technological advances* (pp. 237–247). New York: Plenum Press.

Schroots, J. J. F. (1985a, October). *The art of becoming: Introduction to ontogenetic psychology.* Paper presented to the 1985–86 Seminar on Theories of Aging of the Andrew Norman Institute for Advanced Study in Gerontology and Geriatrics, University of Southern California, Los Angeles.

Schroots, J. J. F. (1985b). Van levenslooppsychologie tot ontogenetische psychologie. In J. J. F. Schroots (Ed.), *Levenslooppsychologie.* Lisse, The Netherlands: Swets & Zeitlinger.

Schroots, J. J. F. (1986, April). *The nature of time.* Paper presented at the 1985–1986 Seminar on Theories of Aging of the Andrew Norman Institute for Advanced Study in Gerontology and Geriatrics, University of Southern California, Los Angeles.

Sheehy, G, (1977). *Passages: Predictable crises of adult life.* New York: Dutton.

Sheldrake, R. (1981a). A new science of life. *New Scientist, 18,* 766–768.

Sheldrake, R. (1981b). *A new science of life: The hypothesis of formative causation.* London: Blond & Briggs.

Stevens, P. S. (1974). *Patterns in nature.* Boston: Little, Brown.

Strehler, B. L. (1977). *Time, cells and aging.* New York: Academic Press.

Thom, R. (1975). *Structural stability and morphogenesis: An outline of a general theory of models.* Reading, Mass.: Benjamin.

Thompson, D'Arcy W. (1961). *On growth and form.* (Abridged edition, edited by J. T. Bonner). Cambridge: Cambridge University Press.

Von Bertalanffy, L. (1968). *General systems theory.* New York: Braziller.

Vygotski, L. S. (1978). *Mind in society*. Cambridge, MA: Harvard University Press.

Waddington, C. H. (1957). *The strategy of the genes*. London: Allen & Unwin.

Waddington, C. H. (1966). *Principles of development and differentiation*. New York: Macmillan.

Waddington, C. H. (Ed.) (1969). *Towards a theoretical biology: 2. Sketches*. Edinburgh: Edinburgh University Press.

Wilden, A. (1980). *System and structure: Essays in communication and exchange*. New York: Tavistock.

Woodcock, A., & Davis, M. (1978). *Catastrophe theory*. Harmondsworth, UK: Penguin Books.

Zeeman, E. C. (1976, April). Catastrophe theory. *Scientific American*, pp. 65–83.

Zeeman, E. C. (1977). *Catastrophe theory, selected papers 1972–1977*. Reading, MA: Benjamin.

PART IV
Social Science Concepts and Theories in Aging

15

Sociological Theories of Aging: Current Perspectives and Future Directions*

Patricia M. Passuth
Vern L. Bengtson

In the past decade there has been a significant growth in the amount of research in the sociology of aging. At the same time, there has also been greater concern for the theoretical underpinnings of aging research. While early social gerontological theories focused primarily on individual difficulties in adjusting to old age, later perspectives have taken into account broader issues regarding social aspects of age and aging. We feel this is an appropriate time for an assessment of current theoretical perspectives as well as prospects for future developments in the sociology of aging.

The purpose of this chapter is to examine the utility of current theories for explaining social aspects of aging and suggest possible directions for future theoretical analysis. In so doing, we will link theoretical perspectives in social gerontology[1] to major theoretical traditions in the field of sociology. While the study of aging has drawn upon sociological theories in general, it has lagged behind in its theoretical development. We will emphasize which per-

*We are especially grateful to Robert Lynott, who provided extensive and insightful comments on several drafts of this paper. We also thank several other colleagues for their comments and suggestions on an earlier draft: James Birren, Dale Dannefer, Anne Foner, John Henretta, Gary Kenyon, Marion Perlmutter, Gary Reker, and Peter Uhlenberg. Preparation of this paper was supported by grants Nos. T32 AG00037 and RO1 04092 from the National Institute on Aging.

spectives show the greatest promise for understanding the aging experience. Moreover, in light of recent interest in the development of a multidisciplinary theory of aging, we will address the problems and prospects for a multidisciplinary perspective. We conclude with a call for a more richly contextualized analysis of the aging process.

Within the field of sociology of aging, theoretical perspectives vary greatly with respect to the relative importance given to a number of factors, including consensus, conflict, the self, social structure, and language use. No single theory explains all social phenomena; each focuses on particular aspects of social behavior, offering minimal explanations for other features of social life. This is evident, for example, in considering the level of analysis examined by each of the various aging theories. While some perspectives focus on macro-structural conditions in seeking to explain the aging process, others are more interested in immediate social relations, or the micro-social level of analysis. In the next section we examine the major sociological theories of aging in terms of their central explanatory focus and assess the ability of each to explain social phenomena associated with aging.

MAJOR THEORETICAL DEVELOPMENTS IN THE SOCIOLOGY OF AGING

Sociological theories of aging have emerged, implicitly or explicitly, from five general sociological perspectives: structural functionalism, exchange, symbolic interactionism, Marxism, and social phenomenology.[2] Figure 15-1 organizes the major theoretical perspectives in social gerontology according to the theoretical traditions in sociology.

As Figure 15-1 shows, structural functionalism informs, to varying degrees, the disengagement, modernization, and age stratification theories of aging. Exchange theory has been directly applied to the experiences of the elderly. Symbolic interactionism has influenced three additional perspectives of old age: activity, social competence/breakdown, and subculture theories. The Marxist tradition is the major influence for a political economy approach to aging. The social phenomenological approach also has been used to study the aging process.[3] We now turn to an analysis of the theories of aging according to the major sociological theories from which they derive.

Structural Functionalist Theories of Aging

Structural functionalism (Parsons, 1951) has been an important influence on theorizing in aging. In part, this has reflected the prominence of functionalism in the development of American sociology during the 1940s and 1950s. The theory argues that social behavior is best understood from the perspective of

MAJOR SOCIOLOGICAL THEORIES   MAJOR THEORIES OF AGING

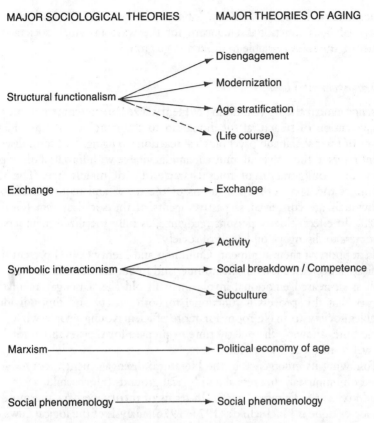

FIGURE 15-1. The influence of sociological theories on theories of aging.

the equilibrium needs of the social system. The approach views social behavior in terms of its function within the structure of society. Key concepts in functionalism include norms, roles, and socialization. Norms are shared rules about appropriate behavior. Roles are the set of behavioral expectations that constitute a particular status. Socialization is the process by which individuals learn and internalize the norms and values of society. Individuals, in turn, become part of the social order, carrying out the needs of the system. As such, the process enables the smooth and efficient functioning of society. In emphasizing the normative aspects of social order, the functionalist perspective focuses on consensus and conformity, rather than conflict, as major features of social order.

Structural functionalist influences on theories in aging can be seen in formulations regarding disengagement (Cumming & Henry, 1961), modernization (Cowgill, 1974; Cowgill & Holmes, 1972), and, to a lesser extent, age stratification (Riley, 1971, 1987; Riley, Johnson, & Foner, 1972). Each of these is informed by a functionalist concern for the ways in which societal norms structure the roles available to different age groups.

Disengagement Theory

Disengagement theory (Cumming & Henry, 1961) represents the most explicit application of structural functionalism to the condition of the elderly in terms of their social and psychological reactions to aging. The term disengagement refers to the universal, mutual, and inevitable withdrawal of older people from the configuration of roles characteristic of middle age. The theory examines the aging process in terms of the needs and requisites of society; individuals are conceived as passive agents of the social system (Gouldner, 1970). In effect, elderly persons recognize, as fully socialized members, their readiness to disengage on behalf of society.

In support of their argument, Cumming and Henry (1961) present data to indicate a decreased level in the number and frequency of social interactions as well as decreased emotional involvement in old age. Disengagement theory argues that this process is functional to both society and the individual; it enables society to make room for more efficient young people while, at the same time, allowing the elderly time to prepare for their eventual total withdrawal from social life – death.

Following its emergence in the literature, disengagement theory was criticized on empirical, theoretical and logical grounds (Hochschild, 1975, 1976; Maddox, 1964; Palmore, 1968). In terms of theory, perhaps the most penetrating critique is Hochschild's (1975, 1976) analysis of the logical flaws in the disengagement presentation. She summarizes these as the "escape clause," the "omnibus variable," and the "assumption of meaning" problems.

The "escape clause" refers to the fact that the theory is unfalsifiable. For example, contrary evidence (which Hochschild found in Cumming and Henry's own data) indicates that a significant proportion of older people do not withdraw from society. However, according to Cumming and Henry (1961), this does not refute the theory since these older people are described as either "unsuccessful" adjusters to old age, "off time" disengagers, or members of a "biological or psychological elite."

The "omnibus variable" problem refers to the overinclusiveness of the variables *age* and *disengagement* in Cumming and Henry's model of aging. That is, age is a broad term that encompasses such multifaceted processes as developmental changes, physical decline, and changes in social relations (e.g., retirement, widowhood). The disengagement variable includes numerous psychological and social processes including, for example, a trend toward fewer, less frequent, and less intense social contacts. Hochschild (1975, 1976) argues that the use of these two variables to explain adjustment to old age obscures the diverse processes that the variables represent.

The "assumption of meaning" problem refers to the theory's preference for imputing compliance without measuring it. For example, the theory argues that elderly individuals willingly withdraw from society; yet Cumming and Henry do not include data addressing the validity of this concept.

Despite the limitations of disengagement theory, it has had a profound effect on the field of social gerontology. It was the first formal theory that attempted to explain the process of growing older. The theory encouraged the development of opposing theories of the aged (Hochschild, 1975) and, eventually, the entire aging process. Disengagement theory's challenge to what was termed activity theory resulted in an enduring interest in explaining the "life satisfaction" or "morale" of older people in social gerontological research. Although the original explication of disengagement theory has been roundly criticized, elements of the perspective—especially society's role in excluding the elderly from valued social roles—have been revived and applied in new ways (see Uhlenburg, this volume).

Modernization Theory

Modernization theory (Cowgill, 1974; Cowgill & Holmes, 1972) attempts to explain variations in age status both historically and across societies. It focuses on the macro-structural conditions of the elderly in varied sociocultural settings. It is a functionalist perspective in that it suggests that the status of the elderly derives from their relationship to evolving systems of social roles which vary across societies depending on the degree of industrialization (or "modernization"). From this perspective, structural changes in a society occur in a particular way, regardless of historical or cultural context.

Modernization theory argues that the status of the aged is inversely related to the level of societal industrialization. Whereas in earlier preindustrial societies the elderly held high status by virtue of their control of scarce resources and their knowledge of tradition, they have lower status in present industrialized societies. In an elaboration of his theory, Cowgill (1974) outlines four elements of modernization—health technology, economic technology, urbanization, and mass education—that result in the lowered status of the aged. Palmore and Manton (1974) found that these elements of modernization were generally related to the status of the elderly in various societies.

Cowgill's evidence is based on 20th-century nonindustrial societies (see Simmons, 1945) that are intended to represent past societies. It has been argued that modernization theory presumes a "golden age of aging" in which the elderly lived in multigeneration households where they held much power, controlled many of the resources in the larger society, and were the source of societal tradition and information. Laslett (1965) refers to this romanticization of the past as "the world we have lost" syndrome. Modernization theory incorporates this popular view into a formal theory of the aged. Recent historical analyses (Haber, 1983; Quadagno, 1982; Stearns, 1982) challenge this belief of an ideal existence for preindustrial elderly as well as the notion of a simple, linear relationship between degree of industrialization and status of the elderly. These histories of old age emphasize variations in the experiences of the elderly depending on gender, race, ethnicity, social class, region, and historical period (Stearns, 1982).

Age Stratification

The age stratification model (Riley, 1971, 1987; Riley, Johnson, & Foner, 1972) has become one of the most influential perspectives in the emerging sociology of aging. Its intellectual roots can be traced primarily to structural functionalism. This model examines the movement of successive birth cohorts across time, known as "cohort flow." A birth cohort is a group of people born at the same time in history who age together. Each cohort is unique because it has its own characteristics (e.g., size, gender, and social class distribution) and each experiences particular historical events which affect its members' attitudes and behaviors. For example, Elder (1974) has shown that the cohort of children who grew up during the Great Depression had different values as adults, depending on such factors as relative economic loss and gender. Research on the age-stratification perspective further argues that the age structure of roles organizes society into a hierarchy, the consequences of which can be viewed much like social class (Riley, 1971). Foner (1974, 1986), in particular, has examined how one's location within an age structure influences opportunities for societal power and rewards (see also Henretta, this volume).

In several ways, the age stratification perspective represents a major advance over previous theories in social gerontology. First, it brings to the study of aging conceptual tools of mainstream sociology, in particular those from the areas of social stratification and demography. Second, the model emphasizes that there are significant variations in older people depending on the characteristics of their birth cohort; this suggests the need for a more explicit analysis of historical and social factors in aging. Third, age stratification's emphasis on the relations of cohorts within the age structure of society offers a useful analytic framework for distinguishing between developmental age changes and cohort historical differences. This has led, in part, to the reexamination of much research on presumed developmental changes including, for example, declines in IQ scores in old age (Schaie, 1979) and greater political conservatism with advanced age (Cutler, 1983).

There are, however, several limitations of the age stratification model. Its analogy to social class overstates the power of age status in explaining the distribution of rewards in society (Cain, 1987; Hendricks & Hendricks, 1986; Streib & Bourg, 1984). Although indicators of social class, such as income, may systematically change with age, it has not been demonstrated conclusively that the age structure [as opposed to, for example, the class system (cf. Olson, 1982)] is the causal mechanism driving the reward structure.

While the concept of cohort is a powerful tool for understanding the experience of aging, it also tends to reify chronological age or birth year. That is, people are defined largely in terms of chronological age per se, ignoring the subjective age dimension [cf. Mannheim's (1928/1952) analysis of generational units]. Age stratification's emphasis on differences between cohorts has resulted in a lack of attention to variations within cohorts (see, e.g., Dannefer, this volume). The assumption of cohort analysis is that people born in a particular year (subdivided by specific intracohort characteristics such as gender, social class, and race) experience age the same way. Accordingly, situational factors in the day-to-day lives of individual members within a given cohort, which may make for very different aging experiences, play little or no role. Yet a number of studies (e.g., Frankfather, 1977; Matthews, 1979; Ross, 1977; Stephens, 1976) have shown that individuals of the same age group often experience age in a wide variety of ways, depending on the relevant social context. These situational variations among cohort members are not seriously taken into account in the age-stratification model.

Life Course Perspective

The life course perspective (Cain, 1964; Clausen, 1972; Elder, 1975; Neugarten & Hagestad, 1976), which has been influenced by the age stratification model, is a recent conceptual development within social and behavioral analyses of aging. Much of the research conducted within this framework incorporates functionalist assumptions about the role of social norms in shaping behavior (e.g., Clausen, 1986; Hogan, 1980, 1981; Neugarten, Moore, & Lowe, 1965). The life course perspective is not a theory per se but a conceptual framework for conducting research and interpreting data. Key elements of this framework include the acknowledgment that (1) aging occurs from birth to death (thereby distinguishing this theory from those that focus exclusively on the elderly); (2) aging involves social, psychological, and biological processes; and (3) aging experiences are shaped by cohort–historical factors.

Hagestad and Neugarten (1985) describe the life course perspective in terms of three research emphases. These are (1) the study of the timing of adult role transitions (e.g., getting married, finishing school, completing military service, and getting a job); (2) the analysis of age norms; and (3) the study of perceptions of age (e.g., at what age is a person "middle-aged"). Recent work within this perspective has suggested the increasing institutionalization of the human life course (Dannefer, 1987; Kohli, 1986; Lawrence, 1984). The lack of explicit links of the life course perspective to sociological theories raises a potential problem in that the term *life course* is used so loosely in the sociology of aging that it is referenced for practically any type of research on adulthood and aging. As such, the perspective, in its current form, loses much of its theoretical explanatory power.

Exchange Theory of Aging

Exchange theory (Blau, 1964; Homans, 1961) applies a rational, economic model to the study of social behavior. From this perspective, social life consists of a collection of individuals involved in ongoing social exchanges. Individuals' reasons for interacting with others depends on their calculations of the costs and benefits they derive from continued social interaction. That is, individuals engage in interactions that are rewarding to them and, conversely, withdraw from interactions that are costly. As such, social order exists as a by-product of "profit-maximizing" individuals.

Exchange Theory

Dowd (1975) draws from Homan's (1961) and Blau's (1964) exchange theory in examining the experiences of the elderly. His analysis attempts to explain why older people tend to withdraw from social interaction. He argues that the aged have less power in encounters with younger people because they possess fewer resources (i.e., lower income, less education, poorer health); continued interactions with the elderly become more costly for younger age groups. The outcome is that older people decrease their participation in social life. Only those elderly who have the necessary resources to sustain a relationship with other age groups remain actively engaged in ongoing social affairs.

Exchange theory adds a new dimension to the study of aging by focusing on the immediate interactions between older people and other age groups. However, the perspective's purely economic, rational model results in certain limitations. While ongoing interactions may indeed include a give-and-take element, the theory sees all interactions from a rational point of view. For example, an attempt is made to redefine nonrational entities, such as love, strictly in economic and behavioral terms [see Blau's (1964) "Excursus on Love"]. Moreover, the theory overlooks the *quality* of exchange relations, defining social interaction solely in terms of the number of interactions initiated. Although Dowd (1975) acknowledges that the subjective dimension is important, he does not attempt to incorporate it. As such, his focus on the quantification of exchanges overlooks the fact that individuals variously define and redefine the meanings of rewards and costs in ongoing exchange relationships.

Symbolic Interactionist Theories of Aging

Symbolic interactionism (Blumer, 1969; Mead, 1934) emphasizes the dynamic and meaningful processes of social interaction. From this perspective, individuals develop a sense of self through interpreting others' responses to their behavior. Individuals attempt to understand how others see their behavior by "taking the role of the other." Social order is contingent on the shared meanings that develop in ongoing interaction. Activity, social competence/breakdown, and subculture theories of aging are influenced, to varying degrees, by symbolic interactionism.

Activity Theory

Activity theory (Cavan, 1962; Cavan, Burgess, Havighurst & Goldhamer, 1949; Havighurst & Albrecht, 1953; Lemon, Bengtson, & Peterson, 1972), in direct contrast to disengagement, argues that the more active elderly persons are, the greater their satisfaction with life. In its original formulation (Cavan et al., 1949; Havighurst & Albrecht, 1953), activity theory was not explicitly framed within a symbolic interactionist perspective. (Indeed, the theory itself was "implicit" until challenged by disengagement theory.) Later analysis (Cavan, 1962), however, has been more directly tied to symbolic interactionism, placing a greater emphasis on ongoing social interaction in the development of self-concept among the elderly.

The activity perspective argues that one's self-concept is related to the roles one holds. With old age comes a loss of roles (e.g., retirement, widowhood). The theory states that in order to maintain a positive sense of self, elderly person's must substitute new roles for those lost in old age. Thus, well-being in late life results from increased activity in newly acquired roles.

Activity theory provides a conceptual justification for a central assumption underlying many programs and interventions for the elderly—that social activity in and of itself is beneficial and results in greater life satisfaction. At the same time, however, the theory assumes that all older persons need and desire high levels of social activity. The activity perspective also overlooks variations in the meaning of particular activities in the lives of older people. Lemon et al. (1972), for example, in their attempt to frame activity theory in terms of symbolic interactionism, found that the relationship between well-being and activity in old age depends on the type of activity: formal, informal, solitary. Moreover, researchers have shown that the effect of activity norms on older people's life satisfaction is related to the age concentration of various environments (Bultena, 1974; Messer, 1967).

Social Competence and Breakdown Theory

Social competence/breakdown theory (Kuypers & Bengtson, 1973) is another application of interactionist theory which attempts to explain both normal and problematic aspects of aging. This perspective borrows from several other theoretical traditions in explaining the interdependence between older people and their social worlds [including labeling theory in sociology and psychiatry, Lawton's (1983) environmental press theory in psychology, and general systems theory]. As originally proposed, the social breakdown syndrome (Zusman, 1966) refers to the process by which a psychologically vulnerable individual receives negative messages from his or her social environment, which are then incorporated into the self-concept, producing a vicious spiral of negative feedback.

Kuypers and Bengtson (1973) have applied these ideas to the social competence of the elderly and to the negative consequences—breakdowns—in competence that can accompany the crises that often occur with advancing age (e.g., loss of health, loss of spouse). They suggest that a negative spiral of feedback can occur: (1) An elderly individual, whose self-concept may already be vulnerable because of role loss or negative stereotypes concerning aging, experiences a health-related crisis; this leads to (2) labeling of the older person as dependent by the social environment—health professionals or family; (3) atrophy of previous competency skills occurs; and (4) the individual adopts the self-concept of sick, inadequate, or incompetent. This leads to further vulnerability, and the negative cycle occurs again, with further consequences to social and psychological competence.

Kuypers and Bengtson (1973) suggest that the spiraling breakdown of competence in elderly individuals can be reversed through what they term a *social reconstruction syndrome*. By improving environmental supports while facilitating an expression of personal strength, a sense of increased competence can be fostered (see also Gubrium, 1973). More recently, Bengtson and Kuypers (1986) have adapted this model to problems facing the aging family. Families are frequently unprepared for the sudden dependency of an aged member, and problems of caregiving (Brody, 1985) create many strains on family competence (as well as on individual competences). However, an awareness of the cyclical nature of individual–environmental interactions affecting the sense of competence can help identify inputs that may improve family functioning, thus reducing the sense of helplessness that many caregivers feel. While useful as a heuristic device (Hendricks & Hendricks, 1986) and for sensitizing practitioners in dealing with problems of aging (Lowy, 1985; Sherman, 1981), the social competence/breakdown model has yet to be tested in empirical studies.

Subculture Theory

Although the subculture theory of aging (Rose, 1964, 1965) includes a functionalist concern for social norms, its main thesis is that these norms develop in interactions with others. The theory holds that the aged are developing their own subculture in American society. This results from (1) older people's exclusion from interactions with other age groups, (2) their increased interaction with each other as a result of age-segregation policies (e.g., retirement, age-homogeneous housing), and (3) their common beliefs and interests (e.g., health care). As a subculture, the elderly create their own norms and values specific to their group. The aged subculture cuts across other status distinctions—gender, race, social class—so that the elderly develop a group identity.

Rose's contention that a subculture is developing can be found in the creation of age-activist groups such as the Gray Panthers and the American Association of Retired Persons (AARP). However, questions arise about whether the elderly constitute a minority group (Streib, 1965). While Rose asserts that the subculture is developing, some research indicates that the aged do not yet share a strong group consciousness, whether measured in terms of voting patterns or similar attitudes and values (Streib, 1985).

Symbolic interactionism is an important addition to the study of aging because it corrects the overly static, passive image of interaction found in functionalist approaches. Symbolic interactionism views the individual as a more active participant in social interaction. An individual does not just become his or her role, as structural functionalist perspectives argue, but rather engages in a process of "role-taking," adjusting his or her behavior depending on the responses of others. Perhaps the major limitation of the symbolic interactionist approach is that its primary focus on the micro level of analysis fails to recognize fully the structural component of social behavior. While individuals are confronted by others' perceptions, the systematic, structural constraints placed upon individual behavior are not addressed (Dannefer, 1984). At the same time, symbolic interactionism, at least as applied to theories of aging, does not seriously examine the ongoing interpretive process in everyday social affairs.[4] This concern, however, is explicitly dealt with by social phenomenology, which we look at later in the chapter.

Marxist Theories of Aging

Marx's (1867/1946) theory of capitalist development emphasizes the constraining features of social order. The perspective argues that the social distribution of power and resources in a capitalist society is embedded within the context of the social relations of production. In the ongoing organization of the economic sphere, people confront the existing social organization of their relations with others (class structure), providing a number of opportunities for some, while excluding the majority of others. The differential class interests make for ongoing strains between competing factions in social life.

The Political Economy of Age

It is only in the last ten years or so that the political economy perspective has been applied to the study of old age. Drawing upon Marxism, this perspective (Estes, 1979; Olson, 1982; Phillipson, 1982; Quadagno, 1982; Walker, 1981) focuses on the state and its relation to the economy in a capitalist society to explain the plight of the elderly. In examining the creation of particular social programs directed toward the elderly, for example, political economists maintain that the effects of such programs have been much more beneficial to capitalist interests than to the elderly themselves, often having adverse effects on older people. Estes (1979) explains the development of government welfare programs for the elderly as helping to increase the number of service-oriented jobs—fueling the capitalist economy—without fundamentally providing for a decent standard of living for needy older people. Other research that has examined the political, social, and economic forces surrounding the conditions of the elderly include Olson's (1982) analysis of the development of a social security system in the United States, Quadagno's (1982) study of the formation of a pension system in England, and Guillemard's (1983) analysis of the welfare state in France.

The political economy perspective is a promising recent addition to the study of aging. In looking at the political and economic conditions that give rise to problems of growing old, this perspective encourages gerontologists to stand back and ask whose interests are really served in the efforts to help the elderly. For example, the issue of generational equity (see, e.g., Kingson, Hirshorn, & Cornman, 1986; Longman, 1985; Preston, 1984) would benefit from a political economic analysis. This debate has been framed in terms of the proportion of Federal monies targeted for children versus the elderly. The political economy perspective, however, would argue that these monies do not directly address the issue of childhood or old-age poverty, given that much of it goes to pay the salaries of those employed by social welfare programs.

While the political economy perspective has expanded the study of aging by focusing on the larger social context of old-age problems, it also tends to overstate the extent to which the elderly, as a whole, are impoverished and disenfranchised—both historically and in advanced industrial societies (Harris & Associates, 1975; Stearns, 1982). Indeed, some researchers suggest that the majority of elderly in contemporary American society constitute a *new old* who are healthier and live in relative economic well-being (Cain, 1967; Neugarten, 1974). Moreover, by focusing on the structure of society itself, the perspective overlooks the role of interpretation and meaning in the everyday experiences of the elderly. As such, the analysis does not address the variety of old-age environments which give rise to their own sets of meanings specific to the elderly's experiences within them (see, e.g., Jacobs, 1975; Myerhoff, 1978; Ross, 1977; Stephens, 1976; Teski, 1979). This issue, however, is explicitly dealt with by another rather recent and promising theoretical development in the sociology of aging—social phenomenology—which we turn to next.

Social Phenomenological Theories of Aging

Social phenomenology is a general term that can be used to encompass a variety of works, in particular the phenomenology of Schutz (1967; 1970) and the ethnomethodology of Garfinkel (1967). The perspective brackets, or puts aside, the question of whether things are real or not and examines the process by which they are socially constructed. While this approach is like symbolic interactionism in that it is concerned with the definitional nature of social life, social phenomenology has a more serious concern with the use of language and knowledge as constitutive elements in everyday realities. For example, researchers have studied the use of developmental discourse by teachers (Cicourel et al., 1974), parents (Speier, 1970), caregivers (Lynott, 1983), social workers and psychiatrists (Pfohl, 1978), among others, in making decisions about other persons' competencies. Their analyses reveal how the course of children's and adults' lives are changed with the interpretive and definitional discussions entered into by decision makers.

Social Phenomenology

As applied to the study of aging, the social phenomenological perspective (Gubrium & Buckholdt, 1977; Hochschild, 1973, 1976; Starr, 1982–1983) examines the emergent, situational, and constitutive features of the aging experience. Gubrium and Buckholdt (1977, p. viii), for example, focus on the practical and ongoing considerations over questions of human development, whereby "the meaning of age is presented and negotiated from moment to moment as people participate in sometimes elusive but serious conversation."

Another focus within the phenomenological perspective has been the critique of positivist research that does not take into account the situated meanings attributed by the social participants. Gubrium and Lynott (1983), for example, have demonstrated that the questions that make up life-satisfaction surveys "instruct" older people to organize their lives in a linear and progressive fashion, regardless of the way they have experienced them. In contrast to the developmental sense of living conveyed in the life satisfaction scales, the authors present evidence from a variety of ethnographic descriptions depicting the contextual and constructed features of life satisfactions among older people. Their critique cautions researchers against findings that do not fit the everyday social realities of elderly persons.

Social phenomenology has brought the study of social construction in everyday life situations to the analysis of the aging experience. Its emphasis on the construction of socially emergent meanings encourages the researcher to pay close attention to ongoing social circumstances. Yet, at the same time, like symbolic interactionism, phenomenology's emphasis on microsocial processes overlooks the structural features of social life. As a result, social phenomenologists tend to minimize the role of power in their analysis of everyday social behaviors (Giddens, 1976).

FUTURE DIRECTIONS IN THEORY BUILDING

Theorizing in the sociology of aging has lagged considerably behind theoretical developments in the field of sociology. There are two primary reasons for this. First, until recently, theoretical development in social gerontology has been dominated by a concern for the predictors of elderly life satisfaction. This was, perhaps, most apparent in the long-running activity-disengagement controversy in the 1960s. As a result of this emphasis on the correlates of life satisfaction, research questions traditionally have been more narrowly focused on the adjustment problems of old age rather than addressing broader theoretical issues concerning the social experiences of aging.

The second reason social gerontology has not kept up with theoretical developments in sociology is that it has been largely dominated by structural functionalism. While the development in social gerontology bears a striking resemblance to the impact of Parsonian functionalism on sociological theorizing in general, its monumental dominance in the field of aging came about much later. As a result, it is only relatively recently that more contemporary perspectives from sociology have been applied to the study of aging.[5] In the remainder of this section we examine two potential directions for future theoretical developments: The prospects for multidisciplinary theories of aging and the promise of a richer, more contextualized analysis of the aging experience.

The Prospects for Multidisciplinary Theories of Aging

More so than many other substantive areas analyzing the human experience, the study of aging has been concerned with the interaction of biological, social, and psychological processes. This has suggested to some the desirability of developing a comprehensive, multiperspective theory of aging. The quest for a grand, interdisciplinary theory encompassing phenomena of aging seems misdirected on several grounds.

There are several obstacles to the formation of multidisciplinary theories of aging. The most critical problem in combining sociological, psychological, and biological approaches is that these disciplines are not unified within themselves. A multidisciplinary approach presumes there is agreement within each discipline concerning how human behavior should be conceptualized. But, as we have shown, there does not exist one sociology (or psychology or biology for that matter). For example, which sociological perspective would one choose in the multidisciplinary study of aging? Structural functionalism? Exchange theory? Symbolic Interactionism? Likewise, which psychological perspective would one choose? Freudianism? Behavioralism? Cognitive theory? Each of these would produce a radically different image of the sociology or psychology of aging. The same is also true, although possibly to a lesser extent, of biology. The existence of many diverse theoretical perspectives in each discipline—and there is little reason to believe this will change in the future—works against the assumption that the social, psychological, and biological influences of aging can be readily combined.

Moreover, the conceptual problems multiply in attempting to merge theoretical perspectives from different disciplines. For example, the individualistic framework of many psychological perspectives is at odds with both macrostructural sociological theories and micro-interpretive perspectives. It is not simply that the theories differ in their units of analysis; their assumptions about human behavior are antagonistic and consequently cannot be combined into a unified theory.

This is not to deny that some psychologists and sociologists share common assumptions about the nature of human behavior. For example, Gergen (1980), a psychologist, and Starr (1982–1983), a sociologist, argue for a similar phenomenological conception of the life course despite their divergent disciplinary training. This example of perspectives that cross disciplinary lines points to one requirement for a comprehensive theory of aging: Self-conscious discussion of the underlying assumptions about human behavior that constitute various theories (see Birren, this volume). Until this discussion is seriously taken up by social theorists of aging, it is probable that any multidisciplinary theory will be combining psychological "apples" with sociological "oranges."

What often occurs with respect to developing a multidisciplinary perspective is that researchers acknowledge the existence of the three processes in aging without fully incorporating each in research. For example, one of the tenets of the life-course perspective is that aging involves biological, social, and psychological processes (Featherman, 1983; Riley, 1987). In practice, however, researchers typically study social factors, less often psychological elements (e.g., Clausen, 1986; Elder, 1974), and rarely incorporate biological variables. Even when researchers do explicitly include the three processes in their models, they typically must oversimplify the concepts contained in each discipline (see, e.g., Brim & Ryff, 1980; Costa & McCrae, 1980; Gutmann, 1974). Thus, psychological processes are subsumed under "personality factors" and sociology is operationalized as "social roles," thereby incorporating a rather superficial, watered-down version of each.

Recent efforts in the social sciences to include sociological, psychological, and biological processes in the study of aging (e.g., Featherman & Lerner, 1985) further illustrate the problems posed by such a comprehensive theory of aging. In their efforts to be inclusive, Featherman and Lerner produce a model that is multidimensional (including social, psychological, and biological variables) but also extremely abstract. Early theories in social gerontology were too simplistic when they attempted to explain the aging process with one variable, whether it be disengagement, activity, or modernization. By the same token, it would be a mistake for future theories to go to the other extreme and develop models that are overly inclusive, explaining little in particular.

An approach that has been relatively fruitful involves empirical research which focuses on one substantive concern (or dependent variable) and studies it from the three disciplines. Research on the combined effects of biological, social, and psychological factors in health and life expectancy (see, e.g., Yates, this volume) have been somewhat successful in incorporating multidisciplinary perspectives. A limitation of this empirical approach is that it cannot deal with more complex social phenomena involving, for example, interactional features of the aging process. In addition, the model's major emphasis on biological factors as the outcome variables results in a narrow vision of what constitutes aging, excluding much gerontological research conducted in sociology and psychology. It is unclear how such models relate to the development of multidisciplinary theories of aging. A model that explains life expectancy is not a theory of aging; it implies that aging can be reduced to one dependent variable. Clearly, aging encompasses more than that.

Toward a Contextual Analysis of Aging

In contrast to the current interest in developing multidisciplinary theories of aging, we believe that a fuller understanding of the social aspects of aging would be a more fruitful direction for future sociological theorizing. Toward this goal, we call for future theoretical directions which concretely analyze the social contexts of aging. By social context we do not mean the kind of analysis commonly done by age stratification and life course researchers, which merely examines statistical comparisons of select cohort demographics. Our concern, rather, is with social *experience*, the fluid and dynamic features of social context.

Political economy and social phenomenology are the most promising theories in this regard. While each focuses on different levels of concern—micro versus macro—and, accordingly, has its respective weaknesses, both provide important insights into the broader contextual features of the aging process. Whether focused on the larger social, political, and economic conditions of society, or the changing social realities in the day-to-day lives of society's members, each perspective, in its own fashion, enables one to stand back and analyze the social dynamics—ideological or socially constructive—involved in understanding aging phenomena.

Consider, for example, how research in social gerontology has strayed too far from people's everyday experiences. A major conceptual issue in social gerontology has focused on the roles and norms applied to the elderly. Rosow (1974), writing from a structural functionalist perspective, argues that old age is characterized by a lack of social roles and norms. That is, unlike other age groups, older people have few social roles to occupy and are not bound by norms of appropriate behavior; old age is thus characterized in terms of a "roleless role" (Burgess, 1960). Hochschild (1973), in her book *The Unexpected Community*, uses a more contextual approach in her analysis of a group of elderly widows living in an apartment complex. Contrary to Rosow's rather bleak view of old age, Hochschild demonstrates that these women lead busy, purposeful lives within their group. She found an elaborate set of newly defined social roles and experiences among the women, which included numerous norms regarding appropriate social behavior. Although Hochschild's approach is not directly phenomenological, her analysis illustrates how the aging experience is variously defined against shifting background relevancies of elderly life. Hochschild's work demonstrates that roles and norms are not only indeed a part of old age, but they are socially constructed within the varied worlds of experience in which older people live. Several other studies have documented similar context-specific social behaviors in a variety of old-age "unexpected" communities (e.g., Eckert, 1980; Frankfather, 1977; Ross, 1977; Teski, 1979). The implication of such studies for the theoretical significance of the political–economic and social phenomenological perspectives is that the two theories' broader social contextualizing features promise to provide yet new insights into, and challenge existing conceptions of, the aging process.

CONCLUSION

The purpose of this chapter has been to assess current sociological theories of aging and propose possible future directions. We have examined the influence of the prominent traditions in sociological theory (structural functionalism, exchange, symbolic interactionism, Marxism, and social phenomenology) on nine theoretical perspectives in the sociology of aging: (1) disengagement, (2) modernization, (3) age stratification (including the life course perspective), (4) exchange, (5) activity, (6) social competence/breakdown, (7) subculture, (8) political economy, and (9) social phenomenology.

We have argued that the current effort to develop multidisciplinary theories of aging is misguided, given the incompatibility not only of theories between the separate disciplines, but also within them. We conclude that the most fruitful areas of analysis for social gerontology lie in a more thorough examination of the contextual features which surround the aging process. This includes historical, political, and economic features as well as the ongoing social construction of everyday aging experiences.

The rapid increase in the older population in recent years has encouraged greater attention to understanding the social aspects of aging. This makes for an exciting period in the sociology of aging, in large part because of the increasing interest in theory development. Theoretically speaking, the study of aging may be coming of age.

NOTES

[1]Throughout this chapter, we will use the term "social gerontology" and "sociology of aging" interchangeably to refer to the study of the social aspects of age, aging, and the aged. See Treas and Passuth (in press) for a fuller discussion of these terms.

[2]We have decided to differentiate theoretical perspectives in this way because these categories are widely recognized within sociology as constituting major theories in the field (see Turner, 1978; Zeitlin, 1973).

[3]We use the term *social phenomenology* to refer primarily to the theoretical work of Schutz (1967, 1970), in the phenomenological tradition, and Garfinkel (1967), in the ethnomethodological tradition. It is distinguished from the phenomenological perspective in psychology discussed by Reker and Wong (this volume).

[4]While Blumer (1969), in his book *Symbolic Interactionism: Perspective and Method*, does examine the ongoing interpretive process, his treatment of symbolic interactionism has not been incorporated into the field of aging.

[5]For example, feminist perspectives are just beginning to be applied to aging issues (e.g., Hess, 1985; Troll, Israel, & Israel, 1977), which is surprising given the predominance of women in the older population.

REFERENCES

Bengtson, V. L., & Kuypers, J. A. (1986). The family support cycle: Psychosocial issues in the aging family. In J. M. A. Munnichs, P. Mussen, & E. Olbrich (Eds.), *Life span and change in a gerontological perspective* (pp. 61–77). New York: Academic Press.

Blau, P. M. (1964). *Exchange and power in social life*. New York: Wiley.

Blumer, H. (1969). *Symbolic interactionism*. Englewood Cliffs, NJ: Prentice-Hall.

Brim, O., & Ryff, C. (1980). On the properties of life events. In P. Baltes & O. Brim (Eds.), *Life-span development and behavior*, Vol. 3 (pp. 65–102). NY: Academic Press.

Brody, E. (1985). Parent care as a normative family stress. *The Gerontologist, 25*, 19–29.

Bultena, G. (1974). Structural effects on the morale of the aged: A comparison of age-segregated and age-integrated communities. In J. Gubrium (Ed.), *Late life* (pp. 18–31). Springfield, IL: Charles C. Thomas.

Burgess, E. W. (1960). Aging in Western culture. In E. Burgess (Ed.), *Aging in Western societies* (pp. 3–28). Chicago: University of Chicago Press.

Cain, L. (1964). Life course and social structure. In R. Faris (Ed.), *Handbook of modern sociology* (pp. 272–309). Chicago: Rand McNally.

Cain, L. (1967). Age status and generational phenomena: The new old people in contemporary America. *The Gerontologist, 7*, 83–92.

Cain, L. (1987). Alternative perspectives on phenomena of human aging: Age stratification and age status. *Journal of Applied Behavior Science, 23*(2), 227–294.

Cavan, R. S. (1962). Self and role in adjustment during old age. In A. Rose (Ed.), *Human behavior and social processes*. Boston: Houghton Mifflin.

Cavan, R. S., Burgess, E. W., Havighurst, R. J., & Goldhamer, H. (1949). *Personal adjustment in old age*. Chicago: Science Research Associates.

Cicourel, A., Jennings, K., Jennings, S., Leiter, K., Mackay, R., Mehan, H., & Roth, D. (1974). *Language use and school performance*. New York: Academic Press.

Clausen, J. (1972). The life course of individuals. In M. Riley, M. Johnson, and A. Foner (Eds.), *Aging and society, Vol. 3. A sociology of age stratification* (pp. 457–514). New York: Russell Sage Foundation.

Clausen, J. (1986). *The sociology of the life course*. Englewood Cliffs, NJ: Prentice-Hall.

Costa, P., & McCrae, R. (1980). Still stable after all these years: Personality as a key to some issues in adulthood and old age. In P. Baltes & O. Brim (Eds.), *Life-span development and behavior*, Vol. 3 (pp. 65–102). New York: Academic Press.

Cowgill, D. O. (1974). Aging and modernization: A revision of the theory. In J. F. Gubrium (Ed.), *Late life* (pp. 123–46). Springfield, IL: Charles C Thomas.

Cowgill, D. O., & Holmes, L. D. (Eds.). (1972). *Aging and modernization*. New York: Appleton-Century-Crofts.

Cumming, E., & Henry, W. E. (1961). *Growing old: The process of disengagement*. New York: Basic Books.

Cutler, N. (1983). Political behavior of the aged. In D. Woodruff & J. Birren (Eds.), *Aging: Scientific perspectives and social issues*, 2nd edition (409–442). New York: Van Nostrand Reinhold.

Dannefer, D. (1984). Adult development and social theory: A paradigmatic reappraisal. *American Sociological Review, 49*, 100–116.

Dannefer, D. (1987). Aging as intracohort differentiation: Accentuation, the Matthew Effect and the life course. *Sociological Forum, 1*, 8–23.

Dowd, J. J. (1975). Aging as exchange: A preface to theory. *Journal of Gerontology, 30*, 584–594.

Eckert, J. (1980). *The unseen elderly*. San Diego: Campanile Press.

Elder, G. (1974). *Children of the Great Depression*. Chicago: University of Chicago Press.

Elder, G. (1975). Age differentiation and the life course. In A. Inkeles, J. Coleman, & N. Smelser (Eds.), *Annual review of sociology*, Vol. 1 (pp. 165–190). Palo Alto, CA: Annual Reviews.

Estes, C. L. (1979). *The aging enterprise*. San Francisco: Jossey-Bass.

Featherman, D. L. (1983). The life span perspective in social science research. In National Science Foundation (Ed.), *Five year outlook on science and technology*, Vol. 2 (pp. 621–648). Washington, DC: National Science Foundation.

Featherman, D. L., & Lerner, R. M. (1985). Ontogenesis and sociogenesis: Problematics for theory and research about development and socialization across the lifespan. *American Sociological Review, 50*, 659–676.

Foner, A. (1974). Age stratification and age conflict in political life. *American Sociological Review, 39*, 1081–1104.

Foner, A. (Ed.) (1975). *Age in society*. Beverly Hills, CA: Sage.

Foner, A. (1986). *Aging and old age: New perspectives*. Englewood Cliffs, NJ: Prentice-Hall.

Frankfather, D. (1977). *The aged in the community*. New York: Praeger.

Garfinkel, H. (1967). *Studies in ethnomethodology*. Englewood Cliffs, NJ: Prentice-Hall.

Gergen, K. (1980). The emerging crisis in life-span developmental theory. In P. Baltes & O. Brim (Eds.), *Life-span development and behavior* (pp. 31–63). New York: Academic.

Giddens, A. (1976). *New rules of sociological method: A positive critique of interpretive sociologies*. New York: Basic Books.

Gouldner, A. (1970). *The coming crisis in Western sociology*. New York: Basic Books.

Gubrium, J. F. (1973). *The myth of the golden years: A socio-environmental theory of aging*. Springfield, IL: Charles C. Thomas.

Gubrium, J. F., & Buckholdt, D. R. (1977). *Toward maturity: The social processing of human development*. San Francisco: Jossey-Bass.

Gubrium, J. F., & Lynott, R. J. (1983). Rethinking life satisfaction. *Human Organization, 42*, 30–38.

Guillemard, A. M. (Ed.). (1983). *Old age in the welfare state*. Beverly Hills, CA: Sage.

Gutmann, D. (1974). Parenthood: A key to the comparative study of the life cycle. In N. Datan & L. Ginsberg (Eds.), *Life-span development crises: Normative life crises* (pp. 167–184). NY: Academic Press.

Haber, C. (1983). *Beyond sixty-five*. Cambridge: Cambridge University Press.

Hagestad, G. O., & Neugarten, B. L. (1985). Age and the life course. In R. Binstock and E. Shanas (Eds.), *Handbook of aging and the social sciences*, 2nd Edition (pp. 35–61). New York: Van Nostrand Reinhold.

Harris, L., & Associates, Inc. (1975). *The myth and reality of aging in America*. Washington, DC: National Council on Aging.

Havighurst, R. J., & Albrecht, R. (1953). *Older people*. New York: Longmans, Green.

Hendricks, J., & Hendricks, C. (1986). *Aging in mass society: Myths and realities*, 3rd Edition. Boston, MA: Little, Brown.

Hess, B. (1985). Aging policies and old women: The hidden agenda. In A. Rossi (Ed.), *Gender and the life course* (pp. 319–331). New York: Aldine.

Hochschild, A. (1973). *The unexpected community*. Englewood Cliffs, NJ: Prentice-Hall.

Hochschild, A. (1975). Disengagement theory: A critique and proposal. *American Sociological Review, 40*, 553–569.

Hochschild, A. (1976). Disengagement theory: A logical, empirical, and phenomenological critique. In J. F. Gubrium (Ed.), *Time, roles, and self in old age* (pp. 53–87). New York: Human Sciences Press.

Hogan, D. (1980). The transition to adulthood as a career contingency. *American Sociological Review, 45*, 261–276.

Hogan, D. (1981). *Transitions and social change: The early lives of American men*. New York: Academic Press.

Homans, G. C. (1961). *Social behavior: Its elementary forms*. New York: Harcourt Brace Jovanovich.

Jacobs, J. (1975). *Older persons and retirement communities*. Springfield, IL: Charles C. Thomas.

Kingson, E. R., Hirshorn, B., & Cornman, J. (1986). *Ties that bind: The interdependence of generations*. Washington, DC: Seven Locks Press.

Kohli, M. (1986). The world we forgot: An historical review of the life course. In V. W. Marshall (Ed.), *Later life: The social psychology of aging* (pp. 271–303). Beverly Hills, CA: Sage Publications.

Kuypers, J. A., & Bengtson, V. L. (1973). Social breakdown and competence: A model of normal aging. *Human Development, 16*, 181–201.

Laslett, P. (1965). *The world we have lost*. London: Methuen.

Lawrence, B. (1984). Age grading: The implicit organizational timetable. *Journal of Occupational Behavior, 5*, 23–35.

Lawton, M. P. (1983). Environment and other determinents of well being in older people. *The Gerontologist, 23*, 349–357.

Lemon, B. W., Bengtson, V. L., & Peterson, J. A. (1972). An exploration of the activity theory of aging: Activity types and life satisfaction among in-movers to a retirement community. *Journal of Gerontology, 27*, 511–523.

Longman, P. (1985, June). Justice between generations. *Atlantic Monthly*, 73–81.

Lowy, L. (1985). *Social work with the aging: The challenges and promises of the later years*. New York: Longman.

Lynott, R. (1983). Alzheimer's disease and institutionalization: The ongoing construction of a decision. *Journal of Family Issues, 4*, 559–574.

Maddox, G. (1964). Disengagement theory: A critical evaluation. *The Gerontologist, 4*, 80–82.

Mannheim, K. (1928, 1952). The problem of generations. In D. Kecskemeti (Ed.), *Essays on the sociology of knowledge* (pp. 276–322). London: Routledge and Kegan Paul.

Marx, K. (1867, 1946). *Das Kapital*. New York: Modern Library.

Matthews, S. H. (1979). *Social world of old women*. Beverly Hills, CA: Sage.

Mead, G. H. (1934). *Mind, self, and society*. Chicago: University of Chicago Press.

Messer, M. (1967). The possibility of an age-concentrated environment becoming a normative system. *The Gerontologist, 7*, 247–250.

Myerhoff B. (1978). *Number our days*. New York: Simon and Schuster.

Neugarten, B. L. (1974). Age groups in American society and the rise of the young old. *Annals of the American Academy of Political and Social Science, 415*, 187–198.

Neugarten, B. L. & Hagestad, G. O. (1976). Age and the life course. In R. Binstock & E. Shanas (Eds.), *Handbook of aging and the social sciences*, 1st edition (pp. 35–55). New York: Van Nostrand Reinhold.

Neugarten, B. L., Moore, J., & Lowe, J. (1965). Age norms, age constraints, and adult socialization. *American Journal of Sociology, 70*, 710–717.

Olson, L. K. (1982). *The political economy of aging*. New York: Columbia University Press.

Palmore, E. B. (1968). The effects of aging on activities and attitudes. *The Gerontologist, 8*, 259–263.

Palmore, E. B., & Manton, K. (1974). Modernization and status of the aged: International correlations. *Journal of Gerontology, 29*, 205–210.

Parsons, T. (1951). *The social system*. New York: Free Press.

Pfohl, S. (1978). *Predicting dangerousness*. Lexington, MA: Lexington Books.

Phillipson, C. (1982). *Capitalism and the construction of old age*. London: Macmillan.

Preston, S. (1984). Children and the elderly: Divergent paths for America's dependents. *Demography, 21*, 435–457.

Quadagno, J. S. (1982). *Aging in early industrial society.* New York: Academic Press.

Riley, M. W. (1971). Social gerontology and the age stratification of society. *The Gerontologist, 11*, 79–87.

Riley, M. W. (1987). On the significance of age in sociology. *American Sociological Review, 52*, 1–14.

Riley, M. W., Johnson, M., & Foner, A. (1972). *Aging and society, Vol. 3: A sociology of age stratification.* New York: Russell Sage Foundation.

Rose, A. M. (1964). A current theoretical issue in social gerontology. *The Gerontologist, 4*, 46–50.

Rose, A. M. (1965). The subculture of aging: A framework for research in social gerontology. In A. M. Rose and W. A. Peterson (Ed.), *Older people and their social world* (pp. 3–16). Philadelphia: F. A. Davis.

Rosow, I. (1974). *Socialization to old age.* Berkeley, CA: University of California Press.

Ross, J. (1977). *Old people, new lives.* Chicago: University of Chicago Press.

Schaie, K. W. (1979). The primary mental abilities in adulthood: An exploration in the development of psychometric intelligence. In P. Baltes & O. Brim (Eds.), *Life-span development and behavior*, Vol. 2 (pp. 68–117). New York: Academic Press.

Schutz, A. (1967). *The phenomenology of the social world.* Introduction by George Walsh. Evanston, IL: Northwestern University Press.

Schutz, A. (1970). *On phenomenology and social relations.* (trans. by H. Wagner). Chicago: University of Chicago Press.

Sherman, E. (1981). *Counseling the aging: An integrative approach.* New York: Free Press.

Simmons, L. (1945). *The role of the aged in primitive society.* New Haven, CT: Yale University Press.

Speier, M. (1970). The everyday world of the child. In J. Douglas (Ed.), *Understanding Everyday Life.* Chicago: Aldine.

Starr, J. M. (1982–83). Toward a social phenomenology of aging: Studying the self process in biographical work. *International Journal of Aging and Human Development, 16*, 255–270.

Stearns, P. N. (1982). *Old age in preindustrial society.* New York: Holmes and Meier.

Stephens, J. (1976). *Loners, losers, and lovers.* Seattle, WA: University of Washington Press.

Streib, G. F. (1965). Are the aged a minority group? In A. Gouldner & S. Miller (Eds.), *Applied sociology* (pp. 311–328). New York: Free Press.

Streib, G. F. (1985). Social stratification and aging. In R. Binstock & E. Shanas (Eds.), *Handbook of aging and the social sciences*, 2nd edition (pp. 339–368). New York: Von Nostrand Reinhold.

Streib, G. F., & Bourg, C. J. (1984). Age stratification theory, inequality, and social change. *Comparative Social Research, 7*, 63–77.

Teski, M. (1979). *Living together.* Washington, DC: University Press of America.

Treas, J., & Passuth, P. (in press). The three sociologies: Age, aging, and the aged. In E. Borgatta and K. Cook (Eds.), *The future of sociology.* Beverly Hills, CA: Sage.

Troll, L., Israel, J., & Israel, K. (1977). *Looking ahead: A woman's guide to the problems and joys of growing older.* Englewood Hills, NJ: Prentice-Hall.

Turner, J. (1978). *The structure of sociological theory* (2nd ed.). Homewood, IL: The Dorsey Press.

Walker, A. (1981). Towards a political economy of old age. *Aging and Society, 1*, 73–94.

Zeitlin, I. (1973). *Rethinking sociology: A critique of contemporary theory.* New York: Appleton-Century-Crofts.

Zusman, J. (1966). Some explanations of the changing appearance of psychotic patients: Antecedents of the social breakdown syndrome concept. *Millbank Memorial Fund Quarterly, 64*, 63–84.

16

What's in a Name? An Account of the Neglect of Variability in the Study of Aging*

Dale Dannefer

> Let the data speak for themselves, they say. The problem . . . is, of course, that data never do speak for themselves.
>
> EVELYN FOX KELLER, *Reflections on Gender and Science*

> We require an education in literature as in the sentiments in order to discover that what we assumed — with the complicity of our teachers — was nature is in fact culture, that what was given is no more than a way of taking.
>
> RICHARD HOWARD, *A Note on S/Z*

SCIENCE AS A SOCIAL ENTERPRISE

Scientific activity is a form of human activity. As such, it is not conducted in a cultural and existential vacuum, but by human actors located in a particular setting and at a particular historical moment. This sociohistorical location

*The author gratefully acknowledges the constructive criticisms and suggestions of several colleagues, some of whom disagree with parts of the argument of this paper. These include, first of all, the members of the Andrew Norman Institute for Advanced Study, 1985–1986. In addition, conversations with Marlee Campbell, Richard Campbell, John Clausen, Neal Cutler, and Harry R. Moody were also helpful in

gives the entire scientific enterprise, as well as the life and work of individual scientists working within in, a distinctive and—in relation to the phenomena it intends to illuminate—a somewhat arbitrary cast. It is not simply the *discovery* of the phenomenon that exists in nature, but the *naming* of it (Keller, 1985, p. 17) in terms comprehensible to the community in which the namer is located. Thus, phenomena can never be intelligibly named and described apart from the structures of language and thought characteristic of the namer's culture. The enterprise of science is a subculture or, more precisely, a system of subcultures that emerge from and are dialectically related to the general society and culture. It is ironic but inescapable that science, which entails discerning the general in the particular, always and necessarily conducts its search from the *particular* vantage point of the individual scientist with a specific sociohistorical location and a unique life history.

If the subject matter of social science is human activity, these considerations describe the compelling need to make scientific activity itself an object of study. The process of inquiry always will be profoundly incomplete if attention to the ways in which the "search for truth" is directed by the perspective of the inquirer is not an integral part of the process. Such analysis is a primary task of the sociology of knowledge, which seeks to understand the relationship of what passes for knowledge and the structure of society (for recent discussions see Collins, 1986; Knorr-Cetina & Mulkay, 1983).

Although it is still a powerful notion in much popular thought and in introductory textbook treatments of the scientific method, the idea that scientific work proceeds in some insulated and pure vacuum of objective discovery has been rejected by several traditions of scholarship, such as intellectual history and the history of science. Without any explicit sociological formalization, these traditions have contributed much to understanding the extent to which the formulation of scientific problems and the interpretation given to findings are shaped by entire classes of extraneous factors that surround any process of inquiry. One class, for example, consists of earlier biographical experiences in the scientist's life course. These have occasionally been analyzed in an explicit sociology-of-knowledge framework. Thus, the relevance of the desire of a young scholar, Freud, to come to terms with his own marginal identity (Cuddihy, 1974) has been hypothesized to be decisive for the later development of the structure of his theory.

A second broad class of factors has to do with professional training. Thus, the intellectual and interpersonal influence of a luminary mentor (Boas) and the desire of a graduate student (Margaret Mead) to please him have been

clarifying some points of the argument; and John Broughton, Elaine Dannefer, Laurence Parker, and Philip Wexler made helpful comments on earlier drafts. They have done all they could; remaining shortcomings are the responsibility of the author.

argued to have influenced greatly the research process and the conclusions of her work (Freeman, 1984; Zuckerman, 1977).

Still another set of forces to be analyzed are the immediate conditions under which scientific activity within a discipline occurs. These include the technical constraints of empirical research, as Campbell and O'Rand (this volume) illustrate. They also include *internal political* dynamics—the realities of the power structure of a discipline, reflecting the paradigm under which "normal science" is conducted (Kuhn, 1962; Miller, 1984); the mechanisms through which dominant paradigms are maintained and would-be competitors are neutralized; and also the realities of interpersonal relations of everyday life in the lab, which can have decisive effects on the direction of scientific knowledge (Koestler, 1971; Miller, 1984). Such analyses provide useful case examples for an analysis of the interaction of scientists in terms of, for example, symbolic interaction and group dynamics. However, a complete sociology-of-knowledge analysis must also attend to the *external* forces that condition scientific activity. These include, of course, such factors as the exigencies of funding agencies (Wheeler, 1980) and the efforts of a discipline to react to threats of encroachment or attack from other disciplines or broader scientific, political, or cultural developments (Noble, 1984).

Finally, an even more fundamental set of constraints can be analyzed as deriving from the particularly characteristic culture of which the scientific enterprise is an extension. A distinct coloration is always given to reality by the broader cultural and linguistic context within which scientific discourse occurs, as illustrated by Keller's (1985) analysis of the effects of the genderedness of language on scientific thought patterns.[1]

Although a sociology-of-knowledge perspective has been used to analyze numerous other areas of social science, few attempts have been made to apply it to the study of aging. Such an application has perhaps been most clearly presaged in sociological analyses of the recently popular stage theories of adulthood. Such analyses have noted the correspondence or "elective affinity" (Weber, 1964) between *development*, as described by such theories, and the kinds of adult career patterns constituted by the processing of employees through contemporary bureaucratic organizations (Dannefer, in press; Rossi, 1980). They note the potentials of such theories to become self-fulfilling prophecies when, as authoritative best-sellers, they describe certain discontents, transitions, or crises that are widely institutionalized aspects of contemporary existence as normal organismically based "development" (Brim, 1976; Dannefer, 1984a; Riley, 1978). Scholarship in allied disciplines has produced findings that contribute directly to a sociology-of-knowledge perspective on aging and development, but the connection is not articulated. For example, Achenbaum (1978) shows how the interaction of technological innovation and demographic shift produces a change in the meaning of being old as it changes one's likelihood of living to become old. Such historical analyses have also been made for other portions of the life course. Thus, Kett (1977) has shown G. Stanley Hall's *Adolescence* was written in response to specific problems of how to deal with youth in an era of great technological change and geographic mobility, and that it found a receptive audience only because it provided a plausible cultural solution to the problem of defining the teenage years in such a period of change — a solution that carried with it the authority of science.

This chapter develops one aspect of a sociology of knowledge of the study of aging. Its analytic perspective and its objectives are sharply delimited. The primary objective is to account for the curious, even anomalous, neglect of an important question of potentially great theoretical importance in the study of aging, the question of the relationship between age and variability, and the related hypothesis of increasing heterogeneity with age. If age categories differ systematically in the amount of variability on a given characteristic, and especially if successive cohorts show similar patterns of variability over the life course, then it is a systematic distortion of the experience of age in a population to focus only on normative and central-tendency measures, as is usually done. A second objective is to explore the implications of this neglect for future theorizing about age.

After describing the growing recognition of the importance of this issue, I will argue that the anomaly of its neglect can be understood through a sociology-of-knowledge analysis. Specifically, I propose that an analysis of the terms of discourse — of the manner in which phenomena are named — of the dominant paradigms used in the study of aging comprises an important set of constraints upon our ability to focus on the issue of variability. The setting of the terms of discourse that guide scientific work are obviously crucial, and they are all the more effective for being nearly invisible, as is often the case. They become taken for granted and regarded as part of "normal science," natural and given components of the objective language of scientific discourse. The impact of language on scientific work is not only important, it is also difficult to discern. The reflective scientist can much more readily discern how his or her childhood experiences or the current politics of the discipline shapes the direction of his or her work than he or she can discern the blinders of a dominant paradigm of scientific thought within which he or she is immersed. If one has been effectively trained in a discipline, the questions one can ask are constrained by its language. As Peter and Brigitte Berger (1979) note, socialization, if it is effective, entails "relative patterns experienced as absolute. . . . The absoluteness with which societies' patterns confront the child is based on two very simple facts — the great power of the adults in the situation, and the ignorance of the child of alternative patterns" (pp. 9–10). The difference between the situation of the child who is learning to live and the graduate student learning a way of doing science is one of degree, not kind. Each is participating in a process of social reproduction from a position of minimum power and knowledge.

The logic of the chapter is as follows. First, it seeks to establish both the past neglect and the logical centrality of variability in any adequate theoretical or descriptive treatment of human aging. Second, the chapter argues that the anomaly of neglect can be understood if it is seen as a product of deeply embedded paradigm assumptions of which it is merely symptomatic. Third, the chapter suggests that the discovery of these problematic assumptions redefines the problem: Addressing the neglect of variability will require a focus on rethinking of the paradigm assumptions that permitted its neglect in the first place. Accordingly, the fourth and final section of the chapter proposes some supplementary concepts which, if integrated at the paradigm level, might help to provide a richer and more adequate conceptual framework for apprehending the phenomenon under study.

AGE AND VARIABILITY: THEORY, RESEARCH, AND COMMONSENSE DISCOURSE IN THE STUDY OF AGING

The Phenomenon of "Aged Heterogeneity" and Its Theoretical Status

A widely acknowledged generalization in the field of gerontology holds that elderly persons are the most heterogeneous of any age stratum with regard to many characteristics. Older people have been thought to be more dissimilar from one another than are younger people in terms of physical health status, intellectual capacity and psychological functioning, material resource availability, and life-style. Although such comparisons are often used to contrast different age groups or strata at one point in time, they also implicitly connote a life-course pattern toward greater heterogeneity among age peers (Bengtson, Kasschau, & Ragan, 1977; Riley, 1980). Thus, members of a cohort are sometimes described as "fanning out" as they age, becoming more unlike each other on any given characteristic (e.g., Baltes, 1979).

In view of the widespread belief in aged heterogeneity, it is surprising that it has been the subject of little systematic research, and even less theorizing. A recent review (Bornstein & Smircana, 1982) claimed that little longitudinal evidence exists that can even address the issue of increasing heterogeneity with age. Medical gerontologists are among those who frequently refer to the reality of heterogeneity, yet there are few good medical studies that systematically explore the issue (Rowe & Kahn, 1987). Survey research in sociology is generally based on strongly designed samples and measures but has seldom been longitudinal in nature. Moreover, analysts who use such data seldom focus on comparisons of differences in individual characteristics among cohorts or age strata in the extent of variability in such characteristics.[2] Recently, scholars from demography (Hogan, 1985; Marini, 1984), sociology (Bielby, 1986; Dannefer, 1984b, 1987; Maddox, 1986), psychology (Perlmutter, 1986), and medicine (Krauss, 1980; Lipson, 1986) have begun identifying the focus on central tendency and concomitant neglect of variability as distorting empirical description and inhibiting theoretical developments in the study of age-related phenomena in these fields.

Despite the history of neglect, a growing body of empirical evidence bears upon the increasing heterogeneity assumption and generally tends to give it more empirical support. Much of this evidence comes from the cumulation of longitudinal and other relevant data sets constructed by those with a specific interest in aging; other evidence comes from studies focused on organizational (e.g., Rosenbaum, 1984), family-related (e.g., Treas & Passuth, 1986), or other issues. It includes cross-sectional (Norris & Shock, 1966; Perlmutter, 1978, 1979, 1985) and longitudinal studies of psychological, physical, and social characteristics (Daatland, 1985; Maddox & Douglass, 1974; Mellstrom, Sundh, & Svanborg, 1985; Thomae, 1985), and synthetic cohort analyses of social characteristics (Mincer, 1974). This research provides considerable evidence of a recurrent pattern of increasing heterogeneity with age. However, the central point to be made here is not the factual status of the generalization, but simply that the issue of the patterning of intracohort variability has received little attention.

In terms of theory, the few references to the phenomenon of aged heterogeneity have for the most part implicitly conceived it as a result of individual-level processes such as accentuation (Feldman & Weiler, 1976) or "canalization" (Jantsch & Waddington, 1976; Schroots, this volume; Waddington, 1960), and sometimes it is even used in a celebratory manner, as representing a kind of "triumph of the individual" over the presumably conformistic influences of the social environment (Hickey, 1980). On many characteristics, however, the greater diversity of the elderly reflects greater prevalence of pathological problems.

In contrast to the view that heterogeneity results from the expression of individuality, recent sociological research has suggested that, for many individual characteristics, the social environment systematically produces *variation*, not conformity, among cohort members as they age (Dannefer, 1987). Although we still lack the comprehensive data needed to chart how life-course trajectories of heterogeneity develop within cohorts, it appears that the trend toward increasing differentiation may be fairly continuous from childhood, at least in bureaucratized societies. Rosenbaum (1976) demonstrated that high school students were more heterogeneous on IQ as 12th-graders than they had been as 9th-graders, a patterned change that appears to be directly linked to the organization-level dynamics of ability grouping and tracking in high school. Such initial differentiation has consequences for college and labor market placement. The pattern of intracohort variation in terms of individual and family income and career rewards appears to diverge from midlife onward until retirement (Rosenbaum, 1984; Treas, 1986); after retirement resources (Henretta & Campbell, 1976; David & Menchik, 1984) and life-style differences (Guillemard, 1982) appear to continue to be highly differentiated in patterned ways. Such findings have led to the argument, elaborated in a recent series of papers (Bengtson & Dannefer, 1987; Dannefer, 1987; Dannefer & Sell, 1986; Maddox, 1986; see also Rosenbaum, 1984), that such increasing heterogeneity can be partially accounted for in terms of social processes, especially those that involve the production of inequality.[3] In view of these recent developments, the long neglect of heterogeneity in the study of aging appears anomalous indeed. Why has it received so little attention from researchers? This question has several possible answers.

One preliminary and partial explanation focuses on the issues arising in the everyday work lives of gerontologists. Among applied gerontologists, the emphasis on heterogeneity has perhaps been greater because of their direct experience of the real people of the diverse older population. Similarly, it appears to have been taken considerably more seriously as an issue for policymaking (Bielby, 1986; Neugarten, 1982), where the exigencies of care provision and planning force attention to it in a way that abstract theorizing and research with small samples may not. However, for the academic study of age, the questions remain: If aged heterogeneity is believed to be a significant aspect of the aging of a population, why has no one bothered to document it? If it is believed to be an empirical reality, why has no one seriously attempted to understand the kinds of dynamics underlying it? If it is an enduring age-related phenomenon, why is it not visibly acknowledged, addressed, and accounted for in theories of human aging?

Factors Involved in the Theoretical Neglect of Heterogeneity

Several partial answers to such questions can be offered without resorting to the fundamental issues of paradigm assumptions. These partial answers arise from a consideration of the state of the study of aging in the social sciences. The past two decades have marked an enormous growth of the field, both conceptually and methodologically. In psychology and biology, age-related psychophysiological mechanisms and processes became a major research emphasis (Birren, 1959, 1964, 1970). In sociology, Ryder's (1965) landmark article introducing the concept of the cohort provided a conceptual foundation for several major paradigmatic developments. The age-stratification perspective (Riley, Johnson, & Foner, 1972) provided a broad conceptual framework within which crucial issues of research design and theory and interpretation became clarified. The life-course perspective (Clausen, 1972; Elder, 1974, 1975) drew additional attention to the problems of disentangling the confounded realities of individual and social change and began a tradition of research focusing on the pivotal consequences of early-life conditions and events. Scholars working in the life-span perspective in developmental psychology (Baltes, 1979; Baltes & Schaie, 1973a) have been concerned with many of the same issues. Given such similarities of concern, considerable energy has been devoted to interdisciplinary collaboration (Baltes & Brim, 1979–1984; Brim & Kagan, 1980; Erikson & Smelser, 1980; Featherman & Lerner, 1985) and to analysis of problems at the interdisciplinary interface (Baltes & Nesselroade, 1984; Dannefer, 1984a,b; Elrod, in press; Perlmutter, 1986; Riley, 1978). This explosion of activity, both within and across disciplines, has meant that there has been no shortage of fresh and emerging ideas for those interested in aging. In short, maybe there just has not been enough time to get around to focusing on heterogeneity until now.

Data requirements also may have contributed to the neglect. The study of variability places stringent requirements upon sampling and other aspects of research design. Since it is intrinsically a collective property, variability can be meaningfully investigated only with a sizable sample of people who are comparable on some orienting dimension, such as year of birth or time of employment. In short, the sample must be said to be able to represent one or more age or entry *cohorts*. To address questions of life-course heterogeneity rather than age-structure heterogeneity, a longitudinal sample is ideally needed. A large longitudinal sample is, of course, expensive and time-consuming to study and poses many technical and procedural challenges for research (see Campbell, Bengtson, & Gilford, 1985, for a recent discussion). In sum, the question of heterogeneity has, at least until quite recently, been a costly one to pursue both temporally and financially, and hence there has been little incentive to pursue it in view of the many other interesting questions a researcher on aging might contemplate.

It is probable that each of these considerations belongs to a complete account of why empirical *research* has not taken up the question of intra-age heterogeneity. It is less clear that these considerations play as strong a role in their *theoretical* neglect. As large longitudinal data sets and others offering possibilities of synthetic cohort analysis have become more plentiful and accessible, there has been no noticeable increase in the attention paid to the heterogeneity issue. To account for the theoretical neglect of the topic, the sociology-of-knowledge hypothesis is proposed: *The question itself does not fit readily within the primary theoretical frameworks* that have guided research in aging. This claim is given support by the fact that the recent calls for more attention to heterogeneity have been pressed by practical concerns (Krauss, 1980; Lipson, 1986) and by conceptual efforts to bring theoretical insights, drawn primarily from other areas of sociological inquiry, to bear upon the subject matter of human aging (Dannefer, 1984a, 1987a; Hochschild, 1975).

ECLIPSE OF THE ISSUE OF VARIABILITY IN THEORIES OF AGING: TWO PROBLEMATIC CONCEPTS

In what follows, two important concepts that have been used in studies of the sociology and psychology of aging are examined: *development* and *socialization*. Each represents distinct intellectual traditions, yet it is suggested that both have the effect of obscuring the entire issue of variability, and even more, of distorting the more general dynamics of human experience and social relations that underlie the production of heterogeneity. The analysis that follows will thus suggest that the neglect of this issue is symptomatic of deep-seated limitations of these concepts in apprehending the phenomena they seek to describe.

Before entering into a critique of these concepts, it is important to acknowledge that something *like* each of them is necessary in the study of aging, for each of them attempts to describe something real and fundamental about human experience over time. Therefore, a responsible effort at criticism cannot simply take the form of negative complaints about what exists but must also seek to propose constructive, supplementary alternatives or reformulations. Some proposed alternatives will be preliminarily explored in the final section of the chapter.

Development

The traditional paradigm of development in the human sciences is anchored in a biologically based model of maturational unfolding. As described by numerous developmental thinkers (Baltes, 1979; Harris, 1957; Lerner, 1976), the basic definition incorporates the following characteristics: sequentiality, unidirectionality, an end state, irreversibility, qualitative-structural transformation, and universality. Recently, numerous representatives of the life-span and related traditions have called for a rethinking of the concept of development along lines that reject these traditional assumptions and in some way reformulate notions of development (Baltes, 1979; Dannefer & Perlmutter, 1987; Featherman & Lerner, 1985; Gergen, 1980; Perlmutter, 1985; Riegel, 1973). The present chapter argues that both the classic formulation of development and the dominant reconceptualized formulations are governed by a logic that systematically deflects attention from the issues related to the heterogeneity of the aged.

In relation to heterogeneity, critique of the concept of development builds on earlier critiques of various applications of the developmental paradigm, especially in adulthood and aging (Brim & Kagan, 1980; Dannefer, 1984a,b; Gubrium & Buckholdt, 1977; Hochschild, 1975; Riley, 1978; Rossi, 1980). Essentially, the substance of these critiques begins by explicating the historical and/or logical affinities of the conventional developmental model with models of growth of lower biological organisms. In such biological systems, patterns of change with age appear to be genetically "hard-wired." Hence, a model of age-related change as an ontogenetic process is appropriate.[4] It is abundantly clear that such a model is fundamentally unable to deal with *human* aging, which has a biological base but is also dialectical, in that it involves the world-producing and self-producing processes fundamental to human activity, processes that also act back upon the aging of the biological human organism in significant ways. As Berger and Luckmann (1967) put it, the human actor both "*is* a body" and "*has* a body," and the humanly created context acts back upon the individual as both — that is, upon both the organism and upon the self. The inappropriateness of some aspects of traditional conceptions of development have been acknowledged and addressed within developmental psychology (Baltes & Schaie, 1973b; Gergen, 1980; Perlmutter, 1985; Riegel, 1973) but without resolution.

The important "revisionist tradition" of life-span developmental theory (Baltes, 1979; Baltes & Reese, 1984; Baltes & Nesselroade, 1984), recognizes human aging as something that changes culturally and historically. However, the life-span paradigm recognizes only the effects of history or social change — mediated through the operation of cohort flow — as systematic social influences on human development ("history-graded"). Within particular cohorts, the life-span paradigm has preserved the emphasis on normativity ("normative age-graded"). This formulation emphasizes diversity between cohorts but obscures it by focusing on central tendency within them.

The paradigmatic centrality of normativity and the concomitant emphasis on central tendency are integral to the neglect of heterogeneity in developmental theory. The continuing emphasis on normativity has several adverse consequences for advancing theory in the study of age and development. These encompass empirical, theoretical, practical, and ideological issues, each of which will be discussed.

First is the issue of adequately representing the empirical reality under consideration. This is a problem with normativity as the *basis for accurate empirical description*. If significant and systematic differences in the extent or patterning of variability do occur, there is no need to interpret them as empirically interesting or theoretically problematic if variation may legitimately be dismissed as error. Such logic imposes upon the data a particular reading, founded on the assumption that normativity is truth. In so doing, this logic deflects attention from the empirical reality of systematic differences in variability.

Beyond the level of description, it is also necessary to consider the deeper paradigmatic assumptions that underlie such a procedural logic. This takes us to the second problem area, *the problem of explanation*. Any discussion of normative differences by age tends to reduce the enterprise from explanation to description. Consider a typical life-course trajectory of age on a given variable in a good longitudinal data set. The omnibus variable *age* (Dannefer, 1984a; Hochschild, 1975; Passuth & Bengtson, this volume) is itself the primary explanatory variable; the cohort trajectory that results from connecting the mean scores of various age categories presumably reveals the effects of aging. No analyses require attention beyond those provided by central tendency by age. Although researchers do, of course, sometimes go further to look at some aspect of diversity or process, these are nonessential aspects of the guiding paradigm — secondary, optional, and residual.

As an omnibus variable, age may predict a great deal, but it offers little in the way of explanation or understanding (Wohwill, 1973). Since age itself is widely recognized to be simply an index variable for a multitude of physical, psychic, and social occurrences that potentially influence the observed age pattern, what the age points on the life-course trajectory of a variable give us is a summated description of the value of the variable at each age (see Perlmutter, 1986, for a closely related discussion). Connecting a succession of such points provides a trajectory of summated descriptions. The emphasis on normativity suggests that the tracking of normative age differences answers the central question of inquiry. The implicit assumption of such a strategy of inquiry is that *age* per se (i.e., birth-anchored, chronologically based, and therefore rooted fundamentally in the life of the individual organism) is the central factor in the production of such patterns, analogous to its role in lower life forms, which are subject to less variability, less profound interactions with the environment, and more genetic control (Dannefer, 1984a; Lewontin, Rose, & Kamin, 1984).[5]

When this is done, the focus of inquiry is inevitably directed toward a description of normative or dominant patterns and toward an attempt to make general statements apply. Further, it has been suggested (Dannefer, 1984a; Perlmutter, 1986) that the focus on central tendency measures has encouraged descriptive work (e.g., mean differences by age) while deflecting attention from the need for a more explanatory emphasis that would seek to identify the processes underlying descriptive outcomes.

For those committed to the traditional emphasis on normativity, the proposal to shift the focus from central tendency to diversity may be seen as unwelcome. The greater the unimodality of the distribution, and the less the diversity, the easier it is to dismiss the effects of all variables other than age as error. A wide or skewed within-age distribution suggests that the cause is not age per se and that other factors must be mobilized to account for the observed outcome. Yet even under such conditions, age may remain a powerful predictor if there are age group differences in mean level. In practice, it may be less a principled commitment to the omnibus variable age than the pragmatic value of its predictive power in research that perpetuates the emphasis on normativity and the concomitant neglect of variability.

In short, in the study of human aging, *normative age* is not properly thought of as an a priori objective of inquiry; rather, normativity is itself both an empirical and theoretical problem. Indeed, the degree of statistical normativity may be regarded as an important variable: Extent of intracohort *age normativity* has varied not only with age but, holding age constant, with culture and historical period as well (Neugarten & Hagestad, 1976; Modell, Furstenberg et al., 1976, 1978). Such differences in normativity have identifiable causes and have significant consequences for the well-being of individuals as they age. Thus, in the study of human aging, normativity ought not to be regarded as a sacred cornerstone of research design but as a variable phenomenon in need of critical analysis and explanation. The ontogenetic paradigm of age research takes for granted a problematic aspect of human aging—the production and distribution of outcomes on a given characteristic, while making problematic what should be secondary—the aggregated mean value on that characteristic.

A third problem area is that of *knowledge and practice in everyday life*. A key problem here is the pervasive and unhappy tendency to equate normativity with normality. Armed only with the naive commonsense assumptions of the general culture with which scientists and social scientists tend to operate in the study of social phenomena, we are subject to ethnocentrism, historiocentrism, and cohort-centrism (Riley, 1978). A representative example is provided by the life-course trajectory of blood pressure, which rises with age in modern Western societies (though not in some traditional societies) and also may become less normative with age even in modern Western societies. Thus, the long-standing presumption that an increase is normal finally has been rejected. The grounds for its rejection might have been discovered much earlier had the logic of inquiry focused on the maximal possibilities for health (i.e., on the life-style, life conditions, and life history of older persons who successfully maintained lower blood pressure) rather than assuming that normativity was equal to health (see Rowe & Kahn, 1987, for a related discussion).

Finally, this chapter will try to illustrate what appears to be the depth of the *ideological dominance of the normative aging idea*. When presenting this material to an interdisciplinary group, one response from a sophisticated developmental psychologist was that psychologists certainly are interested in interindividual differences by age, and these differences are addressed in terms such as *functional age*. In fact, the concept of functional age simply provides another symptom of the dominance of developmental thinking. It cleverly (albeit unwittingly) redefines systematically patterned social differences as age differences. Persons who have the greatest control over life-style and health care—i.e., the most affluent—have a higher probability of long life and enduring good health (see, e.g., Kahn, 1981; Kitagawa & Hauser, 1973). Thus, for example, President Reagan's physician described him as a man of 55 or 60 physiologically. On the other hand, children who lack viable family environments and school opportunities have lower "mental age." The imagery suggested by these examples is that *individuals age differently*.

Sometimes, the diversity of the aged, like diversity more generally, is described in a spirit of celebration. This emphasis discounts the extent to which such differential aging is a result of those individuals having been *differentially allocated* in a historically specific and potentially modifiable system of socially organized experiences, opportunities, and resources. In short, people do not just "age" differently; they are also tracked differently. To reduce processes of social sorting and allocation to a characteristic of the individual is to deny the potentially central role of social stratification and other social processes in producing "aged heterogeneity."

In sum, even the most advanced paradigms of adult development theory have obscured issues of heterogeneity because of their intrinsic emphasis on normativity. It is this intrinsic image of a modal pattern for each age category (around which there is some variation, to be sure, but one hopes it will be in the shape of a normal distribution and hence can be regarded as uninteresting "error" variation) that makes the concept of development inimical to the study of patterns of heterogeneity within a cohort. Although heterogeneity may pose statistical or other methodological problems, it is not theoretically important to developmental logic.

It is ironic that the concept of increasing intracohort heterogeneity with age is acknowledged and depicted in some of Baltes's (1979) major programmatic statements. However, it is not integrated into his central paradigmatic formulation, nor implemented in research and analysis conducted within the life-span tradition even when data that could be brought to bear upon the issue are available. These omissions are indicative of the antipathy of the concept of development to the systematic study of heterogeneity. In spite of the paradigmatic emphasis on normality, some life-span scholars now have begun to explore heterogeneity as an empirical phenomenon (Schaie, in press). The extent to which this will press for a *theoretical* modification of the life-span perspective remains to be seen. What is needed is a conceptual framework that recognizes both maturational processes and the dynamics of differentiation within a cohort. In the concluding section, one direction for the development of such a conceptual base is proposed.

Socialization

Like *development*, *socialization* describes something real and indispensable to an adequate description of human aging: the shaping by social forces of an individual's movement through the life course. And like development, the concept of socialization has taken on connotations that go well beyond this fundamental principle.

One of these connotations is the assumption that socialization is not only a universal social process but also an organic and integrative process for the overall social order. Thus, Bengtson and Black (1973) describe as a dominant emphasis in socialization research the study of "the processes that lead to a uniform cultural product" (p. 212). Similarly, Brim (1966) writes that the function of socialization is to shape individuals into "good working members" of society (p. 5). This general perspective implicitly, and often explicitly, assumes that social order is itself a unitary entity, with requirements for which individuals are prepared and fitted by socialization. These requirements are seen as altogether natural and legitimate. Thus, in discussing adult socialization, Brim (1968) writes: "the socialization experience of childhood is not enough to meet the demands of the later years. . . . Adults must change and be socialized into new roles" (p. 184). Through socialization, individuals thus become responsible members, participants, and contributors. One gets a sense of teamwork, of unity of purpose, of cooperation and consensus among age peers, rendering the divisions and differences existing among them to a secondary, and infrequently examined, level of analysis.

In this general view, the centrality of the assumption of an unproblematic, underlying value consensus is further reflected in the facility with which socialization becomes not just a theoretical construct depicting a basic social process but a legitimate social "need." Adult education is "a response to the need for adult socialization" for adults, including "citizenship class for the immigrant, the programs of employers to retrain their employees . . . family-life education and parent education programs for newlyweds and first-time parents, [and] college programs for women" (p. 194). The central emphasis throughout the corpus of this work, then, is on what Parsons (1964, 1972; Parsons & Platt, 1973) called *inclusiveness*—bringing about an integrated, consensual, and smoothly operating social order. To the extent that such an approach dominates, structured differences within a cohort or age group are given little attention.

In this view, normativity again emerges as a central problematic, deflecting attention from the real-life issues of diversity, but it is normativity of a different sort: It is not the modal patterns of individual characteristics observed in a population (as in the case of developmental psychology) but the presumably *consensual normativity of the social structure*. The theoretical centrality of the social system as an entity to which individuals "contribute," and to the "needs" of which their actions are conformed, renders real differences between individuals tertiary, so long as they have acquired the requisite roles for the smooth functioning of the social order.

Although this conception thus entails normativity of a very different sort, it shares with developmental normativity the underlying image of individuals who are largely undifferentiated except by age stratum or cohort. This affinity is reflected in the uncritical acceptance and adoption of normative developmental conceptions in, for example, disengagement theory (Cumming & Henry, 1961), more recent sociological analyses of adult life change (see Dannefer, 1984a, for a discussion), and, applied to social systems, in family development theory (Duvall, 1975; see also Aldous, 1978, for a more refined treatment).

Ironically, thinkers from these traditions have sometimes discussed some of the costs of such a normative emphasis without identifying them as products of the logic of the functionalist paradigm itself. Thus, Brim (1968) writes that the emphasis in adult socialization has been too heavily focused on upward mobility, a mainstream norm (e.g., Kanter, 1977), while neglecting downward mobility. The present argument suggests that such neglect is not accidental but a systematic consequence of the emphasis on value consensus in traditional conceptions of socialization.

This traditional view of socialization has received extensive criticism from those working from other perspectives, and numerous revisions have been proposed (see Passuth, 1984, for a review). Nevertheless, it is important to consider the logic of this earlier view as it (1) has heavily influenced sociological theorizing in aging and (2) shares some underlying theoretical affinities with the dominant alternative views. For the sociology of aging, the most influential alternative view is symbolic interaction theory, to which this discussion will now turn.

Parsons's (1951) elegant functionalist framework included the kinds of micro-level processes analyzed by symbolic interactionists (see also Toby, 1972). This formulation received relatively little emphasis in the functionalist enterprise, however, apparently because of dominance of macro-level theoretical questions and quantitative research approaches. The elaboration of the micro-processes of socialization by symbolic interactionists has typically been advanced by researchers who claim not to share the value-consensus and implicit passive-individual emphases of the paradigmatic functionalist version of socialization. Based on a research tradition of detailed studies of micro-interaction, their work has contributed to discovering the details of the socialization process, and in particular to the recognition of its bidirectionality and its potentially conflictual character. Thus, the supposed *socializee* is recognized as not just a passive recipient but as a co-socializer (Bengtson & Black, 1973; Denzin, 1973, 1977; Passuth, 1984).

While such views of the process provide welcome corrections to the functionalist conception, symbolic-interaction approaches lack a conception of macro-social structure and processes with which to link the analysis of micro-interaction. The unitary consensus-theory version of social structure is rejected, not to be replaced by a more differentiated and stratified view of structure but as part of an overall rejection of a macro-structural conception of any sort. Since reality is a process of negotiation and social reality is fluid and dynamic, as the argument goes, a conception of social structure will only result in the reification of something that does not exist. Thus, the rejection of a value-consensus view of social structure tends to lead to a denial of social structure altogether.

In the absence of an alternative conception of structure, such formulations permit the consensus version to continue its reign in exile, all the more effective for being unrecognized. The macro-level questions of structure and process are simply not asked. Especially in complex, centralized modern societies, such macro-level processes clearly have a great deal to do with setting the agenda and the parameters of micro-interaction. Both age-grading and tracking within age groups, for example, become principles of mass social organization that shape actors' perceptions and even their interpretive actions in fundamental ways. Yet the symbolic interaction perspective does not make the *sources* of shared perceptions beyond the immediacy of the situation of micro-interaction, or the *extent of generality* of shared perceptions, matters of inquiry. The extent to which larger structures are a *source*—setting parameters upon the expression of creativity and voluntarism in structures—is simply not part of the problem. Nor is the extent to which entire populations are differentiated internally. If macro-structures are not there, of course they cannot be recognized as differentiated in ways that systematically impact individuals as they age. Thus, process-oriented views of socialization that lack a sense of structure perpetuate the twin emphases of (1) an undifferentiated voluntarism in individual action and (2) an undifferentiated macro-social reality.

None of this is to detract from the important contributions of the symbolic-interaction perspective on socialization. It has influenced, directly or indirectly, much valuable research on micro-interaction relevant to understanding aging and development. The only claim here is that its emphasis is one that tends to deflect attention from heterogeneity as an empirical theoretical problem.

When viewed from the vantage point of the dynamics of the larger social order, symbolic-interaction–based versions of socialization thus perpetuate a sense of normativity by default. The micro-interaction perspective logically requires the unarticulated assumption that the overall social order be held together by a kind of consensus; otherwise, persons from California could not interact so freely with those from Nova Scotia or the Netherlands. The neglect of this macro-level structuration logically implies that it is, at least for purposes of the theory, both undifferentiated and unproblematic. From such a view, aged heterogeneity—like social diversity more generally—may be cause for celebration (Gonos, 1977). However, it cannot be recognized for what it is, a systematically produced consequence of social processes.

Ralph Turner's (1976) classic paper "The Real Self: From Institution to Impulse" is symptomatic of this problem in symbolic interaction theory. He argues that, in modern society, personal impulse (i.e., free choice) has replaced the imposition of the institution as the primary determinant of "the real self." Social structure is thus seen as less important as a shaper of the self in the modern world of pluralism and individuality than in traditional societies.

The optimism of such a view is attractive, but held up against the empirical reality of contemporary social life, it appears utopian. The increasing social regimentation and selective deprivation of individuals throughout the modern period and in contemporary society suggest that its mass institutions continue to shape both individual selves and the resources for self-production in decisive ways; indeed, more conformity exists in many aspects of early life than ever before (Modell et al., 1976). The view of the modern self as implementing personal interests or "impulses" reflects the symbolic interactionist emphasis upon personal expression, in contrast to the more structural or institutional paradigm of functionalist theory. It is thus symptomatic of the logic of symbolic interaction theory, which, without a concern for the structural processes, tends to imply that individuals are differentiated mainly by their unique interpretation and action, through which social reality is created in interaction. From such a perspective, heterogeneity is of marginal importance, since it is simply a product of human spontaneity and diversity, and, in any case, is difficult to study systematically because the focus of analysis remains at the micro-level.

It has been noted that socialization is an expression of the ideals of *Gemeinschaft*, of family and village (Wexler, 1983a, p. 135). This is as true in its symbolic interactionist guise, with its emphases on negotiation, mutual influence, and interpretive acts, as it is in the functionalist version, with its emphases on consensus, integration, and inclusiveness. There have been important traditions of research that conceive of socialization as an element in the process of stratification of life conditions and life chances rather than as an aspect of the functional division of labor in a unified social order (Kohn, 1969; Kohn & Schooler, 1983; Rosenbaum, 1976). Such a stratified conception is still quite new to the study of aging. Moreover, terms such as *stratification of socialization* (Rosenbaum, 1976) implicitly point to sense of consensus implicit in the concept of socialization per se.

In sum, statistical normativity is not a central preoccupation in the study of socialization, as it has been in developmental theory, but there is an assumption of normativity of a different kind, the normativity of society. Whether from functionalist or interactionist perspectives, socialization is typically conceived either implicitly or explicitly as a cooperative enterprise accompanied by images of teamwork, unity of purpose, and consensus. The strength of socialization as a unified and consensual concept when applied to adulthood can be seen in its tenacity even when authors explicitly seek to emphasize that socialization is *not* an undifferentiated societal process. Although introductory sociology texts often present socialization in childhood and adolescence as a diverse and culturally variable process, adult socialization is treated largely in an undifferentiated fashion, except for gender differentiation.[6] The division of labor is functional for society but is implicitly or explicitly regarded as trivial for the production of individual differences.

This imposed image of societal uniformity is not required by the essential notion of socialization. It appears to derive from the concept's identification with American functionalism, especially Parsonian functionalism, which has given the concept of socialization its most elegant theoretical expression and integration into a larger theoretical system.[7] Within this framework, the complementary concepts of norm and role share the same dual characteristic of (1) having an essential validity, yet (2) communicating an image of a society that is undifferentiated except on such major functional axes as age and sex.

As articulated within a functionalist model, the image of society as a unitary social order carried by these concepts tends to obscure the entire issue of differentiation within age groups. This is a special application, made at the cohort level, of the more general and frequently made critique of functionalism as obscuring socially structured tendencies toward conflict, inequality, and differentiation that occurs within cohorts.

As in the case of development, these considerations do not affect the general principle underlying the term socialization, the social shaping of the individual. What is needed, then, is a reconceptualization of this process that systematically acknowledges that this social shaping process occurs, not only in a structured fashion but in a structurally differentiating fashion.

CONCLUSION: TOWARD PROCESS AND DIVERSITY IN THEORIES OF AGING

This chapter began with the anomaly of a seemingly obvious and interesting phenomenon—aged heterogeneity—widely neglected by both theory and research in the dominant social science traditions of the study of aging. The analysis offered some reasons for this anomaly and led to more fundamental questions. In the last section, two concepts were discussed, representing distinct traditions of social science inquiry; and it was argued that each of them—despite their diverse theoretical histories—contributes to the consequence of obscuring the reality of heterogeneity as an empirical reality and as a theoretical problem.

Thus, the neglect of heterogeneity was proposed not to be an isolated anomaly, but the product of the systematic logical tendencies deriving from the language and paradigmatic assumptions guiding research on age—in other words, from the particular names given by social science to the phenomena it studies. To the extent that this argument is valid, a reassessment of the concepts and a reformulation of the presuppositions that underlie them are in order. A full development of an alternative view must remain beyond the scope of the present discussion. However, some of the strategies for constructively addressing this problem are quite straightforward.

Clearly, a concern with intra-age variability needs to be made a central question in any inquiry that attempts to *describe* age-related phenomena. Even more important, however, is the issue of *explanation* and its relation to how variability is conceived. Since cohort age trajectories are organized in substantial part by diverse and differentiated social structures and processes of social interaction, intra-age variability in individual characteristics cannot properly be conceived in terms of a statistical artifact, as noise or error randomly distributed around a central pattern, but must be viewed as the product of specific processes linking individuals and social systems.

Similarly, a sociological conception of social shaping cannot be assumed to proceed through normative consensus or in undifferentiated within-age roles but must be described in the language of theory as a systematically stratified and differentiated process. What concepts exist, or can be developed, to address this issue? Although anything approaching an answer to this important question must remain beyond the scope of this brief chapter, two concepts are suggested: *habituation* and *social reproduction*. These represent concepts for a theory of age that give more integral consideration both to variability and to process. It is important to emphasize that these concepts are not proposed as direct substitutes for development and socialization. Although their usefulness remains largely untested in the study of aging, they suggest the potential for an approach to age that is both process-oriented and that avoids normative assumptions.[8]

Kastenbaum (1981, 1984) has proposed the concept of habituation as a partial theory of aging. Habituation is not saddled with a normative bias in either a statistical or an ideological sense. Statistically, it does not assume a normative developmental outcome around which people are randomly distributed by error; the very nature of the construct leads one to expect variation, and it invites analysis of diversity. As conceived by Kastenbaum, habituation is a quantifiable characteristic that, in principle, may be thought of as having an optimal value. The value, however, is determined not by norming a population but by analyzing the potentialities and current levels of functioning of individuals and their relationship to specific activity routines and conditions of life. Thus, habituation avoids the assumption that empirically observable statistical norms reflect the potential for successful aging and invites empirical analysis of diversity.

Habituation also avoids the ideological bias in favor of a *normative condition* that so typically accompanies development. *Normal development* has a positive ring to it; *normal habituation* sounds intrinsically suspicious. The concept does not carry an implicit value message in favor of the status quo. In habituation terms, what has often been assumed to be normal development or aging may be seen as "hyperhabituation"—becoming so habituated that the possibilities of imagination and continued discovery are foreclosed. Such an analysis leaves open the question of what optimal aging really consists of and, because of its transactional nature, of how culture and social structure are related to producing it.

In sum, habituation focuses attention on a *transactionally produced outcome rather than an internal, ontogenetic process.* It seeks to account for a given outcome at a given age in terms of specific activity routines experienced over a long period of time. By illustrating how this interaction may produce age-related outcomes that have often been assumed to be normal aging (and hence inevitable and unproblematic), Kastenbaum's (1981) proposal implies a view of aging that is both more analytical and, ultimately, more optimistic. If "old-like" behavior has its source in hyperhabituation, then it is not entirely clear that it is an inevitable part of the human condition. Habituation thus avoids the normative bias of the traditional developmental notions adopted by students of age, removing strictures on exploring diversity at the same time that it directs attention to processes rather than outcomes.

Social reproduction may, for present purposes, be defined as the ongoing maintenance and reconstitution of society through the activity of its members, which is substantially ordered by "the structure of power relationships and symbolic relationships" (Bourdieu, 1977, p. 71). The term *social reproduction* was initially developed in the tradition of critical social analysis and has always been intended to describe a stratified, or heterogeneous, social order. As in the relation of habituation and development, social reproduction is distinct from socialization in that it avoids emphasizing normativity both methodologically and theoretically.

Integral to the reproduction perspective is an underlying conception of society as a "functioning social system," but unlike traditional functionalism, it is seen as a system in which stratification is regarded as a central and problematic reality with great implications for the lives of the individuals who live within it and are engaged in reproducing it. Actors are differentially located— for example, men and women or upper middle class and working class—and derive rewards that systematically advantage some and disadvantage others, even while the activities of all members of the system are contributing to its ongoing reproduction. Within this framework, it is explicitly recognized that socialization is not a unitary experience in the early years of life nor in adulthood. Schools (Apple, 1982; Brown, 1973; Wexler, 1976), families (Kohn, 1969; Pearlin, 1971; Piotrkowski, 1979; Rubin, 1976), and workplaces are recognized as systematically differentiating individuals in nontrivial ways.[9] A central moment in this process of reproduction is the social shaping of individuals, which socialization has attempted to describe; but set in the context of social reproduction, this process is not described in unitary or normative terms but as an intrinsically differentiated process. Therefore, it avoids the "passive actor" imagery that tended to accompany structural-functional versions of socialization (Brim, 1968; Passuth, 1984; Stryker, 1980; Wrong, 1961).

It should be clear that social reproduction lacks the implicit positive valence of either rendition of socialization. *Adequate* or *successful* socialization are familiar terms in traditional functionalist discourse, as noted earlier. They are taken to mean that the *socializee* has internalized the society's norms and is fit for membership in the collectivity. On the other hand, what would it mean to say that one's child, or perhaps oneself, has been "successfully reproduced"? It sounds intrinsically suspicious. In relation to the symbolic-interactionist formulations of socialization, social reproduction reintroduces the dimensions of structure and power that promise to be helpful in assessing the production of aged heterogeneity.[10]

These suggestions about future theoretical direction are preliminary, partial, and tentative. If together with the foregoing critique they have begun to suggest how the concepts used may influence the nature of research questions and empirical analyses, they will have served a useful purpose. At minimum, I believe they demonstrate the possibilities for shifting the terms of discourse in the study of age to more analytic, critical, and self-critical ground.

NOTES

[1]The question of how sociology-of-science analyses of the types referred to here are exempt from the same kinds of analysis they seek to impose on other people's work may already have occurred to the thoughtful reader. The answer, of course, is that they are not exempt and that any person doing such analysis should welcome a corresponding critique of his or her own work. Logically, this answer raises the specter of an enterprise of inquiry that becomes petrified in an infinite regress, but in practice it has not and cannot work that way. Engagement in the real world keeps returning the question to the real world. Thus, the likely result is a more open process of dialectical progress, in which the ability to get at the essence of the phenomenon under study is enhanced by the clarification of how our views of it are shaped, and perhaps differentially shaped into competing views, by forces that are outside the phenomenon itself.

[2]Social demographers have examined intracohort variability with regard to transition behavior, but their primary focus has been on historical change in cohort homogeneity rather than changes with age in the trajectory of variability among members of one cohort (Glick & Spanier, 1980; Hogan, 1981, 1985; Modell, Furstenberg, & Strong, 1978; Neugarten and Hagestad, 1976).

[3]The basic notion underlying such an argument is, of course, a classic theme in social thought, articulated by Adam Smith as well as Karl Marx. The relevance for

aging and the life course has been noted earlier (Elder, 1969), though the implications have gone largely unnoticed.

[4]In fact, considerable debate exists even among biologists as to the extent to which a "program-driven" genetic model is appropriate to account for aging even for those lower species (Prigogine, 1980; Yates, this volume). However, this debate is irrelevant to the critique of ontogenetic models applied to the human species.

[5]In lower life forms, developmental stages may be genetically programmed in the physiology of the organism or in the selected instinct/learning combinations of group life. Such rigidity, which implies a relatively closed relation with the environment (i.e., corn predictably cross-pollinates, and beavers build dams as regular as clockwork the world over), it may be justifiable to treat variation on a given measure *within* age categories as error [although there is certainly disagreement among biologists about this (see, e.g., Keller, 1985)]. When, as is the case for homo sapiens, the life-world of a species is not governed by such rigid patterns but can take enormously varied forms, and is *dialectical* in that both individual and environment are more or less continuously produced or recreated through profoundly reconstitutive interactions, such assumptions are unjustified.

[6]These assertions are based on a review of all of the recent introductory-level texts I could readily locate, including the following: Broom and Selznick (1970); Conklin (1987), Coser, Nods, Stefan, & Bupard (1987), Johnson (1986); Popenoe (1980), Ritzer, Kenneth, Kammever, and Yetman (1982), Shepard (1984), Stark (1985), Turner (1984). Some notable individual exceptions were found, but the pattern of a brief, undifferentiated treatment of socialization in adulthood was strikingly clear overall.

[7]For thoughtful critiques of Parsons's emphasis on societal value consensus, see, e.g., Gouldner (1970), Heydebrand (1972), or Alexander (1983, esp. Chap. 7). In the context of the present argument, it is interesting to note that Alexander attributes Parsons's more general unifying impulse not to functionalism per se but to "neopositivist ambition" (pp. 193, 429).

[8]For a discussion of these concepts in the context of a more systematic attempt at conceptualizing aging in interactive terms, see Dannefer and Perlmutter (1987).

[9]Within the framework of critical analysis, the "culture industry," the institutions of mass communication and others involved in the production of knowledge for societal consumption — including universities — are often analyzed as key sources of ideological legitimation for the stratified and conflictual social order. Social science concepts such as socialization (Wexler, 1983a) and development (Dannefer, in press) have been argued to be ideological in this sense. Of course, such cultural sources of knowledge also have potential for positive social change as well.

[10]A debate within the tradition of critical analysis and reproduction theory properly concerns the degree to which the reproduction paradigm can adequately capture human *action* — the human actor as agent — as symbolic interaction theory clearly does. Some attempts to do so with the reproduction tradition have been clearly fruitful if less than completely satisfactory. There is a legitimate concern with the adequacy of such a concept on this point, and it deserves debate within the study of aging as elsewhere. This debate necessarily lies beyond the scope of the present chapter.

REFERENCES

Achenbaum, A. (1978). *Old age in the new land: The American experience since 1970.* Baltimore: Johns Hopkins Press.

Aldous, J. (1978). *Family careers.* New York: Wiley.

Alexander, J. C. (1983). *Theoretical logic in sociology; Vol. 4. The modern reconstruction of classical thought: Talcott Parsons.* Berkeley, CA: University of California Press.

Apple, M. (1982). *Cultural and economic reproduction in education: Essays on class, ideology, and the state.* London/Boston: Routledge & Kegan Paul.

Baltes, P. B. (1979). Life-span developmental psychology: Some converging observations on history and theory. In P. B. Baltes & O. G. Brim, Jr. (Eds.), *Life-span development and behavior* (Vol. 2, pp. 256–279). New York: Academic Press.

Baltes, P. B., & Brim, O. G. (Eds.). (1979–1984). *Life-span development and behavior* (Vols. 1–4). New York: Academic Press.

Baltes, P. B., & Nesselroade, S. R. (1984). Paradigm lost and paradigm regained: Critique of Dannefer's portrayal of life-span development. *American Sociological Review, 49,* 841–847.

Baltes, P. B. & Reese, H. W. (1984). The life span perspective in developmental psychology. In M. H. Bornstein & M. E. Lamb (Eds.), *Developmental psychology: An advanced textbook.* Hillsdale, NJ: Erlbaum.

Baltes, P. B., & Schaie, K. W. (1973a). *Life-span developmental psychology: Personality and socialization.* New York: Academic Press.

Baltes, P. B., & Schaie, K. W. (1973b). On life-span developmental research paradigms: Retrospects and prospects. In P. B. Baltes & K. Schaie (Eds.), *Life-span developmental psychology: Personality and socialization* (pp. 366–395). New York: Academic Press.

Bengtson, V. L., & Black, K. D. (1973). Intergenerational relations and continuities in socialization. In P. B. Baltes & K. W. Schaie (Eds.), *Life-span developmental psychology: Personality and socialization* (pp. 207–234). New York: Academic Press.

Bengtson, V. L., & Dannefer, D. (1987). Families, work, and aging: Implications of disordered cohort flow for the 21st century. In R. Ward & S. Tobin (Eds.), *Health and aging: Sociological issues and policy directions.* New York: Springer-Verlag.

Bengtson, V. L., Kasschau, P. L., & Ragan, P. K. (1977). The impact of social structure on aging individuals. In J. E. Birren & K. W. Schaie (Eds.), *Handbook of the psychology of aging* (pp. 327–354). New York: Van Nostrand Reinhold.

Berger, P. L., & Berger, B. (1979). Becoming a member of society. In P. Rose (Ed.), *Socialization and the life course* (pp. 4–20). New York: St. Martins.

Berger, P. L., & Luckmann, T. (1967). *The social construction of reality: A systematic treatise in the sociology of knowledge.* New York: Anchor.

Bielby, D. (1986, April). *Sources of heterogeneity among the aged.* Paper presented at the annual meeting of the Pacific Sociological Association, Denver.

Birren, J. E. (1959). Principles of research on aging. In J. E. Birren (Ed.), *Handbook of aging and the individual: Psychological and biological aspects* (pp. 3–42). Chicago: University of Chicago Press.

Birren, J. E. (1964). *The psychology of aging.* Englewood Cliffs, NJ: Prentice-Hall.

Birren, J. E. (1970). Toward an experimental psychology of aging. *American Psychologist, 29,* 808–815.

Bordieu, P. (1977). Cultural reproduction and social reproduction. In J. Karabel & A. H. Halsey (Eds.), *Power and ideology in education* (pp. 487–511). New York: Oxford University Press.

Bornstein, R., & Smircana, M. T. (1982). The status of the empirical support of the hypothesis of increased variability in aging populations. *The Gerontologist, 22*(3), 258–260.

Brim, O. G. (1966). Socialization through the life cycle. In O. G. Brim & S. Wheeler (Eds.), *Socialization after childhood: Two essays* (pp. 1–49). New York: Wiley.

Brim, O. G. (1968). Adult socialization. In J. A. Clausen (Ed.), *Socialization and society*. Boston: Little, Brown.

Brim, O. G. (1976). Theories of the male mid-life crisis. In N. Schlossberg & A. D. Endive (Eds.), *Counseling adults* (pp. 1–18). Monterey, CA: Brooks/Cole.

Brim, O. G., & Kagan, J. (Eds.). (1980). *Constancy and change in human development*. Cambridge, MA: Harvard University Press.

Broom, L. & Selznick, P. (1970). *Principles of Sociology*. New York: Harper and Rowe.

Brown, B. (1973). *Marx, Freud, and the critique of everyday life: Toward a permanent cultural revolution*. London: Monthly Review Press.

Campbell, M., Richards, L., & Boydston, R. (1985, November). *What time can do to an aging sample: Tracking respondents*. Paper presented at the annual meeting of the Gerontological Society of America, New Orleans.

Clausen, J. (1972). The life course of individuals. In M. W. Riley, M. E. Johnson, & A. Foner (Eds.), *Aging and society: A sociology of age stratification* (Vol. 3, pp. 457–514). New York: Russell Sage Foundation.

Collins, R. (1986). Is sociology in the doldrums? *American Journal of Sociology, 91*(6), 1336–1355.

Conklin, J. E. (1987). *Sociology: An introduction* (2nd ed.). New York: Macmillan.

Coser, L., Nods, S. L., Steffan, P., & Bupard, R. (1987). *Introduction to sociology* (2nd ed.). New York: HGJ.

Cuddihy, J. M. (1974). *Ordeal of civility: Freud, Marx, Levi-Strauss, and the Jewish struggle with modernity*. New York: Delta.

Cumming, E., & Henry, W. E. (1961). *Growing old: The process of disengagement*. New York: Basic Books.

Daatland, S. O. (1985, July). *Social structures and aging*. Paper presented at symposium, Aging and Interindividual Variability, 13th International Congress of Gerontology, New York.

Dannefer, D. (1984a). Adult development and social theory: A paradigmatic reappraisal. *American Sociological Review, 49*, 100–116.

Dannefer, D. (1984b). The role of the social in life-span development, past and future: Rejoinder to Baltes and Nesselroade. *American Sociological Review, 49*, 847–850.

Dannefer, D. (1987a). Aging as intracohort differentiation: Accentuation, the Matthew effect and the life course. *Sociological Forum, 2*.

Dannefer, D. (in press). Choice and fate: Adult development, ideology, and bureaucracy. *Psychology and Social Theory, 5*.

Dannefer, D., & Perlmutter, M. (1987). *Lifelong human development: Toward decomposition of the phenomenon and explication of its dynamics*. Unpublished manuscript.

Dannefer, D., & Sell, R. (1986, August). *Age structure, aged heterogeneity and the life course: Prospects for research and theory*. Paper presented at the annual meeting of the American Sociological Association, New York.

David, M., & Menchik, P. L. (1984). Nonearned income, income instability and inequality: A life-cycle interpretation. In S. Sudman & M. Spaeth (Eds.), *The collection and analysis of economic and consumer behavior data: In memory of Robert Ferber* (pp. 53–73). Urbana, IL: University of Illinois Press.

Denzin, N. K. (1973). *Children and their caretakers*. New Brunswick, NJ: Transaction Books.

Denzin, N. K. (1977). *Childhood socialization*. San Francisco: Jossey-Bass.

Duvall, E. (1975). *Family development*. Philadelphia: J. B. Lippincott.

Elder, G. H., Jr. (1969). Occupational mobility, life patterns and personality. *Journal of Health and Social Behavior, 10*, 308–323.

Elder, G. H., Jr. (1974). *Children of the Great Depression*. Chicago: University of Chicago Press.

Elder, G. H., Jr. (1975). Age differentiation and the life course. In A. Inkeles (Ed.), *Annual review of sociology* (Vol. 1) (pp. 165–190). Palo Alto, CA: Annual Reviews.

Elrod, N. (in press). The wolf in sheep's clothing: A critique of Erik Erikson's portrayal of the American Indians. *Psychology and Social Theory, 5*.

Erikson, E., & Smelser, N. J. (1980). *Themes of love and work in adulthood*. Cambridge, MA: Harvard University Press.

Featherman, D. L., & Lerner, R. M. (1985). Ontogenesis and sociogenesis: Problematics for theory and research about human development and socialization across the life span. *American Sociological Review, 49*, 659–676.

Feldman, K. A., & Weiler, J. (1976). Changes in initial differences among major-field groups: An exploration of the accentuation effect. In W. H. Sewell, R. Hauser, & D. L. Featherman (Eds.), *Schooling and achievement in American society* (pp. 373–407). New York: Academic Press.

Freeman, D. (1984). *Margaret Mead and Samoa*. New York: Viking.

Gergen, K. J. (1980). The emerging crisis in life-span developmental theory. In P. B. Baltes & O. G. Brim (Eds.), *Life-span development and behavior* (Vol. 3, pp. 32–63). New York: Academic Press.

Glick, P., & Spanier, G. B. (1980). The life cycle of American families: An expanded analysis. *Journal of Family History, 12*, 97–111.

Gonos, G. (1977). "Situation" vs. "Frame": The interactional and the structural versions of everyday life. *American Sociological Review, 42*, 854–867.

Gouldner, A. W. (1970). *The coming crisis in Western sociology*. New York: Avon.

Gubrium, J. G., & Buckholdt, D. R. (1977). *Toward maturity: The social processing of human development*. San Francisco: Jossey-Bass.

Guillemard, A. M. (1982). Old age, retirement, and the social class structure: Toward an analysis of the structural dynamics of the latter stage of life. In T. K. Hareven & K. J. Adams (Eds.), *Aging and life-course transitions: An interdisciplinary perspective* (pp. 221–243). New York: Guilford.

Harris, D. B. (Ed.). (1957). *The concept of development*. Minneapolis: University of Minnesota Press.

Henretta, J. C., & Campbell, R. T. (1976). Status attainment and status maintenance: A study of stratification in old age. *American Sociological Review, 41*, 981–992.

Heydebrand, W. (Ed.). (1972). A review symposium of Talcott Parsons. The system of modern societies. *Contemporary Sociology, 1*(5), 387–401.

Hickey, T. (1980). *Health and aging*. Monterey, CA: Brooks/Cole.

Hochschild, A. R. (1975). Disengagement theory: A critique and proposal. *American Sociological Review, 40*, 553–569.

Hogan, D. (1981). *Transitions and the life course*. New York: Academic Press.

Hogan, D. (1985). The demography of life-span transitions: Temporal and gender comparisons. In A. S. Rossi (Ed.), *Gender and the life course* (pp. 65–78). Englewood Cliffs, NJ: Prentice-Hall.

Howard, R. (1974). A note on S/Z. In R. Barthes (Ed.), *S/Z* (pp. *ix–xii*). New York: Hill & Wang.

Jantsch, E., & Waddington, C. H. (Eds.). (1976). *Evolution and consciousness: Human systems in transition*. Reading, MA: Addison-Wesley.

Johnson, A. G. (1986). *Human arrangements: An introduction to sociology*. New York: HGJ.

Kahn, R. (1981). *Work and health*. New York: Wiley.

Kanter, R. (1977). *Men and women of the corporation*. New York: Basic Books.

Kastenbaum, R. J. (1981). Habituation as a model of human aging. *International Journal of Aging and Human Development, 12*(3), 159–170.

Kastenbaum, R. J. (1984). When aging begins: A lifespan developmental approach. *Research on Aging, 6*(1), 105–117.

Keller, E. F. (1985). *Reflections on gender and science*. New Haven, CT: Yale University Press.

Kett, J. (1977). *Rites of passage: Adolescence in America from 1790 to the present*. New York: Basic Books.

Kitagawa, E. M., & Hauser, P. (1973). *Differential mortality in the United States: A study in socio-economic epidemiology*. Cambridge, MA: Harvard University Press.

Knorr-Cetina, K. D., & Mulkay, M. (Eds.). (1983). *Science observed: Perspectives on the social study of science*. Beverly Hills, CA: Sage.

Koestler, A. (1971). *The case of the midwife toad*. New York: Vintage.

Kohn, M. L. (1969). *Class and conformity: A study in values*. Homewood, IL: Dorsey.

Kohn, M. L. & Schooler, C. (1983). *Work & personality: An inquiry into the impact of social stratification*. Norwood, NJ: Ablex.

Krauss, I. K. (1980). Between and within-group comparisons in aging research. In L. W. Poon (Ed.), *Aging in the eighties* (pp. 542–551). Washington, DC: American Psychological Association.

Kuhn, T. S. (1962). *The structure of scientific revolutions*. Chicago: University of Chicago Press.

Lerner, R. M. (1976). *Concepts and theories of human development*. Reading, MA: Addison-Wesley.

Lewontin, R. C., Steven, R., & Kamin, L. J. (1984). *Not in our genes: Biology, ideology, and human nature*. New York: Pantheon.

Lipson, L. (1986). Age & heterogeneity: A medical perspective. Paper presented at the Institute for Advanced Study seminar, Andrus Gerontology Center, University of Southern California, Los Angeles, October, 1986.

Maddox, G. L. (1986, November). *Aging differently*. Robert W. Kleemeier Award Lecture, 39th Annual Scientific Meeting of the Gerontological Society of America, Chicago.

Maddox, G. L., & Douglas, E. R. (1974). Aging and individual differences: A longitudinal analysis of social psychological and physiological indicators. *Journal of Gerontology, 29*, 555–563.

Marini, M. M. (1984). Age and sequencing norms in the transition to adulthood. *Social Forces, 63*, 229–244.

Masson, J. (1983). *Assault on truth*. New York: Farrar, Straus, & Giroux.

Mellstrom, D., Sundh, V., & Svanborg, A. (1985, July). *Interindividual differences in functional measures of age in a longitudinal population study*. Paper presented at symposium, Aging and Interindividual Variability, 13th International Congress of Gerontology, New York.

Miller, A. (1984). *Thou shalt not be aware: Society's betrayal of the child*. New York: Farrar, Straus, & Giroux.

Mincer, J. (1974). *Schooling, experience and earnings*. New York: National Bureau of Economic Research.

Modell, J., Furstenberg, F., & Hershberg, T. (1976). Social change and transitions to adulthood in historical perspective. *Journal of Family History, 1*, 7–32.

Modell, J., Furstenberg, F., & Strong, D. (1978). The timing of marriage in the transition to adulthood: Continuity and change. *American Journal of Sociology, 84*, 120–150.

Neugarten, B. (1982). *Age or need: Public policies and older people*. Beverly Hills, CA: Sage.

Neugarten, B., & Hagestad, G. O. (1976). Age and the life course. In R. H. Binstock & E. Shanas (Eds.), *Handbook of aging and the social sciences* (pp. 25–55). New York: Van Nostrand Reinhold.

Noble, D. (1984). *Forces of production*. New York: Knopf.

Norris, A. H., & Shock, N. W. (1966). Aging and variability. *Annals of the New York Academy of Sciences, 134*(2), 591–601.

Parsons, T. (1951). *The social system*. New York: Free Press.

Parsons, T. (1964). *Social structure and personality*. New York: Free Press.

Parsons, T. (1972). *The system of modern societies*. Englewood Cliffs, NJ: Prentice-Hall.

Parsons, T., & Platt, G. (1973). *The American university*. Cambridge, MA: Harvard University Press.

Passuth, P. M. (1984). *Children's socialization to age hierarchies within the peer group and family*. Doctoral dissertation, Northwestern University, Evanston, IL.

Pearlin, L. (1971). *Class context and family relations: A cross-national study*. Boston: Little, Brown.

Perlmutter, M. (1978). What is memory aging the aging of? *Developmental Psychology, 14*, 330–345.

Perlmutter, M. (1979). Age differences in the consistency of adults' associative responses. *Experimental Aging Research, 5*, 549–553.

Perlmutter, M. (1985). *Cognitive potential in later life*. Paper presented at the Aging Exchange Conference, Brookdale Foundation, New York, September, 1985.

Perlmutter, M. (1986, June). *Cognitive development in life-span perspective: From description of differences to explanation of changes*. Paper presented at the conference on Child Development in Life-Span Perspective, Social Sciences Research Council, Woods Hole, MA.

Piotrkowski, C. (1979). *Work and the family system*. New York: Free Press.

Popenoe, D. (1980). *Sociology*. Englewood Cliffs, NJ: Prentice-Hall.

Prigogine, I. (1980). *From being to becoming*. San Francisco: W. H. Freeman.

Riegel, K. F. (1973). An epitaph for a paradigm. *Human Development, 16*, 1–7.

Riley, M. W. (1978). Aging, social change and the power of ideas. *Daedalus, 107,* 39–52.

Riley, M. W. (1980, October). *Social stratification and aging.* Paper presented at the Wilson Day proceedings, University of Rochester, Rochester, NY.

Riley, M. W., Johnson, M., & Foner, A. (1972). *Aging and society: A sociology of age stratification* (Vol. 3). New York: Russell Sage Foundation.

Ritzer, G., Kenneth, C. W., Kammever, J., & Yetman, N. R. (1982). *Sociology: Experiencing a changing society.* Boston: Allyn & Bacon.

Rosenbaum, J. E. (1976). *Making inequality: The hidden curriculum of high school tracking.* New York: Wiley-Interscience.

Rosenbaum, J. E. (1984). *Careers in a corporate hierarchy.* New York: Academic Press.

Rossi, A. S. (1980). Life-span theory and women's lives. *Signs: Journal of Women in Culture and Society, 6,* 4–32.

Rowe, J. W., & Kahn, R. L. (1987). Human aging: Usual and successful. *Science, 237,* 143–149.

Rubin, L. (1976). *Worlds of pain: Life in the working class family.* New York: Harper Torchbooks.

Ryder, N. B. (1965). The cohort as a concept in the study of social change. *American Sociological Review, 30,* 843–861.

Schaie, K. W. (in press). Individual differences in rate of cognitive change in adulthood. In V. L. Bengtson, & K. W. Schaie (Eds.), *Adult development: The search for meaning.* New York: Springer Publishing Co.

Shepard, J. M. (1984). *Sociology* (2nd ed.). St. Paul, MN: West.

Stark, R. (1985). *Sociology.* Belmont, CA: Wadsworth.

Stryker, S. (1980). *Symbolic interactionism: A social structural version.* Menlo Park, CA: Benjamin/Cummings.

Thomae, H. (1985, July). *Multiple stress experience and belief systems—a psychological approach to the conceptualization of patterns of aging.* Paper presented at symposium, Aging and Interindividual Variability, 13th International Congress of Gerontology, New York.

Toby, J. (1972). A review symposium of Talcott Parsons: The system of modern societies. *Contemporary Sociology, 1*(5), 387–401.

Treas, J. (1986). Postwar perspectives on age & inequality. Paper presented at the annual meeting of the Population Association of America, San Francisco, April, 1986.

Treas, J., & Passuth, P. M. (1986, April). *The three sociologies: Age, aging, and the aged.* Paper presented at the annual meeting of the Pacific Sociological Association, Denver.

Turner, J. (1984). *Sociology: The science of human organization.* Chicago: Nelson-Hall.

Turner, R. (1976). The real self: From institution to impulse. *American Journal of Sociology, 81,* 989–1016.

Waddington, C. H. (1960). *The ethical animal.* New York: Atheneum.

Weber, N. (1964). *The sociology of religion.* Boston: Beacon.

Wexler, P. (1976). *The sociology of education: Beyond equality.* Indianapolis: Bobbs-Merrill.

Wexler, P. (1983a). *Critical social psychology.* London: Routledge & Kegan Paul.

Wexler, P. (1983b). Structure, text and subject: A critical sociology of school knowledge. In M. W. Apple (Ed.), *Cultural and economic reproduction in education* (pp. 275–303). London: Routledge & Kegan Paul.

Wheeler, S. (1980). Selecting and monitoring foundation projects. *Grants Magazine, 3,* 88–98.

Wohwill, J. F. (1973). *The study of behavioral development.* New York: Academic Press.

Wrong, D. (1961). The oversocialized conception of man in modern sociology. *American Sociological Review, 26,* 183–193.

Zuckerman, H. (1977). *Scientific elite: Nobel laureates in the United States.* New York: Free Press.

17

Conflict and Cooperation Among Age Strata

John C. Henretta

The biological facts of birth and death impose important and consequential constraints on the nature of every society. Social structure must integrate persons of different ages, giving rise to an age-stratified society. Every society must also deal with the process of cohort succession as different cohorts move through the sequence of age-stratified social roles. In their different ways, societies do manage to integrate persons of different ages and survive the coming and going of different cohorts, indicating at least some cooperation among age strata. As with other social divisions, such as social class and religion, however, cooperation adequate for societal survival does not imply a lack of conflict.

Although the intuitive meanings of conflict and cooperation are generally applicable to the discussion in this chapter, the terms require further clarification. The age-stratified nature of roles or the nature of human development may lead to age differences in interests or goals that are incompatible. The resolution of these differences is likely to be associated with conflict. Conversely, age differences in roles may promote cooperation between age strata when interests and goals complement each other. The idea of conflict or cooperation between age strata implies a social structure or a developmental process that affects large numbers of persons in a similar way. However, it does not necessarily imply a group process. For example, the "oedipal conflict" is posited to be a universal developmental process, but it does not require shared consciousness among six-year-olds.

Conflict and cooperation represent two polar conceptions of social reality that predate the development of the discipline of sociology (Lenski, 1966). In sociological theory, a focus on cooperation is usually tied to functional theory, which views stratification as producing the complementarity necessary for the smooth functioning of a society. As a result there is a certain "rightness" to stratification and inequality. Conflict theories reject this view and see stratification as reflecting power and control.

Illustrations of the social processes of conflict and cooperation implied by age stratification and cohort succession abound. Generational relations in families are a topic of repeated negotiation between parents and children as their ages and statuses change (see Knipscheer, this volume). In the workplace, formal or informal apprentice and seniority systems, early retirement options, and mandatory retirement rules indicate the tentative nature of negotiated settlements concerning the rights of different age strata. Age-strata conflict and cooperation grow out of very basic social processes and affect most aspects of daily life.

Plan of the Chapter

This chapter discusses the significance of age in social structure and, using that perspective, synthesizes the existing research literature on age conflict and cooperation. The first task involves a presentation of the age-stratification perspective, which in recent years has been a focal point for social scientific thinking about age. Since the extensive theoretical and research literature on aspects of age relations comes from a variety of theoretical perspectives, the second task is to synthesize this literature in a way that focuses on important themes in the age stratification perspective. The goal is twofold: to focus on the insights common to the research literature and to provide a framework that is consistent with age stratification.

AGE STRATIFICATION AS CONCEPTUAL BACKGROUND

In addition to age, other characteristics, such as social class, religion, race, and ethnicity, stratify societies (Lipset, 1960). All are similar in that they affect the nature of daily interaction and bear a close relationship to the distribution of valued things, such as material goods, deference, and respect. It is misleading, however, to take a model for age stratification from these other divisions. Age is different because there is complete "upward" mobility for an individual and no inheritance of status from one generation to the next. As a result, it is very difficult to conceive of age-based antagonism with historical roots. Further, the family is not a basic unit of age stratification but rather a central domain where conflict and cooperation between age strata take place.

The age stratification perspective (Riley, Johnson, & Foner, 1972) provides a formal statement of the nature of age as an element in social structure and differentiates it from other bases of stratification. The three key characteristics of age stratification are (1) the biological base of age that is subject to change through maturation and decay, (2) the existence of age-structured role differentiation at any one time, and (3) the dynamic element of cohort succession or cohort flow as cohorts pass through their individual life courses at different historical times with different age-structured role patterns in force.

Age is similar to other bases of stratification in only the second of these characteristics, and in a static perspective it is reasonable to view age relations as no different from other types. Yet in a dynamic perspective, the other characteristics of age make it unique as a basis of stratification. The biological character of age opens the possibility of a type of conflict—one stemming from developmental processes—that is not found in other types of social divisions. In addition, as Uhlenberg discusses in his chapter (this volume), the relative power and control of a cohort changes in a predictable way over time, with changes in the social roles of its members and their numbers. These changes in role, power, and numbers change the nature of either conflictual or cooperative relationships with other cohorts, since both the cohort members' interests and positions change over time.

The interaction between age and historical period means that age conflict and cooperation may additionally stem from historical and social conditions at a particular time. For example, the coinciding of a relatively large retirement-age cohort and a smaller working-age cohort in a time of economic stagnation may lead to conflict that is an interaction among the age-graded nature of work roles, historical economic conditions, and the relative size of cohorts. The lack of inheritance of age and differing conditions each cohort faces at a particular age mean that such conflicts do not become historically important social divisions.

The age stratification perspective calls for a treatment of age conflict and cooperation that considers the implications of the biological base of age and its inherently dynamic character resulting from individual maturation and cohort flow. These characteristics affect the sources of age conflict. They also affect the character of the conflict because age-stratified social roles are unique among types of stratification. These issues are taken up in the categorization of theory and research on age relationships presented below.

DIMENSIONS OF AGE CONFLICT AND COOPERATION

Discussions of age conflict and cooperation are very diverse and stem from a variety of theoretical perspectives. An important conceptual task is to develop a set of dimensions that usefully characterizes them. This chapter focuses on three such dimensions: underlying ideas concerning what generates age conflict and cooperation, the "domains" where conflict occurs, and the distinction between age-group conflict and conflict about age-related issues.

These are not an exhaustive, analytic set of dimensions for the age conflict literature. They are, however, key distinctions for tying the varied treatments of age relations to the age stratification perspective. The dimensions, taken together, address the distinctive sources and nature of age-based conflict and cooperation.

Sources of Age Conflict

Individual aging or development is subject to two general influences: biological ontogeny and sociocultural or environmental influences. The latter may be derived from social structure in a systematic way or be idiosyncratic. Although the life-span developmental approach (e.g., Baltes & Nesselroade, 1984; Featherman & Lerner, 1985) generally views behavior as a result of an interaction of the two influences, an important difference among approaches to age conflict and consensus is the degree to which behavior is seen as reflecting one or the other influence.

Reese and Overton (1970) outline two divergent "metatheoretical" views of human development: mechanistic and organismic. Mechanistic approaches are most accurately described as addressing behavioral change rather than development. Humans are seen as reactive organisms whose behavior is shaped by reward contingencies in the environment. Although capacity to respond changes with age, there is no sense of behavioral change following a sequence or being directed to a goal. This view is found in behavioral psychology and in psychological reductionism in sociology (e.g., Homans, 1961).

In the mechanistic view, age does not create conflict or cooperation, but there may be a relationship since age is often the basis of social-structural arrangements that determine control of power and resources. Differences in resources do not inevitably lead to conflict, but the two are often related. Dowd's (1980) exchange theory is in the tradition of psychological reductionism, viewing age relations in a mechanistic framework. Social structure places the elderly in a weak position because they have fewer resources to bring to any interaction. The low-power position of the elderly results from the social distribution of power and resources, not from the inevitable character of aging.

Age is often a critical element in defining social-structural divisions in nonliterate societies (e.g., Foner & Kertzer, 1978; Lenski, 1966), though in these cases it is usually the older members of a society who control greater resources. Other theories in this tradition emphasize the social-structural arrangements that allow latent conflict over resources to appear. The subcultural theory of old age protest (Rose, 1962), for example, is one that is free of any ontogenetic process. Social conditions, such as those created by more interaction among the elderly, may lead to conflict that is age-based because they permit communication of grievances that can lead to political mobilization.

The mechanistic view of socialization also involves important instances of conflict and cooperation. Since there is no real role for age in the actual production of conflict or cooperation, age is relevant when an important site for the molding of behavior is age-related. Socialization does not take place only in age-relevant situations, but the "civilizing" of young pleasure-seeking organisms engenders both conflict and cooperation that is age-based. Even if it is viewed as molding of behavior by reward and punishment, socialization is a source of conflict within families and also within communities since schools have taken over some socialization functions that once were performed in primary groups.

Whereas certain "primary" or unconditioned reinforcers (Gewirtz, 1969) presumably have a biological base and the "power" of a cohort varies over its life course because of changes in age-related behavioral potential, the mechanistic approach defaults to social structure—the age-graded nature of social roles—to explain conflict. Many sociological theories of age-strata cooperation and conflict are, by default, in the mechanistic camp to the extent that they view behavior as determined by social structure alone. They are mechanistic *by default* in that there is usually no intent to exclude age or time-dependent (see Featherman & Lerner, 1985) psychological processes, but there is no particular attempt to include them either.

There are many other examples of social-structural factors that affect relations among age strata. For example, changes in the relative size of birth cohorts that are one-time or cyclical (e.g., Easterlin, 1980) can create or reduce conflict over jobs between age groups by affecting the transition to adulthood among young cohorts. Pressure for early retirement can result from economic stagnation and concern over youth unemployment, as it has in Western European countries in recent years.

The other view of development, the organismic view, focuses on age-dependent universal processes. Organismic theories are concerned with the nature of and change over time in unobserved structures. Development is a set of unidirectional changes in these structures that is conceptualized as being directed toward a goal or a final state (Reese & Overton, 1970). In this view, individuals are active manipulators of their environment, striving toward a developmental goal.

The organismic approach does not necessarily exclude a role for environment in development, but organismic theories can be classified according to the role they give to environment. Reese and Overton (1970) contrast the nativistic view that psychological structures are present at birth with the interactionist view that new structures result from an interaction of existing structures, some of which are present at birth, and ongoing activity. It is important to note that this distinction is not the same as the one between the mechanistic and organismic view because it involves only a difference in conception of how psychological structures develop and unfold, not whether they exist. Life-span developmental theory is primarily in the interactionist camp, but there is a lively debate on the relative weight that developmental theory and research have given to the role of environment (Baltes & Nesselroade, 1984; Dannefer, 1984).

Into the general category of organismic theories fall accounts of age-strata relations that focus on age-dependent processes to explain conflict and cooperation. In many theories of child development, for example, there are implications for cooperation because the outcome of socialization is a functioning member of society. The process of identification in psychoanalytic theory is a universal process through which children learn the values of the parent, and morality is passed from one generation to the next (Brown, 1965). The implications for conflict leading to eventual cooperation are also interesting. For example, the oedipal conflict is a specific developmental event that occurs in the predetermined sequence leading to identification. Its successful conclusion requires a change in the child's conception of his parents before psychosocial development proceeds further. In the case of psychoanalytic theory, it is important to distinguish between the content of the superego, which is culturally determined, and the universal process of identification.

The relevance of theories that focus on universal processes is not limited to childhood. Feuer (1969) views youth protests of the 1960s and 1970s as a collective expression of the oedipal conflict, an emphasis that is clear in passages, such as "the students' acts . . . brought into . . . politics all the psychological overtones of sons destroying their fathers . . . the revolt and guilt of the primal sons Freud described" (p. 9). On the other hand, Feuer makes clear the middle-class nature of student movements, indicating the significance of environment in the expression of the underlying conflict. Social-structural components are not just a feature of mechanistic theories.

At the other end of the life course, disengagement theory (Cumming & Henry, 1961), though no longer considered adequate theoretically (Hochschild, 1975), focuses on a posited universal pattern of individual withdrawal. It is a theory of cooperation in the functional tradition (see Passuth and Bengtson, this volume). Disengagement posits gradual withdrawal by the individual, timed by an internal clock. The specific timing of the withdrawal is less important than its programming. The factor that makes this a cooperation theory is that the individual's withdrawal is congruent with society's need to provide for an orderly transition between generations so that the outcome of the transaction between the individual and society is the homeostatic equilibrium of both.

Whereas most theories focus on one explanation, the production of conflict or cooperation is complex and may call for both mechanistic and organismic explanations. The issue of the role of the size of cohorts in age-strata relationships is a particularly interesting and complex example since it is subject to broad biological and social structural influences. As Uhlenberg (this volume) makes clear, the power of a cohort is partly developmentally based. Young children lack the cognitive and physical ability to fulfill many social roles. Among the very old, increased illness and frailty, as well as declining size of the cohort through death, reduce the cohort's power and control in the society, making it less central. Though these outcomes are environmentally modified—as with recent declines in death rates at older ages—the basic process is biological. Yet size of a cohort is also affected by its size at birth, a factor that is determined by historical circumstances. Both of these processes affect the relative size and power of cohorts and may affect conflict.

Domains of Conflict

A second important distinction is the domain of activity. This distinction is critical in defining the nature of age-stratified roles that in turn affect the character of conflict or cooperation. The most important distinction is between cohort and lineage domains. The lineage domain refers to kinship relations, and the cohort domain refers to all age-relevant interaction outside the family (cf. Bengtson, Cutler, Mangen, & Marshall, 1985). The term "generational conflict" refers to a specific variety of cohort-domain conflict that is created by the rise of a "political generation" (e.g., Feuer, 1969; Mannheim, 1928/1952). This distinct kind of cohort conflict is discussed more extensively later.

The reason for distinguishing between lineage and cohort is that they involve distinct kinds of relationships. This difference is captured by Parsons (1951) in the pattern variables, a set of five dimensions that together define the character of interaction. The nature of relations, according to Parsons, varies from affective to affectively neutral, from having a collective orientation to having an individual (or market) orientation, from using universal standards of evaluation to using particularistic standards based on "who someone is," from emphasizing ascribed status to emphasizing achieved status, and from being diffuse interactions to being very specific, limited ones.

The pattern variables can be used to describe actual behavior or normative expectations for different relationships. Consider, for example, the difference between the interaction of a middle-age person with an elderly parent and an older co-worker. In general, the family interaction will have strong emotional overtones that may be positive or negative while relations with co-workers will be less emotionally laden. In the family, actions tend to be taken both in light of others' interests and "for the good of the family." Yet outside the family, market relations are more important; indeed, the American economic system is based on the premise that individual selfish actions will produce the greatest good for all (Smith, 1776/1937). In the family, it is usually appropriate to tailor expectations to individual ability; in the work situation, universal standards are usually evaluated as being most "fair," though they are often not attained. Family relations are wide-ranging, whereas one's relations with co-workers can be limited to work-related tasks. A description of normative expectations should not be an excuse for ignoring variability. For example, much family research explores the effect of variability in the nature of family interaction, and almost everyone has had experience with work or other nonkinship situations that depart from the normative expectation. Yet the central point is still valid: family relations are fundamentally different from most relations outside the family.

A second factor that makes cohort and lineage relations distinct is that there is no necessary correspondence between one's role in the family and cohort membership. Parents of young children or children of elderly parents are of widely differing ages and cohort memberships. More complex family role configurations, such as being both the parent of young children and the child of an elderly parent, confound the relation between cohort membership and family roles even more. Cohort membership and family roles often do not "line up" (see Knipscheer, this volume).

Yet positions in the two domains are related. For the young there is probably the least difference between family and other roles since their age-graded roles provide them little power in any relationship, and there may be little differentiation between the power of parents and the power of adults in other situations. Among adults, it is often hypothesized that family characteristics, such as having grandchildren in school or having an elderly parent receiving Medicare, may affect attitudes on such public issues as school taxes and social security. In addition, both children and adults may take the style of interaction learned in their family of orientation into the wider world.

Though behavior in family and cohort domains is related, there is ample empirical evidence that the two domains operate under different rules. For example, Bengtson (1971) found a smaller perceived generation gap within families than in the society-at-large, though the youngest respondents made the least differentiation between the lineage and cohort domains. A major reason for the smaller perceived family difference might have been that the family relationship was evaluated using much broader criteria even while there was disagreement on political or social issues. In the case of youth protests of the 1960s and 1970s, there is evidence that the conflict found outside the family was not mirrored in the family. Activist young people came from politically active and committed families. While youth protests indicated age-strata conflict in the cohort domain, basic agreement between activist youths and their parents indicated family solidarity; see Braungart & Braungart (1986) for a review of the literature on this point.

Another aspect of the relation of domains is that conflict can move from one to the other. An important contribution of gerontological research over the past 20 years has been the careful documentation of the two-way flow of assistance between generations in the family and the role of family members as primary caregivers for the elderly (e.g., Shanas & Sussman, 1981). Families are important caregivers even though the trend in industrial societies, particularly since the 1930s, has been movement of age strata negotiations concerning economic support of the elderly from the family to the cohort domain (Myles, 1984). The growth of public pensions has drained some of the potential for conflict from the family. The development of private pensions since World War II has furthered this trend.

The cohort domain, in contrast to the lineage domain, is a very gross categorization of a large area of human experience. A full account of age relations requires subdividing it into a number of domains. For example, conflict over retirement rules may be found in public policy discussions, in union-management discussions, in the small work group, or in all three places. The nature of conflict or cooperation may depend not just on the particular domain but also how many domains are affected. Further, an understanding of conflict may require micro-analysis that focuses on variability within a particular domain. For example, employers do not universally benefit from mandatory retirement rules since the firm's interest depends on several issues, such as the relative wage and skill levels of young and old workers (Schulz, 1985). The question of how to subdivide the cohort domain is not pursued further here because the possible domains do not lend themselves to easy classification. In addition, most theoretical discussions relevant to conflict have not developed this idea. Recent life-course literature has emphasized variability within domains and interrelationships of events in different domains. This perspective would result in an important improvement in thinking about age-strata conflict and cooperation.

Conflict about Age-Related Issues

The third distinction is between conflict about age-related issues and conflict between age strata. In the family there are a number of issues that are age-related, such as issues of power and control over younger children or long-term care decisions for older family members. Disagreements on these issues can occur between family members of the same age and family position. In the cohort domain, particularly in the area of public policy, there are many similar examples. There is not necessarily agreement within a cohort, and age-strata allegiances are tempered by other interests.

In recent years, a number of age-related issues have been cast in a "generational equity" framework that focuses on age-strata conflict. The financing of Social Security and Medicare is a common target of this type of analysis (e.g., Longman, 1985). Due to the pay-as-you-go nature of Social Security, it is very likely that the large "baby boom" birth cohort of 1947 to 1959 will pay more in taxes that finance benefits for the elderly than they will receive when they are old. This contrasts with the experience of the cohort that currently is old. The issues raised are real and important ones, but it is important to remember that casting the issues as constituting conflict between age strata is only one possible conceptualization of reality.

For example, consider one of the current generational-equity issues — Medicare. Medicare introduced a prospective reimbursement system in 1983 that pays hospitals a flat fee for each elderly patient, the amount of payment depending on the specific illness. This replaced an earlier system of reimbursing hospitals on an actual cost basis. The effect of this and other changes in Medicare has been to reduce Medicare payments about $40 billion since 1981, or 12% of all federal budget reductions (Iglehart, 1986), though Medicare remains a very expensive program. At first glance, such a reduction would appear to create the strong potential for conflict between age strata since Medicare has been affected more than other programs in an attempt to reduce the federal deficit without a tax increase. As a result of new hospital procedures in response to the prospective reimbursement system, there have been a number of allegations of substandard care resulting from elderly patients' being discharged from acute care hospitals too soon.

However, viewing this issue as one of young versus old is too simple. For example, the changes in Medicare have also threatened federal subsidies of graduate medical education and have reduced hospital employment by about 200,000 since 1983; hospital profit margins, however, appear to have increased (Iglehart, 1986). All of these changes have led to the formation of a coalition of 140 organizations including the American Association of Retired Persons, the American Hospital Association, the American Medical Association, and the American Nurses' Association to influence Medicare legislation (Inglehart, 1986).

Although the non-aging organizations listed are no doubt involved in this effort because of their concern for the welfare of the elderly, the fact remains that the members of these organizations are the "economic constituency" of the elderly and their economic interests are vitally affected by Medicare legislation. In a very complex society, interests of a cohort identified at the macro-level do not simply translate to the same interests at the individual level (e.g., Bengtson, 1986). It is likely that most conflict in the cohort domain that we initially identify as age-strata conflict is really conflict about age-related issues. For this reason, the shift of many issues relating to the elderly from the family to the cohort domain has profound effects not only on the nature of relations between age groups but on the very nature of the society.

A number of other factors operate to turn potential age-strata conflict into conflict over age-related issues by introducing diversity into each cohort. Foner (1986) points to the fact that in the United States many potential age conflicts have been redefined as class issues, so the desire to cut programs for the elderly is strongest among business interests and those with the highest incomes. At the same time, there is the realization among many young persons that the existence of Social Security and Medicare reduces the burden on family members. In addition, the elderly are a diverse group in many characteristics relevant to political behavior (Hudson & Binstock, 1976).

A popular example among those who argue for the potential of age-group conflict is the Townsend movement of the 1930s. Francis Townsend was a physician and founder of a Depression-era organization that demanded $200-per-month pensions for the elderly. Under Townsend's plan, the elderly would be required to spend their pensions within 30 days, and their consumer expenditures would return prosperity to the nation. Older people were attracted to the plan, and as much as 10% of the older population of the United States may have belonged to the Townsend organization at its peak in the mid-1930s (Holtzman, 1963). This level of membership is even more impressive since the Townsend organization was found primarily in California and other western states.

In some important ways, the Townsend organization represented conflict between age groups. The Depression affected the elderly greatly in a period when there was little public income support. Contemporary observers estimated that between one-half and two-thirds of persons over age 65 were dependent on their families or on charity during this time (Holtzman, 1963; Putnam, 1970). The plan promised a return of the status the elderly had lost with the Depression since they were to be the vehicle for returning prosperity to the nation. In this sense, the Townsend plan was a status protest by the elderly (Henretta, 1974).

Yet there are a number of reasons to view the Townsend plan as age-related protest. First, the Depression spawned many recovery plans that today would be labeled "voodoo economics." The Townsend plan was only one of them. Although its special focus attracted the elderly, the plan also attracted support by the young. For example, Holtzman (1963) indicates that up to one-third of the members of Townsend clubs were young or middle-age; and Townsend tried, without much success, to create Townsend Youth Clubs. Further, while some elderly persons received public assistance, much of the economic support burden fell on their families. These younger persons, who were also affected by the Depression, might be expected to support a proposal that would relieve them of the burden. Finally, Holtzman (1963) argues that poll data from the period indicates that low economic status, controlling for age, was a good predictor of support for Townsend.

The distinction between age-strata conflict and conflict about age-related issues suggests the need for a sharpening of the meaning of age stratification. As noted earlier, age stratification is as significant in determining daily activities as any other type of stratification in modern societies. Indeed, knowing someone is 9 years old instead of 45 years old may provide more information than simply knowing someone is rich or poor, black or white. On the other hand, age stratification does not easily translate into age strata conflict. Even in the cohort domain, few issues are so simple as to affect an age group in a uniform way. In addition, age stratification is different from other kinds of stratification in that it cuts across the family. Social scientists have long been aware of the significance of cross-cutting allegiances in reducing conflict, and it is often the "lining up" of several key stratification bases in the same persons that leads to conflict. The increased survival to later ages means that a large proportion of adults will have either young-old or old-old parents or grandparents alive. The long tradition in social research that shows the importance of family support for the elderly means that there is a very strong cross-cutting allegiance that will reduce the potential for age conflict.

EXAMPLES

The three dimensions of age strata conflict that are outlined above provide some perspective on important differences among conceptualizations of age conflict and cooperation. In this section, two examples are discussed in more detail to suggest the interrelations of the elements that have been discussed separately.

Modernization and Aging

The literature on modernization and aging provides the richest example because all of the dimensions that have been discussed are relevant. While the modernization literature has focused on the effects of social structure on patterns of aging, there are important implications for individual developments over the life course; there is a contrast between lineage relations and cohort relations; and finally, there is also a contrast between conflicts between age groups and conflicts about age-related issues.

Some of the influential theorizing on the effect of modernization or industrialization of the "status" of the aged, as well as popular conceptions of social change, argues that the status of the elderly declines with modernization as they lose control over the means of production (Cowgill, 1974), but it may rise again in the most advanced societies (Palmore & Manton, 1974). This argument has been attacked from a number of points of view. For example, Laslett (1976) points to the confusion between our past and less developed societies today. Equating societies that exist today, with their differing cultures and social structures, to Western societies in the past is simply not appropriate. Perhaps more important is the conclusion from a great deal of historical and comparative work (e.g., Foner, 1984; Laslett, 1976; Quadagno, 1982;

Vinoskis, 1982) that there is no unilineal change in the status of the elderly. Rather, the status of the elderly varies with social structure in complex ways, and differences are not highly correlated with industrialization.

One of the unquestioned changes that has occurred in this century has been the increasing public arrangements made for the support of the old (e.g., Myles, 1984). Marshall (1950/1964) discusses this issue in a different context as the general development in Western industrial societies of "citizenship rights" (the things one receives by virtue of citizenship) which supplanted "social class rights" (things one is free to buy). The development of social class rights was the revolution of the 18th century, while citizenship rights were the major transformation of the late 19th and 20th centuries. The right to income support in old age is relatively new citizenship right in Western societies in the same way that universal suffrage, free education, and health care are relatively new developments.

As a result of these changes, the decision about distribution of resources between the young and the old has become, to some degree, a political decision. While it is an oversimplification to see this as necessarily leading to conflict, at the very least the decision about distribution creates a situation in which age-strata cooperation is problematic. There are two important characteristics of this relationship for which the groundwork has been laid in the previous section. First, conflict and cooperation has been moved from the family domain to the cohort domain. Moreover, it has been moved to the public policy domain, which, using the pattern variables to characterize style of interaction, is furthest removed from the family. Second, to a great degree, moving the domain has transformed conflict so that it is about age-related issues but not necessarily a conflict between age strata.

The current situation of the elderly is quite different from those instances in which their economic fate was determined by relations in the family. This statement does not imply that in earlier times the situation of the elderly was better or worse (Laslett, 1976); nor does it deny the important role families play in the care of the elderly today. The change in domain, however, can have important effects.

Take as an example the stem family as described in Ireland in the 1930s by Arensberg and Kimball (1968). Because of developments during the 19th century, including repeated famines, land clearance, repeal of the Corn laws, periodic agricultural depression, and the end of subdivision of land (Kennedy, 1973), Ireland in the 1930s, particularly the western coastal area, had a classic peasant stem family. The major occupation in the country was farming, and there were a limited number of farms that could each support one family. A son's option was to leave or remain a "boy" until his father died or retired. Assuming there were sons, a daughter might leave or hope her father could raise the appropriate dowry. It is easy to overestimate the amount of power this system gave to parents since migration was a very real option for the rural

Irish during the entire period this family system existed. In fact, Kennedy explains high fertility in Ireland at this time as the attempt of parents to have enough children to ensure that one would stay home.

The mere fact that a child remained at home did not necessarily give parents a great deal of power since, depending on circumstance, the child's remaining may have been the result of negotiation between parent and child. The stem system has been found in other places as well (e.g., Goody, 1976). And the elderly had power only as long as the set of circumstances lasted; thus, as urban wages rose, transportation improved, and being a farmer became less attractive, the power of the elderly declined.

While the arrangement is a social-structural one derived from land tenure patterns, the system created the potential for developmentally related conflict. Since young men who did not leave the western rural areas were quite likely to retain the social status of "boy" until well into adulthood, there was the potential for conflict in the family. That such enforced continuation of child-hood was not normative is well illustrated by an anecdote told by Arensberg and Kimball (1968) who report laughter in the Irish Parliament in 1933 when an M.P. used the country idiom to ask for special consideration in the distribu-tion of land to "boys of forty-five and older" (p. 55). This same conflict, cast as an oedipal conflict, is found in Synge's 1907 play, *Playboy of the Western World* (1907/1982), which deals in a literary way with the effects of enforced dependence. The practice of parents' using land ownership to maintain control over their adult children was also quite common in colonial America, though Fischer (1978) speculates that it did not engender conflict.

This kind of family landholding system was far from universal in Europe (Laslett, 1976), and the amount of change in land tenure arrangements some-times observed over relatively short periods of time (e.g., Homans, 1942) indicates that there was not one past, but many. It should be further noted that these arrangements were not necessarily society-wide; they occurred in the special situation of small landholders. The landless rural family, the urban family, or families in other areas of the country with less rigid landholding systems most likely experienced age conflict in different ways. It is reasonable to argue that an older person in the typical situation described by Arensberg and Kimball (1968) had a great deal of power, but it is not at all clear that it is reasonable to extrapolate to old people in general in Ireland. Differences within the preindustrial world could have as much effect on the elderly as changes that occurred with industrialization.

Industrialization had quite variable and unexpected effects on family resi-dence patterns (e.g., Katz, 1982); and recent research on the nature of the life course and career has attempted to tie together events in different domains, particularly work and family careers (e.g., Hogan, 1981; Marini, 1984). Arensberg and Kimball's (1968) account is, in the functional paradigm of its day, the same sort of analysis for a limited segment of Irish society in the 1930s.

The example illustrates the way that relations between age strata can involve important developmental issues and transform conflict about economic support of the elderly into a conflict between age strata as well. The key is a social structure that places the issue in the lineage domain.

Certainly it is not necessary to go so far afield to find an example of the difference in domains, though the Irish example is intensified by the poverty of rural Ireland during this period. It should not be assumed that there is not a possibility of increased conflict of this type in Western industrial societies today. One of the most interesting ironies in current public policy discussions in the United States is the proposal to emphasize family responsibility for nursing home expenditures in order to reduce Medicaid costs. This "solves" the problem by shifting conflict across domains and redefining public issues as personal problems.

Youth Protests

One of the clearest examples of age-strata conflict is the youth protest that has occurred sporadically throughout the 19th and 20th centuries. A discussion of youth protests emphasizes that the conceptual framework for examining age conflict is appropriate for all age groups. More important, a large portion of research and theory on generational conflict has focused on the young. The examination of youth protests brings together the elements that have been discussed in a different context.

There are three aspects of student protests that are important for an examination of conflict and cooperation among age strata. First, they occur sporadically. Second, the active participants constitute a small portion of the members of the cohort, and the protests occur in a context in which most students are relatively conservative (Lipset, 1968). Finally, the issues are not ones that are usually thought of as motivated by self-interest, making this a conflict between age groups but not necessarily about age-related issues.

Braungart (1984) identifies four periods of active youth movements in the 19th and 20th centuries. The most recent was the period of the 1960s and 1970s that in the United States was associated with the Vietnam war. All were periods with relatively large youth cohorts. In each of these cases, only a small portion of the cohort was involved, usually the children of the elite (Feuer, 1969), and protests were of both the left and the right. Youth protests are generally not age-strata conflict in the sense that the protest "represents" the views of the inactive members of a cohort, but only in the sense that the source of the conflict is age-related, either in the social-structural position of youth or through age-dependent development.

Braungart (1984; Braungart & Braungart, 1986) divides explanations of youth protests into two types: "historical" approaches deal with characteristics of social structure that bring fourth protest while "generational" theories focus on development. There are a number of varieties of historical theories. For example, the social discontinuity approach focuses on attempts to reconstitute the social order after social change had made the old normative order inadequate (Smelser, 1962); the "mass society" approach (e.g., Kornhauser, 1959) views protest as arising when traditional social ties have been disrupted and individuals lack their traditional "anchors" to the social structure. It is worth noting that this latter approach is similar to the explanation of development of old age protest in California in the 1950s used by Pinner, Jacobs, and Selznick (1959). Age does not play a particularly central role in these theories, except insofar as it defines the characteristics of the group that is marginal to the society. The crucial role of historical conditions is suggested by the fact that youth protests do not become important forces in a society for every cohort, and the role of social structure at any one time is suggested by the variability in involvement.

In contrast, there are "generational" theories of protest that focus on development processes but also generally acknowledge the role of social structure in creating the situations in which the development process is expressed. Generational theories range from political socialization approaches in which the time of the development of a political outlook in a cohort is age-dependent (e.g., Mannheim, 1928/1952) to traditional developmental theories. Examples of the latter include the psychoanalytic approach of Feuer (1969) and Erikson's (1968) approach to the development of identity.

In the terms being used here, student protests certainly have a developmental aspect, even though they are in the cohort domain. As discussed earlier, it seems most appropriate to view student protests, at least those in the United States in the 1960s and 1970s, as demonstrating family solidarity. Therefore, it is an example in which, according to some theories, developmental tasks are completed outside the family.

The example of student protest is an interesting combination of the dimensions discussed earlier. First, there are approaches that emphasize universal, ontogenetic processes, though allowing a role for social structure, and explanations that focus on social structure. Second, even though one can make a good argument that there is a developmental aspect to such protests, they have occurred in the cohort domain. This suggests the importance of the distinction between source of conflict and the domain in which it occurs. Finally, the significance of the distinction between conflict between age strata and conflict over age-related issues is illustrated. Although only a small part of a cohort is involved, the development aspects of protest make this an age strata conflict even though the issues are not usually age-related.

IMPLICATIONS FOR RESEARCH

There is relatively little general theoretical work on age strata conflict and cooperation per se. Most conceptions of age strata relationships view them in the context of a particular location on the dimensions that have been outlined. In truth, there is no one theory of age strata conflict and cooperation. Instead, behavioral science research is suffused with relevant concepts and examples. Viewing age conflict and cooperation as a single distinct area is possible only through synthesis of widely divergent approaches.

The implications for further research and theorizing on age-strata relationships flow directly from these insights. The major need is to be explicit in relating research on age-strata conflict and cooperation to both the multidisciplinary perspective presented here as well as to existing disciplinary perspectives.

Age conflict and cooperation has not been a natural division of theory and research, so the call for explicit attention to the broad range of research is understandable. Just as important is the potential gain in understanding of age strata conflict and cooperation from specific attention to ideas found in existing disciplinary perspectives. Many of these ideas are reflected in the literature on age relations, but they have not been given adequate emphasis. For example, research on social-structural sources of age conflict and cooperation would benefit from greater consideration of the implications of developmental process for behavior (Featherman & Lerner, 1985). This suggestion is parallel to the call for developmental theory to consider social structure more fully, but it is seldom heard.

As noted earlier, the distinction between lineage and cohort domains and the need to subdivide the cohort domain is consonant with much of the current emphasis in sociological studies of the life course. There is a need to understand the processes that operate in each domain to structure age relations as well as the interrelation among domains.

The distinction between age strata conflict and conflict over age-related issues is also one that can benefit from attention to other areas of sociological theory. Sociologists have always known the difference between "objective" or potential economic class conflict and "subjective" or actual conflict. The specific reasons suggested earlier for variability in interests within each age strata parallel the general categories suggested in the stratification literature.

SUMMARY AND CONCLUSION

Age strata relations are critical in almost any view of social structure since they are associated with the very basic question of how societies are able to reproduce themselves over time. The central argument of this chapter is that age strata conflict and cooperation, which we might at first consider to be a unitary phenomenon, is a very diverse one. There are very diverse views of the causes of conflict, the different domains in which age strata interact operate by very different rules, and conflict over age-related issues does not necessarily imply conflict between age strata. The usefulness of these ideas is illustrated by a discussion of modernization and student protest literatures.

This chapter has unified these dimensions of the age relations literature under the umbrella of the age stratification perspective. The biological basis of age means that universal, age-dependent processes can be the source of conflict. This possibility is reflected in the discussion of the sources of age conflict. In addition, the existence of age-structured social roles that change over time affects the nature of conflict and cooperation between age strata. These ideas are captured in the discussions of domains of conflict and the difference between age strata conflict and conflict over age-related issues. Both discussions address the special characteristics of age-structured roles and the relationship of age stratification to other aspects of social structure.

REFERENCES

Arensberg, M., & Kimball, T. (1968). *Family and community in Ireland* (2nd ed.). Cambridge, MA: Harvard University Press.

Baltes, P. B., & Nesselroade, J. R. (1984). Paradigm lost and paradigm regained: Critique of Dannefer's portrayal of life span developmental psychology. *American Sociological Review, 49*, 841–846.

Bengtson, V. L. (1971). Inter-age differences in perceptions and the generation gap. *The Gerontologist, 11* (Part II), 85–90.

Bengtson, V. L. (1986). Comparative perspectives on the microsociology of aging: Methodological problems and theoretical issues. In V. W. Marshall (Ed.), *Later life: The social psychology of aging* (pp. 304–336). Beverly Hills, CA: Sage.

Bengtson, V. L., Cutler, N. E., Mangen, D. J., & Marshall, V. W. (1985). Generations, cohorts, and relations between age groups. In R. Binstock & E. Shanas (Eds.), *Handbook of aging and the social sciences* (2nd ed.). (pp. 304–338). New York: Van Nostrand Reinhold.

Braungart, R. G. (1984). Historical generations and youth movements: A theoretical perspective. In R. E. Ratcliff & L. Kriesberg (Eds.), *Research in social movements, conflict and change* (Vol. 6, pp. 95–142). Greenwich, CT: JAI Press.

Braungart, R. G. & Braungart, M. M. (1986). Life course and generational politics. *Annual Review of Sociology, 12*, 205–231.

Brown, R. (1965). *Social psychology*. New York: Free Press.

Cowgill, D. O. (1974). Aging and modernization: A revision of the theory. In J. F. Gubrium (Ed.), *Late life communities and environmental policy* (pp. 123–146). Springfield, IL: Charles C. Thomas.

Cumming, E., & Henry, W. H. (1961). *Growing old: The process of disengagement*. New York: Basic Books.

Dannefer, D. (1984). Adult development and social theory: A paradigmatic reappraisal. *American Sociological Review, 49*, 100–116.

Dowd, J. J. (1980). *Stratification among the aged*. Monterey, CA: Brooks-Cole.

Easterlin, R. A. (1980). *Birth and fortune*. New York: Basic Books.

Erikson, E. H. (1968). *Identity: Youth and crisis*. New York: Norton.

Featherman, D. L., & Lerner, R. M. (1985). Ontogenesis and sociogenesis: Problematics for theory and research about development and socialization across the lifespan. *American Sociological Review, 50*, 659–676.

Feuer, L. S. (1969). *The conflict of generations*. New York: Basic Books.

Fischer, D. H. (1978). *Growing old in America*. New York: Oxford University Press.

Foner, N. (1984). *Ages in conflict: A cross-cultural perspective on inequality between old and young*. New York: Columbia University Press.

Foner, A. (1986). *Aging and old age: New Perspectives*. Englewood Cliffs, NJ: Prentice-Hall.

Foner, A., & Kertzer, D. (1978). Transitions over the life course: Lessons from age-set societies. *American Journal of Sociology, 83*, 1081–1104.

Gewirtz, J. L. (1969). Mechanisms of social learning: Some roles of stimulation and behavior in early human development. In D. A. Goslin (Ed.), *Handbook of socialization theory and research* (pp. 57–212). Chicago: Rand-McNally.

Goody, J. (1976). Aging in nonindustrial societies. In R. H. Binstock & E. Shanas (Eds.), *Handbook of aging and the social sciences* (pp. 117–129). New York: Van Nostrand Reinhold.

Henretta, J. C. (1974). *Political protest by the elderly: An organizational study*. Unpublished doctoral dissertation, Harvard University, Cambridge, MA.

Hochschild, A. R. (1975). Disengagement theory: A critique and proposal. *American Sociological Review, 40*, 553–569.

Hogan, D. (1981). *Transitions and social change*. New York: Academic Press.

Holtzman, A. (1963). *The Townsend movement: A political study*. New York: Bookman.

Homans, G. C. (1942). *English villagers of the thirteenth century*. Cambridge, MA: Harvard University Press.

Homans, G. C. (1961). *Social behavior: Its elementary forms*. New York: Harcourt Brace & World.

Hudson, R. B., & Binstock, R. H. (1976). Political systems and aging. In R. H. Binstock & E. Shanas (Eds.), *Handbook of aging and the social sciences* (pp. 369–400). New York: Van Nostrand Reinhold.

Iglehart, J. K. (1986). Early experience with prospective payment of hospitals. *New England Journal of Medicine, 314*, 1460–1464.

Katz, M. B. (1982). Families and early industrialization: Cycle, structure, and economy. In M. White Riley, R. P. Abeles, & M. S. Teitelbaum (Eds.), *Aging from birth to death: Vol. 2. Sociotemporal perspectives* (pp. 139–162). Boulder, CO: Westview.

Kennedy, R. E., Jr. (1973). *The Irish: Emigration, marriage, and fertility*. Berkeley, CA: University of California.

Kornhauser, W. (1959). *The politics of mass society*. Glencoe, IL: Free Press.

Laslett, P. (1976). Societal development and aging. In R. H. Binstock & E. Shanas (Eds.), *Handbook of aging and the social sciences* (pp. 87–116). New York: Van Nostrand Reinhold.

Lenski, G. E. (1966). *Power and privilege: A theory of social stratification.* New York: McGraw-Hill.

Lipset, S. M. (1960). *Political man: The social bases of politics.* New York: Doubleday.

Lipset, S. M. (1968). Students and politics in comparative perspective. *Daedalus, 97,* 1–20.

Longman, P. (1985, June). Justice between generations. *The Atlantic Monthly,* pp. 73–81.

Mannheim, K. (1928; 1952 reprint). The problems of generations. In P. Kecskemeti (Ed.), *Essays on the sociology of knowledge* (pp. 276–322). London: Routledge & Kegan Paul.

Marini, M. M. (1984). Age and sequencing norms in the transition to adulthood. *Social Forces, 63,* 229–244.

Marshall, T. H. (1950; 1964 reprint). Citizenship and social class. In *Class, citizenship, and social development: Essays* (pp. 65–122). Garden City, NY: Doubleday.

Myles, J. (1984). *Old age in the welfare state: the political economy of public pensions.* Boston: Little, Brown.

Palmore, E., & Manton, K. (1974). Modernization and the status of the aged: International correlations. *Journal of Gerontology, 29,* 205–210.

Parsons, T. (1951). *The social system.* New York: Free Press.

Pinner, F. A., Jacobs, P., & Selznick, P. (1959). *Old age and political behavior.* Berkeley, CA: University of California.

Putnam, J. K. (1970). *Old-age politics in California: From Richardson to Reagan.* Stanford, CA: Stanford University Press.

Reese, H. W., & Overton, W. F. (1970). Models of development and theories of development. In L. R. Goulet & P. B. Baltes (Eds.), *Life span development psychology: Research and theory* (pp. 116–149). New York: Academic Press.

Riley, M. W., Johnson, M., & Foner, A. (1972). *Aging and society: Vol. 3. A sociology of age stratification.* New York: Russell Sage Foundation.

Rose, A. M. (1962). The subculture of the aging: A topic for sociological research. *The Gerontologist, 2,* 123–127.

Quadagno, J. (1982). *Aging in early industrial society: Work, family, and social policy in nineteenth century England.* New York: Academic Press.

Schulz, J. (1985). *The economics of aging* (3rd ed.). Belmont, CA: Wadsworth.

Shanas, E., & Sussman, M. B. (1981). The family in later life: Social structure and social policy. In R. W. Fogel, E. Hatfield, S. B. Kiesler, & E. Shanas (Eds.), *Aging: Stability and change in the family* (pp. 211–232). New York: Academic Press.

Smelser, N. J. (1962). *Theory of collective behavior.* New York: Free Press.

Smith, A. (1776; 1937 reprint). *An inquiry into the nature and causes of the wealth of nations.* New York: Modern Library.

Synge, J. M. (1907; 1982 reprint). Playboy of the western world. In A. Saddlemyer (Ed.), *Collected works of J. M. Synge* (Vol. 4, Book 2). Washington, DC: Catholic University of America.

Vinsokis, M. A. (1982). "Aged servants of the Lord": Changes in the status and treatment of elderly ministers in Colonial America. In M. White Riley, R. P. Abeles, & M. S. Teitelbaum, (Eds.), *Aging from birth to death: Vol. 2. Sociotemporal perspectives* (pp. 105–138). Boulder, CO: Westview.

18

Aging and the Societal Significance of Cohorts*

Peter Uhlenberg

Let us begin with a bizarre thought experiment. Suppose that all members of a five-year birth cohort were removed suddenly and permanently from the population. In what ways would the lives of those remaining in the population be altered? Or, alternatively, how much reorganization would occur in the lives of the survivors? Before attempting to answer such questions, at least four vital pieces of information must be provided. First, what age category did the cohort occupy at the time it vanished? Second, what characteristics did the cohort of interest possess? Third, what society is being discussed? Fourth, what is the historical date of the disappearing act? The need for these types of information immediately indicates that the societal significance of a cohort depends upon life-course position, cohort composition, and societal and historical context.

Age plays an important role in determining the degree of control that members of one cohort exert over others in the society. Consider, for example, the removal of those aged 25 to 29 years or 45 to 49 years in contemporary American society. Major reorganization would be required in families (to replace the lost parents of now orphaned children), in work settings (to fill unoccupied critical production slots), in government (to occupy vacated deci-

*This work was completed while the author was a Fellow at the Andrew Norman Institute, Andrus Gerontology Center, at the University of Southern California. I would like to thank James E. Birren, Vern L. Bengtson, and the other fellows at the Andrew Norman Institute for their helpful comments. Matilda Riley and Dale Dannefer were especially helpful in criticizing an earlier draft.

sion-making and administrative positions), in media organizations (to assume open positions as writers, producers, and deliverers of messages), and so on. But what if the cohort was aged 75 to 79? The lives of the other members of society would continue with very little structural reorganization. The loss of this old cohort would not be totally inconsequential, of course. Children, grandchildren, and friends of different ages would experience an emotional loss and some loss of caregiving services. Censuses of hospitals and nursing homes would drop perceptibly, forcing some service providers to make occupational changes. Because of reductions in transfer payments to the aged, government resources would increase slightly, leading to some redistribution of income. But the overall societal readjustments would be minor compared to those resulting from a younger adult cohort being removed. In other words, it is clear that the societal significance of a cohort changes as it ages through time. Indeed, by the time a cohort has only a few remaining members (say, when it is aged 95 to 99) its societal significance is very near zero.

The basic question guiding the development of this chapter concerns the forces that produce changes in the level of societal significance of cohorts as they age through the later years of life. How do social structure and cohort characteristics interact to determine the shape of the societal-significance curve of a cohort over the last phase of its life course? Also, how has the age pattern of societal significance changed between recent cohorts moving through the later years of life? Is the literature on intergenerational equity (e.g., Longman, 1985; Preston, 1984) correct in assuming that the old are gaining power in American society? After examining these questions, the present chapter concludes by considering implications of the level of societal significance for the welfare of older persons.

THE SOCIETAL SIGNIFICANCE OF A COHORT

Psychologists are interested in perceptions of *personal significance* and in the relationship of these perceptions to the mental health of individuals; and social psychologists discuss the role of *significant others* in shaping the behavior of individuals. But the concept of *societal significance* as a property of cohorts has not been developed previously. As used here, the societal significance of a cohort is not measured by aggregating the feelings of significance held by its members, nor is it determined simply by aggregating the frequency with which others identify members of a cohort as significant others. Rather, the societal significance of a cohort refers to the degree of control that members of the cohort exert over the lives and behavior of others in the population.[1] As suggested in the opening paragraph, the significance of a cohort is most clearly revealed by the extent of reorganization that would occur in the lives of others in the society if the cohort suddenly vanished.

To trace the myriad ways in which each individual in a cohort influences and shapes the behavior of others is an impossibly complex method for assessing societal significance. An approach is needed which reveals more simply the most important means by which members of a cohort control and shape the behavior of others. It is also essential that the approach offer some method of measuring the level of control exerted (even if it is crude). In searching for a way to assess a cohort's societal significance, two simple questions provide some direction. First, what are the most important mechanisms that link the lives of individuals in dependent or interdependent relationships? Second, within relationships involving interdependence, who exerts more and who exerts less control? In pursuing answers to these questions there is, of course, no need to assume that the actors are conscious of the controls that exist nor that deliberate manipulation is involved.

Lives of individuals are connected with others through engagement in activities involving direct or indirect interaction.[2] Since most significant social activity can be conceptualized as occurring within social institutions, an examination of institutions that structure relationships is a reasonable starting point. Without attempting to be entirely comprehensive, the most salient social institutions that bring together individuals can be specified. To further simplify the task, attention is restricted to modern Western societies (in particular, 20th-century American society).

Lives are most obviously linked in significant ways within family and work organizations. Within families, the most intense relationships tend to occur within households, where the lives of husbands, wives, and children are closely intertwined. Ideally, other kinship ties cutting across households would also be included, although information on the nature of these is much less readily available. Regarding economic institutions operating outside the household, it is useful to separate those involving the production of goods and services from those involving consumption. In one sense, production and consumption are simply opposite sides of the same coin. However, the determinants of activity in these two spheres are to a large extent independent. One's position as a consumer depends upon possession of economic resources, but economic status is only partially determined by current position in the labor force. Assets, welfare transfers, pensions, intrafamily transfers, and so on all weaken the direct link between income from work and consumption activities.

In addition to family, work, and consumption, there are several other spheres of activity in which lives of individuals are connected. The polity involves elected and appointed officials who exert a variety of controls over the lives of others, while the citizens of a state potentially wield some influence over those in government. Voluntary associations (churches, fraternal and community organizations, clubs, and so on) bring individuals into relationships with others in the society. The mass media, although not involving personal interaction, has become an increasingly important mechanism for connecting individuals to institutions. Finally, the more personal and less structured activities associated with friendship and informal caregiving should be included in a discussion of the ways in which lives are linked. Identifying the major institutions involving social activity is a valuable step in our search for differential levels of societal significance.

The second step is a consideration of the nature of controls exerted within structured relationships. It is obvious that not all actors within a particular domain of social activity have equal control over the others with whom they interact. A hundred random voters do not influence 100 U.S. senators (or even one senator) in the same way that a few senators influence the lives of the citizens and noncitizens. Inequalities exist in relationships between employers and employees, parents and children, network executives and television viewers, priests and churchgoers, and so on. However, these inequalities do not mean that those in the subordinate position have no control over those in the stronger position.

There are several important and interrelated factors associated with inequality in influence. First, to the extent that individuals make decisions that directly regulate the behavior of others, their relative position is strengthened. Second, ability to control how money is spent is directly associated with level of power in a relationship. Third, a residual difference in personal influence may be structured into a relationship by recognized status differences. Aggregating these several potential sources of power over others produces a power hierarchy of individuals within each social institution. To simplify the discussion that follows, this continuum is divided into classes—those with strong positions and those with weak positions. In addition, an individual may not be engaged at all in any particular activity.

Since these various possible positions of influence (strong, weak, uninvolved) may exist within each domain of social activity, we can display the overall picture of how social activities are structured by use of a matrix (see Table 18-1). Examples of roles that would be located within the various cells of the matrix are suggested in Table 18-1. It should be noted that within any domain of activity an individual may be engaged in a number of different relationships, some involving a strong position and others a weak one. The focus of this chapter, however, is upon the overall level of involvement of different cohorts in various spheres of activity. Reflecting upon this view of the organization of social activities, the following proposition is suggested: the more engaged a cohort is in relationships involving others in the society, and the more those engaged occupy strong positions, the greater the societal significance of a cohort.

We will now explore why the relative significance of a cohort changes as the cohort ages. The age stratification of existing social institutions and the demographic characteristics of the cohort are two broad determinants of the societal

TABLE 18-1. The Structure of Social Activities

	Position in activity		
Domain of social activity	Strong	Weak	Uninvolved
Household/family	Head/spouse	Dependent children/other	Single/group quarters
Economic (outside household)			
Production of goods/services	Employer, supervisor, professional	Other workers	Retired
Consumption of goods/services	Consumer with discretionary spending	Poor and near-poor	–
Polity	Executive, policymaker, judge	Active citizen	Inactive
Media	Writer, producer, actor	Consumer	Nonparticipants
Voluntary associations	Professional/leader	Participant	Uninvolved
Friendship/caregiving	Friend/caregiver	Dependent	Loner

significance of a cohort as it occupies a particular phase in the life course.[3] The age stratification of social institutions refers to norms and social expectations that differentially encourage or discourage persons of different ages to occupy positions of power. Since social institutions are dynamic and vary across cultures, the pattern characteristic of modern Western societies cannot be generalized to other societies. Beyond normative forces, it is recognized that various characteristics of a cohort also influence its ability to occupy positions of control within a society. The present chapter will discuss these two important determinants of societal significance and apply this schema in two ways. First, the shape of the societal-significance curve of a cohort journeying through old age in contemporary American society will be examined. Second, recent historical changes in the societal significance of the older population will be assessed.

AGE STRATIFICATION OF SOCIAL INSTITUTIONS

The number of socially recognized age grades, the preferred timing for transitions across age grades, and the expected behavior within each age grade vary widely across cultures and across time. But no society ignores age as a significant variable in structuring life. Although varying in degree of structuredness, a culturally charted life course always exists to guide individuals as they journey from birth to death (Fry & Keith, 1982). In 20th-century American society, old age is clearly recognized as a distinctive phase of life, and it is meaningful to inquire into the present normative structure of this last segment of life.

The goal here is to explicate the general effects of age stratification upon the activities of older persons in the various domains specified in Table 18-1. Later some attention will be given to the direction of change over time in these social institutions and the implications of these changes for the involvement of older cohorts in significant relationships. But first, attention is focused upon changes that are *expected* for a cohort as it moves through old age; or, in other words, on how the age grading of social activities produce changes in participation rates for older cohorts as they age. To separate the force of social structure upon behavior from other influences associated with aging (e.g., biological changes), it is important to identify the changes that are *expected* for the older person who ages with no significant physical or mental impairment.

In order to focus on those aspects of the social structure that most significantly differentiate the behavior of the old from the non-old, it is useful to dispose quickly of all spheres of activity that do not involve strong age norms. With respect to strong positions in activities, several areas lack salient age norms regarding participation by adults: polity, voluntary associations, and friendship/caregiving. To be sure, there may be some bias against the very old, regardless of vigor, in these areas, but it is not very obvious. There are social forces that encourage friendships and caregiving activities to develop within age grades, so the significance of these activities for linking members of different cohorts is limited, but this does not apply uniquely to cohorts in the later years of life. Concerning engagement in activities as weak actors, age norms can be ignored except in the categories of work and family. That is, there are no important structural forces to remove healthy older persons from being engaged as consumers of goods, services, and media products; as active citizens; as recipients of caregiving; or as participants in churches, clubs, and other voluntary associations.

After removing those activities least affected by age norms, the significance of the few remaining ones can be examined more carefully. First is the institution of the family. Within the contemporary American family, norms regulate two activities that strongly connect the lives of individuals. One is the parenting of children from infancy through adolescence. This activity occurs within the household and is largely restricted to young and middle-aged adults, although some grandparents provide substantial care for their grandchildren and function as surrogate parents.[4] The other activity is functioning as a husband or wife. Given the norm for monogamous marriages and negative attitudes toward remarriage of old people (McKain, 1969), the likelihood of being excluded from the role of spouse increases with age throughout later life. The nonparenting engagement of older persons in the lives of their children and grandchildren, although not insignificant, is less intense and more discretionary than the two activities mentioned above. Sharing a household with someone other than spouse or dependent child is not encouraged in this society (Modell & Hareven, 1973; Soldo, 1981). Thus, the social institution that ties the lives of individuals together in the most intimate way is structured in such a way as to progressively reduce the involvement of people as they grow older. As one would expect under this situation, empirical evidence reveals that as cohorts progress through old age, an increasing proportion of their members live alone or in nonfamily group quarters.

The second institution structured in a way that systematically removes old people from active participation is work. The institutionalization of retirement, regardless of an individual's ability to work, has become pervasive and has widespread ramifications. Work outside the home is a major activity for most adults throughout their middle years of life. Removing old people from professional and managerial positions in work organizations means that after a cohort reaches age 65 its influence over younger adults is reduced drastically. Loss of employment in other jobs both removes the old from social activities associated with work and indirectly limits their role as consumers by reducing their income.

It is possible to imagine a social structure that would direct those who retire toward increasing engagement in alternative types of social activity. However, no such structure currently exists in American society, and retirees do not in fact increase their engagement elsewhere (Morrison, 1986; Rosow, 1985). Empirical evidence bearing upon this situation comes from the Retirement History Study, which allows a comparison, on a wide range of activities, between members of a cohort who retired between 1971 and 1975 and those who continued to work. As summarized by Foner and Schwab (1981), this evidence suggests that "the idea that retirees substitute new activities for the loss of their work roles does not appear to be true" (p. 42). The few areas in which retirees were slightly more active than workers in the same cohort tend to involve activities done in isolation—hobbies, taking walks, puttering around the house.

A third institution requiring attention involves the mass communication media. Those employed in generating media products tend to follow the same trajectory as those in other work settings, that is, decreasing involvement with advancing old age. On the other side, as already noted, there is no expectation that aging should reduce one's consumption of media products; perhaps there is even an expectation of increasing consumption due to greater leisure time. But engaging in this activity as a consumer is passive, that is, it does not involve direct engagement with others. Further, the indirect influence upon others of consuming media products is rather minor. The control exerted by consumers of media within a cohort over the strong actors (e.g., producers, writers, performers, advertisers) is especially small if the cohort is perceived to be socially and economically insignificant or uninteresting. When broadcasters and advertisers are guided by profit maximization, the most influential cohorts in shaping their decisions are those expected to purchase most of the goods. While recent improvements in the economic position of the older population are reflected in some retargeting of advertising and programming toward older adults, the dominant market is still younger adults (Powell & Williamson, 1985). What is especially significant about the mass media institution is its role in reinforcing or changing other aspects of the social structure via public opinion. The relatively weak position of the old vis-à-vis those who determine the content of the media restricts their ability to change public attitudes that support existing age stratification norms.

If one simply adds up the areas in which social norms push toward increasing noninvolvement for cohorts as they journey through old age, it appears that not many areas are involved. However, to conclude from this exercise in addition that the social structure does not produce an important decline in the societal significance of cohorts as they age is an error. In terms of what social activities most strongly link individuals to the lives of others, not all institutions are equal. Indeed, the two spheres of life that most significantly structure the lives of adults in modern societies are precisely the ones that most exclude older persons. The declining opportunities and obligations for healthy, vigorous persons to engage in family and work activities as they age from 60 to 100 profoundly diminish the societal significance of cohorts over the later years of life. And further, influence over the media, which significantly shapes attitudes regarding appropriate age-related behavior, also declines for cohorts as they advance through old age.

COHORT CHARACTERISTICS RELATED TO SOCIETAL SIGNIFICANCE

If structural characteristics of society are important determinants of a cohort's societal significance when it occupies a particular age category, so is the membership of the cohort at that time. Cohorts do not consist of uniform collections of individuals who simply conform to a predetermined structure. Rather, the ways in which the members of a cohort engage an existing age-stratified social system depend upon certain characteristics of the cohort. The crucial issue concerns a cohort's characteristics *relative* to those of cohorts simultaneously occupying the other life-course positions. As a cohort ages, its relative characteristics always change. This occurs both because the composition of that cohort changes over time and because the other cohorts in the population are also changing. Thus, a cohort's level of engagement in significant social activities may be expected to change as it ages. Further, since no cohort is an exact replica of the ones that preceded it (and differences between adjacent cohorts can be quite substantial), successive cohorts occupying an age category may vary in their ability to engage in significant social activities involving other cohorts.

Each cohort decreases in size as a function of the inevitability of death to its members. Also, an increasing proportion of each cohort experiences physical and mental disabilities as it ages. Several other cohort characteristics, such as economic resources and useful knowledge, also tend to change with age. How these latter variables change with age, however, depends primarily upon the social structure.

The easiest cohort variable to measure and to discuss is size, or more precisely, relative size. Ceteris paribus, the larger a cohort is relative to the total population, the larger its involvement in activities that directly affect others. This relationship between size and societal significance is a powerful force operating upon cohorts aging in later life, since rate of attrition due to mortality become increasingly large. For example, given current mortality rates, the size of a cohort will be reduced to half of its former level as it moves from age 75 to 85. If the total population is growing over the 10 years it takes a cohort to make this transition in life-course position, then the relative size of the cohort is reduced even further. By the time a cohort arrives at the very oldest ages, say, 100 to 104, it is so small that the entire passing of those left in the cohort would (and does) have no perceptible effect upon the rest of the population. Thus, the dwindling size of each cohort as it ages means that there is an inevitability to the downward slope of the societal-significance curve throughout old age.[5]

Level of physical and mental vigor is a second relevant cohort characteristic affecting involvement in activities. The incidence of physical and mental impairment within a cohort increases as it ages through later life (Chapman, La Plante, & Wilensky, 1986; Davis, 1985). The effect of increasing impairment upon involvement in social activities is not, however, entirely straightforward.

It is clear that the declining vigor of an aging cohort means that fewer members will exercise strong positions in the major social institutions. Of course, if the social structure pushes people to disengage from strong positions prior to experiencing serious disabilities, then these changes in vigor have little actual consequence in these arenas. But loss of health and/or mental acuity also tend to push individuals from weak positions toward nonparticipation in such important institutions as work, church, and political activities.

The effect of declining vigor upon social participation is complex. Disabilities may increase the involvement of individuals as patients and clients of health and welfare services and as recipients of informal caregiving. These are classified as weak positions, but they nevertheless involve interdependence and hence a type of control over the lives of others. If loss of vigor works to remove individuals from certain types of social involvement, while it encourages other types of involvement, what is its net effect upon societal significance? A precise answer to this question requires empirical data that are not presently available (and which would be challenging to obtain). Nevertheless, since any increase in control over others that arises from becoming more dependent must simultaneously increase the control that those others have upon the dependent, it seems likely that increasing disability within a cohort reduces its relative societal significance.

Operating in a way similar to vigor is the possession of wealth and useful knowledge, which is associated with greater access to strong positions in most social activities and to weak positions in such areas as politics, consumerism, and voluntary associations. The opposite of wealth, poverty, leads to greater reliance upon others for support. There is no reason for healthy individuals to experience a loss of income or useful knowledge as they age, and, indeed, some people experience gains on these variables throughout life (see Henry, this volume). But the existing social structure does not lead to this positive outcome for most individuals in a cohort. The age stratification of work and educational institutions, in particular, operates to create obstacles for older persons that do not exist for younger ones. Hence, we observe an increasing proportion of each cohort becoming marginal with respect to income and useful knowledge as it grows older.

In summary, the characteristics of a cohort that influence its overall level of engagement in social activities change as that cohort moves through later life. Biological forces reduce the capacity for societal significance of a cohort by decreasing its relative size and its vigor. Social forces tend to push in the same direction and to amplify the biological forces by reducing a cohort's possession of wealth and useful knowledge. Carefully designed social changes (involving diet, exercise, work conditions, health care, etc.) could certainly ameliorate some of the negative biological forces and improve the income, knowledge, and health characteristics of aging cohorts.

SHAPE OF THE SOCIETAL-SIGNIFICANCE CURVE THROUGH OLD AGE

It is now time to pull together the parts of this discussion in order to see how the societal significance of a cohort changes as it ages in later life. First, a brief review of the argument may be helpful. The total population at any historical time may be viewed as a set of distinct birth cohorts, each occupying a different age category. A variety of social linkages or bonds connects the lives of population members both within and between cohorts. However, cohorts at different places in the life course differ from each other in numerous ways and, consequently, are not equally engaged with other cohorts in the population. Thus we can conceptualize a cohort characteristic called *societal significance*. The societal (or structural) significance of a cohort refers to the degree of control and influence that members of that cohort exert over the lives of others. The greater the societal significance of a cohort, the greater would be the social disorganization resulting from its removal from the society. The discussion thus far has identified the most important variables determining cohort societal significance and the relationship of age to these variables.

Two general categories of variables determine the level of a cohort's societal significance. First are variables that structure the major activities linking individual lives. Especially important in producing different levels of engagement for those in different age categories are the institutions of work and the family. These two institutions, which are dominant in shaping the lives of young and middle-age adults, are structured in ways that encourage decreasing levels of participation throughout the later years of life. Thus, these social forces operate to reduce the societal significance of cohorts, regardless of the characteristics of the cohort members.

The second category of variables producing change in societal significance for cohorts as they age are cohort characteristics. There is an inevitable diminution of the size of a cohort over time. Since all members of a cohort eventually die, the societal significance of any cohort must ultimately be zero. If age had no direct influence upon the degree of social engagement of living individuals, then the downward societal-significance curve of a cohort would be determined simply by the proportion of the total population that was contained within the cohort as it occupied each successively older age category. But of course, being alive is not the only relevant factor, as the discussion of social structure makes clear. In addition, a second biologically based variable is relevant—physical and mental vigor. Deteriorating physical and mental health forces withdrawal from various activities, especially those involving authority, even when no age bias against participation exists. But disability also limits independent living and so forces some increased engagement with others as dependents and patients in caregiving activities. Finally, such socially produced cohort characteristics as possession of wealth and useful knowledge change as a cohort ages, and these also contribute to the shape of the significance curve.

The foregoing arguments leave little doubt concerning the downward trend of the societal significance of a cohort as it journeys through later life. But how rapidly does significance decline? And how much of the decline is due to social rather than biological forces? Precise answers to these questions are not, of course, possible with existing data. Nevertheless, we may be able to draw a crude societal-significance curve for a cohort, showing the approximate contribution of social and biological factors. The curves shown in Figure 18-1 are based upon data, but they are intended to be used only for heuristic purposes. The cohort represented here is the 1910-to-1914 birth cohort (aged 65 to 69 in 1980), with estimates of its position in the future based upon conventional projections.

Four curves are drawn in Figure 18-1, each showing a different pattern of societal significance. In each case, the distance above the horizontal axis represents the cohort's share of the total societal significance of the adult population. The four curves represent the following:

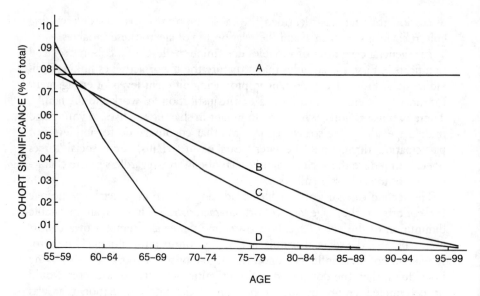

FIGURE 18-1. Alternative cohort societal significant curves. **A**, no change in societal significance with age; **B**, societal significance proportional to cohort's relative size; **C**, societal significance proportional to cohort's relative familial involvement; **D**, societal significance proportional to cohort's relative familial and work involvement.

1. *Curve A* is purely hypothetical and shows an unchanging level of societal significance throughout later life. One way to achieve such a pattern would be for a cohort to age with no attrition and no loss of vigor in an adult population that experiences no growth. Further, it requires that the aggregate engagement of the cohort members in the lives of others in the population does not change as the cohort ages. Such a pattern falls in the range of science fiction and needs no further comment here.

2. *Curve B* shows a more reasonable approximation of an upper boundary for the societal significance curve of a cohort in later life. This curve represents the changing over time of the 1910-to-1914 cohort relative to the total adult population of the United States. Unless there were social forces that increased engagement in social activities with advancing age, the cohort's significance at any age would not be disproportionately larger than its proportion of the total population. The starting point is 1970, when the birth cohort was aged 55 to 59 and constituted about 7.9% of the total population over age 20. As shown by the curve, the relative size of the cohort declines rapidly with age so that by age 75 to 79 it is only 3.5% of the adult population, and by age 95 to 99 (reached in the year 2010) it is 0.3%. These projections assume a continuing decline in age-specific death rates throughout the lifetime

of this cohort, and it would require a major disaster for it to not follow this general course. Thus, the strong impact of biological forces in reducing the societal significance of a cohort are apparent. Another curve, showing the proportion of the total population residing in this cohort that is mentally and physically vigorous, would indicate a somewhat steeper decline, since the prevalence of disability increases with age. Lacking adequate data, and given the mixed effects of disability upon social engagement, no effort is made here to draw this curve.

3. *Curve C* represents the cohort's share of all adults living in families. As argued above, being removed from a household that includes other family members implies some loss of engagement with others. The assumption is that living in an intimate environment with another person tends to increase interdependence between individuals. Although examples of real-life exceptions can be provided easily, the negative relationship between living alone or in group quarters and level of family activity is probably strong. Further, older persons who do live in families tend to be in households with fewer members (since few have children present) than are younger adults, so the extent of their intimate connection with others is less. Living arrangements do change with age, as shown in curve C. The lives of older persons are less connected with others via family and household structures than are those of younger persons, reducing the societal significance of cohorts in old age below the potential level represented by curve B.

4. Finally, *curve D* represents the further reduction in social activities produced by retirement. Separation from work, more than any other social force, progressively removes old people from significant links with other persons. In our current example, age stratification within the institutions of family and work operated to raise the societal significance of this cohort at age 55 to 59 above the average of the entire adult population. Ten years later the cohort's significance, based upon work and family connections, is reduced to about 30% of its potential based upon relative size. By the time it reaches age 75 to 79, the societal significance coming from engagement in both of these activities is near zero. (Of course, the total societal significance of the cohort is not zero at age 75 to 79, since its members are engaged in various other activities.)

This exercise in estimating societal significance of a cohort as it ages leads to two conclusions. First, the biological forces associated with aging (mortality and loss of vigor) reduce the potential significance of cohorts as they grow older. Second, due to the nature of age stratification within major institutions, the actual societal significance of a cohort in old age is far below its potential. If disengagement from intimate family ties and work connections were accompanied by increasing engagement in other social activities, then work and family might not take on so much significance. But old age is not structured in a way that leads to increasing other social activities that link lives in important ways. Indeed, active engagement in other social institutions (polity, voluntary organizations, friendship/caregiving) may also decline as cohorts move past the early phase (age 60 to 69) of old age. There is no reason why the loss of societal significance that is socially produced should be viewed as either inevitable or natural. Further, it may be that a large part of what is now viewed as biologically based loss of health and vigor is in fact socially produced.

HISTORICAL CHANGE IN
SOCIETAL-SIGNIFICANCE CURVES

If it is difficult to develop quantitative estimates for the societal significance of a contemporary cohort in old age, it is even more challenging to provide reasonable historical and prospective comparisons. But since significance depends upon cohort characteristics (which change between birth cohorts) and upon social institutions (which change over time), one should not expect a constant pattern over time. Focusing upon the recent past and the near future, we might, at a minimum, hope to discern the general trend in level of societal significance of aging cohorts. Rather than attempting to compare the whole aging careers of different cohorts, attention is restricted to the situation at three points in time: 1940, 1980, 2020. Cohorts occupying an early phase of old age, those aged 65 to 69 at these three dates, are compared.

To the extent that cohort characteristics influence the shape of a potential societal significance curve through later life, the trend since 1940 clearly has been in an upward direction. Further, the potential societal significance of successive cohorts entering old age will continue to rise through the first third of the next century. The increasing relative size of cohorts born through the baby boom is sufficient to produce this trend. The upper curve in Figure 18-2 shows the changing population significance of the three cohorts beginning their old age careers around 1940, 1980, and 2020, respectively. As expected, each successive cohort exceeds the preceding ones as a proportion of the adult population. This rapid increase in the relative size of older cohorts is a transitory phenomenon in the evolution of societies, reflecting the demographic transition. As a population moves from high to low birth and death rates, the proportion of the population that is in the older ages increases. Once a demographic equilibrium is reached and maintained, however, a cessation of the aging of a population occurs. However, for the period observed for these three cohorts, the growth in the relative size of the older population produces a potential for growing societal significance.

Satisfactory data comparing the overall level of physical and mental health of aged cohorts over the 20th century do not exist. Declining death rates for older persons and improved health technology suggest improvements in physical health but do not directly answer the question about prevalence of disabili-

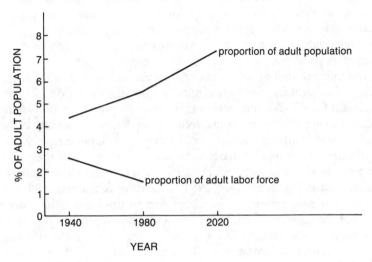

FIGURE 18-2. The proportion of the adult population and the proportion of the adult labor force contained within cohorts aged 65 to 69 in 1940, 1980, and 2020.

ty. There is evidence from health surveys conducted by the National Center for Health Statistics that disabling conditions did not change much in the 1960s and 1970s (Davis, 1985). Although this is a short time span, it adds support to the position that no increase in disability is accompanying the increase in the proportion of each cohort that survives into old age. Looking ahead, there are encouraging signs regarding potential improvements in health related to recent changes in diets, exercise, smoking, occupational safety, and other preventive health care measures. Using these indicators, Matilda Riley and Kathleen Bond (1983) note the possibility that "older people of the future will be better off than today's older people . . . in health" (p. 247). Given these various bits of information, it is reasonable to conclude that no worsening in the vigor of cohorts entering old age is occurring, and there may be some improvement. Thus, the increasing potential for significance provided by the growing size of cohorts as they occupy specific older age categories is not diminished by higher prevalence of disability.

   Possession of useful knowledge is a slippery characteristic to measure, but using education as a crude proxy suggests a rapid improvement in the relative position of older cohorts. The gap in education between cohorts entering old age and younger adults is maximized during periods when the length of time spent in school is increasing, as was the case in the first half of the 20th century. As recently as 1960, only 20% of the population over age 65 had completed 4 years of high school (compared to 43% of the adult population).

But successive cohorts are no longer staying in school longer than the preceding ones, so that by the year 2020 there will be almost no gap in the educational level of older persons compared to younger ones.

The final cohort characteristic considered here is possession of economic resources. A good deal of attention has been given to recent improvements in the economic position of older persons. The establishment of a social security system, subsequent improvements in its benefits, the expansion of other special benefits for the old, and increasing coverage by private pension plans have combined to increase the economic security of persons in later life. Indeed, in the 1970s and 1980s the income of older persons rose more rapidly than did that of other age groups. It needs to be added, however, that the income of older persons *relative* to younger ones declined in the 1950s and 1960s (Clark, Maddox, Schrimper, & Sumner, 1984; Uhlenberg & Salmon, 1986). Comparisons of relative income in the earlier part of this century have not been made, but the increasing retirement rate without compensating pension programs suggests that relative income for persons moving through old age probably had been deteriorating for some time prior to 1950. What situation the baby boom cohorts will experience as they enter old age after 2010 is debatable, but continued improvement in economic status relative to younger cohorts is certainly not guaranteed. It may be that the increasing potential significance of cohorts via increasing relative per capita income is only transitory. Since these changes in economic characteristics are the result of changes in social institutions (primarily work and social policies), it would be useful to examine more closely the historical changes in the social structure.

The most profound change has involved retirement, which contributes greatly to the removal of persons from significant social activities. For each successive cohort entering old age since 1900, retirement has begun at an earlier chronological age and has been increasingly pervasive. The change has been so large that it has more than countered the growing relative size of older cohorts. Figure 18-2 shows that in 1940 the cohort aged 65 to 69 comprised 4.4% of the adult population and contained 2.7% of the members of the labor force. In 1980 the cohort aged 65 to 69 had grown to 5.7% of the adult population, but its share of the labor force had dropped to only 1.7%. Looking ahead to 2020, when the baby boom cohort of 1955 to 1959 will be 65 to 69 years old, this age category will constitute 7.4% of the adult population. Although labor force patterns of the future are unknown, if they follow the path projected by the Bureau of Labor Statistics (U.S. Bureau of the Census, 1984), this cohort will be even less of a factor in the labor force than the preceding ones.

Changes in family and household patterns are also leading to a general decline in the frequency with which the lives of older persons are closely linked with those of younger ones. In 1900 it was uncommon for those over age 65 to live alone (about 11% of those not currently married lived alone); by

1981 this was the typical pattern (involving 66% of the unmarried living in households) (Smith, 1981; U.S. Bureau of the Census, 1984). Another trend, increasing divorce, is likely to accelerate further the frequency of older persons living in environments without intimate linkages to other persons. Whereas about 13% of those aged 65 to 69 in 1970 had their first marriage end in divorce, it is expected that 50% of those reaching old age in 2020 will be in this category (Uhlenberg & Meyers, 1981). Although a majority of those who divorce eventually remarry, the remarriage rate has declined in recent years (Uhlenberg & Chew, 1986). Unless these trends reverse, in the future an increasing proportion of each cohort will be unmarried and living alone in old age.

The conclusion of this brief look at historical changes occurring between cohorts is that the potential societal significance of cohorts in old age is increasing, but their actual significance is not. It is important to note that a continuation of recent trends into the future is not a certainty. It is quite possible for cohorts that are now young to alter the pattern of aging as they move through later life. This could be done by reversing the trends of retirement and/or living alone, or by creating new mechanisms that connect their lives to others in significant ways. If they do not make any of these changes, however, their greater numbers will not be translated into greater societal significance.

CONCLUSION

This chapter has directed attention toward the concept of cohort societal significance and the major biological and social forces that determine the shape of the societal significance curves of cohorts as they age. Cohorts remain a part of the population as long as they exist, but they play a smaller and less integral role in the society as they journey through the later years of life. A portion of this decline in societal significance is biologically produced; another portion is socially produced. The relative contribution of social forces to the decline grows progressively larger as cohorts advance in age. In addition, over time the overall role of social forces in producing a decline in societal significance has grown larger. Whether or not this trend continues has implications for the future well-being of older persons.

Social legislation passed in the 1960s and 1970s treated older persons in a generally benevolent way. Social security benefits were increased, health insurance was introduced, a wide array of new programs was established, anti-age discrimination laws were passed, and funding of gerontological research improved. Over these same years the relative size of the older population increased. Some (e.g., Preston, 1984) have suggested that these two trends are related, that is, the increasing size of older cohorts increased their political power, which in turn led to their improved position in society. If this is a correct interpretation, the next 50 years bode well for older persons, as the proportion of the population that is old will continue to grow. But the link between cohort size and cohort advantage needs to be analyzed more carefully. It is possible that the improvements in the well-being of older cohorts in recent years has occurred in spite of, rather than because of, their growing relative size. And, if this is so, prospects for the future old age of the now younger cohorts may not be especially sanguine.

The potential for increasing the societal significance of older cohorts provided by their growing size and vigor has not been realized. Rather than becoming increasingly involved in significant social activities, older persons have increasingly retired from work and withdrawn from households, including close relationships. Retirement and independent living arrangements are often hailed as victories won by the old, and data show that these two trends reflect preferences expressed by older persons themselves. Probably the societal significance of one's cohort is a completely irrelevant issue in the thinking of most individuals. Nevertheless, the increasing social independence of older persons and the declining societal significance of cohorts in old age may not be a politically irrelevant issue. The severing of work ties and the weakening of intimate family connections, without the addition of new forms of engagement with the younger population, is leaving older cohorts in a particularly vulnerable position.

If a cohort were genuinely self-sufficient in late life, it could afford to become societally insignificant without running any major risk. The old, however, are not economically self-sufficient. Rather, their economic status depends heavily upon transfer payments that are decided upon by political processes. As noted above, the old fared relatively well during the 1960s and 1970s. But as the size of the older population increases, the cost of maintaining the benefits they now enjoy also increases. The suggestion by Neugarten and Neugarten (1986) that we avoid framing the issues in terms of equity among age groups is understandable but unrealistic. A debate over intergenerational equity is underway, and the cost of social programs designed for older persons is already a salient political issue. Given this situation, how can older cohorts respond to protect their own interests? If older persons are removed from strong positions in social institutions, they lack direct control and influence and must rely upon others to make the decisions that affect their welfare. Effective influence upon political decision makers suggests a need for political organization. Whether or not persons can be politically organized on the basis of age is debatable. But even if they can, the result of forming a political bloc of older voters is likely to be disastrous. Why? Because organization on the basis of age to promote self-interest could also occur among other age groups, and it probably would occur if younger adults felt threatened by older ones. If the societal significance of older cohorts continues to decline, they almost certainly will be the losers if genuine conflict along age lines develops.

No one knows how the future old will fare. Blind optimism in the potential of older persons in the future to achieve more successful aging careers is appealing, but wishful thinking will not bring it about. It is conceivable that cohorts could become increasingly economically self-sufficient, so that their declining societal significance in old age would not have adverse consequences. Or it is possible that future cohorts would reduce the gap between their potential and actual societal significance through the restructuring of social institutions. But a continuation of current trends is most unlikely to result in the happy outcome that optimists expect.

NOTES

[1] As used here, *significance* does not refer to the moral value of a cohort. Rather, it concerns level of productive contributions that are valued in the contemporary society. As such, the term *societal significance* could be replaced by *societal importance* or *societal contribution*.

[2] Since attention in this chapter is focused upon the societal significance of a cohort relative to all other cohorts in the society, linkages between members of different cohorts are clearly important. However, the significance of control over others within the same cohort should not be ignored. There is an arbitrariness in how cohorts are defined (1-year, 5-year, etc.), and the notion of a cohort suddenly disappearing is entirely hypothetical. Therefore, relationships within a cohort are also considered as determinants of the overall societal significance of a cohort.

[3] While the distinction between age roles and cohort characteristics is analytically useful, in reality it is difficult to distinguish the two. Matilda Riley (1972, 1985) includes both roles and people within the age stratification system, thereby emphasizing the interrelatedness of the two.

[4] On the basis of about 1,000 interviews, Kornhaber (1985) reports that in approximately 15% of the cases there is "a close emotional bond between grandparent and grandchild" (pp. 159–160). Among black grandmothers, the likelihood of being a caretaker of a grandchild is much higher (Burton & Bengtson, 1985; Cherlin & Furstenberg, 1985).

[5] Because of historical changes in fertility, mortality, and migration, the relative size of successive cohorts occupying the older age categories can vary significantly (Easterlin, 1980; Waring, 1975). Nevertheless, each cohort must move toward extinction as it moves through old age.

REFERENCES

Burton, L. M., & Bengtson, V. L. (1985). Black grandmothers: Issues of timing and continuity of roles. In V. L. Bengtson & J. Robertson (Eds.), *Grandparenthood*. Beverly Hills, CA: Sage. (pp. 61–77).

Chapman, S. H., Laplante, M. P., & Wilensky, G. (1986). Life expectancy and health status of the aged. *Social Security Bulletin, 49*, 24–48.

Cherlin, A., & Furstenberg, F. F. (1985). Styles and strategies of grandparenting. In V. L. Bengtson & J. Robertson (Eds.), *Grandparenthood*. Beverly Hills, CA: Sage. (pp. 97–116).

Clark, R. L., Maddox, G. L., Schrimper, R. A., & Sumner, D. A. (1984). *Inflation and the economic well-being of the elderly*. Baltimore: Johns Hopkins University Press.

Davis, K. (1985). Health care policies and the aged: Observation from the United States. In R. H. Binstock & E. Shanas (Eds.), *Handbook of aging and the social sciences* (2nd ed.). New York: Van Nostrand Reinhold. (pp. 727–744).

Easterlin, R. A. (1980). *Birth and fortune*. New York: Basic Books.

Foner, A., & Schwab, K. (1981). *Aging and retirement*. Monterey, CA : Brooks/Cole.

Fry, C. L., & Keith, J. (1982). The life course as a cultural unit. In M. W. Riley, R. P. Abeles, & M. S. Teitelbaum (Eds.), *Aging from birth to death* (Vol. 2). Boulder, CO.: Westview Press.

Kornhaber, A. (1985). Grandparenthood and the new contract. In V. L. Bengtson & J. Robertson (Eds.), *Grandparenthood*. Beverly Hills, CA: Sage. (pp. 159–171).

Longman, P. (1985). Justice between generations. *The Atlantic Monthly, 255*, 73–81.

McKain, W. C. (1969). *Retirement marriage*. Storrs, CT: University of Connecticut.

Modell, J., & Hareven, T. K. (1973). Urbanization and the malleable household: Boarding and lodging in American families. *Journal of Marriage and the Family, 35*, 467–479.

Morrison, M. H. (1986). Work and retirement in an aging society. *Daedalus, 115*, 269–293.

Neugarten, B. L., & Neugarten, D. A. (1986). Age in the aging society. *Daedalus, 115*, 31–49.

Powell, L. A., & Williamson, J. B. (1985). The mass media and the aged. *Social Policy, 16*, 38–49.

Preston, S. H. (1984). Children and the elderly in the U.S. *Scientific American, 251*, 44–49.

Riley, M. W. (1972). The succession of cohorts. In M. W. Riley, M. Johnson, & A. Foner (Eds.), *Aging and society* (Vol. 3). New York: Russell Sage Foundation.

Riley, M. W. (1985). Age strata in social systems. In R. H. Binstock & E. Shanas (Eds.), *Handbook of aging and the social sciences* (2nd ed.). New York: Van Nostrand Reinhold. (pp. 369–411)

Riley, M. W., & Bond, K. (1983). Beyond ageism: Postponing the onset of disability. In M. W. Riley, B. B. Hess, & K. Bond (Eds.), *Aging in society: Selected review of recent research*. Hillsdale, NJ: Erlbaum. (pp. 243–252).

Rosow, I. (1985). Status and role change through the life cycle. In R. H. Binstock & E. Shanas (Eds.), *Handbook of aging and the social sciences* (2nd ed.). New York: Van Nostrand Reinhold.

Smith, D. S. (1981). Historical change in the household structure of the elderly in economically developed societies. In R. W. Fogel, E. Hatfield, S. B. Kiesler, & E. Shanas (Eds.), *Aging: Stability and change in the family*. New York: Academic Press. (pp. 101–115).

Soldo, B. J. (1981). The living arrangements of the elderly in the near future. In S. B. Kiesler, J. N. Morgan, & V. K. Oppenheimer (Eds.), *Aging: Social change*. New York: Academic Press.

Uhlenberg, P., & Chew, K. S. Y. (1986). Changing place of remarriage in the life course. In D. Kertzer (Ed.), *Family relations in life course perspective*. Greenwich, CT: JAI Press.

Uhlenberg, P., & Myers, M. A. P. (1981). Divorce and the elderly. *The Gerontologist, 21*, 276–282.

Uhlenberg, P., & Salmon, M. A. P. (1986). Changes in relative income of older women: 1960–1980. *The Gerontologist, 26*, 164–170.

U.S. Bureau of the Census. (1984). Demographic and socioeconomic aspects of aging in the United States, *Current population reports*, Ser. P-23, No. 138. Washington, DC: U.S. Government Printing Office.

Waring, J. (1975). Social replenishment and social change: The problem of disordered cohort flow. *American Behavioral Scientist, 2*, 237–255.

19

Temporal Embeddedness and Aging Within the Multigenerational Family: The Case of Grandparenting

Cees P. M. Knipscheer

This chapter is about aging and time. It is not, however, about social time, which refers to institutionalized time patterns in social life. It will not examine timetables constructed on the basis of mean age of consecutive life events and seen as an expression of age norms for these life events (Hagestad & Neugarten, 1985). Rather, it will deal with irreversible human life time (see Schroots, this volume). For this reason, the present chapter will explore the significance of the temporal embeddedness of human beings and human behavior in connection to human aging. Temporal embeddedness refers to the permanent location of human life in a temporal order of past, present, and future and to the specific way human beings are related to this order, which is constantly moving forward.

The irreversibility of human life time does not mean that human beings must always remain in the present. The human mind allows people to go forward and backward perceptually in life time; however, they always start from the mental and physical present, here and now. Thus, humans deal with the capacity to transcend the irreversibility of time by continuously and simultaneously relating to the past, the present, and the future. The focus of the present chapter will be on the social dimension of this temporal embeddedness, that is to say, on how the meaning of the past, present, and future is constructed in the interrelatedness of the individual and the social context. As an organizing approach for this enterprise, the discussion will rely heavily on Mead's time theory, at the core of which the present is the locus of reality (Chappell & Orbach, 1986), and the past is a subjective construction which impacts on this reality.

Focusing on the social dimension of temporal embeddedness presents the opportunity to avoid a totally abstract approach, allowing us to examine the notion of temporal embeddedness in a specific domain of social reality. The domain selected for this chapter is the multigenerational family of Western industrial society. Within the context of the multigenerational family, grandparenthood seems to imply an adequate example of the time dimensions to be analyzed in this chapter. It is important, therefore, to present first a picture of the recently evolved Western multigenerational family, in which the temporal embeddedness of grandparenthood arises.

THE MULTIGENERATIONAL FAMILY

The multigenerational family is one of the main social contexts related to time issues in human life. It presents a social context with a high amount of continuity throughout the life course; its structure itself refers to a range of consecutive stages in the life course that typically are represented in the actual family composition. The whole complex of relationships within the family can be seen as constituting a long-term co-biographical context, a social context of people who are co-authors of each other's biographies (Hagestad & Dixon, 1980).

It is surprising, considering the vast amount of literature on the multigenerational family, that no clear universal definition has been accepted to date. In the present chapter the multigenerational family is defined as at least two generations of adults, including all family members – connected by blood or by marriage – from the oldest generation currently living to the youngest.[1]

In regard to the temporal embeddedness of grandparenthood, two recent changes in the multigenerational family must be stressed: (1) the structural change of the multigenerational family, referred to as the verticalization of the multigenerational family (Knipscheer, 1982), and (2) the shifts in the basis of intergenerational relationships, termed the symbolization of family relationships.

Verticalization of the Multigenerational Family

The verticalization of the multigenerational family is the result of two recent changes in the structure of the family. First, an *intra*generational contraction has occurred due to the decreasing birth rate in the 20th century – there are fewer members per generation in a family. The average size of families by number of children under 18 years of age has decreased from 3.60 in 1950 to 3.26 in 1983. The percentage of families with three or more children decreased by one-third during this period (U.S. Bureau of the Census, 1985). This trend is consistent for most Western industrialized countries. For example, in the Netherlands the birth rate decreased from 31.6 in 1900 to 12.6 in 1978, and the average number of children per family decreased from 4.1 in 1904 to 1.7 in 1974 (Braam, Coolen, & Naafs, 1981).

The second change that resulted in the verticalization of the family is the large *inter*generational extension that has taken place within the multigenerational family—there are more generations per family. Bengtson, Cutler, Mangen, and Marshall (1985) showed that currently 38% of people aged 65 and over have a three-generation family; another 36%, four generations. Starting with the youngest generation, Uhlenberg (1980) demonstrated that "under 1900 mortality conditions, one-fourth of the children would have all grandparents alive at birth; by 1976 it increased to almost two-thirds. The probability of three or more grandparents alive when the child was age 15 increased from .17 to .55" (p. 316).

This verticalization is reinforced by a decreasing interaction between siblings in adulthood and old age so that there is a symbolic verticalization of family ties. Knipscheer (1980), on the basis of data on frequency of interaction and of instrumental support and intimacy, demonstrated that older siblings (65+) in the Netherlands interact infrequently unless one of the siblings does not have children. Thus, the decreasing intensity of relationships among generations has resulted in increased verticalization of significant family ties (see Cicirelli, 1985).

Symbolization of the Multigenerational Family

The second change currently occurring in the multigenerational family is the symbolization of intergenerational relationships. The significance of intergenerational family ties is based increasingly on the quality of the relationships themselves. As is demonstrated in a number of research articles (e.g., Bengtson & Treas, 1980; Knipscheer, 1986), much has changed in the dependency relationships on which past measures of significance were based. For example, the investment that parents make in their children's education now has a far greater bearing on the children's economic situation than has material inheritance. In earlier times this material inheritance could be handled as a claim to keep the family together, whereas well-educated younger generations in today's society seem to be more independent. Similarly, parents' dependency on their children has diminished with the growth of social welfare and the increase of private pension systems. Thus, the customary principle that one must look after one's parents has lost much of its impact, although there are large differences between countries in this respect (for U.S. figures see Ruffin, 1984; Callahan, 1985). With the loosening of the customary pressures and the economic/material sanctions within the intergenerational relationships, the meanings of these relationships have been established more in symbolic terms.

Although the nature of intergenerational relationships is in transition, it is clear that there is frequent interaction between generations within a family (Shanas, 1979; Shanas, Wedderburn, Fries, Milhoy, & Stehouwer, 1968), that these relationships are evaluated highly (Bengtson & Black, 1973; Bengtson & Campbell, 1985), and that socialization processes up and down the generations are intensive (Hagestad, 1985). Also, many forms of care are given by adult children to impaired elderly (Cantor, 1980; Lee, 1985). Nevertheless, the introduction of social security systems and social welfare programs has changed significantly the ways in which older adults are dependent on their children.

While discussing the temporal embeddedness of human life, the present chapter will demonstrate the relevance of recent changes in the multigenerational family, presented here as verticalization and symbolization. The case of grandparenthood will be analyzed as an example of temporal embeddedness and as it is related to the social context of the multigenerational family.

TEMPORAL EMBEDDEDNESS AS INDICATED IN THREE DIMENSIONS OF THE PAST

Maines, Sugrue, and Katovich (1983) analyze the sociological import of the past in their contribution to the recent revival of the sociology of G. H. Mead and, more specifically, his theory of time. They depict four dimensions of the past that are "directly or indirectly" (p. 163) implicated in Mead's theory and utilize these dimensions to analyze the potential of time as a theoretical construct to contribute to sociological investigations. They refer to several areas in the sociology of aging where such constructs can be useful, for example, midlife crisis, life review, and timetables. Here their analysis will be summarized as a foundation for further analysis of grandparenthood utilizing Mead's framework.

The strength of Mead's theory can be seen in the way it fully respects the subjectively perceived reality of the present in the process of human behavior while at the same time acknowledging its temporal and social-structural connections. For Mead (1932), "presents [are] sliding into each other, each with a past which is referable to itself, each past taking up into itself those back of it, and in some degree reconstructing them from its own standpoint" (p. 9). Presents are emerging events. Eames (1973) identifies two aspects of this emergent process: "One aspect . . . is that it is not reducible to its conditions (it is qualitatively unique). The second aspect of the emergent event is that it is a present, and as such is the standpoint of its own perspective from which the past and the future are constructed" (p. 72). The emerging process of the present calls for the "social nature" (i.e., sociality) of the present; the social nature is implied in the process of adjustment of the emerging present in the flow of presents. Thus, "the qualities carried over from the past present must be brought into harmony with the new qualities of the present present" (p. 72).

There is change and continuity in the social nature of the present. Therefore, in the transition of one present to the next, human beings are at the same time in the "old" present and the "new" present. This is called the temporal (or longitudinal) sociality (cf. Eames, 1973, p. 73). In contrast, structural (or latitudinal) sociality refers to the human capacity to take the role of the other. Human intelligence has the capacity to step out of the self and look at the world from another person's point of view, taking the role of significant others or the generalized other (Bergman, 1981, p. 362). In this way, human beings can view the world from the perspectives of several systems at the same time. In the emerging present, the past has to be reconstructed and the future anticipated (temporal sociality) while others' perspectives simultaneously are reflected (structural sociality). Thus, "sociality is the human capacity of being several things at once" (Mead, 1932, p. 49).

Maines et al. (1983) identified four dimensions of the meaning of the past which have special relevance in Mead's theory. The first dimension, and the most easily recognized, is the *symbolically reconstructed past*. This involves "redefining the meaning of past events in such a way that they have meaning and utility for the present" (Mead, 1929, p. 238). The second dimension, the *social-structural past*, has not been dealt with explicitly by Mead himself but is found in the literature on his theory. It refers to the notion that the social context is structured in the past and conditions future activities. Thus, the anticipation of the future as given in the present must take into account the preconditions of this context, settled in the past. The third dimension is the *implied objective past*. This past can be explicated best by a simple example given by Mead himself: "We must have arisen and eaten our breakfast and taken the car, to be where we are. The sense of this past is there as in implication" (p. 238). The fourth dimension, the *mythical past*, is only indirectly implied in Mead's formulation. This dimension refers solely to symbolic creations that are used to manipulate social relationships; they are fictitious, but real in their consequences. Once these "pasts" are legitimated, they get processual validity.

Three of these dimensions of the past are important to the understanding of the context of grandparenthood within the multigenerational family. The implied objective past only impacts to the extent that in grandparenthood there is the supposition of having children and grandchildren. The other three dimensions, to be used in the present chapter, are not strictly separated from each other; they present different levels of analyzing the meaning of the past. The symbolic reconstructed past is primarily related to the personal meaning of grandparenthood, the social structural past is primarily related to the grand-parent behavior, and the mythical past represents a collective belief regarding the grandparenthood role.

The Symbolic Reconstructed Past: Renegotiation of the Past

Human life is like a succession of presents that, one after another, shift into the past. Each emergent present must be realigned with the "new" past. This continu-ous process is especially salient in times of specific transitions. Gubrium and Buckholdt (1977) touch on this issue in stating that "the important questions are not how people respond to life change or proceed through stages, but how they negotiate and generate the reality and meaning of change, stages and development" (p. 261). In the time-conception of Mead, this means a renego-tiation of the past by the self. This self is to be understood "as a reflexive entity of change and continuity, which 'authors' a behavioral biography of successive actions" (Plath, 1982, p. 116). What are the main points of renegotiation in becoming and being a grandparent? How is this reworking of the past related to the individual meaning of grandparenthood? Both questions will be ad-dressed in the present section in order to explicate this complex process of renegotiation.

One of the first areas for an individual becoming a grandparent to renegoti-ate is the relationship to the child who is becoming a parent. For the grandpar-ent, a complete new dimension will be added to the meaning of the child. Research shows that the soon-to-be grandparent gets involved to a greater degree in the life of the child. In this regard, Crawford (1981) cites a recent grandparent: "You don't feel so shut out. You know, when they get married they go, don't they, but when a baby comes along you get more in the picture." Also, more life issues become shared and talked about as the role of parent is shared, and a supportive attitude of the future grandparent to the new parent often is appreciated (Fischer, 1982–1983). In this process, earlier tensions in the relationship will be renegotiated from the emerging present. Not only the relationship to the child is involved in this process; the future grandparent will also review his or her relationship with his or her own parents and, possibly to an even greater degree, relationships with grandparents.

While most studies on grandparenthood have focused on grandparent be-havior, Kivnick (1981) consciously and systematically separates the individu-al's meaning of grandparenthood from that person's behavior as a grandparent. She found a dimension that she termed "re-involvement with personal past." This reworking of the past is implied in statements such as "Being a grandpar-ent has made me think about my own grandparents"; "Part of being a grand-parent is reliving my own, earlier adulthood"; and "When I watch my grand-children do things (like play ball or act in a play), it's just as if I were doing those things, myself." Intergenerational relationships will be reevaluated as an individual becomes a grandparent, not to be copied in their own grandparenthood but to be brought into the creative process of modeling that grandparenthood. One of the outcomes of this process is a personal articulation of the meaning of grandparenthood in view of the individual's own past.

A second dimension Kivnick (1981) identified in the meaning of grandparenthood is that of the "valued elder." Applying this label, *valued elder*, to a grandparent is based on the evaluation of earlier experiences. It refers to grandparenthood in terms of "the activities and attitudes associated with our traditional concept of the wise, esteemed elder in society" (p. 377). Some statements related to this dimension are "I value the fact that my grandchildren confide in me"; "It is important to me to carry on family traditions with my grandchildren"; "It is important to me that my children present me to my grandchildren as someone special"; and "I want to be part of my grandchildren's memories of their childhood years." This dimension seems to prompt people to look back through their lives in a positive way, to look for the valuables in their past. One's view of one's own past seems to be directly involved in the feeling of being of specific value to next generations.

The articulation of one's own meaning of grandparenthood is not a purely individual issue. It is related to the past by temporal sociality and to the multigenerational family and, in a broader sense, to the society by structural sociality. In a continuing communication, both verbal and nonverbal, family members elaborate on the meaning of grandparenthood by sharing each other's viewpoints.

The Social-Structural Past

The social-structural past refers to the fact that future possibilities are structured, conditioned, and/or limited by past activities, events, situations, and/or processes. Social-structural pasts establish only probabilities for what will take place; unanticipated events in the present may ask for adaptation and reorientation. As we have seen, human actors establish the meaning through the construction of social life in the present. However, in this construction, they simultaneously establish parameters for activities that will occur in the future, which are based on the social-structural past and present conditions. In this sense, the social-structural past implies an anticipation of the future.

Maines et al. (1983) restrict their elaboration exclusively to the importance of the past conditions for the future options. The present application of the notion of structural past to grandparenthood will be less rigid. Present events may have the same function, both in the present and in the social-structural past. Elements of the social-structural past and present can be situated at the individual level, the family level, and the societal level. Some events at the family level are termed countertransitions (Hagestad & Dixon, 1980). For example, a daughter becomes a mother; a mother becomes a grandmother.

Maines et al. refer to timetables, timing through the life course, and cohort effects as examples of the social-structural past being important in the sociology of aging. In these examples the social-structural past implies structural variables as well as cultural elements from the past.

The social-structural past aids in anticipation of the future as well as in interpretation of the present. Reaction to events as well as role formation are impacted by this anticipation. For example, the normativity of life-course timetables concerning the best-fitting age range for grandparenthood greatly affects reactions to grandparenthood (Burton & Bengtson, 1985). Thus, early grandmotherhood (grandmothers younger than age 38) in black families has important impacts on the reaction to the role of grandparent. Many early grandmothers relate "an asynchrony between chronological age and family lineage position" (p. 76). This situation creates for many of these young grandmothers tensions and conflicts and a threat for family cohesion and social support. Thus, anticipation and interpretation of norms has a large impact on how role transitions are received.

Of special interest in grandparenting are the attitudes of the parents of the grandchildren as to adequate grandparent behavior. Robertson (1977) has shown the essential intermediary role of the parents as "gatekeepers" in the relationship between grandparent and grandchild. As part of the social-structural past, these attitudes can be anticipated by future grandparents. Recently, Cunningham-Burley (1985) demonstrated this anticipation through interviews with first-time grandparents concerning rules or guidelines that would direct their behavior as grandparents. The point most consistently noted in the anticipated role of grandparent seemed to be not interfering with the family life of the parents, sharing the grandchildren with the other grandparental couple, and not spoiling the grandchildren. "Important for a study of people becoming grandparents is an understanding of this potential for anticipating a role not yet experienced, as a unique mixture of known and unknown elements. Current stock of knowledge, both biographical and intersubjective, are utilized by the prospective grandparents to negotiate this new experience" (Cunningham-Burley, 1985, p. 424). The intersubjective source of anticipated behavior is difficult to locate exactly; it is evolving from prior experience and the current state of family relationships. However, as seen in the example of grandparenthood, this social-structural past is a vital element in understanding behavior.

Likewise, another factor determining grandparent behavior is the marital situation of the parent. Nearly all contributors to the volume by Bengtson and Robertson (1985) refer to the relevance of divorce in the relationship between grandparents and grandchildren. Hagestad (1985) points out that even when the grandchildren are no longer living with their parents, this relationship seems to be at stake. Further, Aldous (1985) shows how the presence of grandchildren directs grandparent behavior in relation to their own children.

Although we can not generalize Aldous's conclusion due to the selectiveness of her data and the small sample size, the data support the hypothesis that parents show greater solicitude for their divorced (not remarried) children who have children. Thus, the extensiveness of the grandparent behavior appears to be dependent on both the marital and the parental situation of the adult child, another factor of the social-structural past.

Many other factors are involved in the social-structural past of grandparent-hood, for example, gender, the occupational role of the grandparents, geo-graphical distance, and so on (Troll, 1985). Further, many of these factors are characteristics of or highly related to the structure and the specific culture of the multigenerational family in which grandparenthood is emerging. The general function of all of the elements of the structural past appears to be to set the options for future behavior, sometimes in a very restrictive way and sometimes opening unprecedented options.

The Mythical Past

The mythical past is based on the distinction made by Mead (1936) between subsistence and existence: "There is a world which subsists, but does not necessarily exist" (p. 336). One definition of a myth is "an unproved collective belief that is accepted uncritically and is used to justify a social institution" (Random House Dictionary, 1966). Some elements in this definition must be elaborated before it can be used to clarify the mythical past as it impacts on present and future behaviors and meanings.

First, a myth is a "collective belief" shared by groups of people with a certain degree of collective identity. The collective belief in the reality of the myth may be one of the grounds on which the group is based. Second, this belief is not proven. That is to say, without being proven, the belief is accepted and its legitimation is not based on fact. In connection with alternative forms of legitimation, Berger and Luckmann (1967) discuss "conceptual machineries of universe-maintenance," mechanisms used in collectivities to maintain specific "universal" beliefs. In this way, mythology, theology, philosophy, and science can be understood as conspicuous types of conceptual machineries (Berger & Luckmann, 1967): "Without proposing an evolutionary scheme for such types, it is safe to say that mythology represents the most archaic form of legitimation generally" (p. 110).

A third essential element in the definition of the myth is the way it is used — as a legitimation of other social realities. For example, for centuries the belief in the inferiority of slaves legitimated inhuman treatment of them. Further, Maines et al. (1983) used this element of the myth to show how Mead's theory of time can be used to analyze power relations. For example, based on their mythical past, the Woodlawn community organization, which succeeded in the early 1960s in organizing a very effective community power movement in Chicago, could afford symbolic power resources for future action.[2]

Before mythical pasts can be effective, they must be legitimated, that is, achieve general acceptance in the collectivity involved and be used as grounds for forthcoming action.[3] Maines et al. (1983) use the term "processual validity." There seem to be boundaries for the (mis)use of the power of mythical pasts. That is to say, the processual validation seems to be continuously at risk, and these kinds of interaction situations mostly demand subtle maneuvering (Knipscheer & Bevers, 1985).

Our example of grandparenthood is particularly relevant in discussing the mythical past. In most societies there seems to be something special about grandparenthood. Many scholars on grandparenthood look for special terms to characterize it. Frazier (1933) talks about the "guardians of generations," Troll (1983) sees them as "watchdogs," Gutmann (1985) uses the term "warden," and Hagestad (1985) calls grandparents the "family national guard." What is expressed by these kinds of descriptions? Is it not some sort of myth about grandparenthood? The mythical past of grandparenting must be viewed as part of many other mythical realities in family life. The following is just one example of the realities in families that are below the surface, not explicitly spoken about, and/or always present in the background, yet strongly influencing family behavior.

"The value system of an entire family can be characterized by certain myths that members have shared throughout generations. . . . Loyalty to the family's value system constitutes an invisible, yet very important, dynamic regarding the accounting of merit in an individual member" (Boszormeni-Nagy & Spark, 1973, p. 84). In reference to the notion of invisible loyalties, Reiss (1981) talks about the kinship code as a loyalty code, "a property of the kindred itself [which] has a central role in regulating the behavior of one member to another" (p. 275). This kinship code stays mostly below the surface.

We now return to our example of grandparenthood and the question: Are there specific myths that can serve grandparenthood? How can mythical pasts create an atmosphere of legitimation, validation, and nurturing? In the conclusion of his book on life stories, Kotre (1984), referring to the life review of older people, writes: "Historical accuracy is not forgotten as they tell their stories to others, but myth enters in the service of narrative truth. If a life is unattached to myth it will nourish no one, but if it does not stand up to a realistic gaze, it will appear hypocritical and collapse under the burden of its mythical accretions" (p. 260). This demonstrates one of the ways grandparents can create a mythical reality and use it in the family context. Through creating this mythical reality, grandparents can impact on their own present and future as well as those of the next generations.

One such dimension of the meaning of grandparenthood is identified by

Kivnick (1983a): "immortality through the clan." This dimension can be interpreted in terms of the mythical past; that is, grandparenthood can be seen as the symbol of family continuity (cf. Neugarten & Weinstein, 1964). Some items in this dimension refer to the patriarchal or matriarchal position of the grandparent in the family; for example, statements like "I feel that my grandchildren belong to me as well as to their parents"; and "As a grandparent I feel I really should look after the whole family." Other items refer to the identification with grandchildren or concern family immortality: "A major way I think of each grandchild is as a new member of our family"; and "It gives me a sense of continuity to know that my grandchildren will have grandchildren and that their grandchildren will probably have children of their own, and on and on." Thus, grandparents look at themselves as family representatives who have borne the torch of the family and transferred it to the next generations.

This picture reminds us of the verticalization and symbolization of the multigenerational family. That is to say, what is transferred in the vertical line of generation to generation is not necessarily the family property or the honored/respected family traditions of the past, but instead the "mythical strength of the sense of loyalty each member feels toward others in the kindred" (Reiss, 1981). Many grandparents feel they deserve to be acknowledged as special representatives of this loyalty, as well as to be nurtured by it. It is within this kind of mythical past that "the effects of grandparenthood can be felt simply from their presence, not their actions" (Hagestad, 1985, p. 44). Through their presence, grandparents offer a legitimated past.

The image of the multigenerational family arising out of the presentation in this section suggests each family is developing its own idiosyncratic mythical elements, mostly based in past experiences and sustained in the ongoing family interactions that reflect as well as confirm this mythical reality. As is shown, grandparenthood can have a special function in this process. Next we will explore what the symbolic reconstructed past, the social-structural past, and the mythical past teach us about aging within the multigenerational family.

AGING WITHIN THE MULTIGENERATIONAL FAMILY: THE THREE DIMENSIONS OF THE PAST

Our focus has been on the importance of the past in human life, with special attention to the case of grandparenthood in the multigenerational family. Based on the social psychology of G. H. Mead, three dimensions of the past—the social reconstructed past, the social-structural past, and the mythical past—have been identified and applied to an analysis of the temporal embeddedness of grandparenthood within the evolving multigenerational family. For Mead, "the past that is remembered and reconstructed is done so from the perspective of the present. . . Similarly the present is responsible for the anticipatory future" (Chappell & Orbach, 1986, p. 85). For example, in the process of becoming and being a grandparent, the personal meaning of grandparenthood emerges from a continuously renegotiated past. The social-structural past—past events, activities, transitions, and processes as perceived in the present—restricts or expands future options of behavior as a grandparent. Finally, the mythical past is the collective belief within the family, of which the grandparent in some ways becomes the most significant representative. Each of these dimensions implies a special relationship to the micro-social context of grandparenthood, the multigenerational family. The emerging process of the meaning of grandparenthood does not happen in isolation; many family members participate in it. In the social-structural past, the lives of other family members have implications for the actual behavior of the grandparents. As well, the mythical past can only be maintained by the support of the whole family. Thus, the past and present interact in the aging process and the formation of grandparenthood. We will now explore and compare these dimensions of the past in the aging process.

Aging, as defined in the present chapter, is the transformation of the (human) organism with time so that the life expectancy decreases while there is a progression of physiological and psychological characteristics involving an increase of the integration of power and intimacy forces, of diversity and heterogeneity, of integrative functions and spiritual commitments, all of which are modulated by society-specific sociological and ecological forces on the micro-, meso-, and macro-level. Our analysis of the temporal embeddedness of grandparenthood has been focused on the interaction of the psychological characteristics and the sociological forces. It presented an analysis of how the interpretive and anticipatory meaning of the past in grandparenthood and the social context of the multigenerational family interact in the formation of behavior in the present and anticipation of the future. The understanding of aging out of this analysis can only be suggestive; no empirical data or theoretical models are available.

The Social Reconstructed Past and Aging

Kohli (1986) has demonstrated that the subjective construction of the life course is related to the specific organization of the social context in which it evolves. He studied the situation of older workers over time and traced how their perspectives on their life course were modeled through the social organization of the specific work situation. The findings of this research can be generalized to the family. From the moment children develop self-awareness, they construct their own perspectives on their life course (Denzin, 1978). This construction, subjective as it is, does not happen in isolation. It occurs in interaction with parents, siblings, and relatives, as well as in other relationships that will not be discussed in the present chapter.

The longer people participate in a web of long-term significant relationships, the more they will profit from this connectedness in developing their own personal meaning of life. The construction of this meaning partially determines present behaviors. This qualifies a special temporal embeddedness with increasing age. The verticalization and the symbolization of the family seem to have enhanced opportunities to increasingly model roles in aging on the basis of the meanings that emerge from the reconstructed past (see Dannefer, this volume). While moving through the multigenerational family from the youngest generation to the oldest one, the commitments to the younger generations get more and more integrated in the symbolic reconstructed past. The current symbolic reconstructed past at any age is based on an accumulation of earlier reconstructed pasts. Although the emerging present dictates new perspectives throughout life, the symbolic reconstructed past of an individual in the fourth generation of a multigenerational family may be different from that of a person in the second generation.

Another example of this phenomenon can be illustrated in the life course of a woman in her seventies who began work as a maid at age 12, married at age 18, and remained a housewife throughout her life. The need for an important reconstruction of her past arose when her daughter entered the work force again after the birth of her second child. A second reconstruction of the meaning of her life course was needed when her granddaughter started an academic study in geography at the age of 18. Her experience of her adolescence and her family household work had not changed, but her interpretation of it was reviewed several times stemming from her family history.

The range of the reference field for the reconstruction of the past in the older generation will be much broader. Also, the development of meanings based on the reconstructed past may have a greater opportunity to form with age; thus, the disruptive quality of emerging presents may decrease. In this way it seems appropriate to suggest an increasing importance of the symbolic reconstructed past with aging, for grandparenthood is partly based on the structural location within the multigenerational family. This would fit with the notion of an increasingly more differentiated and integrated personal meaning system as a function of age (see Reker & Wong, this volume).

The Social-Structural Past and Aging

Aging within the multigenerational family involves moving from the youngest generation through the middle ones to the oldest. As one moves through this process, there is a question of whether the implications of the social-structural past are affected by the position in the generational line. For example, the effect on an adult person's future options when her or his older parents become impaired and must be cared for has a different implication from that when her or his daughter gets divorced and moves back home with a newborn child. The specific effects are dependent on the idiosyncratic situations of the particular multigenerational family. However, generally speaking, choices made in constructing future behaviors will be affected by the direction of the influence from generation to generation.

The developmental stake theory (Kuypers & Bengtson, 1972) indicates a stronger commitment to younger generations in the family than to older generations; this implies a greater impact of the social-structural past related to the younger generations. Further, in the context of the present-day multigenerational family, this implies a larger impact than in earlier days. The more generations there are downward in the vertical line of the family, the more one is confronted with countertransitions resulting from the transitions of younger family members. Thus, the options for future behavior of the older generations in today's society may be more restricted by the many elements of the social-structural past related to the increasing number of younger generations within the family. Aging within the multigenerational family therefore involves an increasing number of commitments to younger family members, family events, and family situations in an increasing number of generations.

In a study of five-generation families, Kruse (1984) demonstrated the complex dynamics in the multigenerational family that are related to different elements of the social-structural past. For example, in families in which the great-great-grandmother was in good shape and performed the role of kinkeeper, the great-grandparents were found to be unable to come to terms with their own aging problems. In contrast, in families in which the great-great-grandmother needed intensive care, the great-grandparent generation was involved in the caring activities and became separated from the rest of the family. Thus, increasing numbers of generations result in increased overlapping of roles. As well, there are increased opportunities for interaction between generations and the effects of the social-structural past in the aging process.

The Mythical Past and Aging

What is the meaning of the mythical past for the aging process in the multigenerational family? As we have seen, each family has in some way or other developed its own myths. The older family members increasingly become the embodiment of these collective beliefs with age. This presents older family members with the opportunity to celebrate their connections with younger generations, to nurture feelings of connectedness, and to represent earlier generations within the family.

There seems to be some analogy between the significance of older generations within the family and of older people in traditional folk societies. As Berger, Berger, and Kellner (1974) point out, through most of human history individuals lived in more or less unified life-worlds. The high degree of integration of this traditional society has evolved over the past centuries into a society segmented in quite differentiated sectors, with discrepant worlds of meaning and experience. In contrast to the pluralization of the public sphere in the modern world—the segmentation of individual lives in connection with the worlds of work and those of large bureaucratic organizations such as public administration, education, health care, and social security maintenance—the private sphere most approaches the unified traditional community. "It is indeed true that the modern individual typically tries to arrange this sphere in such a way that by contrast to this bewildering involvement with the worlds of public institutions, this private world will provide for him an order of integrative and sustaining meanings" (Berger, Berger, & Kellner, 1974, pp. 65–66). However, in order to serve as a meaningful center—a home world for the family members—a large amount of negotiation is required between the marriage partners (cf. Berger & Kellner, 1970) and between the consecutive parent/child generations within the multigenerational family. In comparison to the pluralization of the rest of society, the multigenerational family is characterized by low interpersonal boundaries, as is seen in the flow of socialization up and down generations (Hagestad, 1984). In combination with the long-term shared history family members have in common, this promotes the creation of an idealized image of the family in which the older generations get a special function. Thus, the mythical past, as propagated in the older generations of the multigenerational family, frees the elderly from many practical daily affairs while keeping them involved in the continuity and the well-being of the family.

In four- or five-generation families it may be a challenge to maintain the mythical past in relation to the older generations. Much will depend on the way older generations feature their roles and how younger generations relate to them (Kruse, 1984). It may be that the mythical past of becoming and being a grandparent is temporary, the special flavor of which is connected to the birth and growing up of the grandchildren. Also, this may level off as the grandchildren get older.

The Three Dimensions of the Past and Aging

From the foregoing, some conclusions can be drawn regarding the relative importance of the three dimensions of the past in the aging process. The significance of these dimensions is related to certain concepts that serve as dependent variables in the study of aging: meaning, morale, and life space (see Birren, this volume).

The cumulative character of the symbolic reconstructed past in terms of the continuously expanding field of reference indicates an increasing importance of this dimension with aging. The self as "a reflexive entity of change and continuity" (Plath, 1982) implies in the present of old age a reflection of the whole life course, related directly to meaning. From the negotiation and generation of meaning, which integrates the past and present, the tone of life in old age arises. Thus, there is an increasing importance of the symbolic reconstructed past with aging.

The social-structural past is the dimension most related to behavior. Elements of the social-structural past condition future possibilities and delineate opportunities, and in this way they are related to anticipation of future behavior. Thus, an individual's present is characterized by elements of the social-structural past related to her or his own life as well as to the context of the multigenerational family. A further implication of this is that there are indications that the attitude of people toward elements of the social-structural past changes with age. For example, middle age is seen as a period of shifting perspectives on the life course (Neugarten, 1979), which may imply less impact of the elements of the social-structural past on future behavior. Also, in old age an individual's perspective on the finitude of human life changes (Munnichs, 1966), which may open up opportunities for behavior that would not have been there otherwise. In these examples there is some suggestion that the importance of the social-structural past decreases with increasing age.

The mythical past has two basic elements that are relevant in relation to aging. First, a mythical past must be validated by the group or collectivity in which it is expected to be functional. Thus, the existence of a mythical past reflects the position of the older adult and the significance with which her or his role is viewed. Second, the present mythical past is based on earlier situations and/or activities that legitimate it. This, by definition, relates to aging the effectiveness of the mythical past in influencing behaviors. It is necessary to have a storehouse of fruitful experience and productivity on which the mythical past can be legitimated. This stresses the social context, an indispensable factor in this dimension of the past.

SUMMARY

In irreversible human life time, the present is the locus of reality. However, simultaneously, human beings have the capacity to go forward and backward in time. This creates a special temporal embeddedness. In this chapter this temporal embeddedness has been addressed using three dimensions of the past as implicated in the social psychology of G. H. Mead: the symbolic reconstructed past, the social-structural past, and the mythical past. The process of becoming and being a grandparent has been used as an example to illustrate these dimensions of the past.

The symbolic reconstructed past represents the necessary reconstruction of the meaning of the past with each emerging present. While a new present is emerging, the self renegotiates the meaning of the past to include the older presents. The process of becoming and being a grandparent implies, for example, a reconstruction of the relationship to the child who is becoming a parent. Future grandparents may also review their relationships with their own parents.

The social-structural past represents the specific conditions and events of the past, which, along with the present, delineate the future options of behavior. Social-structural pasts establish probabilities for what will take place; however, anticipated events may still require adaptation and reorientation. The timing of grandparenthood, the intermediary role of the parents in the relationship between grandparents and grandchildren, and the marital status of the parents have been discussed as elements of the social-structural past in grandparenthood.

The mythical past refers to a collective belief that legitimates specific future behaviors of selected individuals or of the collectivity. Mythical pasts are symbolic realities that are based on the past but control future behavior. As discussed, in grandparenthood, the mythical past refers to a collective belief in the family of which the grandparent becomes the most significant representative.

Each of these dimensions of the past is specifically related to the micro-social context, the multigenerational family in the case of grandparenthood. In addition to the elaboration of the three dimensions of the past, this chapter has addressed how these dimensions relate to aging. There is an increasing importance of the symbolic reconstructed past with age. Further, there is some ambiguity as to the relevance of the social-structural past in aging, while it is suggested that the mythical past by definition is related to the later part of life.

NOTES

[1]Although this definition to a certain extent is artificial and streamlined, for the purpose of the present chapter this somewhat superficial treatment will serve the purpose in explicating temporal embeddedness. It is not necessary to go into such details as how stepchildren and/or stepgrandmothers are located in the context of the multigenerational family.

[2]In the structuralist theory of Levi-Straus a somewhat different notion of myth is used. His concern is "ultimately with the extent to which the structures of myths prove actually formative as well as reflective of men's mind: the degree to which they dissolve the distinction between nature and culture. And so his aim, he says, is not to show how men think in myths, but 'how myths think in men, unbeknown to them'" (Hawkes, 1977, p. 41). Our concern is more the phenomenon of myths as well as the content of them.

[3]The question arises as to whether mythical pasts are purposefully created to manipulate social relationships. Although the description given by Maines et al. (1983) seems to imply this, an amendment to this definition is proposed here: Mythical pasts, in the view of the present chapter, are not always purposefully created, nor

are they always created to manipulate social relationships. However, they do control behavior and the people that they concern. Thus, the bearer(s) of the mythical past can celebrate it, nurture it, or profit from it. Likewise, as in the case of slavery, they can suffer from it.

REFERENCES

Aldous, J. (1985). Parent-adult child relations as affected by the grandparent status. In V. L. Bengtson & J. F. Robertson (Eds.), *Grandparenthood* (pp. 117–132). Beverly Hills, CA: Sage.

Bengtson, V. L., & Black, K. D. (1973). Inter-generational relations and continuity in socialization. In P. Baltes & W. Schaie (Eds.), *Lifespan developmental psychology: Personality and socialization* (pp. 207–234). New York: Academic Press.

Bengtson, V. L., & Campbell, M. (1985). *Aging within the family: Current trends, future scenarios*. Paper presented at the 14th annual meeting of the Canadian Gerontological Society, Hamilton, Ontario.

Bengtson, V. L., Cutler, N. E., Mangen, D. J., & Marshall, V. W. (1985). Generations, cohorts and relations between age groups. In R. H. Binstock & E. Shanas (Eds.), *Handbook of aging and the social sciences* (pp. 303–334). New York: Van Nostrand Reinhold.

Bengtson, V. L., & Robertson, J. F. (Eds.). (1985). *Grandparenthood*. Beverly Hills, CA: Sage.

Bengtson, V. L., & Treas, J. (1980). The changing family context of mental health and aging. In J. E. Birren & R. B. Sloane (Eds.), *Handbook of mental health and aging* (pp. 400–428). Englewood Cliffs, NJ: Prentice-Hall.

Berger, P. L., Berger, B., & Kellner, H. (1974). *The homeless mind*. New York: Vantage Books.

Berger, P. L. & Kellner, H. (1970). Marriage and the social construction of reality. In H. P. Dreitzel (Ed.), *Recent Sociology*. London: Collier-MacMillan.

Berger, P. L., & Luckmann, T. (1967). *The social construction of reality*. Garden City, NY: Doubleday.

Bergmann, W. (1981). Zeit, Handlung und Sozialitat bei G. H. Mead. *Zeitschrift fur Soziologie, 10,* 351–363.

Boszormeny-Nagy, I., & Spark, G. M. (1973). *Invisible loyalties: Reciprocity in intergenerational family therapy*. New York: Harper & Row.

Braam, G. P. A., Coolen, J. A. I., & Naafs, J. (1981). *Ouderen in Nederland, sociologie van bejaarden, bejaardenzorg en beleid*. Alphen aan de Rijn, The Netherlands: Samson Uitgeverij.

Burton, L. M., & Bengtson, V. L. (1985). Black grandmothers, issues of timing and continuity of roles. In V. L. Bengtson & J. F. Robertson (Eds.), *Grandparenthood* (pp. 61–78). Beverly Hills, CA: Sage.

Callahan, D. (1985). What do children owe elderly parents? *Hastings Center Report, 15,* 32–37.

Cantor, M. H. (1980). The informal support system: Its relevance in the lives of the elderly. In E. Borgatta & N. McCluskey (Eds.), *Aging and society* (pp. 75–106). Beverly Hills, CA: Sage.

Chappel, N. L., & Orbach, H. L. (1986). Socialization in old age: A Meadian perspective. In V. W. Marshall (Ed.), *Later life, the social psychology of aging* (pp. 75–106). Beverly Hills, CA: Sage.

Cherlin, A., & Furstenberg, F. F. (1985). Styles and strategies of grandparenting. In V. L. Bengtson & J. F. Robertson (Eds.), *Grandparenthood* (pp. 97–116). Beverly Hills, CA: Sage.

Cherlin, A., & Furstenberg, F. F. (in press). *American grandparents.*

Cicirelli, V. G. (1985). The role of siblings as family caregivers. In W. J. Sauer & R. T. Coward (Eds.), *Social support networks and the care of the elderly: Theory, research and practice* (pp. 93–107). New York: Springer Publishing Co.

Crawford, M. (1981). Not disengaged: Grandparents in literature and reality, an empirical study in role satisfaction. *Sociological Review, 29,* 499–519.

Cunningham-Burley, S. (1985). Constructing grandparenthood: Anticipating appropriate action. *Sociology, 19,* 421–436.

Denzin, N. K. (1978). *Childhood socialization.* San Francisco: Jossey-Bass.

Eames, E. R. (1973). Mead's concept of time. In W. R. Corti (Ed.), *The philosophy of George Herbert Mead* (pp. 59–81). Winterthur, Switzerland: Amriswiler Bucherei.

Fischer, L. R. (1982–1983). Transitions to grandmotherhood. *International Journal of Aging and Human Development, 9,* 293–299.

Frazier, E. F. (1939). *The Negro family in the United States.* Chicago: University of Chicago Press.

Gubrium, J. F., & Buckholdt, D. R. (1977). *Toward maturity.* San Francisco: Jossey-Bass.

Gutmann, D. L. (1985). Deculturation and the American grandparent. In V. L. Bengtson & J. R. Robertson (Eds.), *Grandparenthood* (pp. 173–182). Beverly Hills, CA: Sage.

Hagestad, G. O. (1984). Multi-generational families: Socialization, support, and strain. In V. Garms-Homolova, E. M. Hoerning, & D. Schaeffer (Eds.), *Intergenerational relationships* (pp. 105–114). Lewiston, NY: C. J. Hogrefe.

Hagestad, G. O. (1985). Continuity and connectedness. In V. L. Bengtson & J. F. Robertson (Eds.), *Grandparenthood* (pp. 31–48). Beverly Hills, CA: Sage.

Hagestad, G. O., & Dixon, R. A. (1980). *Lineages as units of analysis: New avenues for the study of individual and family careers.* Paper presented at the N.C.F.R. Conference, Portland, OR., October, 1980.

Hagestad, G. O., & Neugarten, B. L. (1985). Age and the life course. In R. H. Binstock & E. Shanas (Eds.), *Handbook of aging and the social sciences* (pp. 35–61). New York: Van Nostrand Reinhold.

Hawkes, T. (1977). *Structuralism and semiotics.* Berkeley, CA: University of California Press.

Kivnick, H. Q. (1981). Grandparenthood and the mental health of grandparents. *Aging and Society, 1,* 365–391.

Kivnick, H. Q. (1983a). Dimensions of grandparenthood meaning: Deductive conceptualization and empirical derivation. *Journal of Personality and Social Psychology, 44,* 1056–1068.

Kivnick, H. Q. (1983b). Grandparenthood and mental health: Meaning, behavior and satisfaction. In V. L. Bengtson & J. F. Robertson (Eds.), *Grandparenthood* (pp. 135–150). Beverly Hills, CA: Sage.

Knipscheer, C. P. M. (1980). *Oude mensen en hun sociale omgeving.* The Hague: Vuga
Knipscheer, C. P. M. (1982). Het familieverband als kontekst van de levensloop. *Tijdschrift voor Gerontologie en Geriatrie, 13,* 232–242.
Knipscheer, C. P. M. (1986). Family care of impaired elderly: Possibilities for innovations. In W. J. A. van den Heuvel & G. Schrijvers (Eds.), *Innovations in care for the elderly* (pp. 137–165). Lochem, The Netherlands: de Tijdstroom.
Knipscheer, K., & Bevers, A. (1985). Older parents and their middle-aged children: Symmetry or asymmetry in their relationship. *Canadian Journal on Aging, 4,* 145–159.
Kohli, M. (in press). Social organization and subjective construction of the life course. In A. B. Sorensen, F. Weiner, & L. Sherrod (Eds.), *Human development and the life course: Multidisciplinary perspectives.* Hillsdale, NJ: Erlbaum.
Kotre, J. (1984). *Outliving the self: Generativity and the interpretation of the self.* Baltimore: Johns Hopkins University Press.
Kruse, A. (1984). The five-generation family, a pilot study. In V. Garms-Homolova, E. M. Hoerning, & D. Schaeffer (Eds.), *Intergenerational relationships* (pp. 115–124). Lewiston, NY: C. J. Hogrefe.
Kuypers, J. A. & Bengtson, V. L. (1973). Social breakdown and competence: A model of normal aging. *Human Development, 16,* 181–201.
Lee, G. R. (1985). Kinship and social support of the elderly: The case of the United States. *Aging and Society, 5,* 19–38.
Maines, D. R., Sugrue, M. N., & Katovich, M. A. (1983). The sociological import of G. H. Mead's theory of the past. *American Sociological Review, 48,* 161–173.
Mead, G. H. (1929). The nature of the past. In J. Coss (Ed.), *Essays in honor of John Dewey* (pp. 235–242). New York: Henry Holt.
Mead, G. H. (1932). *The philosophy of the present.* Chicago: Open Court.
Mead, G. H. (1936). *Movements of thought in the Nineteenth Century.* Chicago: University of Chicago Press.
Munnichs, J. M. A. (1966). *Old age and finitude: A contribution to psychogerontology.* New York: S. Karger.
Neugarten, B. L. (1979). Time, age and the life cycle. *American Journal of Psychiatry, 136,* 887–894.
Neugarten, B. L., & Weinstein, K. K. (1964). The changing American grandparent. *Journal of Marriage and the Family, 26,* 199–204.
Plath, D. W. (1982). Resistance at forty-eight: Old age brinkmanship and Japanese life course pathways. In T. K. Hareven & K. J. Adams (Eds.), *Aging and life course transitions* (pp. 109–125). New York: Guilford Press.
Reiss, D. (1981). *The family's construction of reality.* Cambridge, MA: Harvard University Press.
Robertson, J. F. (1977). Grandmotherhood: A study of role conceptions. *Journal of Marriage and the Family, 39,* 165–174.
Ruffin, M. D. (1984). Contributions of the family to the economic support of the elderly. *Family Economics Review, 4,* 1–11.
Shanas, E. (1979). Social myth as hypothesis: The case of the family relations of old people. *The Gerontologist, 19,* 169–174.
Shanas, E., Wedderburn, D., Fries, H., Milhoy, P., & Stehouwer, J. (1968). *Old people in three industrial societies.* New York: Atherton Press.

Troll, L. E. (1983). Grandparents: The family watchdogs. In T. H. Brubaker (Ed.), *Family relationships in later life* (pp. 63–73). Beverly Hills, CA: Sage.

Troll, L. E. (1985). The contingencies of grandparenting. In V. L. Bengtson & J. F. Robertson (Eds.), *Grandparenthood* (pp. 135–151). Beverly Hills, CA: Sage.

Uhlenberg, P. (1980). Death and the family. *Journal of Family History, 4*, 313, 320.

U.S. Bureau of the Census. (1985). Percent distribution of families by number of children under 18 years old. *U.S. Census Tables*, 1950–1983. Washington, DC: Government Printing Office.

20

Theories of Age and Culture

Christine L. Fry

When looking at culture, a rather obvious conclusion is that differences do count for something. Other people in other places or at other times do things differently. An "ethnographic veto" is a rather powerful caveat against the universality of any generalization. "My people don't do that." A prime example of such a veto is Margaret Mead's study of adolescence in Samoa in the 1920s, which challenged the psychological theory of the day.[1] Age, too, has had its share of ethnographic vetoes. Dramatic accounts of gericide or of gerontocracies and filial piety have canceled out generalizations of universal good or bad treatment of older people. Ethnographic vetoes alone, however, are limited in their productivity unless the reasons are linked to a broader theory of human behavior. Exceptions to the rule must be explained or the rule changed to incorporate the exception. Otherwise, the exceptions become examples to be dusted off occasionally and paraded about, only to be filed away as exotic oddities.

The intent of this chapter is to examine the theoretical advances we have made in understanding the ways in which culture shapes age and is shaped by age. Four major issues organize the chapter. First, we survey the development of anthropological theory on aging, especially within the past 20 years. Second, we consider how culture influences biological maturation and uses differential maturity in defining the life course. Third, theories of cultural transformation are examined which consider the consequences for different cohorts. Finally, we conclude with a consideration of the life course as a cultural unit that is essential to theories of human aging.

AGE IN ANTHROPOLOGICAL THEORY

Over a century ago the concept of *culture* was coined, and it became the central theoretical concept of anthropology. It has not remained a static concept nor the exclusive property of anthropology. Like many other concepts developed in the social sciences, it has permeated other disciplines and even become a part of popular culture. Culture is no longer seen as tradition or a complex of customs people are enculturated into and blindly follow like automatons. Over the past 20 years culture has come to be understood as a phenomenon people use in the practice and negotiation of daily life (Fry, 1985; Ortner, 1984).

In spite of paradigm shifts, three characteristics are the hallmarks of anthropological theory.

1. *Holism*. Intentionally spelled to be jargonistic, holism emphasizes context and continuities. This includes continuities between the biological and cultural sides of humans. It is mandatory that variables and their meanings be grounded in a context *before* they are abstracted in the evaluation of theory.

2. *Comparative*. Theories, to be adequately tested, should not be evaluated on the basis of data from only one culture or culture type. Data from a range of cultures (with known and theoretically salient variation) or from a sample of the 3,000 ± cultures is required. To do otherwise is to ignore the confounds and potentially spurious associations between variables due to uncontrolled and potentially unknown or overlooked conditions that are near constants within one research site or cultural type.

3. *Evolutionary*. Since our species has a nearly 100,000-year history (over 5 million years when we consider the hominid revolution), theories about humans must also be evaluated across time. Temporal comparisons are different from cultural comparisons because they deal with the twin evolutionary processes of (1) change and (2) continuity. The first is the transformation of cultures at both a general and a specific level (Sahlins & Service, 1960). The second is adaptation, or the processes working toward stability and the persistence of the patterns we study (Harding, 1960).

The reasons for holism, comparison, and concerns of stability and change rest in the ambitious agenda of anthropology: to study humans at all times in all places. Humans, in turn, are neither exclusively biological creatures nor have they transcended biology through the superorganic or cultural bases for their behavior. Instead, human behavior and social organization is shaped by both biology and culture. Since maturation and aging is a universal biological characteristic of every human being, every society symbolically encodes age differences and incorporates them into its social organization. Consequently, the holistic, comparative, and evolutionary nature of anthropological theory enables us to ascertain what is universal in the aging process. It also enables us to determine what is unique about how aging is experienced in a particular culture and what conditions are responsible for that situation.

Age and Anthropology

Early anthropology included age because aging is a universal feature of humans. Age, however, never became a major thrust of comparative research. There were other domains to chart, such as kinship or politics, and aging was not a social issue in the late 19th and early 20th centuries. On the other hand, it was not ignored. As early as 1929, Radcliffe-Brown coined the term "age grade" in an effort to clarify age organization terminology. Most ethnographies contained a mandatory chapter on the life cycle, describing the stages of life from infancy to old age. In spite of this, age was not really an integral part of ethnographic descriptions.

The exception to this comes from the ethnographic work in East Africa. There age is an explicit principle organizing males into age sets (e.g., Massai), generation sets (e.g., Boran), age villages (e.g., Nyakyusa), or age regiments (e.g., Zulu). Age organizations—understanding their inner workings and the conditions promoting them—remain a theoretical problem within social anthropology. The import of this theoretical corpus is not limited to this corner of anthropology but provides extreme cases through which to understand broader questions of age stratification, peer relations, and informal age grading (see below). The work on formal age systems also provided much of the foundations for the early work on age norms in the United States (Cain, 1963; Neugarten & Datan, 1973; Neugarten & Hagestad, 1976, 1985; Neugarten, Moore, & Lowe, 1965).

Focused anthropological work on aging began in 1945 with the publication of Simmons's *Role of the Aged in Primitive Society*. This much-cited work received the attention of gerontologists and mathematical anthropologists, but its seed lay dormant within anthropology for nearly two decades. Clark and Anderson's *Culture and Aging* (1967) initiated the past 20 years of intensifying research and theoretical maturation. The development of cultural theories of aging can be divided into three phases defined by the problems of concern: (1) *old* age, (2) ag*ing*, and (3) *age*.

Old Age

Simmons's work was truly pioneering. In the postwar years, the major concern of the fledgling discipline of gerontology was the welfare and well-being of older people. Simmons continued this concern in his use of the then new Human Relations Area Files to investigate the conditions promoting the status and treatment of older people. From these files, which topically ordered materials from existing ethnographies, Simmons assembled data on over 100 sociocultural variables for 71 societies. In spite of the problems inherent in secondary data analysis, his results reveal that aging is a complex phenomenon with goods and bads.

More recently, others have followed in Simmons's footsteps (e.g., Holmes, 1976). A methodology known as holocultural research has defined a sample of world cultures and improved usage of the files for statistical analysis. Questions asked of age parallel Simmons's in focusing exclusively on old people and in looking at status, esteem, prestige, and treatment. As a result of this research we now have more definitive answers on the comparative treatment and position of older adults.

On the good side, the factors promoting esteem of older people are (1) control of resources inclusive of information, (2) continuity in role shifts, (3) responsibility and continued involvement in valued activities, (4) the presence of extended families, and (5) socioeconomic homogeneity (Maxwell & Silverman, 1970; Press & McKool, 1972; Silverman & Maxwell, 1983). Environment and technological control also affect the prestige and treatment of older adults (Lee & Kezis, 1981; Sheehan, 1976). Harsh environments and foraging technology or shifting cultivation do not promote favorable treatment of the old, especially in the marginal or worst seasons (Glascock & Feinman, 1980; Maxwell, Silverman, & Maxwell, 1982).

Simmons's conclusions of the "living liability" of the overage has received substantiation. Killing and forsaking of the old is not that unusual. Contempt, too, is quite common (Maxwell & Maxwell, 1980). What triggers it? The Maxwells report that the loss of family is the most important factor, followed by change in appearance and loss of strength. Deference is not distributed uniformly, women receive less of it (Silverman & Maxwell, 1978). Death and lack of support, however, are not the fate of all old people. Only those who have passed the threshold into "decrepitude" are not supported and their death hastened. Older people who are "intact" are accorded high status and are treated well (Glascock, 1982; Glascock & Feinman, 1981, 1986).

Aging

This phase sees a movement away from status and treatment as the major variables and diversification of questions fueled by primary data collection and analysis. Clark (1967) hailed what she called the "Anthropology of Aging" as a new area for studies of culture and personality. It turned out to be this and more.

A necessary first step for this new wave of research was to go where old people were available. Consequently, the first to be studied were retirement communities, homes for the aged, and high-rise senior housing; older people living in run down hotels of the inner city; and people linked to health care facilities. Questions shifted very quickly from "How are they doing?" to "Why are they doing what they are doing?" For instance, as the empirical evidence mounted from studies of individual retirement communities,[2] it became apparent that the geriatric ghettos that had been forecast had not evolved. In these new developments, which had been intentionally created and marketed (Fry, 1977), residential segregation did not produce the undesirable situation of the old waiting to die alone, together. Instead we found these pioneering older people had created communities [the main exception is Jacobs (1974)]. In understanding why, theory building focused on the community formation process [see Keith (1980b, 1982b) for background and emergent factors promoting community formation].

Parallels are seen in other areas. In the inner city, SRO dwellers have an adaptation of loner, but they are not isolated. Explanations led to consideration of social networks and network maintenance (Cohen & Sokolovsky, 1980; Sokolovsky & Cohen, 1978, 1981). Discovering potentials for survival in these environments resulted in a delineation of their strengths (Bohannan, 1981; Eckert, 1979, 1980). Likewise, ethnicity was no longer viewed as another "tribal difference" in urban societies. Instead, mechanisms at work in these communities became the focus (Cool, 1980, 1981a, 1981b; Cuellar, 1978; Kiefer, 1971). Similarly, Clark and Anderson's work (1967) with mentally well and ill older adults in San Francisco resulted in a theory of developmental tasks and cultural values in late life.

Although the focus of aging research was primarily on the later stages of the life course, the outcome set the stage for the next phase of theory building. Accumulation of empirical data and conflicting conclusions call for theoretical revision and integration. As recently as a decade ago, it was possible to sum up the theoretical work in culture and aging by referring to less than five books and a handful of articles. This is impossible today. A number of volumes and texts have been published, mostly edited (e.g., Amoss & Harrel, 1981; Fry, 1980a, 1981; Holmes, 1983; Keith, 1979; Myerhoff & Simic, 1978; Sokolovsky, 1982, 1983; Sokolovsky & Sokolovsky, 1982). As we survey what we have accomplished, we must ask where we are going. Perhaps the future is already here. In this stage of research we see a transition through what Keith (1981) calls the "back to anthropology movement."

Age

A return to anthropology involves two major steps in theory building. First, we need to bring what we know about the last stages of life to anthropological theory (e.g., see Keith, 1982b). Do old people behave differently, just because they are old? Or are there other principles involved? Second, we must make a more radical shift, from concentrating on old age to a consideration of the entire life span and age or life stage as an integral variable in more traditional anthropological concerns. In spite of the life-span perspective being established well within both psychology and sociology (Featherman, 1981; Neugarten & Datan, 1973; Riley, 1979), its use in anthropological work is only in its infancy.

This phase is off to a good start. In 1981, under the leadership of Matilda White Riley, David Kertzer, and Jennie Keith, a workshop sponsored by the National Institute of Aging was held. Twelve anthropologists representing different perspectives and subfields within anthropology were invited to look at issues in their areas using age and the life span as the "window." The results have been published in *Age and Anthropological Theory* (Kertzer & Keith, 1984). Clearly, the return of the life-span perspective to anthropology will be theoretically productive. As we look at this new phase, it is also apparent that empirically we know very little about age and culture, and there is much work ahead.

MATURATION AND CULTURE

Nature and Culture

"Nature/culture," "raw/cooked," and "private/public" are all familiar dichotomies. At issue is culture, the learned meaningful forms (symbols, norms, technology) by which humans transcend natural vicissitudes and assert control over their existence. Like most constructs, there is no sharp boundary between what is natural and what is cultural. At the more public, cultural, ordered, and artificial end, we find more formal, explicit, standardized rules about behavior. Although the private domestic domain is cultural, it has more informal and implicit standards, with behavior responding to situational factors in daily life. Of the two, it is the public domain, the thing we call "society," that we study, precisely because it is more structured.

Where does age fit? Is it natural or cultural? Each society answers this question as age is incorporated into the social institutions of the society or becomes an institution in and of itself. Just as sex becomes gender differentiation, pedigrees become kinship, or genetic traits become racial castes, age becomes the basis of age grading and age differentiation. No culture ignores the biological base upon which it is built. The biological qualities of people must be incorporated into social life. By being made cultural, age is subject to cultural definition, which shapes the ways in which age is experienced within and across cultures.

Yet age remains a comparatively ignored variable in our studies of social structure. Age has been neglected as an integral part of comparative work for two reasons. First, age is seen as closer to nature and consequently as marginal to sociocultural research (LaFontaine, 1978) except as a demographic variable. Second, when viewed as a principle of social organization, age is seen as a characteristic of the actors. People are differentiated by age, and hence, age becomes a principle of role differentiation. Precisely because age is a biological quality, it is linked to what we call the infrastructure[3] of a culture. Consequently, it is seen as basic and elementary, only to be superseded by more complex and theoretically interesting principles ordering social life (Needham, 1974).

In unraveling age, nature, and culture, we must use the comparative method. We must use it in two ways. The first is to look at age in nature by looking at other social animals (e.g., the nonhuman primates). Second, we look at age in culture by examining both formal and informal age differentiation. The reason is to discover what is uniquely human about the treatment of age.

Age in Nature

Now that the "second generation" of primate studies is well under way, we no longer have the "baboon's-eye view" of the nonhuman primates. This generation not only has taken us beyond zoos and captivity to natural ecological settings but has documented the diversity that is present among our nearest relatives. In spite of diversity, there are generalizations that may be made concerning age. First, these animals live in social groups the members of which differ in maturity. The life stages that primatologists conventionally use in codifying their observations are infant, juvenile, subadult, adult, and old. Although mostly determined by the social context in which the animals are living, these stages are demarcated by changes in hair color, size, or sexual maturity (Jolly, 1985). Of special note is the fact that an old primate is an oddity outside of zoos. For older female monkeys definite roles in troop life have been observed. Postreproductive female macaques ascend the dominance hierarchies, bringing benefits to their offspring, while older langur females defend their "grandchildren"[4] against the attacks of males (Hrdy, 1981).

Comparisons of humans to other primates reveal enormous differences. The two that are most salient to aging are maturation rates and interdependency. Human infants are noted for their helplessness and slowness to grow up. Born 75% less mature than most primates, it takes nearly 100% longer for a human infant to reach maturity than for the slowest-maturing nonhuman primate, the chimpanzee (18 years as compared to 10 years for the chimpanzee) (Washburn, 1981). This slow maturation rate has remarkable implications for the cognitive abilities of the organism and for the information that may be acquired prior to and through maturity.

Length of maturity also has implications for group organization, interdependency, and support available to an individual (Lovejoy, 1981). Nonhuman primates have their mother only until they are weaned. After that point they must forage for themselves. Benefits of group membership include protection from predation, mutual grooming, sociality, and access to mates. Unlike the human group, however, group benefits are not based on exchange between members. In human groups, the blueprint is based on a triadic interdependency. Parents are dependent on each other, and their children are dependent on both parents (not just the mother). After weaning, children continue to receive food and care. All human children can expect to receive food from others, and as they mature they will never forage nor work exclusively for themselves. Humans are involved in networks of exchanges, reciprocity, and food sharing that extend well beyond reproduction. Thus, in human groups, individuals of different maturation levels are supporting each other reciprocally: the mature, the immature, and the postmature. It is the sheer amount of support in human groups produced by this interdependency and resultant division of labor that accounts for the appearance of the postmature or old (Dolhinow, 1984).

Age in Culture

With interdependency as a keystone of human society, a major problem that must be resolved is to keep individuals accumulating *and* discharging social and material capital. One way in which this is done is through the creation and classification of differences and the relationships uniting them. Culturally, people are grouped into social categories. Individuals acquire social identities with reciprocal rights and duties (roles/status) guiding interactions and exchange. Social differences make exchange possible and foster interdependency within the uniquely human divisions of labor. The resulting solidarity may be based on extreme differences (organic) or minimal differences (mechanical) (Durkheim, 1893), but there are differences. Among the axes differentiating individuals, age and gender are universal simply because they are biological attributes. "Youth" and "elder" may be a minimum, with greater refinements in grading the continuum from birth to death being conditioned by cultural understandings of age.

Age joins another principle of differentiation, *ranking*, in stratifying people by age. The age stratification paradigm developed by Riley and her associates (Riley, 1985; Riley, Johnson, & Foner, 1972) represents a major theoretical breakthrough in sociological theories of aging. Age stratification uses biological succession and time to rank individuals by seniority. Stratification by age, however, is unlike other forms of stratification. Strata based on differentials of wealth, access to resources or prestige, and other inequalities limits mobility across strata. In contrast, upward mobility through age strata is universal, reflecting the impermanence of age. Unlike other ascriptive bases of social life (e.g., gender or genetic traits defining caste membership), age is not an enduring characteristic of individuals. Age accumulates or chronologically increases as lives progress through time.

Theoretically the impermanence of age has produced several problems. Most notable are *age-period-cohort effects*, which have been widely discussed (e.g., Baltes, 1968; Riley, 1985; Riley et al., 1985; Schaie, 1965; Uhlenberg, this volume). As time passes, organisms age, social roles change, and societies are transformed, producing rather obvious confounds and analytic headaches for researchers. On another level in building a comparative theory of age, we are faced with the problem that, empirically, we find age as a separate institution only in very few cultures. It may be that an impermanent quality is not the raw material upon which to build institutions.

Building enduring social differences and social organization on changeable characteristics is like running down the up escalator, yet it is done. Extreme cases reveal structure where it seems improbable or, because of its ordinariness, is not apparent. Age differentiation is a formal principle of organization in a small number of world societies, providing a rich natural laboratory to examine age and social differentiation.

Formal Age Grading

As we have learned more empirically about these societies, the variability has proved surprising. Age is clearly quite malleable in its use. Initially, formal age organizations were a part of the ethnography of the East African Cattle Complex. Here men were either initiated into an age set as they approached puberty or joined the generation set at the proper structural distance from their fathers (e.g., in the Gada system this is five sets or 40 years). Once formed, the age mates constitute an egalitarian, corporate group collectively progressing through the social grades. Elsewhere in Africa age villages and age regiments[5] have been reported. In the Americas formal age organization takes a different twist, with age sets being salient only in young adulthood among the Akwe-Shavante of Brazil (Maybury-Lewis, 1967/1974, 1984). On the Great Plains men bought and sold their age societies and the rights to songs and ritual paraphernalia as they progressed through the grades.

In spite of diversity (see Bernardi, 1985, for a typology), we find commonalities. First, formalized age grading is primarily a male phenomenon (Kertzer & Madison, 1981). Second, being male, formalized age grades are cultural and are within or constitute the public domain (Fortes, 1984). Third, formalized age grades are based on structural age (Bernardi, 1985). Structural age is different from physiological age because it is a social category. Actual physiological differences are ignored, with age mates assigned the common identity of age-class membership for the purposes of social organization. Fourth, the age classes constitute a pan-societal hierarchy of seniority, with status and rights assigned to each grade (e.g., initiate, warrior, householder, elder, post-elder). In opposition to the inequality of seniority across age groups, within age classes we find an ethos of equality (Almagor, 1978). Finally, these age systems constitute an integrated political and social system as boys are initiated into a new or recycled age set and as men progress through the grades.

Why take control of time? Why give age the full cultural treatment of categorization, symbols, and ritual? Explanations have focused on three issues. The first has examined the internal workings of age systems and a meta-language to describe these systems (Stewart, 1977). The second comprises a set of functional theories asking what the age groups do for the society in question (Kertzer, 1978; Ritter, 1980). Finally, the third examines the conditions promoting age as an organizing principle (Keith, 1982b). In this chapter we shall consider only the latter.

Primary in promoting age as a basis for group formation is a basic principle that usually sharpens the boundaries between groups and categories. The principle is conflict. Age conflict occurs when younger members must compete with older for basic resources or for what is considered valuable and limited in its availability. With age competition for the material basis of life, age is escalated as a basis for group formation, and conflict becomes collectivized.[6] Age conflict is generated in other social institutions, notably kinship and economics. Kinship is universally an age-heterogeneous institution and is a potential breeding ground for age conflict. This is especially true when descent groups are engaged in a domestic mode of production (Sahlins, 1972).[7] Both production and consumption decisions are made within these units, and sons remain the junior partners until they reach social maturity. Conflict is almost inevitable when son and father want and need the same resources (land, cattle, wives) for their careers—father to advance and son to begin. Formal age groups are a powerful counterbalance. In keeping "good company," generations may be residentially separated (Ottenberg, 1971; Wilson, 1951), or power over a son may be shifted to another man in the formal age organization (Spencer, 1976), and age and kin become important themes in men's lives (Evans-Prichard, 1940; Maybury-Lewis, 1984).

Also, social discontinuities and transitions across age and kinship bring age to the forefront, especially if they are conflictual (Keith, 1985). Age allies are important in bridging discontinuities. The entrance to and exit from social maturity require the most from individuals because they involve shifts between the domestic and public domains. Eisenstadt (1956) hypothesized that age-homogeneous groups appear when "the family or kinship unit cannot ensure, or even impedes, the attainment of full social status by its members" (p. 54).

Conflict does not disappear from these age set societies (Foner & Kertzer, 1978), but it is structured, controlled, and ritualized. Conflict, if unchecked, will destroy the basic fabric of any society. When age conflict is generated by generational succession, it may not have a resolution. Negative reciprocity is the end result of conflict. Combatants cease the giving and taking, and interdependency dissolves. The human costs are high, and fortunately very few societies experience this—one example being the Ik studied by Turnbull (1972).

Informal Age Grading

Extreme cases are instructive, but the majority of cases are not extreme. Most human males are not members of age sets. Age, however, is no less cultural. All humans are age-graded. As in the case of age sets, age grades also involve the classification of differences. What is being classified is a combination of functional age, age statuses, and life stage. Informal age grading is markedly different from formal age grading. Primarily, the grades are not institutionalized into corporate groups, formed by explicit criteria of recruitment, with explicit norms for each grade, that dominate and define public life.[8] Age is not structural age but is functional and reflective of individual life careers. Age-homogeneous groups may be found, but unlike age classes, they are not pan-societal in their membership. Seniority across and equality within age grades may be the rule. However, since the boundaries of age grades are not defined by explicit recruitment and transition criteria, other lines of equality and inequality will blur age alliances and oppositions. Finally, because they are not institutionalized, a prime characteristic of informal age grading is intracultural variation. The numbers of grades are differentiated, and the chronological boundaries of grades are quite variable. Consequently, informal age grading does not result in an integrated social system in and of itself by comparison with age class systems. In spite of the ambiguities involved, informal age grading is the most common form of age stratification.

Precisely because it is so common and ubiquitous, we have comparatively few studies that have empirically attacked the question of informal age grading directly. The earliest studies addressed the question of age norms (Neugarten & Moore, 1968; Neugarten, Moore, & Lowe, 1965). Although age statuses, age identities, and age transitions have emerged as important topics, age grades and the cultural meanings and parameters of age grades have been neglected.[9] Methodologically, the task is complicated once one realizes that the meaning of a simple age category, e.g., *middle age* or *old*, may not be the same for any two people (Jeffers, Eisdorfer, & Busse, 1962). Consequently, one cannot begin with the age grades themselves, but must devise a strategy which delineates culturally significant markers of age and then use these to examine the ways the life course is divided into stages or age grades.

Presently, we have four studies,[10] three in the United States and one in Hong Kong, which have investigated informal age grades. All of these projects employed a common methodology, derived from cognitive anthropology or ethnosemantics,[11] to investigate the meaning of age and the differentiation of adulthood into life stages. A sine qua non of ethnosemantic research is that it systematically investigates the "emic" or the native view. The units are native categories and their semantic structure or defining features. The results from these four studies demonstrate cross-site variability in the cultural markers of age, intracultural variation in age grades, and remarkable similarities across sites on the underlying dimensions of the life course.

Cultural Markers of Age

In order to begin to think like a native, the first question is, "What do I need to know to . . . ?" In this case, we want to make judgments about age groupings, and hence, we need to know what salient information we must have in order to make those judgments. The social attributes that serve as age markers share a good deal of commonality across sites, but there are differences. The similarities are not too surprising since all four communities are parts of industrialized nation states (an international port of trade and, in the United States, a small town, a suburb, and a mid-size city). Information on marital status, children, and work status was required information at all four sites (see Table 20-1). Education and living arrangements proved salient in the U.S. sites. In Swarthmore people needed information on the status of parents, whereas in Momence additional information was required on home ownership and on organizational involvement. To generalize empirically, the social indicators of age are locally defined. This is especially true in contexts in which the social field is smaller. Hong Kong and Lafayette are the most urbanized of the research sites and share a core of age markers. Swarthmore, followed by Momence, are less urbanized, with the markers of age reflecting local concerns, class differences, and community cohesiveness.

TABLE 20-1. Social Characteristics Needed to Make Judgments About Age in Four Study Communities (Ikels, Keith, & Fry, 1987; Fry, 1976, 1980)

Attribute dimension	Momence, 1983 (Fry)	Swarthmore, 1983 (Keith)	Lafayette, 1972 (Fry)	Hong Kong, 1983 (Ikels)
Gender	+	+	+	+
Marital status	+	+	+	+
Children's status	+	+	+	+
Parents' status	−	+	−	−
Living arrangements	+	+	+	−
Housing tenure	+	−	−	−
Education	+	+	+	−
Work status	+	+	+	+
Organization involvement	+	−	−	−

+, information salient; −, information not salient.

Variation

Intracultural variation in age grades is also noted across all sites. Within each site the average number of groups differentiated was five, with most people seeing between three and six groups. The extremes of this variation are notable, ranging from 0 ("it is all one flow" or "age isn't important") to as many as 9, 10, 11 or even 15 divisions of adulthood. Variability and ambiguity prompt several questions. First, what promotes them? Second, what are the consequences of variability in age differentiation? Third, with such variability and potential "noise," is there any order to the age grades?

When considering the questions of causes and consequences, we must note that our generalizations are based on four sites that are parts of industrialized societies noted for internal differentiation. These societies are also literate, keep records, and rely on vital statistics. Thus, age ambiguity disappears when people switch to chronology (to the lament of gerontologists recognizing the insensitivity of the facade of chronological age). Thus, chronology becomes a proxy for social and functional age, with age ambiguity seemingly reduced through the exactitude of calendar years. Empirically, the question of age ambiguity and informal age grading has yet to be resolved for societies that are not literate and do not maintain a census relying on birth and death certificates.

Factors promoting individuals to see more age groups are both structural and situational. Presently, the variables positively associated with greater differentiation in age groups are education, stratification, age, and social networks, especially the age heterogeneity of kin networks (Fry, 1976). The implication is that people see as many age grades as they need, conditioned by their position in the social structure and by circumstance.

Dimensions of the Life Course

Despite differences in salient age statuses across communities and within site variation, the underlying regularities display remarkable agreement. Because respondents within each site were presented with the same stimuli (social persona described by the statuses marking age) and made judgments about age similarity, these data can be analyzed through multidimensional scaling (Kruskal & Wish, 1978). This technique produces a geometric plot of the objects being scaled, which then must be interpreted. These interpretations can then be compared across sites. Here we are extremely fortunate in that we have a similar analysis of data from the Massai (Kirk & Burton, 1977), a society with formal age classes.[12]

Interpretations of the two-dimensional "pictures" of the life course reveal similarities in the dimensions identified (see Table 20-2). The first dimension is clearly related to the developmental cycle of domestic units (family, marriage, children's development and eventual maturation). The second dimension, on

TABLE 20-2. Comparison of Cultural Dimensions Indicated in Two-Dimensional Multidimensional Scaling Plots of Social Persona Representative of Different Positions (Age Status) in the Life Course in Five Communities (Fry, 1980; Keith, Fry, & Ikels, 1984)

Community	Dimension 1 (Family cycle)	Dimension 2 (Engaging in and assuming the responsibility of adult status)
Hong Kong (Ikels)	Domestic cycle	Family burden (responsibility)
Lafayette (Fry)	Reproductive cycle	Engagement
Swarthmore (Keith)	Parental status	Engagement/responsibility
Momence (Fry)	Domestic cycle	Establishment
Massai (Kirk & Burton)	Marriage	Responsibility

the other hand, is linked to involvement in statuses entailing responsibility. The first dimension reflects the domestic or private domain, while the second transects both private and public domains. The concordance in dimensions of the life course is not a total mystery. Age and the social indicators of age are bound to the infrastructure of a culture. Productive and reproductive roles are based on the biological maturity and capacity of individuals performing those roles [see Halperin (1984) for a discussion of age and productive roles in differing economies]. Responsibility reflects the interdependency necessitated by slow-maturing children and the fact that humans do not produce exclusively for themselves.

Gender Differences and Age

Gender, like age, is also bound to the infrastructure of a culture because sex is a biological characteristic of humans. Gender, unlike age, is a permanent quality splitting actors, the roles they perform, and society into male and female halves. Notably, females are closer to nature by being linked to the private or domestic sphere by child rearing, whereas males usually dominate the public domain (Chodorow, 1974; Ortner, 1974). A rather obvious truism, consequently, is that the experience of aging is quite different for men and for women.

Theories about the differences have centered on repeated observations from many unrelated cultures regarding a male/female reversal in late life (Gutmann, 1975). Postreproductive women "become one of the boys." These women become assertive, often drinking and joking with adult males as well as attaining considerable power in public affairs. Older men, on the other hand, become more passive, "domesticated," and turn their attention to spiritual matters. Although there is little argument over the late-life shifts, there is disparity over the explanations. Psychological and social-structural hypotheses explain the male/female reversals in late life.

Psychological Explanations

Through his cross-cultural studies of men, Gutmann (1966, 1968, 1974; Goldstein & Gutmann, 1972; Neugarten & Gutmann, 1958) has documented a systematic shift from "active mastery" to "passive mastery." The shift is in the opposite direction for women. Gutmann (1975) argues this reversal is universal and is linked to the "emergency of parenting." The interdependency required between parents necessitates suppression of certain tendencies. Females surrender aggressive tendencies to provide emotional support while males give up dependency needs that would interfere with physical and instrumental support. Once children mature and assume responsibility for themselves, each gender "recaptures" the characteristics that were repressed.

Social-Structural Explanations

Other researchers have explained the shift through a consideration of social structures and the sources of power available to men and women. Maturation of children changes the status of a woman as she ages. Earlier restrictions guarding her sexuality are reduced, she begins to exercise authority over junior kin, and she becomes eligible for special status (Brown, 1982; Brown & Kerns, 1985). Indeed, the ethnographic literature is full of examples of senior women becoming the managers of the female labor force in large polygamous, extended households. Because the domestic domain is the female domain, women are socialized to be flexible (Cool, 1981b) as they experience variation in gender roles across the life span and endure loss (Klein, 1975; Sinnott, 1977). Men, on the other hand, build their power in the public domain. Consistency is a theme in men's lives, which leaves less opportunity to rehearse or anticipate age-related role losses. Once they can no longer meet the physical demands, men may well find their long-standing influence in the public arena diminished (Cool & McCabe, 1983). In contrast, women can consolidate their power in later life.

Theoretical pluralism is the sign of a maturing science. The merits of multiple hypotheses can be resolved only with empirical data. We need a theory that seeks to specify the conditions under which the male/female reversal occurs and those under which it does not occur. Two studies (one among the Mekranoti of Brazil and the other with the Irish in Chicago) report that the reversal does not occur, since both men and women display more active mastery (Cohler & Leiberman, 1979; Werner, 1981). Second, we need data that incorporates the strategies available to both men and women at different times in their life courses. Third, we need a broader sample of societies to include those differing in degree of gender differentiation.

Age and Cultural Values

Values are the valences of social life: the positives and negatives, the goods and bads. From the time young children learn the rights from the wrongs, values will shape and fuel sentiments for the rest of the life span. Because values are acquired early and entail absolutes, they endure and are more resistant to change than the norms ordering social life. Thus, values are unlikely to change with aging. Yet mental health can be affected by adherence to certain values in the face of declines in old age. These are the values basic to maintaining adult status and interdependence with others: independence and its opposite, dependence.

In their study of mentally well and mentally ill older people in San Francisco, Clark and Anderson (1967) found that those who continued to subscribe to prevailing American values were the ones who experienced difficulties, frustrations, and hospitalizations for mental problems. On the other hand, older adults who had resolved the conflicts between their abilities and values emphasizing independence had fewer problems and better mental health. The adaptive tasks involved in resolving the discrepancies between values and abilities involve recognition of limitations combined with redefinitions, substitutions, reassessments, and reintegration of values and goals. Variables promoting this accommodation are a greater number of social relationships and more active social networks. Significant others with whom one can be *inter*dependent ameliorate the increase in dependence that comes with declining abilities.

The values of interdependency are based on a keystone of human society: reciprocity and exchange. The positive side of this value, independence, is the ability and willingness to give. By giving, however, one creates obligations and may immediately or eventually collect and take back (Mauss, 1925/1967). Others are expected to be independent also. The negative, dependence, is nonreciprocal taking. Nonreciprocity is tolerated in certain roles with definite limitations (Clark, 1972). These are, for example, in times of crisis or illness, during rites of passage, or during infancy and childhood. Chronic dependency borders on freeloading, which in no society receives prestige. If dependency is the companion of old age, then older people are accorded lower status.

Independence, self-reliance, and rugged individualism, however, are not universally the central value of all or even most cultures. American emphasis on independence (Hsu, 1961; Williams, 1970) as an ideal reflects an economic organization that emphasizes productivity and immediacy in balancing reciprocity. This, combined with sufficient wealth to maintain separate households, makes any and all exchanges across household units obvious to those involved. The pain of receiving when one always had and should be giving is felt both by the older recipients and by their children. Dependency in nonindustrial societies has different ramifications (Goody, 1976). Households usually are not as differentiated, and exchanges follow the norm of generalized reciprocity (Sahlins, 1972). The balancing of giving and taking is not calculated in a temporal framework. Thus, in the complicated and delicate process of maintaining interdependency, across-generational reciprocity can be viewed as adult children regarding the care of their parents as reciprocity for their own nurturance in childhood. Regardless of a collectivist or individualist orientation, all cultures must deal with dependency and how individuals who are dependent are evaluated.

Independence/dependence is not the only value dichotomy salient to age. Within family groups the value of filial piety and familism itself shapes the sentiments about intergenerational relations. Filial piety is an ethic requiring children to be obedient, to fulfill obligations, and to show respect for their parents with near-religious devotion during and after their lifetime (Ikels, 1980). Generations are bonded (younger to older, children to parents) in a reciprocal but asymmetrical fashion. Likewise, familism bonds generations. The evaluation of family as the most important of all social groups places the family in the center of the lives of its members, young and old alike (Johnson, 1983). These are values of the domestic sphere and generally benefit the senior generations.

CULTURAL TRANSFORMATION AND CHANGING OPPORTUNITIES

Cultures, like age, are impermanent. Social structures are subject to natural selection in accommodating to environmental variables, resource availability, and population. Cultures are not isolated entities. People interact with members of other cultures, and usually they do not hesitate to borrow whatever they see as beneficial. Also, humans are innovative and playful as they use culture to negotiate their environments and other humans. In addressing the phenomenon of culture change, we must consider three questions. First, what is it that is changing? Second, what is the rate and what are the repercussions of the change? Finally, who benefits from the change? In this section we will examine macro-processes of transformation, namely modernization, and then look at micro-processes of change.

Modernization

Perhaps the greatest social transformation of all time is the advent of stratified societies. Some 5,000 years ago this occurred in what has been called the Urban Revolution. The net effect of this change has been increases in population, social differentiation, inequality, productivity, and wealth. The latest wave of this transformation is the Industrial Revolution, which linked the globe into a world economic system (Wallerstein, 1979). This not only further increased the above trends exponentially but markedly increased societal interdependence through an alteration in production. The use of fossilized fuels and inanimate sources of energy differentiated production from consumption. The basic domestic mode of production was replaced with an industrial mode of production and an extensive division of labor.

Extractive and productive technology requires capital investment, an organization of labor, and a mobilization of labor that is beyond the capabilities of most families. Thus, the labor of family members is exchanged for cash to enable that unit to continue to consume. The advent of industry triggered the process of modernization, which has transformed social life all over the globe, although not equally.

How has modernization affected aging? Population first increased and the age structure altered (Myers, 1985). Advances in medicine, combined with intensified subsistence, more wealth, and a need for labor, reduced mortality and increased fertility. At first the population became young, with older people increasing in absolute numbers but becoming rare in comparison with young adults and children. Following the demographic transition and the reduction of fertility, populations began to age. Older people have become common and are projected to constitute as much as 20% of the total population in most nations. Theoretically, the age composition of a population is an important variable. In its abundance, a cohort, in making demands or by constituting a sizable market through collective purchasing power, can shape culture (e.g., the American youth culture of the 1960s and early 1970s and the senior movement of the 1970s and 1980s) (see also Uhlenberg, this volume). On the other hand, in their scarcity, an age group may become especially valued.

Second, modernization has differentially affected the experience of cohorts. Our earliest research considered the status and treatment of the oldest cohorts. The conclusion is that, as modernization proceeds, the status and treatment of older people decreases (Cowgill & Holmes, 1972). Cowgill has formalized a model isolating demographic variables, medical technology, social organizational and economic factors, and urbanization, as well as education, religion, and values, as the salient variables interacting to depress the status of the aged (see Cowgill, 1974, p. 141; Cowgill, 1986). Over a decade of research has revised modernization theory. Modernization is no longer seen as linearly related to reduced status for the old. Through the addition of more data and a broader sample, our image of the relationship is that of a cycle (Finley, 1982). Initially, the status of the aged increases with the shift from foraging to horticulture. Then there is a decline in the early phases of modernization (Lee & Kezis, 1981), followed by an improvement in the later stages (Palmore, 1976; Palmore & Manton, 1974).

Modernization theory has been sharply attacked on two fronts. The first is concerned with the nature of the process, and the second focuses on the application of the theory to the experience of aging. Modernization is complicated, and to propose it as a universal and uniform process occurring across and within differentiated and ethnically diverse societies may well be an oversimplification (Tipps, 1973). An alternative is the world-system perspective (Wallerstein, 1979), which considers asymmetry in power and exchange between core and peripheral areas. It may be that this latter perspective will prove productive in comparative studies of aging (Hendricks, 1982).

Empirical questions have been raised regarding how well modernization orders the data. From cross-national surveys on attitudes toward older people and modernity of the society we have inconclusive and contradictory results (Arnhoff, Leon, & Lorge, 1964; Bengtson, Dowd, Smith, & Inkles, 1975). The study by Bengtson et al. also revealed that intracultural variation (individual modernity) is not consistent with cross-national variation (societal modernity). Likewise, historical research investigating before/after differences has questioned the process of modernization. The timing and sequencing of proportions of aged (Laslett, 1985), the appearance of retirement (Quadagno, 1982), and the undermining of the authority of the aged (Fischer, 1977) are not consistent with the predictions of modernization theory. The situation of the aged in preindustrial Europe and America (Achenbaum, 1978; Achenbaum & Stearn, 1978) certainly is not consistent with an image of "paradise lost."

Specific Processes

Theories, in generalizing, simplify complex phenomena. Modernization is elegant and parsimonious in capturing the general processes that have shaped the contemporary world. Yet, like most general processes, it can be documented empirically only at the most superficial levels. To empirically investigate change requires data from specific historical and cultural contexts (Laslett, 1976). In these contexts, because of generational succession, cohorts will experience change differently (Foner, 1984) as they take advantage of and manipulate changing opportunity structures. Specific processes differentially affecting cohorts are migration, relocation, barriers to participation, and revivalistic reactions.

Migration

Mobilization of labor results in the migration of the young to the cities, leaving the old in rural villages. Rural populations become old populations and local patterns of interdependency become disrupted because there is an absence of younger personnel to fulfill obligations. Out-migration usually works to the disadvantage of the old. For instance, in Nepal, elderly Sherpas must face their old age alone because the emigration of youngest sons has seriously disrupted the family system. Otherwise active, healthy elders are dissatisfied with their lot (Goldstein & Beall, 1981, 1982). Likewise, a four-fold population decline in western Ireland has devastated the gerontocracy of Irish peasantry reported by Arensberg (1937) in the 1930s. Instead, we have reports of mental illness, a collapse in community cooperation, and a marked reduction in support of the old by the young (Scheper-Hughs, 1983).

Relocation

Creation of an industrial infrastructure sometimes necessitates the removal and relocation of local populations to make way for progress (e.g., highways or hydroelectric dams). The ability to adapt to relocation, to recoup losses, and to regain control of resources may be cohort-specific. In Zambia in the 1950s, resettlement of the Tonga in the Gwembe district because of a hydroelectric project wiped out lineage holdings. In rebuilding and claiming new land, many elders were not able to recoup their losses because of the premium placed on physical strength necessary to clear new fields (Colson & Scudder, 1981).

Barriers to Participation

Altered opportunity favors skills that are more universal in their application. Standard languages are favored over regional dialects. Formal education certifies the acquisition of selected abilities, namely, literacy and mathematics. Lack of skills constitutes an effective barrier to full participation in new opportunities. The cohort most likely affected is the old. In New Guinea, former Asmat head-hunters find the last phase of their lives meaningless. Instead of being *tesmaypit* (big men and leaders), they are now in a ritual void (Van Arsdale 1981a, b). The imposition of national Indonesian rule has favored those who speak Indonesian. Younger men are now the leaders with bilingualism being the key that opens the door to the opportunities within the nation-state. Similarly, as the division of labor changes with demands for a skilled labor force, the lack of an education effectively limits participation and blocks upward mobility. The cohorts most likely to acquire the newer skills and education are the young, since the mature and postmature adults are already well involved in their life careers. Opportunity to acquire these skills, however, may not be restricted by age alone; an even more important factor is position in existing social strata.

Revivalistic Reactions

Change is not always forward-looking nor centered on the material basis of life. People also control information and knowledge of the ideal. When that knowledge is valued, we find it is a resource. On the northwest coast of the United States, the Coast Salish elders have experienced the benefits of an interest in revitalizing the cultural knowledge of the earlier ways (Amoss, 1981a, b). Because of their knowledge of the rituals, the old ways and the traditional culture, older people are being sought out by younger people. They find themselves central and indispensable as they dominate and recreate the revised rituals.

THE LIFE COURSE AS A CULTURAL UNIT

Theoretically age is not an "easy" variable, that is, one to be conceptually and operationally defined with few issues to be resolved. The only thing that makes it appear to be easy is the fact that it occurs in time, and time in industrialized societies is easy to measure because of the tyranny of the clock and the calendar. Age is difficult because, on the level of the individual, it changes through time. Also, it is occurring on several levels simultaneously. Biologically, organisms are conceived, born, grow up, achieve adulthood, and then experience changes in function associated with advanced age. Socially, cohorts move through age status structures of their societies. Psychologically, individuals are changed and incorporate these changes into their identities. With age change occurring on at least three levels simultaneously, we do have difficulty in modeling the timetables that age us (Featherman & Petersen, 1986).

It seems as though we may have a problem with our unit. Units that are impermanent, with change coming in a near-continuum of gradation, present problems. We are forced to divide a unit such as age into stages, periods, or cohorts to create theoretically productive units. Thus, the differentiation of "old" from the continuum of age and the subsequent discussions of how to define it mark the beginning of serious inquiry into aging. The life-course perspective represents further theoretical advances for both psychology and sociology. Adult lives moving through time, social structure, and history define our frame of analysis. However, because time is involved, we must deal with the issues of impermanence and confounds (Nydegger, 1981). Perhaps it is time to push the advances made in life-course research further, to a consideration of the life course as a cultural unit (Fry & Keith, 1981).

As a cultural unit, the life course transcends individuals because it is a part of the superorganic. Consequently, it is a stable unit, although subject to change, as is any part of a culture. A further advantage of the life course as our unit is that it is universal, since all cultures in some way institutionalize the life course. If the life course becomes our unit, we must face basic theoretical issues in modeling social organization. Models of society are scientific attempts to abstract, simplify, and clarify the phenomena under investigation in ways that folk models of the same phenomena do not. Scientific models are more contrived, systematic, and subject to the crucible of empirical evaluation. Being contrived and systematic, they are also developed for an explicit purpose.

For what purposes are we using and can we use the window of the life course in modeling social organization? A rather basic consideration is our reference points. Are we examining the linkages between social units? Or are we studying the linkages between individuals and social units?[13] The life-course perspective can accommodate both, but probably not equally well in all situations. For instance, if linkages between social units are our concern, the cultural unit of the life course may prove most productive in societies with age class systems. Here, age is structural age. Age is the criterion for recruitment and definition of a social unit, age set, generation set, and the like. Relationships within the unit are defined; relationships with junior and senior units are collectively clarified; and relationships to other social institutions (especially kinship) are demarcated.

On the other hand, if our concern is the linkages of individuals to social institutions, the life course may prove to be a productive cultural unit in a wider range of societies. An attractive feature of the life course is that it directly confronts the interface between individuals and society, biology and culture. Maturational changes are socially recognized and culturally become meaningful. The life course is the cultural understanding of age, the time between birth and death. As individuals grow older, they experience more of the life course, and their linkages to and participation in social institutions change.

As a researchable cultural unit, the life course is challenging: if we want to use this unit in our research, we must face issues of theoretical conceptualization. First, how can we conceptualize this unit in such a way that it is seen as a part of the universal pattern of all cultures? Second, in what ways does this unit vary as we begin to ask questions of causes of differing life-course trajectories (both intracultural and cross-cultural) as well as the consequences of these differences?

Conceptualization

At a bare minimum, the life course consists of time, maturation, and cultural definitions and age norms, all of which are subject to cultural interpretation and to change as societies accommodate and respond to circumstance and major historical events. Time, clearly, is a cultural construct. From the vantage point of industrialized societies, time is linear, dominated by the progression of hours, months, and years. This is by no means universal. Other metaphors capture time—circles, cycles—since time consists of a sense of duration, periodicity, and change (Leach, 1961). Likewise, the continuum of maturation is divided into life stages and infused with cultural meaning, social markers, and age norms to define life trajectories. Hence, the life course is a cognitive and normative unit—cognitive in the sense that it is culturally defined and normative in that individuals have expectations about how they should progress through cultural time.

Variability

Life courses, being culturally defined, are variable. Our challenge is to explore the intracultural and cross-cultural variability before we can begin to develop theories about the causes and consequences of differences in the life course. Our research agenda begins with rather basic questions of ways the life course is conceived and evaluated. A few of these questions are as follows:

1. *Perceptions of the life course as a unit.* To what extent is the life course seen, planned for, and evaluated as an integrated unit? Do lives have definite trajectories, or are they seen as an amalgamation of threads in multiple domains? For instance, the Hindu Asram system with its "four stages of life" envisions a life plan for worldly existence and eventual rebirth (Vatuk, 1980). Metaphors capture life careers. Among the Quechua of the Peruvian Andes, vitality is earth. Life unfolds with increasing vigor, to decline only as the "earth supply" is left behind in the climb through life (Holmberg, cited in Smith, Holmberg, Hughes, Rustom, & Rowe, 1961). On the other hand, agreement about the metaphors and the stages of life may be low. Life courses can be seen as responding to circumstance and opportunity with little integration, which suggests that the life course is not institutionalized in such societies.

2. *Uniformity or multiplicity in life pathways.* Is the life course monolithic or is it seen as filled with choice and multiple paths? In Atchatlan, Guatemala, the life course for Indians is monolithic with little room for variation and experimentation. On the other hand, the mestizos of the same village, who are linked to the Guatemalan national social structure, have diverse careers dependent upon contacts, skills, education, opportunities, and goals (Moore, 1973). In contrasting Tahitians with Nepalese, Levy (cited in LeVine, 1978) found Tahitians have no sense of alternative. The Nepalese, contrastingly, view their life courses as filled with branching paths. One hypothesis is that societies that are more differentiated (urban) offer more choice, and consequently the life course is plural in its pathways. This is certainly reinforced by life-course studies in the United States (Neugarten & Hagestad, 1976, 1985).

3. *Parameters of the life course.* What defines the life course? What are the markers of age? What do people need to know to make a judgment about age? Certainly, these are likely to be subject to specific cultural elaboration. Yet our

present evidence suggests that domestic arrangements, reproductive roles, and roles entailing adult responsibilities and work may constitute a minimal core.

4. *Differentiation.* Age grades partition the life course into significant stages. What are the consequences of the degree of differentiation? One study suggests that greater differentiation in age classes reduces age conflict (Nadel, 1952). Social age and physical abilities are more congruent when age grades are more differentiated. Fewer age classes produce incongruency since physically vigorous men arbitrarily become socially old in their mid- to late twenties with considerable resentment.

5. *Transitions across life stages.* Transitions mark the entrances and exits to and from age grades. Empirically, we first need to know what the significant transitions punctuating the life course are. Biology and culture potentially become closely coordinated in life-course transitions. Birth, puberty, reproduction, and death are transformed as ritual superimposes symbols upon biological facts. Do cultures use primarily biology? Do some cultures ignore or skip over some of the biological basics?

Transitions can be abrupt or gradual. Benet (1974) reports continuity and moderation in the lives of long-lived Abkhasians. Similarly, Eskimos see no peak to life, only a gradual curve of increasing respect (Hughes, in Smith et al., 1961). Gradualness and continuity are also reported for the working class of industrialized smaller towns of Germany (Weatherford, 1981). Transitions may also involve choice. Marriage, education, jobs all may involve decisions. On the other hand, puberty and functionality do not involve choice. Even such transitions as parenthood or retirement may not involve much choice on the part of individuals. One hypothesis is that gradualness and control promote more satisfaction with the transition.

6. *Evaluation of life stages.* Life is a mix of goods and bads. To what extent are these age-specific? To what extent are these used to evaluate individuals at different stages? How are the stages themselves evaluated? Which is most preferred and why? Which is least preferred? These are questions for which we have very little empirical work.

CONCLUSION

Since the life course is the cultural framework people use to organize the meaning of time between birth and death, its use as both a framework and as a unit for comparative analysis can only make our theories of aging more powerful and predictive. If one of the tasks of theory building is to discern what is universal about phenomena from what is conditioned by specific social, economic, and cultural conditions, then the life course as our unit is even more attractive. The life course is a unit we know to be variable. It is a unit that examines the linkage between individuals and the social institutions in which their lives are staged. One of the analytic difficulties in aging research is the impermanence of the characteristic we investigate as our subjects move through time and grow old. In many respects, the life course is an institutionalized answer within each culture to the transformations of age and change through time. Also, the life course mediates the tendency for potentially infinite differentiation. Individual lives unfold through time becoming more unique in response to circumstance and experience. It is culture and the meaningful, symbolic structuring of time, maturation, and the courses of life that inform us about age and shape the experience of aging.

NOTES

[1]Mead's (1928) study indicated an absence of stress and turmoil surrounding the transition to adulthood in Samoa. Recently, Freeman has challenged this conclusion, which has generated considerable controversy within and beyond anthropology, concerning adequacy of method and theory across cultures and across time.

[2]These were in California (Byrne, 1974; Johnson, 1971; Hochchild, 1973), Arizona, Wisconsin, Florida, New York (Keith, 1979), France (Keith, 1982a), and Cleveland and England (Francis, 1981, 1984).

[3]This dimension of culture involves the material basis of social life. It reflects the animal nature of humans in that as animals we must eat and reproduce. Consequently, infrastructural concerns are with production (extraction of energy from the environment) and with reproduction, along with the implications for the population making up a culture. Age and gender are linked to infrastructure since human societies are multi-male, multi-female with individuals of differing ages.

[4]Anthropomorphically, these infant langurs can be called "grandchildren" since females of a langur troop constitute its breeding core and share one-eighth or more genes due to common descent.

[5]Age villages and age regiments utilize the principle of age setting for specialized purposes. Age villages exist among the Nyakuysa in that the men of one age set live separately from those of other age sets for the expressed intent of "keeping good company." Age regiments are formed when recruitment into a military force is based on the age set organization. This was the strength of the Zulu army that defeated the English forces in southern Africa.

[6]Foner (1974) has proposed two hypotheses concerning age conflict. The first suggests that age conflict over material issues will be checked by conflict-reducing mechanisms such as membership in age-heterogeneous groups and the inevitability of age. The second suggests that age conflict over ideal issues is not subject to these mechanisms, and hence conflict will follow age lines. In the small-scale, egalitarian societies having formal age classes, neither of the conflict-reducing mechanisms is

effective. Kinship is the only age-heterogeneous institution and often the only institution. Instead of allying kin of different ages in reducing conflict, it is a source of conflict. The inevitability of aging, in the face of limited alternatives and opportunities for the young, sets young against old as the young anxiously await "their turn" and try to terminate a prolonged youth.

[7]A domestic mode of production contrasts markedly with an industrial mode of production. Notably, there is little or no differentiation between production and consumption. Both reside within domestic units that act as if they were domestic corporations. Decisions about production (land and labor) and allocation and consumption of the results are all made within one unit. In contrast, an industrial mode of production is noted for the differentiation between production and consumption. Consuming units (households) send personnel to producing units (factories, corporations) to work in exchange for wages with which they can consume.

[8]Social rights may be institutionalized by age, e.g., pensions and age of majority.

[9]The major exceptions to this have been Neugarten and Peterson (1957) and Cameron (1969), who focused on age parameters of investigator-defined and -labeled age groups.

[10]Three U.S. sites were a mid-size city in the Midwest (Lafayette, Indiana), an eastern suburb (Swarthmore, Pennsylvania), and a small midwestern town (Momence, Illinois). Momence, Swarthmore, and Hong Kong are field sites for Project AGE, a program project (PO1-AG03110) sponsored by the National Institute on Aging. The Lafayette data was collected in conjunction with the author's dissertation research sponsored by the American Association of University Women.

[11]Ethnosemantics emerged from the Cognitive Anthropology movement in the 1950s. Methodologically, the concern is how to chart a culture from the native points of view. This utilizes a linguistic strategy to investigate meaning. The researcher first asks the question of, What do I need to know to . . . ? The answers reveal (1) semantic domains, (2) distinctive features or attributes used to discriminate, and (3) grammatical combinations of features to define categories. Major works in this area are Goodenough (1970), Tyler (1969), and Dougherty (1985). See also Fry (1986) for a discussion of this methodology applied to age.

[12]The Massai data is not directly comparable since a different technique was used for investigating personality descriptors appropriate for the respective age classes. Kirk and Burton (1977) used triad tests to obtain respondents' judgments about appropriate personality characteristics associated with the age sets. The use of multidimensional scaling and the age sets as the frame of reference render the interpretations parallel.

[13]These two questions reflect an important lesson learned in the comparative study of kinship and social organization. Two radically different approaches to kinship systems appeared that became known as *descent* and *alliance* theories. Alliance theory looked at the linkages between descent units as represented in consequences of preferential marriages (e.g., mother's brother's daughter). Descent theory was more individuated, with kinship systems seen as linking egos to more and more inclusive social units (e.g., lineages, clans, phratries, moieties). Since both perspectives can model a number of cases, our modeling of kinship and social organizations was quite muddled until it became clear empirically that quite different kinds of kinship systems were involved (Fox, 1967).

REFERENCES

Achenbaum, W. (1978). *Old age in the new land: The American experience since 1790.* Baltimore: Johns Hopkins University Press.

Achenbaum, W., & Stearns, P. (1978). Essay: Old age and modernization. *Gerontologist, 18,* 307–312.

Almagor, U. (1978). The ethos of equality among Dassanetch age peers. In P. T. W. Baxter & U. Almagor (Eds.), *Age, generation and time* (pp. 69–94). New York: St. Martins Press.

Amoss, P. T. (1981a). Coast Salish elders. In P. T. Amoss & S. Harrell (Eds.), *Other ways of growing old* (pp. 227–238). Stanford, CA: Stanford University Press.

Amoss, P. T. (1981b). Cultural centrality and prestige for the elders: The Coast Salish case. In C. L. Fry (Ed.), *Dimensions: Aging, culture and health* (pp. 47–64). New York: Praeger.

Amoss, P. T., & Harrell, S. (Eds.). (1981). *Other ways of growing old.* Stanford, CA: Stanford University Press.

Arensberg, C. (1937). *The Irish countrymen.* New York: Macmillan.

Arnhoff, F. N., Leon, H. V., & Lorge, I. (1964). Cross-cultural acceptance of stereotypes toward aging. *Journal of Social Psychology, 63,* 41–58.

Baltes, P. B. (1968). Longitudinal and cross-sectional sequences in the study of age and generation effects. *Human Development, 11,* 145–171.

Benet, S. (1974). *Abkhasians: The long-lived people of the Caucasus.* New York: Holt, Rinehart & Winston.

Bengtson, V. L., Dowd, J. J., Smith, D. H., & Inkles, A. (1975). Modernization, modernity and perceptions of aging: A cross-cultural study. *Journal of Gerontology, 30,* 688–695.

Bernardi, B. (1985). *Age class systems: Social institutions and polities based on age.* London: Cambridge University Press.

Bohannan, P. J. (1981). Food of old people in center city hotels. In C. L. Fry (Ed.), *Dimensions: Aging, culture and health* (pp. 185–200). New York: Praeger.

Brown, J. K. (1982). Cross-cultural perspectives on middle aged women. *Current Anthropology, 23,* 143–156.

Brown, J. K., & Kerns, V. (1985). *In her prime: A new view of middle-aged women.* South Hadley, MA: Bergin & Garvey.

Byrne, S. (1974). Arden, an adult community. In G. Foster & R. Kemper (Eds.), *Anthropologists in cities* (pp. 123–152). Boston: Little, Brown.

Cain, L. D. Jr. (1963). *Age status and social structure.* New York: Holt, Rinehart & Winston.

Cameron, P. (1969). Age parameters of young adult, middle age, old and aged. *Journal of Gerontology, 24,* 201–202.

Chodorow, N. (1974). Family structure and female personality. In M. Z. Rosaldo & L. Lamphere (Eds.), *Women, culture and society* (pp. 43–66). Stanford, CA: Stanford University Press.

Clark, M. M. (1967). The anthropology of aging: A new area for studies of culture and personality. *Gerontologist, 7,* 55–65.

Clark, M. M. (1972). Cultural values and dependency in later life. In D. O. Cowgill & L. D. Holmes (Eds.), *Aging and modernization* (pp. 263–274). New York: Appleton-Century-Crofts.

Clark, M. M., & Anderson, B. (1967). *Culture and aging: An anthropological study of older Americans*. Springfield, IL: Charles C. Thomas.

Cohen, C., & Sokolovsky, J. (1980). Social engagement versus isolation: The case of the aged in S.R.O. hotels. *Gerontologist, 20,* 36–44.

Cohler, B., & Lieberman, M. A. (1979). Personality change across the second half of life: Findings from a study of Irish, Italian and Polish-American men and women. In D. E. Gelfand & A. J. Kutzik (Eds.), *Ethnicity and aging* (pp. 245–277). New York: Springer Publishing Co.

Colson, E., & Scudder, T. (1981). Old age in the Guembe District, Zambia. In P. T. Amoss & S. Harrell (Eds.), *Other ways of growing old* (pp. 125–154). Stanford, CA: Stanford University Press.

Cool, L. E. (1980). Ethnicity and aging: Continuity through change for elderly Corsicans. In C. L. Fry (Ed.), *Aging in culture and society: Comparative viewpoints and strategies* (pp. 149–169). New York: Praeger.

Cool, L. E. (1981a). Ethnic identity: A source of community esteem for the elderly. *Anthropological Quarterly, 54,* 179–189.

Cool, L. E. (1981b). Role continuity or crisis in later life? A Corsican case. *International Journal of Aging and Human Development, 13,* 169–181.

Cool, L. E., & McCabe, J. (1983). The scheming hag and the dear old thing: The anthropology of aging women. In J. Sokolousky (Ed.), *Growing old in different cultures — cross cultural perspectives* (pp. 56–68). Belmont, CA: Wadsworth.

Cowgill, D. O. (1974). Aging and modernization: A revision of the theory. In J. Gulbrium (Ed.), *Late life: Communities and environmental policy* (pp. 123–146). Springfield, IL: Charles C. Thomas.

Cowgill, D. O. (1986). *Aging around the world*. Belmont, CA: Wadsworth.

Cowgill, D. O., & Holmes, L. D., (Eds.). (1972). *Aging and modernization*. New York: Appleton-Century-Crofts.

Cuellar, J. (1978). El senior citizens club: The older Mexican-American in the voluntary association. In B. G. Myerhoff & A. Simic (Eds.), *Life's career aging* (pp. 207–230). Beverly Hills, CA: Sage.

Dolhinow, P. (1984). The primates: Age, behavior and evolution. In D. Kertzer & J. Keith (Eds.), *Age and anthropological theory* (pp. 65–81). Ithaca, NY: Cornell University Press.

Dougherty, J. W. (Ed.). (1985). *Directions in cognitive anthropology*. Urbana, IL: University of Illinois Press.

Durkheim, E. (1893). *The division of labor in society* (G. Simpson, Trans.). New York: Macmillan.

Eckert, J. K. (1979). Urban development and renewal: High risk factors for the elderly. *Gerontologist, 19,* 496–502.

Eckert, J. K. (1980). *The unseen elderly*. San Diego, CA: Campanile Press.

Eisenstadt, S. N. (1956). *From generation to generation: Age groups and social structure*. New York: Free Press.

Evans-Prichard, E. E. (1940). *The Nuer*. Oxford: Clarendon.

Featherman, D. (1981). *The life span perspective in social science research*. New York: Social Science Research Council.

Featherman, D., & Petersen, T. (1986). Markers of aging: Modeling the clocks that time us. *Research on Aging, 8,* 339–367.

Finley, G. E. (1982). Modernization and aging. In T. Field (Ed.), *Review of human development*. New York: Wiley-Interscience.

Fisher, D. H. (1977). *Growing old in America*. New York: Oxford University Press.

Foner, A. (1974). Age stratification and age conflict in political life. *American Sociological Review, 39,* 187–196.

Foner, N. (1984). Age and social change. In D. I. Kertzer & J. Keith (Eds.), *Age and anthropological theory* (pp. 195–219). Ithaca, NY: Cornell University Press.

Foner, A., & Kertzer, D. I. (1978). Transitions over the life course: Lessons from age-set societies. *American Journal of Sociology, 83,* 1081–1104.

Fortes, M. (1984). Age, generation and social structure. In D. I. Kertzer & J. Keith (Eds.), *Age and anthropological theory* (pp. 99–122). Ithaca, NY: Cornell University Press.

Fox, R. (1967). *Kinship and marriage*. Harmondsworth, UK: Pelican Books.

Francis, D. G. (1981). Adaptive strategies of the elderly in England and Ohio. In C. L. Fry (Ed.), *Dimensions: Aging, culture and health* (pp. 85–108). New York: Praeger.

Francis, D. G. (1984). *Will you still need me, will you still feed me, when I'm 84?* Bloomington, IN: Indiana University Press.

Fry, C. L. (1976). The ages of adulthood: A question of numbers. *Journal of Gerontology, 31,* 170–177.

Fry, C. L. (1977). The community as commodity: The age graded case. *Human Organization, 31,* 115–123.

Fry, C. L. (1979). Structural conditions affecting community formation among the aged. In J. Keith (Ed.), The ethnography of old age. *Anthropological Quarterly, 52,* 7–18.

Fry, C. L. (1980a). *Aging in culture and society: Comparative viewpoints and strategies*. New York: Praeger.

Fry, C. L. (1980b). Cultural dimensions of age. In C. L. Fry (Ed.), *Aging in culture and society: Comparative viewpoints and strategies* (pp. 42–64). New York: Praeger.

Fry, C. L. (1981). *Dimensions: Aging, culture and health*. New York: Praeger.

Fry, C. L. (1985). Culture, behavior, and aging in the comparative perspective. In J. E. Birren & K. W. Schaie (Eds.), *Handbook of the psychology of aging* (pp. 216–244) (2nd ed.). New York: Van Nostrand Reinhold.

Fry, C. L. (1986). Emics and age: Age differentiation and cognitive anthropological strategies. In C. L. Fry & J. Keith (Eds.), *New methods for old age research* (pp. 105–131). South Hadley, MA: Bergin & Garvey.

Fry, C. L. & Keith, J. (1981). The life course as a cultural unit. In M. W. Riley, R. Abeles, & M. S. Teitelbaum (Eds.), *Aging from birth to death, vol. II: Sociotemporal perspectives* (pp. 51–70). New York: Van Nostrand Reinhold.

Glascock, A. P. (1982). Decrepitude and death-hastening: The nature of old age in third world societies. In J. Sokolovsky (Ed.), *Aging and the aged in the Third World (Part 1)*. Williamsburg, VA: Studies in Third World Societies. Pub. #22.

Glascock, A. P., & Feinman, S. (1980). A holocultural analysis of old age. *Comparative Social Research, 3,* 311–332.

Glascock, A. P., & Feinman, S. (1981). Social asset or social burden: Treatment of the aged in non-industrial societies. In C. L. Fry (Ed.), *Dimensions: Aging, culture and health* (pp. 13–32). New York: Praeger.

Glascock, A. P., & Feinman, S. (1986). Toward a comparative framework: Propositions concerning the treatment of the aged in non-industrial societies. In C. L. Fry & J. Keith (Eds.), *New methods for old age research: Strategies for studying diversity* (pp. 281–296). South Hadley, MA: Bergin & Garvey.

Goldstein, M., & Beall, C. (1981). Modernization and aging in the third and fourth world: Views from the rural hinterland in Nepal. *Human Organization, 40,* 48–55.

Goldstein, M., & Beall, C. (1982). Brief note on demographic aspects of aging in the less developed countries. *Association for Anthropology and Gerontology Newsletter, 3,* 2.

Goldstein, T., & Gutmann, D. (1972). A TAT study of Navajo aging. *Psychiatry, 35,* 373–384.

Goodenough, W. H. (1970). *Description and comparison in cultural anthropology.* Chicago: Aldine.

Goody, J. (1976). Aging in non-industrial societies. In R. H. Binstock & E. Shanas (Eds.), *Handbook of aging and the social sciences* (pp. 117–129). New York: Van Nostrand Reinhold.

Gutmann, D. (1966). Mayan aging—a comparative TAT study. *Psychiatry, 29,* 246–259.

Gutmann, D. (1968). Aging among the highland Maya: A comparative study. In B. L. Neugarten (Ed.), *Middle age and aging* (pp. 444–452). Chicago: University of Chicago Press.

Gutmann, D. (1974). Alternatives to disengagement: The old men of the Highland Druze. In R. LeVine (Ed.), *Culture and personality: Contemporary readings* (pp. 232–245). Chicago: Aldine.

Gutmann, D. (1975). Parenthood: A key to the comparative study of the life cycle. In N. Data & L. H. Ginsberg (Eds.), *Life-span developmental psychology: Normative life crises* (pp. 167–184). New York: Academic Press.

Halperin, R. (1984). Age in cultural economics: An evolutionary approach. In D. I. Kertzer & J. Keith (Eds.), *Age and anthropological theory* (pp. 159–194). Ithaca, NY: Cornell University Press.

Harding, T. G. (1960). Adaptation. In T. G. Harding, D. Kaplan, M. D. Sahlins, & E. R. Service (Eds.), *Evolution and culture.* Ann Arbor, MI: University of Michigan Press. (pp. 45–68).

Hendricks, J. (1982). The elderly in society: Beyond modernization. *Social Science History, 6,* 321–345.

Hochchild, A. R. (1973). *The unexpected community.* Berkeley, CA: University of California Press.

Holmes, L. D. (1976). Trends in anthropological gerontology: From Simmons to the seventies. *International Journal of Aging and Human Development, 7,* 211–220.

Holmes, L. D. (1983). *Other cultures, elder years.* Minneapolis: Burgess.

Hrdy, S. B. (1981). Nepotist and altruists: The behavior of old females among macaques and langur monkeys. In P. T. Amoss & S. Harrell (Eds.), *Other ways of growing old* (pp. 59–76). Stanford, CA: Stanford University Press.

Hsu, F. L. K. (1961). *Psychological anthropology: Approaches to culture and personality.* Homewood, IL: Dorsey Press.

Ikels, C. (1980). The coming of age in Chinese society: Traditional patterns and contemporary Hong Kong. In C. L. Fry (Ed.), *Aging in culture and society: Comparative viewpoints and strategies* (pp. 80–100). New York: Praeger.

Ikels, C., Keith, J. & Fry, C. L. (1987). The use of qualitative methodologies in cross-cultural research. In G. D. Rowles & S. Reinharz (Eds.), *Qualitative gerontology.* New York: Springer Publishing Co.

Jacobs, J. (1974). *Fun City: An ethnographic study of a retirement community.* New York: Holt, Rinehart & Winston.

Jeffers, F., Eisdorfer, C., & Busse, E. (1962). Measurement of age identification: A methodological note. *Journal of Gerontology, 17,* 437–439.

Johnson, C. L. (1983). Interdependence and aging in Italian families. In J. Sokolovsky (Ed.), *Growing old in different cultures* (pp. 92–103). Belmont, CA: Wadsworth.

Johnson, S. (1971). *Idle Haven: Community building among the working class retired.* Berkeley, CA: University of California Press.

Jolly, A. (1985). *Evolution of primate behavior.* New York: Macmillan.

Keith, J. (Ed.). (1979). The ethnography of old age. *Anthropological Quarterly, 52* (Special Issue), 1–69.

Keith, J. (1980a). "The best is yet to be": Toward an anthropology of age. *Annual Review of Anthropology, 9,* 339–364.

Keith, J. (1980b). Old age and community creation. In C. L. Fry (Ed.), *Aging in culture and society: Comparative viewpoints and strategies* (pp. 170–197). New York: Praeger.

Keith, J. (1981). The "back to anthropology" movement in gerontology. In C. L. Fry (Ed.), *Dimensions: Aging, culture and health* (pp. 285–293). New York: Praeger.

Keith, J. (1982a). *Old people, new lives: Community creation in a retirement residence.* Chicago: University of Chicago Press.

Keith, J. (1982b). *Old people as people: Social and cultural influences on aging and old age.* Boston: Little, Brown.

Keith, J. (1985). Age in anthropological research. In R. Binstock & E. Shanas (Eds.), *Aging and the social sciences* (2nd ed.) (pp. 231–263). New York: Van Nostrand Reinhold.

Keith, J., Fry, C. L., & Ikels, C. (1984). Report from Project A. G. E., Discussion Session, Annual Meeting of the Gerontological Society of America, San Antonio, Texas, November, 1984.

Kertzer, D. I. (1978). Theoretical developments in the study of age-group systems. *American Ethnologist, 5,* 368–374.

Kertzer, D. I., & Keith, J. (Eds.). (1984). *Age and anthropological theory.* Ithaca, NY: Cornell University Press.

Kertzer, D. I., & Madison, O. B. B. (1980). African age set systems and political organization: The Latuka of Southern Sudan. *Uomo, 4,* 84–109.

Kertzer, D. I., & Madison, O. B. B. (1981). Women's age-set systems in Africa: The Latuka of Southern Sudan. In C. L. Fry (Ed.), *Dimensions: Aging, culture and health* (pp. 109–130). New York: Praeger.

Kiefer, C. W. (1971). Notes on anthropology and the minority elderly. *Gerontologist, 11,* 26–29.

Kirk, L., & Burton, M. (1977). Meaning and context: A study of contextual shifts in meaning of Massai personality descriptors. *American Ethnologist, 4*, 734–761.

Klein, C. (1975). The socialization of women. *Gerontologist, 15*, 485–492.

Kruskal, J. B., & Wish, M. (1978). *Multidimensional scaling*. Beverly Hills, CA: Sage.

LaFontaine, J. S. (Ed.). (1978). *Sex and age as principles of social differentiation*. London: Academic Press.

Laslett, P. (1976). Societal development and aging. In R. Binstock & E. Shanas (Eds.), *Handbook of aging and the social sciences* (pp. 87–116). New York: Van Nostrand Reinhold.

Laslett, P. (1985). Societal development and aging. In R. Binstock & E. Shanas (Eds.), *Handbook of aging and the social sciences* (2nd ed.) (pp. 199–230). New York: Van Nostrand Reinhold.

Leach, E. R. (1961). *Rethinking anthropology*. New York: Humanities Press.

Lee, G. R., & Kezis, M. (1981). Societal literacy and the aged. *International Journal of Aging and Human Development, 12*, 221–234.

LeVine, R. (1978). Adulthood and aging in cross-cultural perspective. *Items, 31/32*: 1–5.

Lovejoy, C. O. (1981). The origin of man. *Science, 211*, 341–350.

Mauss, M. (1925; 1967 reprint). *The gift* (Ian Currison, Trans.). New York: W. W. Norton.

Maxwell, E. K., & Maxwell, R. J. (1980). Contempt for the elderly. A cross-cultural analysis. *Current Anthropology, 21*, 569–570.

Maxwell, R. J., & Silverman, P. (1970). Information and esteem. *Aging and Human Development, 1*, 127–146.

Maxwell, R. J., Silverman, P., & Maxwell, E. K. (1982). The motive for gerontocide. In J. Sokolovsky (Ed.), *Aging and the aged in the Third World: Part 1*. Williamsburg, VA: Studies in Third World Societies. (Publication No. 22)

Maybury-Lewis, D. (1967; 1974 reprint). *Akwe-Shavante society*. Clarendon: Oxford University Press.

Maybury-Lewis, D. (1984). Age and kinship: A structural view. In D. I. Kertzer & J. Keith (Eds.), *Age and anthropological theory*. Ithaca, NY: Cornell University Press.

Mead, M. (1928). *Coming of age in Samoa*. New York: Morrow.

Moore, A. (1973). *Life cycles in Atchalan: The diverse careers of certain Guatamalans*. New York: Teacher's College Press.

Myerhoff, B. (1984). Rites and signs of ripening: The intertwining of ritual, time and growing older. In D. I. Kertzer & J. Keith (Eds.), *Age and anthropological theory* (pp. 305–330). Ithaca, NY: Cornell University Press.

Myerhoff, B., & Simic, A. (Eds.). (1978). *Life's career: Aging: Cultural variations in growing old*. Beverly Hills, CA: Sage.

Myers, G. C. (1985). Aging and worldwide population change. In R. Binstock & E. Shanas (Eds.), *Handbook of aging and the social sciences* (2nd ed.) (pp. 173–198). New York: Van Nostrand Reinhold.

Nadel, S. F. (1952). Witchcraft in four African societies. *American Anthropologist, 54*, 18–29.

Needham, R. (1974). Age, category, and descent. In R. Needham (Ed.), *Remarks and inventions*. London: Tavistock. (pp. 1–35).

Neugarten, B. L., & Datan, N. (1973). Sociological perspectives on the life cycle. In P.

B. Baltes & K. W. Schaie (Eds.), *Life-span developmental psychology: Personality and socialization* (pp. 53–69). New York: Academic Press.

Neugarten, B. L., & Gutmann, D. (1958). Age and sex roles and personality in middle age: A thematic apperception study. *Psychological Monographs, 72* (No. 17). Washington, DC: American Psychological Association.

Neugarten, B. L., & Hagestad, G. O. (1976). Age and the life course. In R. Binstock & E. Shanas (Eds.), *Handbook of aging and the social sciences* (pp. 35–55). New York: Van Nostrand Reinhold.

Neugarten, B. L., & Hagestad, G. O. (1985). Age and the life course. In R. H. Binstock & E. Shanas (Eds.), *Handbook of aging and the social sciences* (pp. 35–61). New York: Van Nostrand Reinhold.

Neugarten, B. L., & Moore, J. W. (1968). The changing age status system. In B. L. Neugarten (Ed.), *Middle age and aging*. Chicago: Chicago University Press.

Neugarten, B. L., Moore, J. W., & Lowe, J. (1965). Age norms, age constraints, and adult socialization. *American Journal of Sociology, 70*, 710–717.

Neugarten, B. L., & Peterson, W. A. (1957). A study of the American age grade system. In *Proceedings of the Fourth Congress of the International Association of Gerontology* (pp. 497–502). Merano, Italy.

Nydegger, C. (1981). On being caught up in time. *Human Development, 24*, 1–12.

Ortner, S. (1974). Is female to male as nature is to culture? In M. Z. Rosaldo & L. Lamphere (Eds.), *Women, culture and society*. Stanford, CA: Stanford University Press.

Ottenberg, S. (1971). *Leadership and authority in an African society: The Afikpo village group*. Seattle: University of Washington Press.

Palmore, E. (1976). The future status of the aged. *Gerontologist, 16*, 297–302.

Palmore, E., & Manton, K. (1974). Modernization and status of the aged. *Journal of Gerontology, 19*, 205–210.

Press, I., & McKool, M., Jr., (1972). Social structure and status of the aged: Toward some valid cross-cultural generalizations. *Aging and Human Development, 3*, 297–306.

Quadagno, J. (1982). *Aging in early industrial society: Work, family and social policy in nineteenth century England*. New York: Academic Press.

Radcliffe-Brown, A. R. (1929). Age organization-terminology. *Man, 29*, 21.

Riley, M. W. (1979). Introduction. In M. W. Riley (Ed.), *Aging from birth to death: Interdisciplinary perspectives* (pp. 3–14). Bolder, CO: Westview Press.

Riley, M. W. (1985). Age strata in social systems. In R. Binstock & E. Shanas (Eds.), *Handbook of aging and the social sciences* (2nd ed.) (pp. 369–414). New York: Van Nostrand Reinhold.

Riley, M. W., Johnson, M., & Foner, A. (1972). *Aging and society: Vol 3. A sociology of age stratification*. New York: Russell Sage Foundation.

Ritter, M. L. (1980). The conditions favoring age set organization. *Journal of Anthropological Research, 36*, 87–104.

Sahlins, M. D. (1960). Evolution: Specific and general. In T. G. Harding, D. Kaplan, M. D. Sahlins, & E. R. Service (Eds.), *Evolution and culture*. Ann Arbor, MI: University of Michigan Press. (pp. 15–44).

Sahlins, M. D. (1972). *Stone Age economics*. Chicago: Aldine.

Schaie, K. W. (1965). A general model for the study of developmental problems. *Psychological Bulletin, 64*, 92–107.

Scheper-Hughs, N. (1983). Deposed kings: The demise of the rural Irish gerontocracy. In J. Sokolovsky (Ed.), *Growing old in different cultures* (pp. 131–146). Belmont, CA: Wadsworth.

Sheehan, T. (1976). Senior esteem as a factor in socioeconomic complexity. *Gerontologist, 5*, 2–23.

Silverman, P., & Maxwell, R. J. (1978). How do I respect thee? Let me count the ways: Deference towards elderly men and women. *Behavioral Science Research, 13*, 91–108.

Silverman, P., & Maxwell, R. J. (1983). The significance of information and power in the comparative study of the aged. In J. Sokolovsky (Ed.), *Growing old in different societies: Cross-cultural perspectives* (pp. 43–55). Belmont, CA: Wadsworth.

Simmons, L. W. (1945). *The role of the aged in primitive society.* New Haven, CT: Yale University Press.

Sinnott, J. D. (1977). Sex-role inconsistency, biology and successful aging. *Gerontologist, 17*, 459–463.

Smith, R. J., Holmberg, A. R., Hughes, C. C., Rustom, C. & Rowe, W. L. (1961). Cultural differences in the life cycle and the concept of time. In R. Kleemeier (Ed.), *Aging and leisure.* New York: Oxford University Press.

Sokolovsky, J. (Ed.). (1982). *Aging and the aged in the Third World: Part 1.* Williamsburg, VA: Studies in Third World Societies. (Publication No. 22).

Sokolovsky, J. (Ed.) (1983). *Growing old in different societies: Cross-cultural perspectives.* Belmont, CA: Wadsworth.

Sokolovsky, J., & Cohen, C. (1978). The cultural meaning of personal networks for the inner city elderly. *Urban Anthropology, 7*, 323–324.

Sokolovsky, J., & Cohen, C. (1981). Being old in the inner city: Support systems of the S.R.O. aged. In C. L. Fry (Ed.), *Dimensions: Aging, culture and health* (pp. 163–184). New York: Praeger.

Sokolovsky, J., & Sokolovsky, J. (1982). *Aging and the aged in the Third World: Part 2. Regional and ethnographic.* Williamsburg, VA: Studies in Third World Societies. (Publication No. 23).

Spencer, P. (1976). Opposing streams and the gerontocratic ladder: Two models of age organization. *Man, 11*, 153–174.

Stewart, F. H. (1977). *Fundamentals of age-group systems.* New York: Academic Press.

Tipps, T. C. (1973). Modernization theory and the comparative study of societies: A critical perspective. *Comparative Studies in Society and History, 15*, 199–226.

Turnbull, C. M. (1972). *The mountain people.* New York: Simon & Schuster.

Tyler, S. (Ed.). (1969). *Cognitive anthropology.* New York: Holt, Rinehart & Winston.

Van Arsdale, P. W. (1981a). Disintegration of the ritual support network among the aged Asmat hunter-gatherers of New Guinea. In C. L. Fry (Ed.), *Dimensions: Aging, culture and health* (pp. 33–46). New York: Praeger.

Van Arsdale, P. W. (1981b). The elderly Asmat of New Guinea. In P. T. Amoss & S. Harrell (Eds.), *Other ways of growing old* (pp. 111–124). Stanford, CA: Stanford University Press.

Vatuk, S. (1980). Withdrawal and disengagement as a cultural response to aging in India. In C. L. Fry (Ed.), *Aging in culture and society: Comparative viewpoints and strategies.* New York: Praeger. (pp. 126–148).

Wallerstein, E. (1979). *The capitalist world-economy*. New York: Cambridge University Press.

Washburn, S. L. (1981). Longevity in primates. In J. L. McGaugh & S. B. Kiesler (Eds.), *Aging: Biology and behavior* (pp. 2–10). New York: Academic Press.

Weatherford, J. M. (1981). Labor and domestic life cycles in a German community. In C. L. Fry (Ed.), *Dimensions: Aging, culture and health*. New York: Praeger.

Werner, D. (1981). Gerontocracy among the Mekranoti of central Brazil. *Anthropological Quarterly, 54*, 15–27.

Williams, G. C. (1970). *American society: Sociological interpretations*. New York: Alfred A. Knopf.

Wilson, M. (1951). *Good company: Study of Nyakyusa age villages*. London: Oxford University Press.

Subject Index

Name Index*

Abelson, R. P., 183, *212*
Abolafia, J., 73, 77
Abraham, R. H., 92, 104, *114*
Achenbaum, W. A., 5, *16*, 233, *242*, 358, *378*, 465, *473*
Ackerman, B. P., 185, *211*
Adams, N. R., 138, *143*
Adelman, R. C., 119, *126*
Adorno, T., 26, *39*
Albert, M. L., 187, 190, 197, *211*
Albertson, S., 193, 194, 200, *210*
Albrecht, R., 341, *352*
Aldous, J., 370, *378*, 433, 434, *443*
Alexander, J., 20, *37*
Alexander, J. C., 377, *378*
Allison, P. D., 76, 77
Allport, G. W., 224, 225, 233, *242*
Almagor, U., 455, *473*
Almond, R., 221, 235, *242*
Alvolio, B. S., 253, *268*
Alwin, D. F., 51, *54*
Amoss, P. T., 467, *473*
Anderson, B., 451, 462, *474*
Anderson, J. A., 184, *205*
Anderson, J. E., 310, 320, *325*
Anderson, P. A., 179, 183, 194, 199, 200, 204, *210*
Anderson, R. C., 172, *174*, 185, *205*
Antonovsky, A., *294*
Antonucci, T. C., 324, *327*
Apple, M., 375, *378*
Arai, Y., 133, *143*

Arensberg, C., 466, *473*
Arensberg, M., 397, 398, *402*
Arnhoff, F. N., 465, *473*
Aschheim, P., 129, 136, 137, *143*
Atkins, P. W., 91, 100, *114*
Atwood, G. E., 215, *242*

Babloyantz, A., 100, *116*
Baddeley, A. D., 179, 203, *205*
Baer, D. M., 251, *266*
Baird, R. M., 221–223, *242*
Bakan, D., 273, *294*
Baker, T. G., 129, *150*
Baltes, P. B., 8, 9, 10, *17*, 42, 45, 46, 49, 50, 52, *54*, 55, 56, 57, 62, 77, 87, *88*, 161, *174*, 204, *205*, 251, 253, 254, *266*, 360, 363–365, 368, *378*, 388, 390, *402*, 455, *473*
Bandura, A., 251, *266*
Banergi, T. K., 136, *143*
Bannister, D., 226, 236, *242*
Barfield, R. E., 69, 77
Bargmann, R. E., 49, *54*
Barker, L. S., 157, *174*
Barker, R. G., 157, *174*
Barraclough, C. A., 136, *143*
Barrett-Conner, E., 274, *297*
Bartolucci, G., 201, *212*
Battista, J., 221, 235, *242*
Bauman, Z., 31, *37*
Bauneck, E., 131, *146*
Beach, F. A., 128, *144*
Beall, C., 466, *476*
Beasley, D. S., 189, *209*

*Italicized numbers refer to reference list pages.

516